Barcode in Back

Secured Transactions in Personal Property

Cases, Text, and Materials

Fifth Edition

Anthony J. Duggan
Professor of Law
Faculty of Law
University of Toronto

Jacob S. Ziegel
Professor of Law Emeritus
Faculty of Law
University of Toronto

2009
EMOND MONTGOMERY PUBLICATIONS LIMITED
TORONTO, CANADA

Emond Montgomery Publications Limited
60 Shaftesbury Avenue
Toronto ON M4T 1A3
http://www.emp.ca

Printed in Canada.

We acknowledge the financial support of the Government of Canada through the Book Publishing Industry Development Program (BPIDP) for our publishing activities.

Acquisitions editor: Peggy Buchan
Marketing manager: Christine Davidson
Sales manager: James Black
Copy editor: Cindy Fujimoto
Production editor: Cindy Fujimoto
Permissions editor: Jennifer Blackmore
Proofreader: Debbie Gervais

Library and Archives Canada Cataloguing in Publication

Duggan, Anthony J.
    Secured transactions in personal property : cases, text, and materials / Anthony J. Duggan, Jacob S. Ziegel. — 5th ed.

Fourth ed. published under title: Secured transactions in personal property and
    suretyships / Jacob S. Ziegel, Ronald C.C. Cuming, Anthony J. Duggan. First
    published as v. 3 of Commercial and consumer transactions.
ISBN 978-1-55239-340-6

    1. Security (Law) — Canada. 2. Personal property — Canada. I. Ziegel, Jacob S.
II. Title.

KE1042.D83 2009   346.7107'4   C2009-901990-6
KF1050.D83 2009

Preface to the Fifth Edition

This book had its genesis in Part I of the third edition of Jacob S. Ziegel and Ronald C.C. Cuming, *Secured Transactions in Personal Property, Suretyships and Insolvency*, published in 1995. In 2003, Professors Ziegel and Cuming joined with Professor Anthony Duggan to publish a separate volume dedicated to secured transactions in personal property and suretyships. It is six years since the 2003 edition and there have been some significant statutory and case law developments in the meantime. In Ontario, the most important of these was the enactment of the *Securities Transfer Act, 2006*, along with cognate amendments to the *Personal Property Security Act* aimed at facilitating security interests in all kinds of investment property. The PPSA was twice more amended in 2006, the most important changes being the implementation of various law reform proposals made to the government by the Personal Property Security Law Committee of the Ontario Bar Association. We have updated the text to take account of all these changes.

There have also been some significant case law developments, including the Supreme Court of Canada's decision in *Saulnier v. Royal Bank of Canada*, [2008] 3 SCR 166 (on whether a fishing licence is personal property for PPSA purposes), the Ontario Court of Appeal's decision in *1231640 Ontario Inc. (Re)* (2007), 289 DLR (4th) 684 (dealing with the status of an unperfected security interest in the debtor's receivership), and the British Columbia Court of Appeal's decision in *DaimlerChrysler Services Canada Inc. v. Cameron* (2007), 279 DLR (4th) 629 (on the true lease-finance lease distinction in the context of the PPSA, Part V enforcement provisions). We have included extracts from these and other recent cases in this new edition. Chapter 15 incorporates an expanded, though not exhaustive, coverage of international developments in personal property security law, of which the coming into effect of the Protocol on Interests in Aircraft and Aircraft Equipment and the establishment of an international registry for interests in aircraft are probably the most important.

We have omitted the material on suretyships that appeared in earlier editions, and this has created space for fuller coverage of secured transactions topics. We have substantially expanded the commentary and analysis in most chapters of the book, and incorporated new materials focusing on key policy questions. There are now separate chapters dealing with attachment, security interests in proceeds, and conflict of laws issues, while Chapter 6, dealing with the registration system, has been substantially rewritten.

Professor Cuming was not involved in the preparation of this edition, but the book still incorporates many of his contributions to the earlier editions. Professor Ziegel was responsible for Chapter 13 of this edition. Professor Duggan was mainly responsible for the other chapters, in consultation with Professor Ziegel, but the book as a whole remains substantially shaped by Professor Ziegel's inputs to the previous editions.

We owe many debts: to our student research assistants; to our law school for funding assistance; to Cindy Fujimoto, our production editor, for her meticulous work on the manuscript; and to all at Emond Montgomery for encouraging us to persevere and complete the project by the agreed date.

Canada Day, 2009   AJD
                                                                                    JSZ

Acknowledgments

A book of this nature borrows heavily from other published material. We have attempted to request permission from, and to acknowledge in the text, all sources of such material. We wish to make specific references here to the authors, publishers, journals, and institutions that have generously given permission to reproduce in this text works already in print. If we have inadvertently overlooked an acknowledgment or failed to secure a permission, we offer our sincere apologies and undertake to rectify the omission in the next edition.

Aspen Publications.   Grant Gilmore, *Security Interests in Personal Property*, vol. II.

Banking Finance Law Review.   John Cameron, "Secured Transactions Under Ontario's Securities Transfer Act, 2006" (2007), 22 *BFLR* 309.

Business Lawyer.   Homer Kripke, "Should Section 9-307(1) of the Uniform Commercial Code Apply Against a Secured Party in Possession?" (1977) 33 *Bus. Lawyer* 153.

Butterworths LexisNexis Canada.   Jacob S. Ziegel and David L. Denomme, *The Ontario Personal Property Security Act: Commentary and Analysis*, 2d ed. (2000).

Canadian Business Law Journal.   Anthony J. Duggan, "Tracing Canadian Style: Re Graphicshoppe and Other Recent Cases" (2006), 43 *CBLJ* 292.

Canadian Business Law Journal.   Jacob S. Ziegel, "Perfection by Registration, Instruments, Securities, Documents of Title and Personal Property Security Act 1989" (1989), 15 *CBLJ* 242.

Canadian Business Law Journal.   Roderick J. Wood, "The Nature and Definition of Federal Security Interests" (2000), 34 *CBLJ* 65.

Department of Justice Canada.   "Activities and Priorities of the Department of Justice in International Private Law," sections at 8-14, *Uniform Law Conference of Canada, Civil Section, Law Commission of Canada*. Reproduced with the permission of the Minister of Public Works and Government Services Canada, 2009.

Law Commission of Canada.   *Leveraging Knowledge Assets: Reducing Uncertainty for Security Interests in Intellectual Property*, sections at 26-30 (footnotes omitted). Reproduced with the permission of the Minister of Public Works and Government Services Canada, 2009.

Law Commission of Canada.   *Modernizing Canada's Secured Transactions Law: The Bank Act Security Provisions*, sections at 26-30 (footnotes omitted). Reproduced with the permission of the Minister of Public Works and Government Services Canada, 2009."

New York University Law Review.   Homer Kripke, "Suggestions for Clarifying Article 9: Intangibles, Proceeds and Priorities" (1966), 41 *New York University L Rev.* 687.

Saskatchewan Law Review.   R.C.C. Cuming, "Second Generation Personal Property Security Legislation in Canada" (1982), 46 *Saskatchewan L Rev.* 5.

Yale Law Journal.   Thomas H. Jackson and Anthony T. Kronman, "Secured Financing and Priorities Among Creditors" (1979), 88 *Yale LJ* 1143. Reprinted by permission of The Yale Law Journal Company, Inc.

Short Table of Contents

Detailed Table of Contents

Table of Cases

(Page numbers in bold face type indicate that the text of the case or
a significant extract therefrom is reproduced in this volume.)

Table of Abbreviations

A. REFERENCE TEXTS AND FREQUENTLY CITED TREATISES, REPORTS, AND OTHER MATERIALS

BC PPS REPORT	Law Reform Commission of British Columbia, *Report on Debtor-Creditor Relationships* (Project No. 2), Part V—Personal Property Security, LRC 23 (1975)
CATZMAN	F.M. Catzman et al., *Personal Property Security Law in Ontario* (Toronto: Carswell, 1976)
CBAO SUBMISSION	Canadian Bar Association—Ontario, Submission to the Minister of Consumer and Commercial Relations Concerning the Personal Property Security Act, October 21, 1998
CCPPSL[1]	Canadian Conference on Personal Property Security Law
CUMING AND WOOD	R.C.C. Cuming and R.J. Wood, *Alberta Personal Property Security Handbook*, 4th ed. (Toronto: Carswell, 1998)
CUMING AND WOOD	R.C.C. Cuming and R.J. Wood, *British Columbia Personal Property Security Handbook*, 4th ed. (Toronto: Carswell, 1998)
CUMING AND WOOD	R.C.C. Cuming and R.J. Wood, *Saskatchewan and Manitoba Personal Property Security Acts Handbook* (Toronto: Carswell, 1994)
CUMING, WALSH, AND WOOD	Ronald C.C. Cuming, Catherine Walsh, and Roderick J. Wood, *Personal Property Security Law* (Toronto: Irwin Law, 2005)
GILMORE	G. Gilmore, *Security Interests in Personal Property* (Boston: Little, Brown, 1965), 2 vols.

---

1 The Canadian Conference on Personal Property Security Law is an unofficial organization composed of representatives of all jurisdictions in Canada (principally registrars and registry staff) and practising and academic lawyers interested in modern secured financing law.

GOODE   R.M. Goode, *Commercial Law*, 3d ed. (Harmondsworth, Middlesex: Penguin Books, 1998)

GOODE   R.M. Goode, *Legal Problems of Credit and Security*, 3d ed. (London: Sweet & Maxwell, 2003)

GOODE AND ZIEGEL   R.M. Goode and J.S. Ziegel, *Hire-Purchase Law and Conditional Sale: A Comparative Study* (London: British Institute of International and Comparative Law, 1965)

McLAREN   R.H. McLaren, *Secured Transactions in Personal Property in Canada*, 2d ed. (Toronto: Carswell, 1992) (looseleaf, 4 vols.)

PPSL COMMITTEE   See CBAO SUBMISSION.

ZIEGEL AND DENOMME   J.S. Ziegel and David L. Denomme, *The Ontario Personal Property Security Act: Commentary and Analysis*, 2d ed. (Toronto: Butterworths, 2000)

B. FREQUENTLY CITED STATUTES

APA	*Assignment and Preferences Act*, RSO 1990, c. A.33
APPSA	Alberta, *Personal Property Security Act*, SA 1988, c. P-4.05, as am.
OLD ARTICLE 9	Article 9 of the Uniform Commercial Code (now superseded by Revised Article 9)
BANK ACT	*Bank Act*, SC 1991, c. 46
BCPPSA	British Columbia, *Personal Property Security Act*, SBC 1989, c. 36, as am. 1996, c. 359
BIA	*Bankruptcy and Insolvency Act*, RSC 1985, c. B-3
CCAA	*Companies' Creditors Arrangement Act*, RSC 1985, c. C-36
CCQ	*Civil Code of Québec*, SQ 1991, c. 64, as am. (proclaimed January 1, 1994)
CPA	*Consumer Protection Act, 2002*, SO 2002, c. 30, Sch. A
CTA	*Commercial Tenancies Act*, RSO 1990, c. L.7; SO 1999, c. 6 (formerly known as the *Landlord and Tenant Act*)
MPPSA	Manitoba, *Personal Property Security Act*, CCSM, c. P35
MODEL PPSA	Model Personal Property Security Act. Name given to the Act informally adopted by the Canadian Conference on Personal Property Security Law (CCPPSL) and originally drafted by the Western Canada Personal Property Security Act Committee.
REVISED ARTICLE 9	Article 9 of the Uniform Commercial Code, in force as of July 1, 2001
NBPPSA	*New Brunswick Personal Property Security Act*, SNB 1993, P. 7.1, as am.
OPPSA	Ontario, *Personal Property Security Act*, RSO 1990, c. P.10, as am.
RSLA	*Repair and Storage Liens Act*, RSO 1990, c. R.25, as am.
SGA	*Sale of Goods Act*, RSO 1990, c. S.1, as am.

SPPSA   Saskatchewan, *Personal Property Security Act, 1993*, SS 1993, c. P-6.2, as am.

STA   *Securities Transfer Act, 2006*, SO 2006, c. 8

UCC   Uniform Commercial Code (US)

UPPSA   Canadian Bar Association, Uniform Personal Property Security Act 1982[2]

---

2 The Uniform Act was drafted by a joint committee of the Canadian Bar Association and the Uniform Law Conference of Canada and was adopted by these bodies in 1982. It has now been replaced by the Model Personal Property Security Act informally adopted by the Canadian Conference on Personal Property Security Law (CCPPSL).

CHAPTER ONE

Introduction

I. EVOLUTION OF CANADIAN PERSONAL PROPERTY SECURITY LAW

A. Introduction

"Credit" is not a term of art and it is used in different senses in different branches of the law. For the purposes of this casebook, we use it to mean the agreed deferred payment of a debt. It therefore embraces loans of money and the supply of goods and services on a deferred payment basis, regardless of the length of the period of credit.

Credit plays a role even in very simple societies. Not surprisingly, however, its importance grows apace with the industrial and economic development of a country. This is because a country's capital needs expand enormously as it seeks to widen its industrial base and to increase its production of goods and services. At the other end of the spectrum, consumers need credit facilities to enable them to acquire the goods and services produced by the new technology. This is especially true if the cost of the goods and services exceeds consumers' current income. As an industry's capital needs are satisfied, it generates surplus funds that can then be made available to those who are capital seekers, whether within or outside the country. The role of financial intermediaries is to provide efficient means for the reinvestment of such funds.

B. Different Types of Credit Terms

Financial economists usually distinguish between short-term, medium-term, and long-term credit. Short-term credit is credit for a period of up to one year; medium-term credit covers one to five years; and long-term credit represents any duration longer than five years. (These periods, of course, are not written in stone and have no legal significance.)

The most familiar and oldest type of short-term credit is provided by suppliers of goods and services. Typically, depending on the trade custom, the buyer is given 10, 30, or 60 days to pay the account without an *explicit* interest charge and generally without being required to put up security. Revolving lines of credit made available by banks to commercial customers are usually negotiated on a yearly basis. They are an important source of short-term working capital for many businesses and are often secured by a security interest on inventory and/or an assignment of receivables in favour of the bank.

Medium-term credit, both for commercial and consumer purposes, is often used to enable the debtor to acquire new capital items such as equipment, machinery, vehicles for business or professional use, and automobiles, large household appliances, and entertainment units for consumer use. Frequently, the goods being acquired will serve as security (collateral).

Long-term credit serves some of the same purposes as medium-term credit except that typically the goods being acquired (for example, an aircraft or a printing press) are considerably more expensive and the terms of repayment longer. Long-term credit may be a source of permanent or semi-permanent additions to the borrower's capital (and will be treated as such on the borrower's balance sheet), as where a loan is not repayable for 20 years or more. The security required by the lender may be the same as for a medium-term loan. Frequently, however, given the higher degree of risk, the lender will demand a security interest in all of the debtor's assets.

II. CREDITORS' REMEDIES: AN OVERVIEW

A. Unsecured Credit

If C lends D money and D fails to repay the loan in accordance with the terms of the contract, C has an action against D for the money. If the money is lent without any stipulation as to the time of repayment, a present debt is created that is repayable at once without any demand. Typically, though, the parties will either agree that the loan is repayable on demand or they will fix a time for repayment. Where the loan is repayable on demand, the debt does not become due until C makes a valid demand. (A bank overdraft is an example of a loan that is commonly repayable on demand.) If the loan is made for a specified period ("term loan"), repayment is due at the end of the period and, as a general rule, there is no need for C to make a demand. The parties may agree on repayment by installments. Consider the following simple case:

> C lends D $100 for 12 months (unsecured). The $100 is repayable with interest charges of $20 by 12 equal monthly installments of $10. D makes the first three repayments on time but misses the fourth one. What is C's remedy?

Subject to any specific provision in the contract itself, the answer depends on whether D's breach is a repudiation of the contract. To establish a repudiatory breach, C must prove D's intention to dishonour the contract as a whole—that is, that D is not both ready and able to repay the remaining installments. In that case, C may accept D's breach as a repudiation and bring the contract to an end. C can then sue D to recover the outstanding amount of the loan principal plus accrued interest charges and also loss of bargain damages (if any). Typically, loss of bargain damages for breach of a loan contract represent the difference between the interest charges C would have earned if the contract had run its full term and the interest C can earn by relending the money to a substitute borrower for the balance of the term.

In most cases, D's failure to pay a single installment on time is not itself proof of an intention to dishonour the contract as a whole. In other words, subject to any contrary provision in the contract, late payment of a loan installment is not normally a repudiation. This means that C does not have the option immediately of bringing the contract to an end, but is limited to an action for the missed installment. Alternatively, C may serve a notice on D requiring D to pay the missed installment within a reasonable time. The consequence is to make time essential. D's failure to pay within a reasonable time after the date of the notice is a repudiatory breach and C can bring the contract to an end.

The loan contract may include an essential time stipulation—that is, a provision making the time for repayment an essential term. In that case, C may treat D's late payment as a repudiatory breach without the need for any notice of demand. Alternatively, the contract may include an acceleration clause—that is, a provision saying that if D breaches the contract or other named events happen (for example, D becomes bankrupt), the whole outstanding loan balance plus interest charges become immediately due and payable. C can then sue for the accelerated amount as a debt due. The advantage of an acceleration clause is that it allows C to sue D for the total amount outstanding without having to prove that D has repudiated the loan contract as a whole and without the need for C to serve a notice of demand on D making time of the essence. For an example of an acceleration clause, see clause 7 of the standard form security agreement reproduced in the Appendix (Form 2). For a fuller discussion of unsecured creditors' remedies, see *Chitty on Contracts*, vol. II, "Specific Contracts," 30th ed. (London: Sweet & Maxwell, 2008), c. 36. The unsecured creditor's remedies outlined above are personal remedies. They give C a money claim against D but they do not themselves give C rights in D's property. Assume C obtains judgment against D but D fails to pay. There are various methods for the enforcement of judgment debts. These include execution against D's goods or other personal property, execution against land, garnishment, charging orders, and receivership. For a discussion of these processes, see C.R.B. Dunlop, *Creditor-Debtor Law in Canada*, 2d ed. (Toronto: Carswell, 1995), esp. cc. 9-12. The process of execution against goods, the most commonly used alternative for the enforcement of judgment debts, involves the issue of a writ directing the sheriff to seize D's goods to the value of the debt, sell them, and pay the proceeds to C in satisfaction of the debt. If there are two or more execution creditors, the provincial creditors' relief statutes say that any execution proceeds must be shared ratably between them. The common law "first in, best dressed" rule does not apply: see, for example, *Creditors Relief Act*, RSO 1990, c. C.45. For a detailed discussion of the creditors' relief acts, see Dunlop, c. 16.

B. Secured Credit

Consider the following case:

> C lends D $100 for 12 months. The $100 is repayable with interest charges of $20 by 12 equal monthly installments of $10. D gives C a security interest in D's pickup truck to secure repayment of the loan. D makes the first three repayments on time but misses the fourth one. What is C's remedy?

C has the same personal remedies as in the example discussed above. Assume there is an acceleration clause in C's contract with D. As a consequence of D's default, the total outstanding loan balance is now immediately due and payable. C can sue D for this amount. However, the security agreement gives D another option. Instead of suing D, C can enforce its security interest in the pickup truck. Typically this will involve seizure (repossession) and sale of the pickup truck—the sale proceeds being applied to pay down the outstanding loan balance.

What if there is money left over? Under the Ontario *Personal Property Security Act* (OPPSA), the answer is that C must account to D for the surplus. What if the sale proceeds are less than the amount of D's debt? Under the PPSA, the answer is that C can sue D for the deficiency.

C's right to enforce its security interest in the pickup truck is a real remedy. It is a real remedy in the sense that it is exercisable against a specific asset belonging to D. By contrast, as mentioned earlier, a personal remedy gives C a money claim against D but it does not itself give C a property right in any of D's assets.

So, to recapitulate, in the case of an unsecured loan contract, C has personal remedies if D defaults. In the case of a secured loan contract, C has both personal remedies and real remedies. Why might C want to take security? Some traditional explanations are as follows. (1) There is a risk that the debtor may go bankrupt. A recession sharply increases the risk of non-payment for both commercial and consumer debts. An unsecured creditor can expect to receive only a small dividend (on average five cents on the dollar) from the realization of the bankrupt's assets, and frequently will receive nothing at all. Even where a secured creditor's recovery is limited to the value of the collateral, if the secured creditor is first in line, realization of 60 to 70 percent of the claim is quite common, and may be higher. (2) Even if the debtor does not become insolvent, having to sue the debtor to recover the amount owing and to levy execution on the debtor's property is time consuming and expensive.

A secured creditor, on the other hand, is free in many of the provinces, and generally under federal law, to seize the collateral and dispose of it without needing prior judicial authorization. (3) If the creditor does not take security, there is always the danger that a subsequent creditor will demand it and, thereby, acquire priority in the event of non-payment of both debts. Again, the debtor may be tempted to sell some of its assets to generate cash. Obviously this will reduce the volume and value of assets available for distribution among the debtor's creditors. (4) A secured creditor is often given power in the security agreement to monitor the debtor's affairs and such monitoring is more effective with the benefit of security than without it. The secured creditor can also threaten to seize the collateral if the debtor fails to make payment or otherwise fails to meet its obligations under the security agreement. These traditional explanations have been challenged by finance economists, who argue that the reduced risk to C from taking security is not cost-free. Typically, C will have to pay D for it in the form of a lower interest rate. C's reduced risk will be matched by an increased risk to D's other creditors and so they can be expected to raise their interest rates correspondingly. In other words, secured lending is a zero-sum game. From this perspective, the prevalence of secured lending in advanced economies is a puzzle. For a fuller discussion of the secured lending puzzle, see Part VIII, below.

C. Issues in Secured Transactions Law

Some of the key issues in secured transactions law are as follows:

1. Formal requirements—for example,
   - Does the security agreement have to be in writing?
   - Does it have to be signed?
   - Is there particular information it must contain?
   - What are the consequences if the formal requirements are not complied with?

2. Registration—for example,
   - Does the security agreement or the security interest have to be registered in a public register?
   - If so, which is the relevant register?
   - What are the consequences of failure to register?

3. Rights of the parties (C and D) between themselves—for example,
   - Is the security agreement unenforceable for non-compliance with the formal requirements?
   - Does the agreement contain particular terms that the law prohibits?
   - Is the collateral prohibited? (Common examples of prohibited collateral include after-acquired consumer goods and wages.)

4. Rights of third parties—for example,
   - If D fraudulently sells the pickup truck to T without C's consent, does T take the pickup truck free of, or subject to, C's security interest?
   - If C and C1 both have security interests in the pickup truck and D defaults, which of them has first claim on the pickup truck for satisfaction of its debt?
   - Does C's security interest have priority over D's execution creditors outside bankruptcy or over D's trustee if D becomes bankrupt?

5. Default and enforcement—for example,
   - Must C give D notice before enforcing its security interest?
   - Are there any procedural limits on C's right of seizure (repossession)?
   - If C seizes the pickup truck, must it give D a chance to redeem it before going ahead with the sale?
   - Are there any procedural limits on C's right of sale?
   - What obligations does C have to account to D or third parties for the collateral sale proceeds?
   - Apart from seizure and sale, what are the other methods open to C for enforcing its security interest?

III. PRE-PPSA FORMS OF SECURED TRANSACTION

Pre-PPSA, there were numerous forms a secured transaction might take. These formal differences mattered because they affected legal outcomes in relation to the kinds of questions listed above. The main pre-PPSA forms of secured transaction were the chattel mortgage, the pledge, the charge (or lien), the conditional sale agreement, and the various kinds of hire and purchase arrangement. The text below briefly describes these transactions, as well as accounts receivable financing and security interests in circulating assets.

A. Chattel Mortgage

A mortgage is a transfer by D to C of the collateral (the pickup truck) coupled with a provision that the mortgage will terminate when D has met his obligations to C. In other words, the mortgage is a form of conditional assignment. (This is the language the pre-PPSA bills of sale laws used.) The assignment is a conditional one because of the assignee's covenant to reassign (retransfer). In the case of a legal mortgage (a mortgage of legal title), C is the owner of the pickup truck during the term of the security agreement though typically the mortgage agreement will provide for D to have possession for as long as D is not in default. In the case of an equitable mortgage (a mortgage of an equitable interest), C has beneficial ownership during the term of the agreement.

Following the mortgage to C, D retains an equitable interest in the collateral. This is the so-called equity of redemption. The equity of redemption is founded on D's right to specific performance of C's covenant to retransfer the collateral to D at the end of the term. The equity of redemption is a proprietary interest. A second mortgage is a mortgage by D to a second creditor of D's equity of redemption. A second mortgage, as the name implies, is a second-ranking security interest in the collateral, behind C's. If D defaults, C gets first claim on the pickup truck for repayment of its mortgage debt. The secured creditor has rights with respect to any "equity" left over.

The mortgagee's historical remedy was to foreclose. Foreclosure is a court order that extinguishes D's equity of redemption. The mortgagee ends up as the outright owner of the collateral, which it takes in full satisfaction of the mortgage debt. An alternative remedy is the power of sale. The mortgagee may acquire a power of sale by: (1) agreement, (2) court order, or (3) statute. In contrast to foreclosure, exercise of the power of sale does not extinguish the mortgage debt. This means that, as a general rule, the mortgagor remains personally liable for any shortfall. The mortgagee's sale has replaced foreclosure as the standard method of enforcement. A standard form chattel mortgage agreement is reproduced in the Appendix.

B. Pledge

A pledge involves transfer by D to C of possession coupled with a right to sell the collateral if D defaults on its loan obligations. There are at least three noteworthy differences between the pledge and the mortgage. (1) The mortgage involves transfer of title by D to C, but usually not possession, whereas the pledge involves transfer of possession but not title. In other words, the mortgage is a non-possessory security interest and the pledge is a possessory security interest. (2) The mortgagee has a right of foreclosure and typically also a power of sale. At common law, the pledgee has a power of sale but no right of foreclosure. (3) In the case of a mortgage, C's right to enforce its security interest is linked conceptually to its ownership of the collateral. In the case of a pledge, C does not own the collateral and its power of sale derives from an express or implied term in the pledge agreement.

The above account describes a pledge of goods. As Ziegel explains in the extract, below, the pledging of chattels at least for commercial purposes has disappeared almost completely. However, documentary pledges still play an important role in short-term financing. The documentary pledge usually consists of negotiable instruments, securities, or documents of title (for example, bills of lading or warehouse receipts). The *Uniform Warehouse Receipts Act* explicitly establishes a negotiable type of receipt when the receipt is so marked and it spells out the consequences of its negotiability. A standard form documentary pledge agreement is reproduced in the Appendix (Form 5).

C. The Charge

There are three ways a charge (or lien) may be created: (1) agreement between the parties, (2) court order, or (3) statute. These comments focus on charges created by agreement. D by agreement gives C the right to seize and sell the collateral (the pickup truck) if D defaults and to use the sale proceeds to pay down the outstanding debt. The mortgage is a transfer form of security. By contrast, the charge is a "hypothecation." In other words, C's rights derive not from the fact of ownership, but from an express or implied term in its contract with D that C may appropriate the value of the collateral to satisfy the secured obligation in the event of D's default. In contrast to the mortgage, the chargee has no right of foreclosure because there is no equity of redemption to extinguish. The pledge is a possessory security interest. The charge—like the mortgage—is a non-possessory security interest. The charge is an equitable device. This means that, apart from statute, the chargee's interest is liable to be defeated by a bona fide purchaser of the collateral for value without notice.

D. The Conditional Sale Agreement

Consider the following case:

> C agrees to sell D a pickup truck for $100. D does not have the cash and C agrees to finance the purchase over 12 months in return for a $20 charge. D agrees to pay C the $120 by equal monthly installments. C wants security for payment.

There are various ways C and D could structure the transaction. One option would be for C to lend D the money and take a mortgage or charge over the truck. Another option would be for C to include in the contract of sale a provision reserving title in the pickup truck until D pays the last installment. D gets immediate possession of the pickup truck, but ownership stays with C for the duration of the payment period. This is the so-called conditional sale agreement. If D defaults, C can assert its right of retained ownership and claim back the pickup truck. The conditional sale agreement is a close functional equivalent of the mortgage or charge. The main difference is that it depends on title retention. By contrast, the mortgage depends on title transfer, while the charge is an hypothecation. (For the implications of this difference, pre-PPSA, see Michael G. Bridge et al., "Formalism, Functionalism and Understanding the Law of Secured Transactions" (1999), 44 *McGill LJ* 567, at 587-98.) The genesis of the conditional sale agreement lay in the bills of sale legislation. The bills of sale laws were enacted in England in the mid-19th century and the Canadian provinces enacted similar laws. Roughly speaking, a bill of sale, as defined in the legislation, is an "assurance" of chattels by D to C under which D remains in possession but C has a power of seizure and sale if D defaults in his obligations. The legislation imposed onerous registration and documentation requirements on the parties. The conditional sale agreement was a way of avoiding the bills of sale legislation. The legislation caught chattel mortgages and the like, but it did not catch conditional sale agreements. The reason is that C's power to seize the goods derives not from any grant by D, but from the fact that C retains title: *McEntire v. Crossley*, [1895] AC 457.

Pre-PPSA, conditional sale agreements in Canada were subject to provincial conditional sale agreement (CSA) statutes. The CSAs restricted the seller's enforcement rights and imposed mandatory registration requirements. In both respects, the CSAs moved the law governing conditional sale agreements closer to the law governing chattel mortgages. The PPSAs supersede both the bills of sale laws and the CSAs.

A standard form conditional sale agreement is reproduced in the Appendix (Form 1). Note that the agreement appears under the Canadian Imperial Bank of Commerce logo and it contemplates an "assignment and transfer" by C to CIBC. Typically, a dealer (C) will not have the resources to provide financing itself. A solution is for C to have a standing arrangement with a financial institution for the assignment of its conditional sale agreements. The financial institution acquires C's rights under the conditional sale agreement in exchange for a cash payment to C. (In the trade, this type of transaction is referred to as the dealer's "discounting" of its (chattel) paper and, in the United States, for many years, there was keen competition among finance companies to purchase the paper from dealers, especially in the auto trade.)

E. Hire-Purchase and Lease Agreements

D may agree to hire or rent or lease the pickup truck from C ("hire," "rent," and "lease" all mean the same thing). For example, the agreement may say that D is to lease the pickup truck from C for a monthly rental of $x. Beyond this basic agreement there is a range of possible variables. For example:

1. The agreement may require D to buy the pickup truck at the end of the lease period. This is an "in substance" conditional sale agreement because C has promised to sell the pickup truck and D has agreed to buy it. The parties may call the agreement a hiring agreement and they may describe the payments as rentals, but the language they use does not determine the legal characterization of the transaction: *Lee v. Butler*, [1893] 2 QB 318. This point matters because, under the *Factors Acts*, a buyer in possession may in certain circumstances transfer clear title in the goods to a third party.

2. The agreement may give D the option of buying the pickup truck and impose financial penalties if D fails to take up the option or, more typically, the agreement may give D an option to buy with no penalties attached. These are forms of a hire-purchase agreement. They are not a sale because C does not promise to sell D the goods and D does not promise to buy them until the option is exercised. Because they are hiring agreements and not sales they avoid the *Factors Acts*: *Helby v. Matthews*, [1895] AC 471.

3. There may be no express option to buy, but the agreement may be structured on the tacit understanding that D will buy the pickup truck for a predetermined price ("residual value") at the end of the lease period. This is the so-called finance lease. The finance lease is commonly used in commercial dealings to facilitate the acquisition of vehicles and other equipment. It has income tax advantages if the goods are for use in a business enterprise, because rentals may be claimed as tax deductions provided that D uses the leased equipment for the production of assessable income. The lessor, C, (usually a financial intermediary of some description) benefits from being able to claim depreciation of the goods as a tax deduction and being able to pass on that benefit in the form of a reduced interest rate to the lessee, D.

4. The agreement may simply provide for D to return the truck to C at the end of the lease period. This is a simple contract of hire.

Pre-PPSA, the provincial CSAs applied to cases (1) and (2), but not (3) and (4). The Ontario PPSA applies to cases (1) to (3), but not (4). The other provincial PPSAs apply to all four cases if the term of the lease is more than one year. For further discussion of lease agreements in the OPPSA context, see Chapters 2 and 13.

F. Accounts Receivable Financing

Accounts receivable or "receivables" or "book debts" are trade debts owing to D by D's account customers (as where D sells goods to O for $100 on 30, 60, or 90-day terms). There are two main ways D can raise money on its outstanding receivables: (1) It can assign them outright ("discount" them) to C. Assume D discounts to C for $90 the $100 debt O owes D. C and D are both better off. C acquires the right to $100 later in exchange for the payment of $90 now. Correspondingly, D gets $90 now in exchange for the right to $100 later. C and D may enter into a one-off discounting transaction. Alternatively, they may have a standing arrangement for the discounting of D's receivables from time to time (that is, a "factoring" agreement). (2) The alternative is for D to borrow money from C against D's receivables: for example, D borrows $90 from C and gives C a security interest in O's $100 debt to secure repayment of the loan. The security interest means that if D defaults on the loan, C can look to O's obligation as a source of payment.

The two forms of transaction described above (security and non-security assignments) are functionally alike. An important difference is that, in the first case (the non-security or outright assignment), C bears the risk of O's non-payment whereas in the second case (the security assignment) D bears the risk. The risk is with C in the first case because, unless there is a provision in the contract to say otherwise, if O fails to pay, C cannot call on D to pay instead. The risk is with D in the second case because, if O fails to pay, C can sue D on D's personal obligation under the loan contract. In the first case (the non-security or outright assignment), C may bargain for a right of recourse against D. In other words, the agreement may say that if O fails to pay, C may look to D for payment instead. In effect, D guarantees to C the performance of O's payment obligation. A recourse agreement like this eliminates the difference identified above. In other words, in the case of both a non-security or outright assignment with recourse and a security assignment it is ultimately D, not C, who bears the risk of O's non-payment. Following the US Article 9 lead, the application of the PPSAs extends to non-security assignments. The usual justification is the functional similarity between security and non-security assignments. For a contrary view, see Michael G. Bridge et al., "Formalism, Functionalism and Understanding the Law of Secured Transactions" (1999), 44 *McGill LJ* 567, at 580-87, arguing that: (1) "sale and security remain distinct transactions even in a functionalist world"; and (2) "the only really persuasive justification for including both sale and security assignments ... within Article 9 and the PPSAs is that they both fall within the general regulatory objectives underlying the Article 9 and PPSA perfection and priority framework." Article 9 is discussed later in this chapter.

C and D may negotiate an assignment on either a notification or non-notification basis. In the case of a notification assignment, C or D notifies O of the assignment and O pays C on the due date. In the case of a non-notification assignment, the parties do not notify O and, if all goes well, O will never learn of the assignment. O pays D on the due date and D accounts to C for the payment. In substance, D acts as C's collection agent. Before the PPSAs were enacted, notification had legal consequences. (1) Notification was one of the require- ments for a valid assignment at law of a chose in action. Non-notification assignments were valid only in equity. The difference had procedural implications. (A "chose in action" is a right to recover a sum of money. A debt is a chose in action.) (2) Notification was relevant in the case of a priority dispute by virtue of the rule in *Dearle v. Hall* (1823), 3 Russ. 1. According to the rule in *Dearle v. Hall*, if there is a competition between two or more as- signees of the same chose in action, priority turns in part on which assignee is first to notify O of its interest. (Under the PPSAs, notification is no longer relevant in either of these senses.) Why might D prefer not to notify O? One possible reason is because a non- notification assignment does not disturb existing payment arrangements between D and its account customers. Another possible reason is a desire for secrecy—D may worry that if outsiders find out that D is factoring its receivables, they may infer, rightly or wrongly, that D is in financial difficulty. A third reason may be that C lacks collection facilities.

G. Security Interests in Circulating Assets

Consider the following case:

> D is a trader. D wants to borrow money from C to finance its business. D has fixed assets, including plant and equipment. It also has circulating assets, specifically: (1) its stock- in-trade ("inventory") and (2) its accounts receivable ("accounts"). D's inventory and ac- counts are circulating assets in the sense that, unlike fixed assets, D does not intend them to remain in the business. D's intention is to turn them over to generate new wealth: sales of inventory generate accounts; collection of accounts generates liquid proceeds (cash and the like); the proceeds allow D to purchase new inventory and the cycle starts again.

Can circulating assets be used as collateral? There are two potential problems: (1) the after-acquired property problem; and (2) the right of disposal problem.

1. The After-Acquired Property Problem

Circulating assets circulate. This means that C's security interest must cover not just the in- ventory D has in stock at the date of the security agreement but also D's future inventory. Likewise, it must cover not just C's present accounts but future ones as well. This raises the question, how can D give C an interest in property that D does not presently own? At com- mon law, the *nemo dat quod non habet* idea was a major obstacle to dealings in future or after-acquired property: the common law could not conceive of a seller or mortgagor pass- ing title in goods it did not yet own. However, equity came to the rescue. Assume C and D enter into a security agreement on September 1 covering D's present and after-acquired in- ventory. On September 15, D gets in a new batch of inventory (the "new inventory"). At common law, C has no interest in the new inventory on September 1 because, at that date, D has nothing to transfer (*nemo dat quod non habet*). Nor does C acquire any interest on

September 15 without some further act of assurance on D's part. In equity, C likewise acquires no interest on September 1. However, it may acquire an interest on September 15 as soon as the new inventory comes into D's hands. This is on the basis of the maxim, "equity deems as done what ought to be done." If C has given value pursuant to its agreement with D in exchange for D's promise of a security interest in the new inventory, this is normally enough to attract the operation of the maxim: *Tailby v. Official Receiver* (1888), 13 AC 523; cf. *Holroyd v. Marshall* (1861-62), 11 EE 999, 10 HLC 191. The upshot, pre-PPSA, is that by virtue of the September 1 agreement, C on September 15 acquires an equitable security interest in the new inventory without the need for any further assurance on D's part. The PPSAs substitute statutory rules for equitable doctrine with the aim of facilitating security interests in after-acquired property.

2. The Right of Disposal Problem

Where the collateral is circulating assets—for example, inventory—the security agreement must either expressly or by implication give D a right to dispose of the collateral in the ordinary course of D's business. Why? Because if C's security interest prevents D from selling its inventory, then the inventory will cease to be circulating assets and D's business will likely grind to a halt. This is also the case, if C and D enter into a receivables financing agreement on a non-notification basis. In that case, it will be self-defeating if C's security interest prevents D from collecting its accounts and putting the proceeds back into the business. This raises the question, how can D give C a security interest in its inventory, accounts, and the like, but at the same time reserve a right of disposal?

In *Benedict v. Ratner*, 268 US 353 (1925), the US Supreme Court struck down a non-notification receivables financing agreement on the ground that a transfer of property that reserves a right of disposal to the transferor is void as against D's creditors under the fraudulent conveyance laws. The parties cannot have it both ways. Either D intends to assign the collateral to C or it does not. The reservation to D of a right of disposal is inconsistent with an intention to assign. D must either give up "dominion" over the collateral or run the risk of a court concluding that the assignment is not a genuine one. To escape the decision, future lenders were forced into exercising dominion over their security. What came to be the standard practice in non-notification receivables financing was for the assignor to remit the collection proceeds daily to the assignee, subject to re-remittance to the assignor at a later date. The reasoning in *Benedict v. Ratner* applied equally to inventory financing agreements and, again, to avoid the decision, financers were forced to exercise dominion over the collateral. Field warehousing was one method of meeting this requirement. There were others. This and other artificial forms of transaction that were devised with the same end in view persisted until the advent of Article 9 of the Uniform Commercial Code. Article 9 abolishes the dominion rule and reverses *Benedict v. Ratner*.

Anglo-Canadian law took a different path. The English courts developed the floating charge in response to the right of disposal problem and the Canadian courts followed suit. The floating charge is an equitable charge (or lien), typically over assets such as inventory and accounts and their proceeds. Recall that a charge is a form of hypothecation. It gives C the right to claim payment out of a particular fund or asset belonging to D. What makes the floating charge distinctive is that so long as D does not default, the charge does not attach to any particular asset. Instead it "floats" over D's shifting mass of assets. While the floating charge remains in this suspensory state, D is free to deal with the collateral, subject to any restrictions the agreement may stipulate. There is no interference with C's rights because C has no rights to any specific asset. The picture changes when D defaults. Subject to the terms of C and D's agreement, default causes the floating charge to "crystallize." Crystallization brings to an end the suspensory state of the charge. It converts the floating charge into a fixed charge over whatever collateral D happens to own at that point and it deprives D of its freedom to deal with the collateral. C's usual remedy upon crystallization is to appoint a receiver.* The receiver's function is to take control of D's business, collect in and liquidate the collateral and pay over the sale proceeds to C in full or partial satisfaction of D's debt. For a simple floating charge agreement, see the standard form demand debenture reproduced in the Appendix (Form 4). The floating charge is still widely used in England. In Canada, the PPSAs incorporate a statutory set of rules that to some extent mimic floating charge outcomes with a view to facilitating security interests in circulating assets. However, it is now settled that the English-style floating charge itself is dead in the PPSA jurisdictions. See Chapter 4. On the other hand, receiverships remain alive and well and are expressly recognized in the PPSAs: see Chapter 13, Part VII.

IV. PRE-PPSA PATTERNS OF REGULATION

Jacob S. Ziegel, "Canadian Chattel Security Law: Past Experience and Current Developments"
in J.G. Sauveplanne, ed., *Security Over Corporeal Moveables* (Leiden: A.W. Sijthoff, 1974), 71, at 83-86 (footnotes omitted)

I have already described the use to which particular security devices are put in Canada. In the present section I should like to draw attention to some of the more salient features of the principal devices and the extent to which they are subject to statutory regulation. This brief discussion will also provide an introduction to the shortcomings of the existing Canadian law, a theme that is more fully developed in a subsequent section.

1. The Pledge. As elsewhere, this is the oldest of our security devices and, as has been previously explained, documentary pledges still serve an important role in short term financing. Their importance is partly recognized in the Uniform Warehouse Receipts Act which was adopted by the Canadian Uniformity Commissioners in 1945 and is now in force in six provinces. The Act explicitly establishes a negotiable type of receipt when the receipt is so marked and spells out the consequences of its negotiability.

Apart from these exceptions, there has been little attempt to put the documentary pledge to new uses. The ingenious field warehousing receipt invented in the US is sparingly used in Canada and its status is still unsettled. A probable reason for this reticence

---

* There was no rule against the secured party enforcing the charge itself, but it was not recommended because of the strict "anti-waste" rules that 19th-century courts applied against the charge. Receivership provisions overcome this difficulty by deeming the receiver to be the debtor's agent.

is that less expensive and reasonably effective security devices are available for inventory financing purposes, which was not true of American law at the time when field warehousing was first introduced there. For obvious reasons the pledging of chattels for commercial purposes has disappeared almost completely. Even pawnbroking has suffered a marked decline as standards of living have improved and more sophisticated methods of consumer financing have taken its place.

2. Conditional Sale Agreements, Hire-Purchase Agreements, and Equipment Leases. The conditional sale agreement first became common in Canada around the 1860s and it still enjoys high popularity among sellers and sales finance companies as a purchase money security device. The Canadian common law early adopted the principle of English law that the parties to a sale agreement are free to postpone the vesting of title of goods in the buyer until a future time and this rule was subsequently enshrined in the provincial Sale of Goods Acts. However, it seemed wrong to the commercial community that a buyer should enjoy the appearance of ownership without its reality and thus from 1882 onwards legislation was adopted by the provinces requiring conditional sale agreements to be registered in a designated public office. These requirements still exist. Some provinces permitted the seller to attach his name and address to the goods as a substitute for registration but this alternative fortunately has now been dropped. In 1922 the Conference of Commissioners on Uniformity of Legislation in Canada adopted a Uniform Conditional Sales Act and this Act was subsequently revised in 1947 and 1955. In its original or revised form the Uniform Act has been copied, wholly or in part, by many of the provinces.

The major difficulty about the conditional sale agreement has been with respect to its characterization. From the start there has been an almost continuous seesaw battle between those courts that regarded it as merely a short form of chattel mortgage, those who saw it as an executory agreement of sale, and those courts who could not quite make up their minds one way or the other. Surprising as it may seem, the various conditional sales acts never put to rest this important controversy.

The definition of conditional sale agreement in most of the provincial acts is wide enough to catch any bailment of goods with an option to purchase, but hire-purchase agreements of the English type are not common in Canada. Equipment leases, on the other hand, have grown rapidly in popularity and the courts have held that they are not governed by the conditional sales acts in the absence of an option to purchase even though in other respects the lease may be only a disguised conditional sale. As in the UK, lessors have sought to protect themselves against premature termination of the agreement by various types of deficiency or minimum payment clauses. By and large the Canadian courts have uncritically applied the English jurisprudence and in this way reached the same unsatisfactory results.

3. The Chattel Mortgage and Floating Charge. The chattel mortgage is a much more flexible instrument than the conditional sale agreement since, first, it can be used to secure a sale on credit as well as a straight loan, secondly, because it is available to cover future as well as present advances and, thirdly, because it may cover after-acquired as well as existing collateral. These features are of course very important in inventory financing where the parties are engaged in a continuous series of transactions and there is a constant flow of goods in and out of the debtor's premises.

The disadvantages of the chattel mortgage as it has evolved in Canada are almost as great as its advantages. Registration requirements began to be adopted in Canada as early as 1849 and were subsequently enshrined by the Uniformity Commissioners in the Uniform Bills of Sale and Chattel Mortgage Act of 1928. What made the statute particularly onerous was the necessity to append to each agreement two highly technical affidavits of bona fides and execution. The courts have often applied the affidavit requirements with Draconian severity and many a secured lender has met his Waterloo on this particular battleground! A second shortcoming was the doubt, which still exists, whether and to what extent future advances can be secured under the Acts and the need to file a new document each time a new agreement is concluded between the parties. A further and equally serious shortcoming arises out of the decision in *Joseph v. Lyons*, which has been followed in Canada.

It was held by the Supreme Court of Canada in *Gordon Mackay & Co. Ltd. v. J.A. Larocque Ltd.* that the Ontario Bills of Sale Act then in force applied to a corporate debenture secured by a fixed and floating charge. This result was felt to be inconvenient. All the provincial acts require chattel mortgage filings to be renewed every two or three years whereas many corporate securities are of a long term character and may not mature for twenty years or more. To overcome the effects of the decision the Uniformity Commissioners adopted in 1931 a Uniform Corporation Securities Registration Act. This does not however dispose of all the problems. One of the persistent difficulties which the Canadian courts have experienced is to draw a satisfactory distinction between a specific mortgage coupled with a licence to carry on business by the debtor and a floating charge in the English sense. The difference may materially affect the position of the secured creditor vis-à-vis third parties. In my opinion, the problem can only satisfactorily be dealt with by legislation, although it is by no means clear that this has happened in the Ontario Personal Property Security Act.

4. Inventory Financing and the Section 88 Security [now s. 427]. The American trust receipt was never adopted in Canada but we have a close analogue in Section 88 of the federal Bank Act. In several respects it is a superior instrument to the inventory financing device sanctioned in the Uniform Trust Receipts Act because it is much less technical and more flexible.

It was a widely held dogma in Canada in the last century that the only forms of security suitable for banking loans were those which were highly liquid in character and easily realizable in an emergency. Goods and merchandise not represented by documents of title or warehouse receipts did not fall into this category and the banks were prohibited from taking this form of collateral as security. The prohibition threatened to impede the development of the important agricultural, lumber and extractive industries. To meet their needs for working capital a series of exceptions were made beginning in 1861. The earliest exceptions made use of a fiction and permitted a warehouseman and other specified classes of persons to issue and pledge warehouse receipts even though the issuer of the receipt was also the owner of the goods. In 1890 the fiction was abandoned and banks were now permitted to grant loans against the security of the inventory of manufacturers and certain types of wholesalers without the pretence of a documentary pledge. Over the next seventy years the range of acceptable collateral was gradually expanded to include various forms of farmers' and fishermen's assets but the stock-in-trade of merchants and retail stores generally remained outside the charmed circle.

The section of the Bank Act containing these exceptions is Section 88 and the security taken pursuant to it is generally referred to as a "Section 88" security. The Bank Act was completely revised in 1967, but the Section 88 provisions were left unaltered.

From the legal point of view the special significance of the section resides in its perfection requirements. Originally all that was required was a short document signed by the borrower granting the bank a Section 88 security interest in the goods, present or future, which could be described in the most general terms. The effect of the agreement was to vest in the bank a legal title in the collateral which took priority over all subsequently created security interests. Until 1923 nothing was required to be filed, but since that time the bank's security interest is not perfected until a 'notice of intention to give a Section 88 security' has been filed in one of the regional offices of the Bank of Canada. This one-page document is even briefer than the agreement to which it relates and is a model of simplicity. It represents in fact the Canadian counterpart of notice filing and corresponds closely to the Notice of Intention formerly required to be filed under the Uniform Trust Receipts Act and now continued in Article 9 of the Uniform Commercial Code.

One of several shortcomings about Section 88 is that it does not deal with the bank's rights with respect to the proceeds of the disposition of the inventory. However, a recent decision of the Supreme Court of Canada has bridged the gap to some extent by holding that the bank's security shifts automatically from the inventory to the proceeds and is not dependent on any new agreement between the parties.

5. *Assignment of Book Debts (Accounts Receivable Financing).* Reference has already been made to the important position which accounts receivable financing occupies in Canada. Its popularity is explained in part by the liquid character of the security and the relative simplicity of the statutory formalities. Until 1919 such assignments were not subject to any registration requirement although the secured party's priority was (and still is) liable to be defeated under the rule in *Dearle v. Hall.* An amendment to the federal Bankruptcy Act adopted in that year avoided general assignment of book debts against a trustee in bankruptcy unless the debt had been paid at the time of the bankruptcy or the assignment had been registered in accordance with provincial requirements. The provinces responded with a Uniform Assignment of Book Debts Act which was first adopted by the Uniformity Commissioners in 1928. This Act, like Section 43 of the English Bankruptcy Act, applies to any assignment of present and future book debts other than an assignment of book debts due at the date of assignment from specific debtors "or becoming due under specified contracts."

Two major difficulties confront the accounts receivable financer under existing Canadian law. The first is to know whether the courts will treat the assignment as a floating charge or as a specific charge. As we have seen, the identical problem arises in the inventory financing field. The second is the rule in *Dearle v. Hall,* which may cause him to lose his priority to a subsequent assignee who gives notice of the assignment to the account debtor before he does. Obviously the general assignee cannot be expected to give notice to an account debtor who may not even exist at the time of the original assignment. Even if he could give notice the common law requirement is commercially quite unreasonable. The failure to deal with this hiatus constitutes a serious blemish on the Canadian law. A further difficulty may be mentioned and this is that the accounts receivable financer may not always have notice of a proceeds clause under an inventory financing agreement since, as previously noted, the agreement does not have to be registered under the Assignment of Book Debts Acts.

V. ARTICLE 9 OF THE AMERICAN UNIFORM COMMERCIAL CODE

American chattel security law in the pre-Article 9 period suffered from the same shortcomings as its Canadian counterpart and from a good many more. In general, American state law was not as generous to secured creditors as Canadian law. In particular, many states imposed significant restrictions on the validity of "after-acquired" property clauses or did not recognize them at all. The doctrine in *Benedict v. Ratner*, 268 US 353 (1925), held that an accounts receivable financer (and by inference an inventory financer as well) could not enforce its security interest against the debtor's creditors unless the secured party also carefully policed the debtor's collection of receivables and required the debtor to account for them. American common law never adopted the English-style fixed and floating charge. The *Uniform Trust Receipts Act*, adopted in 1933 by the National Conference of Commissioners on Uniform State Law (NCCUSL), was designed to facilitate inventory financing in domestic transactions, but the Act itself was highly technical and difficult to interpret.

In 1942 the NCCUSL launched its ambitious Uniform Commercial Code project in conjunction with the American Law Institute. The revision and integration of the uniform laws on chattel security comprised an important part of this effort. Professor Grant Gilmore of the Yale Law School and Professor Allison Dunham of the University of Chicago Law School were appointed joint reporters of what became Article 9 of the Code. After attempting to deal separately with different forms of secured financing, they independently reached the conclusion that this was unnecessary and that all forms of financing and the different types of security devices could be accommodated in a single article of the *Code on Secured Transactions*.

The first version of the Code was completed in 1951. A revised *Official Text* appeared in 1962. A further revision, adopted in 1972, incorporated important changes recommended by the Article 9 Review Committee. Smaller changes, conforming to those made in Article 8, were added in 1978 to take account of certificateless securities. In 1987, the Code's sponsors added a new article to the Code, Article 2A—Leases—which is concerned with personal property leases. At the same time, the definition of "security interest" in UCC 1-201(37) was completely recast. Article 9 has just been through a major revision process. Revised Article 9 was drafted over a six-year period by a drafting committee established by the Code's sponsors and it was approved by the sponsors in 1998. It came into effect on July 1, 2001 and it has been approved by all states and the District of Columbia. The following passages are extracted from Jacob S. Ziegel and David L. Denomme, *The Ontario Personal Property Security Act: Commentary and Analysis*, 2d ed. (Markham, ON: Butterworths, 2000), lix-lxi. They identify the features of revised Article 9 that are likely to be of most interest to Canadian lawyers.

American Developments—New Article 9

The adoption of a totally revised Article 9 is undoubtedly the single most important development in the US New Article 9 was drafted in the remarkably short space of 6 years by a drafting committee established by the Code's sponsors, and was approved by the sponsors in 1998. Article 9 will come into effect on July 1, 2001. As of August 2000, it had been approved by 27 states and in the District of Columbia, and is expected to be approved by most of the states by the operative date.

New Article 9 is much longer and more complex than its predecessor, the 1972 revised Article 9. The sections have also been reorganized to follow what the drafters believed to be a more logical sequence, and a new Part 4 has been added. Despite the many changes, the organizing principles and concepts of new Article 9 remain the same as in old Article 9, though to a Canadian reader approaching new Article 9 for the first (or even a second) time it may sometimes be difficult to see the wood for the trees. In the space at our disposal, it is impossible to provide even an adequate summary of the many changes appearing in new Article 9 and we therefore confine ourselves to a brief description of those features likely to be of greatest interest to Canadian lawyers.

- *Expanded Scope.* New Article 9 for the first time allows a security interest in a deposit account unlike old Article 9 which only recognized a security interest in a deposit account as proceeds from dealings in other collateral. The definition of "account" in new Article 9 has been greatly expanded to include many new types of rights to payment of a monetary obligation. A new class of collateral, "payment intangible," defined as a general intangible under which the account debtor's principal obligation is a monetary obligation, has been created but only applies to sales. Apparently, the purpose of the new classification is to legitimate sales of loan participations and to ensure that sales of payment intangibles are not required to be perfected by registration: rather such security interests are deemed to be automatically perfected once the security interest has attached. New Article 9 also brings within its scope non-possessory statutory agricultural liens, "true" consignments-bailments for the purpose of sale by the consignee, supporting obligations to a debt or other liability (such as a guarantee or letter of credit) and property securing rights to payment and the assignment of commercial tort claims.
- *Choice of Law Provisions.* The single most important change in this area involves the rules governing the perfection of non-possessory security interests in collateral. For most purposes, new Article 9 requires perfection in compliance with the law of the jurisdiction where the debtor is located. In the case of a "registered organization," such as a corporation or limited liability company, this means the state under whose law the debtor is organized. This rule is designed to make it much easier to determine the location of business debtors and optimally to ascertain from a single search what non-possessory security interests have been given by a registered organization.
- *Perfection of Security Interests in Deposit Accounts.* From a Canadian perspective, a striking feature of the new Article 9 perfection rules is that a security interest in deposit accounts can generally only be perfected by the secured party taking control of the deposit account. A secured party is deemed, *inter alia*, to have control of an account when, with the consent of the debtor, the secured party obtains the depository bank's agreement to act on the secured party's instructions or when the secured party is itself the depository bank.

- *New Priority Rules.* New Article 9 contains several new priority rules relating to banks and deposit accounts that are very favourable to depository institutions. Of particular interest is Section 9-340(a) which, subject to the exception noted below, confers on a bank with which a deposit account is maintained the right to exercise a right of recoupment or set-off against a secured party that holds a security interest in the deposit account. The exception applies where the secured party has perfected its security interest in the deposit account by control, as that term has been previously explained.

New Article 9 also clarifies the scope of purchase money security interests in *non*-consumer goods transactions by allowing a PMSI interest to enjoy a dual status, and by expanding the scope of PMSIs for inventory financing purposes by recognizing a revolving PMSI for this type of collateral.

- *Contents of Financing Statements.* New Part 5 of Article 9 addresses some of the same problems that Canadian courts have had to contend with in interpreting the provincial PPSAs. Section 9-503 spells out the rules for identifying the debtor's name in a financing statement but it is not clear whether, and to what extent, these rules can be supplemented by regulations. Section 9-506(a) retains the rule in old Section 9-402(8) that an error or omission in a financing statement does not invalidate the financing statement unless the defect is seriously misleading. Pursuant to Section 9-506(b) and (c) a financing statement that fails to state the debtor's name in conformity with Section 9-503(a) is seriously misleading unless a search of the records of the filing office under the debtor's correct name, using the filing office's standard search logic, would disclose the financing statement with the given name description.
- *Default and Enforcement.* Part 6 of new Article 9 (Part 5 of old Article 9) considerably expands the old provisions by spelling out much more fully the parties entitled to receive notification of the secured party's intention to dispose of the collateral, the rights and duties of a secondary obligor, and the effect of noncompliance by the secured party with the Part 6 requirements in consumer and non-consumer transactions. Section 9-620(a) is of particular interest in so far as it permits a secured party to accept collateral in partial as well as in full satisfaction of the obligation secured. Section 9-622(b) clarifies the effect of such a foreclosure on the rights of junior secured parties.

VI. THE CANADIAN PPSAs

In 1959, the then attorney general of Ontario invited a committee of the Canadian Bar Association to review the provincial registration statutes and to make recommendations for their improvement. The committee's attention was drawn to Article 9. It liked what it saw and endorsed the Article 9 approach. The committee then set about to prepare an Ontario version of Article 9. The task was completed in 1963 and, after various reviews, the *Personal Property Security Act* was enacted by the Ontario legislature in 1967. However, only that part of the Act involving the establishment of a central registry came into effect on royal assent to the Bill. The rest of the Act, the major part, was not proclaimed until 1976.

The Ontario initiative was followed with interest in the other provinces. In 1964 the Canadian Bar Association established a special committee to determine whether or not it was feasible to adapt the then proposed Ontario Act so that it could be a model for similar legislation in other provinces. The committee decided to prepare a model *Personal Property Security Act* that would serve as the basis for reform of personal property security law throughout the country. The committee published the *Uniform Personal Property Security Act* in 1969. This was adopted by the Canadian Bar Association in 1970 and provided the pattern for the 1973 Manitoba Act.

While the 1969 Uniform Act adopted most features of the 1967 Ontario Act, it differed in some important respects. Thereafter, the committee monitored the operation of the Ontario Act and developments in the United States. The very substantial revisions of Article 9 of the Uniform Commercial Code that were made in 1972 and the weaknesses in the Ontario Act and the 1969 Uniform Act induced the committee to prepare a second draft of the Uniform Act. In the meantime the Saskatchewan Law Reform Commission published a report in 1971 proposing a *Personal Property Security Act* for Saskatchewan based in part on the Uniform Act, but containing a number of significant new features. The Saskatchewan Legislature responded by enacting a *Personal Property Security Act* in 1980. The *Model Uniform Personal Property Security Act*, adopted by the Canadian Bar Association and the Uniform Law Conference in 1982, replicated many of the features of the Saskatchewan Act.

When it became clear in 1984, with the release of the *Report of the Minister's Advisory Committee on the Personal Property Security Act* that Ontario would not adopt the 1982 *Uniform Personal Property Security Act* as a model for further reform of personal property security legislation in that province, the Western Canada Personal Property Security Act Committee was formed. The goal of the committee was to develop a model for adoption by jurisdictions in western Canada. This model ultimately provided the basis for the British Columbia, Alberta, and Northwest Territories Acts and the new Saskatchewan and Manitoba Acts. In 1991, the Western Canada Personal Property Security Act Committee was reconstituted as the Canadian Conference on Personal Property Security Law (CCPPSL).

In autumn 1988, the Alberta Legislature enacted a *Personal Property Security Act* and in the early summer of 1989 the BC *Personal Property Security Act* was passed. Minor housekeeping amendments were made to both of these Acts before they came into force in 1990. Saskatchewan adopted a revised PPSA in 1993 (SS 1993, c. P-6.2), which came into force on April 1, 1995. Manitoba also adopted a new Act in 1995, but it was only recently proclaimed, on September 5, 2000. New Brunswick enacted a statute based on the CCPPSL Model Act in 1993 (SNB 1993, c. P-7.1) and it came into force on April 18, 1995. The other maritime provinces and Newfoundland and Labrador have all since followed suit: SNS 1995-1996, c. 13 (in force, November 3, 1997); SPEI 1997, c. 33 (in force April 27, 1998), SNL 1998, c. P-7.1 (in force February 12, 1999). The maritime regimes share common computer facilities and their registries are administered by a common administrator.

The Ontario position has not remained static. In 1976, the minister of consumer and commercial relations established an advisory committee on the PPSA to prepare a revised Act in the light of the 1972 amendments to Article 9 and the work of the Model Uniform PPSA committee. The advisory committee reported in June 1984 with an accompanying draft revised Act. See *Report of the Minister's Advisory Committee on the Personal Property Security Act* (Toronto, June 1984). The committee issued a supplementary report in January 1986 incorporating changes in the draft Act and responding to the many briefs received by it on its original report. The new legislation, the *Personal Property Security Act, 1989*, was enacted in March 1989 and came into force in October 1989. The new Act closely follows the recommendations of the advisory committee except in one important respect. The Ontario government did not follow the committee's recommendation that leases of goods for a year or more and commercial consignment agreements be included in the scope provisions of the Act, whether or not the lease or consignment agreement was a true security agreement. In October 1998, the Canadian Bar Association—Ontario Committee on Personal Property Security Law made a submission to the minister of consumer and commercial relations recommending reforms to the Ontario PPSA. The CBAO submission contains 28 specific recommendations and 7 general recommendations (details of the main recommendations are discussed in the following chapters of this book according to the context to which they relate). Legislation giving effect to the committee's "non-controversial" recommendations was enacted in 2000. Most of the remaining recommendations were implemented by legislation enacted in 2006. These changes go some way toward narrowing the gap between the Ontario Act and the PPSAs of the other provinces. However, they will not achieve full uniformity. While favouring the greatest possible degree of harmonization between Ontario and the other provinces, the committee did not think it was realistic to expect Ontario to repeal its Act in favour of the CCPPSL Model Act and it did not favour such a step: Canadian Bar Association—Ontario, *Submission to the Minister of Consumer and Commercial Relations Concerning the Personal Property Security Act* (Toronto: CBAO, 1988), 4.

The *Securities Transfer Act*, SO 2006, c. 8 (STA) makes major changes to the law governing the purchase and sale of investment property and, simultaneously with its enactment, cognate provisions were incorporated in the OPPSA to deal with security interests in investment property. The *Securities Transfer Act* is based on Article 8 of the United States Uniform Commercial Code and the cognate OPPSA reforms derive from Revised Article 9. The other provinces have enacted, or are in the process of enacting, corresponding laws with the aim of achieving uniformity across Canada.

In Quebec, the new *Civil Code*, with its completely recast provisions on security interests in movables, came into effect on January 1, 1994. The new Code adopts a generic non-possessory hypothec for movables. In this, and in other respects, the new regime has been significantly influenced by Article 9 concepts. However, the assimilation is not a complete one and the Quebec provisions are quite distinctive. Among other important differences, the Code does not treat conditional sale agreements, equipment leases, and similar quasi-security devices as creating a hypothec, though they are subject to registration requirements.

At the national level, the Canadian Conference on Personal Property Security Law provides a forum for the exchange of information on PPS issues and for discussion of provincial and international developments. The conference undertook a study of revised Article 9 with a view to determining which of its features are suitable for adoption in Canada as part of a future package of amendments to the CCPPSL Model *Personal Property Security Act*: R.C.C. Cuming and Catherine Walsh, "Potential Changes to the Model Personal Property Security Act of the Canadian Conference on Personal Property Security Law, Part 1 (ss. 1-41)" (paper presented at the Montreal annual CCPPSL conference, May 27-31, 2000 and in revised form at the annual meeting of the Uniform Law Conference of Canada, Victoria, BC, August 2000). There is also a project under way to achieve greater harmonization between the Ontario PPSA and the legislation in other provinces that is based on the CCPPSL Model Act.

VII. LEGISLATIVE OBJECTIVES

Before focusing on the detailed features of the *Personal Property Security Act*, it is important to consider the legislative objectives underlying it. The Act contains an elaborate and detailed system for the regulation of personal property security transactions. It is not just a consolidation of prior law. Not only does it employ new concepts and legislative approaches, but, in addition, embedded in its provisions are important policy choices that affect credit grantors, credit users, unsecured creditors, and buyers dealing with credit users. The full implications of these concepts, approaches, and policy choices and the significance of the differences in approach and choices among the Acts are becoming progressively clearer as experience is gained by their practical operation.

A comparison of the *Personal Property Security Act* with the personal property security law it replaced highlights several of its most important features: structural integration, conceptual unity, comprehensiveness, legal predictability, accommodation of modern business financing techniques, and detailed regulation of default rights and remedies.

A. Structural Integration

The Act prescribes a single system of law in place of the disparate and sometimes conflicting structures of common law, equity, and statutory law relating to security agreements existing before its enactment. While the Act does not completely pre-empt common law and equitable principles, it leaves little scope for the continued recognition of differences between the traditional types of security agreements such as conditional sales contracts, equitable chattel mortgages, legal chattel mortgages, assignment of choses in action, and floating charges.

B. Conceptual Unity

Structural integration was made possible by the legislative recognition of a single generic concept as the central feature of all security agreements providing for an interest in property to secure performance of an obligation.

At common law and equity, the primary mechanisms for securing obligations involved the security transfer of title (legal or equitable) in the obligor's personal property in favour of the secured party, the retention of title by the seller where the obligation arose out of the sale of property, or the creation of equitable charges and special property interests. The fact that different types of interests were involved dictated that differences would exist among the various types of security devices with respect to both *inter partes* and priority rights. It also prevented the consistent and rational development of personal property security law.

Neither form nor locus of title to collateral plays a significant role as a determinant of the application of the PPSA or the rules applicable to a particular transaction. So long as it creates or provides for an interest in personal property to secure payment or performance of an obligation, a transaction falls within the scope of the Act (see OPPSA s. 1(1) "security agreement" and s. 2 "security interest"). The Act does draw distinctions between types of transactions, but not on the basis of form or locus of title. Purely functional considerations provide justification for differential treatment. For example, security agreements providing for purchase-money security interests (PMSIs) (OPPSA ss. 1(1) "purchase-money security interest" 20(3) and 33) or security interests in chattel paper (OPPSA ss. 1(1) "chattel paper" and 28(3)) are given, for public policy and commercial reasons, a special priority status if prescribed conditions are met.

C. Comprehensiveness

The PPSA is not a code of law in the sense that it is totally self-contained. Nevertheless, it is much more complete than anything existing before its enactment. The statutory personal property security law that the Act replaced focused primarily on forcing public disclosure of the existence of security interests. Loss of priority to other persons claiming interests in the collateral was the consequence of non-compliance with public disclosure requirements. Apart from this, priority issues were left to be resolved by common law and equity principles.

The PPSA deals with a wide range of matters involving personal property security transactions, including the form of a security agreement (OPPSA ss. 9, 11(2), 12-17, 59); the creation of a security interest (OPPSA ss. 11-13); perfection of the security interest and registration rules (OPPSA ss. 22-46, 41-57); a complete set of rules to determine priorities among competing interests (OPPSA ss. 27-37); the rights and remedies of the secured party in the event of the debtor's default (OPPSA ss. 57.1-66); and choice of law rules governing the validity and perfection of foreign security interests (OPPSA ss. 5-8).

D. Legal Predictability

The ability to predict accurately the relative priority position a credit grantor will occupy in the event it is required to rely on a security interest is often an important consideration in the initial decision to grant credit. The lack of a single, integrated system of priority rules that characterized prior law meant that a decision whether or not to grant credit often had to be made in the context of considerable legal uncertainty about the outcome of a priority dispute involving other claims to the collateral. The much more complete priority system of the PPSA not only ensures greater consistency in court decisions dealing with priority disputes, but also facilitates more accurate assessment of the legal risks involved in granting credit.

E. Accommodation of Modern Business Financing

While equity facilitated business financing through its recognition of equitable interests in after-acquired property, much more was required to bring the law abreast of the needs of modern business financing. The PPSA was designed to do this. The Act permits parties to a security agreement a large measure of freedom to tailor their agreement to fit their particular circumstances (OPPSA s. 9). A security interest can be taken in a revolving line of inventory (OPPSA s. 12). A line of credit can be secured without fear of loss of priority to intervening interests (OPPSA ss. 13, 30(4)). Special priority rules are included to deal with the distinctive features of the purchase and sale of chattel paper (OPPSA s. 28(3)). Perhaps the most important feature of the Act in this context is the flexibility supplied by the notice filing registration system (OPPSA ss. 45-46, 18).

F. Regulation of Default Rights and Remedies

Under prior law the relative rights of the secured party and the debtor in the event of default by the debtor depended upon the type of security agreement involved and the terms of the agreement. Proceeding from the premise that all security agreements are designed to accomplish the same end, PPSA prescribes a detailed system for the regulation of default rights and remedies that is designed to provide consistency and fairness in the enforcement of security interests (OPPSA ss. 57.1-66).

The Acts based on the CCPPSL model contain provisions dealing with several important aspects of receiverships. See, for example, BCPPSA ss. 64-66. The OPPSA does little more than recognize the use of receiverships and provide for general judicial supervision of the conduct of receivers (OPPSA s. 60).

VIII. THE SECURED LENDING PUZZLE

John Armour, "The Law and Economics Debate About Secured Lending: Lessons for European Lawmaking?"
(2008), 5 *European Company and Financial L Rev.* 3, Part 2

General theories of secured credit

What does secured credit do?

The grant of a security interest may be understood from a functional perspective as conferring upon the lender two sets of entitlements, which relate respectively to *priority* of payment and to *control* of the collateral. The control rights are what economists call "state contingent," because their extent is contingent on whether the debtor continues to meet their obligations under the loan. Provided the debtor is not in default, the secured creditor's control is of a purely negative variety, consisting of the ability to veto sales of the collateral. If the debtor is in default, then the secured creditor has a positive right (subject to any procedural restrictions imposed by insolvency law) to control the liquidation of the collateral. Moreover, the secured creditor is entitled to priority of repayment out of the proceeds of sale of the collateral.

From the point of view of the secured creditor, a grant of security lowers default risk. All other things being equal, a creditor may therefore be expected to offer a debtor more advantageous terms—for example, a reduced interest rate—when lending on a secured than an unsecured basis. However, the priority accorded to a secured creditor means that unsecured creditors will now fare worse in insolvency. They may therefore be expected to demand terms that are correspondingly less advantageous for the debtor—for example, an increased interest rate. From the debtor's point of view, these adjustments in borrowing terms might be expected, in markets in which creditors adjust perfectly to the risks they undertake, to cancel each other out. Moreover, a grant of secured credit creates costs for the debtor—in terms of restrictions over alienation of assets—that are not present in an unsecured borrowing arrangement. The early literature on secured credit viewed these stylised facts as giving rise to a "puzzle" over why debtors grant security: if the effect of security on a debtor's aggregate cost of capital is neutral (secured creditors reduce rates, unsecured creditors increase them), and there are costs to the debtor associated with a grant of security, why bother?

Various theories were advanced to explain why debtors might nevertheless be motivated to offer security to their creditors. These fall into two broad categories. "Efficiency" theories of secured credit suggest that its use generates benefits not present in an all-unsecured capital structure, such that the total cost of credit goes down. "Redistributive" theories, on the other hand, suggest that a reduced overall cost of credit is obtained at the expense of creditors who do not adjust their terms to reflect the fact that a grant of security has reduced the expected value of their claims. We will now briefly review each of these theories.

Security and signalling

Two principal theories—with diametrically opposed empirical predictions—were advanced to suggest that security interests could enhance efficiency in credit markets characterised by asymmetric information. The first, the "signalling" theory, viewed security as a "hostage" offered by a debtor to a creditor to demonstrate the seriousness of the debtor's commitment to repayment. If security is something that would be more costly for a "low-quality" borrower to offer than a "high-quality" borrower, then willingness to offer it can be a credible signal of quality. In a market characterised by asymmetric information, the ability to use a signal can assist creditors in reducing their costs of screening potential borrowers. The prediction of the signalling theory is therefore that more creditworthy borrowers will be more willing to offer security. This is, however, contrary to available empirical evidence on the use of security, which finds that it tends to be granted more frequently by younger, and smaller firms—both known proxies for lower creditworthiness.

The problem with the application of signalling theory to secured credit lies in a simplistic interpretation of the cost of granting security. It is assumed that a grant of security is costly for a debtor, because the debtor runs the risk of losing the collateral, and that this cost is greater (in expected value terms) for a less creditworthy debtor, because the risk of losing the collateral is greater. But from the debtor's point of view, there is no difference in the consequences of default as between secured and unsecured borrowing: *in either case*, the debtor's assets will be seized by creditors. The benefit of being a secured creditor under such circumstances is not vis-à-vis the debtor, but against other creditors—the secured creditor has priority as regards repayment. The difference between secured and unsecured borrowing, as perceived by the debtor, will rather be felt in states of the world in which default does *not* occur. Secured borrowing involves giving creditors rights to control the alienation of assets that are not present in unsecured lending. This means that the marginal cost to the debtor of granting security, as opposed to borrowing unsecured, is therefore *decreasing* with the probability of default, because the "cost" is only incurred so long as the debtor does not default. In other words, the early application of the signalling model in the literature was mis-specified, deriving the inverse prediction. In fact, properly specified, willingness on the debtor's part may actually be a signal of *lack* of quality.

Security and monitoring and bonding

A second theory posits social benefits from the use of secured credit as a means of preventing debtors from engaging in acts harmful to creditors' interests. Security is thought to be able to assist creditors in lowering "financial agency costs"; that is, the costs of conflicts of interest between shareholders and creditors. For example, if the business is financially distressed, shareholders—or managers acting on their behalf—may have incentives to pursue highly risky strategies that actually have a negative net present value, simply because they stand to benefit from the upside in the unlikely event that the strategy is successful. By restricting the ability of a debtor to alienate collateral, security enables the creditor to prevent the debtor from selling assets of stable value to fund more risky business ventures. Security also restricts the debtor's ability to borrow to fund such ventures. By granting existing lenders priority to the firm's assets, security forces new lenders to look primarily to the value generated by the ventures they fund, and thereby to scrutinise more carefully the purposes for which the debtor is borrowing.

On the agency costs view, the grant of security is thus a bond by the debtor not to engage in wealth-reducing transactions. Such a bond is valuable to the debtor, because by "tying its hands" to prevent itself entering such transactions *ex post*, it increases its borrowing capacity *ex ante*. This theory views security as closely related in function to loan covenants and contractual priority arrangements, which also impose restrictions on the debtor's freedom of action that may be justified as bonds against wealth-reducing transactions. In each case, we would expect these arrangements only to be agreed to if the benefits to the debtor outweigh the costs—hence riskier firms, which we might expect to be more prone to financial agency costs, would be more likely to use loan covenants and security.

In this context, the utility of secured credit is a function of its advantages over and above contractual covenants. The key to the difference lies in the consequences if the debtor ultimately defaults. As security creates proprietary rights, it is "self-enforcing," whereas loan covenants are not. Security also has another difference from loan covenants: it allocates control (subject to restrictions imposed by insolvency law) over the enforcement process. This permits creditors to allocate control over enforcement to those best-placed to maximise the value realised, and to deter other creditors from engaging in a wasteful "race to collect" when the debtor is in financial difficulty. We would therefore expect security to be used by those firms which are riskiest, or about which creditors have least information. Risky firms are more likely to default, and hence more likely to go into insolvency proceedings. In keeping with these predictions, empirical studies from a number of jurisdictions establish that security tends to be used principally in relation to smaller, younger, and riskier firms.

On this view, the ability of corporate debtors to grant security has the potential to yield social benefits extending beyond the parties to the security agreement (that is, "positive externalities"). *Ex ante*, by facilitating bonding and monitoring activity, security lowers the probability that the debtor will engage in wealth-reducing transactions, and helps to reduce the probability of default. This increases the value of all creditors' claims. *Ex post*, by facilitating efficient enforcement, it can increase the overall "size of the pie" for distribution.

Security and redistribution

A third theoretical explanation for the use of secured credit posits that it is or can be a mechanism for the transfer of wealth from one party to another. The mechanism for such wealth transfers depends on the presence of so-called "non-adjusting" creditors: that is, creditors whose decision to extend credit does not fully reflect the increased risk (to them) associated with the fact that the debtor has granted security. The intuition is that, all other things being equal, a loan made on a secured rather than an unsecured basis will carry with it a lower rate of interest, reflecting the reduction in risk that the lender will bear. Correlatively, an unsecured creditor is worse off if his debtor has granted security to another creditor. Thus unless unsecured creditors "adjust" the terms of their credit to reflect the increased risk it brings for them, a grant of security may result in a transfer of wealth—in an expected-value sense—from unsecured debtors to the borrower. By borrowing on a secured basis, the debtor obtains a lower interest rate; by failing to adjust, the "cost" is borne by unsecured creditors.

This claim does not necessarily imply that the benefits of security discussed in the previous section do not exist. Yet at the very least it implies that, even if such benefits exist, the possibility of such wealth transfers will lead debtors to take "too much" security. The costs of granting such "unnecessary" security will be wasted. Moreover, non-adjusting creditors who thereby end up bearing the additional risk may be poorly diversified and so least well-placed to bear it. Determining the extent to which these theories account for the use of secured credit is, however, an empirical question, and so we now turn to the empirical literature.

Empirical studies

Doubt has sometimes been cast on propositions made in the theoretical literature regarding secured credit about interest rate reductions. Each of the theories about security—whether they characterise it as efficiency-enhancing or redistributive—posits that a debtor grants security because it receives an interest rate reduction for doing so. Yet empirically, it appears that secured loans granted by banks in the UK, Germany and France are associated with interest rates no lower than for unsecured loans. This leads some to question the extent to which the theories describe reality. However, it is important to note that the theoretical claims about interest rate reductions are made *ceteris paribus*—that is, all other things being equal. Both the agency costs theory and the redistribution theory predict that security will tend to be most valuable in relation to more risky borrowers. This means that when comparing secured and unsecured interest rates, all other things are not likely to be equal. Riskier borrowers would be likely to incur higher interest rates. So both security *and* increased interest rates are associated with riskier borrowers. Because of this selection effect, a comparison of interest rates for secured and unsecured loans may associate secured loans with higher interest rates. However, the appropriate comparison is rather with the terms on which borrowers with similar levels of credit risk to those observed to borrow on a secured basis would be offered *unsecured* credit. Studies which have sought explicitly to take this selection effect into account have found that borrowing on a secured basis tends to lower the cost of credit for debtors.

Having clarified this point, we may now consider which of these theories derives most support from empirical studies of use of secured credit. As we have seen, in developed countries, security tends to be granted by firms which are at relatively greater risk of default. This is consistent with the predictions of both the agency costs and redistribution theories. The benefits of policing a debtor so as to reduce their likelihood of default will clearly increase with the debtor's riskiness. At the same time, the expected value of the "insolvency share" of unsecured creditors, which the critics of security argue it permits to be "sold" to secured creditors, also increases with the probability of the debtor's default. Evidence on the types of firm that obtain secured credit is therefore inconclusive: it could be explained by reference to either, or a combination of both, effects.

More specific studies allow us to draw some distinctions between the theories of secured credit. A recent study by Yair Listokin [(2008), 58 *Duke LJ* 1037] sets out to test the redistributive theory directly. Listokin examines the capital structures of firms of a type that are likely to have significant numbers of tort non-adjusting creditors: US tobacco manufacturers. The redistributive theory would predict that these firms, likely to be on the receiving end of mass tort litigation, would be likely to carry more secured credit than the average borrower. This is because the tort victims are unable to adjust the terms on which they become creditors to reflect their subordination to secured claims. As such, tobacco firms ought, if security is used to transfer wealth from non-adjusting creditors, to load up with secured debt. Yet Listokin finds the opposite: tobacco companies actually use *less* secured debt than average. This strongly contradicts the redistributive theory.

Other findings emerge from empirical studies that also tend to contradict the redistributive theory and support the agency costs view. Franks and Sussman, in a study of relations between UK banks and troubled borrowers [(2005), 9 *Rev. of Finance* 65], report that the presence of a secured corporate loan is correlated with the grant of personal guarantees by company directors. Such guarantees assist the creditor in controlling debtor misbehaviour. Mokal [(2002), 22 *Oxford J of Legal Studies* 687] argues that their presence also tends to contradict the view that security is granted in order to transfer value from non-adjusting creditors to the debtor. This is because, to the extent that a grant of corporate security precipitates a grant of personal security by the debtor company's directors, the latter incur a cost by granting corporate security.

More generally, it seems unlikely that there are significant numbers of "nonadjusting" creditors, at least for firms outside the reach of US mass tort litigation. On the one hand, tort claims sufficient to bankrupt a defendant are rare outside the US. On the other, the interests of tort victims are well-protected in the UK and in some other jurisdictions through systems of mandatory insurance for the most empirically significant categories of tort claim, coupled with statutory provisions that transfer an insolvent company's claim against a liability insurer to the injured party.

Those claiming that security is used to transfer wealth typically assume that trade creditors' adjustment is only partial, on the basis that they face relatively high information and transaction costs relative to the amount at stake. Yet we have seen that security tends to be ubiquitous amongst smaller, younger firms. *A priori*, it would be surprising if trade creditors could not use these borrower characteristics as readily observable proxies for whether or not security had been granted. Moreover, the assumption that trade creditors only adjust to a limited extent does not seem consistent with empirical data. Whilst trade creditors do tend to offer the same *terms* to all "borrowers" (that is, customers who purchase on credit), the non-adjustment idea is contradicted by evidence that trade creditors tend to adjust the *amount* of trade credit granted in accordance with the debtor's creditworthiness and the scope for misbehaviour by the debtor.

Thus, whilst it is possible that some grants of security may be harmful to non-adjusting creditors, it seems likely that the beneficial aspects of security are empirically more significant.

IX. THE STRUCTURE OF THE ONTARIO ACT

A. Structure and Terminology

The OPPSA is divided into seven parts, preceded by a definition section (s. 1):

Part I   (ss. 2-8) "Application and Conflict of Laws," deals with the scope of the Act and conflict of laws rules.

Part II   (ss. 9-18) "Validity of Security Agreements and Rights of Parties," deals with the creation of the security interest.

Part III   (ss. 19-40) "Perfection and Priorities," deals with the steps required to make a security interest effective against a third party and with the priority rules among competing security interests or between a security interest and a third party.

Part IV   (ss. 41-57) "Registration," provides for a province-wide unified system for the registration of financing statements.

Part V   (ss. 58-66) "Default Rights and Remedies," sets out the secured party's rights and remedies on the debtor's default.

Part VI   (ss. 67-74) "Miscellaneous," deals with judicial supervision of the exercise of rights and remedies given by the Act, compensation for non-compliance with statutory requirements, service of notices, what constitutes knowledge, interface with other statutes, and regulation-making powers.

Part VII   (ss. 75-86) "Application, Transition, Amendments, Repeals, Commencement" deals with the transition from prior registry statutes, an amendment to the Execution Act relating to the seizure of security interests and the repeal of Acts replaced by the new Act.

The PPSA introduces into the legal lexicon of personal property security law a few new terms (for example, OPPSA s. 11, "attach" and s. 19, "perfected") that are undefined. It gives statutory definition to other terms that had been in general use in secured financing arrangements but that had no legal meaning (for example, OPPSA s. 1(1), "chattel paper," "proceeds," "purchase-money security interest," and "security interest"). Other commonly used terms (for example, OPPSA s. 1(1), "consumer goods," "debtor," "equipment," and "inventory") have been converted into legal terms of art.

Since the PPSA was designed to implement a highly integrated, structurally complete system of law for the regulation of personal property security transactions, a proper understanding of it requires careful attention to the meanings ascribed by the Act to the key words used in its provisions.

B. The Personal Property Registry

A central feature of the OPPSA is protection of third parties who may deal with a debtor in the mistaken belief that personal property in the possession or control of such a debtor is unencumbered by security interests. One, and by far the most important, of the measures prescribed by the Act for this purpose is to require public disclosure of the existence or potential existence of security interests as a prerequisite to recognition of the priority of these interests over competitive claims to the property in which the interests are held. This approach is not new; the province of Canada established a registry for chattel mortgages taken in Upper Canada as far back as 1849. However, the system prescribed by the PPSA for public disclosure of security interests is modern and, compared with the systems it displaced, efficient but necessarily complex. The details of its structure and the rules that must be met by secured parties seeking perfection of their interests by registration are set out in Part IV (OPPSA ss. 41-57) of the Act and in the Minister's Order under the OPPSA.

C. Classification of Collateral

(All references are to the OPPSA.)

With several minor exceptions (see ss. 4(1)(c), 4(1)(d), 4(1)(e)), the OPPSA encompasses security interests in all types of personal property (collateral—s. 1(1)). However, different rules apply to different types of collateral. Note the relevance of collateral type in the context of the following:

- Conflicts of laws (see ss. 5(1) and 5(2)).
- Consumer protection (see ss. 12(2)(b), 45(2), 51(5) and 65(1), and 66(2)).
- Perfection by possession (see s. 22).
- Perfection by registration (see s. 23 and Minister's Order).
- Temporary perfection (see s. 24).
- Special priority rules (see, for example, ss. 28, 33, 34, and 35).
- Default rights and remedies (see ss. 61 and 62(b)).

Special attention should be directed to the ways in which the Act deals with goods collateral. Note that the classification of goods as consumer goods, inventory, or equipment does not depend upon any essential characteristic of the goods involved, but upon the use being made of the goods at the relevant time by the debtor in possession. Accordingly, a truck would be "consumer goods" if used by the debtor for personal, family, or household purposes; "inventory" if held by the debtor for sale or lease; or "equipment" if it is being used by the debtor as other than "consumer goods" or "equipment." Note too that, under the Minister's Order, goods may be described on a financing statement (and, therefore, in the computerized record of the registry) according to the use being made of the goods by the debtor. Under the Acts based on the CCPPSL model, with the exception of inventory, goods must be described specifically or generically. See, for example, BC reg. s. 13. The significance of this difference is addressed in Chapter 6, Part IV.

The PPSA adopts a second method of classifying collateral—a method based not on the characteristics of the collateral and not on the use being made of it by the debtor, but on the way in which the debtor acquires rights in the collateral. Personal property or a fixture in any form acquired by the debtor as a result of any dealing with the (original) collateral is described as "proceeds" in s. 1(1). Note that "proceeds" includes proceeds of proceeds (sometimes referred to in the literature as "second-generation proceeds"). This category of collateral is the subject matter of a special priority regime (s. 25) designed to permit a security interest to extend beyond the original collateral to personal property received in place of the original collateral or in part payment of its price.

In some situations, property that would otherwise fall within two categories of collateral is limited by exclusion to one category. An instrument taken as part of a secured installment contract ("chattel paper" s. 1(1)) is not an "instrument" (s. 1(1)) for the purposes of the Act. Again, an intangible in the form of an account that is an aspect of chattel paper is not an "intangible" or an "account" (s. 1(1)).

PROBLEMS

1) A car dealer uses a bank loan to purchase a stock of new cars. The bank takes a security interest in the cars. The cars are sold on secured credit by the dealer as follows:
   a) to a businessperson for use in a business;
   b) to an individual for family purposes;
   c) to a doctor for use partly for family purposes and partly in his or her profession;
   d) to another car dealer for the purpose of resale;
   e) to a rental company for the purpose of renting out to customers.
What is the PPSA classification (i) of the cars in the hands of the original car dealer; and (ii) of each car in the hands of each purchaser? Describe the types of proceeds collateral the car dealer might obtain from the sales of the new cars.

2) A refrigerator is sold on credit in return for:
   a) a promissory note signed by the buyer;
   b) a promissory note signed by the buyer, taken together with a security agreement signed by the buyer giving the seller a security interest in the refrigerator;
   c) a contract obligation by the buyer to pay the price;
   d) a "conditional sale contract" under which the seller retains full title to the refrigerator until complete discharge of the buyer's obligation;
   e) cash.
What category of collateral does each of the five items fall into?

3) A lender takes a security interest in the assets of a farmer including dairy cows, beef cattle, milking machinery, grain held to be fed to cattle, and grain held for sale to grain buyers. Categorize the collateral for registration and priority purposes.

CHAPTER TWO

The Scope of the Act

I. INTRODUCTION

The scope of the PPSA is stated in very broad and imprecise terms. Section 2 of the OPPSA states that the Act applies to (1) "every transaction" (2) that "in substance creates" a security interest (3) in personal property. The "transaction" referred to is a "security agreement." The section provides some important, albeit essentially negative, information as to what a security agreement is and what is involved in the creation of a security interest. There must be a concluded agreement, otherwise the Act will not apply. For example, in *Ellingsen (Trustee of) v. Hallmark Ford Sales Ltd.* (2000), 190 DLR (4th) 47 (BCCA), extracted in Chapter 3, the parties entered into a contract for the sale of a truck "subject to credit approval." The seller allowed the buyer to take immediate delivery but the buyer ended up being unable to obtain finance. A question arose as to whether the seller had a security interest. The court held that it did not because there was no contract: the "subject to credit approval" stipulation was a condition precedent that remained unfulfilled.

The agreement must "in substance" create a security interest. A security agreement is essentially a hypothecation that involves the following pattern. The debtor has an *in rem* interest in personal property. By agreement between the debtor and the obligee, that interest is charged with or encumbered by an interest granted in favour of the obligee for the purposes of securing performance of an obligation of the debtor. This concept is not new, it was a feature of Roman law (*hypothec*) and was recognized in equity (equitable charge). However, the focus of s. 2 is more on pragmatism than on conceptual purity. The role of subparagraph (a)(ii) of the section is to bring within the regime of the Act not only traditional types of secured financing agreements but also other devices, such as conditional sales contracts and leases, that function as security devices but do not have the characteristics of a hypothecation. The legislative policy underlying s. 2 is to merge separate streams of secured financing law into a single system. What is common to the forms of transactions brought within the scope of the Act is that they all entail the recognition that a person to whom an obligation is owed has an interest in personal property that would permit that person to look to the property as a source of compensation should the obligation not be performed. The effect of the transaction, not its form or the way in which the interest arises, is determinative. This approach involves re-characterization of transactions such as conditional sales contracts and leases.

The list of transactions referred to in s. 2 is not exhaustive. Other types of transactions not mentioned fall within the scope of the Act. Among other things, the Act applies to trusts, but only to those trusts that are functionally equivalent to a security agreement: *Re Skybridge Holidays Inc.* (1999), 173 DLR (4th) 333 (BCCA), extracted in Part IV, below.

In summary, since the Act applies to every transaction that "in substance" creates a security interest, the form of the agreement is of little significance. Likewise, the use of terminology found in a traditional type of agreement that, under prior law, did not indicate a security device (for example, "lease," "lessor," "lessee," and "lease payments") is not determinative. Correspondingly, it is not necessary for the parties to state expressly that the transaction is a security agreement, provided that it is clear from a reading of the agreement as a whole that their intention is to create a security interest. For example, in *356447 British Columbia Ltd. v. Canadian Imperial Bank of Commerce* (1998), 157 DLR (4th) 682 (BCCA), extracted in Chapter 3, Part II, the borrower agreed to repay the lender from a certain fund. The court held that the agreement was tantamount to a charge on the fund, and so the lender held a security interest.

The scope of the Act is also limited by the requirement that the security interest must be in "personal property." It follows that, as a general rule, the Act does not apply if the collateral is land, and s. 4(1)(e) confirms this point while at the same time identifying a couple of exceptions. It also follows that the Act does not apply unless the supposed collateral qualifies as "property." This is a matter of first principle because the collateral must have the attributes of property if the secured party is to acquire rights in it. There is an ongoing issue as to whether a statutory licence, such as a taxi cab licence, a nursing home licence, or a fishing licence, can be used as collateral and, if so, what rights the secured party acquires: see *Saulnier v. Royal Bank of Canada*, [2008] 3 SCR 166, extracted in Part II, below.

Another issue relates to the nature of the rights an investor acquires when she purchases corporate securities through the indirect holding system. An investor may hold shares in Company C either directly or indirectly. For example, assume Investor A pays $200 for 100 shares in Company C. This is a direct holding. Now assume that Intermediary X buys 10,000 shares in Company C and Investor A pays X $200 in return for an investment in X's holding. This is an example of an indirect holding. The example is a simplified one, in part because there is usually a chain of intermediaries, not just one. One of the main advantages of the indirect holding system is that it facilitates the transfer of investments.

If Investor A holds 100 Company C shares in the direct holding system and wants to sell them into the market, she has to sign a transfer form and deliver up the share certificates to her broker. Assume Investor B buys the shares. B will have to take delivery of the share certificates and the transfer form, and lodge them with Company C so C can register B as the new owner. By contrast, in the indirect holding system, if A wants to sell her investment, everything can be done by computerized book entries in Intermediary X's accounts: to continue with our simplified example, X will simply debit A's account for the shares and pay her out.

The *Securities Transfer Act, 2006* (STA), SO 2006, c. 8 makes major changes to the law governing the purchase and sale of investment property in both the direct and indirect holding systems. Previously, the property rights of investors in the indirect holding system were uncertain. Assume that, in our example, the following further transactions occur:

- Investor M pays $5,000 for an undivided share of X's holding,
- Investor N pays $10,000 for an undivided share of X's holding, and
- Investor O pays $6,000 for an undivided share of X's holding.

Note that the fund is now oversubscribed to the tune of $1,200. To make matters worse, X's principal absconds with 2,000 shares from the fund. Shortly afterward, X goes into bankruptcy. There are 8,000 shares left in the fund and four investors claiming a total of 10,600 shares. Who gets what? Prior law gave no clear answer to this question. This uncertainty had knock-on effects for secured transactions. Assume that Investor A wants to borrow $100 from Bank and offers Bank her investment with X as security. Will Bank accept the investment as security? Under prior law, the answer would quite possibly have been "no," because Bank had no way of knowing what its rights would be if Investor A defaulted and X was insolvent.

Under the new laws, Investor A holds what is called a "security entitlement." STA Part VI specifies that Investor A has a proportionate proprietary interest in X's fund. It also gives A a set of personal rights exercisable against X if it breaches its duties to investors. These rights, in combination, make up the "security entitlement" and they are what Investor A gets in return for her $200. Cognate reforms to the PPSA are aimed at facilitating security interests in investment property. Note that the PPSA definition of "investment property" expressly includes a security entitlement. Other parts of the Act spell out the rules for attachment of a security interest in a security entitlement and other kinds of investment property. They also stipulate what the secured party should do to perfect its security interest in investment property and they enact special priority rules for disputes between the holder of a security interest in investment property and competing claims. The STA is modeled on Article 8 of the US Uniform Commercial Code (UCC) and the cognate PPSA amendments derive from Revised Article 9. Similar reforms have been enacted, or are in process, in the other provinces. The extract in Part III, below, explains the difference between the direct and indirect holding systems, discusses the meanings of "security" in the context of the direct holding system and "security entitlement" in the context of the indirect holding system, and identifies the nature of the investor's rights in the indirect holding system.

The OPPSA applies to every transaction that in substance creates a security interest in personal property. It also applies to certain transactions that are not in substance security agreements, namely: (1) the outright transfer of an account or chattel paper; and (2) a lease of goods for a term of more than one year: see Part V, below. However, the Act does not apply to the transactions listed in s. 4: see Part VI, below.

II. WHAT IS "PERSONAL PROPERTY"? THE LICENCE ISSUE

Saulnier v. Royal Bank of Canada
[2008] 3 SCR 166

BINNIE J:

I. Facts

...

[5] The appellant Saulnier holds four fishing licences (lobster, herring, swordfish and mackerel). Like most fishers, he required loans to finance his business. Accordingly, in April 1999, he signed a General Security Agreement ("GSA") with the Royal Bank. In January 2003, he signed a guarantee (limited to $215,000) to the Royal Bank for the debts

of the appellant Bingo Queen, a company of which he was the sole owner. At that time, Bingo Queen also entered into a GSA. The standard form GSA gave the Bank a security interest in: "all ... present and after acquired personal property including ... Intangibles ... and in all proceeds and renewals thereof." The GSA also specified that the term "intangible" would be interpreted according to its definition in the *PPSA*. The GSA contemplated a listing of specific property in Schedule C but in the case of both GSAs in question Schedule C was left blank.

[6] In 2004, the appellants' fishing business faltered. As of July 6, Mr. Saulnier owed the Bank $120,449, and Bingo Queen owed $177,282. On July 8, Saulnier made an assignment in bankruptcy. His Statement of Affairs under the *BIA* [*Bankruptcy and Insolvency Act*, RSC 1985, c. B-3] showed liabilities of $400,330, of which about $250,000 was owed to the Royal Bank. The trial judge found that according to the evidence, Saulnier's four fishing licences had a market value in excess of $600,000. This amount, if available to creditors, would be sufficient to discharge all debts and provide a surplus.

[7] On November 18, 2004, four months after the bankruptcy, Saulnier purported to lease his lobster licence to Horizon Fisheries Limited, whose principal owner was his common law spouse. In March 2005, the receiver and the trustee in bankruptcy signed an agreement to sell Saulnier's fishing licences and other assets to a third party for $630,000 (the sale was conditional on the trustee being able to effect a transfer of the licences). Saulnier refused to sign the necessary documents. The trustee in bankruptcy and the Royal Bank brought the present application for declaratory relief.

...

III. Judicial History

A. Supreme Court of Nova Scotia (2006), 241 NSR (2d) 96, 2006 NSSC 34

[9] Kennedy CJSC found that "the fair and correct approach is to characterize the federal fishing licences based on the reality of the commercial arena" (para. 49). He added that "[t]o accept the argument ... that there can be no property in these licences in the hands of the holder, because of ministerial control would ... foster an unrealistic legal condition based on an historic definition of property that ignores what is actually happening in the commercial world that the law must serve" (para. 53). In his view, the bundle of rights conferred by the licences "constitute marketable property capable of providing security" (para. 54) and also "property for purposes of the *BIA*" (para. 57).

B. Nova Scotia Court of Appeal (Bateman, Hamilton and Fichaud JA)
(2006), 246 NSR (2d) 239, 2006 NSCA 91

[10] Fichaud JA, writing for the court, found that while commercial reality and the market value attached to licences "may be a determinant in the accounting or appraisal contexts" (para. 17), the legal issue should be determined with reference to the definitions of "property" and "personal property" in the *BIA* and the *PPSA*.

[11] Based on his consideration of ss. 2 and 16(1) of the *Regulations*, he concluded that the licence itself is the property of the Crown, and not of the holder. However, "during the term of a license a licensee has a beneficial interest in the earnings from use of the

license. That interest, and the right to those earnings, pass to the trustee in bankruptcy of the license holder" (para. 38). An important issue, in his view, was whether Mr. Saulnier had any rights relating to the renewal or reissuance of his licences, and whether these rights pass to the trustee. He considered it important that the holder of a fishing licence not only had the right to request a renewal but a right not to be arbitrarily denied it. In these circumstances

> [t]he license holder has a legally recognized right—limited though it may be—that constitutes intangible personal property. ... The security holder or trustee in bankruptcy takes the license holder's limited legal right or beneficial interest. The security holder or trustee takes [it] subject to all the risks of non-renewal that applied to the license holder—i.e., non-renewal on grounds that are not arbitrary. This ensures that the interest of the security holder or trustee in bankruptcy does not degrade the regulatory scheme of the [fisheries] legislation. ... [para. 49]

[12]   Fichaud JA cited cases in which bad-faith ministerial decisions had given rise to damages or had been judicially reviewed by the courts including *St. Anthony Seafoods Limited Partnership v. Newfoundland and Labrador (Minister of Fisheries and Aquaculture)* (2004), 245 DLR (4th) 597, 2004 NLCA 59. On the strength of these decisions, he found that "[a] legal right to damages or to set aside a ministerial decision is, in my view, intangible personal property under the broad definition in s. 2 of the *BIA*" (para. 52). Moreover, while "[t]he PPSA's framework to define 'intangible' is less substantial than in the *BIA*," the result concerning the fishing licences is the same (para. 61). The holder's rights in the fishing licences are also personal property ("intangibles") for the purposes of the *PPSA*, in his view.

IV. Analysis

[13]   A commercial fisher with a ramshackle boat and a licence to fish is much better off financially than a fisher with a great boat tied up at the wharf with no licence. Financial institutions looking for readily marketable loan collateral want to snap up licences issued under the federal *Regulations*, which in the case of the lobster fishery can have a dockside value that fluctuates up to a half a million dollars or more. Fishers want to offer as much collateral as they can to obtain the loans needed to acquire the equipment to enable them to put to sea.

[14]   The Minister's claim to more or less unfettered discretion to renew or not to renew fishing licences each year is based on the legislation as interpreted in *Comeau's Sea Foods Ltd. v. Canada (Minister of Fisheries and Oceans)*, [1997] 1 SCR 12. In that case Major J wrote for the Court:

> Canada's fisheries are a "common property resource," belonging to all the people of Canada. Under the *Fisheries Act*, it is the Minister's duty to manage, conserve and develop the fishery on behalf of Canadians in the public interest (s. 43). Licensing is a tool in the arsenal of powers available to the Minister under the *Fisheries Act* to manage fisheries. [para. 37]

Nevertheless, the fact is that the stability of the fishing industry depends on the Minister's predictable renewal of such licences year after year. Few fishers expect to see their loans paid off with the proceeds of a single year's catch. In an industry where holding one of a very restricted number of licences is a condition precedent to participation, the licence unlocks the value in the fishers' other marine assets.

[15] Yet the appellants are correct to say that just because a "right" or "power" to fish has commercial value, it does not follow that licences also constitute property within the scope of the *BIA* or *PPSA*. Earlier trial level decisions in Nova Scotia had held that fishing licences were not property and were not claimable by the trustee in bankruptcy. See e.g. *Re Jenkins* (1997), 32 CBR (4th) 262 (NSSC), and *Re Townsend* (2002), 32 CBR (4th) 318 (NSSC). We cannot wish away the statutory language however much practical sense is reflected in the result reached by the courts below.

A. A Question of Statutory Interpretation

[16] The questions before the Court essentially raise a dispute about statutory interpretation. We are not concerned with the concept of "property" in the abstract. The notion of "property" is, in any event, a term of some elasticity that takes its meaning from the context. The task is to interpret the definitions in the *BIA* and *PPSA* in a purposeful way having regard to "their entire context, in their grammatical and ordinary sense harmoniously with the scheme of the Act, the object of the Act, and the intention of Parliament" (R. Sullivan, *Sullivan and Driedger on the Construction of Statutes* (4th ed. 2002), at p. 1). Because a fishing licence may not qualify as "property" for the general purposes of the common law does not mean that it is also excluded from the reach of the statutes. For particular purposes Parliament can and does create its own lexicon.

[17] In determining the scope of the definition of "property" in a statutory context, it is necessary to have regard to the overall purpose of the *BIA*, which is to regulate the orderly administration of the bankrupt's affairs, keeping a balance between the rights of creditors and the desirability of giving the bankrupt a clean break: *Husky Oil Operations Ltd. v. Minister of National Revenue*, [1995] 3 SCR 453, at para. 7. The exemption of designated property from distribution among creditors under s. 67(1) is to allow the bankrupt to continue a living pending discharge and, when discharged, to make a fresh start. Those exemptions do not, it seems to me, bear much similarity to the proposed "exempting" of a valuable asset such as a commercial fishing licence. If Saulnier had "sold" his licences prior to discharge the cash proceeds would, it seems, be after-acquired property that would be divided amongst his creditors under s. 67(1)(c) of the *BIA*.

[18] Within this overall purpose an appropriate interpretation must be given to the following definition of "property" in s. 2 of the *BIA*:

> "property" means any type of property, whether situated in Canada or elsewhere, and includes money, goods, things in action, land and every description of property, whether real or personal, legal or equitable, as well as obligations, easements and every description of estate, interest and profit, present or future, vested or contingent, in, arising out of or incident to property.

[19] The *PPSA*, on the other hand, is designed to facilitate the creation of a security interest to enable holders of personal property to use it as collateral, and to enable lenders to predict accurately the priority of their claims against the assets in question ...

[20] Within that overall purpose, an interpretation must be given to the somewhat circular definitions given in s. 2 of the *PPSA*:

(w) "intangible" means personal property that is not goods, a document of title, chattel paper, a security, an instrument or money;

...

(ad) "personal property" means goods, a document of title, chattel paper, a security, an instrument, money or an intangible.

[21] Of course a creditor/lender who enters into a security agreement that is not registerable under the *PPSA* may still have contractual rights against the borrower. However, the objective of lenders is to achieve priority (or to know in advance what priority they *can* achieve) over other claimants. Otherwise a miscreant could enter into a series of unregistered financing agreements purporting to use and re-use the same boat and licence as collateral.

B. The Interest Conferred by a Fishing Licence

[22] The fishery is a public resource. The fishing licence permits the holder to participate for a limited time in its exploitation. The fish, once caught, become the property of the holder. Accordingly, the fishing licence is more than a "mere licence" to do that which is otherwise illegal. It is a licence coupled with a proprietary interest in the harvest from the fishing effort contingent, of course, on first catching it.

[23] It is extremely doubtful that a simple licence could itself be considered property at common law. See generally A.M. Honoré, "Ownership," in A.G. Guest, ed., *Oxford Essays in Jurisprudence* (1961). On the other hand, if not property in the common law sense, a fishing licence is unquestionably a major commercial asset.

[24] Successive Ministers of Fisheries have issued policies underscoring their support for stability in the fishing industry, which necessitates continuity in the ranks of licence holders. Despite a policy favouring stability and continuity, the Minister's *Commercial Fisheries Licensing Policy for Eastern Canada, 1996* seeks to guard against any notion that such licences should be read as conferring a property interest on licence holders, which could possibly impose a fetter on the exercise of the Minister's "absolute discretion" in their issuance. Thus s. 5(a) of the *Licencing Policy* states:

[a] "licence" grants permission to do something which, without such permission, would be prohibited. As such, a licence confers no property or other rights which can be legally sold, bartered or bequeathed. Essentially, it is a privilege to do something, subject to the terms and conditions of the licence.

The Minister's statement of policy expresses a departmental position that has no regulatory status and which, in the eye of the law, does not add to or subtract from his "absolute discretion" under s. 7(1) of the *Fisheries Act* to issue licences. Nor does this informal policy determine whether the licence can be construed as "property" for the purposes of the *BIA* and *PPSA*. The reality, as found by the courts below, is that the commercial market operates justifiably on the assumption that licences can be transferred on application to the Minister with the consent of the existing licence holder, that licences will be renewed from year to year, and that the Minister's policy will not be changed to the detriment of the existing licence holders. Thus, despite the Minister's protestations, the market attributes a high market value to what might otherwise be seen, as some of the cases put it, as a "transitory and ephemeral" right.

[25] The jurisprudence indicates a number of different approaches.

(i) The Traditional "Property" Approach

[26] The appellants rely on the decision of the Ontario Court of Appeal in *National Trust Co. v. Bouckhuyt* (1987), 61 OR (2d) 640. In that case, the court dismissed the trust company's claim that a valuable tobacco quota listed in a chattel mortgage could properly be made the subject of Ontario *PPSA* registration. Cory JA, as he then was, referred to some traditional *indicia* of rights of property and concluded that renewal of the tobacco quota year to year was subject to the "unfettered discretion of the [Tobacco B]oard" and that the quota itself was "transitory and ephemeral" (pp. 647-48). Accordingly, the quota did "not constitute intangible personal property as that term is utilized" in the Ontario *PPSA* (p. 649). The Quebec Court of Appeal reached a similar conclusion under the *BIA* in relation to a fishing licence in *Re Noel (Syndic)*, [1994] QJ No. 978 (QL) (CA).

[27] The *Bouckhuyt* approach has been followed in some of the Ontario *PPSA* cases; see e.g. *Canadian Imperial Bank of Commerce v. Hallahan* (1990), 69 DLR (4th) 449 (Ont. CA), and *Bank of Montreal v. Bale* (1992), 4 PPSAC (2d) 114 (Ont. CA), but it has been criticized as insufficiently sensitive to the particular context of personal property security legislation, which (so the critics say) commands a broader concept of intangible property if the purposes of that legislation are to be achieved. See e.g. J.S. Ziegel and D.L. Denomme, *The Ontario Personal Property Security Act: Commentary and Analysis* (1994), at pp. 40-42. As discussed below, more recent cases have tended to restrict *Bouckhuyt* to its facts. Even in the "regulatory cases" the courts now adopt a more purposeful approach to the definitions in the *BIA* and in personal property security legislation, and consider traditional common law notions of property as less of a stumbling block to recognition of licences and quotas as "property" for statutory purposes. I agree with this evolution.

[28] In any event, there is a significant difference between a quota (as in *Bouckhuyt*) and a fishing licence, which bears some analogy to a common law *profit à prendre* which is undeniably a property right. A *profit à prendre* enables the holder to enter onto the land of another to extract some part of the natural produce, such as crops or game birds (B. Ziff, *Principles of Property Law* (2nd ed. 1996), at pp. 333-34; *The Queen in Right of British Columbia v. Tener*, [1985] 1 SCR 533; and M.J. Mossman and W.F. Flanagan, *Property Law: Cases and Commentary* (2nd ed. 2004), at p. 545). Equally, a "profit of piscary" (being a type of *profit à prendre*) is recognized as a property right to fish in the privately owned waters of another.

[29] Fichaud JA in the court below noted numerous cases where it was held that "during the term of a license the license holder has a beneficial interest to the earnings from his license" (para. 37). See also: *Waryk v. Bank of Montreal* (1991), 85 DLR (4th) 514 (BCCA), at pp. 521-24; *British Columbia Packers Ltd. v. Sparrow*, [1989] 4 CNLR 63 (BCCA), at p. 68; and *Buston v. Canada*, [1993] 2 CTC 2720 (TCC), at pp. 2733-34. This is another way of expressing substantially the same idea. The earnings flow from the

catch which is lawfully reduced to possession at the time of the catch, as is the case with a *profit à prendre*.

[30] Some analytical comfort may be drawn in this connection from the observations of R. Megarry and H.W.R. Wade on *The Law of Real Property* (4th ed. 2008), at p. 779:

> A licence may be coupled with some proprietary interest in other property. Thus the right to enter another man's land to hunt and take away the deer killed, or to enter and cut down a tree and take it away, involves two things, namely, a licence to enter the land and the grant of an interest (a *profit à prendre*) in the deer or tree.

And at p. 822:

> A right to "hawk, hunt, fish and fowl" may thus exist as a profit, for this gives the right to take creatures living on the soil which, when killed, are capable of being owned.

• • •

[33] … A fishing licence is, no doubt, a creature of the *Fisheries Act* and its *Regulations*. Our Court has already emphasized the broad scope and discretion of the Minister in relation to such licences in *Comeau's Sea Foods*. Nevertheless, there are important points of analogy between the fishing licences issued to the appellant Saulnier and the form of common law property called a *profit à prendre*, which may include a profit of piscary. If the question were whether a fishing licence *is* a *profit à prendre*, the answer would almost certainly be no. But that is not the question. The question before us is whether the fishing licences thus conceived can satisfy the statutory definition of the *BIA* and *PPSA*, purposefully interpreted.

[34] My point is simply that the subject matter of the licence (i.e. the right to participate in a fishery that is exclusive to licence holders) coupled with a proprietary interest in the fish caught pursuant to its terms, bears a reasonable analogy to rights traditionally considered at common law to be proprietary in nature. It is thus reasonably within the contemplation of the definition of "property" in s. 2 of the *BIA*, where reference is made to a "profit, present or future, vested or contingent, in, arising out of or incident to property." In this connection the property in question is the fish harvest.

[35] Of course, the holder's rights under a fishing licence are limited in time, place and the manner of their exercise by the *Fisheries Act* and *Regulations*. To say that the fishing licence is *coupled* with a proprietary interest does not encumber the Minister's discretion with proprietary fetters. The analogy used for present purposes does not prevail over the legislation. The licence is no more and no less than is described in the relevant legislation. Nevertheless, during its lifetime, however fragile, the fishing licence clearly confers something more than a "mere" permission to do something which is otherwise illegal.

(ii) The Regulatory Approach

[36] *Bouckhuyt* resulted in a line of cases in which licences and quotas were held to be intangible property (or not) according to the degree of renewal discretion vested in the issuing authority. In *Sugarman (in trust) v. Duca Community Credit Union Ltd.* (1999), 44 OR (3d) 257 (CA), the court distinguished *Bouckhuyt* on the basis that the authority issuing nursing home licences was bound to grant licences to operators that

qualified, with little discretion to refuse, and an administrative appeal procedure in the event issuance or renewal *was* refused. See also *Re Foster* (1992), 89 DLR (4th) 555 (Ont. Ct. (Gen. Div.)), at pp. 564-65. The Nova Scotia Court of Appeal in the present case adopted a variant of the "regulatory" approach in holding that a licence holder's ability to request a renewal or reissuance of a licence to its designate, and to resist an arbitrary denial by the Minister, forms part of a "bundle of rights" which collectively constitute a type of property in which a security interest can be taken. ...

[37] In my view, the debate about the extent to which licences are "transitory and ephemeral" is of limited value. A lease of land for one day or one hour is undeniably a property interest, as is a lease terminable at pleasure. A third party may be willing to pay "key money" to take over a shop lease that is soon to expire in the expectation (reasonable or not) that a renewal will be forthcoming. Uncertainties of renewal do not detract from the interest presently possessed by the holder, but nor does an expectation of renewal based on a Minister's policy which could change tomorrow, transform a licence into a property interest.

[38] A difficulty with the "regulatory approach" is that there are no clear criteria to determine how much "fetter" on the issuing authority's discretion is enough to transform a "mere licence" into some sort of interest sufficient to satisfy the statutory definitions in the *BIA* and the *PPSA*. In *Bouckhuyt*, the fetters on the authority issuing tobacco quota were considered too weak, the discretion too great, to qualify the tobacco quota as Ontario *PPSA* "property." In *Sugarman* and *Foster* the "fetters" placed on the issuing authorities of nursing home licences and taxi licences, respectively, were thought to be enough to confer a proprietary interest within the terms of the Ontario *PPSA*. The regulatory frameworks in all three cases were different to be sure, but at what point does a licence that does not qualify under personal property security legislation become transformed into a qualifying licence? ... The cases do not suggest an answer. No doubt criteria will emerge more clearly as cases that rely on a "regulatory approach" evolve. In this respect, however, I do not believe the "judicial review" paradigm offered by the Nova Scotia Court of Appeal in this case is helpful. The *Regulations* permit *anyone* to apply for a fisheries licence and *everyone* is entitled to a ministerial decision that complies with procedural fairness. I cannot agree that these elements are capable, as such, of constituting a licence "property" in the hands of a holder.

[39] In any event, I agree with the observation adopted by Major J in *Comeau's Sea Foods* that he could not find in the fisheries legislation any legal underpinning for the "vesting" of an interest in a licence "beyond the rights which it gives for the year in which it was issued" (p. 25). ... To the extent the regulatory cases are considered relevant here they do not assist the appellants, in my opinion. Section 7(1) of the *Fisheries Act* says that the Minister's discretion is "absolute."

[40] However, I do not believe the prospect of renewal, whether or not subject to an "unfettered" discretion, is determinative. For present purposes the appellants do not have to prove a renewal or even the reasonable prospect of it. The question under the *PPSA* is whether the holder (in this case the appellant Saulnier) had a qualifying interest in the licence either *at the time he entered into a General Security Agreement* with the Royal Bank in April 1999, or at the time the Bank sought to realize on Saulnier's after-acquired

property, and the question under the *BIA* is whether he had a qualifying interest within the meaning of that Act *when he made an assignment in bankruptcy* on July 8, 2004.

(iii) The "Commercial Realities" Approach

[41] This approach is well illustrated by the trial decision of Kennedy CJSC in this case, who put the argument succinctly:

> That evidence confirms my understanding, that on the east coast of Canada fishing licenses, particularly for lobster, are commonly exchanged between fishermen for a great deal of money.
> Fishing vessels of questionable value are traded for small fortunes because of the licences that are anticipated to come with them.
>
> ...
>
> To ignore commercial reality would be to deny creditors access to something of significant value in the hands of the bankrupt. That would be both artificial and potentially inequitable. [paras. 51-52 and 58] ...

[42] The criticism of this approach is that many things that have commercial value do not constitute property, while the value of some property may be minimal. There is no necessary connection between proprietary status and commercial value. ... I agree with the Court of Appeal that "commercial realities" cannot legitimate wishful thinking about the notion of "property" in the *BIA* and the *PPSA*, although commercial realities provide an appropriate context in which to interpret the statutory provisions. The *BIA* and the *PPSA* are, after all, largely commercial statutes which should be interpreted in a way best suited to enable them to accomplish their respective commercial purposes.

(iv) The Preferred Approach

[43] As described above, the holder of a s. 7(1) licence acquires a good deal more than merely permission to do that which would otherwise be unlawful. The holder requires the right to engage in an exclusive fishery under the conditions imposed by the licence and, what is of prime importance, a proprietary right in the wild fish harvested thereunder, and the earnings from their sale. While these elements do not wholly correspond to the full range of rights necessary to characterize something as "property" at common law, the question is whether (even leaving aside the debate about the prospects of renewal) they are sufficient to qualify the "bundle of rights" the appellant Saulnier *did* possess as property for purposes of the statutes.

(a) Fishing Licences Qualify as Property Within the Scope of Section 2 of the BIA

[44] ... The terms of the [*BIA* definition of "property"] are very wide. Parliament unambiguously signalled an intention to sweep up a variety of assets of the bankrupt not normally considered "property" at common law. This intention should be respected if the purposes of the *BIA* are to be achieved.

[45] Reliance was placed on s. 16 of the *Regulations* which provides that a fishing licence is a "document" which is "the property of the Crown and is not transferable." From

this it was inferred that the licence, in its commercial dimension, is declared by the *Regulations* to be a property right in the hands of the Crown. I think s. 16 merely says that the *Regulations* contemplate that the *documentation* of the licence (as opposed to the licence itself) is the property of the Crown, in the same way that a Canadian Passport is declared to be the property of the Crown, not the holder: *Veffer v. Canada (Minister of Foreign Affairs)*, [2008] 1 FCR 641, 2007 FCA 247, at para. 6. A fisher whose licence is suspended or revoked cannot refuse the Minister's demand for a return of the documentation on the basis the Minister gave it to him and it is now his property.

[46] I prefer to look at the substance of what was conferred, namely a licence to participate in the fishery coupled with a proprietary interest in the fish caught according to its terms and subject to the Minister's regulation. As noted earlier, the *BIA* is intended to fulfill certain objectives in the event of a bankruptcy which require, in general, that non-exempt assets be made available to creditors. The s. 2 definition of property should be construed accordingly to include a s. 7(1) fishing licence.

[47] It is true that the proprietary interest in the fish is contingent on the fish first being caught, but the existence of that contingency is contemplated in the *BIA* definition and is no more fatal to the proprietary status for *BIA* purposes than is the case with the equivalent contingency arising under a *profit à prendre*, which is undeniably a property interest.

[48] Counsel for the Attorney General of Canada was greatly concerned that a holding that the fishing licence is property in the hands of the holder even for limited statutory purposes might be raised in future litigation to fetter the Minister's discretion, but I do not think this concern is well founded. The licence is a creature of the regulatory system. Section 7(1) of the *Fisheries Act* speaks of the Minister's "absolute discretion." The Minister gives and the Minister (when acting properly within his jurisdiction under s. 9 of the Act) can take away, according to the exigencies of his or her management of the fisheries. The statute defines the nature of the holder's interest, and this interest is not expanded by our decision that a fishing licence qualifies for inclusion as "property" for certain statutory purposes.

[49] It follows that in my view the trustee was entitled to require the appellant Saulnier to execute the appropriate documentation to obtain a transfer of the fishing licences to the third party purchaser.

[50] It may well be that in the course of a bankruptcy the fishing licence will expire, or has already expired. If so, the trustee will have the same right as the original holder of an expired licence to go to the Minister to seek its replacement, and has the same recourse (or the lack of it) if the request is rejected. The bankrupt can transfer no greater rights than he possesses. The trustee simply steps into the shoes of the appellant Saulnier and takes the licence "warts and all."

(b) The Fishing Licence Is Also "Personal Property" Within the Meaning of Section 2 of the PPSA

[51] … The [PPSA] definition of "intangible" simply describes something that otherwise constitutes "personal property" but is not one of the listed types of *tangible* personal property. "Intangible" would include an interest created by statute having the characteristics of a licence coupled with an interest at common law as in the case of a *profit à pren-*

dre. Again, to repeat, I do not suggest that a fishing licence constitutes a *profit à prendre* at common law, for clearly there would be numerous conceptual objections to such a characterization. Our concern is exclusively with the extended definitions of "personal property" in the context of a statute that seeks to facilitate financing by borrowers and the protection of creditors. In my view the grant by the Fisheries Minister of a licence coupled with a proprietary interest as described above is sufficient to satisfy the *PPSA* definition.

[52] In this respect, the registration is therefore valid to include the s. 7(1) fishing licence and, in the absence of any other *PPSA* defence, the respondent bank is entitled to proceed with its *PPSA* remedies.

• • •

Appeal dismissed.

NOTES AND QUESTIONS

1) Does the Supreme Court's decision in *Saulnier* resolve the debate about whether a statutory licence is property for the purposes of the PPSA? Would a taxi licence qualify as "property" on Binnie J's approach? What about a milk quota, or a nursing home licence? What would the answers to these questions have been if the court had adopted the reasoning of: (i) the trial judge; or (ii) the Court of Appeal? Do you agree with Binnie J's reasons for rejecting both these approaches? For a critical analysis of the Supreme Court's decision, see Anthony Duggan, "In the Wake of the Bingo Queen" (2009), 47 *CBLJ* 225. For an account of the lower court decisions in *Saulnier* and the earlier case law, see Thomas G.W. Telfer, "Statutory Licences and the Search for Property: The End of the Imbroglio" (2007), 45 *CBLJ* 224.

2) Saskatchewan is the only province so far to have enacted a legislative response to the licence question. The Saskatchewan *Personal Property Security Act* (SPPSA) s. 2(w) defines "intangible" to include a "licence," and the s. 2(z) defininition of "licence" reads as follows:

> (z) "licence" means a right, whether or not exclusive:
>> (i) to manufacture, produce, sell, transport, or otherwise deal with personal property; or
>> (ii) to provide services;
> that is transferrable by the grantee with or without restriction or the consent of the grantor.

In Ontario, the Personal Property Security Law (PPSL) Committee recommended in 1998 and again in 2006 an amendment to the definition of "intangible" in the OPPSA to make it clear that it includes a licence. However, the Ontario government has not yet adopted the recommendation.

3) *Saulnier* deals with statutory licences. Licences can also be granted by contract. A contractual licence is a form of agreement under which licensor A gives licensee B permission to use A's property. Licensing is a common method for the sharing of intellectual property rights (patents, copyrights, trademarks, and the like). In form, a contractual licence is a promise by A to B that B may use the property for the duration of the agreement. Is a patent or copyright licence personal property?

The definition in SPPSA s. 2(w) is clearly wide enough to cover both statutory and contractual licences, but it is limited to transferable licences. In the case of a statutory licence, the definition means that if the governing legislation absolutely prohibits transfers, the PPSA will not apply, but the fact that transfers are subject to the licensing authority's discretion does not take the licence outside the PPSA definition. In the case of a contractual licence, the definition means that if there is an anti-assignment provision, the PPSA will not apply, but the fact that transfers are subject to the grantor's consent does not take the licence outside the PPSA definition. Enforcement of a security interest in a licence will typically involve sale of the licence to a willing buyer, along with the business to which the licence relates. In this connection, SPPSA s. 57(3) provides that the secured party may seize the licence upon giving notice to the debtor and also to the grantor of the licence or the grantor's successor in title, while s. 59(18) provides that the licence may be disposed of only in accordance with the terms and conditions under which the licence was granted. This provision is relevant to the case of a statutory licence where transfers are at the licensing authority's discretion, and also to a contractual licence where transfers require the grantor's consent.

The Saskatchewan provisions are to be contrasted with the approach taken in Revised Article 9, which provides that a term in a licence that prohibits or restricts the transfer of the licence is ineffective to the extent that the term would impair the creation, attachment, or perfection of a security interest: UCC 9-104(a). In the case of a statutory licence, this provision means that even an absolute prohibition on transfers in the governing statute does not itself prevent the taking of a security interest in the licence. Correspondingly, in the case of a contractual licence, the provision means that an anti-assignment provision does not preclude security interests. The Revised Article 9 approach is based on an assessment that facilitating access to credit is more important than, in the case of a statutory licence, whatever public benefit there might be in prohibiting security interests altogether and, in the case of a contractual licence, the value to the grantor of prohibiting security interests.

The Saskatchewan approach is based on the opposite assessment. The choice between these competing views is a matter for empirical observation and it cannot be determined on an *a priori* basis. However, it might be noted in passing that the SPPSA takes a different view of anti-assignment provisions in relation to accounts, stipulating that an anti-assignment provision in the contract that creates the account is ineffective to prevent the creation of a security interest in the account: s. 41(9) (compare OPPSA s. 40(4)). The Article 9 approach at least has the virtue of consistency in this regard.

In 2005, a Study Committee of the Uniform Law Conference of Canada tentatively recommended PPSA amendments along the lines of the Revised Article 9 approach, but to date nothing has come of this initiative: *Papers on PPSA Harmonization*: "Background Paper 5: Licences."

In 1998, the Canadian Bar Association—Ontario recommended amendments to the OPPSA along the lines of the Saskatchewan model: Canadian Bar Association—Ontario, *Submission to the Minister of Consumer and Commercial Relations Concerning the Personal Property Security Act* (October 21, 1998). As Justice Binnie was later to do in *Saulnier*, the submission stressed that the proposal constituted no threat to the grantor's interests because the secured party takes its security interest "warts and all":

> Whatever restrictions exist in the terms of the license or in the relevant legislation imposing regulatory requirements will continue to apply. The explicit inclusion of licenses simply means

that the OPPSA applies to a security interest in a license. It leaves it up to the secured party, as a matter of commercial judgment, to decide whether the license is suitable collateral having regard to the contractual or statutory restrictions in the license. [at p. 7]

The proposal was not adopted, apparently because some government stakeholders, including the Ministry of Agriculture, Food and Rural Affairs, opposed it on the ground that Ministries responsible for the issue of government licences and quotas should have exclusive responsibility for the transfer, assignment, and creation of interests in them. This concern apparently overlooks the warts and all qualification. In any event, the same proposal was put to the government again in 2006 and, again, it was rejected. It appears that, at the political level, the warts and all idea is a hard one to get across.

The Ontario Bar Association Business Law Section's Personal Property Security Law Committee is currently working on a new draft proposal. As previously, the proposed amendment would specify that the statute applies subject to any prohibition in the statute or the licence agreement on transfers or the creation of security interests. However, in contrast to the Saskatchewan model, the effect of such a prohibition on transfers would be simply to prevent the secured party from enforcing its security interest by selling the licence and not to prevent the creation of the security interest at all. The thinking is that the licence itself may be viable collateral even if it is non-transferable because, for example, it may allow the secured party's receiver to operate the business. On the other hand, the proposed reform would allow the licence grantor to prevent the creation of security interests altogether by expressly prohibiting them in the licensing statute or the licence agreement, as the case may be. The chances of this proposal being adopted are uncertain, but the fate of the earlier proposals does not provide much ground for optimism. Given the political challenges of selling the case for statutory reform, *Saulnier*'s failure to unambiguously resolve the matter assumes added significance.

III. SECURITY INTERESTS IN INVESTMENT PROPERTY

John Cameron, "Secured Transactions Under Ontario's Securities Transfer Act, 2006"
(2007), 22 *BFLR* 309, at 309, 310-11, 316-18, 335-39 (footnotes omitted)

Ontario's new *Securities Transfer Act, 2006* came into force on January 1, 2007. It creates a complex set of rules to govern the rights and obligations of issuers, securities intermediaries, investors and secured parties, relating to the transfer of securities. Despite this complexity, the new rules will greatly facilitate the use of securities as collateral.

This article describes the provisions that are most relevant to secured transactions.

A summary of the important rules appears at the beginning of this article. The summary includes a description of the difference between the *direct* holding system and the *indirect* holding system. Understanding this difference is essential to any understanding of the new rules.

...

Direct and Indirect Holding Systems

In Canada and the United States, securities are held under two systems: the direct holding system and the indirect holding system. The direct holding system applies where a direct relationship exists between an issuer and an investor. For example, the direct holding system applies to the relationship between a private company and its shareholders. The indirect holding system applies to the indirect relationship between an issuer and an investor, where the securities are held through a securities intermediary such as CDS Clearing and Depository Services Inc. (CDS), a bank or trust company acting as custodian, or a securities dealer. The indirect holding system depends in part on the direct holding system because for every security held in the indirect holding system, a direct relationship exists between an issuer and a person registered as the owner of a security or holding a bearer security, such as CDS.

The most common types of secured lending transactions that lawyers in private practice deal with occur under the direct holding system. For example, when a corporate borrower pledges the shares of its subsidiaries to secure a credit facility, and delivers the duly endorsed share certificates to the lender at closing, the direct holding system applies. Although the terminology used in the PPSA has changed slightly, the substance of the relevant rules applicable to secured transactions in the direct holding system remains largely unchanged by the STA. The most significant changes arise in the context of the indirect holding system, under which secured parties now have a new ability to perfect their security interest by way of a "control agreement" between the securities intermediary, the secured party and the debtor (i.e., the investor).

...

Direct Holding System

...

The direct holding system applies to direct dealings in a security. A security can be represented by a certificate (defined as a "certificated security") or not represented by a certificate (defined as an "uncertificated security"). The direct holding system applies to both types of securities.

Security is defined in the STA using very similar language to the definition of security in the PPSA prior to the STA amendments, with one key exception—the new definition focuses on an "obligation" of an issuer or a "share, participation or other interest" (i.e., the intangible rights created by a security) instead of the approach embodied in the old PPSA, which focused on a "document." ...

"Issuer" is very broadly defined, and with the definition of person includes (among other things) any individual, partnership, trust, corporation, government and any other legal or commercial entity. As noted in the Comment,* the definition of security has three components. First, the obligation or interest must be "fully transferable, in the sense that the issuer either maintains transfer books or the obligation or interest is represented by a certificate in bearer or registered form." Second, the obligation or interest

---

* Comments that accompanied the *Uniform Securities Transfer Act* approved at the Uniform Law Conference of Canada annual meeting, August 22-26, 2004.

must be part of a class or series, or must be divisible. This requirement distinguishes a security from obligations governed by ordinary contract law or typical instruments governed by the *Bills of Exchange Act*, which do not form part of a class or series and are not, by their terms, divisible into a class or series. The Comment expressly states that "securities issued in book-entry only form meet the divisibility test because the underlying intangible interest is divisible via the mechanism of the indirect holding system, ... even though the clearing agency is the only eligible direct holder of the security." Third, there is a functional test that generally turns on whether the obligation or interest is, or is of a type, dealt in or traded on securities markets or securities exchanges. However, there is an opt-in provision in clause (c)(ii) of the definition of security that permits the issuer of an obligation or interest, which meets the requirements of paragraphs (a) and (b), to specify that it is a security for the purposes of the STA.

Other sections of the STA clarify that a share or similar equity interest issued by a corporation, business trust or similar entity and a mutual fund security are each a security. According to the Comment, the specific reference to a share of a "corporation" (defined to mean any body corporate, wherever incorporated) clarifies that shares of private companies qualify as a security, whether or not the particular issue of shares is dealt in or traded on securities exchanges or in securities markets. Section 12 of the STA provides that an interest in a partnership or limited liability company is not a security unless (among other things) "that interest is dealt in or traded on securities exchanges or in securities markets" or "the terms of that interest expressly provide that the interest is a security for the purposes of this Act." Because section 12(a) excludes limited partnership units and shares in a limited liability company unless they are, in fact, traded on securities exchanges or in securities markets, section 12(b) allows an issuer to explicitly opt in by specifying that the units or shares are securities for the purposes of the STA. This flexibility is designed to (among other things) facilitate the use of partnership units and shares of limited liability companies as collateral for secured loans. The Comment notes that in the case of a share in a limited liability company, section 12 is intended to override section 10, which states that a share of a body corporate is a security.

Other sections of the STA exclude from the definition of security a bill of exchange or promissory note to which the BEA applies, a depository bill or depository note to which the *Depository Bills and Notes Act* applies, a clearing house option and a futures contract. However, any such bill of exchange, promissory note, depository bill or depository note, or any partnership unit and share of a limited liability company will qualify as a financial asset for the purposes of the indirect holding system if it is held in a securities account. The meaning of those phrases is discussed below under the heading "Indirect Holding System." This means that although the delivery of those excluded obligations or interests to CDS is not governed by the STA, the creation and pledging of a security entitlement in respect of those obligations or interests is governed by the STA and the PPSA.

···

Indirect Holding System

The indirect holding system applies where a securities intermediary (such as CDS, a bank or trust company acting as custodian, or a securities dealer) holds securities and other financial assets in a securities account for a person. The bundle of property and other rights (each of which is specifically described in the STA) in relation to the securities and other financial assets held in a securities account is known as a "security entitlement." The "security entitlement" (described in detail below) is at the heart of the indirect holding system.

A "securities intermediary" is a person that in the ordinary course of its business maintains securities accounts for the benefits of others and is acting in that capacity. The most common examples of securities intermediaries are clearing agencies (such as CDS) holding securities for their participants, banks or trust companies acting as securities custodians, and securities dealers holding securities on behalf of their customers.

A "securities account" is defined to mean "an account to which a financial asset is or may be credited in accordance with an agreement under which the person maintaining the account undertakes to treat the person for whom the account is maintained as entitled to exercise the rights that constitute the financial asset." According to the Comment, "[w]hether an arrangement between a firm and another person concerning a security or other financial asset is a 'securities account' under [the STA] depends on whether the firm has undertaken to treat the other person as entitled to exercise the rights that comprise the security or other financial asset." The Comment also notes:

> There are many arrangements between institutions and other persons concerning securities or other financial assets that do not fall within the definition of "securities account" because the institutions have not undertaken to treat the other persons as entitled to exercise the ordinary rights of an entitlement holder specified in the Part [6] rules. For example, the term securities account does not cover the relationship between a bank and its depositors or the relationship between a trustee and the beneficiary of an ordinary trust, because those are not relationships in which the holder of a financial asset has undertaken to treat the other as entitled to exercise the rights that comprise the financial asset contemplated by the Part [6] rules.

Paraphrasing the STA, a "financial asset" is defined to mean any of four types of property, as follows:

- any security;
- any share or obligation that "is, or is of a type, dealt in or traded on financial markets" or "is recognized in any other market or area in which it is issued or dealt in as a medium for investment"—e.g., commercial paper, bankers acceptances, partnership units, and shares of a limited liability company;
- any property held in a securities account that a securities intermediary and the person for whom the account is maintained have agreed is to be treated as a financial asset;
- a credit balance in a securities account unless the securities intermediary and the person for whom the account is maintained have agreed is not to be treated as a financial asset.

Although there is a circularity to these definitions, the key to solving this puzzle is found in Part VI of the STA, which defines the "rights and property interests" enjoyed by the person for whom the securities account is maintained by the financial intermediary.

A securities account will exist where those rights and property interests found in Part VI of the STA are appropriate for that relationship.

Security Entitlements

Section 1(1) of the STA defines "security entitlement" to mean "the rights and property interest of an entitlement holder with respect to a financial asset that are specified in Part VI" of the STA. In most cases, the security entitlement is created when a securities intermediary credits a financial asset to a person's securities account, even if the securities intermediary does not itself hold the financial asset. One of the components of the security entitlement is a *property interest in the underlying security or other financial asset*, if any, held by the securities intermediary together with various *cut-off rules*. The other component consists of *in personam rights against the securities intermediary*.

In Personam Rights

Those *in personam* rights consist of five core duties of a securities intermediary, as follows:

- *Duty to maintain financial assets:* A securities intermediary has a duty to obtain and maintain a financial asset in quantity corresponding to the aggregate of all security entitlements that the securities intermediary has established for its entitlement holders with respect to that financial asset.
- *Duty to obtain payments or distributions:* A securities intermediary has a duty to take action to obtain a payment or distribution made by the issuer of a financial asset, and to account to the entitlement holder for payments or distributions received by the securities intermediary.
- *Duty to exercise rights as directed:* A securities intermediary has a duty to exercise rights with respect to a financial asset if directed to do so by the entitlement holder.
- *Duty to change security entitlement into another form of holding:* A securities intermediary has a duty to change a security entitlement into another available form of holding for which the entitlement holder is eligible, or to cause the financial asset to be transferred to a securities account of the entitlement holder with another securities intermediary.

Property Rights and Cut-off Rules

As mentioned above, a security entitlement includes certain property rights and related cut-off rules, including the following:

- *Basic principle:* As stated succinctly by leading US commentators, "The baseline property principle of the indirect holding system is that financial assets held by a securities intermediary are held for its customers, to the extent necessary for the securities intermediary to satisfy all security entitlements against it to those financial assets" and "[o]nly the excess, if any, belongs to the securities intermediary." As to each financial asset in a securities account, the entitlement holder has a proportionate property interest in all of those financial assets held by the securities intermediary, regardless of when the security entitlement was created or the financial asset acquired. However, the property interest may be enforced against the securities intermediary only by exercise of the last four core *in personam* rights described above (created by sections 99 to 102 of the STA).

- *Rights against unsecured creditors of securities intermediary:* "Unsecured creditors of a securities intermediary cannot reach the financial assets held by the intermediary to the extent that the intermediary needs them to satisfy the related security entitlements against it."
- *Rights against secured creditors of securities intermediary:* Subject to two significant exceptions, secured creditors of a securities intermediary who have a security interest in financial assets held by that intermediary cannot reach those financial assets to the extent that the intermediary needs them to satisfy the related security entitlements against it even though section 19.2(2) of the PPSA provides that a security interest in investment property created by [a] broker or securities intermediary is perfected when it attaches. The two significant exceptions are as follows: (i) A secured creditor who has a security interest in a financial asset held by a securities intermediary and who has control over that financial asset has priority over the claims under the related security entitlements. (ii) A creditor of a clearing agency (e.g., CDS) has priority over the claims of entitlement holders.

IV. SECURITY INTEREST AND TRUSTS

Re Skybridge Holidays Inc.
(1999), 173 DLR (4th) 333 (BCCA)

GOLDIE JA: On 2 June 1998 Mr. Justice Mackenzie (as he then was) dismissed an application by the Trustee in Bankruptcy for directions regarding the claims of certain creditors of the bankrupt. This is an appeal from that dismissal.

Mr. Justice Mackenzie described the nature of the application in these terms:

> Skybridge Holidays Inc. filed for bankruptcy while holding monies received from travellers for travel services to be arranged through Skybridge. Skybridge's trustee in bankruptcy asks for direction as to the applicability of the provisions of the *Personal Property Security Act*, RSBC 1996, c. 359 ("PPSA") to the funds so held. For the purposes of the application, I have been asked to assume that the monies were deposited pursuant to a term, express or implied, that the funds would be held in trust for the traveller until the tickets or other travel receipts purchased were delivered. This assumed trust is separate from the statutory trust created by s. 7 of the *Travel Agents Act*, RSBC 1996, c. 459. By earlier order of this court, the statutory trust is not enforceable against the assets of Skybridge in bankruptcy. (I shall refer to the *Personal Property Security Act* as the "PPS Act.")

> • • •

Notwithstanding this loss of the provincial statutory trust the Registrar of Travel Agents, on behalf of the creditors in question, asserts they are the beneficiaries of a common law trust underlying the statutory trust and claims for them the benefit of paragraph (a) of s. 67(1) of the *Bankruptcy and Insolvency Act*, RSC 1985, c. B-3, as amended (the "Bankruptcy Act") which provides in part:

> 67(1) The property of a bankrupt divisible among his creditors shall not comprise:
> (a) property held by the bankrupt in trust for any other person,

It was in this circumstance that the Trustee applied for directions. The relief sought was couched in these terms:

> … for an order that a direction that the Trustee should not accept the claim of any traveller who asserts a non-statutory trust claim against any asset of the Bankrupt but who had not perfected that trust for claim by registration at the Personal Property Registry up to the date of bankruptcy;
>
> …

In summary then:

(a) The class of creditors in question paid monies to the bankrupt towards the purchase of travel monies;
(b) no declaration of trust by the bankrupt existed in respect of those monies; and
(c) the monies were identifiable by reason of their deposit in three segregated bank accounts of the bankrupt referred to in the order of 23 April 1998.

The Trustee admits for the purposes of this application the existence of the underlying trust—the so-called "assumed trust"—but relies on paragraph (i) of s-s. 20(b) of the PPS Act which provides that a security interest in collateral is not effective against:

> (i) a trustee in bankruptcy if the security interest is unperfected at the date of the bankruptcy …

It is common ground no security interest was registered in respect of the interest of the creditors in question here to the funds in the three segregated bank accounts.

The substantial question is whether the interest in the deposited funds of the class of creditors in question here is a security interest.

Section 2 of the PPS Act provides:

> 2(1) Subject to section 4, this Act applies:
> (a) to every transaction that in substance creates a security interest, without regard to its form and without regard to the person who has title to the collateral, and
> (b) without limiting paragraph (a), to a chattel mortgage, a conditional sale, a floating charge, a pledge, a trust indenture, a trust receipt, an assignment, a consignment, a lease, **a trust**, and a transfer of chattel paper if they secure payment or performance of an obligation.
>
> …

The Trustee's position is that the PPS Act has replaced the varieties of ways creditors formerly secured what was owed them with one comprehensive security interest, determined as to its effect by the substance of the transaction and registered in accordance with one statutory scheme in one registry.

Ms. Pike, for the Trustee, contended the true nature of the deposit made by the traveller was security for the performance by the bankrupt of its obligation to obtain the bargained-for travel service. She submits the intention of the parties is irrelevant and that the passing of title is no longer a consideration. These contentions and the overriding effect of paragraph (i) of s. 20(b) of the PPS Act are alluded to in *Re Giffen* (1998), 155 DLR (4th) 332 (SCC), at 344 where Mr. Justice Iacobucci, speaking for the Court, said:

> The Court of Appeal did not recognize that the provincial legislature, in enacting the PPSA, has set aside the traditional concepts of title and ownership to a certain extent. T.M. Buckwold and R.C.C. Cuming, in their article "The Personal Property Security Act and the Bankruptcy and Insolvency Act, Two Solitudes or Complementary Systems?" (1997), 12 *Banking & Finance L Rev.* 467, at pp. 469-70, underline the fact that provincial legislatures, in enacting personal property security regimes, have redefined traditional concepts of rights in property:
>
> > Simply put, the property rights of persons subject to provincial legislation are what the legislature determines them to be. While a statutory definition of rights may incorporate common law concepts in whole or in part, it is open to the legislature to redefine or revise those concepts as may be required to meet the objectives of the legislation. This was done in the provincial PPSAs, which implement a new conceptual approach to the definition and assertion of rights in and to personal property falling within their scope. The priority and realization provisions of the Acts revolve around the central statutory concept of "security interest." The rights of parties to a transaction that creates a security interest are explicitly not dependent upon either the form of the transaction or upon traditional questions of title. Rather, they are defined by the Act itself.

The chambers judge applied *Re Giffen* in observing that it is the substance of the transaction, rather than its form, that was normally determinative. Ms. Pike submitted he erred, however, in saying neither the travellers nor the travel agent would have considered their relationship to be one of creditor and debtor. Ms. Pike suggests the very existence of the assumed trust acknowledged risk of default on the part of the travel agent and so evidences an objectively determined intention to provide security in the collateral (the monies deposited) in the event of non-performance.

What they subjectively considered was in her submission irrelevant as the principle and purpose of the PPS Act, manifested in unambiguous language, would be eroded if an unperfected security interest was accorded a priority in bankruptcy.

But this, with all respect, begs the question as its premise is that the nature of the relationship between a traveller and the travel agent is analogous to that of debtor and creditor. Once that assumption is made the characterization of the arrangement as a security interest is inevitable.

In my view the analysis does not start with this premise. I agree with what the chambers judge said in the following portion of his judgment:

> The fact that the travellers' interest is a beneficial interest in a trust does not determine the issue. The PPSA is explicit that a trust interest is a security interest if the purpose is to secure payment or performance of an obligation. The substantive nature of the trust is critical. The travellers in this case are consumers not lenders and they become creditors unintentionally

as a result of the unforeseen bankruptcy. Skybridge received the funds as agent to purchase travel services and not as part of a security transaction.

Mr. Butler, for the Registrar of Travel Services, contended that the appropriate analysis must begin with an examination of the relationship in the case at bar, with particular reference to cases in which the critical factor was the characterization of the relationship. I agree with this approach and turn to some of these authorities.

In *Gervais v. Yewdale* (1993), 6 PPSAC (2d) 62 (BCSC) a judgment creditor garnished funds in the hands of the judgment debtor's solicitors. On an application for summary determination of the garnishee's liability the judgment creditor contended the funds attached consisted of the unearned portion of a retainer. The issue was whether the PPS Act converted the law firm's interest in these fund into a security interest. Madam Justice Huddart (as she then was) said this of a true retainer at 65:

> The Personal Property Security Act does not transform a solicitor-client relationship into a debtor-creditor relationship, a retainer into a debt. The issue is the true nature of the alleged retainer and whether that retainer can be legally garnished, not the priorities between a security interest in money and the interest of a garnisher in the same money. The Personal Property Security Act does not turn collateral into debt and thus create the right to garnishment where no debt existed by agreement or otherwise at common law or equity.

In *Graff v. Bitz (Trustee of)* (1991), 2 PPSAC (2d) 262 (Sask. QB) the relationship was one of agent and principal. The principal had given the agent money to buy a particular type and model of an automobile in the United States. The agent did so, registering it in his own name. Upon the agent's bankruptcy he did not list the vehicle as an asset and the principal claimed the bankrupt held the vehicle in trust for him. The court held the elements of a resulting trust were established. There was no evidence of a loan or business relationship. The agreement between the principal and the bankrupt was not a security interest.

In *Re Berman* (1979), 1 PPSAC 81 (Ont. CA) a lender's right to repayment from the proceeds of the bankrupt's debtor's registered retirement savings plan, of which the lender was the trustee, was upheld according to the law of trusts. The lower court was reversed in its holding that the lender, having failed to comply with the *Personal Property Securities Act*, was not entitled to recoup its advances. See also *Re Bronson* (1995), 10 PPSAC (2d) 164 (BCSC).

...

As I have said, the chambers judge was asked to assume the existence of the elements of the underlying trust. The Trustee accepted the burden of demonstrating the trust was a security interest. The chambers judge concluded this could not be done by simply applying the words of the PPS Act to the circumstances. What he did was to adopt an approach which, if there had been a disguised utilization of the trust as a security instrument, would have revealed that fact. He looked at the purpose of the transactions; the role and relationship of the parties; the practicality and commercial reality; and the intention of the parties with respect to the transactions.

We were referred to a number of other authorities, including writings of experts in this field. I have found it unnecessary to refer to these as I am satisfied the chambers judge's analysis was principled and in accord with the law in this jurisdiction.

I would dismiss the appeal.

NOTES AND QUESTIONS

1) Note that the BCPPSA (and all of the other non-Ontario PPSAs) make specific reference to "trust" as a method of creating a security interest. Does the absence of this reference from the OPPSA result in a different approach being applied in Ontario? In *Re Hounsome* (1991), 4 CBR (3d) 32 (Ont. SCJ), Rosenberg J refused to recognize that a trust could be used to circumvent the registration requirements of the OPPSA and defeat a trustee in bankruptcy. He said (at 37-38):

> From my analysis of the cases it appears that where the funds are never the property of the assignor, then the trust arrangement does not require a registration of a statement under the *Personal Property Security Act*. However, in cases where the receivable or property is that of the assignor at the time of making the assignment, then the assignment must be registered by filing a financing statement under the *Personal Property Security Act*. ...
>
> In addition, the statutory provisions are designed to protect the public so that they can regulate their affairs knowing what security interests are held. If the creating of [the] trust agreement of this kind could avoid the necessity of filing under the *Personal Property Security Act*, then the proposed creditor could not act prudently with knowledge of the true state of affairs of the debtor.

2) As to the use of the tracing rules of equity to earmark proceeds, see Chapter 12.

3) Does the following transaction give rise to a security interest? A loans money to B for the express purpose of paying specified creditors of B. The money is held by B as trustee under the terms of an implied trust that the money will be used to pay the creditors. If the money is not used for this purpose, it is subject to an implied trust requiring its return to A. See *Gignac, Sutts v. National Bank of Canada* (1987), 5 CBR (4th) 44 (Ont. SC). See also *Barclays Bank Ltd. v. Quistclose Investments Ltd.*, [1970] AC 567 and *Twinsectra Ltd. v. Yardley*, [2002] 2 AC 164 (HL). These cases have been the focus of considerable academic analysis. See, for example, D.R. Klink, "The Quistclose Trust in Canada" (1994), 23 *CBLJ* 45 and "Recharacterizing the *Quistclose* Trust: Lord Millett's *Obiter Dicta* in *Twinsectra*" (2005), 42 *CBLJ* 427; and M. Bridge, R. MacDonald, R. Simmonds, and C. Walsh, "Formalism, Functionalism, and Understanding the Law of Secured Transactions" (1999), 44 *McGill LJ* 567, at 616.

4) The trust is just one context in which it may be necessary to consider whether the transaction is in substance a security agreement. The question may arise in numerous other contexts as well. For example, which of the following transactions create security interests?

a) A loan agreement in which the borrower undertakes not to encumber some or all of his assets until the indebtedness is paid (generally described as a "negative covenant").

b) A subordination agreement under which a party (the senior creditor) agrees to postpone its rights against the debtor until the claim of the other party (the junior creditor) is satisfied. See OPPSA ss. 38 and 50, and Chapter 7, Part VII. In some subordination agreements, the senior creditor merely waives or postpones its rights in favour of the junior creditor; in others, the senior creditor surrenders rights to the junior creditor that are taken by the latter to secure payment of the obligation of the common debtor.

c) A contractual right of distress contained in a real property lease.

d) A contractual right given by A to B under which B is entitled to set off any obligations owing by A to B against the obligation of B to A.

V. DEEMED SECURITY INTERESTS

A. Transfers of Accounts and Chattel Paper

OPPSA s. 2(b) provides that the Act applies to a transfer of an account or chattel paper even though the transfer may not secure payment or performance of an obligation. As a result, a sale of an account or chattel paper falls within the perfection, priorities, and conflict of laws provisions of the Act. For example, Wilma sells goods to Barney for $100 on 90-day terms. Fred loans Wilma $90 and takes a security interest in Barney's account to secure repayment. This is a transfer of an account that secures payment or performance of an obligation and the Act applies. Now assume that, instead of taking a secured loan, Wilma sells Barney's account outright to Fred for $90. This is a non-security transfer, but the Act still applies by virtue of s. 2(b).

Why does the PPSA apply to non-security transfers of accounts and chattel paper? Part of the answer is that pre-PPSA, there was legislation requiring the registration of assignments of book debts and this applied to both security and non-security assignments. The PPSA continues this policy. Another part of the answer is as follows. In the two examples, the methods of transacting distribute the risk differently. In the first case, Wilma bears the risk of Barney's non-payment, because whether or not Barney pays, Wilma is still liable to Fred on the loan contract. In the second case, Fred bears the risk of Barney's non-payment, because Fred has bought the account outright and he takes the bad with the good. Fred could protect himself by negotiating a guarantee of payment with Wilma. This kind of arrangement is quite common. It is sometimes called a "with-recourse" assignment. It is with recourse in the sense that, if Barney defaults in payment, Fred has recourse against Wilma instead. A with-recourse outright assignment or transfer is functionally the same as a security transfer.

An assignment of accounts may be done on either a notification basis or a non-notification basis. In other words, the account debtor (Barney) may or may not be told about the assignment. If he is told, then his obligation will be to pay Fred. If he is not told, then his obligation will be to pay Wilma and it will be up to Fred to collect from Wilma: see s. 40(2). Assume the contract between Wilma and Barney contains a provision prohibiting assignment (an "anti-assignment clause"). Does the clause invalidate Wilma's assignment to Fred? Section 40(3) deals with this question. The answer is "no": the assignment remains effective, but Barney can sue Wilma for breach of contract, claiming damages for any loss. There are two competing policy considerations at stake here: (1) freedom of contract as between Wilma and Barney; and (2) the importance of facilitating the use of accounts receivable as a source of finance. Section 40(3) favours the second consideration.

B. Leases

Much of the interest in leasing as a financing device has been induced by taxation laws. Often, lessees are companies that do not have a great deal of taxable income, but need to acquire new equipment for which an accelerated capital cost allowance can be claimed. Leases have been used as vehicles to trade this capital cost allowance for a reduced finance charge. Under a leasing arrangement, the financer buys the equipment from the supplier and leases it to the lessee at a credit cost to the lessee below what it would pay if it borrowed the purchase price of the equipment. As to the test applied by Revenue Canada to determine whether a true lease or security lease is involved, see Department of National Revenue, Taxation, *Interpretation Bulletin* IT-233R, February 11, 1983.

The use of equipment leases as financing vehicles triggered a torrent of litigation in Ontario because the Ontario courts used a variety of tests to determine whether the agreements were genuine leases or only disguised security agreements, and therefore subject to the OPPSA. Some Ontario courts looked at the length of the lease and the size of the lease payments required to be made by the lessee compared to the regular price of the goods (mostly vehicles). Other courts were concerned to see whether the lessee was obliged to pay a "residual" sum at the end of the lease and how that sum was arrived at. Still other courts focused on whether the lessor or the lessee was obligated to pay for the cost of repair and maintenance of the leased goods during the period of the lease; and still another group of courts felt a near conclusive test was whether the lessor was genuinely engaged in the leasing of goods or whether the lessor was simply serving a financing function. See further, Ziegel and Denomme, 2d ed., §2.2.3.

The other provinces avoided these difficulties by adopting the rule that a lease of goods for more than a year (broadly defined) falls within the Act, other than for Part V purposes, whether or not the lease secures payment or performance of an obligation. In Ontario, the Personal Property Security Law Committee of the Ontario Bar Association recommended in a 1998 *Submission to the Minister of Consumer and Commercial Relations Concerning the Personal Property Security Act* the adoption of a similar provision in the Ontario Act, but it took the Ontario government until 2006 to implement the recommendation. See SO 2006, c. 34, Sched. E, s. 2, effective August 1, 2007. New OPPSA s. 2(c) provides that the Act applies to a lease of goods under a lease for a term of more than one year even though the lease may not secure payment or performance of an obligation. Note the definition of "lease for a term of more than one year" in PPSA s. 1(1). Despite s. 2(c), Part V of the Act, which deals with enforcement of security interests, applies only to transactions that secure payment or performance of an obligation: s. 57.1. This means that the lease characterization problem will remain important—and divisive—for this purpose. See further, Chapter 13, Part VIII.

So far as the adoption of new s. 2(c) is concerned, the PPSL Committee's Report based its recommendation on the following grounds: OPPSA s. 2(c) provides that the Act applies to a lease of goods under a lease for a term of more than one year, even though the lease may not secure payment or performance of an obligation. Note the definition of "lease for a term of more than one year" in PPSA s. 1(1). This is a recent provision: it was introduced in 2006 and came into effect on August 1, 2007. Previously, what s. 2 said was that the Act applied to a lease if it secured payment or performance of an obligation, but not otherwise. The amendment was based on a recommendation contained in a 1998 *Submission to the Minister of Consumer and Commercial Relations Concerning the Personal Property Security Act* by the Canadian Bar Association—Ontario, which read in part as follows:

> As we stated in our 1993 Submission, since the introduction of personal property security legislation in Ontario, no single issue has generated more litigation and controversy than the question of whether a particular lease is one to which the OPPSA applies. This question has not only been the subject of much litigation but has also been the subject of numerous articles in Canadian legal publications. A great amount of court time has been spent attempting to come to grips

with this problem and, for every court case which has been reported, there are undoubtedly many other disputes which have been settled one way or another outside the court. Disputes as to whether a lease is one governed by the OPPSA continue to be a source of costly litigation.

This issue was previously considered by the Minister's Advisory Committee in its *Report* of 1984 and in its *Supplementary Report* of 1985. That Committee recommended that the OPPSA apply to all leases of more than a year, whether or not such leases amounted to security leases. Despite such recommendation, the proposed change was not included in the 1989 version of the OPPSA.

In our view, it is now time to clarify the law and to move toward uniformity with *Personal Property Security Acts* in other provinces. To this end, we recommend that Ontario follow the western model, and adopt the definition of "lease for a term of more than one year," with all necessary related changes. While the OPPSA should thus apply to all leases, the default provisions set out in Part V of the OPPSA should only apply to those leases which in substance create a security interest. In other words, where there is a "true" lease, the rights and remedies of the parties after default should continue to lie outside the OPPSA.

With such amendments, it is hoped that certainty and predictability will be brought into this area and we will no longer need to focus on the identity of the lessor, the value of purchase options, intentions of parties, and so on, in determining whether registration of a financing statement or other perfection step is necessary to protect the interest of the lessor. [at pp. 8-9]

The reason for the one year cut-off rule is to exclude short-term rentals, such as the hire of a car for a weekend. The premise is that short-term rentals are typically not financing transactions, whereas longer-term rentals are more likely to be. Assume a lease for a term of less than one year that, as it happens, is a financing transaction. Does the Act apply? Section 2(c) does not catch the transaction because it is for a term of less than one year. However, s. 2(a)(ii) catches the transaction because it is a lease that secures payment or performance of an obligation.

The main practical implication of s. 2(c) is that longer-term lessors need to register a financing statement under the PPSA. Consider the following case:

SP is an equipment lessor. D is a road-builder. SP leases earth-moving equipment to D for an 18-month project. During the currency of the lease, D sells the equipment to T who has no knowledge of SP's interest. If SP fails to register, T will get title and SP's title will be extinguished: PPSA s. 20(1)(c) (see Chapter 5).

Contrast the following case:

SP is a garden equipment rental company. It rents a lawnmower to D for the weekend. D sells the lawnmower to T who has no knowledge of SP's interest. SP learns about the sale and claims the lawnmower from T.

The PPSA does not apply because the lease is a non-security lease and it is for a term of less than one year. This means that: (1) there is no requirement for SP to register a financing statement; and (2) the common law priority rules apply. At common law, the *nemo dat* rule (*nemo dat quod non habet*) governs and so SP's claim will succeed. This may seem unfair because, without a registration facility, there is no easy way for T to discover SP's interest. Why not extend the PPSA to all hiring agreements, regardless of length? One answer is that the PPSA is a secured transactions statute; extending its application to longer term hiring agreements can be justified on the ground that longer term transactions are more likely to be, in substance, security agreements. The same justification cannot be given for short-term rentals. Besides, the problem in the above example is one of ostensible ownership and hiring agreements are not the only source of the problem. Any proposal to bring hiring agreements at large within the scope of the Act would raise questions about the need for bringing in other transactions that create ostensible ownership problems as well; for example, trusts and bailments (other than contracts of hire). Another reason for not requiring registration of all hiring agreements is the burden it would impose on short-term hirers and the likelihood that a prospective third-party buyer would not search the register anyway, particularly if the goods are low value.

Professor Mooney is a strong opponent of registration requirements for leases in the United States. See "The Mystery and Myth of Ostensible Ownership and Article 9 Filing: A Critique of Proposals to Extend Filing Requirements to Leases" (1988), 39 *Ala. L Rev.* 683; and "Filing Requirements for Personal Property Leases: A Comment and Response to Professor Ziegel" (1990), 16 *CBLJ* 419. In "Should Canada Adopt an Article 2A Type Law on Personal Property Leasing?" (1990), 16 *CBLJ* 369, Professor Ziegel answers in detail Professor Mooney's principal objections to registration. In a study of the practices of lawyers who work in the areas of secured financing in Ontario, it was found that 70.4 percent of respondents to a questionnaire supported the inclusion of long-term leases within the scope of the registration, priorities, and conflict of laws provisions of the OPPSA. The survey also revealed that 54.9 percent of respondents always, and an additional 28.7 percent often registered financing statements relating to chattel leases in the Ontario Personal Property Registry. See Ziegel and Denomme, "How Ontario Lawyers View the Personal Property Security Act: An Empirical Survey" (1992), 20 *CBLJ* 90, at 102-4.

In the United States, arguments like Professor Mooney's have prevailed and Article 9 does not apply to true leases. Instead, UCC 1-203 incorporates a set of statutory rules for distinguishing a lease from a security interest, as follows:

(a) Whether a transaction in the form of a lease creates a lease or security interest is determined by the facts of each case.

(b) A transaction in the form of a lease creates a security interest if the consideration that the lessee is to pay the lessor for the right to possession and use of the goods is an obligation for the term of the lease and is not subject to termination by the lessee, and: (1) the original term of the lease is equal to or greater than the remaining economic life of the goods; (2) the lessee is bound to renew the lease for the remaining economic life of the goods or is bound to become the owner of the goods; (3) the lessee has an option to renew the lease for the remaining economic life of the goods for no additional consideration or for nominal additional consideration upon compliance with the lease agreement; or (4) the lessee has an option to become the owner of the goods for no additional consideration or for nominal additional consideration upon compliance with the lease agreement.

(c) A transaction in the form of a lease does not create a security interest merely because: (1) the present value of the consideration the lessee is obligated to pay the lessor for the right to possession and use of the goods is substantially equal to or is greater than the fair market value of the goods at the time the lease is entered into; (2) the lessee assumes risk of loss of the goods; (3) the lessee agrees to pay, with respect to the goods, taxes, insurance, filing, recording, or registration fees, or service or maintenance costs; (4) the lessee has an option to renew the lease or to become the owner of the goods; (5) the lessee has an option to renew the lease for a fixed rent that is equal to or greater than the reasonably predictable fair market rent for the use of the goods for the term of the renewal at the time the option is to be performed; or (6) the lessee has an option to become the owner of the goods for a fixed price that is equal to or greater than the reasonably predictable fair market value of the goods at the time the option is to be performed.

(d) Additional consideration is nominal if it is less than the lessee's reasonably predictable cost of performing under the lease agreement if the option is not exercised. Additional consideration is not nominal if: (1) when the option to renew the lease is granted to the lessee, the rent is stated to be the fair market rent for the use of the goods for the term of the renewal determined at the time the option is to be performed; or (2) when the option to become the owner of the goods is granted to the lessee, the price is stated to be the fair market value of the goods determined at the time the option is to be performed.

(e) The "remaining economic life of the goods" and "reasonably predictable" fair market rent, fair market value, or cost of performing under the lease agreement must be determined with reference to the facts and circumstances at the time the transaction is entered into.

In a 1999 report entitled *A Discussion Paper on Potential Changes to the Model Personal Property Security Act of the Canadian Conference on Personal Property Security Law*, presented to the Civil Law Section of the Uniform Law Conference of Canada, Professors Ronald Cuming and Catherine Walsh proposed a similar set of guidelines for inclusion in the PPSAs. See also Cuming, "True Leases and Security Leases under Canadian Personal Property Security Act" (1982), 7 *CBLJ* 251. The Cuming and Walsh proposal is relevant to PPSA, Part V (Default—Rights and Remedies), which, as noted above, as a general rule applies to a security interest only if it secures payment or performance of an obligation.

C. Consignments

A true consignment has many of the characteristics of a principal–agent relationship—not so much the characteristics of a sale. The owner of goods delivers possession of the goods to another person whose role it is to sell the goods as agent for the owner. While the consignee-agent will have obligations to the consignor-principal under this arrangement and may well be a trustee of property of the consignor-principal, these obligations are not secured either by the retained ownership of the consignor-principal in the consigned goods or by the beneficial interest he or she acquires under the trust. They are inherent in the principal–agent relationship. If, however, the consignee is obligated to pay the price of the goods and, consequently, does not have a right to return them to the consignor, a security agreement is involved. For a good review of the authorities, see *Access Cash International, Inc. v. Elliot Lake and North Shore Corporation for Business Development* (2000), 1 PPSAC (3d) 209 (Ont. SCJ).

The OPPSA applies to a consignment, but only if it secures payment or performance of an obligation. By contrast, in the other provinces the Act (except Part V) applies to all commercial consignments, whether or not they secure payment or performance of an obligation. The rationale is to avoid expensive litigation over the distinction between a true consignment and a security consignment.

In its 1998 *Submission to the Minister of Consumer and Commercial Relations Concerning the Personal Property Security Act*, the Canadian Bar Association—Ontario, stated (at page 9):

> [In addition to leases for a term of more than one year] we have also considered whether the OPPSA should be amended to apply also to commercial consignments, as is the case with the western model, and as was previously recommended by the Minister's Advisory Committee. While it would be logically consistent to include such consignments, on balance the Committee is of the view that this is not a pressing issue. We are also concerned that such a change could be a trap for unwary individuals such as artisans or craftspersons who consign goods on a regular basis to retail merchants, and who would not likely be aware of the perfection requirements.

VI. EXCLUSIONS FROM THE SCOPE OF THE ACT

A. Liens Given by Statute or Rule of Law: Section 4(1)(a)

Commercial Credit Corp. Ltd. v. Harry Shields Ltd.
(1981), 32 OR 703 (CA)

WEATHERSTON JA: This appeal raises a question as to the priority between a chattel mortgagee (the appellant) and a landlord who distrained for arrears of rent (the respondent). The chattel mortgage was properly registered in accordance with the provisions of the *Personal Property Security Act*, RSO 1970, c. 344. The landlord on its part had distrained properly for arrears of rent some time after the chattel mortgagee had sent a notice claiming possession of the secured property for default in payment.

Section 3(1)(a) [now s. 4(1)(a)] of the *Personal Property Security Act* exempts from the application of that Act "a lien given by statute or rule of law." A distress is the right of a landlord to take and hold possession until rent is paid, plus the statutory right to sell the distrained goods. We agree with the trial Judge that a distress, when made, confers on the landlord a lien within the meaning of s. 3(1)(a) of the *Personal Property Security Act* notwithstanding that it has other legal incidents. The effect of this is twofold. First of all the landlord's rights after making of a distress need not be registered in accordance with the *Personal Property Security Act*; and secondly, s. 68 has no application to the case. Section 68 provides that:

> 68. ... where there is conflict between a provision of this Act and a provision of any general or special Act ... the provision of this Act prevails.

At common law a landlord could levy a distress on all goods found on the demised premises. That right is limited by s. 31(2) of the *Landlord and Tenant Act*, RSO 1970, c. 236, to the tenant's goods unless "title is derived ... by way of mortgage." So here the appellant's title having been derived by way of mortgage, the appellant does not have the benefit of s. 31(2) and the landlord therefore has priority as found by the trial Judge.

Appeal dismissed.

NOTES AND QUESTIONS

1) As the *Harry Shields* case makes clear, the landlord's right of distress, once exercised, converts to a lien given by statute or rule of law to which the OPPSA s. 4(1)(a) exception applies. See also *859587 Ontario Ltd. v. Starmark Property Management Ltd.* (1998), 40 OR (3d) 481 (CA), extracted in Chapter 9, Part II.C. For other examples of liens that fall within the s. 4(1)(a) exception, see Chapter 10. Given that, in *Harry Shields*, the landlord's lien fell within the s. 4(1)(a) exception, clearly the court could not rely on the PPSA priority rules to determine the dispute. The court turned instead to the statute that created the lien, namely the *Landlord and Tenant Act* (now *Commercial Tenancies Act*, RSO 1990, c. L.7). Section 31(2) limits the right of distress to the tenant's goods unless title is derived by way of mortgage; in other words, the landlord may distrain against: (1) the tenant's own goods; and (2) goods title to which is in a secured party by virtue of a mortgage given by the tenant. So understood, s. 31(2) answered the question that was before the court. See also *Leavere v. Port Colborne (City)* (1995), 22 OR (3d) 44 (CA), extracted in Chapter 10, where, as in *Harry Shields*, the PPSA s. 4(1)(a) exception applied and the court turned to the statute creating the lien for the applicable priority rule.

2) Assume that in *Harry Shields*, the dispute had been between the landlord and the seller of goods to the tenant pursuant to a conditional sale agreement. Would the landlord have been allowed to distrain? Is there any justification for different outcomes depending on the form of the transaction between the tenant/debtor and the secured party? Should the landlord have priority over the secured party in any event? For example, assume the goods are inventory and the secured party financed the purchase. If the landlord's right of distress has priority over the secured party, the consequence may be to increase the cost of inventory finance, thereby potentially reducing the tenant/debtor's profitability. This is not in the landlord's interests, at least *ex ante*, because the tenant's reduced profitability increases the risk of non-payment of rent. Several provinces have amended their landlord and tenant acts to provide specific priority rules dealing with conflicting claims of distraining landlords and secured parties holding security interests in tenants' personal property. See, for example, *The Landlord and Tenant Act*, RSS 1978, c. L-6, s. 25.

3) In its 1998 *Submission to the Minister of Consumer and Commercial Relations Concerning the Personal Property Security Act*, the Canadian Bar Association—Ontario stated (at page 33):

> Jurisprudence in Ontario is to the effect that a landlord's right of distress against the tenant's goods gives rise to a "lien" arising by operation of law that is outside the scope of the OPPSA. As a result, no priority rule in the OPPSA will resolve a dispute between a landlord's right to distrain and a PPSA security interest. Our courts have endeavored to resolve such a priority dispute by giving effect to subsection 31(2) of the *Commercial Tenancies Act* (Ontario) (formerly named the *Landlord and Tenant Act*). Unfortunately, the statutory provision is not clear because it is expressed in pre-PPSA terminology and does not take into account the generic "security interest." The landlord and tenant legislation in some provinces has been amended to afford purchase-money security interests priority over the distraint rights of landlords.
>
> With a view to clarifying the law in Ontario in this regard, we recommend changes both in the *Commercial Tenancies Act* and the OPPSA. The changes to the *Commercial Tenancies Act* in essence would provide that a landlord would not be entitled to distrain upon goods which are

subject to a perfected purchase-money security interest at the time the landlord purports to distrain. It is necessary also to make complementary changes to subclause 20(1)(a)(i) of the OPPSA concerning the subordination of an unperfected security interest, in light of the fact that the OPPSA provides statutory "grace" periods in favour of security parties with respect to the time for perfection by registration of a purchase-money security interest. Hence, even if the secured party has not perfected its purchase-money security interest at the time the landlord exercises its distraint rights, if the purchase-money security interest is perfected within the "grace" period permitted by the OPPSA, the purchase-money security interest should not be subordinated. The recommended changes to the OPPSA, when read together with clause 4(1)(a) of the OPPSA, are not intended to change the law substantively in this area but only to clarify it.

To date, these recommendations have not been acted upon by the Ontario legislature.

4) There is a wide range of liens created by statute and rules of law, and the list of statutory liens continues to expand at an impressive and (from the secured parties' points of view) alarming rate. Most of the provincial PPSAs do not apply to these liens, although they all contain a priority rule dealing with repairers' liens. See, for example, OPPSA s. 31. The OPPSA stands alone, however, to the extent that it contains a more general (and controversial) priority rule governing the competition between an *unperfected* security interest and a lien created by statute or arising at common law: OPPSA ss. 4(1)(a) and 20(1)(a)(i).

These provisions do not address the most important question in this context: what are the respective priority positions of a lien holder and a secured party with a *perfected* security interest? The issue has attracted a very large, complex and expanding volume of litigation. The answer depends in part on the terms of the statute creating the lien and in part on whether the question arises before or after the debtor's bankruptcy. See, for example, the *Leavere* case, extracted in Chapter 10.

5) Section 4(1)(d) of the OPPSA excludes from the scope of the Act "a transaction under the *Pawnbrokers Act*." What justification is there for this exclusion? A pawn transaction (pledge) is a security agreement with ancient and respectable lineage. The Acts based on the CCPPSL model apply to pledge transactions, but exclude them from the enforcement (seizure and sale) provisions. Which approach is more consistent with the policies underlying the PPSA?

B. Insurance: Section 4(1)(c)

Stelco Inc. (Re)
(2005), 253 DLR (4th) 524 (Ont. CA)

WEILER JA: [1] This appeal raises two issues. First, when an insured has fully paid for a policy of insurance and assigns its right to receive a refund of any unearned premiums, is this a *security interest* that is *transferred*? Second, is it necessary to file notice of the security interest under the *Personal Property Security Act*, RSO 1990, c. P.10 ("PPSA") or is the security interest exempt from registration by virtue of a combination of s. 4(1)(c) of the PPSA and s. 138 of the *Insurance Act*, RSO 1990, c. I.8, or at common law?

Facts

[2] CAFO Inc. ("CAFO") finances insurance premiums for businesses under a standard form Premium Instalment Contract (a "PIC"). A purchaser will give an insurance company a down payment on the premiums due to the insurer. Under the PIC, the purchaser agrees to pay the rest of the premiums to CAFO over time and CAFO pays the insurer that remaining sum up front in exchange for an assignment of the right to receive payment of any amounts due from the insurer, such as unearned premiums. This assignment functions as security for the total amount that CAFO pays to the insurer.

[3] Stelco Inc. ("Stelco") and CAFO signed two PICs. The first concerned insurance for which the total premiums including taxes was $8.8 million. Stelco made all payments under this PIC. Stelco and CAFO also signed a PIC on June 11, 2003, under which funds were advanced for an insurance policy with Royal Sun Alliance Insurance. The premiums and taxes totalled $1.8 million; the down payment was $0.36 million and the balance plus service charge totalled $1.5 million. Stelco defaulted on this PIC in March 2004.

[4] Before the default, on January 29, 2004, Farley J made an order under the *Companies' Creditors Arrangement Act* ("CCAA") staying all actions by Stelco's creditors. Notice of the PIC was not registered under the PPSA because it was believed, based on the practice in the industry, that under s. 138 of the *Insurance Act* and s. 4(1)(c) of the PPSA, notice was not required to perfect the security. CAFO brought a motion asking Farley J to permit it to enforce its security under the PIC. However, Farley J refused, holding that the effect of s. 138 and s. 4(1)(c) did not create a perfected security interest in unearned insurance premiums unless notice of the PIC was filed under the PPSA. In holding that s. 4(1)(c) does not apply to exempt premium financing contracts, the motion judge essentially affirmed the opinion he had previously expressed in obiter in *Re Ivaco Inc.* (2004), 1 CBR (5th) 204 (Ont. SCJ). Farley J also suggested that a security interest might not arise under the PIC until the underlying insurance policy is cancelled, calling the timing of the security into question.

[5] Before this appeal was heard, the insurance policy underlying the PIC expired such that CAFO could no longer claim any unearned premiums and such that Stelco no longer had an interest in the litigation. Therefore, this court made a representation order requiring CAFO to pay the costs of the appeal on a substantial indemnity basis and appointing counsel to oppose CAFO's arguments.

Analysis

[6] Section 4(1) of the PPSA provides:

This Act does not apply,

...

(c) to a transfer of an interest or claim in or under any policy of insurance or contract of annuity.

[7] CAFO submits that the insured's right to obtain a refund of any unearned premiums coupled with the transfer of the insured's right to cancel the insurance policy operate so as to "transfer" an "interest" "in or under" any policy. As a result, the exemption

created by s. 4(1) applies and exempts CAFO from the need to register its interest under the PPSA.

[8] Farley J rejected this submission. His most important reason for holding that CAFO's security interest does not fall within the exemption is that the right to a potential refund of unearned premium arises under the premium instalment financing agreement. He concluded at para. 17 of his judgment:

> It would seem to me that one would need stronger and more specific language to reasonably conclude that the context of s. 4(1)(c) of the PPSA was intended to encompass the return of unearned premiums since what one is looking at is the enforcement of rights under a financing agreement—and in theory, such a financing agreement could be used for any other item of commerce.

[9] CAFO submits that the insurance premium financing agreement is not like other items of commerce. In most financings, security is taken in a property, most often a property that already exists. Here, CAFO's advance of funds creates the property: a fully paid-up insurance policy. Yet CAFO takes no interest in the underlying property. Nor does CAFO take any security against other assets owned by the insured. CAFO's only security is in the remaining unearned premiums on the policy. Items of commerce such as tangible wasting assets can be sold so that their value is "frozen" or preserved for all secured creditors. The insurance policy continues to run so that the value of the unearned premiums continues to decline and cannot be frozen by a quick sale.

[10] In any event, s. 4(1)(c) deals specifically with transfers of interests or claims in insurance policies. It does not deal with "other items of commerce" and these are not exempted.

[11] Insofar as the language of s. 4(1) is concerned, I am of the opinion that the wording does encompass the return of unearned premiums. The word "transfer" in s. 4(1)(c) includes an assignment. Black's Law Dictionary defines the word transfer as embracing:

> [E]very method—direct or indirect, absolute or commercial, voluntary or involuntary—of disposing of or parting with ... an interest in property, including retention of title as a security interest and foreclosure of the debtor's equity of redemption.
>
> ...
>
> The four methods of transfer are by [e]ndorsement, by delivery, by assignment, and by operation of law.

[12] The next question is whether assignments of unearned premiums create an "interest" in property. In the concluding line of para. 13, Farley J observed, "one may reasonably question the proposition that 'the unearned premiums come into existence when the policy is funded, not when the policies are cancelled.'"

[13] It would be more accurate to say that a right to any unearned premiums is created when the policy is funded but the realization of that interest is contingent on the happening of a future event, namely, the non-payment of premiums and the cancellation of the policy. Nevertheless, the right is an "interest." For example, Black's Law Dictionary defines an interest as an aggregate of rights and further states that an interest "refers to any one right, privilege, power or immunity." Were it otherwise, even if CAFO was sub-

ject to the PPSA, CAFO would have nothing to register until a default occurred and by then it would likely be too late for CAFO to become a secured creditor.

[14] With respect to whether the transfer of an interest is "in or under" the policy of insurance as opposed to the premium financing contract, Black's Law Dictionary indicates that the preposition "in" does not only mean "contained in." "In" also means "under or based upon the law of." The premium financing company's right to a refund is under the insurance contract in the sense that the premium financing agreement identifies the insurance contract giving rise to the buyer's right to a refund: See Jacob Ziegel, in *Unearned Insurance Premiums as Security Interests under The Canadian Personal Property Security Acts* (2004) 1 CBR (5th) 173 at 179.

[15] The wording of the exclusion in s. 4(1)(c) is clear and should be read as including the assignment of unearned premium under a policy of insurance.

[16] My conclusion is also consistent with American jurisprudence. Farley J considered six American cases that were cited to him: Re Redfeather Fast Freight, Inc., 1 BR 446 (Bankr. NE 1979); Re Maplewood Poultry Co., 2 BR 550 (Bankr. ME 1980); Re Auto-Train Corp., 9 BR 159 (Bankr. DC 1981); Re Air Vermont, 40 BR 335 (Bankr. VT 1984); Re RBS Industries, Inc., 67 BR 946 (Bankr. CT 1986); and Re U.S. Repeating Arms Co., 67 BR 990 (Bankr. CT 1986). He distinguished or rejected each of them, either because the particular state in question had specific PIC financing legislation or because the case contained little or no analysis and simply followed other cases. He also noted that the wording in Article 9-104 of the *Uniform Commercial Code (UCC)* is slightly different than s. 4(1)(c) of the PPSA.

[17] I agree with the application judge that Canadian courts should not simply follow American courts when interpreting similar legislative provisions. That said, I do not agree with him that the difference in wording between s. 4(1)(c) and the corresponding language in the American *UCC*'s article 9-104(g) is significant. Article 9-104(g) provides:

9-104 This Article does not apply

...

(g) to a transfer of an interest in a claim in or under any policy of insurance, except as provided with respect to proceeds (Section 9-306) and priorities in proceeds (Section 9-312).

The application judge observed that the *UCC* expressly excludes from the scope of s. 9-104 an insurance claim as proceeds whereas s. 4(1)(c) does not. However, the difference in wording is not significant because the definition of "proceeds" in s. 1(1) of the PPSA accomplishes the same result: See Ziegel, *supra*, at p. 178 of his article on Unearned Premiums, *supra*.

[18] There are two reasons why resort should be had to American jurisprudence in this case. The PPSA in Ontario and in other Canadian common law jurisdictions is closely patterned on Art. 9 of the *UCC* and American jurisprudence should, therefore, provide helpful guidance. Secondly, the PPSA was enacted in the various common law jurisdictions to make the law uniform and to facilitate business in more than one jurisdiction: *Gimli Auto Ltd. v. BDO Dunwoody Ltd.* (1998), 219 AR 166 (CA) at paras. 15-16.

[19] The values of certainty, uniformity, and ease of commerce are promoted if s. 4(1) of the PPSA is construed so as to exempt CAFO from having to register its interest in any

unearned premiums. Such an interpretation is consistent with the purpose and objective of the personal property security regimes enacted across the country and in the United States: *GMAC Commercial Credit Corp.-Canada v. TCT Logistics Inc.* (2004), 70 OR (3d) 321 at para. 20.

[20] Further not all of the cases can be distinguished on this basis. Cases from states that do not have such legislation include Re U.S. Repeating Arms, *supra*, Re Big Squaw Mountain Corp., 122 BR 831 (Bankr. ME 1990) at 9-10, Re Maplewood Poultry Co., *supra*, at 4 and Re Auto-Train, *supra*, at 8. In those cases, the first step was to hold that the transaction was excluded from the operation of Art. 9 of the *UCC* registration regime and then to look at the common law to determine the result.

[21] In Ontario, interpreting s. 4(1) as exempting CAFO from registering its right to receive any unearned insurance premium leads one to s. 138 of the *Insurance Act*. It states:

> 138(1) Where an insured assigns the right to refund of premium that may accrue by reason of the cancellation or termination of a contract of insurance under the terms thereof and notice of the assignment is given by the assignee to the insurer, the insurer shall pay any such refund to the assignee despite any condition in the contract, whether prescribed under this Act or not, requiring the refund to be paid to the insured or to accompany any notice of cancellation or termination to the insured.
>
> (2) Where the condition in the contract dealing with cancellation or termination by the insurer provides that the refund shall accompany the notice of cancellation or termination, the insurer shall include in the notice a statement that in lieu of payment of the refund in accordance with the condition the refund is being paid to the assignee under this section.

[22] This is not to say that s. 138 gives CAFO the right to priority over other secured lenders. To determine priorities, resort to the common law or to the provisions of the *Bankruptcy and Insolvency Act*, RSC 1985, c. B-3, would be necessary and that issue awaits another day. I do note, however, that in Re Maplewood Poultry Co., *supra*, the court held that a transfer of the insurance policies in question there could not be accomplished without placing the transferee on notice of the existence of a premium finance agreement because the policies contained explicit references to the premium finance agreements. Thus the exemption from registration under Art. 9 of the *UCC* did no harm to public policy.

[23] CAFO argues that no harm is done to public policy in any event because it is the proceeds of any insurance policy rather than the unearned premiums that form part of a lender's security. Clearly, however, the lender would have an interest in knowing if the insurance policy could be cancelled and unearned premiums remitted to the financier of a PIC. The exemption from the PPSA and its policy of providing notice to lenders about the state of the assets in which they will take security should not to be taken as a licence to keep lenders in the dark about the actual state of affairs. It behooves CAFO, and those who finance premium insurance contracts, to ensure that the policies contain explicit references to the insurance premium finance agreement itself and to the right of cancellation. In any event, when a judge decides whether to exercise his or her discretion to lift the stay under the CCAA and allow a premium financing company to obtain a refund of

unearned premium, one consideration would be whether the policy clearly contained an explicit reference to the premium finance agreement.

[24] Accordingly, I would allow the appeal and hold that CAFO has an interest in the unearned premiums that were transferred to it by virtue of the PICs and that that security interest was exempt from registration by virtue of a combination of s. 4(1)(c) of the PPSA and s. 138 of the *Insurance Act*.

NOTE

Re Stelco confirms that the OPPSA s. 4(1)(c) exception extends to insurance premium financing. Insurance premium financing works as follows. Insurance polices against fire, theft, property damage, etc., are for a fixed term, usually 12 months. The insured pays the premium up front and that buys 12-months' coverage. At the end of the 12 months, the insured pays another premium to renew the policy and that buys another 12-months' coverage. Assume that the insured cancels the policy part way through the term. Typically, the policy will give the insured a right to a refund for the unearned part of the premium. For example, if the insured cancels the policy three months in, she will normally get 75 percent of the premium back. If she cancels nine months in, she will get 25 percent back. The premium refund entitlement is assignable. *Insurance Act* s. 138 provides that if the insured assigns her refund entitlement and notifies the insurer, the insurer must pay the refund to the assignee. Insurance premium financing is a method of financing the premium where the financer takes a security interest in the premium refund entitlement. Typically, the insured pays the insurer a downpayment. The financer pays the rest. The insured agrees to repay the financer by installments over the life of the policy. The agreement provides that, if the insured defaults, the financer may cancel the policy and claim the premium refund. The installments are calibrated to the declining value of the premium refund. For example, if the insured defaults three months in, the 75 percent premium refund will be just enough to cover the nine months' installments still owing. Likewise, if the insured defaults nine months in, the 25 percent premium refund will be just enough to cover the three months' installments still owing. Are there good policy reasons for excluding such arrangements from the scope of the PPSA?

GE Canada Equipment Financing G.P. v. ING Insurance Company of Canada
(2009), 94 OR (3d) 321 (CA)

CRONK JA: [1] This appeal involves a priority dispute between a secured creditor who holds perfected security interests under the *Personal Property Security Act*, RSO 1990, c. P.10 (the "PPSA") in two highway tractor trucks and an automobile insurer who is entitled to salvage rights in the same vehicles under statutory condition 6(7) in *Statutory Conditions—Automobile Insurance*, O. Reg. 777/93 passed under the *Insurance Act*, RSO 1990, c. I.8, as amended (the "Insurance Act"). At issue is the interplay between s. 4(1)(c) of the PPSA, which excludes "a transfer of an interest or claim in or under any policy of insurance" from the application of the PPSA, and statutory condition 6(7) of the

Insurance Act, which affords an insurer the right to salvage in an insured vehicle in certain circumstances. ...

I. Facts

(1) The Parties and the Events

[2] The appellant, GE Canada Equipment Financing G.P. ("GE"), an asset-backed lender, leases or conditionally sells various types of collateral, including highway tractor trucks. The respondent, ING Insurance Company of Canada ("ING"), offers a range of insurance products and services to the public, including automobile insurance. At the relevant time, Brampton Leasing and Rentals Limited ("Brampton") was in the vehicle leasing and rental business, operating as a Hertz car and truck rental agency.

[3] GE financed the purchase of numerous vehicles for use by Brampton in its leasing and rental business. In particular, on September 18, 2002 and November 18, 2004, GE entered into two conditional sale agreements (the "CSAs") with Brampton, whereby GE financed Brampton's acquisition of two highway tractor trucks manufactured in 2003 and 2005 (referred to in these reasons as the "2003 Truck," the "2005 Truck" or, collectively, the "Trucks").

[4] Under the terms of the CSAs: (i) GE was named as the "assignee" and Brampton was named as the "purchaser" of the Trucks; (ii) GE remained the owner of and held title to the Trucks until they were paid for in full; (iii) Brampton was required to place and maintain comprehensive first party all risks insurance on the Trucks for their full replacement value, to name GE as a beneficiary in the insurance policies so obtained, and to ensure that the policies contained a waiver of subrogation clause in favour of GE; and (iv) while not in default under the CSAs, Brampton was entitled to the quiet use and enjoyment of the Trucks.

[5] By the end of November 2004, GE had taken all necessary steps under the PPSA to perfect its purchase money security interests ("PMSIs") in the Trucks and their proceeds.

[6] In accordance with its obligations under the CSAs, Brampton obtained comprehensive general liability insurance policies on the Trucks from Zurich Insurance Company, naming GE as loss payee thereunder. In addition, in February and May 2005, when Brampton leased the Trucks to two separate third parties, each lessee obtained automobile insurance on its leased vehicle under a policy of insurance issued by ING (the "ING policies"). The third parties were named as the insureds and lessees, and Brampton was named as the lessor and loss payee under the ING policies. No mention was made of GE in the ING policies.

[7] After the ING policies were issued, both Trucks were stolen. As a result, in September 2005 and May 2006, the third party lessees completed loss claims and Brampton submitted proof of loss forms to ING in respect of the stolen Trucks. In the latter documents, Brampton falsely represented in relation to the Trucks: "[N]o person, firm, or corporation, other than the Insured, has had any interest therein, and there is no lien, chattel mortgage, or conditional sales agreement thereon."

[8] In consideration for the receipt of the ING insurance proceeds, Brampton also purported to transfer title to the Trucks to ING in circumstances of a vehicle total loss claim (the "Transfer"). The proof of loss forms stated:

> Payment of this claim to [the insured and Brampton] is hereby authorized and in consideration of such payment the Insurer is discharged forever from all further claim by reason of the said loss or damage. All rights to recovery from any other person are hereby transferred to the Insurer which is authorized to bring action in the Insured's name to enforce such rights. *All right, title and interest in the vehicle or any part or equipment thereof is hereby transferred to the Insurer only in the event that this claim is based upon the whole value of the vehicle because it has been lost, destroyed or damaged beyond economical repair and the Insured agrees immediately to notify the Insurer in the event of its recovery.* [Emphasis added.]

The record does not reveal how the Transfer contemplated by this provision was actually made.

[9] ING accepted the loss claims and discharged its indemnity obligations under the ING policies by paying the cash value of the stolen Trucks jointly to Brampton and the third party lessees, less applicable deductibles. As a result, as I discuss later in these reasons, ING became entitled to salvage rights in the Trucks under statutory condition 6(7) of the Insurance Act.

[10] ING did not conduct PPSA searches prior to issuing the ING policies, paying the ING insurance proceeds, or accepting title to the Trucks from Brampton.

[11] Both Trucks were later recovered and ING took possession of them. ING then sold the 2005 Truck to an unrelated party. As a result of this litigation, ING has retained possession of the 2003 Truck and the proceeds from the sale of the 2005 Truck.

[12] Brampton did not notify GE of the theft of the Trucks. On the contrary, it continued to make payments to GE under the CSAs for some months after the Trucks were stolen. Similarly, GE received no notice of the terms of the ING policies, the claims made thereunder by Brampton and the third party lessees, the payment to them of the ING insurance proceeds, or the Transfer. None of the ING insurance proceeds was remitted to GE.

[13] Brampton defaulted in its payment obligations under the CSAs in December 2006 and filed an assignment in bankruptcy on March 1, 2007. GE learned of the theft of the Trucks when it attempted to exercise its remedies on default under the CSAs. On March 14, 2007, GE obtained used vehicle information packages for the Trucks from the Ministry of Transportation, which indicated that ING was the registered owner of the 2003 Truck and that it had owned, and subsequently sold, the 2005 Truck. The packages also identified GE as a "secured party" and a registered lienholder in relation to both Trucks.

[14] There is no suggestion that the third party lessees or ING knew of GE's PMSIs in the Trucks prior to the end of March 2007, when GE wrote to ING and informed it of GE's perfected PMSIs in the Trucks. Brampton, of course, knew of GE's PMSIs throughout.

(2) Relevant Statutory Provisions

[15] The following statutory provisions are central to the issues on appeal:

A. The PPSA:

[Sections 4(1)(c), 9(1), 25(1), 28(1).]

B. Statutory Condition 6(7) of the Insurance Act:
There shall be no abandonment of the automobile to the insurer without the insurer's consent. If the insurer exercises the option to replace the automobile or pays the actual cash value of the automobile, the salvage, if any, shall vest in the insurer.

(3) The Litigation

[16] Despite demand therefor, ING refused to surrender possession of the 2003 Truck or to pay the proceeds from the sale of the 2005 Truck to GE. As a result, GE commenced proceedings against ING, applying for declarations that: (i) its PMSIs in the Trucks had priority over ING's rights to salvage in the same vehicles; and (ii) it was entitled to the return of the Trucks or, in the case of the 2005 Truck, to the proceeds of sale thereof, from ING.

[17] ING resisted GE's application on two grounds. It maintained that its salvage rights flowed from the ING policies, which incorporated statutory condition 6(7) of the Insurance Act, and that the PPSA did not apply to its interests in the Trucks by virtue of s. 4(1)(c) of the PPSA and statutory condition 6(7) of the Insurance Act. ING also argued that as the Transfer was a "[sale] in the ordinary course of business," the PPSA did not apply by operation of s. 28(1) of the PPSA. On both grounds, ING asserted that it took title to the Trucks free from GE's pre-existing perfected PMSIs in the Trucks.

[18] By order dated February 4, 2008, the application judge dismissed GE's application and, on consent, awarded costs to ING in the total amount of $15,000, plus interest. The core of his reasoning was as follows:

> As a matter of priority, the PPSA, in effect, has stated that GE is not to have priority over transfers of interest to ING by reason of the operation of Statutory Condition 6(7) which is incorporated into insurance policies.

> *Conclusion*
> I find that GE's interest in the vehicles *vis a vis* ING is not protected by the PPSA for the reason that [the] PPSA does not apply to a transfer of an interest under a policy of insurance [s. 4(1)(c) of the PPSA]. There was such a transfer of an interest by virtue of Statutory Condition 6(7).

[19] Given this conclusion, the application judge regarded it as unnecessary to address ING's s. 28(1) PPSA argument. In contrast to its position on this appeal, ING did not rely on s. 25(1) of the PPSA in the proceeding before the application judge.

II. Issues

[20] I would frame the issues on appeal this way: do ING's salvage rights in the Trucks have priority over GE's pre-existing perfected PMSIs in the Trucks and their proceeds by operation of: (i) s. 4(1)(c) of the PPSA and statutory condition 6(7) of the Insurance Act; (ii) s. 28(1) of the PPSA; or (iii) s. 25(1) of the PPSA?

III. Analysis

[21] GE advances two main arguments in support of its claim that its PMSIs have priority over ING's salvage rights. It submits that the application judge erred by concluding that the combined operation of s. 4(1)(c) of the PPSA and statutory condition 6(7) of the Insurance Act resulted in title to the Trucks vesting in ING free from GE's perfected PMSIs in the Trucks and their proceeds. GE also asserts that neither s. 28(1) nor s. 25(1) of the PPSA are engaged in this case since, in the case of s. 28(1), the Transfer was not a "[sale] in the ordinary course of business" and, in the case of s. 25(1), GE did not expressly or impliedly authorize the Transfer. I will address these arguments in turn.

...

(1) Section 4(1)(c) of the PPSA and Statutory Condition 6(7) of the Insurance Act

[23] The application judge concluded that the combined effect of s. 4(1)(c) of the PPSA and statutory condition 6(7) of the Insurance Act was to deprive GE of the priority protection otherwise afforded to its PMSIs under the PPSA. With respect, I disagree.

...

[28] Section 4(1)(c) of the PPSA excludes transfers of "an interest or claim in or under any policy of insurance" from the application of the PPSA. Jacob S. Ziegel and David L. Denomme, in *The Ontario Personal Property Security Act: Commentary and Analysis*, 2nd ed. (Toronto and Vancouver: Butterworths, 2000) at p. 82, citing F.M. Catzman, Q.C., *Personal Property Security Law in Ontario* (Toronto: Carswell, 1976) at p. 35, explain the rationale for the s. 4(1)(c) exclusion in this fashion:

> The drafters of the original Ontario Act rationalized the exclusion of security interests in insurance policies on the ground that the insurer maintains records of title and claims to policies and contracts issued by it and that there was no need for a separate registry.

See also *Rektor (Re)*, [1983] OJ No. 957 (HCJ), at para. 11.

[29] Thus, the purpose of s. 4(1)(c) is to avoid the unnecessary duplication of notice systems concerning transfers that create interests or claims in or under insurance policies. This is achieved by excluding such interests or claims from the PPSA notice and registration scheme. Simply put, notice under the PPSA is not required to perfect a security interest falling within the ambit of s. 4(1)(c).

...

[31] The effect of s. 4(1)(c) in this case ... was to relieve ING of the obligation to protect its interests under the ING policies by providing notice of those interests in the

PPSA registry. But s. 4(1)(c) did no more. It did not relieve ING of the requirement to be mindful of the PPSA-protected interests of secured creditors. Nothing in the language of s. 4(1)(c) suggests that it is intended to resolve priority disputes between creditors, including priority competitions between a creditor with a perfected security interest under the PPSA (like GE) and a creditor whose interest in collateral is exempt from the notice and registration requirements of the PPSA (like ING).

• • •

[35] Section 4(1)(c) of the PPSA is modelled after Article 9 of the Uniform Commercial Code (the "UCC"), which establishes exceptions from similar personal property registration schemes in the United States. UCC 9-109(d)(8) provides:

> 9-109(d) This article does not apply to:
>
> (8) a transfer of an interest in or an assignment of a claim under a policy of insurance …

[36] Prior to July 1, 2001, the wording of UCC 9-104(g)—the predecessor provision to current UCC 9-109(d)(8)—was identical to that of s. 4(1)(c) of the PPSA. The ambit of UCC 9-104(g) was interpreted by American courts as limited to direct interests created in an insurance policy by making the policy itself the collateral securing the transaction in question. Thus, for example, in *Paskow v. Calvert Fire Insurance Co.* 579 F2d 949, 953 (5th Cir. 1979), the court explained that UCC 9-104(g) was "directed not at the insurance of collateral but the creation of a security interest *in an insurance policy*" (emphasis added). See also *PPG Industries v. Hartford Fire Ins. Co.* 531 F2d 58, 60 (2nd Cir. 1976).

[37] The Transfer in this case was not a secured transaction—it did not create an interest that secured payment or performance of an obligation. Nor did it create a security interest "in or under an insurance policy," including in respect of amounts payable under an insurance policy, so as to trigger the application of s. 4(1)(c) of the PPSA. Rather, it involved the purported transfer of ownership in the Trucks to ING in exchange for full indemnification under the ING policies on the basis of a total loss claim.

[38] I note that GE makes no claim to the ING policies or their proceeds. Its claims are to the collateral secured by the CSAs—the Trucks—and, in the case of the 2005 Truck, to the proceeds of sale realized by ING, in respect of which GE holds PPSA-protected security interests. GE's claims, therefore, are unaffected by s. 4(1)(c). Its claims are based on "PPSA security interests" in the Trucks and, in respect of the 2005 Truck, in its proceeds. In contrast, ING's interests in or under the ING policies and its salvage rights in the Trucks are "non-PPSA interests."

[39] In all these circumstances, I agree with GE's submission that s. 4(1)(c) does not operate in this case to determine the priorities between GE's PPSA security interests in the Trucks and their proceeds and ING's non-PPSA salvage rights in the Trucks. Section 4(1)(c) simply has no bearing on that key issue.

[40] However, that does not end the matter. In the application judge's view, it was the combined operation of s. 4(1)(c) and statutory condition 6(7) that determined this priority contest. Recall that he held that GE's interest in the vehicles, "is not protected by the PPSA for the reason that [the] PPSA does not apply to a transfer of an interest under a

policy of insurance" and "There was such a transfer of an interest by virtue of Statutory Condition 6(7)." I turn now to consideration of statutory condition 6(7).

...

[41] Under s. 234(1) of the Insurance Act, statutory condition 6(7) forms part of the standard form automobile insurance policy in use in Ontario. Statutory condition 6(7) is concerned with automobile total loss cases. In such cases, an insurer is entitled to the salvage, if any, in the lost automobile where it elects to replace or pay the actual cash value of the automobile. In *David Polowin Real Estate Ltd. v. Dominion of Canada General Insurance Co.* (2005), 76 OR (3d) 161, at para. 54, leave to appeal to SCC refused, [2005] SCCA No. 388, this court explained that statutory condition 6(7) affords an insurer three options where an insured vehicle is a total loss:

> First, the insurer can replace the insured's car and take title to the salvage. It is entitled to the salvage because otherwise, its insured will be over-indemnified. Second, it can pay the actual cash value of the car and take title to the salvage. Again, the insurer claims entitlement to the salvage to prevent over-indemnification. Third, it can elect to leave the salvage with the insured, in which case the insured's loss would not be the actual cash value of the car but its diminution in value.

[42] In this case, the Trucks were lost through theft. On proof of loss, ING exercised the second option described in *Polowin*—it paid Brampton and the third party lessees the actual cash value of the Trucks, less applicable deductibles, in exchange for the Transfer. Having satisfied its indemnity obligations under the ING policies in full, ING became entitled under statutory condition 6(7) to title to any salvage in the Trucks. But this does not mean that statutory condition 6(7) operates to vest title to the salvage in ING, free and clear of pre-existing perfected security interests in the Trucks. I say this for several reasons.

[43] First, the concepts of priority and salvage are not the same. Statutory condition 6(7) does not refer to priorities, the interests of secured creditors, or the PPSA. It refers to the right to salvage in respect of a total loss insured vehicle. A plain reading of statutory condition 6(7) offers no support for ING's contention that it is intended, alone or in combination with s. 4(1)(c) of the PPSA, to extinguish a creditor's pre-existing perfected security interest in a vehicle that becomes the subject of a total loss claim. For example, statutory condition 6(7) does not contain the words "notwithstanding any security interest in the vehicle." It is, of course, open to the legislature to create a right that extinguishes or subordinates the pre-existing perfected security interests of third parties. But if this were the intent of statutory condition 6(7), it could easily have been accomplished by the use of explicit priorities language.

...

[46] Second, and importantly, statutory condition 6(7) represents a statutory codification of the common law right of subrogation. In *Polowin*, Laskin JA, writing for a unanimous court, held at para. 82 that an insurer's right to claim salvage under statutory condition 6(7), "amounts to the exercise of the right of subrogation after fully indemnifying the insured for the insured's loss." He later added at para. 100: "Once an insured has been fully indemnified for the loss, the right to salvage is simply the exercise of the right of subrogation to prevent over-indemnification [of the insured]."

[47] Subrogation is a derivative right that rests on the principle of indemnification. It contemplates that on full indemnification of an insured by an insurer for an insured loss, the insurer becomes entitled to exercise a right belonging to the insured. ...

[48] In other words, under the principle of subrogation, the insurer succeeds only to the exact right otherwise enjoyed by its insured. This is not a new proposition. It has long been recognized that under the right of subrogation, the insurer must be placed in the position of its insured. For this reason, the discussion in *Polowin* of an insurer's exercise of the right of subrogation under statutory condition 6(7) recognizes that prior to the insurer's election to trigger statutory condition 6(7), the right to salvage in an insured vehicle is a property right of the insured. Where, however, the insurer pays the insured's total loss claim in respect of the insured vehicle, it becomes entitled to all the salvage rights that the insured possessed in respect of the insured vehicle. Statutory condition 6(7), therefore, is concerned with an insurer's right to salvage as against its insured.

···

[52] Where—as here—salvage is available, the principle of subrogation that underlies statutory condition 6(7) and the requirement of indemnification on which that principle rests, mandate that an insurer who replaces or pays the actual cash value of an automobile in a total loss case steps into the shoes of the insured in relation to the right to salvage. The insurer is only entitled under the subrogation principle to the salvage right that was enjoyed by its insured prior to the insurer's decision to invoke statutory condition 6(7).

[53] In this case, Brampton's interests in the Trucks were subject to GE's perfected PMSIs. Statutory condition 6(7) conferred on ING only those rights to salvage possessed by Brampton prior to ING's payment of the actual cash value of the Trucks. Absent express statutory language to the contrary, statutory condition 6(7) should not be interpreted so as to confer on Brampton's insurer greater rights to salvage in the Trucks than were held by Brampton.

···

[60] I would summarize my conclusions concerning s. 4(1)(c) of the PPSA and statutory condition 6(7) of the Insurance Act as follows:

(i) Section 4(1)(c) and statutory condition 6(7) do not address priorities. ... On the facts of this case, GE's PMSIs in the Trucks are effective as against ING under s. 9(1).

(ii) Under s. 4(1)(c), ING was relieved of the obligation to provide notice of its interests under the ING policies in the PPSA registry. However, while s. 4(1)(c) freed ING from the need to protect its own interests under the PPSA, it did not relieve it of the requirement to be mindful of the PPSA-protected interests of other parties in the same collateral.

(iii) The reach of ING's salvage rights under statutory condition 6(7) is determined by Brampton's salvage rights as they existed before ING triggered statutory condition 6(7). Brampton's salvage rights in the Trucks did not extinguish or displace the priority of GE's PMSIs in the Trucks and their proceeds. As against GE, therefore, ING is in no better position in respect of its salvage rights than was Brampton.

···

(4) Concluding Observations

[79] I end with these observations. This case involves the balancing of the competing interests in collateral of two 'innocent' parties. GE took all necessary steps to perfect its PMSIs under the PPSA. It had no knowledge that the Trucks had been stolen until its own inquiries led to discovery of the thefts. Nor did it know of Brampton's misrepresentations to ING. ING had no involvement in the thefts or Brampton's misrepresentations, and it did not know of GE's security interests in the Trucks until after it had paid the proceeds under the ING policies.

[80] On the other hand, measures were available to both parties that might have avoided this dispute. GE did not require that Brampton cause its third party lessees to name GE as an insured, a loss payee or a beneficiary under any third party insurance policy obtained on the Trucks. Nor did GE require Brampton to provide it with copies of any third party insurance policies. These options were available to GE. However, their success was dependent on the reliability of Brampton and its lessees.

[81] For its part, ING did not conduct any PPSA searches in this case. It defends this omission by pointing to what it describes as standard insurance industry practice: in reliance on s. 4(1)(c) of the PPSA, no PPSA searches are performed by insurers or insurance brokers prior to the issuance of automobile insurance policies. But, as I have said, the effect of s. 4(1)(c) of the PPSA is to relieve an insurer from the necessity of protecting its own interests in respect of an insurance policy by providing notice of those interests in the PPSA registry. Section 4(1)(c) does not insulate insurers from the PPSA-protected claims of third party secured creditors.

[82] And the means of ascertaining the existence of GE's PMSIs in the Trucks were readily available to ING by the simple device of conducting a PPSA search before issuing the ING policies, before paying the ING insurance proceeds, before requesting and receiving the Transfer from Brampton and, in the case of the 2005 Truck, before disposing of the insured collateral. Notice of GE's security interests was also provided in the used vehicle information packages available from the Ministry of Transportation. ING did not avail itself of any of these opportunities to determine if its interests would be subject to the protected priority position of another claimant. Unlike the preventative options available to GE, which I have described above, the measures available to ING to protect its interests were not dependent on the reliability of its insured or a third party.

[83] I note also that the potential existence of secured creditors with claims regarding the insured collateral was within ING's contemplation. The ING policies provided for the identification of lienholders and the protection of their interests on payment of the ING insurance proceeds. This record is silent as to what steps ING took, if any, to determine if secured claims existed in respect of the Trucks prior to settling Brampton's claim for indemnification under the ING policies.

[84] In these circumstances, I view it as unreasonable that a creditor in GE's position should lose its priority in secured collateral because it failed to foresee that its debtor would actively mislead its involved insurers. To hold otherwise would impose a protectionist obligation on GE and similarly situated secured lenders that could undermine normal good faith collateral financings.

[85] I therefore conclude that, as between GE and ING, the consequences of Brampton's misrepresentations must be borne by ING. It is ING, therefore, who must look to Brampton for satisfaction. This result is consistent with the proposition, which I endorse, that an insured or its named loss payee who has derived the benefit of an insurance policy, must make good to the insurer any loss occasioned to it by the insured's or the loss payee's lack of good faith or honesty.

…

Juriansz and MacFarland JJA agreed.

Appeal dismissed.

NOTE

The court rejected ING's s. 28(1) argument on the grounds that: (1) the transfer from Brampton to ING was not a "sale" within the meaning of the provision; and (2) the transfer was not in the ordinary course of Brampton's business. Section 28(1) is dealt with in Chapter 11. ING's s. 25(1) argument was that GE's security interest did not "continue as to the collateral" because GE "expressly or impliedly authorized" Brampton's transfer of the collateral to ING. The court rejected this contention. Section 25(1) is dealt with in Chapter 12.

C. Interests in Real Property: Section 4(1)(e)

Re Urman
(1984), 3 DLR (4th) 631 (Ont. CA)

WEATHERSTON JA: A receiving order was made against Nathan N. Urman on August 13, 1980. He was a mortgage broker whose principal business seems to have been the purchase and sale of mortgages. Sometimes he sold mortgages outright, in which case he would simply assign them to the purchasers. We are concerned in this appeal with the priorities in respect of two mortgage transactions that were somewhat more complicated.

Urman financed his transactions by means of a revolving line of credit with the Canadian Imperial Bank of Commerce. The bank had as security a general assignment of book debts, dated April 21, 1976, and duly registered under the *Personal Property Security Act*, RSO 1980, c. 375, the material parts of which were as follows:

FOR VALUABLE CONSIDERATION the undersigned Nathan N. Urman of 161 Kenwood Avenue, Toronto, Ontario hereby assign(s) and transfer(s) all debts, accounts, claims, moneys and choses in action which now are or which may at any time hereafter be due or owing to or owned by the undersigned, and also all securities, bills, notes and other documents now held or owned or which may be hereafter taken, held or owned by the undersigned or anyone on behalf of the undersigned in respect of the said debts, accounts, claims, moneys and choses in action or any part thereof, and also all books and papers recording, evidencing or relating to said debts, accounts, moneys and choses in action or any part thereof (all of the foregoing being herein called the "assigned premises") to CANADIAN IMPERIAL

BANK OF COMMERCE (herein called the "Bank") as a general and continuing collateral security for payment of all existing and future indebtedness and liability of the undersigned to the Bank wheresoever and howsoever incurred and any ultimate unpaid balance thereof, and as a first and prior claim upon the assigned premises. ...

> 5. All moneys collected or received by the undersigned in respect of the assigned premises shall be received as trustee for the Bank and shall be forthwith paid over to the Bank.

At all material times the bank was aware that Urman, in the ordinary course of his business, was acquiring mortgages for the most part for resale and the revolving line of credit was provided for this purpose. Repayment was expected to be from the sale of mortgages, payments on the mortgages and profits on the sale of mortgages.

By a document dated April 24, 1979, entitled "Assignment of Mortgage as Security," Urman assigned to Kreindel Investments Limited two second mortgages as security for a loan by Kreindel to Urman of $65,000. In form, the document was an absolute assignment of the mortgage debts, and a conveyance of the mortgaged lands, but it contained the following proviso:

> Provided that if the Assignor shall pay to the Assignee the sum of $65,000 together with interest thereon at the rate of 11% per annum ... then the Assignee shall, at the request and cost of the Assignor, reassign the said Mortgage to the Assignor giving trustee covenants only.

This assignment was registered in the registry office but no financing statement was registered under the *Personal Property Security Act*. On April 24, 1979, Kreindel gave notice to the mortgagors of its assignment, requiring them to make payments to Urman until notified of default by Urman. In July, 1980, Kreindel notified them of Urman's default and required mortgage payments to be made to their solicitors. The bank notified the mortgagors of its assignment of book debts on August 29, 1980.

The other mortgage transaction with which we are concerned involved a second mortgage for $160,000 from Phyllis Eckhardt to Nathan N. Urman dated March 1, 1978. The principal sum secured by the mortgage was advanced by Urman on March 1, 1978. At various times between May 9, 1978 and April 30, 1979, clients of Urman paid him sums of money to participate in the mortgage loan. In each case Urman signed a "Trust Agreement," the terms of which I shall set out later.

No financing statement was registered under the *Personal Property Security Act* in respect of these Trust Agreements. Urman continued to collect the mortgage payments, depositing them in a trust account at the bank, and, from time to time, forwarding to the trust claimants "T5" statements of investment income in respect of payments made by him to them for their respective shares of mortgage payments. The bank gave the mortgagor notice of its assignment on August 29, 1980.

On a motion for advice to determine the respective interests and priorities of the bank, the trustee in bankruptcy and of Kreindel and the trust claimants, Steele J held that the bank had waived its rights under its assignment of book debts, and that the Kreindel assignment and the Trust Agreements created security interests within the meaning of the *Personal Property Security Act* which, since no financing statement was registered, were unperfected and so subordinate to the interest of the trustee in bankruptcy [128 DLR (3d) 33, 1 PPSAC 340, 38 CBR (NS) 261].

Steele J was of the opinion that because a mortgage is personal property, the *Personal Property Security Act* applied both to the assignment of a mortgage and to a debt secured by a real property mortgage. The effect of his ruling is that anyone acquiring an interest in a real property mortgage would be required to search under the *Personal Property Security Act* as well as under the *Registry Act*, RSO 1980, c. 445, or the *Land Titles Act*, RSO 1980, c. 230.

By s. 2 of the *Personal Property Security Act*, it is provided that the Act applies:

(a) to every transaction without regard to its form and without regard to the person who has title to the collateral that in substance creates a security interest, including, without limiting the foregoing,

(i) a chattel mortgage, conditional sale, equipment trust, floating charge, pledge, trust deed or trust receipt, and

(ii) an assignment, lease or consignment intended as security; and

(b) to every assignment of book debts not intended as security, but not to an assignment for the general benefit or creditors to which the *Assignments and Preferences Act* applies.

Section 1 has the following definitions:

(y) "security interest" means an interest in goods, other than building materials that have been affixed to the realty, fixtures, documents of title, instruments, securities, chattel papers or intangibles that secures payment or performance of an obligation, and includes an interest arising from an assignment of book debts; ...

(m) "intangible" means all personal property, including choses in action, that is not goods, chattel paper, documents of title, instruments or securities;

A mortgage, by which a mortgagor mortgages his land to secure a debt, creates an interest in land. It does not create a "security interest" as defined by the Act, and so the Act does not apply to it. But mortgages are said to have a dual character, and the right of the mortgagee to receive the mortgage money is treated in equity as personal property and is therefore an "intangible." An interest in an intangible that secures payment or performance of an obligation is a "security interest." However, an absolute assignment of a mortgage does not secure payment or performance of an obligation and does not create a "security interest." It absolutely transfers the mortgagee's interest in the mortgage; it does not create an interest in the right to receive the mortgage money (an intangible) that secures payment or performance of an obligation. So the Act does not apply to the absolute assignment of a mortgage.

Here, the Kreindel assignment was not absolute. The mortgages were assigned as security for the mortgagee's own debt. The mortgagee's right to receive the mortgage moneys was an intangible that secured payment or performance of an obligation, and so, on its literal wording, the Act can be said to apply to this assignment.

But the dual character of real estate mortgages has not been universally applied. By a rule established as long ago as 1804, a mortgage debt is not to be separated from the land on which it is secured for the purpose of determining priority between competing assignees. In *Taylor v. London & County Banking Co.; London & County Banking Co. v. Nixon*, [1901] 2 Ch. 231, Stirling LJ said, at 254-55:

Although a mortgage debt is a chose in action, yet, where the subject of the security is land, the mortgagee is treated as having "an interest in land," and priorities are governed by the rules applicable to interests in land, and not by the rules which apply to interests in personalty. The reason is thus stated by Sir William Grant in *Jones v. Gibbons* [(1804), 9 Ves. Jun. 407 at 410-1, 32 ER 659]: "A mortgage consists partly of the estate in the land, partly of the debt. So far as it conveys the estate, the assignment" that is, of the mortgage "is absolute and complete the moment it is made according to the forms of law. Undoubtedly it is not necessary to give notice to the mortgagor, that the mortgage has been assigned, in order to make it valid and effectual. The estate being absolute at law, the debtor has no means of redeeming it but by paying the money. Therefore he, who has the estate, has in effect the debt; as the estate can never be taken from him except by payment of the debt."

Jones v. Gibbons, referred to by Stirling LJ, is remarkably similar to the present case. A West Indies merchant was in financial difficulties, and an arrangement was made with his creditors whereby he assigned to trustees several securities for debts due to him, including mortgage debts, as security for his own debts. He remained in possession of the assets, and the assignments of mortgages were not registered. Later, he became bankrupt, and a contest arose between the trustees for the creditors on the one hand, and the assignees in bankruptcy on the other hand, who attacked the earlier assignment as being fraudulent and void against the general creditors. The attack was resisted as to the mortgage debts. Sir William Grant MR held that the other debts and chattels covered by the assignment to trustees, since they remained in the possession, order and disposition of the bankrupt at the time of the bankruptcy, passed to the assignees in bankruptcy. Then came the passage in his judgment as to the mortgage debts that was quoted by Stirling LJ. He held that they passed by the assignment of the mortgages to the trustees for the first creditors, and the general creditors were not entitled to any account of them [at 411]:

With regard to the objection, that these deeds were not registered, the Registry Acts have no effect as between those claiming by conveyance and the assignees of the bankrupt, who made the conveyance. It was never held bad, because not registered; the object being purely for the protection of subsequent purchasers.

These two cases are sufficient authority to hold that the Kreindel assignment, although in effect a mortgage of a mortgage, is to be treated as an interest in land and not in an intangible, and, accordingly, the Act did not apply to it. Kreindel is entitled to priority over the trustee in bankruptcy to the extent of its security interest in the mortgages.

After Steele J had given judgment on the motion before him, the Legislature enacted s. 3(1)(e) by the *Personal Property Security Amendment Act (No. 2)*, 1981 (Ont.), c. 58, s. 1, by which it was provided that the Act does not apply

(e) to the creation or assignment of an interest in real property, including a mortgage, charge or lease of real property ...

This enactment must now be taken as merely a declaration of the existing law.

· · ·

Appeal allowed.

NOTES

1) Section 4(1)(e), by negative inference, brings within the scope of the OPPSA the assignment of a right to payment under a mortgage, charge, or lease where the assignment does not convey or transfer the assignor's interest in real property. See also, ss. 36(1) and 54(1)(b). Are these sections to be taken as a legislative reversal of the legal conclusion of the Court of Appeal that a mortgage debt cannot be separated from the land on which it is secured for the purposes of determining priority between competing assignees? Note that these provisions were enacted before the Court of Appeal's decision. Professor Geva, also writing before the Court of Appeal decision, concluded:

> Read alone, new s. 3(1)(e)(ii) [now s. 4(1)(e)] seems to raise the possibility of a split priority between a debt and the right to a real estate mortgage securing it. Yet, read in conjunction with new section 36a(2) [now s. 36(2)], new s. 3(1)(e)(ii) makes more sense. The combined effect of the two provisions is that the registration of a specific assignment in the proper land registry office will put the assignee ahead of a secured party who subsequently registered his PPSA security interest in the land registry office under new section 54(1)(b). The assignee's priority will be with respect to the land as well as to the debt.
>
> What is the position of a security interest in a right to payment under a real estate mortgage to which the PPSA will apply under Bill 163, vis-à-vis the interest of an assignee of a specific real estate mortgage, where the latter registered the mortgage assignment after a notice of the security interest had been registered in the proper land registry office? The negative implication from new section 36a(2) is that priority is given to the security interest in the right to payment governed by the PPSA. But does this priority extend to the real estate mortgage securing the right to payment? A positive answer is suggested if one recalls that the mortgage follows the debt. Nonetheless, is not this rule explicitly rejected by proposed section 3(1)(e)(ii)? Does this mean a split priority? Does this mean that real estate law determines priority? I do not know.

See Geva, "Security Interests on Secured Obligations" (1982), 60 *CBR* 151, at 170-71 and cf. Ziegel (1981-82), 6 *CBLJ* 107, at 118-26.

2) For the most part, the Acts in the other provinces exclude from their scope real property interests or rights to payment that arise in connection with a real property interest. Consequently, assignments of mortgage payments or rentals are excluded. See, for example, BCPPSA ss. 4(f) and 4(g).

3) However, in Saskatchewan, an assignment of rental payments is deemed to be a transfer of an interest in land with the result that priorities among successive assignees are determined under *The Land Titles Act, 2000*, SS 2000, c. L-5.1, s. 144.

CHAPTER THREE

Validity and Enforceability of the Security Interest

I. INTRODUCTION

The validity and enforceability of a security interest depend on the following requirements:

First, there must be a concluded security agreement: see Part II, below.

Second, the agreement must comply with the Statute of Frauds requirements specified in OPPSA s. 11(2)(a)-(d), otherwise the security interest will be unenforceable against third parties: see Part III, below.

Third, there must be attachment: see Chapter 4.

Fourth, the security interest must be perfected, typically by the secured party either taking possession of the collateral or registering a financing statement, otherwise it will be subordinate to or ineffective against the parties listed in OPPSA s. 20(1): see Chapter 5.

II. VALIDITY OF THE SECURITY AGREEMENT

Ellingsen (Trustee of) v. Hallmark Ford Sales Ltd.
(2000), 190 DLR (4th) 47 (BCCA)

DONALD JA: [1] Hallmark Ford Sales Ltd. agreed to sell a truck to Greg Allan Ellingsen and let him take the truck to his logging operations without paying for it. Hallmark transferred ownership to Ellingsen on the expectation that the deal would be financed by a bank. Ellingsen would cover the balance by a trade-in.

[2] Various delays occurred in the financing arrangements. Three months after taking the truck Ellingsen went into bankruptcy. The Trustee now has the truck (or its sale proceeds) and asserts that it is an asset forming part of the general estate of the bankrupt.

[3] The Trustee brought a motion in the Supreme Court of British Columbia in bankruptcy for an order that the truck is vested in the Trustee free and clear of any claims by Hallmark and for an order that Hallmark discharge a registration against the truck in the Personal Property Registry. The latter refers to a registration filed in desperation by Hallmark after the bankruptcy occurred.

[4] On 29 September 1997 the motion was granted on the terms sought by the Trustee. Hallmark appeals from this decision on several grounds, including the contention that the chambers judge erred in failing to find a remedial constructive trust in its favour. As I would allow the appeal on that ground, I do not propose to discuss the other grounds of appeal. In my judgment, a constructive trust is necessary to prevent an unjust enrichment.

[5] The deal in question took place on 2 January 1997 at Hallmark's lot in Surrey. Hallmark agreed to take back a used truck it had earlier sold to Ellingsen under an incorrect declaration that the truck had not been in an accident involving more than $2,000 damage. In arranging the sale of the new truck Hallmark ascribed a trade-in value to the old truck as though it had not been previously damaged. To complete the purchase Ellingsen needed financing to pay out the outstanding balance of approximately $27,500 due under a conditional sales contract in favour of the Bank of Nova Scotia and to cover the balance of the purchase price of the new truck, $12,105.11.

[6] Ellingsen completed the required credit application, and advised Johann Halldorson, the salesman, that if the credit application was not approved, his own bank in Penticton, the Bank of Nova Scotia, would be willing to finance the deal. He said he needed to conclude the transaction quickly as he had to return to work up north in the bush. The credit application was left with Randy Jenks, the business manager of Hallmark.

[7] Jenks attempted to obtain financing on behalf of Ellingsen for the transaction. He initially called the Bank of Nova Scotia and determined the amount required to pay out the conditional sales contract and then called the Hongkong Bank to seek credit approval for the required amount of $39,641.10. He also spoke to the manager of Ellingsen's bank in Penticton, who indicated that he was prepared to work with Hallmark on the deal, but he wanted to see Ellingsen and receive the deal information first.

[8] Approximately three hours later that same day, Ellingsen returned to the dealership and was told by Jenks that financing had not yet been obtained. Ellingsen put pressure on Hallmark to complete the transaction as he was eager to leave for his job in the north. Jenks deposes that as a result of the pressure and based on the expectation that approval of financing would be forthcoming, he agreed to permit the delivery of the new truck to Ellingsen and to transfer the new truck into his name. Before doing so, Jenks had Ellingsen sign a Motor Vehicle Purchase Agreement dated 2 January, 1997; a Hongkong Bank Conditional Sales Agreement bearing the same date; a blank Scotia Bank Buyer's Statement and two blank Scotia Bank Conditional Sales Agreements; a blank Motor Vehicle Purchase Agreement; and a blank Credit Application for the Hongkong Bank of Canada. He also had Ellingsen sign a transfer form transferring the old truck to Hallmark which Jenks intended to process upon completion of the financing for the new truck. Jenks asked Ellingsen to sign the above noted documents in blank in case they were needed as part of the financing package. Hallmark executed the transfer but none of the other documents.

[9] Jenks then arranged for Ellingsen's insurance and Ellingsen left the dealership with the new truck. Jenks claims that the sale was conditional upon the financing being obtained, and says that although he never expressed to Ellingsen what would happen if the financing was not obtained, it was clear that the transaction was subject to the obtaining of financing. He maintains that it was always understood that Hallmark had not

agreed to finance the transaction and that it was obvious that in the event financing approval was not obtained, Ellingsen would be required to return the new truck.

[10] The Motor Vehicle Purchase Agreement dated 2 January, 1997 signed by Ellingsen stipulated that the transaction was "subject to credit approval." Under "Purchaser Declarations" it said:

> Purchaser understands that this agreement does not become binding on the parties hereto until accepted and executed by a duly authorized official of the Dealer. Salespersons do not have this authority. Deposits, partial payments and down payments are non-refundable.

[11] Ellingsen denies that it was ever expressed to him that the sale was conditional, and agrees that the issue of what would happen if the financing was declined was never discussed, as he had not anticipated there would be a problem.

[12] On 8 January 1997 the Hongkong Bank advised Hallmark that it would finance the transaction provided Ellingsen made a downpayment of $5,000. Jenks called Ellingsen and told him about the approval subject to a downpayment, and Ellingsen advised that he could not make that payment until he arrived from his work up north. Jenks responded that this would be acceptable, and that he needed Ellingsen to sign a new Hongkong Bank Conditional Sales Agreement showing the downpayment. Ellingsen agreed to sign and return the document on receipt. Jenks sent the documents out, and when he did not receive them back, he made numerous unsuccessful attempts to reach Ellingsen.

[13] On 15 March 1997 Ellingsen called Hallmark to ask that it "pay out the lien" on the old truck, and if it did not, Hallmark would have to come and get the new truck. Halldorson told Ellingsen that Jenks needed the contract, referring to the $5,000 downpayment, signed and returned. Approximately one week later, Ellingsen spoke to Jenks, who informed him again that Hallmark could not pay out the lien on the old truck until the financing contract was signed and returned, and that the old truck had been sitting on Hallmark's lot since January and that Hallmark could not process the transfer until the financing on the new truck had been concluded. Ellingsen told Jenks, as he had told Halldorson earlier, that he would return from the bush in April and he would deal with the paperwork then.

[14] On 11 April 1997 Jenks received a call from an employee of the Bank of Nova Scotia about payment of the lien on the old truck. Jenks informed her that he could not pay out the amount owed until he had received the financing documentation on the new truck, and that if he had not received it within two weeks, he was going to try to find the new truck and bring it back to Hallmark. On the same day, Ellingsen filed an assignment into bankruptcy. After the bankruptcy, the Bank of Nova Scotia seized the old truck from the Hallmark lot pursuant to its conditional sales contract which had been registered at the Personal Property Registry.

[15] Shortly after the assignment into bankruptcy, a representative of the Trustee advised Hallmark that Hallmark had no claim on the new truck as a Financing Statement under the *Personal Property Security Act* had not been filed. Without obtaining legal advice, Hallmark then filed a financing statement in the Personal Property Registry.

[16] In the court below Hallmark framed its argument on the law of trust in the manner described by the chambers judge:

[11] Hallmark's position is that there was never a concluded sale of the new truck to Ellingsen, and that beneficial ownership of the new truck did not ever pass. Hallmark says that Ellingsen held only bare legal title, and was a trustee of the beneficial interest in the new truck in favour of Hallmark. Hallmark further says that there was no security interest which existed and could be registered in this case given the nature of the transaction, and consequently, the PPSA has no application. Finally, Hallmark says that the trustee has no interest in the new truck, given the express provisions of the BIA [*Bankruptcy and Insolvency Act*], and particularly s. 67 of the same, which provides that the property of the bankrupt shall not comprise property held by a bankrupt in trust for another.

[17] The chambers judge concluded that the transaction was a sale rather than a creation of a trust. She held that the unpaid sales price gave rise to a security interest which could have been registered and had it been registered it would have protected Hallmark from the bankruptcy. Her reasoning went as follows:

> [12] I cannot accept that the nature of the transaction between Hallmark and Ellingsen in January of 1997 was the creation of a trust. On the facts, Ellingsen must have considered that he had purchased, and that he owned, the new truck, even though the purchase price had not as of yet been paid. It is inconceivable that, as Hallmark now argues, Ellingsen could have driven the new truck in his work up north for more than three months, and then simply returned the new truck to Hallmark, or that he could have resisted an action by Hallmark for the purchase price of the new truck, on the basis that no deal had been made between the parties.
>
> [13] Further, Hallmark did not conduct itself in a way that would be consistent with a trust relationship, with mere legal title to the new truck having passed. Hallmark was aware, within weeks of the transaction, that there was a problem with financing. Hallmark made no effort to obtain possession of the truck, or to even demand return of the truck. The only interest Hallmark had at that time was to receive payment for the truck from someone, whether it be Ellingsen, or a finance company, or a combination of the two.
>
> [14] I have concluded, on these facts, that the nature of the transaction was a sale, with payment anticipated and agreed by the parties to be made shortly after the transfer of title and possession. The transaction created what was in substance a security interest, as that term is defined in s. 1 and s. 2 of the PPSA, on the part of Hallmark, which Hallmark could, and given what happened should, have registered in the Personal Property Registry. Given that Hallmark did not register, and thereby perfect, its security interest prior to the date of bankruptcy, I find that the new truck forms part of the bankrupt's estate, and is available for distribution to the estate's creditors.

[18] With respect, I do not think the evidence reasonably supports the finding that this was a sale and that Hallmark retained a security interest after it released the truck. The deal was subject to financing by a third party which never materialized. There was no enforceable instrument on which Hallmark could sue Ellingsen for the purchase price. As Hallmark did not sign the Motor Vehicle Purchase Agreement it was never brought into effect. Ellingsen did not agree to pay cash for the new truck and at no time did Hallmark agree to finance the deal itself. The documents make it plain that credit was to be approved by a lending institution.

[19] Hallmark imprudently transferred ownership registration to Ellingsen and therein lies the problem. On the surface the transfer implies that a concluded contract of purchase and sale took place and that the relationship between the parties was one of debtor and creditor. But on a full appreciation of all the circumstances I think the only reasonable conclusion is that the proposed sale never occurred because a condition precedent, the proposed financing, was not fulfilled. The transfer facilitated acquisition of insurance and moved the transaction along but it did not complete it.

[20] The Trustee argues that if the term "subject to credit approval" was a condition precedent Hallmark waived it by transferring ownership registration. With respect, I do not think that conforms to the fact that the financing continued to be a problem after the transfer. I note, in particular, that the Hongkong Bank was not prepared to finance the deal as written and insisted that Ellingsen put $5,000 down.

[21] The Trustee further argues that the Motor Vehicle Purchase Agreement and the Hongkong Bank Conditional Sales Agreement are structured so that the financing obligation is primarily between the seller and the purchaser with the bank taking the paper as assignee. This is said to establish a debtor-creditor relationship independent of the bank's involvement. While it is true that the full cost of borrowing and the payment schedule are set out in the sales agreement and that the conditional sales agreement is between the seller and purchaser with the bank as assignee, the fact remains that neither agreement was executed. They were not executed because financing was not concluded and so we return to the position that Ellingsen had a truck that he had no right to keep when he was unable to meet the conditions of financing.

[22] The more difficult area for analysis in this case is the relationship between the *Personal Property Security Act* (PPSA) and the law of remedial constructive trusts. Hallmark's case for a constructive trust can be broken down this way:

1. The contract of sale was ineffective through non-fulfillment of a condition precedent.

2. Hallmark is entitled to a proprietary remedy (return of the truck), on meeting three conditions:

   (a) no transaction effective to vest property rights has taken place;
   (b) it must be possible to trace the property;
   (c) against the actual holder of the property it is unjust that the claimant not be allowed to re-take it: G.H.L. Fridman and J.G. McLeod, *Restitution* (Toronto: Carswell, 1982) at 568-9.

3. Hallmark meets all three conditions: the contract was ineffective because no financing was arranged; the truck was still in Ellingsen's possession at time of bankruptcy; and Hallmark did not extend credit to Ellingsen. Not having extended credit, Hallmark occupies a different position from that of the general creditors of the bankrupt estate who did extend credit. The creditors would unfairly enjoy a windfall if the truck formed part of the assets available to them: P.D. Maddaugh and J.D. McCamus, *The Law of Restitution* (Aurora: Canada Law Book, 1990) at 137.

4. Section 67(1)(a) of the *Bankruptcy and Insolvency Act* (BIA) provides that the property of the bankrupt should not comprise property held by a bankrupt in trust for another:

> 67.(1) The property of a bankrupt divisible among his creditors shall not comprise
> (a) property held by the bankrupt in trust for any other person.

5. A trust in the form of a constructive trust should be imposed to prevent an unjust enrichment with the order taking effect just prior to the bankruptcy so that s. 67(1)(a) of the BIA is engaged.

6. Since the trust is constructed as a remedy by the court on the doctrine of unjust enrichment it falls within an exclusion provided in s. 4(a) of the PPSA as an "interest given by a rule of law." Section 4(a) of the PPSA reads:

> Except as otherwise provided in this Act, this Act does not apply to the following:
> (a) a lien, charge or other interest given by a rule of law or by an enactment unless the enactment contains an express provision that this Act applies;

[23] Hallmark must find an exclusion from the PPSA because if its interest was "a security interest" within the meaning of the PPSA (such interest can include a "trust" if the trust secures payment or performance of an obligation: (s. 2(1)(b)), then unless the interest is perfected by registration it is not effective against the trustee in bankruptcy: s. 20(b)(i). Section 2(1) of the PPSA reads:

[See OPPSA s. 2(1).]

[25] The Trustee submits that this transaction comes within the PPSA and that the interest held by Hallmark is an unperfected interest and thereby ineffective against the Trustee under s. 20(b)(i). The argument is founded on two conditions on the reverse side of the Motor Vehicle Purchase Agreement which are said to reserve rights to Hallmark in the event of a default by the purchaser. They are conditions 3(a) and 7(a):

3. If any cheque or other bill of exchange tendered as payment of any amount due as set out on the reverse side hereof is dishonoured, such cheque or bill of exchange shall be deemed not to be payment and shall be null and void and of no effect. If any such dishonoured cheque or bill of exchange forms all or part of the amount due by the Purchaser to the Dealer, then:
> (a) the Purchaser agrees that the Dealer shall have immediate possession of the motor vehicle as if the Dealer had never parted with possession and the Dealer may exercise all rights to possession; …

7. Subject to paragraph 3 of this Agreement, if the Purchaser defaults in the payment of any amount due hereby or defaults in the performance or observance of any other matter or thing required to be observed or performed by the Purchaser or if any proceeding is commenced by or against the Purchaser under any bankruptcy or insolvency laws, then
> (a) the entire amount due by the Purchaser to the Dealer shall become immediately due and payable at the option of the Dealer.

[26] The difficulty with this argument is that it is premised on a concluded contract which is absent here. Hallmark's right to recover the truck does not arise, and could not arise, on the conditions quoted above; Hallmark's remedy lies outside the document and is found in the power of the court to provide a restitutionary remedy.

[27] The Trustee submits, in the alternative, that any equitable interest supporting a trust in the circumstances amounts to a security interest for the purposes of the PPSA, in the sense that that interest only existed as a method for securing payment of the truck.

[28] I think this argument goes to the kind of trust, implied or resulting, for which Hallmark argued below and which formed part of Hallmark's alternative submissions before us. As I apprehend the position, an implied or resulting trust arises from an understanding that Ellingsen would hold the truck in trust for Hallmark until financing was completed. But I am not concerned with these other trusts having been persuaded that the appropriate remedy is the constructive trust. I do not know how it could be said that a constructive trust secures a payment or the performance of an obligation; rather its purpose is to prevent an unjust outcome. The chambers judge inquired whether the behaviour of the parties "was consistent with a trust relationship." That can only refer to an implied or a resulting trust and is not relevant to the question whether a constructive trust should be imposed.

[29] The final point raised by the Trustee in relation to the PPSA is that s. 20(b)(i) provides a "juristic reason" for the deprivation of Hallmark and the corresponding enrichment of the general creditors of the estate. This refers to the classic three-part formula for determining unjust enrichment. McLachlin J (now CJC) put it this way in *Peter v. Beblow*, [1993] 1 SCR 980 at 987:

> The basic notions are simple enough. An action for unjust enrichment arises when three elements are satisfied: (1) an enrichment; (2) a corresponding deprivation; and (3) the absence of a juristic reason for the enrichment. These proven, the action is established and the right to claim relief made out.

[30] If Hallmark's interest is a security interest the consequences of not registering the interest are prescribed by s. 20(b)(i) of the PPSA. The collateral goes into the general estate by operation of statute and hence a juristic reason exists for the enrichment. It is necessary to repeat, in order to deal with this point, that in my opinion Hallmark's interest was not a security interest within the meaning of the Act. There was nothing to register. The truck was not collateral to any enforceable contract. The substance of the transaction, not its form, must determine whether a security interest was created: see *Skybridge Holdings Inc. (Trustee of) v. British Columbia (Registrar of Travel Services)* (1999), 173 DLR (4th) 333, 68 BCLR (3d) 209 (CA). It follows that s. 20(b)(i) does not provide a juristic reason in answer to a claim of unjust enrichment.

[31] Is this an appropriate case for a remedial constructive trust? Two issues arise for discussion. First, why should equity intervene in a commercial transaction where Hallmark could have protected itself contractually? Second, is it appropriate to use a constructive trust to alter the priorities amongst creditors in a bankruptcy?

...

[Donald JA answered both questions in the appellant's favour and continued:]

[41] For these reasons I would allow the appeal and impose a constructive trust on the truck in favour of Hallmark with effect from 15 March 1997. I understand that by agreement the truck has been sold and the proceeds held by the Trustee pending the

decision on this appeal. The restitutionary remedy I intend will be satisfied by payment of those proceeds plus costs.

McEACHERN CJBC (dissenting): [42] I have read the Reasons for Judgment of Mr. Justice Donald on this appeal. I regret that I am unable to agree with the conclusions he has reached. I am, however, content to accept the careful statement of the facts that he has prepared and I need not repeat what he has said in that regard.

[43] In my judgment, Mr. Ellingsen purchased the new truck from Hallmark by turning in his old truck, by assuring Hallmark that his bank would finance the purchase if the dealer's financing resources were not fruitful, by signing a Motor Vehicle Purchase Agreement setting out conditions of sale, by accepting registration of the new truck in his name and by taking possession of the new truck.

[44] The Purchase Agreement signed by Mr. Ellingsen provided that the purchase balance would be payable "… in 60 equal monthly installments of $709.05 commencing on the 18 day of Feb. '97 with a final balance of $709.05 to be paid on the 18 day of Jan. 2002 …" (clause 8).

[45] It is true this Agreement to Purchase, a printed form, stated "SUBJECT TO CREDIT APPROVAL." The Agreement, however, also provided remedies for the repossession of the truck in the event of non-payment, and Hallmark was at all times the unpaid vendor of the truck. Pending the completion of financing, the obligation of Mr. Ellingsen was to carry out the terms of the agreement. It is unthinkable that Mr. Ellingsen could retain the truck without completing the financing or that Hallmark would be without remedies. Either under the Agreement or at common law, Hallmark was entitled to be paid or to have the truck back. Hallmark, at least, waived the subject clause when it transferred title to Mr. Ellingsen. Mr. Ellingsen, in turn, must be taken to have waived the clause when he retained the truck without arranging the financing. However one analyzes this transaction, mutual obligations arose as soon as Mr. Ellingsen took possession of the truck.

[46] Accordingly, I have no doubt that this Purchase Agreement, or the mutual obligations undertaken by the parties, created a security interest in favour of Hallmark as defined in the *Personal Property Security Act*, RSBC 1996, c. 359 (the Act). In fact, Hallmark registered it as such after Mr. Ellingsen had filed for bankruptcy and declared the new truck as a part of his estate at the time of his assignment in bankruptcy.

[47] Mr. Casey, in his able argument, conceded that he had to rely upon a trust analysis in order to escape the consequences of the Act. Mr. Justice Donald has undertaken such an analysis and concludes that there was no completed sale, and that it would be an unjust enrichment to the estate if Hallmark were deprived of its property interest in the new truck. He relies in part on the classic definition of a constructive trust furnished by McLachlin J (now CJC) in *Peter v. Beblow*, [1993] 1 SCR 980 at 987:

> … An action for unjust enrichment arises when three elements are satisfied: (1) an enrichment, (2) a corresponding deprivation, and (3) the absence of a juristic reason for the enrichment. These proven, the action is established and the right to claim relief made out.

[48] With respect, there are good juristic reasons for this enrichment (if such it is) in the provisions of the Act, which is intended to provide the certainty that is so necessary

in the commercial law. It is probably unnecessary to point out that the assertion of a constructive trust based on unjust enrichment could become commonplace, with unfortunate commercial consequences, if such a remedy is made available upon a failure to make the necessary filings under the Act.

[49] Assuming for the moment that there was no completed purchase agreement in this case, which I do not accept, it becomes necessary to analyze further the position of Hallmark to see whether its then rights would prevail against a trustee in bankruptcy. This requires a closer examination of the Act.

[50] As already mentioned, there is no doubt Mr. Ellingsen agreed to purchase the truck and pay for it by trading in his old truck and by financing the balance at his own bank if necessary. On this basis, he took possession (and title) to the truck. There was no thought or discussion of a trust.

[51] What happened, obviously, was that Hallmark took a chance that the purchase price would be paid by or on behalf of Mr. Ellingsen, and Hallmark neglected to perfect its security interest by the appropriate filing until after the bankruptcy of Ellingsen.

[52] This is precisely the kind of case the Legislature had in mind when it enacted the Act.

[53] A "security interest" under the Act means "an interest in goods ... that secures payment or performance of an obligation ..." At the very least, this transaction, even if characterized as a failed Purchase Agreement, entitled Hallmark to a return of the vehicle or to a debt and a corresponding obligation on Mr. Ellingsen to return the truck or pay for it. I need say no more about debt because such a debt would not prevail over a trustee in bankruptcy. If Hallmark's entitlement was to a return of the vehicle, that interest could only be protected by an appropriate filing under the Act.

[54] This is because, subject to section 4, the Act applies:

> ... to every transaction that in substance creates a security interest, without regard to its form ... (section 2(1)(a)).

[55] Under this definition the obligation to return the truck creates a security interest in Hallmark.

[56] Turning to s. 4, the Act does not apply to interests "given by a rule of law" which could include a constructive trust, although I have serious reservations about the introduction of such concepts into consumer transactions. However, I have already concluded that there are strong juristic reasons militating against the recognition of an unjust enrichment or a constructive trust in the circumstances of this case.

[57] For these reasons, whether or not the Purchase Agreement was a completed agreement, Hallmark must fail in its attempt to establish an unregistered interest in this vehicle that survives a bankruptcy. I would dismiss this appeal.

Appeal allowed.

[A concurring majority judgment was delivered by Lambert JA.]

NOTES

1) For a critical discussion of *Ellingsen*, see Ziegel, "The Unwelcome Intrusion of the Remedial Constructive Trust in Personal Property Security Law: *Ellingsen (Trustee of) v. Hallmark Ford Sales Ltd.*" (2001), 34 *CBLJ* 460. Professor Ziegel agrees with the majority judgments that the PPSA did not apply because there was no binding agreement between the parties and that delivery of possession by a prospective vendor is not sufficient to trigger the PPSA. Do you think the PPSAs should be amended to cover situations like that in *Ellingsen*?

2) Professor Ziegel also queries why it was necessary for the majority in *Ellingsen* to invoke principles of unjust enrichment at all. If title never passed to *Ellingsen*, it remained with Hallmark, and Hallmark was entitled at common law, under the detinue remedy and under the BIA (s. 81), to recover the vehicle from the trustee. Definitionally, the remedy of unjust enrichment can apply only where the plaintiff has conferred a benefit on the defendant that the defendant should not be allowed to retain. According to the majority judgments, what was the benefit that Hallmark was trying to recover from *Ellingsen*?

994814 Ontario Inc. v. RSL Canada Inc. and En-Plas Inc.
(2006), 20 CBR (5th) 163 (Ont. CA)

ROULEAU JA:

Overview

[1] This appeal involves a contest over three pieces of equipment that were located on the premises of RSL Canada Inc. (RSL), a company in receivership. The contest is between En-Plas Inc., the supplier of the equipment, and 994814 Ontario Inc. (the appellant), a company holding a general security agreement (GSA) over all of the assets and undertakings of RSL, including after-acquired equipment. The GSA was perfected under the *Personal Property Security Act*, RSO 1990, c. P.10 (PPSA).

[2] The appellant submits that the motion judge erred in his analysis and application of the PPSA. It also argues that there are palpable and overriding errors in the motion judge's findings of fact. Although I agree with the appellant that certain portions of the motion judge's analysis and application of the PPSA are problematic, I find no basis to interfere with his findings of fact. Based on those findings, I conclude that the appeal should be dismissed.

Facts

[3] En-Plas is the Canadian representative for Nissei, a manufacturer of injection molding machines used in the production of plastic products throughout Canada. These machines are very large and can weigh several tons. They are manufactured in Japan. En-Plas imports these machines, providing technical services and advice for their installation and startup at the customer's production facility. In many instances, the machine is shipped directly from the manufacturer in Japan to the customer's premises, and any additional work to be done to make the machine operational is done on site.

[4] En-Plas proposed to sell, as a package deal, three molding machines to RSL. The appellant is the parent and secured creditor of RSL.

[5] On July 28, 2004, En-Plas sent a quote to RSL. The terms of the quote included:

    (a) that En-Plas retain title in the equipment until payment in full was received; and

    (b) that startup was to be performed by En-Plas.

[6] The quote also set out, in bold print with double underlining, the words "Electrical Safety Approved."

[7] Two of the machines had never previously been sold in Canada. En-Plas had been advised by the Ontario Electrical Safety Authority on April 29, 2004, that modification to the design of these two machines (the NEX machines) was required before they could be approved for operation under the Ontario Electric Safety Code. At the time, En-Plas thought that a solution could quickly be found and the requisite modifications carried out. En-Plas did not, therefore, tell RSL about this issue at that time.

[8] On July 29, 2004, RSL issued a purchase order for the three machines at a cost of $373,000 US with ten percent down and net 180 days. The purchase order also set out "[a]ll other terms and conditions per En-Plas Quote # 'Q0019814.'" The ten percent down payment was paid in early August 2004.

[9] The machine that En-Plas had in stock was shipped from En-Plas on August 4, 2004 and made operational thereafter. The other two machines were, as frequently occurs, shipped from Japan directly to RSL's premises on December 15, 2004. They required modifications and these would be made on site. Both the shipping orders and purchase order included the title retention language as noted above.

[10] At the time the motion was heard, one or two of the machines had still not met the electrical safety authority standards. Accordingly, En-Plas could not provide the necessary safety certification for the sale and operation of these machines in Ontario. En-Plas did not consider that delivery to RSL of the machines could occur until this condition was met. As a result, RSL had not been invoiced and no debt had yet been recorded in the books.

[11] On February 8, 2005, on application by the appellant as secured creditor of RSL, RSM Richter Inc. (Richter) was appointed interim receiver of RSL pursuant to an order of Farley J. The registered GSA provided the appellant with security over inventory and equipment.

[12] As full payment had not been made, En-Plas initially took the position that it was the owner of the three machines. En-Plas requested that the balance owing be paid, or that arrangements be made for the return of the machines. The solicitors for the appellant responded that the secured creditor had taken possession of all of the assets and that En-Plas was simply an unsecured creditor of RSL. Later En-Plas advised Richter that it held title to the machines for reasons related to safety, and that, in fact, two of the machines had not yet received Electrical Safety Authority approval and were not operational. By this time Richter had obtained an order from Ground J approving the sale of the machines to Depco International Inc., a company associated with RSL. In light of the position being taken by En-Plas, Richter obtained an undertaking from Depco that it would not resell the machines and would return them to Richter if a court determined that En-Plas had priority with respect to them. On July 7, 2005, En-Plas moved to vary

Ground J's order, set aside the sale of the machines and declare that the machines were the property of En-Plas or, in the alternative, conduct a trial of an issue.

[13] The motion judge found that the conditions of sale had not been satisfied and, as a result, the sale had not been completed. The machines therefore remained the property of En-Plas and title had not passed. No debt had been created and, because RSL was not a debtor, a security interest could not attach to the machines. Thus, the PPSA regime was not yet engaged.

Position of the Parties

[14] The appellant argues that the motion judge erred in his interpretation of the PPSA. The fact that En-Plas had stipulated that it retained title until all payments were received is of no relevance. The PPSA applies to "every transaction without regard to its form and without regard to the person who has title to the collateral that in substance creates a security interest" [PPSA s. 2(a)]. Subsection 2(a)(i) of the Act specifically provides that it applies to conditional sale agreements.

[15] The appellant submits that the equipment was purchased by RSL from En-Plas pursuant to a conditional sale agreement. Once RSL entered into that agreement, the appellant acquired a security interest in that piece of equipment which attached pursuant to s. 11 of the PPSA. The GSA entered into between RSL and the appellant had been registered and the security interest in that machine therefore had been perfected as required by the PPSA.

[16] To obtain protection under the PPSA, En-Plas would have had to perfect its security interest in the machine through registration. It never did and, as a result, the appellant argues that it should be found to have priority.

[17] En-Plas argues that the sale was never completed and no debt was ever created. RSL therefore never got possession, and the appellant could not obtain a security interest. In addition, title never passed to RSL so as to bring the PPSA into play.

Analysis

[18] The appellant referred the court to various passages contained in the motion judge's reasons that suggest that he misconstrued or misapplied the PPSA. Although there may be merit in that argument, I need not address it. The question is not whether the trial judge's interpretation of the PPSA was correct but rather whether, based on the findings of fact, the motion judge was correct in concluding that the PPSA regime had not yet been engaged. In my view he was.

[19] As is apparent from the reasons of Brook JA in *Guaranty Trust Co. of Canada v. Canadian Imperial Bank of Commerce* (1993), 6 PPSAC (2d) 51 (Ont. CA) aff'g (1989), 2 PPSAC (2d) 88 (Ontario HC), a court must initially determine if and when an agreement of purchase and sale was reached. This is because a security interest in equipment cannot attach until a transaction occurs which gives the debtor rights in the equipment.

[20] On this issue, the motion judge made important findings. After considering all of the documentation exchanged between the parties and the affidavits and cross-examinations filed, the motion judge found:

[28] En-Plas does not show RSL as an account receivable but it does show a liability to RSL in relation to the deposit paid as En-Plas would be required to return the deposit if it was unable to complete delivery and installation.

...

[38] ... The agreement was for a total package price for the delivery and installation of three Machines. Delivery and installation of the Machines was not complete on the date of the Receivership, February 8, 2005. The NEX 6000 was not operational and the NEX 2000 had not received the necessary electrical and safety certification for safe and legal operation.

[39] RSL and En-Plas had not recorded the transaction in their accounting records so as to create a debtor–creditor relation. The obligation was still pending to RSL and RSL was still in a position to reject the goods. En-Plas was not in a position to demand payment.

[21] The appellant argues that there is no basis for the motion judge's findings set out above and that they constitute palpable and overriding error. In particular, the appellant points out that, because En-Plas did not advise RSL of the electrical safety issue regarding the machines, En-Plas could not rely on this as delaying the completion of the delivery and installation. I disagree. The motion judge's reasons show that he was well aware of the fact that En-Plas had not advised RSL of the electrical safety issues. The findings I have quoted are fully supported by the record, including the language of the documentation, the nature of the property in issue, En-Plas's obligation to obtain electrical certification and make the machines operational, as well as the fact that the books and records of RSL and En-Plas are consistent with the machines being entirely the property of En-Plas at the relevant time.

[22] Although the motion judge did not put it this way, I take his findings quoted above, when read in the context of the balance of his reasons, to mean that on the particular facts of this case, RSL had not yet acquired an interest in the machines. The documentation exchanged between the parties did not give RSL rights in the equipment to which the appellant's GSA could attach. RSL acquired nothing until the machines were "Electrical Safety Approved" and En-Plas had made them operational. Since this never occurred, RSL never became a debtor and never acquired any rights in the three machines, a prerequisite for the creation of a security interest.

Conclusion

[23] For these reasons, I would dismiss the appeal and award costs to the respondent fixed at $18,000 inclusive of GST and disbursements.

Doherty and Goudge JJA agreed.

NOTES

1) The *RSL Canada* case is similar to *Ellingsen*: in both cases, the alleged conditional sale agreement in issue was subject to a condition precedent that remained unfulfilled. The consequence in the *RSL Canada* case was that RSL never acquired any interest in the disputed machines, and so the appellant's security interest never attached. En-Plas was entitled to the machines because it still owned them while the appellant, for its part, had no interest in

them. If the condition precedent had been satisfied, then: (1) ownership of the machines would have passed to RSL; (2) En-Plas would have acquired a security interest in the machines; and (3) the appellant's security interest would have attached to the machines. The outcome of the dispute would then have turned on the rules in the PPSA governing priorities between competing security interests in the same collateral; specifically, since En-Plas had not registered a financing statement, its unperfected security interest would have been subordinate to the appellant's perfected security interest (PPSA s. 20(1)(a)(i)): see Chapter 5.

2) Section 9 of the OPPSA provides that, "Except as otherwise provided by this or any other Act, a security agreement is effective according to its terms between the parties to it and against third parties." This section is of great conceptual significance. It embraces the principle of freedom of contract for security agreements. Its importance is greater for US law than for Anglo-Canadian law, since, as we saw in Chapter 1, for more than a century, Anglo-Canadian law has generally been very accommodating to chattel security agreements.

Section 9 seems so far to have generated only a small amount of important case law. Nevertheless, it raises some difficult interpretational issues. The parties' contractual freedom is limited by contrary provisions in "this or any other Act." The PPSA restrictions appear throughout the Act and are of two principal kinds. *First*, there are those that apply to all security interests and agreements. These include the requirements for the attachment and perfection of a security interest, and the rules in Part V of the Act that govern the enforcement of the security interest. *Second*, there is a group of limitations applicable only to consumer transactions or consumer goods. See, for example, OPPSA ss. 12(2)(b), 14(2), 45(2), 57, 65(1), 66(2), and 73. These are largely based on comparable provisions in Article 9. There have been intermittent discussions about whether they should be deleted and re-enacted in consumer protection legislation. In Ontario, at any rate, they are likely to stay in the Act for the time being—their number was actually increased in the current Act.

What is the rationale for retaining the restrictions on security agreements in *non*-PPSA Acts? Does it not dilute the PPSA aim to present a comprehensive statement of the modern law? Catzman et al., at 50, claim that:

> The reference to other Acts in the first phrase of s. 9 is for all intents and purposes superfluous because s. 68 [s. 73 in current Act] of the Act deals with the effect of this Act vis-à-vis the provisions of other Acts and lays down the rule that with the exception of The Consumer Protection Act, the provisions of The Personal Property Security Act prevail over the provisions of any other general or special Act in the event of a conflict.

Is this correct? Does s. 73 override s. 9?

What of common law restrictions on the validity of security agreements? They too fall into two groups. First, there are the restrictions common to all contracts—for example, capacity, requirements of consideration, effects of misrepresentations and stipulations contrary to public policy, etc. Presumably these continue to apply. UCC 1-103 expressly so provides for all Code transactions. In the current Ontario Act, s. 72 contains a similar provision, as do the other provincial acts.

The second group of common law restrictions are those particular to security agreements—for example, clogs on the equity of redemption. Is there an equally valid argument for their retention, or does it depend on whether the restriction conflicts with a specific provision or the general philosophy of the PPSA?

3) A further implication of s. 9 is that the parties do not have to say expressly in their agreement that their intention is to create a security interest. It is sufficient if their intention can be derived by implication from a reading of the agreement as a whole. The following case illustrates the point.

356447 British Columbia Ltd. v. Canadian Imperial Bank of Commerce
(1998), 157 DLR (4th) 682 (BCCA)

NEWBURY JA: [1] By an agreement dated March 17, 1989, the respondents 356557 [sic] British Columbia Ltd. ("356447") and Noordin Sayani agreed to advance certain funds to 347202 B.C. Ltd. ("347202") and/or its controlling shareholder, Zarina Sayani. The purpose of the loan was to enable 347202 in turn to pay certain indebtedness it had incurred to the Bank of Credit and Commerce in order to acquire a 40 percent interest in the "Georgian Court Joint Venture." More than six years later, on May 26 and June 1, 1995, the respondents filed notices of their purported security interest in the Personal Property Registry. By then, the Canadian Imperial Bank of Commerce (the "Bank"), had obtained a judgment against Ms. Sayani and issued a writ of seizure with respect to her shares in 347202. The Bank then applied to the Registrar under s. 50(3) of the Personal Property Security Act, SBC 1989, c. 36, for the discharge of the respondents' security—an application the Registrar granted. The respondents in turn petitioned to Supreme Court under s. 50(8) of the Act for an order that their purported security be "maintained" on the register.

[2] The discrete issue raised by this proceeding, then, is whether the Agreement was one that created or provided for a "security interest" within the meaning of the Personal Property Security Act. Counsel are agreed that the question turns solely on the construction of paragraph 8 of the Agreement of March 17, 1989. It provided:

8. As consideration for the subsequent loan, Zarina and [347202] agree with Noordin and 356447 to:
(i) to pay all funds derived from the Georgian Hospitality Joint Venture to Noordin and 356447;
(ii) provide personal covenant of Zarina for any shortfall due Bank of Credit and Commerce;
(iii) indemnify and save harmless Noordin and 356447 from any and all losses, penalties, costs, damages including loss due to any adverse tax consequences;
it being the intent and understanding at all material times that Noordin and 356447 shall in turn apply such payments to reducing the indebtedness to Bank of Credit and Commerce until the subsequent loan is fully paid out, and in priority to any other application of proceeds so derived.

The Bank contends that this language is not sufficient to create a security interest, even though it concedes the parties to the Agreement intended to create such an interest. In Mr. Grieve's submission, although the Agreement may be binding on the conscience of and be enforceable against 347202 and Ms. Sayani, it does not create a proprietary right enforceable as against the Georgian Court Joint Venture. At most, it constitutes a promise that if and when Ms. Sayani or 347202 receive funds from the joint venture, such funds shall be paid over to the respondents.

[3] The Chambers judge in the court below did not accede to this argument, [1995] BCJ No. 2244. Applying what he referred to as the "substance test," he concluded that:

> ... the transaction here was one in which [Ms. Sayani] and 347202 gave an interest in their property to secure payment or performance of their obligation to repay Noordin [Sayani] and 356447 the monies advanced to the Bank of Credit and Commerce. In substance its purpose was to secure payment of an obligation. It falls within the first definition of "security interest" contained in paragraph (a) of the definition.
>
> I conclude, as well, that the language of paragraph 8 effects a transfer to Noordin [Sayani] and 356447 of an account due to [Ms. Sayani] and 347202. Paragraph 8 requires the payment of all funds derived by [Ms. Sayani] and 347292 [sic] from the Georgian Hospitality Joint Venture to Noordin [Sayani] and 356447. Such a transfer falls within the second definition contained in paragraph 1(b) of the Act. The transfer of an account such as this does not require the securing of payment or performance of an obligation to fall within the provisions of the Act. [para. 17-18]

Analysis

[4] As noted by the Chambers judge, s. 50(3) of the Act provides that if a financing statement is registered and no security agreement exists between the secured party and the debtor, a person in the position of the Bank may require that the registration be discharged. Section 1 defines the phrase "security agreement" to mean:

> ... an agreement that creates or provides for a security interest and, if the context permits, includes:
>
> (a) an agreement that provides for a prior security interest, and
>
> (b) writing that evidences a security agreement;

The phrase "security interest" in turn is defined to mean in part:

> (a) an interest in goods, chattel paper, a security, a document of title, an instrument, money or an intangible that secures payment or performance of an obligation, ...
>
> (b) the interest of
>
>   (i) a transferee arising from the transfer of an account or a transfer of chattel paper ...
>
> whether or not the interest secures payment or performance of an obligation;

[5] Section 10 of the Act states that subject to s-s. (2) thereof, a security interest is "only enforceable against a third party" where:

> (a) the collateral is in the possession of the secured party, or
>
> (b) the debtor has signed a security agreement that contains
>
>   (i) a description of the collateral by item or kind, or by reference to one or more of the following: goods, securities, instruments, documents of title, chattel paper, intangibles, money, crops or licences,

(Presumably the section should more properly have read "Subject to subsection (2), a security interest is enforceable against a third party only if. ...") Strictly speaking, however, we are not here concerned with s. 10 or the enforceability of any security interest that may have been created by the Agreement against the third party in this case, the Georgian Court Joint Venture. The Bank did not argue on this occasion that the document dated March 17, 1989 was not an "agreement" for purposes of the Act, nor that the receivable which 347202 apparently holds from the joint venture does not come within the ambit of the types of personal property listed in the definition of "security interest." Thus the sole question for this court is whether the Chambers judge was correct in concluding that the Agreement creates an interest that comes within either subparagraph (a) or (b) of the definition of "security interest" quoted above. If his conclusion was correct, then the Agreement creates or provides for a "security interest" and is clearly a "security agreement" the registration of which must be maintained until all the debtor's obligations thereunder have been performed or the respondents agree to release all or part of the collateral described in the financing statement. (See s. 50(3)(a) and (b) of the Act.)

[6] Section 2(1)(a) of the Act provides some assistance in construing agreements in these circumstances: it states that the Act applies "to every transaction that in substance creates a security interest, without regard to its form and without regard to the person who has title to the collateral." Consistent with this, R.C. Cuming and R.J. Wood, authors of the *British Columbia Personal Property Security Act Handbook*, observed in the first edition of their book in 1990:

> The actual label used by the parties is irrelevant: a transaction termed a lease is nevertheless a security agreement if its purpose is to secure payment or performance of an obligation. Nor is any particular form of words required in order create a security agreement. The Act eliminates the need to recite in the agreement that the debtor transfers title to the secured party or that a seller retains title to the goods sold. ...
>
> The substance test of s. 2 ignores both title and form as factors in characterizing transactions. If a transaction is one under which a party gives or recognizes that someone else has an interest in his or her property in order to secure payment or performance of an obligation, it is a security agreement. [at 29-31]

and further at 34:

> The definition of a "security interest" requires that there be an interest created in personal property. This suggests that the creditor must obtain a real right in the property, i.e. a right exercisable not only against the debtor, but against third parties as well. A mere contractual licence to seize and sell the debtor's property does not create an interest in the property enforceable against strangers and therefore should not be regarded as a security agreement.

This wording also appears in the [1996] edition of the Handbook at 47.

[7] Accepting, then, that no particular wording is required to create a security interest, did the undertaking of Ms. Sayani and 347202 to "pay funds derived" from the joint venture, to the respondents give them a proprietary right exercisable against the joint venture, or only a contractual right exercisable against the grantors? No case authority of direct assistance was cited to us on this question, although I note that in *Gontel v. Kocian, Ward and Bank of Nova Scotia* [1985] 6 WWR 458 (Man. QB), it was held that an

acknowledgment by a debtor that he owed his creditor a stated sum plus interest for a 1979 GMC truck, with serial number specified, was sufficient to satisfy the requirements of the Act in the particular circumstances of that case.

[8] Of more relevance is the older law to the effect that "an engagement ... to pay a sum of money out of a specified debt or fund constitutes an equitable assignment": *Halsbury's Laws of England* (4th ed., v. 6) at para. 30, citing *Durham Brothers v. Robertson* [1898] 1 QB 765 (CA) at 769 and *Yeates v. Groves* (1791) 1 Ves. 280 and *Re Rowe, Ex parte South* (1818) 3 Swan 392. Thus in *Riccard v. Pritchard* (1855) 1 K & J 277, Vice-Chancellor Wood noted:

> I apprehend that, if A tells B that he expects that 10,000 is coming to him by a given day, and agrees out of that to pay B 5,000, that is good agreement to constitute a charge upon the fund. That is substantially the agreement in this case. In *Rodick v. Gandell* [citation omitted] Lord Truro collects the result of numerous authorities, summing them up by saying that two things were established: "the extent of the principle to be deduced," he says, "is that an agreement between the debtor and the creditor that the debt owing shall be paid out of a specific fund coming to the debtor, or an order given by a debtor to his creditor upon a person owing money or holding funds belonging to the giver of the order, directing such person to pay such funds to the creditor, will create a valid equitable charge upon such fund, in other words, will operate as an equitable assignment of the debts or fund to which the order refers. [at 279-80]

[9] A more recent case is *William Brandt's Sons & Co. v. Dunlop Rubber Company, Limited* [1905] AC 454 (HL), which concerned a letter written by the Dunlop Company to Brandt's stating:

> Herewith we beg to confirm that we shall remit, subject to approval of goods, the amount of invoice [details omitted] received to-day from Messrs. Kramrisch & Co., Liverpool, when due, direct to your good selves for account of Messrs. Kramrisch & Co.
>
> Yours faithfully. [at 456]

The letter was delivered pursuant to an earlier undertaking by Dunlop that it would grant Messrs. Kramrisch & Co. "the sole and absolute lien on said goods and their proceeds" until they obtained full payment of credit they had extended. Their Lordships concluded that the letter in question constituted an equitable assignment even though it did not "purport to be an assignment nor use the language of an assignment." Lord Macnaghten reasoned:

> An equitable assignment does not always take that form. It may be addressed to the debtor. It may be couched in the language of command. It may be a courteous request. It may assume the form of mere permission. The language is immaterial if the meaning is plain. All that is necessary is that the debtor should be given to understand that the debt has been made over by the creditor to some third person. If the debtor ignores such a notice, he does so at his peril. [at 462]

[10] *Dunlop* was applied to an equitable assignment by way of gift in *Letts v. Inland Revenue Commissioners* [1956] 3 All ER 588 (Ch. Div.). Further, in *Re Dalton* [1962] 2

All ER 499 (Ch. Div.), the court found that an equitable assignment had been created when the solicitors for a debtor wrote to a creditor confirming that they had their client's instructions to pay the creditor out of the proceeds of sale of certain goods.

[11] Applying these cases to paragraph 8 of the Agreement, it appears that the wording used would have been sufficient to create a valid equitable assignment of any funds received by 347202 or Ms. Sayani from the Georgian Court Joint Venture. The introduction of the Personal Property Security Act has subjected assignments of choses in action to a new registration scheme, but no reason was suggested to us why words that created a valid assignment at equity should not be construed as creating a "security interest" for purposes of the new regime. In this regard, I note that s. 68(1) of the Act purports to preserve the principles of equity except insofar as they are inconsistent with the statute.

[12] I therefore conclude that the Agreement "created or provided for" a security interest properly registrable under the Act. In reaching this conclusion, I make no comment on the question of whether the assignment was valid and enforceable as between the Georgian Court Joint Venture and the respondents in the absence of notice of the assignment having been given to the joint venture. Prior to the enactment of the Act such notice would have been necessary to make the assignee's title effective against the debtor or fundholder: see *Halsbury's, supra*, at para. 42. It may be that the Act does away with this requirement and replaces it with the requirement of perfection by registration of a financing statement against the debtor; however, counsel did not raise this point and we were told that in any event there was no evidence as to whether the "third party" had received notice.

...

Appeal dismissed.

NOTES

1) Would the case have been decided differently if there had been no pre-PPSA rule recognizing equitable assignments of choses in action? Could the case have been decided more simply by reference to BCPPSA s. 9 (OPPSA s. 9), stating that, "Subject to this and any other enactment, a security agreement is effective according to its terms"?

2) Newbury JA notes that, at common law, notice to the account debtor was a prerequisite to the perfection of an equitable assignment. Perfection requirements under the PPSAs are dealt with in Chapter 5. Suffice it to say at this point that perfection usually involves the secured party taking possession of the collateral or filing a financing statement in a public registry. Notice to the account debtor in the case of the assignment of an intangible is never sufficient by itself. Notice to the account debtor may, however, be relevant in determining that party's rights of set-off. See OPPSA s. 40 and comparable provisions in the other PPSAs.

III. "STATUTE OF FRAUDS" REQUIREMENTS

The "Statute of Frauds," or writing, requirements are in OPPSA s. 11(2)(a)-(d). In summary, the requirements are that, unless the secured party takes possession of the collateral (or, where the collateral is investment property, has control over it), the security agreement must be in writing and signed by the debtor, and it must contain a description of the collateral sufficient to identify it. Failure to comply means that the security agreement is unenforceable against third parties.

The policy behind the writing requirements is to prevent a party from falsely asserting the existence of a security agreement. For example, consider the following case:

> Fred owns a pickup truck. He goes into bankruptcy and his trustee in bankruptcy claims the truck as part of the estate. Barney is Fred's business associate. Fred tells the trustee that Barney has a non-possessory security interest in the truck and Barney supports Fred's story. How can Fred's trustee in bankruptcy verify Fred and Barney's story?

The obvious first step is for the trustee to check the PPSA register. However, even if Barney has registered a financing statement, this is not conclusive proof of the security agreement's existence. Except where the collateral is consumer goods, the secured party may register a financing statement before the security agreement is concluded: PPSA s. 45(3). Consequently, registration is no more than a warning to third parties that there *might be* a security interest in the collateral. It is possible that Barney registered a financing statement just before Fred went into bankruptcy, but without ever concluding a security agreement.

In summary, the function of the writing requirements is to corroborate the parties' assertion that there is a security agreement: see the *MacEwen Agricentre* case and the *Atlas Industries* case, both extracted below. There is no need for a written agreement if the secured party takes possession of the collateral. The reason is that possession serves as an alternative form of corroboration.

To satisfy the writing requirement, the document has to contain a description of the collateral that is sufficient to enable it to be identified. Assume that the secured party takes a security agreement in the debtor's pickup truck. The agreement describes the collateral as "pickup truck." Is this a sufficient description? Having regard to the corroborative function of the writing requirements, the answer may depend on the circumstances; for example, whether the debtor owns more than one pickup truck. If he does, more information may be necessary to identify the particular pickup truck. If the collateral is a security entitlement, securities account, or futures account, the description requirement is more specific: s. 11(2)(a)(ii) provides that the agreement may describe the collateral by any of those terms or as investment property or it may describe the underlying financial asset or futures contract.

With a view to greater certainty, the PPSAs in the other provinces go into more detail than the OPPSA on the required description. For example, s. 10(1)(d) of the Saskatchewan PPSA specifies:

> 10(1)(d) ...
>> (i) a description of the collateral by item or kind or by reference to one or more of the following:
>>> (A) "crops";
>>> (B) "goods";

(C) "chattel paper";

(D) "investment property";

(E) "documents of title";

(F) "instruments";

(G) "money";

(H) "intangibles";

(ii) a description of collateral that is a security entitlement, securities account, or futures account if it describes the collateral by those terms or as "investment property" or if it describes the underlying financial asset or futures contract;

(iii) a statement that a security interest is taken in all of the debtor's present and after-acquired personal property; or

(iv) a statement that a security interest is taken in all of the debtor's present and after-acquired personal property except specified items or kinds of personal property or except personal property described by reference to one or more of the following:

(A) "crops";

(B) "goods";

(C) "chattel paper";

(D) "investment property";

(E) "documents of title";

(F) "instruments";

(G) "money";

(H) "intangibles."

Section 10(3) provides that a description is inadequate if it describes the collateral as consumer goods or equipment without further reference to the item or kind of collateral and s. 10(4) provides that a description of collateral as inventory is adequate only while it is held by the debtor as inventory.

MacEwen Agricentre Inc. v. Bériault et al.
(2002), 61 OR (3d) 63 (SCJ)

AITKEN J:

Nature of Proceedings

[1] Norman MacLennan is a farmer in Eastern Ontario, who in recent years has fallen on some difficult times. By the spring of 2001, he owed $129,476.73 to MacEwen Agricentre Inc. ("MacEwen"), his long-time supplier of seed, fertilizer and equipment. Some of that debt related to supplies for the 2000 growing season. In 2000, Mr. MacLennan was unable to meet his contractual obligations with his grain dealer, Lucien Bériault, and ended the season owing him $23,673.35. By the end of the 2001 season, this sum had increased to $32,715.10. Through the sale of soybeans grown by Mr. MacLennan in 2001 and sold through Mr. Bériault, Mr. MacLennan received $33,125.45. The question in this litigation is to whom those proceeds of sale should be paid: MacEwen Agricentre Inc. or Lucien Bériault. The funds have been sitting in the trust account of Mr. Bériault's lawyer.

Mr. MacLennan acknowledges that he is indebted to both parties; he does not seek any portion of the proceeds for himself.

Foundation of Claim by MacEwen Agricentre Inc.

[2] In January 2001, James MacEwen, the President of MacEwen Agricentre Inc., was concerned about the size of the debt owing to his company by Norman MacLennan, and he asked Mr. MacLennan for security in the form of a land mortgage. This request was renewed in April 2001. On both occasions, Mr. MacLennan stated that he could not provide such security because, due to a recent separation, his wife would not consent to any mortgage. At Mr. MacEwen's request, on April 19, 2001, Mr. MacLennan did sign a promissory note payable on demand in favour of the company in the amount of $129,476.73 to reflect the outstanding debt at that time owing to the company.

[3] At Mr. MacEwen's subsequent request, Mr. MacLennan met with him on July 27, 2001 to again discuss the issue of security for the outstanding debt. At some point before that meeting, Mr. MacLennan had suggested to Mr. MacEwen that he could give him crop security. At the time of the meeting, Mr. MacEwen asked Mr. MacLennan details concerning his financial situation. Mr. MacLennan advised him that he also owed money to the Farm Credit Corporation and to the Caisse Populaire and that he had two contracts with Lucien Bériault in regard to the sale of a specified amount of soybeans at a fixed price. Mr. MacLennan also advised Mr. MacEwen that he had not given crop security to anyone else.

[4] In April 2001, Mr. MacLennan had been considering applying for a loan through the Agricultural Commodity Corporation, and he had partially completed an application form in this regard entitled "Loan Application Booklet for Grain and Oilseed Producers, Potato, Dark Fired Tobacco, Air-Cured Tobacco and Burley Tobacco Growers." One page of that application form was entitled "Location of Secured Crops." Mr. MacLennan had completed that sheet in detail. It contained detailed information as to the location of his corn and soybean crops. Mr. MacLennan gave this sheet to Mr. MacEwen. Mr. MacEwen made notes on the back of the sheet in regard to Mr. MacLennan's financial information. Mr. MacLennan then signed the sheet to indicate that the information contained thereon was accurate and complete. Mr. MacLennan then rewrote this sheet so that it would be neater, and he signed the Loan Application Booklet. Mr. MacEwen advised him that he would give the document to his lawyer. Mr. MacLennan was under the impression that he would be receiving a further document from Mr. MacEwen's lawyer that would have to be signed to evidence the security agreement; but he acknowledged that Mr. MacEwen never told him this. No further document was ever signed by Mr. MacLennan.

[5] I find that Mr. MacLennan left Mr. MacEwen's office with the signed Loan Application Booklet and Mr. MacEwen only kept the single sheet showing the location of the crops MacLennan had signed. On January 17, 2002, Mr. MacLennan gave the full document to Mr. MacEwen, when Mr. MacEwen discovered that he did not have it on his file.

[6] The Agricultural Commodity Corporation document, as completed by Mr. MacLennan, contained his name and address, information concerning his financial institutions and outstanding debts, and information concerning his crops and crop locations. The document referred to a general and continuing security for the payment of all exist-

ing and future indebtedness that the Producer (in this case identified as Norman Mac-Lennan) was giving, and it specifically identified crops and the proceeds of sale of crops as assets that were being secured. Reference to the Agricultural Commodity Corporation in the document had not been struck out and replaced with the name MacEwen Agricentre Inc. The only place in the document that the applicant's name appeared was under the listing of existing creditors.

[7] When no further payments had been made on the MacEwen Agricentre debt by harvest time, Mr. MacEwen had his lawyer register a financing statement under the *Personal Property Security Act*, RSO 1990, c. P.10, as am. ("PPSA") to evidence what he considered was a security interest his company had in Mr. MacLennan's crops. This was done on November 7, 2001. At no subsequent time has Mr. MacLennan ever argued that MacEwen had no right to register the financing statement. MacEwen Agricentre personnel also contacted Mr. Bériault to advise him of the company's security interest and to instruct him to send the proceeds of sale of Mr. MacLennan's soybean crop to MacEwen. On January 17, 2002, Mr. MacLennan signed a Direction to Lucien Bériault confirming his earlier oral directions that Mr. Bériault should pay to MacEwen the entire proceeds of sale of his soybeans and/or corn, without deduction, because of the security interest which he had given to MacEwen. Mr. Bériault never forwarded the proceeds to MacEwen.

[8] Based on Mr. MacLennan's affidavit evidence and his responses to questions when examined by MacEwen's counsel and Mr. Bériault's counsel, I find that on July 27, 2001, Mr. MacLennan intended to give MacEwen Agricentre Inc. a security interest over all of his 2001 crops in order to secure his indebtedness to that company. I find that James MacEwen, on behalf of the company, believed that was what the company was receiving on that date. I find that both James MacEwen and Norman MacLennan conducted themselves subsequent to July 27, 2001 on the assumption that such a security interest had been given. I note in particular the following excerpts from Mr. MacLennan's Affidavit:

> I signed the second page of the list of crops and it is my belief that what I had agreed to at that time was that I had given to the Applicant my 2001 crop as security for money owing to the Applicant. ...
>
> In early November 2001 I received a copy of the PPSA registration and I was somewhat surprised at the time because I believed that I had given this security to the Applicant on July 27, 2001 when I met Mr. MacEwen at his office.

[9] Mr. Bériault's counsel argues that Mr. MacLennan's answers on his cross-examination are more consistent with his signing documents on July 27, 2001 just to indicate the information on those documents was accurate, and not to signify in any respect that he was providing MacEwen with a security interest in his crops. I find that Mr. MacLennan signed the documents for both purposes; they are not inconsistent purposes. I note that most of the questions put to Mr. MacLennan by Mr. Champagne [Lucien Bériault's lawyer] were leading questions inviting Mr. MacLennan to agree with Mr. Champagne. As well, many of the questions contained numerous questions within the same sentence, thereby making it impossible to determine to what aspect of the question a "yes" or "no" answer applied. When Mr. MacLennan was given the opportunity to

express himself in his own words, he made it clear that he assumed on July 27, 2001 that he had given MacEwen a security interest over his crops.

[10] MacEwen takes the position that it had a security interest in Mr. MacLennan's 2001 crops by virtue of the security agreement entered July 27, 2001, and that this security agreement was effective against Lucien Bériault by virtue of the provisions in the PPSA.

Foundation of Claim by Lucien Bériault

[11] Lucien Bériault is a grain dealer who acts as an intermediary between the grain producers and the grain brokers. He agrees to purchase a certain amount of grain of a particular quality from a farmer at a fixed price per tonne. He had been purchasing grains from Mr. MacLennan since 1999.

[12] Due to poor weather conditions, Mr. MacLennan was unable to meet his obligations to Mr. Bériault under their contracts for the year 2000 crops. As a result, Mr. Mac-Lennan was charged certain replacement costs under those contracts, which he had then been unable to pay.

[13] On July 6, 2001, Mr. MacLennan agreed to sell to Mr. Bériault 375 tonnes of soybeans at a fixed price. On July 10, 2001, he agreed to sell him 210 tonnes of soybeans at a fixed price. During their meetings, Mr. MacLennan also agreed with Mr. Bériault that the proceeds he received from the first harvest of soybeans in 2001 would be credited on the amounts owed to Mr. Bériault in regard to the unsatisfied 2000 contracts.

[14] In November 2001, Mr. MacLennan supplied to Mr. Bériault some, but not all, of the soybeans which he had undertaken to provide pursuant to the two contracts with Mr. Bériault, thereby resulting in a further penalty of $4,840. By January 2002, Mr. Mac-Lennan owed Mr. Bériault $32,715.10.

[15] As of December 10, 2001, Mr. Bériault owed Mr. MacLennan $33,125.45 for the soybeans he had purchased under the July 2001 contracts. However, he wished to claim a set-off against these proceeds of the sums then owing to him by Mr. MacLennan. On January 12, 2002, Mr. Bériault went to see Mr. MacLennan with two cheques payable to Mr. MacLennan representing the moneys owing to him under the contracts. At that time, Mr. Bériault asked Mr. MacLennan to endorse the cheques over to him. He explained that his grain dealer's licence was up for renewal and it was important that he have a clean slate. Mr. Bériault assured Mr. MacLennan that the moneys would be deposited into his lawyer's trust account pending a determination of who, between himself and MacEwen, was entitled to receive the proceeds. Mr. MacLennan willingly endorsed the cheques because he did not want Mr. Bériault to have any problems renewing his licence. In doing so, he was not choosing between Mr. Bériault and MacEwen. It is very clear that he felt it was up to the court to decide which of his creditors had priority over the proceeds.

[16] Mr. Bériault takes the position that MacEwen did not have a security interest in Mr. MacLennan's 2001 soybean crop, and even if it did, that security interest was created by what was only a verbal agreement. Such a security interest was not enforceable against Mr. Bériault as a third party, because it had not attached, as that term is used in s. 11(1) and 11(2) of the PPSA. Furthermore, Mr. Bériault takes the position that when Norman

MacLennan purportedly gave a security interest in his 2001 crops to MacEwen on July 27, he could not give a security interest in something which he did not own at the time, namely the soybeans he had already agreed to sell to Mr. Bériault by virtue of the July 6 and 10 contracts.

Analysis

...

Did a Security Interest Exist in Favour of MacEwen?

[18] A security agreement can be oral or in writing or some combination thereof. (*1329207 Ontario Inc. v. D & R Custom Millwork Ltd.*, [2000] OJ No. 2485 (Quicklaw) (SCJ), upheld [2001] OJ No. 5435 (Quicklaw) (Div. Ct.); *Garry v. Sternbauer Estate*, [2000] OJ No. 2704 (Quicklaw) (SCJ); *977380 Ontario Inc. v. Roy's Towing Co.* (1997), 13 PPSAC (2d) 201 (Ont. Gen. Div.)). This flows from the definition of "security agreement" in the PPSA. It also flows logically from s. 10 of the Act, which is prefaced by the phrase: "where a security agreement is in writing, ..." If the security agreement is oral, there is still a requirement for the terms of the agreement to be clear (*1329207 Ontario Inc. v. D & R Custom Millwork Ltd.*, *supra*).

[19] There can be more than one document forming the written part of a security agreement. (*Universal Handling Equipment Co. v. Redipac Recycling Inc.*, [1992] OJ No. 1763 (Quicklaw) (Gen. Div.) per Rosenberg J, as he then was.) Again, this flows from the definition of "security agreement" in the PPSA, where a security agreement can include a document *evidencing* a security interest. This wording suggests that any document which corroborates the existence of a security interest, even though it might not contain all the terms of the security agreement, falls within the definition of "security agreement." This interpretation is consistent with the terms of s. 11(2)(a) of the PPSA where it describes the security agreement required to satisfy that clause as being one "that contains a description of the collateral sufficient to enable it to be identified." This implies that not all documents described as "security agreements" under the PPSA will contain detailed descriptions of the collateral forming the subject matter of the agreement.

[20] I find that a security agreement was created on July 27, 2001 at the time that Norman MacLennan met with James MacEwen and they discussed Mr. MacLennan providing MacEwen Agricentre Inc. with crop security. I find that the terms of the agreement were that Mr. MacLennan was pledging his 2001 crops (including his soybean crop) as security for his outstanding indebtedness with MacEwen in the approximate amount of $129,500. The understanding was that MacEwen was entitled to receive the entire proceeds from the sale of those crops—up to the maximum of what was owed to MacEwen at the time. The understanding was that there were no security interests in the crops ahead of that of MacEwen. At the time, Mr. MacLennan had some unsecured debtors only. As well, the understanding was that Mr. MacLennan had committed to sell a certain quantity of his 2001 soybean crop to his usual dealer, Lucien Bériault, as part of the normal course of doing business. The understanding was that the proceeds from this transaction would be paid to MacEwen.

[21] I find that this security agreement was primarily oral, but it was also partially written. Most importantly, there was the document entitled "Location of Secured Crops" which set out very clearly a description of the crops that were forming the collateral; namely where the crops were being grown, the acreage involved, the legal description of the land, the nature of Mr. MacLennan's interest in the land, the name of the landlord or mortgagee and whether any lease or mortgage payments were up to date. This document was signed. There was also the entire Agricultural Commodity Corporation Application for Loan Booklet in which reference was made to crop security, along with many other extraneous terms. Finally, there was the promissory note in the amount of $129,476.73 in favour of MacEwen Agricentre Inc., dated April 19, 2001 and signed by Norman Mac-Lennan. This document set out the parties to the agreement, the amount of the indebtedness, the interest payable and the fact that the indebtedness was payable on demand. What the promissory note did not do was refer to any security interest. Therefore standing alone, it would not fall within the definition of "security agreement" under the PPSA.

Attachment of Security Interest

(a) Signing Security Agreement

[22] There is no dispute that for a security interest to be enforceable against a third party, it has to be attached, as that term is used in the PPSA. For attachment to occur when the secured party does not have possession of the collateral, at least part of the security agreement must be in writing, the part that is in writing must contain provisions relating to security, and that portion of the documentation must be signed. (*Astral Communications Inc. v. 825536 Ontario Inc. (Trustee of)* (2000), 46 OR (3d) 477, 183 DLR (4th) 455 (CA); *Universal Handling Equipment Co. v. Redipac Recycling Inc., supra.*)

[23] Since MacEwen did not have possession of the crops or of the proceeds from the sale of the crops, MacEwen's security interest in the crops would only have attached when Mr. MacLennan signed a security agreement that contained a description of the collateral sufficient to enable it to be identified. The issue is whether the document entitled "Location of Secured Crops" together with the document entitled "Agricultural Commodity Corporation Application for Loan Booklet," both of which were signed by Mr. Mac-Lennan on July 27, 2001, constituted a security agreement, as described in s. 11(2)(a). Mr. Bériault's lawyer argues that they did not, because neither document indicated who the secured creditor was and what was being secured.

[24] Mr. Bériault proffered the expert opinion evidence of Yves Ménard, a commercial lawyer, to the effect that these documents do not constitute a signed security agreement because they do not identify the name of the secured party, they do not identify the essential terms of the security, and they do not contain the signature of the debtor in relation to a security agreement with MacEwen Agricentre Inc. Lawyers are not normally asked to give expert opinion evidence on the law of Ontario in regard to the very point to be decided by the court.

[25] Both counsel were asked to make further submissions on the question of whether the documents signed by Mr. MacLennan, when considered together, could satisfy the requirements of s. 11(2)(a). Both were given the opportunity of seeking further case law

that might be of assistance to the court, but both felt that they had provided whatever case law was applicable. Nevertheless, another case has come to my attention, that of *Garry v. Sternbauer Estate*, [2000] OJ No. 2704 (Quicklaw) (SCJ), a decision of Gillese J (now of the Ontario Court of Appeal). That case is very similar to the one at hand and also involved the question of whether a creditor had a secured interest in a farmer's soybean crop.

[26] Over time, Gladys Garry loaned various amounts of money to her friend, Philip Sternbauer, a soybean farmer. At the time of his death in 1999, he owed her approximately $135,600. On most occasions, both Ms. Garry and the deceased signed notes evidencing the loans. As the loans increased, Ms. Garry sought and received assurance from Mr. Sternbauer that she would be repaid her loans in full when the 1999 soybean crop was sold. He told her that the soybean crop was her security. The soybean crop was subject to a harvest contract with a company, "Thompsons," pursuant to which Mr. Sternbauer had an obligation to grow, harvest and deliver the soybean crop to Thompsons. After Mr. Sternbauer's death, Ms. Garry's lawyer registered a financing statement under the PPSA. Thompsons subsequently harvested and sold the crop. Mr. Sternbauer's landlord attempted to distrain in regard to rent owing on the property after Mr. Sternbauer's death. The case concerned the competing interests of the landlord, the Estate and Ms. Garry in regard to the proceeds of sale of the crop.

[27] One of the notes signed by Mr. Sternbauer and Ms. Garry on March 18, 1999 read as follows:

> I Philip Sternbauer of R.R. 3 Tillsonburg Ont. N4G 4G8 subtenant of 1110 acres leased from Schwab's Meat Products Ltd. head office at 5410 Huron Church Line Rd. Windsor Ontario N9H 1H6 give as security to Gladys Garry of 1635 Hamilton Rd. London Ont. N6M 1G5 967 acres of soya bean crop for 1999 as security for a loan of $45,000.

> 1 check for $20,000 p No. 964. 2 check for $25,000—No. 965

> To be paid by December 1/1999 or sooner.

[28] Ms. Garry took the position that she was a secured creditor holding a perfected interest in the whole of the soybean crop; that the security interest was created by a security agreement that was partly oral and partly written; that her claim to the soybean crop extended to the entire net proceeds of its sale; that her security interest was enforceable against third parties because it had attached; and that it was perfected when it attached and all steps required for perfection had been completed. In other words, the position she took is the same position as is being taken by MacEwen in the case at hand.

[29] After dispensing with any problems created by s. 13 of the *Evidence Act*, RSO 1990, c. E.23, the parol evidence rule and the landlord's distraint claim, Gillese J (as she then was) found that Ms. Garry's security interest in the soybean crop attached on March 18, 1999, even though the note signed on that date referred only to $45,000 and the amount Ms. Garry was claiming was well in excess of that sum. Gillese J was satisfied that the security agreement in that case consisted of the March 18, 1999 note together with the oral agreement to grant a security interest in the crop for the full extent of the deceased's indebtedness, including future advances.

[30] Implicit in this finding is a recognition that the security agreement required under s. 11(2)(a), containing a description of the collateral sufficient to enable it to be identified, will not necessarily contain all of the terms of the security agreement between the parties.

[31] However, the *Garry* case is distinguishable from the case at hand in that the March 18, 1999 note with the description of the collateral at least named the parties to the security agreement and confirmed that a security interest was being given from the debtor to the creditor. Those two pieces of information are not explicitly given in the documents signed by Mr. MacLennan on July 27, 2001. This is an important distinction as there is no explicit reference in the documents signed on July 27, 2001 tying them in with a security agreement between Mr. MacLennan and MacEwen. The purpose of the s. 11(2)(a) requirement is to enable one creditor to be able to identify that another creditor has a security interest in identifiable collateral. That could not be accomplished through reference to the documents Mr. MacLennan signed on July 27.

...

(b) Value

[33] The second requirement for a security interest to attach is that value be given. There is no dispute in this case that value was given by MacEwen to Mr. MacLennan.

(c) Debtor Has Rights in Collateral

[34] Counsel for Mr. Bériault argued that on July 27, 2001, Mr. MacLennan did not have any rights in his soybean crops due to the July 6 and July 10, 2001 purchase orders he had signed with Mr. MacLennan. I do not accept this argument.

[35] All that was agreed to in the purchase orders was that Mr. Bériault would purchase a certain quantity of a certain quality of soybeans from Mr. MacLennan by a certain date for a fixed price, with there being certain financial repercussions if such soybeans were not delivered, as required under the purchase order. Mr. MacLennan was not obliged to provide those soybeans from any particular crops. If Mr. Bériault did not receive the soybeans from Mr. MacLennan as contemplated in the purchase orders, Mr. Bériault did not have the right to harvest Mr. MacLennan's crops so as to get the soybeans. Put another way, the sale of Mr. MacLennan's soybeans to Mr. Bériault did not take place on July 6 and July 10. The documents signed that date simply evidenced an agreement for a sale at a particular price to occur at a later date, with liquidated damages payable if the sale did not proceed as anticipated.

[36] In these circumstances, Mr. MacLennan's soybean crops remained his property on July 27, 2001, and he was in the position to pledge them as collateral to MacEwen.

Conclusion

[37] As between Norman MacLennan and MacEwen, a security interest in Mr. MacLennan's 2001 soybean and corn crops existed in favour of MacEwen, pursuant to an oral security agreement between the parties negotiated on July 27, 2001, as evidenced in part by the list of crops provided to Mr. MacEwen on that date. However, that security interest

did not attach as required under s. 11(1) of the PPSA so as to be enforceable against third parties, such as Mr. Bériault.

[38] The application is dismissed.

Atlas Industries v. Federal Business Development Bank: S.K.T.N. Farm and Truck Equipment Ltd. (Debtor)
(1983), 3 PPSAC 39 (Sask. QB)

NOBLE J: The applicant is a manufacturer and as a result of four orders received from the debtor dated July 29, August 11, 16 and 20 all in 1982, manufactured and delivered certain equipment parts to the debtor. All of the equipment parts so ordered were delivered to the debtor as they were manufactured and delivery was completed prior to October 25, 1982. On that date the applicant became aware that the "bank" had decided to realize on the security it had on the assets of the debtor by way of a registered debenture, by appointing a receiver to take control of the debtor's business. On October 27, 1982 the applicant delivered four invoices to the bank's receiver recovering the goods described in the four work orders already mentioned. On each invoice the applicant stamped the following words:

> Title to property described on this invoice retained by vendor until payment in full. Vendor has right of repossession on default. Power to forceably retake. This is a security agreement.

The bank, under date of February 9, 1981 had acquired a debenture to secure a loan of $150,000 from the debtor. The debenture was duly registered pursuant to the *Corporation Securities Registration Act*, RSS 1978, c. C-39 [subsequently repealed 1979-80, c. 18, s. 2] on February 26, 1981. Without going into detail, the said debenture represented a floating debenture which forms a charge, *inter alia*, "on all chattels now owned or hereafter acquired by the Company (debtor) … ."

The applicant now seeks, pursuant to the *Personal Property Security Act*, SS 1979-80, c. P-6.1, an order firstly that it has a security interest in the equipment parts sold to the debtor by virtue of the work orders and the invoices; and secondly, that such security interest takes priority over the bank's debenture and is enforceable.

The first issue is whether or not the debtor's work orders, when combined with the applicant's invoices, represent a security agreement as defined by the Act. Section 2(mm) of the Act defines security agreement as "… an agreement that creates or provides for a security interest, and includes a document evidencing a security agreement when the context permits." The applicant argues that the work orders taken together with the invoices can be read together to fall within the definition of a security agreement. The work orders are a request to supply certain equipment parts which the applicant agrees were ordered for resale by the debtor. They contain a signature of someone who was apparently authorized to place such orders. The chattels were, as indicated, delivered as they became available with the invoices being issued later on October 26, 1982. As I understand the applicant's argument, notwithstanding that the debtor was unaware of the applicant's intention to reserve title to the goods until the invoices were delivered, the documents taken together represent a security agreement based on the terms of the invoices in particular. In my opinion it is clear that the applicant attempted to create a security agreement after it became apparent that the bank was about to swallow up the equipment parts as part of the inventory of the debtor covered by the debenture security. The fact is that it was open to the applicant to search the Personal Property Registry even before it delivered the goods to the debtor, and had it done so, would no doubt have discovered the bank's security on all chattels including those "hereafter acquired." It might then have insisted on cash or made a separate arrangement for payment which would circumvent the floating charge of the bank. It is, in my opinion, a little late to claim a security interest after the fact and in circumstances which make it clear the buyer of the goods was not aware of the terms of the transaction at the time the goods were delivered. So I am drawn to the conclusion that the documents evidencing the transaction between the applicant and the debtor do not represent a security agreement as defined by the statute. In my opinion, the sale by the applicant to the debtor was on the basis of goods and chattels delivered pursuant to an order on an open account. On this basis alone the applicant's motion fails.

However, even if I am wrong in this conclusion, the applicant fails because the documents of the sale (i.e., the work orders and the invoices) do not comply with s. 10 of the statute and are not therefore enforceable as against a third party:

> 10(1) No security interest is enforceable against a third party unless:
>
> (a) the collateral is in the possession of the secured party; or
>
> (b) the debtor has signed a security agreement that contains a description of the collateral which enables the type or kind of collateral taken under the security agreement to be distinguished from types or kinds of collateral which are not collateral under the security agreement, and, in the case of a security interest taken in all of the debtor's present and after-acquired property, a statement indicating that a security interest has been taken in all of the debtor's present and after-acquired property is sufficient.

The flaw in the documents, even if one could find them to be a security agreement, is that they are not signed by the debtor. It is true that a signature appears on each of the four work orders, but there is no evidence as to whether that person was in fact authorized to sign on behalf of the debtor company. Even if one assumes that the signature on each work order is an authorization which binds the debtor, it cannot be said to be a signature as contemplated by s. 10(1)(b) of the Act. As counsel for the bank argued, a purchase order is delivered without conditions and in this instance was delivered to the debtor in the ordinary course of business so that the debtor could acquire the equipment parts for its inventory. While the signature authorizes the delivery of the goods, it would be absurd to suggest that it was intended to authorize delivery upon any terms the applicant chose to impose as to price, security or payment. Thus, if there is to be an agreement that the applicant shall retain title to the goods once they were delivered, that condition should be imposed before the transaction is finalized, and in any event it cannot be said that the signature on the work order somehow authorized the unknown condition in advance. So I am inclined to agree that even if it could be successfully argued that the applicant had a "security agreement" and thereby acquired a security interest in the equipment parts, it is not enforceable as against the bank's security in any event. In this regard *Pickles Tents & Awnings Ltd. v. Joseph Group of Cos.*, [1981] 6 WWR 300, 10 Man. R (2d) 19, 2 PPSAC 1, 127 DLR (3d) 176 (CA) and the case of *Roynat Inc. v. United Rescue Services Ltd.*, [1982] 3 WWR 512, 2 PPSAC 49 (Man. CA) in McLaren's *Secured Transactions in Personal Property in Canada*, seem to support the bank's position.

Application dismissed.

NOTE

The *Atlas Industries* case is a good example of the situation that the s. 9 writing requirement is aimed at. Atlas was trying to protect itself against the bank by conjuring up a security agreement after the event. In effect, the attempt failed for lack of evidence to corroborate Atlas's assertion that there was a security agreement.

CHAPTER FOUR

Attachment

I. INTRODUCTION

"Attachment" and "perfection" are the OPPSA's two central concepts. Broadly speaking, attachment marks the point at which the secured party's security interest materializes, while perfection relates to the publication of the security interest. Perfection is a function of attachment, in the sense that a security interest cannot be perfected unless it has first attached to the collateral: OPPSA s. 19. This chapter deals with attachment. Chapter 5 deals with perfection.

The requirements for attachment are set out in s. 11. Broadly speaking, the requirements are that: (1) there must be (a) a security agreement, which (b) satisfies the Statute of Frauds requirements (see Chapter 3); (2) the secured party must give value; and (3) the debtor must have rights in the collateral or the power to transfer rights in the collateral to a secured party. The security interest attaches once all these requirements have been met, but the parties may agree to postpone the time for attachment. Section 11.1 enacts special rules for the attachment of a security interest in favour of a securities intermediary and a security interest in a certificated security.

According to s. 11(1), a security interest is not enforceable against a third party unless it has attached. This is misleading because it implies that a security interest may be enforceable between the parties themselves whether or not it has attached. However, as a matter of first principles, non-compliance with requirement (1)(a), (2), or (3) above must lead to the conclusion that the secured party does not have a security interest at all (see further below). Therefore, a more accurate statement of the consequences of non-attachment would be that if the security interest has failed to attach due to non-compliance with requirement (1)(b), the security interest is unenforceable against third parties but remains enforceable between the parties themselves; however, if the security interest has failed to attach due to non-compliance with requirement (1)(a), (2), or (3), the secured party has no enforceable rights, *qua* secured party, even against the debtor.

II. SECURITY AGREEMENT

The first requirement for attachment is that there must be a security agreement. This proposition derives by implication from OPPSA s. 11(2)(a). The reason for the requirement is obvious. The attachment rules presuppose a consensual security interest, as opposed to a security interest (or lien) arising by operation of law, and there cannot be a consensual security interest without a contract. *Ellingsen (Trustee of) v. Hallmark Ford Sales Ltd.* (2000), 190 DLR (4th) 47 (BCCA) and *994814 Ontario Inc. v. RSL Canada Inc. and En-Plas Inc.* (2006), 20 CBR (5th) 163 (Ont. CA), extracted in Chapter 3, illustrate the point.

III. VALUE

There is a definition of "value" in OPPSA s. 1(1): value means "any consideration sufficient to support a simple contract … ." So, for example, if SP makes a loan to D, the loan is value. Likewise, if SP promises to make a loan to D, the promise is value. The reason for the value requirement is straightforward: the value is the consideration SP gives in exchange for the security interest. In the absence of consideration, there can be no security agreement and without a security agreement, SP cannot have a security interest.

IV. RIGHTS IN THE COLLATERAL

A. Introduction

The third requirement for attachment is that the debtor must have rights in the collateral or at least the power to transfer rights. Again, the reason for this requirement is straightforward: if the debtor has no rights in the collateral, she has nothing to give the secured party: *nemo dat quod non habet*. The *RSL Canada* case (see above), extracted in Chapter 3, is a good illustration of this proposition. Recall that there, the debtor, RSL, contracted with En-Plas for the purchase of some machines, but the contract was never concluded. The appellant held a security interest in all RSL's present and after-acquired personal property and it claimed the machines. The court held that since RSL had no rights in the machines, given the non-conclusion of the purchase contract with En-Plas, the appellant's security interest did not attach to them and so it had no claim.

B. After-Acquired Property

Section 12 provides that a security interest may cover after-acquired property, subject to exceptions for crops and consumer goods. The mechanism for taking a security interest in after-acquired property is simple: all it requires is a provision in the security agreement specifying that the collateral includes after-acquired property (for example, "Debtor's present and after-acquired factory equipment," "Debtor's present and after-acquired accounts receivable," or "all Debtor's present and after-acquired personal property").

Consider the following case:

> On June 1, 2007, D, a retailer, enters into an agreement assigning all D's present and after-acquired accounts receivable to SP. The agreement is in writing and signed by D, and SP gives value in the form of a promise to pay for the accounts in batches from time to time. (Note that, although this is an outright assignment, for PPSA purposes, SP holds a security interest (s. 2(b)).) On September 1, D sells goods to O for $100 on 90-day terms. When does SP's security interest attach to O's account?

The answer is, on September 1, the date the account comes into existence, because that is the date on which D acquires rights in the account. This outcome replicates pre-PPSA case law (see, for example, *Holroyd v. Marshall* (1861-1862), 11 EE 999, 10 HLC 191 and *Tailby v. Official Receiver* (1888), 13 AC 523, discussed in Chapter 1).

Section 12(2)(a) of the OPPSA (crops) is based on UCC 9-204(4)(a) (1962 text), which in turn was inspired by the one-year limitations on after-acquired property (AAP) clauses in crop mortgages that were common in pre-Code US state law. See Gilmore, vol. II, §32.4, at 864. AAP clauses do not appear to have caused comparable problems in Canadian crop mortgages—why, we do not know, although the well-established role of Canadian banks in providing current crop financing under s. 427 of the *Bank Act* may have something to do with it.

OPPSA s. 12(2)(b) (consumer goods) is also of Code origin—in this case, UCC 9-204(4)(b) (1962 text). Gilmore (vol. I, §11.6, at 357) explains that the Code provision is "one of the vestiges of the original plan, later abandoned, to include in Article 9 a full-scale treatment of the problems of consumer finance." He also notes that existing state retail installment sales acts frequently contain more extensive prohibitions on "add-on" clauses than those in UCC 9-204(4)(b).

Why are AAP clauses objectionable in consumer security agreements? Is it because of concern that an unscrupulous lender will tie up all the debtor's household goods? If this is the basis of the objection, would it not be better to prohibit mortgages altogether on household goods? See, for example, the *Exemptions Act*, RSS 1978, c. E-14, ss. 2 and 5. Should a distinction be drawn between a purchase-money security interest in consumer goods and other security interests?

Note that s. 12(2)(b) applies only to consumer goods, not to other types of collateral. Presumably, a consumer is free to pledge his or her future rights under an RRSP, a trust, or a will. Is the distinction justified? What of a wage assignment? In most provinces it is expressly outlawed under separate legislation, except for assignments in favour of a credit union or similar cooperative. See, for example, *Wages Act*, RSO 1990, c. W.1, s. 7(2). Wages, however, do not include the fees earned by a self-employed professional: *Re Kryspin* (1983), 40 OR (2d) 424 (SC).

C. The Floating Charge

The opening words of OPPSA s. 11(2) provide that a security interest, including a security interest in the nature of a floating charge, attaches when the requirements of the section are satisfied. As pointed out in Chapter 1, the floating charge was a mechanism developed by the English courts to facilitate security interests in circulating assets, such as inventory and accounts receivable.

To recapitulate, the floating charge is an equitable charge (or lien), typically over assets such as inventory and accounts and their proceeds. What makes the floating charge distinctive is that so long as the debtor does not default, the charge does not attach to any particular asset. Instead it "floats" over the debtor's shifting mass of assets. While the floating charge remains in this suspensory state, the debtor is free to deal with the collateral, subject to any restrictions the agreement may stipulate. This does not interfere with the secured party's rights because the secured party has no rights to any specific part of the pledged assets as distinct from a charge on the mass of shifting assets.

The picture changes when the debtor defaults. Subject to the terms of the security agreement, default causes the floating charge to "crystallize." Crystallization brings to an end the suspensory state of the charge. It converts the floating charge into a fixed charge over whatever collateral the debtor happens to own at that point and it deprives the debtor of its freedom to deal with the collateral. Simultaneously, subject to the terms of the agreement, the secured party becomes entitled to enforce the charge by seizing and realizing on the relevant collateral.

The PPSA does away with the need for floating charges. Post-PPSA, if the parties want a security interest in the debtor's circulating assets, all they have to do is specify in the security agreement that the debtor gives the secured party a security interest in the debtor's present and after-acquired inventory or its present and after-acquired accounts or all its present and after-acquired personal property (as the case may be) and to make it clear, expressly or by implication, that, in the absence of default, the debtor remains free to deal with the collateral in the ordinary course of its business. Subject to any express restrictions in the security agreement, the courts are likely to imply the debtor's right to dispose of inventory collateral in the ordinary course of business because, without this facility, the debtor's business would grind to a halt. OPPSA s. 25(1) provides that where collateral gives rise to proceeds, the security interest (a) continues as to the collateral unless the secured party expressly or impliedly authorized the dealing with the collateral free of the security interest and (b) extends to the proceeds. Assume that Debtor gives Secured Party a security interest in all Debtor's present and after-acquired inventory. Debtor sells an item of inventory to Customer in the ordinary course of business on 90-day terms. The legal consequences are as follows: (1) Customer takes the item free of Secured Party's security interest (s. 25(1)(a)) (this is because if not expressly, then at least by implication, Secured Party authorized the sale to Customer free of the security interest); (2) Secured Party acquires a security interest in Customer's account as proceeds of the inventory (s. 25(1)(b)); and (3) Secured Party's security interest attaches to the account at the point of Customer's purchase (which is when the account comes into existence and Debtor acquires rights in it) (OPPSA s. 11(2)).

Note that what the Act gives Secured Party is a fixed (legal) security interest, not a floating (equitable) one. Immediately before Debtor's sale to Customer, Secured Party has a fixed security interest in the inventory item. The sale extinguishes Secured Party's security interest in the item and triggers its replacement with a fixed security interest in Customer's account. To continue the analysis one step further, assume that Debtor collects on Customer's account and uses the funds to buy another item of inventory. At that point, Secured Party loses its security interest in the account (which, upon collection, ceases to exist) and, by virtue of the after-acquired property clause in the security agreement, obtains instead a security interest in the new item of inventory, which attaches upon Debtor's acquisition (s. 11(2)).

As the foregoing implies, the PPSA makes it unnecessary for parties wanting a security interest in circulating assets to use floating-charge language anymore. On the other hand, there is nothing to prevent parties from continuing to use floating-charge documentation if they want to. Suppose that Secured Party and Debtor enter into a floating-charge form of agreement covering Debtor's present and after-acquired inventory. Specifically, the agreement describes Secured Party's security interest as a floating one, and it provides for crystallization upon the happening of prescribed defaults. The agreement is signed on June 1 and Secured Party makes a loan to Debtor on the same date and registers a financing statement. On July 1, Debtor acquires a new item of inventory. On August 1, Debtor defaults and Secured Party appoints a receiver. In the meantime, on July 15, Judgment Creditor levies execution against the July 1 item of inventory. Who has priority in relation to the July 1 item of inventory: Secured Party or Judgment Creditor?

The governing provision is OPPSA s. 20(1)(a)(ii), which provides that an unperfected security interest is subordinate to an execution creditor who has assumed control of the collateral. Attachment is a condition of perfection (OPPSA s. 19). In other words, Secured Party's registration on June 1 is not enough to perfect its security interest. There has to be attachment as well. So the question becomes, when does Secured Party's security interest attach? If the ordinary attachment rules in s. 11(2) apply, the answer would be July 1, the date Debtor acquired rights in the new inventory. On the other hand, it could be argued that by using floating-charge language, Secured Party and Debtor have agreed to postpone the time for attachment until crystallization (that is, August 1). The opening words of s. 11(2) tell against this argument: they suggest that the use of floating-charge language is not enough to displace the ordinary attachment rules and that if the parties do want to displace the ordinary rules, they must use clear language. The following cases address this issue.

Access Advertising Management Inc. v. Servex Computers Inc.
(1993), 15 OR (3d) 635 (Gen. Div.)

SAUNDERS J: This is a motion under rule 60.08(16) of the Rules of Civil Procedure for an order setting aside a notice of garnishment and declaring that the funds held in court to the credit of this matter be paid to the moving party. The issue is whether funds collected under a notice of garnishment are subject to the interest of the moving party under a security agreement.

The background facts are as follows:

1. By agreement in writing executed on April 6, 1992 (the "guarantee agreement") Everex Systems (Canada) Inc. ("Everex-Canada") guaranteed the indebtedness, liabilities and obligations of Everex Systems, Inc. ("Everex-US") to the CIT Group/Credit Finance, Inc. ("CIT").

2. In support of the guarantee, Everex-Canada executed an agreement (the "security agreement") with CIT on April 6, 1992 whereby, as continuing security for its obligations under the guarantee agreement, Everex-Canada created a security interest in all its present and after-acquired personal property "together with ... all deposit accounts."

3. A financial statement with respect to the security interest created by the security agreement was registered on April 14, 1992 pursuant to the Personal Property Security Act, RSO 1990, c. P.10 (the "PPSA").

4. On January 4, 1993, Everex-US filed a voluntary petition pursuant to c. 11 of the United States Bankruptcy Code. Everex-US as borrower and CIT as lender had entered into an agreement executed on June 4, 1991 (the "loan agreement"). Under the loan agreement any petition or any application for relief under the bankruptcy laws of the United States is an event of default. Under the guarantee agreement, upon the occurrence

of any default under the loan agreement, the obligations under the guarantee agreement become immediately due and payable. Also under the security agreement, the security constituted thereunder becomes enforceable at the option of CIT upon the occurrence of any event of default under the loan agreement.

5. On January 5, 1993, the solicitors for CIT wrote to Everex-Canada advising of the default, terminating the right of Everex-Canada to receive proceeds and directing Everex-Canada that all such property was to be received by it in trust for CIT pursuant to the terms of the security agreement.

6. On January 6, 1993, CIT sent to Everex-Canada, described as an insolvent person, a notice of intention to enforce the security under the security agreement pursuant to s. 244(1) of the Bankruptcy and Insolvency Act, RSC 1985, c. B-3 (the "BIA"), as amended.

7. On January 7, 1993, Price Waterhouse Limited was appointed interim receiver by order of this court on an application under s. 47 of the BIA.

8. On January 12, 1993, the creditor, Access Advertising Management Inc. ("Access"), obtained judgment against Everex-Canada in the amount of $54,437.35. On January 14 Access issued a notice of garnishment against the Bank of Nova Scotia (the "Bank"). The notice was served on the Bank on the same day. On January 15 the Bank debited the account of Everex-Canada by the amount of the judgment and remitted the funds to the sheriff. The funds were subsequently paid into court to the credit of this matter pursuant to court order.

9. On January 17, 1993, CIT appointed Price Waterhouse Limited as receiver pursuant to the terms of the security agreement.

Price Waterhouse Limited claims the money in court on the basis that CIT had a perfected security interest on the moneys in the account at the Bank which interest had priority over the notice of garnishment. Access submits that the floating charge of CIT did not crystallize until Price Waterhouse Limited was appointed receiver on January 17, 1993, and that by that time the moneys had been removed from the account and were beyond the reach of the receiver: see *Royal Bank of Canada v. Mohawk Moving & Storage Ltd.* (1985), 49 OR (2d) 734, 16 DLR (4th) 434 (HCJ).

Section 19 of the PPSA provides: ...

And s. 11(2) of the PPSA provides: ...

There is agreement that the security interest of CIT is in the nature of a floating charge. The collateral described in the security agreement includes "all deposit accounts." That description in my opinion is sufficient to identify the funds in the account of Everex-Canada at the Bank. Property subject to a floating charge changes from time to time. Assets are acquired and disposed of between the time the charge is given and the time it is discharged or converted into a specific charge. In such circumstances, collateral can only be described in general terms. For example, a floating charge on the inventory of a dealer in appliances could not describe the collateral by serial number or even by make or model. It is sufficient if the property in question (here a deposit account at a bank) falls within the general description of collateral in the security agreement: see McLaren, *Secured Transactions in Personal Property in Canada*, 2nd ed. (1992), pp. 2-8 and 2-29.

It was argued that because the security was a floating charge there was an agreement to postpone attachment until crystallization.

The security agreement provides otherwise. The charge on deposit accounts is described as a floating charge. The security agreement provides that the security interests created by it attach to the collateral when Everex-Canada has rights in the collateral. CIT and Everex-Canada in the agreement acknowledge that the security interests created pursuant to it have not been postponed.

A security agreement was signed, value was given and Everex-Canada had rights in the deposit accounts at the Bank. When all those three events occurred the security interest in the collateral in issue attached. The security interest was perfected by registration of the financing statement. The possibility that attachment did not occur until crystallization does not have to be dealt with. As indicated subsequently I consider the time of crystallization to be a crucial matter for determination. The security interest attached at the latest upon crystallization of the charge. As registration had already been done, the charge was also perfected no later than the time of crystallization.

The effect of perfection was that the floating charge was not subordinate to the interest of Access who assumed control of the funds on deposit through the garnishment (see PPSA s. 20(1)(a)(ii)). It did not follow that CIT by attaining perfection acquired priority over the garnishment by Access. To acquire priority the floating charge must have become specific. There must have been crystallization: *Royal Bank of Canada v. Mohawk, supra*; and *Re Standard-Modern Technologies Corp.* (1992), 6 OR (3d) 161, 87 DLR (4th) 442 (CA).

The critical issue, therefore, is the determination of when the charge crystallized. There is no dispute that there was crystallization on January 17, 1993 when the receiver was appointed. The issue is whether crystallization occurred at an earlier date. If crystallization occurred before the funds left the hands of the Bank, the claim of Price Waterhouse Limited prevails over the claim of Access. On the other hand, if crystallization occurred after that time the claim of Access prevails.

Part XI of the BIA dealing with secured creditors and receivers came into force on November 30, 1992 (SC 1992, c. 27). Where the debtor is an "insolvent person" (as defined in s. 2) a secured creditor who intends to enforce a security on all or substantially all of the property of the debtor must give the debtor notice of that intention in the prescribed form and manner (s. 244(1)). Subsection 244(2) provides that the creditor shall not enforce the security until the expiry of 10 days after sending the notice unless the insolvent person consents to an earlier enforcement. In order to protect the property covered by its security where a notice has been sent, an interim receiver may be appointed with wide powers to take such action as the court considers advisable (s. 47). The powers that may be given to an interim receiver under s. 47 are broader than those that may be given to such a receiver after the filing of a petition for a receiving order (see s. 46).

• • •

It would appear to be settled that a default rendering a security in the form of a floating charge enforceable at the option of the chargee does not of itself cause the charge to crystallize. There must be some intervention by the chargee to enforce the security: *Evans v. Rival Granite Quarries*, [1910] 2 KB 979, 79 LJKB 970 (CA); *R v. Consolidated Churchill Copper Corp.* (1978), 30 CBR (NS) 27, 90 DLR (3d) 357 (BCSC); and *Bayhold Financial Corp. v. Community Hotel Co. (Receiver of)* (1991), 86 DLR (4th) 127, 10 CBR (3d) 159 *sub nom. Bayhold Financial Corp. v. Clarkson Co.* (CA). Crystallization may be brought about in various ways. An appointment of a receiver crystallizes a charge. A demand for payment of the money secured does not: *Evans, supra*.

There has been some uncertainty as to when a floating charge crystallizes. It has been the position of some that an event which involved no action by the chargee could nevertheless crystallize a charge. As indicated, it now appears settled that there must be some intervention by the chargee. The question is to determine how much intervention is required.

There are sound policy reasons for requiring some intervention. If no intervention were required, a chargee in an event of default could do nothing and allow the chargor to continue carrying on business. If in the course of that business a claim arose such as a garnishment, the chargee could rely on crystallization resulting from the earlier default to establish priority.

There are equally sound policy reasons for protecting a chargee who is entitled to enforce his security and has determined to do so but is prevented from taking immediate action. Under the BIA, if the chargor is insolvent, the chargee must give notice of his intention and wait 10 days. If he is uncertain about the insolvency, it would still be prudent to follow the BIA procedure.

In my opinion the sending of the notice pursuant to s. 244(1) of the BIA was sufficient intervention to crystallize the charge. It was not necessary to actually enforce the security by appointing a receiver in order to effect crystallization and, as I have said, that could not be done until the 10-day period had expired. To hold otherwise would mean that secured creditors with a floating charge security would be exposed during the 10-day period to subsequent claims which would have priority over their security. Secured creditors should not be so prejudiced because of the requirements of the BIA.

The BIA would have no application if Everex-Canada was not an insolvent person within the meaning of that statute. Nevertheless, if such were the case, the notice effectively communicated the intention of CIT to enforce its security. The sending of the notice was sufficient intervention to effect crystallization. Whether or not Everex-Canada was insolvent made no difference.

The charge crystallized on January 6, 1993 when the notice pursuant to s. 244(1) of the BIA was sent. The security had attached and was perfected. The charge had priority over the subsequent garnishment of Access.

There will be an order setting aside the notice of garnishment issued to the Bank and a declaration that Price Waterhouse Limited as receiver of Everex-Canada has priority over Access to the funds in court to the credit of this matter.

. . .

Order accordingly.

Credit Suisse Canada v. Yonge Street Holdings
(1996), 28 OR (3d) 670 (Gen. Div.)

DAY J: This is an application by Credit Suisse Canada ("Bank") for an order for:

(a) the determination of the rights of the Bank pursuant to an assignment of rents ("assignment") granted to it by the respondent 1133 Yonge Street Holdings Limited ("Holdings"); and

(b) interim and interlocutory orders restraining the respondent Euromart Management Group Ltd. ("Euromart") from disposing of any funds constituting the rents or proceeds from the rents derived from property known municipally as 1133 Yonge Street in Toronto ("property") pending the disposition of this application.

Facts

1. The Loan and the Assignment

By letter dated December 8, 1986 (the "commitment") the Bank agreed to make a loan ("loan") of $7 million (or the Swiss franc equivalent) to Holdings. The loan proceeds were used to purchase the property. The commitment provided that the loan matured on November 30, 1994, and it was repayable in full on that date. The loan was evidenced by a promissory note and was secured by a collateral security agreement ("CSA") and by a mortgage on the property ("mortgage"). The loan was also secured by the assignment. Money was advanced and the assignment was signed on January 21, 1987 and registered against title to the property in the registry office on January 22, 1987. A financing statement giving notice of the assignment was filed on January 22, 1987 under the *Personal Property Security Act*, RSO 1990, c. P.10 (the "PPSA"). A subsequent financing statement was filed on July 19, 1990.

The salient provisions of the assignment are ss. 2, 11, 7, and 6, in that order. They read as follows:

2. The Mortgagor hereby assigns, transfers and sets over to the Mortgagee, the full benefit and advantage under all Existing and Future Leases, of all covenants, provisos and agreements therein named to be observed, kept and performed, all rents and monies reserved or payable under all Existing and Future Leases owing and the full benefit and advantage of all rights against any guarantors of the Lessees' obligations under such Existing and Future Leases.

11. The Mortgagor acknowledges and agrees with the Mortgagee that this assignment is an effective, present assignment, provided and it is expressly understood and agreed, anything herein contained to the contrary notwithstanding, that the Mortgagee shall not exercise any of the rights or powers herein conferred upon it until a default shall occur under the terms and provisions of this assignment, the Commitment Letter or under the Mortgage.

7. Until notified to the contrary in writing, the Mortgagor shall be entitled to, and the lessee under any lease shall pay to the Mortgagor, all rents and other amounts then due under such lease and thereafter accruing. All lessees are hereby irrevocably authorized to rely upon and comply with (and shall be fully protected in so doing) any notice or demand by the Mortgagee for any payment to the Mortgagee of any rental or other sums which may be or thereafter become due under any lease, or for the performance of any lessee's undertakings under any lease and they shall have no right or duty to inquire as to whether any default under the Mortgage or this assignment has actually occurred or is then existing. Any notice provided for hereunder may be effectively given by sending the same by registered mail to any lessee at its premises located on or in the Premises or by delivering same personally to any lessee, or any officer of such lessee.

6. In the event:

    (a) The Mortgagor is in default under the Mortgage;

    (b) The Mortgagor is in default under the Commitment Letter;

(c) The Mortgagor is in default of any covenant contained in this assignment which is not in the opinion of the Mortgagee acting reasonably capable of being cured; or

(d) The Mortgagor is in default of any covenant contained in this assignment which is in the opinion of the Mortgagee acting reasonably capable of being cured and such default has not been cured within 15 days of the date the Mortgagor has received written notice of such default if such default can reasonably be cured within 15 days or if such default cannot reasonably be cured within 15 days the Mortgagor is not diligently proceeding to cure such default within a reasonable time period, determined by the Mortgagee;

Then, upon the occurrence of any such event, the mortgagor shall be in default hereunder and under the mortgage.

2. Holdings and Euromart

Holdings is owned in varying proportions by seven individuals or entities ("owners"). Holdings holds title to the property in trust for the owners. This is set out in para. 1 of the affidavit of Klaus Vogel sworn March 10, 1995 and substantiated by the 1993 financial statements for the 1133 Yonge Street joint venture located on p. 6 at Tab 2-G of the respondents' motion record. There is no evidence to the contrary; so this is accepted as a fact.

In mid-1994 the owners appointed the respondent Euromart Management Group Ltd. ("Euromart") to manage and administer the property and the business affairs of Holdings. Euromart was required to collect rent and pay expenses in respect of the property. Euromart opened an account with the Toronto-Dominion Bank (the "T-D account") which it operated solely for the purposes of depositing rents and paying expenses relating to the property.

3. Disposition of Rental Proceeds

Euromart was directed by the owners to distribute any surplus from the T-D account quarterly. Euromart, as trustee, had no discretion in this matter. Euromart was obligated to transfer the quarterly surpluses as directed by the owners.

On the specific directions of the owners, Euromart actually transferred the surplus monthly from the T-D account into an account at the Bank of Nova Scotia ("BNS account"). The BNS account contained only surpluses from the property, via the T-D account and interest income on those surpluses. The uncontested evidence of Mr. Vogel is that the funds in the T-D account and the surpluses in the BNS account were held in trust for the owners. Thus, this is accepted as a fact.

The BNS account was managed by Greater Canada Finance Corporation ("GCFC"), the owners' investment adviser. The BNS account was GCFC's current account. However, the account's statement indicates that Holdings is the account holder of the BNS account. This I find to be held in trust for the same reasons as above noted.

The owners directed GCFC as to the investment of the surplus in the BNS account. As at November 30, 1994, when the loan matured, virtually the entire amount (the "accrued surplus") from the BNS account, approximately $550,000, had been transferred into a

Bank of Nova Scotia GIC. Holdings was the registered owners of the GIC. This I also find to be in trust for the same reasons above noted.

4. *Default on the Loan and Demands Under the Assignment*

The loan matured on November 30, 1994 without being paid. Holdings and the owners agreed that Holdings defaulted on the loan. As at the maturity of the Loan SFr 4,841,817.72 and US $1,421,919.90 were owing and outstanding.

On December 1, 1994, the Bank made written demand for payment of the loan. At the same time they gave notice of intention to enforce security pursuant to s. 244(1) of the Bankruptcy and Insolvency Act, RSC 1985, c. B-3 (the "BIA"). The notice under s. 244(1) of the BIA provides in s. 1 as follows:

> Credit Suisse Canada, a secured creditor, intends to enforce its security on the Property of the insolvent person described below: [Instead of identifying Holdings as the insolvent person the following is inserted]
>
> (a) the leases of the real property Municipally known as 1133 Yonge Street, Toronto, Ontario, and all rents payable thereunder.

Notwithstanding what appears to be a technical flaw, it would appear that the notice under s. 244(1) of the BIA would have been met in spirit.

Subsection 4 of the notice provides:

> The secured creditor will not have the right to enforce the security until after the expiry of the ten-day period following the sending of the notice, unless the insolvent person consents to an earlier enforcement.

The next surplus of rental income minus expenses on the property was generated commencing at the beginning of December 1994 in the amount of approximately $120,000 (the "December surplus"). The December surplus was held by Euromart in the T-D account. As at January 31, 1995, Euromart held approximately $100,000 from the December surplus in a Toronto-Dominion term deposit and the balance in the T-D account.

Negotiations regarding a structured loan facility continued after December 1, 1994. In the meantime, on December 8, the owners instructed GCFC to remove the accrued surplus from the BNS account and related GICs and to transfer it pro rata to seven separate Euromart trust accounts, one for each owner at the Toronto-Dominion Bank (the "individual accounts").

The restructuring negotiations were unsuccessful. By letter dated December 29, 1994, the Bank demanded that all rents, proceeds and other payments from the tenants of the property, whether then in Holdings' possession or under its control or received in the future, be turned over to the Bank forthwith pursuant to the Assignment. The Bank also notified Holdings and Euromart that any moneys held by Holdings or Euromart relating to the property which arose or were proceeds from the leases or rents from the property were held in trust for the Bank.

The Bank issued a notice of sale under mortgage on January 27, 1995. By order of Winkler J dated February 20, 1995 (the "order"), the Bank was granted leave to commence this application. The order also granted an interim injunction restraining Euromart from disposing of the accrued surplus or the December surplus (together the "surpluses") for ten days.

5. Current Status

As at January 26, 1995, and subject to any accounting of other complaints by Holdings, Holdings' indebtedness to the Bank under the loan amounted to nearly $7 million. The property was not sold and the loan remains in default. The December surplus is still held by Euromart in the T-D account and related term deposit and the accrued surplus is still held by Euromart in the individual accounts and related term accounts pursuant to an undertaking to preserve those funds pending disposition of this application.

Issues

1. Does the concept of crystallization continue to apply under the PPSA?
2. Applying the PPSA, does the Bank's security interest under the assignment extend to the surpluses?
3. Is the owners' trust claim relevant?

The Parties' Submissions

The Bank takes the position that the concept of crystallization has no application under the PPSA and that its security interest, having attached and been perfected, is fully enforceable. The Bank also submits that its interest is not restricted to the original collateral but also extends to the proceeds of the collateral. It further states that, if a trust exists as the respondents claim, it does not impede the continued application of the assignment to the proceeds or a proper basis for defeating the Bank's claim.

Holdings claims that the PPSA only gives priority to properly registered security interests once they have crystallized and, at that point, rights are created only in the property which is then owned by the debtor. Holdings further submits that the rental proceeds are held in trust for the owners and the Bank's claim to a security interest in the proceeds is thus invalid.

...

Analysis

1. Crystallization

Both counsel initially advised the court that the concept of crystallization of a floating charge under the PPSA had never been adjudicated. As it turns out, this issue has been the subject of considerable judicial and academic comment that, in my view, amply supports the Bank's position. Rather than turning immediately to the case-law, I think it would first be useful to briefly review the history and purpose of the PPSA.

The PPSA is modeled on art. 9 of the Uniform Commercial Code. The revolutionary nature of art. 9 is described by Professor Jacob Ziegel, a leading academic in the area of commercial law, in "The New Provincial Chattel Security Law Regimes" (1991), 70 *Can. Bar Rev.* 680, at pp. 685-86, in the following terms:

The distinctive feature of Article 9 is that it abolishes the pre-Code distinctions between the multiplicity of common law, equitable and statutory security devices and replaces them with the generic concept of a "security agreement" creating a "security interest." This radical solution derived from the drafters' profound insight that all security interests serve the same function—to secure payment or performance of an obligation—and that there was no justification for the retention of the old divisions and the large baggage of discrete rules and doctrines that accompanied them. Instead, they could be replaced by a common set of prescriptions covering the successive stages in the life of a security interest—its creation and perfection and the consequences of non-perfection, the rules governing priorities between competing security interests in the same collateral and, if the debtor defaults, the enforcement of the security interest. Article 9 retains some important distinctions but they are based on functional and not historical or doctrinal considerations.

There is little doubt that the distinctive nature of this reform is carried forward in the PPSA. As Fred Catzman states in *Personal Property Security Law in Ontario* (Toronto: Carswell, 1976), at pp. 1-2:

The main feature of *The Personal Property Security Act* ... is its overall consolidation and harmonization of the law of personal property as security for debts. The Act applies to all transactions that are intended to create a security interest in personal property and fixtures. It supplies to the law and to the economy a comprehensive and integrated statute where none now exists ...

In summary, the Act is designed to supplant substantially all existing security devices related to personal property and fixtures that fall within the jurisdiction of the Legislature of the Province of Ontario.

A key aspect of the reform brought about by the PPSA, in other words, was the rationalization of existing chattel security law through the creation of a single security interest which, regardless of its form, is subject to a common set of rules. This purpose is readily apparent in s. 2 of the PPSA:

2. Subject to subsection 4(1), this Act applies to,
   (a) every transaction without regard to its form and without regard to the person who has title to the collateral that in substance creates a security interest including, without limiting the foregoing,
      (i) a ... floating charge ...

Moreover, although floating charges were unknown to US law and therefore not contemplated by the drafters of the Uniform Commercial Code, the specific enumeration of floating charges in s. 2(a)(i) of the PPSA removes any doubt, by its very language, that floating charges fall squarely within the scope of the legislative reform and are governed by the rules set out in the PPSA. This point is succinctly made by Professors R.C.C. Cuming and R.J. Wood in the *British Columbia Personal Property Security Act Handbook*, 2nd ed. (Toronto: Carswell, 1993), at p. 30, speaking in relation to a similar provision in the British Columbia legislation:

Section 2(1)(b) enumerates a non-exclusive list of traditional pre-PPSA security devices. It does so merely to confirm they are within the scope of the Act. It remains open for the parties to continue using these devices. Their use will not, however, have the effect of invoking the traditional law governing such transactions. For example, the use of a floating charge in a security agreement will not have the effect of resurrecting the notion of crystallization and the peculiar priority rules that governed this device. Instead, the priority rules that govern will he those set out in the PPSA.

The legislative evolution of the attachment provision of the PPSA provides further support for this view. As originally enacted in SO 1967, c. 73, the attachment provision provided that:

> 12(1) A security interest attaches when,
>> (a) the parties intend it to attach;
>> (b) value is given; and
>> (c) the debtor has rights in the collateral.

The requirement that a security interest attaches when the parties intend it to attach, as set out in cl. (a), generated considerable controversy in the early years of the PPSA. In particular, because floating charges under the pre-PPSA law did not become specific until crystallization, the argument was raised in several cases that the use of what amounted to an interest in the nature of a floating charge demonstrated the parties' intention to postpone attachment until crystallization: see, e.g., *Royal Bank of Canada v. Inmont Canada Ltd.* (1980), 1 PPSAC 197 (Ont. Co. Ct.), at pp. 205-07; *Irving A. Burton Ltd. v. Canadian Imperial Bank of Commerce* (1982), 36 OR (2d) 703 at pp. 706-07, 134 DLR (3d) 369 (CA); *First City Capital Ltd. v. Arthur Anderson Inc.* (1984), 46 OR (2d) 168 at p. 171, 9 DLR (4th) 117 (HCJ); and *Canadian Imperial Bank of Commerce v. Otto Timm Enterprises Ltd.* (1991), 2 PPSAC (2d) 58 (Ont. Gen. Div.) at pp. 73-74, reversed (1995), 26 OR (3d) 724 at p. 730, 130 DLR (4th) 91 at p. 95 (CA). Although this argument met with little success in the courts, the attachment provision was subsequently amended in 1989 to remove any ambiguity on this point. For ease of reference, the relevant subsection now provides:

> 11(2) A security interest, including a security interest in the nature of a floating charge, attaches when,
>> (a) the secured party or a person on behalf of the secured party other than the debtor or the debtor's agent obtains possession of the collateral or when the debtor signs a security agreement that contains a description of the collateral sufficient to enable it to be identified;
>> (b) value is given; and
>> (c) the debtor has rights in the collateral,
> unless the parties have agreed to postpone the time for attachment, in which case the security interest attaches at the agreed time.

The *Report of the Minister's Advisory Committee on the Personal Property Security Act* (Ministry of Consumer and Commercial Relations, June 1984) explains at p. 34 that the reason for adding the words "including a security interest in the nature of a floating charge" to the attachment provision was to make it clear that the general rules for attachment applied to a security interest in the nature of a floating charge. While this report cannot be used by the court to interpret the PPSA, it does indicate the legislature's intention to subject security interests in the nature of floating charges to the general PPSA regime. This is consistent with the language of the PPSA. It would therefore be contrary to the clear language of the PPSA to impose, in addition to the requirements of attachment and perfection, the old terminology and principles associated with floating charges.

I thus agree with Professor Ziegel in "Floating Charges and the OPPSA: A Basic Misunderstanding" (1994), 23 CBLJ 470, at p. 478, that there is little doubt the legislative drafters of the PPSA intended the floating charge to be absorbed in the new legislation and to be replaced by the new statutory security interest. However, despite what is mandated by the clear language of the PPSA, many courts, particularly in Ontario, have displayed considerable reluctance in abandoning the old terminology and principles. On the whole, however, I am of the view that my conclusion is correct and supported by the case-law.

For example, in the recent case of *National Bank of Canada v. Grinnell Corp. of Canada* (1993), 5 PPSAC (2d) 266 (Ont. Div. Ct.), the Divisional Court displayed no aversion to accepting and applying the plain language of the PPSA in according the bank's general security agreement, characterized by the trial judge as an interest in the nature of a floating charge, priority over a subsequent notice of garnishment. O'Driscoll J, writing for the court, stated at p. 268:

> In our view, the security agreement attached and was perfected prior to the garnishment proceedings of August 1991.
>
> The definition of proceeds in s. 1(1) of the PPSA, together with ss. 11(2) and 25 of the Act, extended the bank's security interest to the insurance proceeds of Moore's inventory.
>
> Section 11(2) makes specific reference to a floating charge attaching upon occurrence of three events:
>
> (a) the signing of a security agreement containing a description of the collateral sufficient to identify it;
>
> (b) value is given;
>
> (c) the debtor has rights in the collateral.
>
> Here all these requirements were met and there was no agreement to postpone attachment.

Thus, attachment of the security interest in accordance with s. 11(2), coupled with the perfection of the interest by registration, resulted in the bank's general security agreement having priority over the subsequent garnishment. The argument that use of a floating charge delayed attachment until crystallization was rejected by the court. Moreover, the Divisional Court did not find it necessary that the bank engage in some overt act of crystallization before its floating charge could gain priority over the subsequent garnishment.

A contrary approach was adopted by Saunders J in *Access Advertising Management Inc. v. Servex Computers Inc.* (1993), 15 OR (3d) 635, 21 CBR (3d) 304 (Gen. Div.), again involving a dispute between a secured creditor, CIT, and a third party, Access, over money paid into court pursuant to a notice of garnishment. Saunders J found that the security interest of the secured creditor was in the nature of a floating charge and that this interest had attached and been perfected. However, in his view, the crucial issue was whether the interest had crystallized. He stated at p. 639:

> The effect of perfection was that the floating charge was not subordinate to the interest of Access who assumed control of the funds on deposit through the garnishment (see PPSA, s. 20(1)(a)(ii)). It did not follow that CIT by attaining perfection acquired priority over the garnishment by Access. To acquire priority the floating charge must have become specific. There must have been crystallization: *Royal Bank of Canada v. Mohawk* [(1985), 49 OR (2d) 734 (HCJ)] and *Re Standard-Modern Technologies Corp.* (1992), 6 OR (3d) 161, 87 DLR (4th) 44 (CA).

Thus, in addition to attachment and perfection, Saunders J required the secured creditor to crystallize its security interest if it were to achieve priority. This approach has been criticized by Professor Ziegel in "Floating Charges and the OPPSA: A Basic Misunderstanding," supra, at pp. 474-80. As Professor Ziegel notes, the cases relied on by Saunders J do not support the proposition advanced in the case. The PPSA was not mentioned by Anderson J in *Royal Bank of Canada v. Mohawk Moving & Storage Ltd.* (1985), 49 OR (2d) 734, 16 DLR (4th) 434 (HCJ). In *Re Standard-Modern Technologies Corp.* (1992), 6 OR (3d) 161, 87 DLR (4th) 442 (CA), the parties conceded, perhaps wrongly, that the PPSA did not apply. It also does not appear that Saunders J's attention was directed to the Divisional Court's decision in *National Bank of Canada v. Grinnell Corp. of Canada*, supra. Further, as outlined at the beginning of my reasons, a review of the PPSA's history reveals that traditional personal property security law has been superseded by the PPSA including abolition of the distinction between fixed and floating charges. Consequently, I conclude that the concept of crystallization is irrelevant under the PPSA regime.

This view has also been adopted by the courts in other provinces where personal property security legislation has been enacted. In *Royal Bank of Canada v. G.M. Homes Inc.* (1982), 4 PPSAC 116, 25 Sask. R 6 (CA), for example, the argument was raised that use of a security interest in the nature of a floating charge indicated the parties' intention to postpone attachment until crystallization. The Saskatchewan Court of Appeal had no difficulty in rejecting this argument, stating at p. 124:

> The purpose of the *Personal Property Security Act* is to create a complete commercial code which provides a system of priorities for security interests in personal property in consensual transactions when security interests are granted. The Act specifically sets out when a security interest attaches to collateral. The use by the parties of a floating charge in a consensual transaction does not, in my opinion, raise a presumption that the parties intended the security interest to attach to the collateral at a later time. This form of security alone is not, without more, evidence of the intention of the parties that the security interest would not attach to the collateral at the time of execution. The Act, in my opinion, contemplates that for attachment to occur at a time other than on the execution of the security agreement, there must be a contrary contained intention in the agreement itself.

Similarly, in *Affinity International Inc. v. Alliance International Inc.* (1994), 8 PPSAC (2d) 73, 96 Man. R (2d) 200 (QB), affirmed (1995), 9 PPSAC (2d) 174, 100 Man. R (2d) 223 (CA), the garnishing creditor argued that it was entitled to the funds paid into court because the bank's security interest was in the nature of a floating charge which had not attached at the time of the garnishment. Beard J rejected this view, stating at p. 81 that the provision of a floating charge does not create an intention on the part of the parties to postpone attachment until there is some overt act by the secured party amounting to crystallization. The same approach was also adopted in *Transamerica Commercial Finance Corp. Canada v. Karpes* (1994), 8 PPSAC (2d) 86 (BCSC), with respect to a dispute between a third party and secured creditor over entitlement to funds received from the sale of the debtor's inventory, which was the subject of a floating charge. Clancy J held at p. 93 that, since the necessary steps for attachment had taken place and the interest was perfected, it was enforceable and the priorities between the parties fell to be determined in accordance with the provisions of the PPSA. In each of these cases, attachment and perfection alone were sufficient to give the secured creditor an enforceable security interest; no further overt act of crystallization was required.

Most recently, in *Rehm v. DSG Communications Inc.* (1995), 33 CBR (3d) 65, 9 PPSAC (2d) 114 (Sask. QB), the plaintiff argued that until the bank had crystallized its security interest, it had only a floating interest in the customer's account and thus no priority to the money paid into court. After reviewing the applicable law, Hunter J concluded (p. 73):

> To continue to use the language of floating charges and crystallization which do not exist in the PPSA causes confusion in the interpretation of the unambiguous provisions of the PPSA. This confusion has been contributed to by the continued use of this archaic language in the cases cited by Rehm, namely, *Access Advertising Management Inc. v. Servex Computers Inc.* (1993), 21 CBR (3d) 304 (Ont. Gen. Div.); *Canadian Imperial Bank of Commerce v. Otto Timm Enterprises Ltd.* (1991), 79 DLR (4th) 67 (Ont. Gen. Div.); and *A & B Landscaping & Interlocking Ltd. v. Bradsil Ltd.* (1993), 6 PPSAC (2d) 141 (Ont. Gen. Div.).
>
> The concept of a floating charge does not exist in the PPSA. The PPSA provisions apply and as clearly stated in *Affinity International Inc.*, in the headnote, the reasoning is as follows:
>
>> "Attachment" occurs when all the steps necessary to create a security interest in the collateral as between the immediate parties to the security agreement have been completed. "Perfection" occurs after attachment and requires the creditor to take additional steps to acquire rights as against third parties. Attachment is a prerequisite to perfection. An agreement's provision of a floating charge does not create an intention by the parties to postpone attachment until there is some overt act by the creditor amounting to crystallization. Here, the charge contained in the security agreement had attached and was perfected when the company's account with the debtor came into effect. That being the last step necessary to complete attachment under the Act, the bank was entitled to the funds in court.

I echo these comments. As Professor Richard McLaren states in *Secured Transactions in Personal Property in Canada*, 2nd ed. (Supp.) (Toronto: Carswell, 1992), at p. 2-38:

> There is no historical need or justification for carrying the concept [of floating charges and crystallization] forward into the Act. The Act has created a flexible single security interest which can meet the needs of the business community as they arise. It should not be burdened with a concept designed to serve the needs of the financial community of the nineteenth century.

The PPSA requires only attachment and perfection. It does not contemplate, nor require, any further act of crystallization. The PPSA applies to security interests in the nature of floating charges in the same fashion and manner that it applies to other security interests.

[Day J went on to find that the bank was entitled to the rental payments collected on behalf of the debtor company and/or received by the company's shareholders, and he made an order to this effect. On appeal, the Ontario Court of Appeal (below) affirmed Day J's judgment on the issue of crystallization and reversed his judgment on the bank's right to follow part of the proceeds. This latter aspect of the Court of Appeal's judgment is reproduced below.]

Credit Suisse Canada v. 1133 Yonge Street Holdings Ltd.
(1998), 41 OR (3d) 632 (CA)

BLAIR J (ad hoc):   1133 Yonge Street Holdings Limited appeals from the judgment of the Honourable Mr. Justice Day dated April 16, 1996 (reported (1996), 28 OR (3d) 670). Day J gave judgment declaring that the respondent, Credit Suisse Canada, holds a valid security interest in certain net rental proceeds paid to Holdings by commercial tenants at 1133 Yonge Street in Toronto. Day J ordered that the proceeds (the "surplus funds"), which amount to approximately $550,000 plus interest, be paid to Credit Suisse.

Construction of the commercial premises at 1133 Yonge St. had been financed through a $7 million loan facility arranged between Holdings, as borrower, and Credit Suisse as lender. The security interest in question—an assignment of leases and rents granted to Credit Suisse by Holdings on January 2, 1987 (the "assignment")—was one of several security instruments executed in connection with the loan transaction. The assignment was duly registered under the Personal Property Security Act, RSO 1980, c. 375 ("PPSA") [now RSO 1990, c. P.10].

Under the loan commitment and the related security documentation, Holdings (the borrower) was to make monthly payments of $60,000 to Credit Suisse (the lender) and the lender was to hold these payments in an interest-bearing account and was to pay interest and principal payments out of that account. The lender had the right to call for an increase in such monthly payments (although it never did). The excess funds in this account were called "the cash collateral account," and were secured by a separate security interest in that account in favour of Credit Suisse. As well as this security, and the assignment mentioned above, Credit Suisse also held a first collateral mortgage on the property.

Under the assignment, Holdings assigned to Credit Suisse the full benefit and advantage of all existing and future leases, including all rents. The assignment was acknowledged to be an effective, present assignment. Paragraph 11 stated:

> 11. The Mortgagor (Holdings) acknowledges and agrees with the Mortgagee (Credit Suisse) that this assignment is an effective, present assignment, provided and it is expressly understood and agreed, anything herein contained to the contrary notwithstanding, that the

Mortgagee shall not exercise any of the rights or powers herein conferred upon it until a default shall occur under the terms and provision of this assignment, the Commitment Letter or under the Mortgage.

Default under the assignment was defined to include not only defaults of varying kinds under the assignment itself, but also any default under the property mortgage or the commitment letter.

Paragraph 7 of the assignment is of central importance to this proceeding. The pertinent part provides as follows:

> 7. Until notified to the contrary in writing, the Mortgagor *shall be entitled to*, and the lessee under any lease shall pay to the Mortgagor, all rents and other amounts then due under such lease and thereafter accruing.

(Emphasis added.)

From the inception of the transaction until the end of November 1994, all requisite payments of principal and interest were made. The parties operated on a pattern whereby all rents were paid into a separate account from which expenses (and moneys required to freshen up the cash collateral account) were paid, and the surpluses were then paid out to accounts for the benefit of Holdings or its owners.

The loan matured on November 30, 1994 without being paid. On December 1, 1994 Credit Suisse made written demand for payment and served notice of its intention to enforce its security, under s. 244(1) of the Bankruptcy and Insolvency Act, RSC 1985, c. B-3, as amended. The loan has been in default since that date.

As at November 30, 1994, the approximate sum of $550,000 was deposited in accounts which could be traced from such net rental proceeds. The moneys are held in trust either for Holdings or for its several owners (as some payments have been made to shareholders who, in turn, have given directions as to the funds). It is these amounts, plus interest, which are at issue on this appeal. A December 1994 surplus of approximately $100,000 is no longer at issue, since it is conceded that it represented moneys paid after default had occurred.

On the argument before Day J much attention was paid to the question whether the concept of crystallization continues to apply to securities granted under the PPSA. Credit Suisse argued, as it does here, that crystallization has no application, and that their security interest—having attached and been perfected under the PPSA legislation—was fully enforceable, and, further, that the security extended not simply to the original collateral (the rents) but also to the proceeds of that collateral (its various traceable forms in other bank accounts). Day J reviewed the law regarding the crystallization question and concluded, correctly, that the concept of crystallization is irrelevant under the PPSA regime. Appellate jurisprudence has confirmed the correctness of that decision: see *Canadian Imperial Bank of Commerce v. Otto Timm Enterprises Ltd.* (1995), 26 OR (3d) 724, 130 DLR (4th) 91 (CA); *Royal Bank of Canada v. Sparrow Electric Corp.*, [1997] 1 SCR 411, 143 DLR (4th) 385.

Section 11(2) of the PPSA stipulates that attachment occurs under the Act when the three elements set out in that subsection have been satisfied "unless the parties have agreed to postpone the time for attachment." Having concluded that Credit Suisse had an attached and perfected security interest in the rents following registration of the assignment on January 22, 1987, Day J commented (at p. 685) that in his view the portion of cl. 7 of the assignment which allows Holdings to deal with the rents until default was not sufficient to establish a contrary intention that attachment would take place at another time. He decided that Credit Suisse's statutory right to the rental proceeds existed "independently of any entitlement Holdings had to deal with the original rents" (at p. 685). In speaking of an entitlement to deal with rents, it may be that Day J also had in mind the language of s. 25(1) of the PPSA, which was relied upon by counsel for Credit Suisse, too, and which states:

…

In my respectful view, Day J erred in coming to these conclusions. He misapprehended the combined effect of that portion of para. 7 of the assignment cited above, and s. 9(1) of the PPSA. Section 9(1) specifies:

> 9(1) Except as otherwise provided by this or any other Act, a security agreement is effective according to its terms between the parties to it and against third parties.

By these provisions, the PPSA has preserved the principle of freedom of contract as between the parties in securities transactions, subject to any restrictions appearing in the PPSA itself or in other provincial legislation: see Ziegel and Denomme, *The Personal Property Security Act: Commentary and Analysis* (1994), pp. 104-05; Richard H. McLaren, *The 1989 Ontario Personal Property Security Act* (Toronto: Carswell, 1997), at p. 61. There is nothing to override the freedom of contract principle in the circumstances of this case.

Here, the parties have agreed by their contract that Holdings "shall be entitled to … the rents … due [under the leases]," until notified to the contrary in writing, and that Credit Suisse "shall not exercise any of the rights or powers … conferred upon it until a default shall occur." The security agreement itself, therefore, not only entitles the borrower, Holdings, to deal with the security prior to default—the rents are the "security" in question under the assignment—but it entitles Holdings to the security, prior to such event.

The word "entitlement" must be given its plain and ordinary meaning, namely, "to give a rightful claim," or "to give a right or legal title." *Black's Law Dictionary* (West Publishing Co., 1979), for instance, contains the following definitions, at p. 477:

> Entitle. In its usual sense, to entitle is to give a right or legal title to.

> Entitlement. Right to benefits, income or property which may not be abridged without due process.

Jowitt, *The Dictionary of English Law* (London: Street & Maxwell, 1959) says this with respect to "entitle" (p. 718):

> In its usual sense, to entitle is to give a right; therefore a person is said to be entitled to property when he has a right to it.

Thus, in my view, to be "effective in accordance with its terms" the assignment is to be interpreted in a fashion which recognizes the right of Holdings—during the currency of the loan term and provided that the borrower is not in default—to take for its own use and benefit the net rental proceeds from the leases. The effect of this is to discharge and release the lender's security in such proceeds, i.e., with respect to that "collateral" and the "proceeds" of that collateral. The security is discharged, however, only with respect to those amounts which are paid over prior to default. It continues to be attached and enforceable under the PPSA, and "effective according to its terms between the parties."

Day J concluded that because Credit Suisse had an attached and perfected security interest in the rents as at January 22, 1987, that security interest extended to the proceeds of those proceeds, and to successive generations of proceeds, by virtue of s. 25(1)(b) of the PPSA, and that the lender was entitled to claim the funds which consume the surplus provided the funds were identifiable or traceable as proceeds of the rents. In the end, he was satisfied that the funds could be traced, and he granted judgment accordingly.

The real question in these proceedings, however, is whether the assignment by its terms enables the lender retrospectively to reach the net rental proceeds paid to Holdings during the loan period but prior to default. For the reasons I have indicated. I do not think it does. While the security interest "attaches," within the meaning of the PPSA, its "effect" is to permit the borrower to deal with the net rents for its own account until default occurs and it is "notified to the contrary in writing." In short, the security interest of the lender, in so far as it attaches to the net rental proceeds, is released or discharged with respect to such proceeds once they are paid out to the borrower in accordance with the terms of the agreement. Consequently, to the extent that the net rentals are discharged upon payment to the borrower, the issue of whether attachment and perfection of the security causes the security to extend to the proceeds of the collateral—which is what s. 25(1) is about—is not engaged.

Counsel for the respondent submitted that to interpret the assignment in this fashion would be tantamount to re-introducing the concepts of the floating charge and crystallization to PPSA matters, contrary to what has recently been clarified in cases such as *Royal Bank of Canada v. Sparrow Electric Corp.*, supra, and *Canadian Imperial Bank of Commerce v. Otto Timm Enterprises*, supra. I do not agree. It can be equally as misleading and confusing to suggest that a given security structure created by the parties should not be recognized because to do so would re-invoke the concepts of old forms of security. Such an argument—a sort of *in terrorem* response—runs the risk of precluding the legitimate creativity of parties to tailor their agreements to meet their particular circumstances. There is ample scope within the provisions of the PPSA to permit debtors to deal with collateral in various fashions—including dealing with it on their own account—notwithstanding that the creditor's security interest in the collateral has attached and been perfected. It is not the purpose of the PPSA to render security transactions inflexible or, indeed, to prevent the parties from agreeing to security structures which may well accomplish the same kind of protection that older forms of security—such as floating charges—seek to provide.

· · ·

In each case, it is a matter of examining the terms of the security interest in question to determine what precisely are its terms as between the parties, because s. 9(1) of the PPSA makes it clear that the security instrument is only effective in accordance with those terms. There is nothing which prevents commercial parties from negotiating terms which may, in practical terms, have similar commercial consequences to those encompassed in older forms of security. Such flexibility is required.

Indeed, to interpret the assignment of leases and rents in this case in the fashion sought by the respondent might well lead to commercial instability, in my view. Debtors who are entitled under security instruments to take the collateral and deal with it as their own pending default or notification to the contrary—and who do so—should not be subjected to the risk and uncertainty of the funds representing the collateral or its proceeds being taken from them retrospectively at some time in the future in the event that such a default occurs or notification is given. Relying upon their right to utilize the funds, to take but one example, they might in turn have used those funds—assuming they are not otherwise encumbered—as security for other commercial transactions, or to purchase other identifiable assets. I do not think that such authorized transactions should be placed in jeopardy simply because of the happenstance that the funds or proceeds remain in some identifiable or traceable form and remain within the jurisdiction. The situation becomes even less tenable when, as here, the debtor pays out the funds to shareholders or other third parties but they, in turn, utilize the funds in a fashion in which they remain identifiable or traceable.

I do not mean to suggest by these remarks that the nature of a security instrument can be determined by the use which the debtor makes of the collateral. Collateral, or the proceeds of collateral, which the security instrument is "effective" to reach, continue to be caught by the security instrument and cannot be utilized by the debtor in a way that ignores the security interest. Where, as here, however, the debtor is entitled to the collateral itself, subject to certain events occurring, and where the parties conduct themselves over the period of the loan transaction in a fashion which acknowledges the debtor's right to use the funds representing the collateral on its own account, circumstances of great commercial ambivalence would exist if the lender were able at the end of the day to undo what had been done. At the very least, Credit Suisse is estopped from taking such a position in the circumstances of this case: PPSA, s. 72.

...

Order accordingly.

NOTES

1) *Access Advertising Management Inc. v. Servex Computers Inc.*, above, has been reproduced in this chapter because it illustrates the confusion about the status of English-style floating charges under the OPPSA that obtained in Ontario before Day J's definitive judgment in *Credit Suisse Canada v. Yonge Street Holdings* laid to rest the heresy that the Ontario Act has retained any aspect of the conceptual structure of the English-style floating charge.

2) Regarding *Credit Suisse*, it may seem odd that a secured party would allow the debtor untrammelled use of proceeds (here, rentals from commercial property) before default, but in the commercial mortgages area it appears to be very common. In fact, without access to the rental payments, the mortgagor would not be able to cover the running costs of the mortgaged property. Moreover, realty mortgages rely primarily on the realty security and, it appears, only secondarily on the rentals generated by the mortgaged property and then only from the time of default. Credit Suisse's misfortune was that there was a cataclysmic drop in

the Toronto real estate market in the early 1990s, which affected the property mortgaged to the bank. See further, J.S. Ziegel, "Freedom of Contract and the Right to Claim Proceeds Under the OPPSA" (1999), 31 *CBLJ* 299. What advice would you give mortgage lenders in light of the Ontario Court of Appeal's decision?

3) The effect of s. 2 of the Ontario Act, coupled with s. 11(2), is to restore the early 19th-century concept of a security interest in inventory and accounts receivable as a fixed interest with an implied licence to the debtor to continue to carry on business until the debtor defaults. The same constructional rule applies, but only more so, where the debtor has given a general security interest in all of its assets. Obviously, in such a case, a strong licence to continue to carry on business must be implied in the debtor's favour, since without it, the debtor's business would come to a halt. Of particular importance in this context is the Supreme Court's judgment in *Royal Bank of Canada v. Sparrow Electric Corp.*, extracted below, where the judges were sharply divided in their analyses of the issues.

Royal Bank of Canada v. Sparrow Electric Corp.
[1997] 1 SCR 411

[The Royal Bank secured a loan made to Sparrow Electric with a general security agreement (GSA) covering Sparrow's present and after-acquired property and with *Bank Act* security (BAS) created by an assignment of inventory under s. 427 of the *Bank Act*. When Sparrow experienced financial difficulties, a standstill agreement was executed. This agreement allowed Sparrow to continue its business, but permitted the bank, on default, to appoint a receiver and enforce its security. A receiver was appointed in November 1992, at which time it was discovered that Sparrow had not been remitting its payroll deductions as required by s. 153 of the *Income Tax Act* (ITA). It is probable that these defaults had occurred in 1992. In January 1993, the receiver received court permission to sell Sparrow's assets. An amount from the proceeds of sale equivalent to that owing to the federal government was ordered to be held in trust pending resolution as to entitlement. The bank claimed priority based on its GSA and its BAS, which entitled it to inventory proceeds. The federal government's claim was based on the s. 227 ITA deemed trust provisions, which created a deemed statutory trust in the monies deducted from wages but not remitted to Her Majesty.

All the members of the Supreme Court agreed (1) that s. 227(5) of the ITA was not retroactive in its effect and, therefore, could not override the bank's security interests, which were created and attached before the deemed trust arose in favour of the Crown; and (2) that the security interests created under the Alberta PPSA and s. 427 of the *Bank Act* were specific security interests and not floating charges. For the PPSA aspects of this question, see the text preceding the *Access Advertising* case, above; for the s. 427 aspects, see Chapter 15. However, the members of the court were divided over the question of whether the terms of the GSA, authorizing Sparrow to continue to carry on its business, conferred an express or implied licence on Sparrow to use proceeds from the sale of its inventory to meet Sparrow's operating expenses, including payment of employee wages. If there was such a licence it would also enure for the benefit of the Crown to the extent that Sparrow had not remitted tax deductions relating to such wages.

The relevant provisions in the parties' security agreements included the following:

So long as this Security Agreement remains in effect Debtor covenants and agrees:

(a) to defend the Collateral against the claims and demands of all other parties claiming the same or an interest therein; to keep the Collateral free from all Encumbrances … ; provided always that, until default, Debtor may, in the ordinary course of Debtor's business, sell or lease inventory and, subject to Clause 7 hereof, use Money available to Debtor,

...

(e) to pay all taxes, rates, levies, assessments and other charges of every nature which may be lawfully levied, assessed or imposed against or in respect of Debtor or Collateral as and when the same become due and payable;

Additionally, under the credit facilities agreement between Sparrow and the bank, dated January 22, 1992, Sparrow covenanted as follows:

(3) it will promptly pay when due all business, income and other taxes properly levied on its operations and property and remit all statutory employee deductions when due;

The following extracts from the judgments reflect the divergent opinions of Gonthier J, dissenting (supported by La Forest and Cory JJ), and Iacobucci J, writing for the majority of the court.]

GONTHIER J (dissenting): … [72] Looking at these express provisions of the contractual arrangements between Sparrow and the bank, I conclude that the payment of payroll deductions would be a usage to which the bank contemplated Sparrow would use the proceeds of inventory sold in the "ordinary course of … business." My conclusion in this respect is buttressed when the nature of the dealings between Sparrow and the bank, and all the surrounding circumstances, are observed.

[73] The bank was Sparrow's primary lender; it held a security interest in most, if not all, of Sparrow's assets. In particular, the bank held various security interests in Sparrow's inventory. It was of course in the bank's best interest that Sparrow function as a viable economic unit. To do so, Sparrow was required to sell its services as an electrical contractor and, necessarily, sell its inventory. From the sales of the inventory, Sparrow could generate revenues to, inter alia, pay its outstanding operating debts. If it failed to do so, Sparrow could be petitioned into bankruptcy, with the result that Sparrow could no longer generate the profits necessary to pay its loan obligations to the bank in the long term. One of Sparrow's ongoing obligations, its costs of doing business, was the paying of wages. In order to stay in business, and operate as a profitable business enterprise, Sparrow would have to pay its employees. This is a necessary requirement of continuing in business. It would be reasonable that the bank expect, taking into consideration all the circumstances of this arrangement, that revenue from the sale of inventory would be used to pay wages.

[74] From these observations, I consider the licence to sell inventory in the ordinary course of business in this case necessarily included a licence to sell inventory to pay wages, and remit wage deductions, in the course of its business. Where, as here, the secured party has security over the majority of the assets of the debtor, the security interest over the inventory must permit the debtor to sell the inventory and put it to the general

use of its business, including towards the payment of wages. Indeed, the express terms of the licence intimates this, providing Sparrow could, "in the ordinary course of … business, … use Money available." The scope of the licence can thus be ascertained either from the express terms of the security agreement, or from the nature of the agreement and the conduct of the parties. To be clear, however, the scope of the licence in this case flows not merely from a right to sell inventory per se. Instead, it is the licence to sell inventory in the "ordinary course of [Sparrow's] business … and use [the proceeds]" which renders it of such a quality as to include a right to use the proceeds to pay wages. …

[75] In summary, the true test of whether the licence to sell inventory includes the right to pay wages must therefore be a matter of interpreting the contractual arrangement between the parties. The focus is not so much on the circumstances of the selling of inventory, but rather the permitted usage of the proceeds of inventory. As in Professor Wood's example, where the licence has a limited scope, that licence may not include the right to use proceeds to pay wages. However, the expression of a limited use for proceeds of inventory cannot prevail if the arrangement between the parties is such as to allow, in practice, the debtor to use the inventory proceeds in the course of its business. In this respect, I agree with Professor Wood's comments regarding the appropriate test for determining whether a licence to sell inventory includes permission to pay wages with the proceeds ("Revenue Canada's Deemed Trust Extends Its Tentacles: Royal Bank of Canada v. Sparrow Electric Corp.," [10 *BFLR* 429], at pp. 435-36):

> This is not to say that the analysis should hinge on the existence of a trust proceeds clause or other contractual provision requiring the debtor to remit proceeds. A contractual provision of this type should not govern if the real arrangement between the parties is such that the debtor has the freedom to use the proceeds of inventory in the ordinary course of business. …
>
> To make any sense at all, the licence theory must, at the very least, be restricted to cases where the secured party permits the debtor to pay employees either out of its collateral or out of the proceeds of its collateral. This permission cannot be derived merely from the existence of a licence to sell inventory. The test should be whether the debtor had the freedom to use these funds in the ordinary course of business as opposed to being under an obligation to remit them to the secured party.

[76] In the case at bar, the GSA contained an express licence permitting Sparrow to sell inventory in the course of its business and use the proceeds available; the BAS contained an implied licence to this effect. While it is true that the GSA contained a trust proceeds clause, I find that this cannot have the effect of limiting the scope of the licence where the real arrangement between the parties was, as expressly stated, that Sparrow could use the proceeds of inventory in the course of its business. The bank in this case was not a small inventory financier who required Sparrow to immediately remit proceeds of inventory to it. To the contrary, the bank was a large scale lender who permitted Sparrow to use inventory sales to maintain the viability of its enterprise. For these reasons, applying Professor Wood's test, I find that under the licence to "sell … inventory" "in the ordinary course of … business" and "use [the] [m]oneys available" the bank permitted Sparrow to sell inventory to pay wages and, necessarily, payroll deduction obligations.

[77] For all these reasons, through the application of the licence theory, it is my conclusion that the appellant's s. 227(5) deemed trust must take priority over the bank's security interests in the disputed collateral. The trust fund representing the deducted amounts, while without identified subject matter from the date of its inception, is capable of identifying property subject to that trust *ex post facto*. To reiterate, the bank consented to the reduction in its security in inventory in order to pay wage deductions at the time those deductions were made, and s. 227(5) ITA has the effect of carrying forward that consent to the time of receivership. By consenting to the payment of wages out of the proceeds of inventory during the course of Sparrow's business, the bank *ipso facto* consented to the statutory scheme under the ITA designed to cover unpaid wage deductions. In short, in the present case the licence to deal with inventory proceeds coupled with the statutory scheme in s. 227(4) and (5) ITA gives priority to Her Majesty's claims for statutory wage deductions. This result is obtained both in regard to the bank's GSA, and its BAS.

                                         ...

[79] I add as a final matter that in addition to providing certainty in disputes between consensual and non-consensual security interests, the licence theory has the virtue of achieving fairness in commercial law. Here, the respondent bank had permitted Sparrow to sell its inventory in the course of its business in order to, among other things, pay wages and wage deductions. To this extent, therefore, the bank permitted the reduction in the value of its security interest in Sparrow's inventory, during the ordinary course of Sparrow's business. Implicit in the bank's consent is the assumption that in so doing, Sparrow would generate profits from the conversion of inventory into revenues; this economic process, as I noted above, ensures that interest payments owing to the bank would be paid to them on a sustainable basis. In short, the bank benefitted in a general sense from Sparrow's carrying on its business operations, an endeavour which required Sparrow to pay wages and wage deductions. More specifically, however, when Sparrow stopped paying its wage deductions, as required, the bank could be said to benefit from the artificial increase in Sparrow's working capital, allowing an extension of the life of Sparrow's business.

[80] Now, when Sparrow's business is no longer a viable enterprise, the bank says that it is entitled to the very payments which allowed Sparrow, in part at least, to stay in business longer than was legally economical. In essence, the bank is willing to accept the benefits of Sparrow's non-payment of statutory deductions, and can be said to have reasonably permitted the use of its collateral to pay these deductions at the time they should have lawfully been paid, but refuses to accept the burden of Sparrow's unlawful action at the time of its receivership. In my view, it should be the policy of the law that the respondent bank be held accountable for Sparrow's outstanding statutory obligations. The licence theory, as I have developed it, ensures that in appropriate circumstances this result will obtain. In this way, in my opinion the licence theory is grounded not only in legal principles, but also in sound policy.

                                         ...

IACOBUCCI J: ... [91] My colleague disposes of this appeal on the basis of the so-called "licence theory." Briefly, the licence theory holds that a bank's security interest in a debtor's inventory, though it be fixed and specific, is subject nevertheless to a licence in the

debtor to deal with that inventory in the ordinary course of business. Consequently, says
the theory, the bank's claim to the inventory must give way to any debts incurred in the
ordinary course of business. The leading articulation of the licence theory appears in
McLachlin JA's (as she then was) reasons in *R in Right of BC v. FBDB*, [1988] 1 WWR 1
(BCCA) ... , at p. 40.

[92] The theoretical basis of the licence theory seems to be that a creditor who has
granted a licence to sell inventory has thereby consented to the subjection of his security
interest to other obligations that may arise "in the ordinary course of business." My colleague says this in his reasons, at para. 68:

> In short, where the bank has consented to the reduction in the value of its security in order
> to pay statutory deductions at the time those deductions are made, they have to the same
> extent, by virtue of s. 227(5) [ITA], consented to the reduction in their security at the time
> of receivership.

This is sensible, because it is only if the licence is understood as a kind of tacit lessening
of the creditor's security interest that the appellant's cause is advanced. Certainly the actual operation of the licence is not relevant, because in this case the inventory in question
was never actually sold pursuant to the licence. Rather, the receiver sold it by court order.
If the licence is to have anything to do with the disposition of this appeal, it must be by
virtue of the evidence it affords of the respondent's intention to take less than an entire
security interest in the inventory.

[93] In my view, the licence affords no such evidence. My colleague seems to think
that the potential sale of the inventory amounts to an actual limitation of the security interest. For my part, I do not see what the one thing has to do with the other. There is a
great difference between saying, on the one hand, that if a debtor sells inventory and applies the proceeds to a debt to a third party, then the third party takes the proceeds free
of any security interest and saying, on the other hand, that because a third party could
take the proceeds free of any security interest, no security interest exists in the proceeds
as against that third party. A licence to sell inventory in the ordinary course of business
is a condition of the former kind. The consequent (defeasance of the security interest)
follows only if the antecedent (sale of the inventory and application of proceeds to an
obligation to a third party) is satisfied. In other words, the security interest in the inventory disappears only if the debtor actually sells the inventory and applies the proceeds to
a debt to a third party.

[94] That this is so is suggested by s. 28(1) [of the Alberta] PPSA [OPPSA s. 25.1],
which provides:

...

In accordance with this provision, the result of a sale of inventory is to give the purchaser
an unencumbered interest in the inventory and the licensor a continuing security interest in the proceeds of the sale. It is only if the debtor subsequently uses the proceeds to
satisfy an obligation to a third party that the proceeds will be removed from the scope of
the licensor's security interest in them. Accordingly, what a security agreement with a licence to sell creates is a defeasible interest; but the event of defeasance is the actual sale
of the inventory and the actual application of the proceeds against an obligation to a
third party.

[95] I recognize that the operation of s. 28(1) PPSA is not necessarily inconsistent with the broad interpretation of the licence to sell that my colleague advances. However, it seems to me that this is an appropriate case for the invocation of the maxim *expressio unius est exclusio alterius*. The statute prescribes certain consequences for the security interest that follow a dealing with inventory. In particular, the statute contemplates defeasance of the interest if the debtor actually sells the inventory and applies the proceeds to an obligation to a third party. Significantly, the statute does not contemplate a defeasance on the happening of any other event. In my view, the statute occupies the field and crowds out other possible interpretations of the licence, including the one that Gonthier J favours.

[96] Because in this case there was no actual sale of the inventory in question, let alone any disposition of the proceeds, the licence can have had no effect on the respondent's security interest. What the debtor might have done with the licence does not matter.

[97] If it were otherwise, the licence to sell inventory would entirely eviscerate the respondent's general security agreement. The satisfaction of any legitimate debt or obligation, whenever incurred, is arguably "in the ordinary course of business." Certainly the payment of creditors is a permissible "use" of the proceeds of a sale of inventory. Following my colleague's reasoning, this would mean that every subsequent claim should prevail over the respondent's general security agreement, because every rival claim might have been satisfied out of the proceeds of a hypothetical sale of the inventory. Moreover, the priority rules of the PPSA, whose general policy is to assign priority to the earliest registered security interest, would be turned on their head. Presuming that every charge against inventory is subject to a licence to sell—a presumption that accords with the interest of creditors in ensuring the debtor's continued vitality—the last security interest would take priority over all earlier ones, because only the last interest would not be subject to some charge arising in the ordinary course of business. In answer to this objection, it might be said that as between two PPSA securities, the rules in the Act should be applied to determine priority. However, such an answer would not be consistent with the licence theory, which supposes that the original security interest in the inventory ends where obligations incurred in the ordinary course of business begin. The subsequent interest would prevail because the earlier interest would disappear before it.

[98] It is open to my colleague to distinguish the fact situation in this appeal from the hypothetical priority contests I have mentioned on the ground that the Crown's interest in the inventory is unlike other charges against inventory in that it depends on the fictional device of deeming. What makes this case different, it might be said, is that the ITA deems to have been done what could have been done. On this understanding, it does not matter that the inventory was not actually sold and the proceeds were not actually remitted to the Receiver General, because s. 227(4) and (5) ITA deem these things to have been done. But in my view, this answer cannot succeed because the inventory was not an unencumbered asset at the moment the taxes came due. It was subject to the respondent's security interest and therefore was legally the respondent's and not attachable by the deemed trust. As Gonthier J himself says (at para. 39):

> ... [s. 227(4)] does not permit Her Majesty to attach Her beneficial interest to property which, at the time of liquidation, assignment, receivership or bankruptcy, in law belongs to a party other than the tax debtor.

[99] The deeming is thus not a mechanism for undoing an existing security interest, but rather a device for going back in time and seeking out an asset that was not, at the moment the income taxes came due, subject to any competing security interest. In short, the deemed trust provision cannot be effective unless it is first determined that there is some unencumbered asset out of which the trust may be deemed. The deeming follows the answering of the chattel security question; it does not determine the answer.

[100] Indeed, Gonthier J does seize on the peculiar nature of the deemed trust as a possible ground for distinguishing the Crown's interest from rival interests. However, his argument differs from the one I have outlined to the extent that it emphasizes the deemed performance of the obligation to the Crown. It appears to be my colleague's position that the licence to sell represents a reduction in the value of the security interest only with respect to performed obligations but not with respect to unperformed ones. In his view, this represents a sufficient check on the licence theory. I agree that, if the distinction between performed and unperformed obligations were maintainable, then the likelihood of the licence consuming the security interest would be greatly reduced. However, in my view, the distinction cannot be maintained. As Gonthier J says more than once in his reasons, the licence theory rests on the consent of the parties. But the parties to this case consented to the sale of inventory "in the ordinary course of Debtor's business." The language is unqualified. No distinction is drawn between performed and unperformed obligations. The only performance that is contemplated in the licence is the actual sale of the inventory and the application of the proceeds to a debt. And, as I have already argued, the deeming mechanism does not furnish the needed actual sale. Accordingly, I conclude that if the words of the licence are to be given their due as an indicium of the parties' intent, then there can be no distinction between performed and unperformed obligations.

[101] My colleague places great emphasis on the fact that the debtor covenanted, in the general security agreement, "to pay all taxes, rates, levies, assessments and other charges of every nature which may be lawfully levied, assessed or imposed against or in respect of Debtor or Collateral as and when the same become due and payable." But this covenant is not part of the licence. And in any event, it is merely a covenant to obey the law. It adds nothing to s. 153(1) ITA. Furthermore, it does not prescribe the outcome of a priority contest. What is more, the covenant to pay taxes is only one of several in the agreement. Another covenant provides that the debtor shall "carry on and conduct the business of Debtor in a proper and efficient manner." Presumably the debtor might incur subsequent debts in the course of carrying on and conducting its business. Gonthier J advances no principle that might permit the settlement of priority disputes as between the Crown and subsequent lenders. In the event of a dispute, both would have the benefit of the licence to sell inventory and of express covenants, so that some other criterion would have to be found to determine which takes priority. Here, as before, the prospect of a reversal of the ordinary priority rules is immediate and troubling.

...

[107] Though I consider the above legal arguments sufficient to dispose of this appeal, I observe that policy considerations also tell in favour of the conclusion I have reached.

[108] In this respect, the first thing to notice is that the security agreement that the debtor and the respondent had in this case is an example of a very common and important financing device. To a considerable extent, commerce in our country depends on the vitality of such agreements. As several leading academics have observed, the amounts at stake run into the billions of dollars each year. And though not every creditor seeks security, the incentives to do so are powerful. See Jacob S. Ziegel, Benjamin Geva and R.C.C. Cuming, *Commercial and Consumer Transactions* (Rev. 2nd ed. 1990), at pp. 957-60. Accordingly, tinkering with security interests is a dangerous business. The risks of judicial innovation in this neighbourhood of the law are considerable.

[109] Chief among these is the risk that attends legal uncertainty. If the legal rule is not clear, then inventory financiers will have to provide against the risk that their security interest might be defeated by some rival claim. The danger is particularly acute where as here, the language is as broad as "in the ordinary course of business." In this regard, I agree with what Professor Roderick J. Wood said in his article ("Revenue Canada's Deemed Trust Extends Its Tentacles: Royal Bank of Canada v. Sparrow Electric Corp." (1995), 10 BFLR 429, at p. 429) that my colleague cites:

> … there is little controversy with the proposition that a priority rule should be capable of producing reasonably predictable results. An unclear priority rule imposes a number of social costs. It means that creditors must plan their affairs against less certain outcomes. Uncertain rules generate more litigation than clear rules. Over time an uncertain rule is sometimes transformed into a clear rule through the process of judicial interpretation. However, this is a piecemeal approach which often occurs at a glacial pace.

[110] Indeed, the consequences of my colleague's approach might be more dire than even Professor Wood supposes. For, as I have observed, almost any subsequent financial arrangement might be in the ordinary course of business. Accordingly, the possibility is real that my colleague's proposed rule would effectively obliterate the PPSA charge against inventory. As insurance against this outcome, the costs of financing would presumably increase. I agree that if Parliament mandated this outcome, the courts must perforce accept it. However, judges should not rush to embrace such a weighty consequence unless the statutory language requiring them to do so is unequivocal.

[111] Moreover, and for reasons I have already given, there is every likelihood that a broad interpretation of the licence theory would do violence to the PPSA. The Act clearly contemplates that inventory financing will be an important commercial device. But allowing the mere potential operation of a licence to sell to defeat a security interest in inventory would deprive the interest of all efficacy. It would not be any sort of security against subsequent obligations.

···

Appeal dismissed.

NOTES

1) For a detailed discussion of *Sparrow*, see Kevin Davis, Comment (1998), 29 *CBLJ* 145. See also Anthony Duggan and Jacob Ziegel, "Justice Iacobucci and the Canadian Law of Deemed Trusts and Chattel Security" (2007), 57 *UTLJ* 227. Does Iacobucci J fairly state

Gonthier J's position? Did Gonthier J suggest that the licence given to Sparrow included a right to create consensual security interests having priority over the bank's security interests? Is there any inconsistency, as Iacobucci J suggests there is, between the bank's consent to the sale of inventory in the ordinary course of business and Gonthier J's restriction of the use of the proceeds of sale to actually performed obligations?

2) Was Iacobucci J also correct in suggesting that Gonthier J's reading of the licence would lead to evisceration of the bank's security interest? Seemingly, he overlooks the fact that the bank had a general security interest in all of Sparrow's personal property and, therefore, was not relying solely on Sparrow's inventory for its security. Equally significant is the fact that, as Sparrow's banker, the Royal Bank would have known Sparrow's financial condition on a daily basis and, given the usual terms of a demand loan, would have been able to enforce its security interest at almost any time without waiting for Sparrow's complete financial collapse.

Jacob S. Ziegel and David L. Denomme, *The Ontario Personal Property Security Act: Commentary and Analysis*, 2d ed.
(Markham, ON: Butterworths, 2000), §25.3 (footnotes omitted)

§25.3. Scope of Express and Implied Licences. Apart from the majority and minority judgments of the Supreme Court of Canada in *Royal Bank of Canada v. Sparrow Electric Corp.* ("*Sparrow Electric*"), there has been little discussion in the PPSA cases of express and implied licences conferred on a debtor to deal with collateral, and the proceeds arising from the disposition of collateral, of which third parties may avail themselves to defeat an otherwise superior claim of the secured party. *Sparrow Electric* was very fact specific and addressed only some of the many permutations that may arise in practice. It may be helpful therefore to provide a broader overview of the different scenarios that may require consideration in practice. We believe the following propositions are justified by the authorities and the underlying principles and structure of the Ontario Act:

  i. The burden is on the party averring it to show that an express or implied licence was given the debtor to support the third party's claim in defeasance of the secured party's interest, assuming of course that the secured party had a perfected security interest to begin with. This basic principle derives from the fact that the OPPSA only recognizes fixed security interests and that the Act has abolished the equitable fixed and floating charge.
  ii. The Ontario Act itself confers no express or implied licences in the debtor's favour. Rather, it provides that, unless otherwise provided in the Act or other legislation, every security agreement is effective according to its terms.
  iii. General security agreements and inventory financing agreements regularly grant the debtor an express licence to deal with some or all of the collateral. In the case of inventory financing agreements, the agreement will commonly authorize the debtor to dispose of the inventory in the ordinary course of business but will require the debtor to hold the proceeds on trust for the secured party. The scope of the power of sale conferred under such agreements has not attracted significant case law,

presumably because the third party can usually avail itself of the broader buyer in ordinary course protection available under subss. 28(1) and (2) of the Act.

iv. Because they encompass all or most of the debtor's personal property, general security agreements will usually confer a broader range of licences on the debtor. There is no common format since so much will depend on the size of the debtor's business, the lender's character, the amount of the indebtedness, the terms of repayment, the ratio of the indebtedness to the value of the collateral, whether the collateral supports a public issue of bonds, and many other factors. The security agreement may authorize the debtor to continue to carry on business generally or limit the power to the disposition of inventory. It may (somewhat incongruously) require the debtor to hold the proceeds on trust for the secured party even though the agreement also entitles the debtor to use the proceeds in its business. The court will then be called upon to resolve the conflicting clauses.

v. General security agreements also frequently authorize the debtor to give a PMSI for the acquisition of new inventory and may expressly subordinate the GSA to the PMSI. It goes without saying that such provisions do not entitle the debtor to create non-purchase money security interests ranking pari passu with or in priority to the existing security interest.

vi. The language in which the power to deal with collateral and its proceeds is expressed may make a significant difference. In *Credit Suisse Canada v. 1133 Yonge Street Holdings Ltd.*, *supra*, this chapter, a real estate mortgage in the bank's favour also contained an assignment of the benefit of leases in the building and of the rents payable under the leases. Paragraph 7 of the security agreement provided that "Until notified to the contrary in writing, the Mortgagor shall *be entitled to*, and the lessee under any lease shall pay the Mortgagor, all rents and other amounts then due under such lease and thereafter accruing." The Ontario Court of Appeal held that para. 7 meant that prior to default the debtor was absolutely entitled to retain the rents as its own and that the parties' freedom to fashion the security agreement in accordance with their wishes overrode the secured party's presumptive entitlement to proceeds under s. 25(1)(b).

vii. If a GSA authorizes the debtor to use proceeds from the disposition of collateral in its business, the proceeds may be used to pay employee wages and to settle any deemed trusts arising under the federal *Income Tax Act* and other legislation in respect of deductions and remittances required to be made to the federal or provincial Crowns. However, this authorization only extends to payments actually made by the debtor prior to the debtor's default and commencement of enforcement proceedings by the secured party. Once enforcement proceedings are initiated and in the absence of overriding legislation, federal or provincial, the debtor loses its authority to disburse any proceeds. The unmet claims will thereafter be treated as enjoying no priority over the secured party's claim whether or not the claims are supported by non-consensual liens under the fiscal legislation. This was the conclusion reached by a strongly divided Supreme Court in *Sparrow Electric*. It seems however from Iacobucci J's majority judgment that he would admit an exception if the events attracting the non-consensual lien are closely connected to the sale of the collateral. However, there are other decisions, decided outside the PPSA, which take a broader view of the impact of non-consensual liens in relation to the debtor's authorized activities.

viii. The existence and scope of any *implied* licence will depend on the character of the security agreement and other surrounding circumstances. The Supreme Court of Canada held as far back as 1883 that where a chattel mortgage includes inventory the debtor has an implied licence to continue to realize the inventory since otherwise the debtor would have no means of repaying the secured creditor. Such an implied licence, it is important to note, does not extend to the debtor's entitlement to deal with the proceeds of disposition; they will enure for the secured creditor's benefit unless the security agreement provides otherwise. A licence to use proceeds to meet normal business expenses will be implied much more readily in the case of a GSA because without this authority the debtor would have to close its business. Again however it is important to emphasize that debts not paid by the debtor prior to default, even if incurred in the ordinary course of business, will rank as unsecured claims after default unless controlling legislation provides otherwise. This will be true even if an unpaid creditor has obtained judgment against the debtor and has issued a writ of execution prior to the secured party's enforcement of its security interest since an implied licence to pay ordinary course business debts does not extend to satisfying an involuntary judgment, at least not where the implied licence is terminated before the judgment has been satisfied.

ix. Even if the third party cannot rely on an express or implied licence in the debtor's favour, the third party may still be able to defeat the secured party's interest by bringing itself within one of the important exceptions in ss. 28-29 and 31 of the Act. It may also be able to invoke common law principles of estoppel if it can show that the secured party has knowingly acquiesced in the debtor holding itself out as having an unencumbered title to its property. Section 25 does not advert to these provisions but no adverse inferences should be drawn from the omission; the omission no doubt reflects the Article 9 drafters' preference (shared at least to some degree by the Minister's Advisory Committee) to avoid statements of the obvious and to rely on the reader's ability to follow a principle through to its logical conclusion.

As will be seen from the above list, most of the difficulties are likely to arise in construing the scope of express and implied licences given the debtor in the case of a GSA. Although, conceptually, the express and implied licence route *is* different from the common law treatment of floating charges, the practical results are not that much different. In both cases the debtor will ordinarily be entitled to pay ordinary course business debts prior to the initiation of enforcement proceedings by the secured party or the crystallization of the floating charge. In both cases, too, debts not paid before these events will enjoy no priority over the security interest after the debtor's default even though the debtor might have been entitled to pay them before default. The implied licence in a GSA differs from a floating charge in at least two respects: first, it does not entitle the debtor to create security interests ranking pari passu or in priority to the existing security interest and, second, it does not confer a priority in respect of judgment or other liens attaching to the collateral, at least not if the liens are not satisfied before the secured party intervenes. However, as indicated, the status of non-consensual liens arising out of authorized activities by the debtor requires further clarification. It must also be confessed that there is an element of artificiality to resolving these competing priorities through the prism of implied licences given that at bottom the court is addressing issues of public policy.

D. Conditional Sales and the Like

Kinetics Technology International Corp. v. Fourth National Bank of Tulsa
705 F2d 396 (CCA 10 1983)

SEYMOUR Circuit Judge: Kinetics Technology International Corporation (KTI) brought this diversity action seeking damages for an alleged conversion of goods by Fourth National Bank of Tulsa (the Bank). The Bank admits taking possession of the goods from the custody of a third party, Oklahoma Heat Transfer Corporation (OHT), but claims a right to the goods arising under the Oklahoma version of the Uniform Commercial Code (hereinafter UCC or Code), Okla. Stat. tit. 12A, §1-101 to 11-107 (1981). For the reasons set out below, we affirm in part and reverse in part.

OHT, now defunct, was a manufacturer specializing in constructing heat exchangers to specifications supplied by its customers. On May 25, 1977, the Bank issued OHT a line of credit for $600,000, taking a security interest in OHT's inventory. On June 1, the Bank filed a financing statement covering, *inter alia*, "[a]ll inventory now or hereafter owned by the Debtor." Rec., vol. I, at 37.

KTI is a company that designs and supplies process furnaces for the refinery and petrochemical industry. On August 18, 1977, it entered into a contract with OHT under which OHT was to build eight furnace economizers to KTI's specifications, in part from materials supplied by KTI, and in part from materials supplied by OHT. KTI was to ship to OHT certain specially designed and manufactured goods consisting of finned tubes, castings, fittings, and anchors (hereinafter referred to as the KTI Goods). OHT was to build eight box units (hereinafter referred to as the Box Units) from materials out of OHT's inventory, and then install the KTI Goods into the Box Units, resulting in eight completed furnace economizers. KTI agreed to make progress payments to OHT at various stages in the process. The purchase order form, supplied by KTI, provided that title to goods delivered to OHT by KTI would remain in KTI. Title to goods acquired by OHT from other sources for use in the KTI contract would pass to KTI upon the first progress (or other) payment made by KTI to OHT. KTI did not file under the UCC.

KTI procured the goods specified in the contract (the KTI Goods), and had them delivered to OHT. Delivery was complete by January 25, 1978. OHT began work on the contract. During this time, OHT's financial situation deteriorated, and it became necessary to seek additional financing from the Bank. The Bank agreed to make additional loans (separate from the line of credit), secured in part by specified accounts receivable of OHT. A loan was made to OHT on January 10, 1978, secured by the progress payments specified in the KTI-OHT contract. The Bank instructed KTI to make the first two progress payments directly to the Bank.

OHT's work on the contract reached the point at which OHT was entitled to the first two progress payments, a total of $42,600. Both payments, which KTI made on January 10 and January 19, 1978, were received by the Bank. OHT began work on the Box Units, but prior to their completion OHT management determined that the business' financial state could not support continued operation. On January 27, OHT shut down, and on January 30, OHT's management delivered the plant keys to the Bank. At that time, the Bank took possession and control of the plant where OHT's inventory, the Box Units, and the KTI Goods were located.

KTI demanded the surrender of the Box Units and the KTI Goods, but the Bank refused on the strength of its security interest in OHT's inventory, offering instead to sell the Box Units and the KTI Goods to KTI. Consequently, KTI filed this suit for conversion. A prolonged series of negotiations culminated in KTI's purchase of the Box Units and the KTI Goods on March 20, 1978. KTI reserved the right to litigate all issues. After a trial to the bench, the court found that KTI was entitled both to the KTI Goods and to the Box Units, and awarded damages in the amount of $156,272.30 plus interest. Although we reach a similar result, we do so by a different route.

The Bank's argument for reversal is based on its status as a holder of a perfected security interest on OHT's inventory. The Bank asserts that both the KTI Goods and the Box Units were inventory collateral in OHT's hands, to which the Bank was entitled when OHT defaulted on the line of credit. The Bank contends that KTI's interest in the Box Units and in the KTI Goods amounted only to an unperfected security interest over which the Bank's perfected security interest had priority. KTI argues that the Bank's security interest was ineffective as to the goods at issue because, under the contract, KTI retained title and ownership rights in the KTI Goods and acquired title and ownership rights in the Box Units when it made the progress payments. The Bank asserts alternatively that even if the trial court was correct on the issue of liability, it erroneously computed the amount of damages.

I. Bank Security Interest in the KTI Goods

The Bank's claim to the KTI Goods is based on its perfected security interest in OHT's inventory. The Bank argues that when KTI had the KTI Goods delivered to OHT and OHT began work on the contract, the goods became inventory for the purposes of the Bank's security interest. The Bank insists that KTI's rights in the KTI Goods at most amounted to a retained, unperfected security interest. KTI bases its claim on its ownership of the goods as evidenced by the title retention clause in the contract, arguing that OHT was in the position of a bailee. Thus, KTI asserts, the goods were never part of OHT's inventory, and therefore never became subject to the Bank's security interest.

The trial court examined the transaction between KTI and OHT to determine whether a "sale" by KTI to OHT had occurred when the KTI Goods were delivered to OHT. Finding none, it concluded that "Article Two has no application, and §2-401(1) cannot operate to convert KTI's retention of title into a security interest under Article Nine." Rec., vol. I, at 252. The court held additionally that, as a matter of law, "OHT has never had any interest in KTI's Goods other than that of a bailee." Id., at 253. The court concluded that KTI was entitled to possession of the KTI Goods notwithstanding the Bank's security interest.

In order for the Bank's security interest to include the KTI Goods and be enforceable, it must have attached to the goods. Tit. 12A, §9-203(1). A security interest attaches to collateral when (1) the debtor (here OHT) has signed a security agreement describing the collateral, (2) value has been given, and (3) the debtor has "rights in the collateral." *Id.* The first two requirements are met in this case. The issue here is whether OHT had sufficient rights in the collateral to meet the third requirement. The parties' disagreement is centered on whether OHT was a mere bailee of the KTI Goods, or instead had a greater property interest in them.

The phrase "rights in the collateral" is not defined in the UCC. The Code clearly does not require that a debtor have full ownership rights. See, *e.g.,* tit. 12A, §9-112. The Seventh Circuit has said that the requirement of "rights in the collateral" illustrates the general principal that "one cannot encumber another man's property in the absence of consent, estoppel, or some other special rule." In *re Pubs, Inc.,* 618 F2d 432, at 436 (7th Cir. 1980) (quoting *First National Bank & Trust Co. v. McElmurray,* 120 Ga. App. 134, at 138, 169 SE 2d 720, at 724 (1969)).

In *Amfac Mortgage Corp. v. Arizona Mall,* 127 Ariz. 70, 618 P2d 240 (Ct. App. 1980), the debtor Mall had contracted with a third party for the construction of a shopping mall. The contract specified that the contractor would obtain the needed materials, and that title to the materials would pass to the Mall upon satisfaction of various conditions, including payment. Amfac loaned money to the Mall, taking a security interest in all materials to be incorporated in the Mall. The contractor acquired the materials and had them delivered, but prior to their incorporation and before any payments were made by the Mall to the contractor, the enterprise folded. Amfac brought an action to recover the unincorporated steel. The court, in deciding whether the Mall had had sufficient rights in the steel for Amfac's security interest to attach, stated that a debtor acquires sufficient rights when the debtor obtains possession of collateral pursuant to an agreement with the seller or manufacturer. Possession with contingent rights of ownership was held to be sufficient with or without payment on the contract. See *Evans Products Co. v. Jorgensen,* 245 Or. 362, 421 P2d 978, at 981 (1966) (en banc).

In *Manger v. Davis,* 619 P2d 687 (Utah 1980), a consignment case, the Utah Supreme Court found that a debtor's "rights" in collateral must be in the nature of authority to subject the property to a security interest, and looked to the law of agency to resolve the issue. *Id.,* at 690. In *Connecticut Bank & Trust Co. v. Schindelman (In re Bosson),* 432 F. Supp. 1013 (D. Conn. 1977), the court found that under prevailing case law a debtor had sufficient rights when the debtor acquired possession of collateral pursuant to a sales contract or like agreement. The court looked to principles of law external to the Code to find if such "rights" existed. *Id.,* at 1018.

Thus, it is clear that for a security interest to attach, a debtor must have some degree of control or authority over collateral placed in the debtor's possession. The Oklahoma Supreme Court, in a case factually similar to the case before us, has said that the requisite authority exists "where a debtor gains possession of collateral pursuant to an agreement endowing him with any interest other than naked possession." *Morton Booth Co. v. Tiara Furniture, Inc.,* 564 P2d 210, at 214 (Okl. 1977). But see *Chrysler Corp. v. Adamatic, Inc.,* 59 Wis. 2d 219, 208 NW 2d 97, at 104 (1973) (bailee's possessory interest for limited purpose of repair not sufficient "rights in the collateral"). The *Morton Booth* definition strongly supports the Article Nine purpose of promoting certainty in commercial loan transactions. See UCC, §9-101, Official Comment. Otherwise, if a debtor received collateral from a third party under an agreement giving the debtor authority to exercise any outward indicia or manifestations of ownership or control, a would-be creditor could easily be misled into making a loan under an ineffective security agreement. For example, in *Morton Booth*, the debtor, Tiara, contracted to build gun cabinets from materials supplied primarily by Morton Booth, and then sell the completed products to Morton Booth. Tiara, a furniture manufacturer, subsequently sought and received financing from the Small Business Association, giving the participating banks a security interest in Tiara's present and after-acquired inventory, which apparently consisted of the same types of materials that were supplied it by Morton Booth. See 564 P2d, at 211. Had the court found that Tiara lacked sufficient "rights" in the Morton Booth-supplied collateral for the banks' security interest to attach, the bank's claim to the goods upon Tiara's default would have been defeated by the sort of hidden-title subterfuge the Code was intended to prevent.

This reason for the *Morton Booth* result is supported by another feature of Article Nine. In this context, buyers such as Morton Booth and KTI finance a debtor's operation by supplying materials rather than money with which to buy materials. Such a buyer-lender could easily protect itself from after-acquired property creditors of its contractor by filing an Article Nine purchase money security interest in the goods supplied by it to the contractor, as well as those purchased or otherwise identified in the contract by the contractor. See tit. 12A, §§9-107, -312(3). Requiring buyers such as KTI to take this additional step—done easily and at minimal cost—thoroughly advances the Code policy of providing notice and certainty to inventory lenders.

In accordance with *Morton Booth Co.*, we conclude contrary to the district court that the Bank's perfected security interest in OHT's collateral attached to the KTI Goods.

[The court went on to find that since the debtor's business consisted of custom fabricating steel pursuant to contractual terms with its customers, the sale from OHT to KTI was in the ordinary course of OHT's business and as such was authorized by the bank's security agreement. KTI therefore took the goods free of the bank's security interest.]

Affirmed in part, reversed in part and remanded.

R v. Canadian Imperial Bank of Commerce
(2000), 51 OR (3d) 257 (CA)

BY THE COURT: [1] The appellant served as the banker to Mr. A. Obront, the perpetrator of a massive fraudulent telemarketing scheme wherein many victims in the United States were induced to purchase gemstones at inflated prices. Mr. Obront pled guilty and received a sentence of four years in penitentiary. A forfeiture order was also made. One of the assets ordered forfeited to the Crown was a US dollar bank account at the Canadian Imperial Bank of Commerce (CIBC) in the amount of US $28,809.37 in the name of Royal International Collectibles (RIC), the corporate vehicle of Mr. Obront. The bank account had been frozen by order of Roberts J made on January 20, 1997 and served on the bank on January 21, 1997. The bank appeals that portion of the forfeiture order.

[2] The forfeiture order was made by Kelly J on October 30, 1998. The portion of his reasons dealing with the issue are as follows:

> As far as the US account is concerned, I must confess, this gave me more difficulty than some of the other issues. There is a *Personal Property Security Act* security which was taken by the bank, apparently in good faith, and among other assets, this US account, formed part of the security. On the other hand, there is no doubt that the proceeds, which the bank is claiming out of this account, are proceeds of crime and as such, cannot be given or dealt with given as security by Mr. Obront.

[3] The sections of the *Criminal Code*, RSC 1985, c. C-46, which allow these orders to be made are ss. 462.37(1) and (2) which provide:

> 462.37(1) Subject to this section and sections 462.39 to 462.41, where an offender is convicted, or discharged under section 730, of an enterprise crime offence and the court imposing sentence on the offender, on application of the Attorney General, is satisfied, on a balance of probabilities, that any property is proceeds of crime and that the enterprise crime offence was committed in relation to that property, the court shall order that the property be forfeited to Her Majesty to be disposed of as the Attorney General directs or otherwise dealt with in accordance with the law.
>
> (2) Where the evidence does not establish to the satisfaction of the court that the enterprise crime offence of which the offender is convicted, or discharged under section 730, was committed in relation to property in respect of which an order of forfeiture would otherwise be made under subsection (1) but the court is satisfied, beyond a reasonable doubt, that that property is proceeds of crime, the court may make an order of forfeiture under subsection (1) in relation to that property.

[4] Section 462.41 requires that before a forfeiture order is made, notice must be given to any person "who, in the opinion of the court, appears to have a valid interest in the property." Section 462.41(3) says:

> 462.41(3) Where a court is satisfied that any person, other than
>
>   (a) a person who is charged with, or was convicted of, an enterprise crime offence or a designated substance offence, or
>
>   (b) a person who acquired title to or a right of possession of that property from a person referred to in paragraph (a) under circumstances that give rise to a reasonable inference that the title or right was transferred for the purpose of avoiding the forfeiture of the property,
>
> is the lawful owner or is lawfully entitled to possession of any property or any part thereof that would otherwise be forfeited pursuant to subsection 462.37(1) or 462.38(2) and that the person appears innocent of any complicity in an offence referred to in paragraph (a) or of any collusion in relation to such an offence, the court may order that the property or part thereof be returned to that person.

[5] The appellant's position is that it has a valid interest in the bank account and that Kelly J erred by ordering the moneys in the account forfeited to the Crown. First, the

bank submits that Kelly J erred by holding that because the "proceeds" in the account are proceeds of crime, they could not be given as security by the perpetrator of the fraud.

[6] The appellant's submission is correct. The bank was a secured creditor of RIC pursuant to a security agreement dated May 2, 1995 and registered under the *Personal Property Security Act*, RSO 1990, c. P.10 (PPSA), which agreement secured credit facilities provided to RIC by the bank. The Crown's submission is that s. 11 of the PPSA provides that a security interest only attaches when the debtor acquires rights in the collateral, and that RIC never acquired rights in the funds of the victims because the funds were obtained by fraud, an application of the *nemo dat* rule, which says essentially that you cannot give what you do not have. The argument is that RIC never acquired any interest in the funds of the victims because they were obtained by fraud.

[7] The Crown relies on the case of *Chrysler Credit Canada Ltd. v. MVL Leasing Ltd.* (1993), 5 PPSAC (2d) 92 (Ont. Gen. Div.). That case involved a stolen car, and is distinguishable from the case at bar. There was never any intent by the owner of the car to transfer ownership to the rogue. In this case, the victims of the gem scam did not know they were victims and intended to forward their funds to RIC in exchange for the gemstones which they received. The interest of RIC in the funds was voidable but not void *ab initio*. The security interest of the bank was therefore able to attach to the funds deposited into the account.

[8] Because of the trial judge's error, he did not go on to consider whether to exercise his discretion under s. 462.41 of the Code and allow the bank to retain for itself the balance in the bank account. On appeal, this court may exercise the discretion conferred by that section on the sentencing judge: (s. 686(8) and s. 462.44 of the Code).

• • •

[14] The court has a discretion under s. 462.41 of the Code whether to return part of any proceeds of crime to an innocent person with an interest in those proceeds. Although we are satisfied that the bank has a security interest in all the moneys in the account pursuant to its security agreement, we would not exercise the court's discretion in favour of the bank in these circumstances in respect of any of the US $27,374.08 of new victims' money deposited on January 21, 1997. Those moneys are identifiable proceeds of crime which should be returned to the victims.

[15] In the result, the order of Kelly J is set aside, and instead, an order will go forfeiting to the Crown the amount of US $27,374.08. The balance shown in the account of US $1,435.29 is to be returned to the bank.

Appeal allowed in part.

NOTES

1) The Official Comment to old UCC 9-203 (1990 edition) casts no light on the intended meaning of the requirement in UCC 9-203(1)(c) that the debtor "has rights in the collateral." Gilmore (vol. I, at 353) acknowledges that Article 9 does not specify the quantum of rights that a debtor must have in collateral to support a security interest in it, but he suggests that something less than full legal title will do.

2) Was the court in *KTI v. Fourth National Bank* correct in holding that, so long as the debtor has some rights in the collateral, a security interest given by the debtor will bind the owner of the collateral? Do old UCC 9-203(1) or the comparable provisions in the PPS Acts support this interpretation? Was the court influenced in its ruling by the fact that the materials supplied by KTI appeared to form part of OHT's inventory, thus misleading a potential lender to OHT? Does this mean that every customer that orders goods to its specifications and supplies part of the components is at risk so long as the components are in the debtor's possession? The PPS Acts, like old UCC 9-203(1), all require the debtor to have "rights" in the collateral. Does this preclude the invocation of estoppel principles or of statutory provisions such as SGA ss. 25(1) and (2) and s. 2 of the *Factors Act*? Revised Article 9, UCC 9-202(b)(2) provides that the security interest attaches when the debtor has rights in the collateral "or the power to transfer rights in the collateral to a secured party."

3) What do you make of the following observation by White and Summers, 3d ed., at 990:

> One final caveat: There is good reason to believe that judges do not often mechanically apply the phrase "rights in the collateral." Nor do they mechanically determine when those rights arise. Rather, equities between competing claimants may be fought out in the name of this phrase. And the time when a court determines that the debtor acquired rights in the collateral may not only depend on such equities, but also on the nature of the competing parties and the kind of law involved.

V. INVESTMENT PROPERTY

John Cameron, "Secured Transactions Under Ontario's Securities Transfer Act, 2006"
(2007), 22 *BFLR* 309, at 318-20 and 343-44 (footnotes omitted)

Attachment in Direct Holding System

[For an account of the direct and indirect holding systems, see Chapter 2, Part III.] The criteria for attachment of a security interest under the direct holding system have not changed much. Apart from a statutorily created security interest of very limited application, a security interest attaches to collateral only when three conditions are met:

1. Value is given. The PPSA defines "value" as "any consideration sufficient to support a simple contract and includes an antecedent debt or liability."
2. The debtor has rights in the collateral or the power to transfer rights in the collateral to a secured party. Previously, attachment required that the "debtor has rights in the collateral" without reference to the power to transfer.
3. (i) The debtor must have signed a security agreement containing a description of the collateral sufficient to enable it to be identified; or (ii) in the case of a certificated security in registered form, the security has been delivered to the secured party in accordance with section 68 of the STA; or (iii) in the case of investment property, which includes a security, the secured party has obtained "control" ... under the debtor's security agreement.

As to the criterion described in paragraph 3(ii) above, section 68(1) of the STA provides for delivery of a certificated security to a "purchaser" (defined broadly to include a person who takes by, among other things, sale, security interest, gift or any other voluntary transaction that creates an interest in property) by (i) the secured party acquiring possession of the security certificate, or (ii) another person (other than a securities intermediary) acquiring possession of the security certificate on behalf of the secured party, or that person having previously acquired possession, acknowledging that the person holds the security certificate for the secured party. There is also a provision allowing for a securities intermediary to acquire possession of a security certificate on behalf of a secured party, but only where it is registered in the name of the secured party, payable to the order of the secured party or specially endorsed to the secured party without being endorsed to the securities intermediary or in blank. Unlike the possession sufficient for the purposes of attachment in the case of other collateral (such as goods), there is no rule precluding perfection through an agent of the debtor.

... [S]ection 11.1(2) of the PPSA creates by statute a security interest in (among other things) a certificated security that is (among other requirements) delivered between persons in the business of dealing in securities, against payment, in order to secure the obligation to make payment. More specifically, section 11.1(2) provides the following:

> (2) A security interest in favour of a person that delivers a certificated security or other financial asset represented by a writing attaches to the security or other financial asset if,
>
> (a) the security or other financial asset is,
>
> (i) in the ordinary course of business transferred by delivery with any necessary endorsement or assignment, and
>
> (ii) delivered under an agreement between persons in the business of dealing with such securities or financial assets; and
>
> (b) the agreement calls for delivery against payment.

The existence of this rule will not normally present issues in connection with a typical secured lending transaction where the collateral consists of securities and the secured party seeks to obtain "control" ... of the securities.

...

Attachment in Indirect Holding System

Similar to the direct holding system, the criteria for attachment of a security interest under the indirect holding system have not changed much. Apart from a statutory recognition of the common law broker's lien, a security interest attaches to collateral in the indirect holding system only when three conditions are met:

1. Value is given.
2. The debtor has rights in the collateral or the power to transfer rights in the collateral to a secured party.
3. (i) The debtor must have signed a security agreement describing the collateral as a security entitlement or a securities account, or describing the underlying financial asset held in the securities account; or (ii) in the case of investment property (which includes, among other things, a security entitlement or a

securities account), the secured party has obtained "control" ... under the debtor's security agreement.

Attachment of a security interest in a securities account is also attachment of a security interest in the security entitlements carried in the securities account. This rule corresponds to Revised UCC Article 9 §9-203(h), the Official Comment to which indicates that it makes "clear that attachment of a security interest in a securities account ... is also attachment in security entitlements ... carried in the [account]."

As mentioned above, the PPSA recognizes the common law broker's lien. Section 11.1(1) of the PPSA creates by statute a security interest in favour of a securities intermediary, which attaches to a customer's security entitlement if the customer buys a financial asset through the securities intermediary and is obligated to pay the purchase price to the securities intermediary at the time of purchase, and the securities intermediary credits the financial asset to the customer's securities account before receiving payment of the purchase price. Section 11.1(4) states that the security interest so created secures the customer's obligation to pay for the financial asset.

As with the direct holding system, the rules for attachment of a security interest in proceeds of any collateral (including investment property) remain unchanged.

CHAPTER FIVE

Perfection

I. INTRODUCTION

Broadly speaking, perfection relates to the publication of a security interest. Possession is one method of publication, and the pledge, the oldest form of security device, is built on this idea: see Chapter 1, Part III. Pledgees usually carried on a recognized business and it was assumed that the transfer of possession to the pledgee gave sufficient notice of the pledge to the pledgor's creditors. This meant that creditors could safely extend credit to the pledgor on the strength of the goods in his possession. In *Twyne's* case, 3 Co. Rep. 806, 76 Eng. Rep. 809 (Star Chamber, 1601), the debtor, Pierce, conveyed a flock of sheep to Twyne as security for a loan, but remained in possession. A judgment creditor levied execution against the sheep to enforce payment and a dispute arose between him and Pierce over who was entitled to the sheep. The court held that the transaction between Pierce and Twyne was a fraudulent conveyance and so it was void against the judgment creditor. According to the law of fraudulent conveyances, if a debtor transfers property with the intention of defeating creditors, the transfer is void. *Twyne's* case stands for the proposition that if the debtor transfers ownership, but not possession, that creates a presumption of intention to defeat creditors. The thinking was that if the debtor stayed in possession, the transfer cannot have been a genuine one and, therefore, the most likely purpose was to defeat creditors.

There is a second policy consideration behind *Twyne's* case; namely, that if D transfers goods to SP, but SP leaves D in possession, this creates a false appearance of ownership and third parties may be misled. That is exactly what happened in *Twyne's* case: the judgment creditor assumed that Pierce owned the sheep and, acting on the strength of that assumption, he went to the trouble and expense of taking execution proceedings. *Twyne's* case had the consequence of preventing non-possessory security interests. In the wake of the decision, if SP wanted a security interest in D's goods, he had to take possession: in other words, the pledge was the only valid form of security in tangible collateral. This may have been a workable rule in an agrarian economy, but it is impractical in the modern world because, typically, D needs the goods to earn income to repay SP's loan.

There are two opposing policy considerations: (1) the need to facilitate non-possessory secured lending; and (2) the need to protect third parties from being misled. Registration provides a way of reconciling these two policies by giving interested third parties the means of discovering a non-possessory security interest in advance of a transaction involving the collateral. The English and US *Bills of Sale Acts*, enacted in the mid-19th century, were an early form of registration statute and they were copied in Canada. For a short account of this legislation and its deficiencies, see Chapter 1, Part IV. The PPSAs are the direct successors of the bills of sale legislation. The PPSA registration system is different in both scope and design from the bills of sale system (see further, Chapter 6), but the underlying policy objective is the same.

The publicity concern that underpins *Twyne's* case is not limited to goods; it applies to all forms of collateral, including intangibles (accounts receivable and the like). The problem is that, while a possession requirement may be feasible for security interests in tangible collateral, for obvious reasons the law cannot insist on possession of intangibles. *Dearle v. Hall* (1823), 3 Russ. 1 was an early attempt to facilitate dealings in intangibles. According to the rule in *Dearle v. Hall*, if there was a competition between two or more assignees of the same chose in action, priority turned in part on which assignee was the first to notify the account debtor of its interest. The rule had the effect of conscripting the account debtor into the role of surrogate register and it gave prospective assignees an incentive to consult the "register." The assumption was that the account debtor would tell the prospective assignee about any prior assignment. Subject to possible dishonesty on the account debtor's part, his "all clear" to the assignee meant one or the other of two things—that there was no prior assignment, or that the prior assignee had failed to give notice—and either way the prospective assignee was safe. One shortcoming of the rule in *Dearle v. Hall* is that it only worked for the assignment of an existing debt; if the assignment concerned a future chose in action, for obvious reasons notification of the account debtor was impossible. For discussion of this and other limitations, see Chapter 1, Part IV. Legislation providing for the registration of assignment of book debts was enacted in England in the 19th century to supplement the rule in *Dearle v. Hall* and complement the bills of sale acts, and similar legislation was enacted in Canada in the early part of the 20th century. (For a brief account of this legislation and its shortcomings, see Chapter 1, Part IV.) The PPSAs supersede these earlier laws.

According to s. 19 of the OPPSA, "a security interest is perfected when, (a) it has attached; and (b) all steps required for perfection under any provision of this Act have been completed." Like its source, old UCC 9-303(1), the definition is circular since perfection is defined partly in terms of itself. This unfortunate result has come about because perfection is used in two senses in the Act: first, in terms of the *procedural steps* required to give public notice of an existing or future security interest (usually by registering a financing statement or by the secured party taking possession of the collateral), and, second, to describe the *status* of a security interest that has attached under s. 11(1) and that meets the procedural requirements. The double meaning has not so far given rise to reported difficulties and it is usually fairly straightforward to determine whether a section refers to perfection in the first sense or the second. Thus, in ss. 20, 28, and 34-35 it is used in the status sense, whereas in such sections as 21-24, 30, and 45 it is used in the procedural sense.

The Act recognizes four types of perfection: (1) perfection by possession; (2) perfection by registration; (3) perfection by control; and (4) temporary perfection.

Perfection by possession is regulated in OPPSA s. 22. As will be seen, only tangible things, including specific documentary expression of rights, *viz.* chattel paper, instruments, certificated securities, letters of credit, and advices of credits and negotiable documents of title, can be perfected by possession. (Most of these terms are defined in s. 1(1).) Can you see the reason for this restriction? Perfection by possession is dealt with in Part II, below.

Perfection by registration. OPPSA s. 23 provides that "Registration perfects a security interest in any type of collateral." It will be apparent from the foregoing why the Act treats registration and possession as alternative methods of perfection. The details of the registration system are dealt with in Chapter 6.

Perfection by control. Section 22.1 provides that a security interest in investment property may be perfected by control of the collateral. Broadly speaking, control means that the secured party has the ability to transfer the investment property without further action by the debtor. Perfection by control is dealt with in Part III, below. As will be seen, the main advantage of perfection by control is that it trumps perfection by all other methods, including registration.

Temporary perfection exists when a security interest is protected even though no financing statement has been registered and the secured party is not in possession of the collateral. OPPSA s. 24 enumerates two such cases. However, the Act recognizes a number of other situations where the secured party is given a grace period within which to perfect an as yet unperfected security interest or to reperfect a security interest that has or may become unperfected by reason of a change of circumstances. See, for example, ss. 20(3), 25(4), 48(2) and (3), and 6(2), 6(5), and 7(2). The reason for these derogations from the normal rules is that it is not always practicable or possible for the secured party to perfect its security interest immediately, and in the case of very short-term security interests (those covered in s. 24), it is unreasonable to require it to do so.

Where more than one method of perfection is permissible, the secured party is free to switch from one method to the other without interrupting the continuity of perfection: see OPPSA s. 21 (Part IV, below).

II. PERFECTION BY POSSESSION

Re Raymond Darzinskas
(1981), 34 OR (2D) 782 (SC)

STEELE J: The trustee brings this application to declare that the security interest of Joel Morgenstern, as evidenced by a chattel mortgage dated January 24, 1979, is subordinate in interest to that of the Trustee in Bankruptcy. Council agree that the financing statement, registered under the Personal Property Security Act, RSO 1980, c. 375 (the PPSA), was improperly registered and therefore the sole issue before the Court is whether the security of Morgenstern was perfected by possession.

The property in question is a heavy piece of manufacturing equipment. There is no evidence that it was attached to the real property. It was located within the building and was connected with heavy electrical wiring for its use. It was not a fixture.

By reason of a default under the security, Morgenstern instructed a bailiff to seize the equipment which was done on July 28, 1981, in the presence of both the bailiff and Morgenstern. The lien warrant was served on the landlord of the premises occupied by the bankrupt. The bankrupt himself was not present at the time. Because of the size of the equipment, it was not removed from the premises, nor were any operative parts of the equipment removed therefrom. On or about August 4, 1981, the bailiff re-attended at the premises and requested that the bankrupt bring the chattel mortgage into good standing but no money was forthcoming.

An affidavit filed by the Trustee upon information received from the bankrupt is to the effect that because the equipment was not removed or placed in a non-working condition the bankrupt was permitted to use the equipment in the ordinary course of business. However, the affidavit does not say that the bankrupt in fact used the equipment. It merely states that as a result of promises of payment Morgenstern permitted the bankrupt to use the equipment some time in late July 1981. Morgenstern's affidavit is much clearer. Apart from confirming the seizure by the bailiff and the re-attendance by the bailiff, he states that on or about August 12, 1981, he was approached by the bankrupt who advised him that he was arranging finances to pay off the chattel mortgage which money would be available within a few days, and that in view of those circumstances he, Morgenstern, consented to the bankrupt using the equipment. When no refinancing was arranged, Morgenstern proceeded to file the petition for a receiving order which was dated August 17, 1981.

Based on the above evidence, I find that the bailiff in fact seized the property on July 28, 1981, and that the bankrupt did not use the equipment thereafter until August 12, 1981, when he was given permission so to do by Morgenstern. In *Johnson v. Pickering*, [1907] 2 KB 437, at 443-44, it was stated as follows:

> Now it is clear that a sheriff may seize goods and chattels without actually laying his hands upon them; it is sufficient if he enters upon land on which the goods and chattels are and announces his present intention of seizing all the goods and chattels upon that land: *Gladstone v. Padwick* (1871), LR 6 Ex. 203.

I am therefore satisfied that the bailiff seized the goods in question, notwithstanding the fact that the bankrupt was not present. I particularly find this in view of the uncontradicted affidavit of Morgenstern that at a later date the bankrupt approached him requesting permission to use the goods.

The question is, is this seizure an effective possession under the provision of s. 24 of the PPSA.

Section 24 provides as follows [see now OPPSA s. 22]:

> 24. Except as provided in section 26, possession of the collateral by the secured party, or on his behalf by a person other than the debtor or the debtor's agent, perfects a security interest in,
>
> > (a) chattel paper;
> > (b) goods;
> > (c) instruments;
> > (d) securities;
> > (e) letters of credit and advices of credit; or
> > (f) negotiable documents of title,
>
> but subject to section 23, only during its actual holding as collateral.

I am of the opinion that the intention of the Act is to provide notice to persons dealing with the property or with the owner thereof that the secured party claims an interest in the goods. This can be effected by constructive notice, by registration or by actual notice by possession. In the present case Morgenstern had constructive possession by reason of his seizure but he did not have actual possession. He left the equipment in full working order on the premises. Section 58 of the Personal Property Security Act provides for the right to take possession or where there has been perfected registration to render the equipment unusable without removal upon default. I am of the opinion that s. 24 of the Act requires actual physical possession to be taken and the goods held by the secured party to perfect his security interest in order to give notice to all persons dealing therewith. This possession is required even more where the security interest was not perfected by registration. No such physical possession was taken in the present case and therefore Morgenstern's possession was not perfected. Therefore, his interest is subordinate to the interest of the Trustee by virtue of s. 22 of the PPSA.

Declaration in favour of trustee.

Sperry Inc. v. Canadian Imperial Bank of Commerce
(1985), 17 DLR (4th) 236 (Ont. CA)

MORDEN JA: The defendants, Canadian Imperial Bank of Commerce and Thorne Riddell Inc., appeal from a judgment of Montgomery J [reported at 40 OR (2d) 54, 2 PPSAC 225, 44 CBR (NS) 69, 141 DLR (3d) 119] declaring that the plaintiff, Sperry Inc. (Sperry) "is entitled as against the defendants to title and delivery of the goods covered by its Dealer Security Agreement free from any claims by either of the defendants." The appeal involves the resolution of the competing claims of Sperry and the bank to farm equipment sold by Sperry to a dealer. There is also a cross-appeal respecting expenses incurred by Sperry in maintaining a letter of credit filed with the Court.

The basic facts, apart from the relevant terms of the competing security documents, are set forth in the trial judgment which, as indicated, is reported and, accordingly, I shall not repeat them in detail. The following outline is sufficient to deal with the issues on which this appeal turns.

W.J. Allinson Farm Equipment & Supplies Limited [Allinson] was a dealer in farm equipment and supplies in Kingston. On August 27, 1976 it entered into a dealer security agreement with Sperry. The material provisions of this document read as follows:

> 1. It is anticipated that Company [Sperry] in its continuing sole discretion, from time to time may sell its goods on credit to Dealer [Allinson] and purchase Lien Notes and Conditional Sales Contracts from Dealer. Dealer agrees to pay Company for such credit sales of Company goods in the manner and at the times prescribed in the Terms of Sale or Terms of Sale Schedules published from time to time by Company and in effect at the time of sale.
>
> 2. In order to induce Company to make such sales, and to purchase such Lien Notes and Conditional Sales Contracts, *Dealer hereby grants to Company a security interest under the Personal Property Security Act in the collateral described in Paragraph 3 below to secure all present and future obligations* and liabilities of Dealer to Company, including but not limited to contingent liabilities and future advances made for taxes, levies and repairs to or maintenance of the collateral (all of which obligations and liabilities together are herein called the "indebtedness").

3. The word collateral, as used in this Agreement, shall mean: (a) Dealer's entire inventory now owned or hereafter acquired by Dealer from Company comprising new and used agricultural equipment, industrial equipment, other machinery, equipment and supplies, repair parts therefor, twine and wire; (b) all replacements, attachments and additions thereto; and (c) all proceeds thereof.

...

5. *Dealer represents and warrants that: (a) at the time Company's security interest attaches with respect to any collateral, the Dealer shall be the owner of said collateral* with good rights to sell, transfer, assign or pledge the same, free from any lien, security interest, encumbrances or other right, title or interest, other than that of Company; ... [The italics are mine.]

On September 9, 1977 Allinson entered into a general security agreement with the bank. The terms of the agreement which are relevant to the issues on this appeal are as follows:

1. As a general and continuing collateral security for payment of all existing and future indebtedness and liability of the undersigned [Allinson] to Canadian Imperial Bank of Commerce (the "Bank") wheresoever and howsoever incurred and any ultimate unpaid balance thereof, *the undersigned hereby charges in favour of and grants to the Bank a security interest in the undertaking of the undersigned and all property of the kinds hereinafter described of which the undersigned is now or may hereafter become the owner* and which, insofar as the same consists of tangible property, is now or may hereafter be in the place or places designated in paragraph 14 hereof; and the undersigned agrees with the Bank as hereinafter set out.

2. In this agreement ...
"Collateral" means and includes all of the above mentioned undertaking and property whether now owned or hereafter acquired, and whether tangible or otherwise; ...

3. *Description of Property*
01. *Inventory* All goods now or hereafter forming part of the inventory of the undersigned including, without limiting the generality of the foregoing, the following: goods held for sale or lease; ...

4. *Ownership of Collateral*
The undersigned represents and warrants that, except for the security interest created hereby and except for purchase money obligations, the undersigned is, or with respect to Collateral acquired after the date hereof will be, the owner of the Collateral free from any mortgage, lien, charge, security interest or encumbrance. "Purchase money obligations" means any mortgage, lien or other encumbrance upon property assumed or given back as part of the purchase price of such property, or arising by operation of law or any extension or renewal or replacement thereof upon the same property, if the principal amount of the indebtedness secured thereby is not increased. ...

9. *Default*
01. Upon default by the undersigned in payment of all or any part of the indebtedness or liability of the undersigned to the Bank or in the performance or observance of

any of the provisions hereof (in this agreement called "default") the Bank may appoint in writing any person to be a receiver (which term shall include a receiver and manager) of the Collateral, including any rents and profits thereof, and may remove any receiver and appoint another in his stead, and such receiver so appointed shall have power to take possession of the Collateral and to carry on or concur in carrying on the business of the undersigned, and to sell or concur in selling the Collateral or any part thereof. *Any such receiver shall for all purposes be deemed to be the agent of the undersigned.* The Bank may from time to time fix the remuneration of such receiver. All moneys from time to time received by such receiver shall be paid by him first in discharge of all rents, taxes, rates, insurance premiums and outgoings affecting the Collateral, secondly in payment of his remuneration as receiver, thirdly in keeping in good standing all liens and charges on the Collateral prior to the security constituted by this agreement, and fourthly in or toward payment of such parts of the indebtedness and liability of the undersigned to the Bank as to the Bank seems best, and any residue of such moneys so received shall be paid to the undersigned. The Bank in appointing or refraining from appointing such receiver shall not incur any liability to the receiver, the undersigned or otherwise. ...

18. *General*
... The security interest created or provided for by this agreement is intended to attach when this agreement is signed by the undersigned and delivered to the Bank. ... [The italics are mine.]

Initially, the security interests secured by each of these agreements were duly perfected by registration under the Personal Property Security Act, RSO 1970, c. 344, as amended (the Act). For reasons that are not material to this appeal both of these perfections lapsed, that of the bank early in 1979 and that of Sperry in September 1979.

On or about the 14th day of March 1980 the bank appointed Thorne Riddell Inc. to act as receiver and manager of Allinson's business. Thorne Riddell took immediate possession of Allinson's premises and of all of its property, equipment and undertaking, including the inventory supplied by Sperry which is in issue in this appeal. On or about March 14, 1980 Sperry learned that the bank had appointed a receiver and manager and within a few days, apparently on or before March 17, 1980, its representative attended at the Allinson premises. They were not permitted to remove the inventory in dispute. They valued it at $246,256.64. On March 17, 1980 Thorne Riddell wrote to Sperry as follows:

This is to confirm that a representative of your firm has counted the Sperry New Holland equipment on the premises of W.J. Allinson (Equipment) Limited on March 17, 1980.

We further confirm that the above equipment will not be sold or removed from the premises by us until the security agreements are reviewed by the lawyers appointed by the Canadian Imperial Bank of Commerce.

The evidence on behalf of the bank and the receiver was that the receiver "elected to run the business on a day to day basis until Friday, March 21, 1980." There is no evidence that the security agreements were "reviewed." The next dealing with the Sperry equipment appears to be its delivery to Sperry under the court order to which I shall refer shortly.

On March 25, 1980 Sperry filed a renewal of its financing statement with a view to perfecting its security interest in the inventory.

In May 1980 Sperry commenced this action against the bank and Thorne Riddell asserting its rights under the dealer security agreement and claimed "[a] declaration that as against both defendants the plaintiff is entitled to title and delivery of the goods covered by its Dealer Security Agreement free from any claims by both defendants." As indicated above, the trial Judge granted judgment in favour of Sperry in these terms.

Very soon after the action was commenced, Master Garfield made an order, on consent, in a motion brought by Sperry that upon the delivery by Sperry to the accountant of the Court of a letter of credit in a specified form the bank was to deliver to Sperry the inventory in dispute. The bank and Thorne Riddell counterclaimed against Sperry for the value of the goods returned. In this appeal they seek what is said to be the sum owing to the bank as of the time of trial ($220,798.04) with interest at 15 per cent per annum from then to date.

Sperry cross-appealed for an order that the costs of maintaining the letter of credit (said to be some $8,000 at the time of the trial) be awarded to it. The trial Judge had refused to make such an order.

At the trial the two basic issues were: (1) did the bank have a security interest in the inventory covered by the dealer security agreement between Sperry and Allinson? and (2), if it did, which party's claim was entitled to priority? The learned trial Judge resolved the first issue against the bank and this was sufficient for Sperry's claim to succeed. He went on to express the opinion that if he were wrong with respect to the scope of the bank's security interest and the case were to be determined on the basis of who had priority then he would have decided in favour of the bank on the basis that its possession of the inventory on March 20, 1980 was a perfection of its interest under s. 24 [now s. 22] of the Act. I shall in due course refer to the trial Judge's reasons relating to the date March 20, 1980. ...

[Morden JA found that the trial judge had erred on the first issue, and continued:]

The next issue is—which party has priority? The relevant provision is s. 35(1) of the Act [now s. 30], which provides:

> 35(1) If no other provision of this Act is applicable, priority between security interests in the same collateral shall be determined.
>
> (a) by the order of registration, if the security interests have been perfected by registration;
>
> (b) by the order of perfection, unless the security interests have been perfected by registration; or
>
> (c) by the order of attachment under subsection 12(1), if no security interest has been perfected.

The bank relies on s. 35(1)(b) to support its claim for priority on the basis of its perfection by possession under s. 24 of the Act. Sperry relies on s. 35(1)(c) on the basis of the earlier attachment of its security interest.

As indicated earlier in these reasons the trial Judge was of the view that if the case were to be determined on the basis of which party had priority he would have decided in favour of the bank on the basis that its possession of the inventory on and after March 20, 1980 (I think he meant March 21) was a perfection of its interest under s. 24 of the Act. The trial Judge was concerned with the effect of the provision in para. 9 of the bank's general security agreement that the receiver "shall for all purposes be deemed to be the agent of [Allinson]." He quoted the following passage from the judgment of Houlden JA for this Court in *Peat Marwick Ltd. v. Consumers' Gas Co.* (1980), 29 OR (2d) 336, 1 PPSAC 149, 11 BLR 114, 35 CBR (NS) 1, 113 DLR (3d) 754, at 344 [29 OR (2d)]:

> It seems to me that the receiver and manager in a situation, like the present, is wearing two hats. When wearing one hat, he is the agent of the debtor company; when wearing the other, the agent of the debenture holder. In occupying the premises of the debtor and in carrying on the business, the receiver and manager acts as the agent of the debtor company. In realizing the security of the debenture holder, notwithstanding the language of the debenture, he acts as the agent of the debenture holder, and thus is able to confer title on a purchaser free of encumbrance.

The trial Judge then said [2 PPSAC, at 235]:

> Thorne Riddell acted as agent for Allinson from the time it took possession on March 14, 1980 until March 20, 1980. On March 20, a decision was made to realize on the security and liquidate the assets. At that point the receiver was acting as agent of the Bank notwithstanding the wording of the security agreement. ...
>
> If I had not found there was no attachment under s. 21 because of the failure of the Bank to comply with s. 12, possession by the Bank's agent would have given the Bank priority of perfection of its general security agreement.
>
> It is helpful at this point to set out the relevant parts of s. 24:
>
> > 24. Except as provided in section 26, possession of the collateral by the secured party, or on his behalf by a person other than the debtor or the debtor's agent, perfects a security interest in, ...
> >
> > (b) goods;
> >
> > but subject to section 23, only during its actual holding as collateral.

The bank initially submitted that the trial Judge was correct in concluding that perfection took place on March 20 but, when the query was raised whether a mere decision to realize on the security could amount to perfection and, in any event, whether there was any evidence respecting a decision to realize on the Sperry inventory, the bank submitted that it had perfected on March 14.

Several issues arise with respect to the bank's claim to have perfected its security interest by possession but it is not necessary to deal with all of them. I do not need to deal with Sperry's contention that "repossession" of collateral on default cannot amount to possession for the purpose of s. 24. There is a helpful discussion of this issue in J.A. Carfagnini, "Statutory Requirements for Perfection by Possession under the Ontario Personal Property Security Act" (1982), 7 *CBLJ* 234. The requirement in s. 24 that perfection by possession is "only during its actual holding as collateral" would have to be addressed. However, it need not be in this case because I think it turns on more basic considerations.

In my view the bank never perfected its security interest in the Sperry-supplied inventory in contention. The bank seeks to minimize the effect of the agency provision in its general security agreement. It submits that the taking of possession of Allinson's assets was an act taken by the receiver as agent for the bank and was the initial act of realization.

The apparent logic of the first part of the bank's submission ignores the effect of the agency provision in the general security agreement under which Thorne Riddell was appointed. This term bound not only the parties to the agreement but was "effective ... against third parties" (Act, s. 9). The possession required by s. 24 of the Act should be unequivocal. Expressly, it cannot be by the debtor's agent (s. 24). I have difficulty seeing how the receiver's possession could be to a person informed of the basic facts that "reasonable, clear and actual possession" of the creditor which satisfies one of the main objects of perfection—to inform outsiders: see Catzman, F.M., *Personal Property Security Law in Ontario* (1976), at 121. The bank is really seeking the best of both worlds and in this respect the following words of Houlden JA in *Peat Marwick* are apposite [29 OR (2d), at 346]:

> If the bank chooses to provide in its debenture that the receiver and manager shall be deemed to be the agent of the debtor company, then it must not only take the benefits, but it must also accept detriments which flow from such a provision.

I turn now to the trial Judge's opinion that the bank took possession of the inventory on March 20 when "a decision was made to realize on the security and liquidate the assets." The trial Judge in this passage was adverting to the passage in the judgment in *Peat Marwick* which I have just quoted. With respect, I think the trial Judge applied the analysis in *Peat Marwick* beyond its proper scope. It is only "in realizing" that the receiver acts as the creditor's agent—to give commercial efficacy to the security agreement, i.e., so that title may be conferred on the purchaser free of encumbrance. The mere decision to realize falls short of realizing on the security.

In any event, I think the evidence does not support a conclusion in favour of either the realization or a decision to realize on Sperry's inventory. I have earlier quoted Thorne Riddell's letter of March 17, 1980 to Sperry. It clearly indicated that as of that date no decision had been made to realize on the Sperry inventory and there is nothing of sufficient weight in the subsequent evidence to deflect the inference that this position continued to the commencement of the action. Further, it may be noted that if the bank or receiver had decided to sell the Sperry inventory it did not manifest this decision in the form of a notice to Sperry under s. 59(5) of the Act.

Appeal dismissed.

NOTES AND QUESTIONS

1) In *Re Darzinskas*, Steele J notes the contrasting provisions in ss. 24 and 58(b) of the Act (now ss. 22 and 62(b)), but without deciding whether a secured party's taking possession of the collateral on the debtor's default also satisfies the perfection requirements in s. 24. The point was also left open by Morden JA in *Sperry v. CIBC*. In his "Comment" in (1982-83), 7 *CBLJ* 234, J.A. Carfagnini argues that the perfection requirements in s. 24 should not be satisfied. He relies heavily on the requirement in the concluding lines of s. 24 that possession perfects a security interest "only during its actual holding as collateral" (this has changed slightly in s. 22 of the new Act, and now reads: "but only while it is actually held as collateral," but no change in substance was intended). He reasons that collateral that is seized on default is possessed for purposes of realization and is not to be held as collateral. Do you find this reasoning persuasive? It appealed to Nobleton J in *Deloitte, Haskins & Sells Ltd. v. Folden* (1986), 6 PPSAC 102 (Sask.), but it was rejected, at least implicitly, in *Re Charron* (1984), 4 PPSAC 228 (Ont.), *Re Olmstead* (1984), 4 PPSAC 220 (Ont.), and in *Sifton Credit Union Ltd. v. Barber* (1986), 6 PPSAC 9 (Man.). In all these cases, seizure of the collateral on the debtor's default was held to perfect the security interest by possession.

The Ontario Advisory Committee was also not persuaded by Carfagnini's distinction, but thought the position should be clarified. Accordingly, s. 22 of the new Act speaks of "possession or repossession" of the collateral by the secured party as perfecting a security interest in the described collateral.

2) However, this amendment does not resolve the question of the meaning of "but only while it is actually held as collateral." This qualifier does not appear in UCC 9-305 and US courts have held that it does not matter in which capacity the secured party holds the collateral so long as he is lawfully in possession of it. See, for example, *Raleigh Industries of America Inc. v. Tassone*, 141 Cal. Rep. 641 (1977), and *In re Chapman*, 5 UCCR 649 (Ref. Bkcy WD Mich. 1968). Do you find these rulings objectionable? Should the concluding words in s. 22 be deleted? Catzman, at 121, suggests their purpose is to establish the time of perfection where the secured party held the collateral in an earlier capacity before the security agreement was concluded—for example, goods held by a bailee. Is this persuasive? Is s. 22 concerned with the *time* of perfection?

3) SP, a truck dealer, has sold a truck to D on a conditional sale basis. D returns the truck to SP for a checkup under the manufacturer's warranty. While the truck is in the dealer's possession, D becomes bankrupt. Does SP have a perfected security interest by possession under the Ontario Act?

4) Note the provisions in s. 26 with respect to perfection by possession where the goods are in the hands of a bailee. For the distinction between a negotiable and non-negotiable warehouse receipt, see, for example, *Warehouse Receipts Act*, RSO 1990, c. W.3, ss. 19-24. See also Ziegel and Duggan, *Commercial and Consumer Sales Transactions*, 4th ed. (Toronto: Emond Montgomery, 2002), c. 11. None of the provinces has adopted comprehensive legislation on documents of title comparable to Article 7 of the UCC.

5) *Field warehousing.* Perfection by possession is sometimes used in the United States in connection with an inventory type of financing referred to as "field warehousing." Part of the debtor's business premises is cordoned off into a locked area under the exclusive control

of an agent of the secured party and appropriate notices are posted around the area. The agent issues warehouse receipts (a type of "document of title" as defined in OPPSA s. 1(1)) to the secured creditor for goods supplied to the debtor and placed in the area (called a "field warehouse"). The secured party advances money to the debtor against the warehouse receipts. Since the secured party holds the warehouse receipts, the debtor cannot deal with the goods without his consent. Besides providing a method of perfection, field warehousing thus also provides an effective means of protecting the inventory financer against unauthorized dealings with the collateral. Field warehousing has occasionally been used in Canada. For early examples, see *Banque Nationale v. Royer* (1910), 20 Que. KB 351 and *In re Wedlock Ltd.*, [1926] 2 DLR 263 (PEI). As to field warehousing in general, see D.M. Friedman, "Field Warehousing" (1942), 42 *Colum. L Rev.* 991. See also *Bostian v. Park National Bank of Kansas City*, 226 F2d 753 (8th Cir. 1955), and in particular its discussion as to whether access to the field warehouse by the debtor destroys the exclusiveness of the secured party's possession and the perfection of his security interest.

III. PERFECTION BY CONTROL

John Cameron, "Secured Transactions Under Ontario's Securities Transfer Act, 2006"
(2007), 22 *BFLR* 309, at 310-14, 321-26, and 344-347 (footnotes omitted)

Summary of Important Rules

There is an enormous amount of detail and nuances in the STA [*Securities Transfer Act*, SO 2006, c. 8], together with the related PPSA amendments. Simplifying greatly, I summarize the most important rules in practice as follows:

1. *Methods of Perfection:* Apart from some special rules, there are three methods to perfect a security interest in investment property (which includes securities):

(a) *Control:* "Control" (defined below) is the best method to perfect a security interest in both the direct and indirect holding systems [for an explanation of the direct and indirect holding systems, see Chapter 2, Part III].

(b) *Possession:* Possession of a certificated security can perfect a security interest in the direct holding system.

(c) *Registration:* Registration of a financing statement can perfect any security interest in investment property in both the direct and indirect holding systems.

2. *Meaning of "Control":* In essence, "control" means the secured party has the ability to transfer the investment property without further action by the debtor.

3. *Control in the Direct System:* The method to obtain "control" varies, depending whether the security is certificated or uncertificated:

(a) *Certificated Securities:* If the security is evidenced by a certificate, a secured party obtains control through delivery to it of the certificate plus (if the certificate is in registered form) (i) an appropriate endorsement, or (ii) arranging for the issuer to register the security in the name of the secured party. Mere possession of a security certificate in registered form suffices to perfect a security interest, but "control" is much better. ...

(b) *Uncertificated Securities:* If the security is not evidenced by a certificate, control is obtained by (i) arranging for the issuer to register the security in the name of the secured party, (ii) obtaining a control agreement from the issuer, or (iii) someone else having control for the benefit of the secured party.

(c) *Control Agreement:* In the direct holding system, a control agreement is an agreement between the issuer, the secured party and the debtor under which the issuer agrees that it will comply with instructions from the secured party without further consent of the debtor.

(d) *Not Necessarily Exclusive Control:* A control agreement need not give exclusive control to a secured party. A debtor can retain rights to give instructions, and other secured parties can obtain (or may already have) a concurrent right to give instructions.

4. *Security Entitlements:* Where securities are held by a securities intermediary, the investor acquires a bundle of property and contract rights when the securities intermediary records that it holds a security or other financial asset in the investor's account. That bundle of rights is called a "security entitlement." A security entitlement is not bought or sold. Instead, when an investor sells a security in the indirect system, the securities intermediary extinguishes the investor's security entitlement, and (if the related security remains in the indirect system), a new security entitlement is created in favour of the purchaser.

5. *Control in the Indirect System:* A secured party obtains "control" of a security entitlement by (i) arranging for the securities intermediary to record the secured party as the entitlement holder, (ii) obtaining a control agreement from the securities intermediary, or (iii) someone else having control for the benefit of the secured party.

(a) *Control Agreement:* In the indirect holding system, a control agreement is an agreement between the securities intermediary, the secured party and the debtor under which the securities intermediary agrees that it will comply with instructions from the secured party without the further consent of the debtor.

(b) *Not Necessarily Exclusive Control:* A control agreement need not give exclusive control to the secured party. A debtor can retain rights to give instructions, and other secured parties can obtain (or may already have) a concurrent right to give instructions.

6. *Key Priority Rules:* The key rules are:

(a) *Control Trumps Non-Control:* A security interest perfected by control has priority over another security interest perfected otherwise than by control.

(b) *Two Security Interests Perfected by Control:* If two or more security interests are perfected by control, they rank in priority by first in time to obtain control.

(c) *Securities Intermediary Priority:* Despite the above rules, in the indirect holding system a securities intermediary with a security interest in a security entitlement created by it has priority over other secured parties, unless the intermediary otherwise agrees.

...

Perfection in Direct Holding System

In order for a security interest to be perfected, the PPSA requires that the security interest must be attached, and that all steps necessary for perfection under the PPSA have been completed. Apart from a special rule for automatic perfection of a security interest created by a broker or securities intermediary and a special rule for automatic perfection of the security interest created by statute when a certificated security is delivered between persons in the business of dealing in such securities, a security interest in a security may be perfected by three methods:

(a) "control" of the security;

(b) in the case of a certificated security, delivery of the security to the secured party under section 68 of the STA; or

(c) registration of a financing statement under the PPSA.

Each of these three methods of perfection is described further below.

Perfection by "Control" in Direct Holding System

As the Comment* notes, obtaining "control" means a secured party has taken whatever steps are necessary to place itself in a position where it can have the securities sold, without further action by the owner. The necessary steps depend on the nature of security, and the manner in which it is held.

Certificated Securities: The rules for a secured party to obtain control of a certificated security are set forth in section 23 of the STA, as follows:

(1) A purchaser has control of a certificated security that is in bearer form if the certificated security is delivered to the purchaser.

(2) A purchaser has control of a certificated security that is in registered form if the certificated security is delivered to the purchaser and,

(a) the security certificate is endorsed to the purchaser or in blank by an effective endorsement; or

(b) the security certificate is registered in the name of the purchaser at the time of the original issue or registration of transfer by the issuer.

In the case of a bearer security, "control" occurs when the steps necessary for delivery of the certificated security to the secured party have been completed, as described in section 68 of the STA ... . In the case of a registered security, there are two requirements. First, the certificated security must be delivered to the secured party, as described in section 68(1) of the STA. Second, the certificated security must be either endorsed to the secured party or in blank, or registered in the name of the secured party by the issuer. The rules governing the effectiveness of an endorsement are set forth in sections 29 to 32 of the STA.

---

* Comments accompanying the Uniform Securities Transfer Act approved at the Uniform Law Conference of Canada Annual Meeting, August 22-26, 2004.

Unlike the rule in section 22(1) of the PPSA for perfection by possession of other collateral (such as goods), section 22(2) of the PPSA and section 68(1) of the STA do not preclude perfection by possession of a certificated security on behalf of a secured party through an agent of the debtor.

Uncertificated Securities: The rules for a secured party to obtain control of an uncertificated security are set forth in section 24 of the STA. Section 24(1) provides that:

> (1) A purchaser has control of an uncertificated security if,
> (a) the uncertificated security is delivered to the purchaser; or
> (b) the issuer has agreed that the issuer will comply with instructions that are originated by the purchaser without the further consent of the registered owner.

A secured party obtains control of an uncertificated security by delivery if the issuer registers the secured party as the owner, or another person (other than a securities intermediary) either becomes the registered owner on behalf of the secured party or, having previously become the registered owner, acknowledges that the person holds the security for the secured party.

A secured party can also obtain control of an uncertificated security which remains registered in the name of the debtor, if the issuer agrees that it will comply with the secured party's instructions without the further consent of the debtor. That agreement would be embodied in a "control agreement" between the issuer, the secured party and the debtor (as registered owner). Together with the new priority rules in the PPSA, these new rules will facilitate the perfection of a security interest in mutual fund units, which are typically uncertificated securities.

The Comment notes that, for a secured party to have control under section 24(1)(b), "… it is essential that the issuer … actually be a party to the agreement" and that a power of attorney authorizing the secured party to act in the name of the debtor is not sufficient, without the issuer's agreement. It is also clear that more than one person may have control of the same uncertificated security at the same time, where control is obtained by way of a control agreement.

Section 24(2) of the STA clarifies that a secured party can obtain perfection by way of a control agreement even though the debtor is permitted to make substitutions, give instructions to the issuer, or otherwise deal with the uncertificated security. Section 24(2) provides that:

> (2) A purchaser to whom subsection (1) applies in relation to an uncertificated security has control of the uncertificated security even if the registered owner retains the right,
> (a) to make substitutions for the uncertificated security;
> (b) to originate instructions to the issuer; or
> (c) to otherwise deal with the uncertificated security.

The Comment also notes that there is no "… requirement that the [secured party's] powers be unconditional, provided that further consent of the [registered owner] is not a condition."

Perfection by Delivery of Certificated Security in Direct Holding System

As noted above, the PPSA allows a secured party to perfect a security interest in a certificated security by delivery. The rules for a secured party to obtain delivery of a certificated security are set forth in section 68(1) of the STA ... . Mere "delivery" differs from "control" of a registered security in the sense that the security certificate is not endorsed to the secured party or in blank, nor registered in the name of [the] secured party.

Perfection by Registration in Direct Holding System

The PPSA rules governing registration of a financing statement remain unaffected by the STA. However, the explanatory notes which accompany the first reading version of Bill 152 indicate that the system for classifying collateral, which involved checking up to five boxes on the financing statement (i.e., "consumer goods," "inventory," "equipment," "accounts" and "other") will be replaced with a system that requires the secured party to use a narrative description that describes the collateral by item or type. These rules will require a secured party to exercise more care when filing a financing statement, but will make it easier for persons searching for PPSA registrations to determine the scope of the security interests perfected by registration. The Ministry has indicated that it will take some period of time (perhaps a year or more) to change the PPSA computer system.

· · ·

Priority in Direct Holding System

The PPSA provides a set of rules to govern the priority among security interests in the same collateral. The STA and PPSA also provide a set of "cut-off" rules which cut-off the claims of others, the most significant of which is the "protected purchaser" rule.

· · ·

The priority rules for security interests in "investment property" (which includes a "security") are set forth in section 30.1, summarized as follows:

- A security interest of a secured party having control of investment property has priority over a security interest of a secured party that does not have control of the investment property.
- A security interest in a certificated security in registered form which is perfected by taking delivery under subsection 22(2) and not by control under section 22.1 has priority over a conflicting security interest perfected by a method other than control. In this situation, the secured party to whom the certificated security has been delivered has not arranged (i) for the security certificate to be endorsed to the secured party, or in blank, or (ii) for the security to be registered in the name of the secured party.
- Where two or more secured parties each have control of a security, the security interests rank according to priority in time.
- In all other cases, priority among conflicting security interests in investment property is governed by section 30 of the PPSA.

The definition of "purchase-money security interest" has been amended to exclude investment property. Consequently, a secured party cannot rely on the PMSI rules in section 33 of the PPSA to obtain priority over other secured creditors.

In summary, control of a security offers the best protection for a secured party, especially if the means of control excludes the possibility of another secured party obtaining control of the same security.

...

Perfection in Indirect Holding System

As with the direct holding system, in order for a security interest to be perfected, the PPSA requires that the security interest must be attached, and that all steps necessary for perfection under the PPSA have been completed. Apart from a special rule for automatic perfection of a security interest created by a broker or securities intermediary and a special rule for automatic perfection of the security interest created by statute when a certificated security or other financial asset in writing (e.g., money market instruments, commercial paper, certificates of deposit and bankers acceptances) is delivered between persons in the business of dealing in such securities or financial assets, a security interest in investment property may be perfected by two methods:

(a) "control" of the investment property; or
(b) registration of a financing statement under the PPSA.

Each of these two methods of perfection is described further below.

Section 19.1(1) provides that perfection of a security interest in a securities account also perfects a security interest in the security entitlements carried in the securities account. This rule corresponds to the rule for attachment in section 11(4) of the PPSA, and like that rule presumably exists just for greater certainty.

Perfection by "Control" in Indirect Holding System

Clause 1(2)(c) of the PPSA indicates that a secured party has control of a security entitlement if the secured party has control in the manner provided under section 25 or 26 of the STA. Clause 1(2)(e) of the PPSA states that a secured party having control of all security entitlements in a securities account has control over the securities account.

Three methods of obtaining control—Section 25(1) of the STA provides as follows:

(1) A purchaser has control of a security entitlement if,
    (a) the purchaser becomes the entitlement holder;
    (b) the securities intermediary has agreed that it will comply with entitlement orders that are originated by the purchaser without the further consent of the entitlement holder; or
    (c) another person has control of the security entitlement on behalf of the purchaser or, having previously obtained control of the security entitlement, acknowledges that the person has control on behalf of the purchaser.

The rules in section 25 allow the secured party to obtain control in any one of three ways: (a) the secured party can become the entitlement holder; (b) the secured party, the securities intermediary and the debtor can enter into a control agreement (discussed below) under which the securities intermediary agrees to comply with entitlement orders from the secured party without any further consent of the debtor; or (c) a third party may obtain control on behalf of the secured party (or, if the third party has control, it may acknowledge that it has control on behalf of the secured party).

Automatic control for a securities intermediary—If the securities intermediary is the secured party in respect of its own entitlement holder, it has control automatically by virtue of section 26 of the STA, which provides:

> If an interest in a security entitlement is granted by the entitlement holder to the entitlement holder's own securities intermediary, the securities intermediary has control of the security entitlement.

Control agreements—A control agreement exists where a securities intermediary agrees with a secured party that the securities intermediary will comply with instructions originated by the secured party to deal with a security entitlement without the further consent of the entitlement holder. The entitlement holder should be a party to the agreement because, among other reasons, section 28(1) of the STA prohibits a securities intermediary from entering into a control agreement without the consent of the entitlement holder. It is clear that more than one person may have control of a security entitlement at the same time—i.e., control need not be exclusive in order to comply with the STA.

Section 25(2) of the STA clarifies that a secured party retains control even if the entitlement holder retains the right to make substitutions, continue to give entitlement orders or otherwise deal with the security entitlement, as follows:

> (2) A purchaser to whom subsection (1) applies in relation to a security entitlement has control of the security entitlement even if the entitlement holder retains the right,
>
> > (a) to make substitutions for the security entitlement;
> >
> > (b) to originate entitlement orders to the securities intermediary; or
> >
> > (c) to otherwise deal with the security entitlement.

The Comment also notes that there is no "... requirement that the [secured party's] powers be unconditional, provided that further consent of the [registered owner] is not a condition." In particular, example 11 in the Comment confirms that a secured party retains control even if its right to give an entitlement order to the securities intermediary is conditioned on the debtor's default. The Comment states that because the securities intermediary's agreement to act on the secured party's entitlement orders is not conditioned on the debtor's further consent, the secured party has control of the securities entitlement.

Beyond these essential elements for perfection by control, there are several issues which a secured party and its lawyers will wish to consider including in a control agreement to protect the interests of a secured party. Some of these will require negotiation, especially with the securities intermediary. ...

Perfection by Registration in Indirect Holding System

As mentioned above, the PPSA rules governing registration of a financing statement remain unaffected by the STA. However, the explanatory notes which accompanied Bill 152 indicate that the system for classifying collateral, which involved checking up to five boxes on the financing statement (i.e., "consumer goods," "inventory," "equipment," "accounts" and "other") will be replaced with a system that requires the secured party to use a narrative description that describes the collateral by item or type. These rules will require a secured party to exercise more care when filing a financing statement, but will make it easier for persons searching for PPSA registrations to determine the scope of the security interests perfected by registration. As mentioned above, it will be some period of time (perhaps over a year) before the Ministry completes the computer changes necessary for these new rules.

...

Priority in Indirect Holding System

The PPSA provides a set of rules to govern the priority among security interests in the same collateral. ... The PPSA priority rules are summarized below.

The priority rules for security interests in a security entitlement and security account are set forth in section 30.1, summarized as follows:

- A security interest of a secured party having control of investment property has priority over a security interest of a secured party that does not have control of the investment property.
- Subject to the special priority for a security interest held by a securities intermediary (described in the next "bullet point"), where two or more secured parties each have control of a security entitlement, the security interests rank according to priority in time of (i) the secured party becoming the entitlement holder, (ii) the securities intermediary's agreement to comply with the secured party's entitlement orders, or (iii) the secured party obtaining control through another person who holds the security entitlement on behalf of the secured party. This means, for example, if two secured parties have obtained control in the same security entitlement by way of a control agreement, then the first secured party to obtain a control agreement has priority over the other secured party.
- A security interest in favour of a securities intermediary in a security entitlement created by it or a securities account maintained by it has priority over a conflicting security interest held by another secured party.
- Conflicting security interests granted by a broker or securities intermediary which are perfected without control rank equally.
- In all other cases, priority among conflicting security interests in investment property is governed by section 30 of the PPSA.

As noted above, the PMSI rules in section 33 of the PPSA are no longer available for investment property.

In summary, control of a security entitlement offers the best protection for a secured party, especially where the secured party becomes the entitlement holder.

IV. CONTINUITY OF PERFECTION

OPPSA s. 21(1) provides as follows:

> 21(1) If a security interest is originally perfected in any way permitted under this Act and is again perfected in some way under this Act without an intermediate period when it was unperfected, the security interest shall be deemed to be perfected continuously for the purposes of this Act.

Section 30(2) provides that:

> 30(2) … a continuously perfected security interest shall be treated at all times as if perfected by registration, if it was originally so perfected, and it shall be treated at all times as if perfected otherwise than by registration if it was originally perfected otherwise than by registration.

Consider the following example.

SP1 takes a security interest in D's truck and perfects by possession on May 1. On June 30, SP1 registers a financing statement and gives the truck back to D. Meanwhile, on June 15, SP2 takes a security interest in the same truck and registers a financing statement. On August 31, D defaults against both SP1 and SP2 and they both claim the truck. Who has priority?

The analysis goes as follows. As a consequence of ss. 21(1) and 30(2), SP1's security interest is deemed to have been continuously perfected by possession from May 1. SP2's security interest was perfected by registration on June 15. The governing priority rule is in s. 30(1), rule 2 which provides, more or less, that in a competition between a security interest perfected by registration and a security interest perfected otherwise than by registration, priority turns on the order of events. Since, in our example, SP1's security interest was perfected by possession before SP2 registered a financing statement, SP1 has priority. The justification for this outcome is straightforward: since SP1's security interest was at all relevant times perfected, the switch in methods of perfection does not prejudice third parties.

> Now assume that SP1 gives the truck back to D on June 30, but does not get around to registering a financing statement until August 15 (all other facts remaining the same). Note that SP2 is not prejudiced by SP1's delay in registration, because SP1 was perfected by possession on the date of SP2's transaction with D and this should have been enough to alert SP2 to SP1's security interest. But does s. 21(1) apply?

Section 30(6) provides in part as follows:

> where a security interest that is perfected by registration becomes unperfected and is again perfected by registration, the security interest shall be deemed to have been continuously perfected from the time of first perfection.

> Can SP1 rely on this provision? If neither s. 21(1) nor s. 30(6) apply, what is the outcome of the dispute? (Section 30(6) is discussed further in Chapter 7, Part VI.)

Section 21(2) provides that an assignee of a security interest succeeds in so far as its perfection is concerned to the position of the assignor at the time of the assignment. Consider the following example.

Seller supplies Debtor with a truck under a conditional sale agreement and registers a financing statement on May 1. On June 1 Seller assigns the chattel paper to SP1. On August 31, Debtor gives SP2 a security interest in the truck and SP2 registers a financing statement. Debtor defaults against SP1 and SP2 and they both claim the truck. Who has priority?

By virtue of s. 21(2), SP1 inherits Seller's perfected status in relation to the truck. Seller perfected by registration on May 1. SP2 perfected by registration, but only on August 31. Therefore, SP1 has priority over SP2 (s. 30(1), rule 1). The thinking behind s. 21(2) is that SP1 should not have to register a new financing statement in relation to the truck, because there is no potential prejudice to third parties. For example, if SP2 had done a register search, it would have discovered Seller's security interest and further inquiry would have revealed the assignment.

Note that while SP1 does not have to register a financing statement for *the truck*, it does need to perfect its security interest in *the chattel paper* either by taking possession of the chattel paper or otherwise by registration. Otherwise SP1 will be at risk if Seller assigns the chattel paper a second time to SP3. For treatment of the rules relating to disputes over chattel paper, see Chapter 11.

V. CONSEQUENCES OF NON-PERFECTION

A. Introduction

Non-perfection does not result in avoidance of the security interest altogether. Instead, failure to perfect means that the security interest will be "subordinate to" or "ineffective against" the categories of claimant listed in s. 20(1), namely: (1) a person holding a perfected security interest in the same collateral; (2) lienholders and persons having priority under any other Act; (3) execution creditors and such like; (4) a trustee in bankruptcy and other creditors' representative; and (5) a transferee of the collateral.

B. Lienholders

In this context, "lienholder" means a person holding a non-consensual security interest; in other words, a security interest given under a statute or rule of law. The reason for subordinating an unperfected security interest to the holder of a perfected security interest in the same collateral is reasonably self-evident. But what is the reason for preferring lienholders over an unperfected security interest? Is it assumed to prejudice the lienholder whose lien arises before the security interest is perfected? How is a government agency that is given a statutory lien for monies owing to it by the debtor prejudiced by an unperfected security interest? "Lien" is not defined but presumably means the right to retain or seize all or some of the debtor's assets and to sell them to satisfy the debtor's obligation to the lienholder. Note, too, s. 20(2) on the time of attachment of a statutory lien.

C. Trustee in Bankruptcy

OPPSA s. 20(1)(b) provides that an unperfected security interest is not effective against a person who represents the creditors of the debtor, including an assignee for the benefit of creditors and a trustee in bankruptcy. This provision is initially puzzling. A trustee in bankruptcy has no dealings with the debtor on the strength of what the register may or may not say. In other words, non-perfection does not prejudice the trustee. This makes the trustee different from the other categories of claimant listed in s. 20(1) (competing secured creditors, purchasers, execution creditors, and so on). It is easy enough to understand why an unperfected security interest should be ineffective against these parties. But why should it be ineffective against the trustee? *Re Giffen*, extracted below, provides the answer and also deals with the constitutional implications of the provision.

Re Giffen
[1998] 1 SCR 91

IACOBUCCI J: [1] The principal question raised by this appeal is whether s. 20(b)(i) of the *Personal Property Security Act*, SBC 1989, c. 36 ("PPSA"), can render a lessor's unperfected security interest in personal property ineffective against the rights acquired in the property by the trustee in bankruptcy, which finds its authority under the *Bankruptcy and Insolvency Act*, RSC, 1985, c. B-3 ("BIA"). I conclude that s. 20(b)(i) operates, on the present facts, to defeat the unperfected security interest of the respondent Telecom Leasing Canada (TLC) Limited (the "lessor"), in favour of the interest acquired by the appellant R. West & Associates Inc. (the "trustee").

[2] Constitutional questions were raised in this appeal; however, in my view of the case, it is not necessary to address these issues. A reading of the provisions of the BIA and the PPSA in question reveals that no conflict arises in the operation of the legislation.

1. Facts

[3] On October 27, 1992, the lessor leased a 1993 Saturn car to the BC Telephone Company, which in turn leased the car to one of its employees, Carol Anne Giffen (the "bankrupt"). The bankrupt and her employer were parties to the agreement of lease entitled "Employee Agreement Personal Vehicle Lease Program/Flex Lease Program." The term of the lease was for more than one year. The lease gave the bankrupt the option of purchasing the vehicle from the lessor.

[4] Although the lessor was not a party to the agreement, it played an important role in the arrangement contemplated by the agreement. More specifically, the lessor received a deposit from the bankrupt, it fixed the lease rates, and it was entitled to receive payments directly from the lessee/bankrupt if her employer stopped paying her. Further, the

lessor and the bankrupt were named as the owners of the vehicle in the registration and insurance documents relating to the vehicle; the lessor was described as the "lessor" and the bankrupt was described as the "lessee."

[5] The bankrupt made an assignment in bankruptcy on October 12, 1993. Neither the lessor nor the BC Telephone Company had registered financing statements under the PPSA in respect of their leases. The failure to register meant that the lessor's security interest in the car was not perfected, as defined in the PPSA, at the time of the assignment in bankruptcy.

[6] The appellant was appointed as the trustee in bankruptcy. The lessor seized the vehicle and sold it with the trustee's consent; proceeds of $10,154.54 were held in trust by the lessor's counsel. The trustee subsequently brought a motion for an order that it was entitled to the proceeds of sale relying on s. 20(b)(i) of the PPSA. The lessor opposed the claim on the grounds that the bankrupt never owned the car and that the trustee could not have a better claim to the car than the bankrupt had.

[7] Hood J of the Supreme Court of British Columbia held that, by virtue of s. 20(b)(i) of the PPSA, the unperfected security interest of the lessor was of no effect as against the trustee. Hood J ordered that the proceeds from the sale of the vehicle be paid over to the trustee. The lessor appealed to the Court of Appeal for British Columbia; the Attorney General of British Columbia was granted leave to intervene as a party respondent in the appeal. The Court of Appeal allowed the appeal and held that the proceeds properly belonged to the lessor.

2. Relevant Statutory Provisions

[8] *Personal Property Security Act*, SBC 1989, c. 36

2(1) Subject to section 4, this Act applies

(a) to every transaction that in substance creates a security interest, without regard to its form and without regard to the person who has title to the collateral, and

(b) without limiting the generality of paragraph (a), to a chattel mortgage, a conditional sale, a floating charge, a pledge, a trust indenture, a trust receipt, an assignment, a consignment, a lease, a trust, and a transfer of chattel paper where they secure payment or performance of an obligation.

3. Subject to sections 4 and 55, this Act applies to

(a) a transfer of an account or chattel paper,

(b) a commercial consignment, and

(c) a lease for a term of more than one year

that do not secure payment or performance of an obligation.

20. A security interest …

(b) in collateral is not effective against

(i) a trustee in bankruptcy if the security interest is unperfected at the date of the bankruptcy, …

21. Where the interest of a lessor under a lease for a term of more than one year or of a consignor under a commercial consignment is not effective against a judgment creditor under section 20(a) or a trustee or liquidator under section 20(b), the lessor or consignor is deemed, as against the lessee or consignee, as the case may be, to have suffered, immediately

before the seizure of the leased or consigned goods or the date of the bankruptcy or winding-up order, damages in an amount equal to

(a) the value of the leased or consigned goods at the date of the seizure, bankruptcy or winding-up order, and

(b) the amount of loss other than that referred to in paragraph (a) that results from the termination of the lease or consignment.

Bankruptcy and Insolvency Act, RSC, 1985, c. B-3

30(1) The trustee may, with the permission of the inspectors, do all or any of the following things: …

(k) elect to retain for the whole [or] part of its unexpired term, or to assign, surrender or disclaim any lease of, or other temporary interest in, any property of the bankrupt; …

67(1) The property of a bankrupt divisible among his creditors shall not comprise

(a) property held by the bankrupt in trust for any other person,

(b) any property that as against the bankrupt is exempt from execution or seizure under the laws of the province within which the property is situated and within which the bankrupt resides,

but it shall comprise

(c) all property wherever situated of the bankrupt at the date of his bankruptcy or that may be acquired by or devolve on him before his discharge, and

(d) such powers in or over or in respect of the property as might have been exercised by the bankrupt for his own benefit.

71(1) A bankruptcy shall be deemed to have relation back to, and to commence at the time of the filing of, the petition on which a receiving order is made or of the filing of an assignment with the official receiver.

(2) On a receiving order being made or an assignment being filed with an official receiver, a bankrupt ceases to have any capacity to dispose of or otherwise deal with his property, which shall, subject to this Act and to the rights of secured creditors, forthwith pass to and vest in the trustee named in the receiving order or assignment, and in any case of change of trustee the property shall pass from trustee to trustee without any conveyance, assignment or transfer.

72(1) The provisions of this Act shall not be deemed to abrogate or supersede the substantive provisions of any other law or statute relating to property and civil rights that are not in conflict with this Act, and the trustee is entitled to avail himself of all rights and remedies provided by that law or statute as supplementary to and in addition to the rights and remedies provided by this Act.

(2) No receiving order, assignment or other document made or executed under the authority of this Act shall, except as otherwise provided in this Act, be within the operation of any legislative enactment in force at any time in any province relating to deeds, mortgages, judgments, bills of sale, chattel mortgages, property or registration of documents affecting title to or liens or charges on real or personal property.

81(1) Where a person claims any property, or interest therein, in the possession of a bankrupt at the time of the bankruptcy, he shall file with the trustee a proof of claim verified by affidavit giving the grounds on which the claim is based and sufficient particulars to enable the property to be identified.

(2) The trustee with whom a proof of claim is filed under subsection (1) shall within fifteen days thereafter or within fifteen days after the first meeting of creditors, whichever is the later, either admit the claim and deliver possession of the property to the claimant or give notice in writing to the claimant that the claim is disputed with his reasons therefor, and, unless the claimant appeals therefrom to the court within fifteen days after the mailing of the notice of dispute, he shall be deemed to have abandoned or relinquished all his right to or interest in the property to the trustee who thereupon may sell or dispose of the property free of any lien, right, title or interest of the claimant.

(3) The onus of establishing a claim to or in property under this section is on the claimant.

(4) The trustee may give notice in writing to any person to prove his claim to or in property under this section, and, unless that person files with the trustee a proof of claim in the prescribed form within fifteen days after the mailing of the notice, the trustee may thereupon with the leave of the court sell or dispose of the property free of any lien, right, title or interest of that person.

(5) No proceedings shall be instituted to establish a claim to, or to recover any right or interest in, any property in the possession of a bankrupt at the time of the bankruptcy, except as provided in this section.

(6) Nothing in this section shall be construed as extending the rights of any person other than the trustee.

136(1) Subject to the rights of secured creditors, the proceeds realized from the property of a bankrupt shall be applied in priority of payment as follows. ...

3. Judicial History

A. British Columbia Supreme Court (1994), 90 BCLR (2d) 326

[9] Hood J held that the trustee was entitled to the proceeds from the car. He began his analysis by examining the relationship between the parties and found that the respondent was the lessor and the bankrupt was the lessee of the car, even though the respondent was not party to the lease agreement. He also found that the lease agreement, which was for a period of more than one year, was a "security interest" for the purposes of the PPSA.

[10] Hood J analysed the holding of the Saskatchewan Court of Appeal in *International Harvester Credit Corp. of Canada Ltd. v. Bell's Dairy Ltd. (Trustee of)* (1986), 61 CBR (NS) 193. The Saskatchewan Court of Appeal found that a trustee in bankruptcy may acquire a higher interest in property than that enjoyed by the bankrupt through the operation of the PPSA. The court also concluded, in accordance with the Saskatchewan PPSA, that a lessor's security interest is subordinate to the interest of a trustee in bankruptcy where the lessor failed to perfect its interest. Hood J added that the trustee's claim in the present case was even stronger than that of the trustee in *International Harvester* since s. 20(b)(i) of the PPSA provides that an unperfected security interest will be "not effective against" a trustee in bankruptcy whereas the Saskatchewan equivalent provides

that an unperfected security interest will be "subordinate to" the interest of a trustee in bankruptcy.

[11] Hood J held that the PPSA applied on the facts and in so doing he rejected the lessor's argument that this was a matter of exclusive federal jurisdiction governed by the BIA. He noted that the constitutionality of the PPSA was not in issue before him, and that in *Paccar Financial Services Ltd. v. Sinco Trucking Ltd. (Trustee of)*, [1989] 3 WWR 481 (Sask. CA), the Saskatchewan equivalent to s. 20(b)(i) was held to be constitutionally valid.

[12] The learned trial judge rejected the lessor's argument that the trustee had disclaimed the property by failing to elect to retain the lease under s. 30(1)(k) of the BIA. He found that this argument ignored the statutory rights granted to the trustee under s. 20(b)(i) of the PPSA. Hood J also dismissed the lessor's argument that a resulting trust existed between the bankrupt and the lessor, and therefore the vehicle did not form part of the bankrupt's estate, as provided by s. 67(1)(a) of the BIA. In Hood J's view, the equitable principle of resulting trust could not usurp the clear provisions of the PPSA and the rights it conferred upon the trustee. The lessor had also argued that the trustee was estopped from claiming that the vehicle was part of the bankrupt's estate, given that the bankrupt signed a statement of affairs which referred to the vehicle as "fully encumbered." Hood J stated that the bankrupt's conduct or view of her interest was not determinative of the question of law at issue.

[13] Hood J concluded that the trustee was entitled to the net sale proceeds from the vehicle, together with an accounting.

B. British Columbia Court of Appeal (1996), 16 BCLR (3d) 29

[14] Finch JA, Macfarlane and Wood JJA concurring, overturned Hood J and held that the lessor was entitled to the proceeds of the car.

[15] Finch JA disagreed with the reasoning and the result in *International Harvester*, which had been followed by the trial judge. In his view, both *International Harvester* and Hood J's decision in the case on appeal failed to account for the role of the BIA in the circumstances of a bankruptcy. Section 67 of the BIA provides that the trustee in bankruptcy shall receive only the "property of the bankrupt" thus there was no legitimate basis for granting to a trustee in bankruptcy a greater claim to the property than that which the bankrupt enjoyed. Finch JA held (at p. 40) that to allow the trustee a greater claim to the property than the bankrupt had would "overlook fundamental concepts of bankruptcy law" as expressed in *Fleeming v. Howden* (1868), LR 1 Sc. & Div. 372 (HL), and *Flintoft v. Royal Bank of Canada*, [1964] SCR 631.

[16] Finch JA rejected the Saskatchewan Court of Appeal's characterization of the trustee as "a representative of the creditors of the bankrupt," and he found that the Saskatchewan Court erred in relying on *Re Perepeluk; Canadian Imperial Bank of Commerce v. Touche Ross Ltd.*, [1986] 2 WWR 631 (Sask. CA), as authority for that proposition. He did not find that *Perepeluk* "[laid] down any broad statement of principle to the effect that the trustee's obligation is to the creditors as opposed to the bankrupt" (p. 42). Further, Finch JA noted that the Saskatchewan Court of Appeal failed to consider that a

trustee is an officer of the court, appointed to stand in the bankrupt's shoes and to represent the bankrupt's interests, even where those interests are adverse to the interests of the creditors. With these principles in mind, Finch JA underlined that the trustee could only succeed to the rights of the bankrupt.

[17] Finch JA distinguished *Robinson v. Countrywide Factors Ltd.*, [1978] 1 SCR 753, which the appellant Attorney General cited in support of the argument that assets other than those of the bankrupt may be distributed upon bankruptcy. Finch JA held that recovering for a bankrupt's estate property which the bankrupt had unlawfully concealed is not comparable to the present circumstances where provincial legislation operates to add to the bankrupt's estate property which never belonged to the bankrupt.

[18] Finch JA also considered *Husky Oil Operations Ltd. v. Minister of National Revenue*, [1995] 3 SCR 453, where this Court held that valid provincial workers' compensation legislation was inoperative where it conflicted with federal priorities as established by the BIA. The lessor argued that *Husky Oil* stood for the proposition that provincial legislation can neither remove nor add something to a bankrupt's estate owing to the primacy of the priority scheme of the BIA. Finch JA reviewed Gonthier J's comments in *Husky Oil* regarding the analysis which must be undertaken to determine whether two laws are in operational conflict. He then found that s. 20(b)(i) and the BIA do conflict since s. 20(b)(i) purports to define the property of the bankrupt in a way which is inconsistent with the definition provided in the BIA. He further found that s. 20(b)(i) is inconsistent with the BIA since it permits property which does not belong to the bankrupt to be distributed among the bankrupt's creditors.

[19] Finch JA stated that the real question at issue is who holds title to the car. That is, did the bankrupt or the trustee in bankruptcy obtain title to the vehicle by reason of the lessor's failure to register its security interest? The bankrupt acquired only a right to use the car and a contingent future right of purchase. The learned judge concluded that s. 20(b)(i) cannot possibly have the effect of transferring title from the lessor, the true owner, to the trustee in bankruptcy because this would give the trustee greater proprietary rights in the car than the bankrupt enjoyed.

[20] Finch JA rejected the argument that *Re Nishi Industries*, [1978] 6 WWR 736 (BCCA), in which the British Columbia *Conditional Sales Act, 1961*, SBC 1961, c. 9, was held to be constitutionally valid and was found to give a trustee in bankruptcy priority over a secured creditor, supported the trustee's position. He distinguished that case on the basis that, under a conditional sale or chattel mortgage, the mortgagee or the purchaser acquires a property interest, whereas in the present case the lessee does not acquire a property interest in the collateral. Rather, the bankrupt held only the right to possess the car while payments were being made.

[21] Finch JA also dismissed the lessor's argument based on s. 30(1)(k) of the BIA, under which a trustee may elect to retain a lease. Finch JA found that s. 30(1)(k) applied only to leases of property belonging to the bankrupt and had no application where the bankrupt has leased the property of another.

[22] Finding it unnecessary to address the other issues raised by the lessor or to deal with the constitutional questions raised by the Attorney General, Finch JA allowed the appeal and directed that the proceeds be paid to the lessor.

4. Issues

[23] There is one principal issue in the present appeal: can s. 20(b)(i) of the PPSA extinguish the lessor's right to the car in favour of the trustee's interest, or is the operation of s. 20(b)(i) limited by certain provisions of the BIA?

[24] In my view, this issue can be resolved through a normal reading of the relevant provisions of both the PPSA and the BIA, buttressed by the policy considerations supporting these provisions.

5. Analysis

A. The Locus of Title Is Not Determinative

[25] At the outset, it is important to note that the Court of Appeal's holding in the present appeal rests on the principle that the "property of the bankrupt" shall vest in the trustee (s. 71(2) BIA) and that only the property of the bankrupt shall be distributed among the bankrupt's creditors (s. 67(1) BIA). In the opinion of the Court of Appeal, the bankrupt, as lessee, did not have a proprietary interest in the car, and since the trustee obtains its entitlements to the contents of the bankrupt's estate through the bankrupt, the trustee cannot assert a proprietary interest in the car. In my view, the Court of Appeal, with respect, erred fundamentally in focussing on the locus of title and in holding that the lessor's common law ownership interest prevailed despite the clear meaning of s. 20(b)(i).

[26] The Court of Appeal did not recognize that the provincial legislature, in enacting the PPSA, has set aside the traditional concepts of title and ownership to a certain extent. T.M. Buckwold and R.C.C. Cuming, in their article "The Personal Property Security Act and the Bankruptcy and Insolvency Act: Two Solitudes or Complementary Systems?" (1997), 12 *Banking & Finance L Rev.* 467, at pp. 469-70, underline the fact that provincial legislatures, in enacting personal property security regimes, have redefined traditional concepts of rights in property:

> Simply put, the property rights of persons subject to provincial legislation are what the legislature determines them to be. While a statutory definition of rights may incorporate common law concepts in whole or in part, it is open to the legislature to redefine or revise those concepts as may be required to meet the objectives of its legislation. This was done in the provincial PPSAs, which implement a new conceptual approach to the definition and assertion of rights in and to personal property falling within their scope. The priority and realization provisions of the Acts revolve around the central statutory concept of "security interest." The rights of parties to a transaction that creates a security interest are explicitly not dependent upon either the form of the transaction or upon traditional questions of title. Rather, they are defined by the Act itself.

[27] In *International Harvester*, supra, the Saskatchewan Court of Appeal recognized that the regime put in place to regulate competing interests in personal property does not turn on title to the collateral (at p. 204):

> There is nothing in the language of the section [s. 20 of the Saskatchewan PPSA which is the equivalent of s. 20 of the British Columbia PPSA], or its relationship with other sections, or indeed in the overall scheme of the Act to suggest, for example, that an unperfected security

interest, because it is rooted in and attached to the title of particular goods in the possession of a debtor, should be treated as superior to the more generally derived and broadly attached interest which an execution creditor comes to have in a debtor's goods. Indeed, the very opposite is suggested not only by the language of the section, but by the overall thrust of the Act.

[28] The Court of Appeal in the present appeal did not look past the traditional concepts of title and ownership. But this dispute cannot be resolved through the determination of who has title to the car because the dispute is one of priority to the car and not ownership in it. It is in this context that the PPSA must be given its intended effect and it is to this question that I now wish to turn.

B. Definition of "Security Interest"

[29] The PPSA applies to "every transaction that in substance creates a security interest, without regard to its form and without regard to the person who has title to the collateral" (s. 2(1)(a)).

[30] Section 1 of the PPSA defines "security interest," in part, as "an interest in goods, chattel paper, a security, a document of title, an instrument, money or an intangible that secures payment or performance of an obligation." This definition is elaborated upon by paragraph 1(a)(iii) of the PPSA, which provides that "security interest" means the interest of "a lessor under a lease for a term of more than one year, whether or not the interest secures payment or performance of an obligation." Further, s. 3 of the PPSA deems certain agreements, which do not secure payment or performance of an obligation, to be security agreements for the purposes of the PPSA. Section 3 includes leases "for a term of more than one year that do not secure payment or performance of an obligation."

[31] The elements of the definition of "security interest" explicitly include within the definition of "security interest" leases for a term of more than one year. The lessor's interest in the car is the reservation of title in the car; this interest, created by the lease agreement, falls within the ambit of the PPSA.

C. The Nature of the Lessor's Interest in the Car

[32] A security interest is valid and enforceable when it attaches to personal property. Section 12(1)(b) of the PPSA provides that a security interest "attaches" when the debtor acquires "rights in the collateral." Section 12(2) states explicitly that "a debtor has rights in goods leased to the debtor ... when he obtains possession of them in accordance with the lease." Thus, upon delivery of the car to the bankrupt, the lessor had a valid security interest in the car that could be asserted against the lessee and against a third party claiming a right in the car. However, the lessor's security interest remained vulnerable to the claims of third parties who obtain an interest in the car through the lessee including, trustees in bankruptcy. In order to protect its security interest from such claims, the lessor must therefore perfect its interest through registration of its interest (s. 25), or repossession of the collateral (s. 24). The lessor did not have possession of the car, and it did not register its security interest. Thus, prior to the bankruptcy, the lessor held an unperfected security interest in the car. This brings us to the BIA.

D. The Bankrupt's Interest in the Car Vests in the Trustee

[33] Section 71(2) of the BIA provides that, upon an assignment into bankruptcy, the bankrupt's "property ... shall, subject to this Act and to the rights of secured creditors, forthwith pass to and vest in the trustee." Section 2 of the BIA defines "property" very broadly to include "every description of estate, interest and profit, present or future, vested or contingent, in, arising out of or incident to property."

[34] In my opinion, the bankrupt's right to use and possession of the car constitutes "property" for the purposes of the BIA and the trustee, by virtue of s. 71(2) of the BIA, succeeds to this proprietary right. I find support for this conclusion in *Paccar Financial Services*, supra, where the Saskatchewan Court of Appeal held that "property" as it is used in the BIA is "broad enough to include a leasehold interest" (at p. 494, citing *Re Cadieux* and *Jas. A. Ogilvy's Ltd.* (1952), 33 CBR 15 (Que. Sup. Ct.), at p. 16).

[35] The trustee assumes the bankrupt's possessory interest in the car through the operation of s. 71(2); it is upon this basis that the trustee can assert a claim to the car.

[36] I note that s. 12(2) of the PPSA also recognizes that a lessee obtains a proprietary interest in leased goods. Section 12(2) states explicitly that "a debtor has rights in goods leased to the debtor ... when he obtains possession of them in accordance with the lease." Thus, s. 12 operates to "deem or recognize that a lessee has a proprietary interest" (Buckwold and Cuming, supra, at p. 471). The Saskatchewan Court of Appeal considered a provision similar to s. 12 of the British Columbia PPSA in *International Harvester* and held that (at p. 206):

> ... a trustee in bankruptcy, upon whom there devolves a chattel in the possession of the bankrupt under a commercial lease for a term exceeding a year, succeeds to the contractual or "possessory" interest of the bankrupt in that chattel, as well as the bankrupt's statutory or "proprietary" interest therein as conferred upon the debtor by s. 12 of the Act.

[37] From the perspective of both the PPSA and the BIA the bankrupt, as lessee, can be described as having a proprietary interest in the car.

E. The Priority Contest and the Operation of Section 20(b)(i)

(i) Purpose of Section 20(b)(i)

[38] The Saskatchewan Court of Appeal explained the theory behind s. 20 of the Saskatchewan PPSA in *International Harvester* (at pp. 204-5). A person with an interest rooted in title to property in the possession of another, once perfected, can, in the event of default by the debtor, look to the property ahead of all others to satisfy his claim. However, if that interest is not perfected, it is vulnerable, even though it is rooted in title to the goods (at p. 205):

> A third party may derive an interest in the same goods by virtue of some dealing with the person in possession of them, and ... he may become entitled to priority. That is, he may become entitled, ahead of the person holding the unperfected security interest, to look to the goods to satisfy his claim.

Public disclosure of the security interest is required to prevent innocent third parties from granting credit to the debtor or otherwise acquiring an interest in the collateral.

However, public disclosure of the security interest does not seem to be required to protect a trustee who is not in the position of an innocent third party; rather, the trustee succeeds to the interests of the bankrupt. In one authority's opinion, trustees are given the capacity to defeat unperfected security interests because of the "representative capacity of the trustee and the effect of bankruptcy on the enforcement rights of unsecured creditors" (R.C.C. Cuming, "Canadian Bankruptcy Law: A Secured Creditor's Heaven" (1994), 24 *Can. Bus. LJ* 17, at pp. 27-28).

[39] Prior to a bankruptcy, unsecured creditors can make claims against the debtor through provincial judgment enforcement measures. Successful claims will rank prior to unperfected security interests pursuant to s. 20. Once a bankruptcy occurs, however, all claims are frozen and the unsecured creditors must look to the trustee in bankruptcy to assert their claims. Cuming describes the purpose of s. 20(b)(i) (at p. 29):

> In effect, the judgment enforcement rights of unsecured creditors are merged in the bankruptcy proceedings and the trustee is now the representative of creditors who can no longer bring their claims to a "perfected" status under provincial law. As the repository of enforcement rights, the trustee has status under s. 20(b)(i) of the BCPPSA to attack the unperfected security interest.

[40] The purpose behind granting a trustee in bankruptcy the power to defeat unperfected security interests was recognized by the Saskatchewan Court of Appeal in *International Harvester* (at p. 206):

> Indeed, the fact that a trustee in bankruptcy is a representative of creditors serves to shed light on more than one aspect of the issue. It explains—or at least assists in the explanation of—why a trustee in bankruptcy is included in s. 20, as well as why a trustee is not necessarily confined to the interest of the bankrupt.

[41] The Saskatchewan Court of Appeal again acknowledged the representative role of the trustee in bankruptcy in *Paccar Financial Services*, which also involved a priority contest between a trustee and the unperfected security interest of a lessor. The court stated that the trustee, after bankruptcy, acts as the representative of the unsecured creditors of the bankrupt and asserts "the claim of the unsecured creditors to the goods and possessions of the bankrupt pursuant to the priorities established for competing perfected and unperfected security interests. It is simply a contest as between an unsecured creditor and the holder of an unperfected security interest" (p. 490).

[42] The Court of Appeal erred, in my view, in not recognizing that the purpose of s. 20(b)(i) is, at least in part, to permit the unsecured creditors to maintain, through the person of the trustee, the same status vis-à-vis secured creditors who have not perfected their security interests which they enjoyed prior to the bankruptcy of the debtor.

(ii) The Present Appeal and Section 20(b)(i)

[43] In the present appeal, the trustee's possessory interest in the car, acquired through the bankrupt under the authority of the BIA, comes into competition with the unperfected security interest of the lessor. Section 20(b)(i) of the PPSA states explicitly that a security interest in collateral "is not effective against a trustee in bankruptcy if the

security interest is unperfected at the date of the bankruptcy." On a plain reading of s. 20(b)(i), the lessor's interest in the car is ineffective against the trustee.

[44] Section 20(b)(i) does not grant title or any other proprietary interest to the trustee, but it prevents the lessor from exercising rights against the trustee. Admittedly, the effect of s. 20(b)(i), on the present facts, is that the trustee ends up with full rights to the car when the bankrupt had only a right of use and possession. The Court of Appeal refused to accept this result because, in its view, it violated fundamental concepts of bankruptcy law. In this respect, the Court of Appeal cites *Fleeming*, supra, and *Flintoft*, supra, in support of the proposition that a trustee in bankruptcy cannot receive a greater interest in the property than the bankrupt had at the time of the bankruptcy.

[45] With respect, I disagree with the Court of Appeal for two reasons: first, *Fleeming* and *Flintoft* can be distinguished; and second, s. 20(b)(i) modifies the principle that a trustee is limited to the rights in the property enjoyed by the bankrupt.

• • •

[50] I accept that there is a principle which provides that a trustee in bankruptcy cannot obtain a greater interest to the goods than the bankrupt (beyond the context of a trust where the goods are not property of the bankrupt). However, s. 20(b)(i) itself modifies that principle. Cases decided prior to the Court of Appeal decision in the case on appeal have consistently accepted that s. 20(b)(i), or its equivalent, can give the trustee a greater interest in the disputed property than that enjoyed by the bankrupt.

[51] In *International Harvester*, the lessor of vehicles failed to register one security interest and improperly registered another. The lessee went bankrupt. The Saskatchewan Court of Appeal had to determine the nature of the interest that the trustee had in the vehicles. The Saskatchewan PPSA had a provision very similar to s. 20(b)(i), except it provided that an unperfected security interest shall be "subordinate to" the interest of a trustee in bankruptcy (as opposed to "not effective against"). The lessor argued that this provision could not be interpreted to permit the trustee to acquire a greater interest in property than the bankrupt had.

[52] The court acknowledged that federal bankruptcy legislation provides that a trustee shall step into the shoes of the bankrupt and "as a general rule acquires no higher right in the property of the bankrupt than that which the bankrupt enjoyed" (p. 200). The court then considered the policy considerations supporting the PPSA regime and the potential for mischief which arises in security transactions where title to property is separated from possession of that property. Provincial legislatures, faced with a policy choice involving the competing interests of the true owner and those of third parties dealing with the ostensible owner, have decided that the true owner must forfeit title, when faced with a competing interest, if she failed to register her interest as required. The court also noted that true leases were not regulated by the personal property regimes until recently. Thus, "as a general rule the common law did not allow the lessor's title to leased goods to be defeated through some dealing of the lessee. However, the Personal Property Security Act has effected far-reaching changes to the law" (p. 201).

[53] The court stated that to find that the trustee in bankruptcy cannot have a greater claim to the goods than the bankrupt enjoyed would (at p. 205)

> require resort to traditional common law concepts, to form over substance, to a technical construction of the term "interest," and to the defeat of the policy choice made by the legis-

lature in choosing, as it did, to include within the scope of the Act a true lease of goods. It would render the section largely, if not wholly, ineffective in this instance. ...

...

F. The Trustee Can Confer Clear Title

[57] Title could not defeat the trustee's claim under s. 20(b)(i) of the PPSA, but does the lessor's retention of title and the principle of nemo dat quod non habet prevent the trustee from selling the car, conferring clear title, and distributing its proceeds under the BIA?

[58] Section 81 of the BIA provides a procedure through which third parties can file claims with the trustee against "property ... in the possession of a bankrupt at the time of the bankruptcy." Subsection 81(2) provides that where the trustee disputes a claim, and the claimant does not appeal within the prescribed time period, then the claimant is "deemed to have abandoned or relinquished all his right to or interest in the property to the trustee who thereupon may sell or dispose of the property free of any lien, right, title or interest of the claimant." Section 81 does not specifically deal with the circumstances where a claimant's claim is defeated, but presumably the trustee would be able to sell the good free of the claim.

[59] The lessor could have made a claim under s. 81 of the BIA. This claim would have been defeated by the trustee in reliance on s. 20(b)(i) of the PPSA. In my view, both the defeat of a claim and the failure to make a claim under s. 81 result in the effective abandonment or relinquishment of any claim to the car; the trustee can therefore sell the car and confer good title.

G. The Federal Priority Scheme, Which Is Subject to the Rights of Secured Creditors, Is Not Disturbed

[60] Section 136 of the BIA sets out a priority scheme for the division of the property of the bankrupt; the interests of the various creditors are all "[s]ubject to the rights of secured creditors." Section 67 describes that which constitutes the property of the bankrupt.

[61] This Court has held on a number of occasions that provincial legislatures cannot enact legislation which operates to interfere with the priority of distribution set out in the BIA, nor can they confer secured creditor status on a class of creditors not entitled to such status under the BIA. A very recent example is *Husky Oil*, supra, where a majority of the Court held that s. 133 of the *Workers' Compensation Act, 1979*, SS 1979, c. W-17.1, was inapplicable in a bankruptcy because it operated to secure the Workers' Compensation Board's claim against the bankrupt's estate in violation of the priority of the Board's claim as set out in s. 136 of the BIA.

[62] Previous to *Husky Oil* were the so-called "quartet" of judgments on this issue. In *Deputy Minister of Revenue v. Rainville*, [1980] 1 SCR 35, and *Deloitte Haskins and Sells Ltd. v. Workers' Compensation Board*, [1985] 1 SCR 785, this Court held that a province cannot claim to be a secured creditor in a bankruptcy pursuant to provincial legislation where the Crown claim is listed as a preferred claim with a particular ranking in the BIA. In *Federal Business Development Bank v. Quebec (Commission de la santé et de la sécurité du travail)*, [1988] 1 SCR 1061, the Court held that, where a secured creditor liquidates his security outside the bankruptcy proceedings, the property constituting the security

is still property of the bankrupt and payment from the proceeds must be determined by the federal bankruptcy priorities and not in accordance with provincial law. Finally, in *British Columbia v. Henfrey Samson Belair Ltd.*, [1989] 2 SCR 24, the Court held that the province cannot deem a statutory trust to remove property from the estate of a bankrupt and thereby create its own priorities.

[63] The Court of Appeal applied this Court's decision in *Husky Oil* to conclude that a provincial law cannot add to the estate of a bankrupt property which the bankrupt never had. In my view, the Court of Appeal erred in its characterization of s. 20(b)(i). Section 20(b)(i) of the PPSA does not offend the priorities set out in the BIA as interpreted by the quartet and *Husky Oil*; rather, s. 20(b)(i) is but one element of the provincial legislation which serves to define the rights of the parties involved in a bankruptcy. More particularly, s. 20(b)(i) serves, on the present facts, to define the rights of the lessor and indicates that for the purpose of the bankruptcy, the lessor does not have the status of a secured creditor.

[64] Even though bankruptcy is clearly a federal matter, and even though it has been established that the federal Parliament alone can determine distribution priorities, the BIA is dependent on provincial property and civil rights legislation in order to inform the terms of the BIA and the rights of the parties involved in the bankruptcy. Section 72(1) of the BIA contemplates interaction with provincial legislation.

[65] This Court has recognized the important role that provincial legislation plays in the event of bankruptcy in *Husky Oil*. Gonthier J stated, at p. 481:

> It is trite to observe that the Bankruptcy Act is contingent on the provincial law of property for its operation. The Act is superimposed on those provincial schemes when a debtor declares bankruptcy. As a result, provincial law necessarily affects the "bottom line," but this is contemplated by the Bankruptcy Act itself.

And I stated the following for the minority in *Husky Oil*, at p. 531:

> [P]rovincial legislation is deeply involved in determining the priority, registration, and amount of indebtedness in the bankruptcy process. In fact, the proprietary and contractual rights that are regulated by the bankruptcy process are usually created by virtue of provincial law.

[66] J.S. Ziegel lucidly underlined the role which provincial law plays in bankruptcy in his article "Personal Property Security and Bankruptcy: There Is No War!" (1993), 72 *Can. Bar Rev.* 44, at p. 50:

> The answer is confirmed by the opening words of section 136(1), "Subject to the rights of secured creditors ... ." How are those rights (and obligations) to be determined? Since the Bankruptcy [and Insolvency] Act does not spell them out the reply must surely be: by consulting the law that gave them birth, and that law, in the absence of conflicting federal prescriptions, also determines what conditions and restrictions are imposed on the recognition and enforceability of the security interest.

[67] Section s. 20(b)(i) does not reorder federal priorities. Compliance with the perfection requirements of the PPSA is a precondition to maintaining secured creditor status under the BIA. In the event of bankruptcy, the consequences of a failure to perfect are

spelled out in s. 20(b)(i). In effect, the secured party with an unperfected security interest becomes an unsecured creditor of the bankrupt:

> ... any secured party with a security interest in personal property, who fails to meet the requirements of the Act for perfecting its security interest prior to the date a petition is filed or an assignment is made, loses the status of a secured creditor in the bankruptcy and is relegated to unsecured status.

(Cuming, supra, at pp. 25-26).

...

6. *Conclusion and Disposition*

[73] In accordance with s. 20(b)(i), the lessor's unperfected security interest is ineffective against the possessory interest acquired by the trustee in bankruptcy. The trustee's interest in the car takes priority over that of the lessor; the trustee is therefore entitled to the proceeds of the car.

Appeal allowed.

NOTES

1) The Supreme Court's decision in *Re Giffen*, above, illustrates the critical interaction of provincial law and federal bankruptcy law in the chattel security area. A trustee in bankruptcy wears several hats. For some purposes, the trustee wears the bankrupt's hat, most particularly for succeeding to whatever rights the bankrupt has to property wherever located. See BIA s. 67(3), s. 2, definition of property, and s. 71(2).

For other purposes, the trustee is the creditors' representative because the trustee's obligation is to gather in the debtor's estate and to distribute the proceeds among the creditors according to the BIA's distribution scheme. It is for this reason that chattel security legislation in all common law jurisdictions has long subordinated unperfected security interests to the claims of a trustee in the same way that fraudulent conveyancing and fraudulent preference legislation entitles a creditors' representative to attack prebankruptcy transactions prejudicial to creditors' interests.

From Lord Coke's day onward, a secret sale by a debtor not in the ordinary course of business and not accompanied by an open and "notorious" transfer of possession of the chattels to the buyer was regarded as a badge of fraud under 13 Eliz., c. 5, and therefore voidable at the trustee's or other creditors' representative initiative. With the introduction of bills of sale legislation in Canada and England in the 19th century, it was natural that trustees should explicitly be given the status to challenge unrecorded bills of sale and, later, other types of secured transactions, on the ground that the (frequently quite draconian) registration requirements had not been complied with. US law was, and remains, even more rigorous than Canadian law in championing a trustee's right to challenge fraudulent conveyances and unperfected security interests. For contemporary examples, see Revised Article 9, UCC 9-317. For further discussion of *Re Giffen*, see Anthony Duggan and Jacob Ziegel, "Justice Iacobucci and the Canadian Law of Deemed Trusts and Chattel Security" (2007), 57 *UTLJ* 227.

2) Section 20(2)(b) provides that the rights of a person under s. 20(1)(b) in respect of the collateral are to be determined as of the date from which the person's representative status takes effect. Section 71(1) of the pre-1997 *Bankruptcy and Insolvency Act*, RSC 1985, c. B-3, provided that "[t]he bankruptcy shall be deemed to have relation back to and to commence at the time of the filing of the petition on which a receiving order is made or of the filing of an assignment with the official receiver." The effect of this section on old OPPSA s. 22(2) was held to be that "the date from which the status of the trustee had effect was the date of filing of the petition": *Re Hillstead Ltd.* (1979), 103 DLR (3d) 347, at 349 (Ont. SC—Bktcy.). In this case, it was held that registration of a financing statement after the filing of the petition in bankruptcy but before the receiving order was made too late to save the security interest from subordination to the trustee in bankruptcy. BIA s. 71(1) was repealed in 1997 with the result, apparently, that there is nothing now to prevent perfection of a security interest after bankruptcy proceedings have been commenced against a debtor and before the bankruptcy order has been made. There may have been sound reasons for the repeal of s. 71(1), but this particular effect appears to have been overlooked.

3) Section 20(1)(b) refers to "a person who represents the creditors of the debtor, including ... a trustee in bankruptcy." Section 20(1)(b) replaces an earlier provision which said that "an unperfected security interest is subordinate to ... the interests of a person ... who represents the creditors of the debtor as ... trustee in bankruptcy or receiver." The change originated in a recommendation of the Catzman Committee (*Report of the Minister's Advisory Committee on the Personal Property Security Act* (April 18, 1984)). The Catzman Committee Report does not explain why the reference to receivers was dropped, but according to Catzman himself, the term "receiver" is a generic one, covering both privately-appointed and court-appointed receivers, and it is only a court-appointed receiver that can be said to represent the interests of creditors: Catzman et al., *Personal Property Security Law in Ontario*, at 114. This statement provides a clue to the committee's thinking: the purpose, apparently, was to make it clear that the section did not apply to a privately appointed receiver, but that it did apply to a court-appointed receiver as a person who represents the creditors. However, in *1231640 Ontario Inc. (Re)*, extracted below, the Ontario Court of Appeal concluded otherwise.

1231640 Ontario Inc. (Re)
2007 ONCA 810

FELDMAN JA: [1] When the appellant bank sought the appointment of an interim receiver of the debtor company, it held a perfected security interest over the assets of that company. However, during the receivership the appellant allowed its registration under the *Personal Property Security Act* ... (the "*PPSA*") to lapse. The appellant did not reperfect its security interest before the interim receiver assigned the debtor into bankruptcy, following which, a significant tax refund came into the debtor's estate.

[2] The appellant asserts priority under ss. 20(1)(b) and 20(2)(b) of the *PPSA* over the tax refund and some other undistributed funds, on the basis that the date when the receiver was appointed is the date for determining priority, and on that date, the appellant's security interest was perfected. In contrast, the trustee in bankruptcy says that the

relevant date for determining priority is the date of the assignment into bankruptcy. Because on that date the appellant's security interest was unperfected as against the trustee, the appellant ranks as an unsecured creditor, *pari passu* with other unsecured creditors.

[3] The motion judge dismissed the appellant's claim. For the reasons that follow, I agree with the motion judge and would dismiss the appeal.

Background

[4] The appellant held a first registered general security interest over the personal property of State, the debtor, and sought to enforce its security by seeking the appointment of an interim receiver under s. 47(1) of the *Bankruptcy and Insolvency Act* … (the "*BIA*"). A court order appointing the respondent, PricewaterhouseCoopers Inc. ("PWC"), as interim receiver was issued on November 14, 2001. Following its appointment, the interim receiver sold the substantial assets of State in three sales. In accordance with the vesting orders of the court, the interim receiver distributed the proceeds of the first two sales to the creditors according to their respective priorities at the time of the sales. As part of the first sale on November 14, 2001, the receiver sold State's name [to 1231640 Ontario Inc.] triggering s. 48(3) of the *PPSA* [reperfection required following debtor's name change].

[5] On January 31, 2002, in accordance with the terms of the order appointing it as interim receiver, PWC assigned the debtor into bankruptcy and PWC was appointed the trustee in bankruptcy of the debtor's estate. Following the assignment, the trustee in bankruptcy received an income tax refund of $4.325 million from the Canada Revenue Agency.

[6] Before the date of the debtor's assignment into bankruptcy (and before the third sale of assets) both the appellant bank and St. Paul Guarantee Insurance Company ("St. Paul"), a subsequent secured creditor, had knowledge of the sale of the debtor's name and failed to register a financing change statement. Therefore, both of their secured debts had become unperfected in accordance with s. 48(3).

[7] Following the debtor's assignment into bankruptcy, the appellant bank asserted a first priority right to the income tax refund and some other funds held by the trustee by filing a proof of claim, which included a secured claim in the amount of $20 million, with PWC as trustee in bankruptcy. In response, the trustee in bankruptcy brought a motion for the advice and direction of the court as to whether the appellant bank's security interest, which was unperfected at the date of the bankruptcy, remained effective against it as trustee.

...

[11] In his submissions, counsel for the appellant characterized the effect of ss. 20(1)(b) and 20(2)(b) to be that when a representative of creditors is appointed, "the music stops" under the *PPSA*, meaning that the priority rights of all parties are frozen for the purpose of distribution of the estate of the debtor.

[12] The appellant's position is that an interim receiver, appointed by the court under s. 47(1) of the *BIA*, is "a person who represents the creditors of the debtor" within the meaning of s. 20(1)(b) of the *PPSA*. The appellant submits that upon the appointment of the interim receiver, the priority interests of all creditors of the debtor are frozen and the

interim receiver is to distribute the assets or proceeds of the assets of the debtor, no matter when they are realized or distributed, in accordance with the respective priority positions of the creditors as of the date of the receiver's appointment.

[13] To the extent that the security interest of a secured creditor may become unperfected under s. 48(3) of the *PPSA* following the appointment of a representative of creditors, submits the appellant, this post-appointment event has no bearing on the secured creditor's priority for the purpose of the distribution of assets of the debtor's estate. Or, put another way, the effect of the order appointing the interim receiver was to exempt the appellant from the requirement of complying with s. 48(3). Consequently, the fact that the appellant failed to file a financing change statement before the date of the debtor's assignment into bankruptcy and the appointment of the trustee in bankruptcy did not affect the appellant's entitlement to continue to be paid from the assets of the estate in accordance with its priority position as it stood on the date of the appointment of the interim receiver, at which time its security interest was perfected.

[14] I summarize my reasons for rejecting the appellant's position as follows. First, although an interim receiver may represent the creditors of the debtor for some purposes, it is not "a person who represents the creditors of the debtor" within the meaning and purpose of ss. 20(1)(b) and 20(2)(b), and the term "receiver" should not be read in to these subsections. Unlike a trustee in bankruptcy, a receiver does not obtain the debtor's proprietary interest in the collateral and obtains no priority rights under ss. 20(1)(b) or 20(2)(b) in the collateral, or in respect of the collateral, and thus is not in a priority contest with any creditor on behalf of unsecured creditors. The purpose of these subsections is to allow the representative of creditors to defeat unperfected security interests on behalf of unsecured creditors whose rights to collect outstanding debts from the debtor are statutorily stayed, such as on bankruptcy or assignment for the benefit of creditors. Unlike on a bankruptcy or assignment for the benefit of creditors, creditors' priority rights are not statutorily stayed on a receivership. Although such rights may be stayed by the order appointing the receiver, a creditor may apply to lift the stay in order to commence or continue proceedings to collect its debt.

[15] Second, the effect of ss. 20(1)(b) and 20(2)(b) is to determine the priority rights of creditors at a particular time, but not to freeze priorities for all time, or, in the words of appellant's counsel, to "stop the music." Neither these subsections nor the order appointing the interim receiver had the effect of exempting the appellant from the requirement of complying with s. 48(3). Consequently the appellant's security interest became unperfected by its failure to file a financing change statement within the time period specified by s. 48(3). Because it also failed to re-register under s. 30(6) before the debtor's assignment into bankruptcy, the appellant's security interest is not effective against the trustee in bankruptcy.

Analysis

Issue 1: Did the order appointing the interim receiver give the appellant an exemption from complying with s. 48(3) of the PPSA?

[16] The motion judge found that the order appointing the receiver did not exempt the appellant from complying with s. 48(3), nor did the stay provisions of the order pre-

vent the appellant from seeking to lift the stay in order to file a financing change statement. My colleague concludes that the motion judge was correct on this issue and I
agree. In my view, the consequence of this conclusion is that the appellant's failure to
comply with s. 48(3) caused its security interest to become unperfected and to be ineffective against the trustee in bankruptcy under ss. 20(1)(b) and 20(2)(b).

**Issue 2: *Did the appellant's failure to file a financing change statement result in a
loss of its priority as a secured creditor?***

(i) Subsection 20(1) of the PPSA

[17] Subsection 20(1) prescribes the effect of perfection of a security interest in collateral in relation to other claims against the same collateral and defines the rules for
determining priority between the holder of an unperfected security interest and others
with a claim to, or an interest in, the collateral. Under s. 20(1)(a), an unperfected security
interest "is subordinate to" perfected security interests in the same collateral as well to
the interests of lienholders and of unsecured creditors who have seized the collateral
through legal processes.

[18] In contrast, under ss. 20(1)(b), (c) and (d), an unperfected security interest "is
not effective" against a person who represents the creditors of the debtor, including an
assignee for the benefit of creditors and a trustee in bankruptcy, and against certain
transferees of the debtor's property. The different language is used because s. 20(1)(a) orders the priority among secured creditors and other creditors with a realized interest in
the collateral, while under ss. 20(1)(b), (c) and (d), an unperfected security interest is
treated as an unsecured interest as against the named persons.

[19] In order to interpret the meaning and scope of the term "a person who represents the creditors of the debtor" in s. 20(1)(b) of the *PPSA*, one must examine the
language of ss. 20(1)(b) and 20(2)(b), since both clauses work together, as well as the
purpose of the provisions, which I will discuss later in these reasons.

[20] Clause 20(1)(b) states that a security interest in collateral, until perfected, "is not
effective against a person who represents the creditors of the debtor, including an assignee for the benefit of creditors and a trustee in bankruptcy." Before this provision was
amended in 1989, it provided that an unperfected security interest in collateral was ineffective against three named representatives: a trustee in bankruptcy, an assignee for the
benefit of creditors, and a receiver. See *Personal Property Security Act*, RSO 1980, c. 375,
s. 22(1)(a)(iii). While in amending the provision the legislature specifically removed the
reference to a "receiver," it also added the term "including," which now precedes "assignee
for the benefit of creditors" and "trustee in bankruptcy." The appellant argues that because the legislature used the word "including," the removal of the reference to a "receiver" does not indicate an intention by the legislature to exclude receivers from the ambit
of the provision.

[21] I disagree. The legislature's removal of a receiver from s. 20(1)(b) means the appellant cannot succeed without showing that an interim receiver is a "person who represents the creditors of the debtor" in the sense that fits the language and purpose of both
ss. 20(1)(b) and 20(2)(b). There is no question that, in carrying out its functions and
duties, an interim receiver can act in a representative capacity on behalf of some or all of

the creditors. The issue in this case is whether an interim receiver is the type of representative of creditors that is referred to in these two clauses.

(ii) A receiver does not obtain the debtor's proprietary interest in the collateral

[22] The first relevant difference between a receiver and a trustee in bankruptcy or an assignee for the benefit of creditors is that a receiver does not obtain the debtor's proprietary interest in the collateral. In their text *Personal Property Security Law* (Toronto: Irwin Law Inc., 2005), Professors Cuming, Walsh and Wood, at pp. 441-42, begin their discussion of the interface between s. 20 of the *PPSA* and the *BIA* by explaining that the vesting of the debtor's personal property in the trustee in bankruptcy under s. 71(2) of the *BIA* gives the trustee the independent status to defeat unperfected security interests in that property under s. 20:

> The *PPSA* provides that a security interest is not effective against a trustee in bankruptcy if the security interest is unperfected at the date of bankruptcy. The effect of this is to give to the debtor's trustee in bankruptcy an independent status to defeat unperfected security interests in personal property that vests in the trustee as provided by *BIA* [sub]section 71(2). [Citations omitted.]

[23] The two creditors' representatives named in s. 20(1)(b) share an important characteristic: by virtue of statute (s. 71 of the *BIA* and ss. 7 and 8 of the *Assignments and Preferences Act*, RSO 1990, c. A.33), upon their respective appointments, the proprietary rights of the debtor in the collateral vest in these representatives.

•••

[26] As a result, these representatives hold the debtor's proprietary interest in the collateral. This is to be contrasted with the role and legal status of a receiver, whether privately or court-appointed. I will discuss court-appointed receivers because in this case, PWC is a court-appointed receiver and a court-appointed receiver has statutory authority.

[27] One important difference between a court-appointed receiver and a trustee in bankruptcy (or assignee for the benefit of creditors) is that a receiver obtains its powers from an order of the court. These powers allow the receiver to administer the business and assets of the debtor, and to effect a sale of the debtor's assets pursuant to a vesting order of the court. However, the debtor's property rights in the assets, whether the debtor has full or partial title or merely a right of possession, do not devolve onto the receiver as they do onto a trustee in bankruptcy by statute under s. 71 of the *BIA*. ...

[28] The receiver is solely an administrator accountable to the court and to all stakeholders in the receivership, appointed to ensure that the debtor's assets are realized in an orderly manner and for the maximum realizable value, and then to distribute the proceeds to creditors and other claimants in accordance with their respective priorities. It is in that way that a receiver may represent creditors. As the motion judge pointed out, a debtor could retain possession and remain in business during a receivership, and, subject to the terms of the order appointing the interim receiver, could borrow additional funds and create additional security that would continue after the termination of the receivership. In some circumstances the debtor could retain the business following the discharge

of the receiver. The debtor is not stripped of all of its interest in the collateral upon the appointment of an interim receiver.

[29] The fact that ss. 20(1)(b) and 20(2)(b) deal with proprietary rights is reflected in the language and effect of s. 20(2)(b) ... . The effect of s. 20(2) is to define the time from which the rights of statutory lienholders under s. 20(1)(a)(i) and of representatives of creditors under s. 20(1)(b) are to be determined. The effective timing of the other rights under ss. 20(1)(a), (c) and (d) is built into the description of those rights. ...

[30] However, the wording of s. 20(2)(b) also tells us that s. 20(1)(b) has conferred "rights ... in respect of the collateral" on the representative of creditors and that those rights are to be determined "as of" the effective date of the representative's appointment. Although the term "rights," standing alone, is used in s. 60 of the *PPSA* to mean the right to take administrative steps, "rights ... in respect of the collateral" are rights that indicate a proprietary or priority interest in the collateral that entitles the holder of such rights to be paid out of the proceeds of that collateral in accordance with its priority.

(iii) A receiver does not assert the claim of the unsecured creditors against competing security interests

[31] A trustee in bankruptcy, unlike a receiver, represents the creditors in another way beyond administering the estate: the trustee holds the debtor's proprietary interest in the assets on behalf of the unsecured creditors. As Iacobucci J stated in *Re Giffen*, [1998] 1 SCR 91 at para. 41 (referring to the Saskatchewan Court of Appeal decision in *Paccar Financial Services Ltd. v. Sinco Trucking Ltd. (Trustee of)*, [1989] 3 WWR 481 at 490):

> [T]he trustee, after bankruptcy, acts as the representative of the unsecured creditors of the bankrupt and asserts "the claim of the unsecured creditors to the goods and possessions of the bankrupt pursuant to the priorities established for competing perfected and unperfected security interests."

[32] Consequently, a trustee occupies a priority position for the purpose of distribution of the proceeds of the debtor's estate. In that sense, a trustee in bankruptcy is in competition with other creditors for its priority position among creditors, and its rights in the collateral are in competition with the rights of other creditors in the collateral. In contrast, a receiver is not in competition with creditors and has no priority position itself because any rights it has in the collateral are administrative but not proprietary. It is merely an administrator who pays out the proceeds to the creditors, both secured and unsecured, if there are sufficient funds, in the order of their priority.

[33] In *Re Giffen*, Iacobucci J ... explained that the reason why the *PPSA* provides that a trustee in bankruptcy defeats an unperfected security interest is because, before bankruptcy, an unsecured creditor can take steps to obtain and enforce a judgment against the debtor through execution proceedings that will rank ahead of an unperfected security interest under s. 20(1)(a)(i). However, once bankruptcy occurs, "all claims are frozen and the unsecured creditors must look to the trustee in bankruptcy to assert their claims." *Re Giffen, supra* at para. 39. As Anthony Duggan and Jacob Ziegel explain when discussing *Re Giffen* in their article, "Justice Iacobucci and the Canadian Law of Deemed

Trusts and Chattel Security" (2007), 57 UTLJ 227 at 231: "If the debtor becomes bankrupt while the execution process is still in train, the execution creditor loses this priority by virtue of the stay provisions in the *BIA*, ss. 69.3 and 70."

...

[35] In their discussion of *Re Giffen*, Professors Duggan and Ziegel, *supra* at 231-34, explain how bankruptcy law works with the *PPSA* to preserve creditors' relative priority entitlements post-bankruptcy. The authors comment that Iacobucci J's decision in *Re Giffen* confirms "the complementary relationship between the federal bankruptcy statute and the provincial PPSAs": *supra* at 249.

[36] It follows from *Re Giffen* that a receiver is not intended to be included as a "person who represents the creditors of the debtor" for the purpose and therefore within the meaning of ss. 20(1)(b) and 20(2)(b) of the *PPSA*. The reasons for this conclusion are: (a) unlike in a bankruptcy, a receiver, including a court-appointed interim receiver, does not stand in for unsecured creditors in a priority contest with any other creditor; (b) a receiver is not the "repository of enforcement rights" of unsecured creditors with any status to "attack the unperfected security interest" (*Re Giffen*, *supra*, at para. 39); and (c) in a receivership, unlike in a bankruptcy, there is no statutory stay causing execution creditors to lose their priority and ability to realize on their debt.

(iv) Personal Property Security Acts of other provinces

[37] The conclusion that a receiver is not a person who represents the creditors of the debtor under s. 20 is also consistent with the correlative sections of the Personal Property Security Acts of the other common law provinces. The comparable provisions in British Columbia, Alberta, Saskatchewan, Manitoba, Nova Scotia, New Brunswick, Prince Edward Island and Newfoundland do not include a receiver. Only the relevant sections of the Manitoba and Ontario Acts formerly referred to a receiver, but both have since been amended to remove this reference.

[38] The Manitoba statute contained a provision with language identical to the previous version of the Ontario section ... . Manitoba's replacement provision does not use the term "includes," but instead lists only two representatives of creditors, neither of which is a receiver.

[39] The Manitoba courts considered the effect of the former wording of s. 22 in the context of a court-appointed receivership in the case of *RoyNat Inc. v. Ja-Sha Trucking & Leasing Ltd. (Receiver of)*, [1991] 6 WWR 764 (QB), aff'd (1992), 94 DLR (4th) 611 (CA). The court had appointed a receiver of the debtor trucking company at the request of a secured creditor, Roynat. Another secured creditor, Paccar, had a prior purchase-money security interest in some of the trucks, but had inadvertently failed to renew its *PPSA* registration and was unperfected on the date of the appointment of the receiver. Paccar sought an extension of time to re-perfect its security under s. 65 of the Manitoba *PPSA*, which provided that when an extension is granted "the rights of other persons accrued up to the time of the registration of the order made under this section are not affected by the order." The receiver opposed Paccar's motion. It took the position that on its appointment as a receiver, by operation of ss. 22(1)(a)(iii) and 22(2), it had accrued the rights referred to in s. 65.

[40] In the Court of Queen's Bench, Scollin J rejected the position of the receiver. He explained that even though a receiver was referred to in s. 22, the rights and interests of a receiver are not the same as those of a trustee in bankruptcy. He concluded at 768 that:

> [T]he provisions of s. 22 can be sensibly reconciled with the provisions of s. 65 by recognizing that the only rights of the creditor which should be subordinated to the interest and rights of the receiver are those which necessarily conflict with the due exercise of the rights of the receiver as representative of the creditors in executing the mandate of the court. The status of a receiver does not bring with it a cornucopia of rights. ... Beyond his mandate, the receiver has no status. Unless his rights or interests are affected, no issue of subordination even arises. In this case he has demonstrated no diminution of his rights or interest and no prejudice to any creditor. To recognize the substantive security interest of Paccar causes no injustice or prejudice to the receiver or to other creditors and permits full recognition of and harmony between ss. 22 and 65 of the Act. Absent prejudice, the receiver's rights or interest do not extend to defeating an application which, but for his appointment, would be effective to relieve against an inadvertent lapse.

[41] The Court of Appeal dismissed the appeal. Twaddle JA acknowledged that Scollin J may have been correct in his view, distinguishing a trustee in bankruptcy from a receiver, that while a trustee in bankruptcy does acquire a priority property right on appointment, a receiver does not. However, he said he was not required to decide the issue because he could dismiss the appeal based on his interpretation that s. 22 did not defeat the remedial effect of s. 65. He stated at p. 615:

> An order made under s. 65 re-perfects the security interest as though it had never lapsed, subject only to the rights of those who have dealt with the debtor in the meantime and who would be prejudiced by permitting the order under s. 65 to have retroactive effect.

[42] In my view, Scollin J's analysis of the rights of a receiver was correct and consistent with the conclusion reached on the appeal. Furthermore, his understanding was given full effect when s. 22 was repealed and replaced in Manitoba in 1993 with the new provision that excludes a receiver from its ambit. As mentioned above, the equivalent statutory provisions of the other common law provinces do not make reference to a receiver.

(v) The effect of a court-ordered stay

[43] Other case law has also considered the issue of re-perfecting a security interest following the appointment of a receiver or of a monitor under s. 11.7 of the *Companies' Creditors Arrangement Act*, RSC 1985, c. C-36. This case law arises because when a receiver (or monitor) is appointed, unlike in a bankruptcy, the debtor does not lose all rights and interest in the collateral and the rights of creditors are not statutorily frozen. Although an order appointing a receiver will normally stay all proceedings against the interests of the debtor, the court can always lift the stay to allow a creditor to take certain steps to enforce its rights or perfect its security against the debtor, subject to considering competing rights acquired by other creditors in the interim.

[44] Subsection 30(6) of the Ontario *PPSA* provides:

> Where a security interest that is perfected by registration becomes unperfected and is again perfected by registration, the security interest shall be deemed to have been continuously perfected from the time of first perfection except that if a person acquired rights in all or part of the collateral during the period when the security interest was unperfected, the registration shall not be effective as against the person who acquired the rights during such period.

Using s. 30(6), a secured creditor with a security interest that is originally perfected by registration but becomes unperfected, can re-perfect by registration and regain its priority standing as against all other creditors except as against someone who "acquired rights in all or part of the collateral" while the creditor's security interest was unperfected.

[45] ... [O]n appointment, a receiver does not acquire any rights in the collateral that are in competition with the rights of any creditor. In other words, a receiver does not obtain the right to receive any portion of the proceeds of the estate of the debtor. Consequently, a secured creditor whose security interest had been perfected at some point but was unperfected on the date of the appointment of a receiver may re-perfect under s. 30(6) and retain its priority, regardless of the appointment of a receiver in the interim, by obtaining a lift-stay order from the court, if necessary.

. . .

[52] In fact, the new Standard Template Receivership Order of the Commercial List—which is to be used when a receiver is appointed by the Superior Court of Justice—clearly excepts registrations under the *PPSA* from the effect of the stay. Paragraph 9, which contains the stay order, specifically provides that nothing in that paragraph prevents "the filing of any registrations to preserve or perfect a security interest." This paragraph clearly describes the understanding of the bench and bar that the "music" does not stop on the appointment of a receiver because the ongoing need to register and to perfect security is recognized and acknowledged. There would be no cause or purpose in doing so if priorities were frozen on the date of the order.

. . .

Conclusion

[59] I agree with the motion judge that a receiver is not a representative of creditors within the meaning of ss. 20(1)(b) and 20(2)(b) of the *PPSA* and the term "receiver" should not be read in to the legislation. Because the appellant's security interest became unperfected as a result of the operation of s. 48(3), and because it did not re-perfect its security interest before the assignment of the debtor into bankruptcy, it was unperfected on the date of the appointment of the trustee and its security interest is therefore ineffective against the trustee.

[60] The unfortunate result for the appellant, and apparent windfall for St. Paul, is that the appellant loses its priority over St. Paul, and even though St. Paul also lost its secured standing, they rank *pari passu* as unsecured creditors in the bankruptcy. This result flows from the fact that both were unperfected on the date of the appointment of the trustee and both their security interests are therefore ineffective against the trustee.

[LA FORME JA concurred. WEILER JA dissented in part, pointing out that there was nothing in the history of s. 20(1)(b) to indicate that the Ontario legislature meant to exclude receivers and arguing that the normal rule of statutory construction should be applied, *viz.*, that where subsequent legislation uses the same expression as an earlier Act (here "person who represents the creditors of the debtor"), it is assumed to have the same meaning as in the earlier legislation.]

NOTES

1) St. Paul apparently thought it was better off arguing that both security interests were ineffective, because that way it would end up with a pro rata share of the disputed funds. Both parties appear to have overlooked OPPSA s. 30(1), rule 4 ("where priority is to be determined between unperfected security interests, priority shall be determined by the order of attachment"). OPPSA s. 20(1)(b) provides that an unperfected security interest is "not effective against ... a trustee in bankruptcy." It does not say that an unperfected security interest is not effective *at all* once the debtor has become bankrupt. The bank could have argued that, by virtue of s. 20(1)(b), both parties were relegated to unsecured creditor status vis-à-vis the trustee, but by virtue of s. 30(1), rule 4, the bank still had priority over St. Paul. In other words, the bank was entitled to St. Paul's pro rata share of the disputed funds in the same way as if the parties had entered into a subordination agreement.

2) In the Saskatchewan PPSA, the governing provision is s. 20(2), which provides in relevant part that a security interest in collateral is not effective against a trustee in bankruptcy if the security interest is unperfected at the date of bankruptcy. The other provincial and territorial PPSAs contain a provision similar to the SPPSA version. This wording leaves less room for argument that the provision applies in a receivership, and in *Brookside Capital Partners Inc. v. RSM Richter* (2006), 25 CBR (5th) 273 (Alta. QB), Lo Vecchio J held that it does not.

3) Does OPPSA s. 20(1)(b) apply in *Companies' Creditors Arrangement Act* proceedings? See *PSINet Ltd., Re* (2002), 30 CBR (4th) 226 (Ont. SC); aff'd. (2002), CanLII 1209 (Ont. CA) and *TRG Services Inc., Re* (2006), 26 CBR (5th) 203 (Ont. SCJ). For a critical analysis of these decisions and discussion of the policy considerations, see Anthony Duggan, "The Status of Unperfected Security Interests in Insolvency Proceedings" (2008), 24 BFLR 103.

D. Transferee of Collateral

1. Introduction

OPPSA ss. 20(1)(c) and (d) provide that an unperfected security interest

20(1)(c) in chattel paper, documents of title, instruments or goods is not effective against a transferee thereof who takes under a transaction that does not secure payment or performance of an obligation and who gives value and receives delivery thereof without knowledge of the security interest;

(d) in intangibles other than accounts is not effective against a transferee thereof who takes under a transaction that does not secure payment or performance of an obligation and who gives value without knowledge of the security interest.

Consider the following example:

SP has an unperfected security interest in D's pickup truck. D sells and delivers the pickup truck to T without SP's authority. T does not know about SP's security interest.

Section 20(1)(c) applies and so T takes the truck free of SP's security interest. The *ex post* justification is that SP's failure to perfect left T without the means of discovering SP's security interest and it is reasonable that SP should pay the price. The *ex ante* justification is to give SP the incentive to perfect its security interest with a view to avoiding the dispute.

Now consider the following case:

SP1 has an unperfected security interest in D's pickup truck. Later, D gives SP2 a security interest in the same pickup truck. The security agreement is in the form of a mortgage, and SP2 registers a financing statement. D defaults against SP1 and SP2 and they both claim the truck, which is still in D's possession. SP1 argues that s. 20(1)(c) applies because SP2 is a transferee pursuant to the mortgage and that, therefore, SP1 has priority because SP2 did not take delivery of the collateral. SP2 argues that s. 20(1)(a)(i) applies and that, because SP1's security interest is unperfected, SP2 has priority.

SP2 is correct. Section 20(1)(c) does not apply because SP2 took "under a transaction that ... secures payment or performance of an obligation." As this example demonstrates, the purpose of the quoted words is to avoid overlap between ss. 20(1)(a)(i) and 20(1)(c) and potentially contradictory outcomes.

Section 20(1)(c) applies where the collateral is a tangible. Section 20(1)(d) enacts a parallel rule for intangibles. The provisions are the same except that s. 20(1)(d), for obvious reasons, leaves out the requirement that the transferee must take delivery, because intangibles cannot be delivered.

2. *Accounts*

Section 20(1)(d) applies to all intangibles except accounts. Why the exception for accounts? Consider the following example (Case 1):

SP holds an unperfected security interest in D's accounts. D makes an outright assignment of the same accounts to T, who registers a financing statement. SP and T both claim the accounts. Who has priority?

Section 20(1)(d) does not apply because the collateral is accounts. Instead, s. 20(1)(a)(i) is the governing provision. Section 20(1)(a)(i) applies because T's interest is a deemed security interest by virtue of s. 2(b) (see Chapter 2, Part V.A). Therefore, since T has registered a financing statement, it has priority over SP. Assume that T had not registered a financing statement. Then, notionally at any rate, the competition would have been between two unperfected security interests; however, as a matter of practice, in these circumstances one or both parties will belatedly register a financing statement. If both parties register, priority will turn on the first to register rule in s. 30(1), rule 1, and if only one party registers, priority will turn on s. 20(1)(a)(i).

But for the exclusion of accounts, the rule in s. 20(1)(d) would apply as well because the transaction between D and T does not secure payment or performance of an obligation. If s. 20(1)(d) applied, T would have priority over SP regardless of whether it registered a financing statement, but only if it transacted without knowledge of SP's unperfected security interest. The purpose of excluding accounts from s. 20(1)(d) is to avoid overlap with s. 20(1)(a)(i) and the potentially contradictory outcomes that might result.

3. Chattel Paper

Now consider the following example (Case 2):

> SP holds an unperfected security interest in D's chattel paper. D makes an outright assignment of the chattel paper to T, who either takes possession of the chattel paper or registers a financing statement. SP and T both claim the chattel paper. Who has priority?

Section 20(1)(a)(i) applies on the same footing as in Case 1: this means that, since T has perfected its security interest, it has priority over SP. However, s. 20(1)(c) applies as well because the transaction between D and T does not secure payment or performance of an obligation. The upshot is that T has priority over SP, but only if it received delivery of the chattel paper without knowledge of SP's security interest. In summary, s. 20(1)(a)(i) and s. 20(1)(c) potentially lead to different outcomes and the statute fails to indicate which provision takes precedence.

4. Knowledge

Consider the following example (Case 3):

> Assume that SP holds an unperfected security interest in D's pickup truck. D sells the pickup truck to T. SP and T both claim the truck. Who has priority?

Section 20(1)(c) applies because the collateral is goods and the transaction between D and T does not secure payment or performance of an obligation. On this basis, T has priority, but only if it receives delivery of the pickup truck without knowledge of SP's security interest. Why should T's state of knowledge matter if the collateral is goods (Case 3), but not if the collateral is accounts (Case 1) or chattel paper (Case 3)? By the same token, why should knowledge matter in the case of a dispute over goods between the holder of a security interest and a third-party buyer (OPPSA s. 20(1)(c)), but not in the case of a dispute between the holders of competing security interests (OPPSA s. 20(1)(a)(i))?

In the context of OPPSA s. 30, the cases make it clear that priority turns on the first to perfect, regardless of knowledge. There are two main justifications: (1) a lack of knowledge requirement would reduce the incentive to perfect by diluting the consequences of non-perfection; and (2) a lack of knowledge requirement would increase litigation costs (see the Baird and Jackson extract in Chapter 7, Part III). Section 52 of the *New Zealand Personal Property Securities Act 1999* provides as follows:

A buyer or lessee of collateral who acquires the collateral for value takes the collateral free of an unperfected security interest in the collateral, unless the unperfected security interest was created or provided for by a transaction to which the buyer or lessee is a party.

This provision is the counterpart of OPPSA s. 20(1)(c), but it omits the reference to delivery and it also omits the reference to the transferee's state of knowledge. The thinking is that the policy considerations stated above are not limited to disputes between competing secured parties but apply equally where the dispute is between a secured party and a third-party buyer.

5. Value

Consider the following case (Case 4):

SP holds an unperfected security interest in D's pickup truck. D agrees to sell the truck to T on June 1, with payment due on June 8. In the meantime, on June 3, SP registers a financing statement. T tenders payment on June 8. Does T take the truck free of C's security interest?

PPSA s. 1(1) defines "value" to mean any consideration sufficient to support a simple contract. On this basis, T's promise to pay made on June 1 is "value," and the requirements of s. 20(1)(c) are met at that point.

However, it has been held that, for the purposes of s. 20(1)(c), "value" means executed consideration, and in Case 4, T does not give value in this sense until June 8 when he tenders payment. Since SP is perfected by that point, s. 20(1)(c) does not apply, and so T takes the truck subject to SP's security interest: *Royal Bank of Canada v. Dawson Motors (Guelph) Ltd.* (1981), 30 CBR (NS) 304 (Ont. Co. Ct.). The rationale is that T should not be allowed to complete the purchase once it knows or has the means of discovering SP's security interest. The decision puts the onus on T to search the register a second time before making payment. However, the case was decided under the old Act. OPPSA s. 46(5)(a) now provides that registration does not constitute constructive notice or knowledge of a security interest, while s. 69 defines knowledge in a way that seems to preclude constructive notice. These provisions limit *Dawson Motors'* application: the decision now only matters in the case where T acquires actual knowledge of SP's security interest before the payment date.

Nevertheless, in this case, *Dawson Motors* puts s. 20(1)(c) further out of kilter with s. 20(1)(a)(i). Section 20(1)(a)(i) also requires the giving of value because value is a requirement for attachment, which, in turn, is a requirement for perfection. However, here it seems clear that the s. 1(1) definition applies. Why should the meaning of value vary between the two provisions? Ziegel and Denomme suggest that the appropriate solution in Case 4 fact situations would be to allow T to complete the purchase on paying the balance of the agreed consideration to SP: Ziegel and Denomme, p. 167. See also Ziegel, Comment (1981-1982), 6 *CBLJ* 507.

CHAPTER SIX

Registration

I. INTRODUCTION

Public disclosure of security interests through registration has long been a feature of personal property security law in common law jurisdictions in Canada. The Legislature of the Assembly of the Province of Canada enacted legislation in 1849 requiring public registration of chattel mortgages as a condition of their enforceability against subsequent interests in mortgaged property acquired from mortgagors. By the turn of the 20th century, all common law jurisdictions required chattel mortgages to be registered, and all but Manitoba extended registration requirements to conditional sales contracts. The enactment of a *Bankruptcy Act* in 1919 forced provinces to enact registration requirements for general assignment of book debts by providing that a general assignment of book debts was void as against the trustee in bankruptcy unless registered in a provincial registry.

A few jurisdictions included provisions in companies legislation for the registration of secured corporate bonds, debentures, floating charges, and other corporate securities. Much of the early legislation of this kind was patterned on s. 14 of the English *Companies Act* of 1900. In 1932 the Uniform Law Conference of Canada, a semi-official organization established in 1918 by the Canadian Bar Association to encourage uniformity of provincial law, put forward the *Uniform Corporation Securities Registration Act* that, shortly thereafter, was adopted in several provinces, including Ontario. Starting in 1922, the Uniform Law Conference of Canada adopted a series of uniform acts in the area of personal property security law. These acts dealt primarily with registration of security agreements and, while not implemented in all jurisdictions, were influential in shaping chattel security legislation in several common law provinces.

The enactment of PPSAs resulted in the repeal of separate registry statutes dealing with chattel mortgages, conditional sales contracts, assignment of book debts, and corporate securities. Three, and in many cases, four separate, antiquated and disparate systems were replaced by a single modern system applicable to all types of security interests. However, not all of the PPSA registry systems are identical. While the various provincial systems are coming closer together, largely as a result of the efforts of the Canadian Conference on Personal Property Security Law (CCPPSL), it is not yet possible to assume that the requirements of one system are identical to those of others. The differences among the systems are a product of a number of factors, including policy choices. The systems in the Atlantic provinces are entirely electronic, while other systems permit the use of "hard copy" financing statements or financing change statements as alternatives to electronic financing statements or financing change statements. (Ontario was until recently in this latter group, but it has now moved to a fully electronic system.) Collateral description requirements in financing statements and financing change statements are very different under the Acts based on the CCPPSL model from those of the Ontario Act. In particular, the requirements for specific collateral identification by serial number are much broader under the CCPPSL Acts. (The Ontario government has signaled its intention to adopt the collateral description requirements of the other provinces, but at the date of writing it is uncertain when the change will be implemented.)

In this chapter, the basic features of a central, computerized notice registration system are examined. The primary focus is on the Ontario Personal Property Registry. Significant features of other systems, based on the CCPPSL model, that differ from the Ontario system are noted.

II. THE FUNCTION OF REGISTRATION

Douglas G. Baird, "Notice Filing and the Problem of Ostensible Ownership"
(1983), 12 *Journal of Legal Studies* 53, at 59-67 (footnotes omitted)

The drafters of article 9 considered abandoning filing systems altogether and replacing them with rules to protect potential creditors from debtor misrepresentations. A secured creditor would have been obliged "to use due diligence to see that his debtor's financial statements made full disclosure of the security interest; creditors and purchasers misled by improper statements were to have a right of recovery, to the extent of loss caused by good faith reliance, not only against the issuer of the statement but against a secured party who had failed to perform his policing duty." To the drafters' surprise, however, the representatives of secured lenders, who generally favored relaxing the stringent precode filing rules, objected to the abolition even more violently than the representatives of unsecured creditors.

Why did secured creditors oppose the change? They had complained that the early filing systems were burdensome; they should have been glad to escape the burden of filing altogether. Perhaps secured creditors preferred a filing system to the proposed change. A duty to file only once might have seemed less onerous than a general duty of diligence. An article 9 filing is easy to make and costs only a few dollars. A general duty of diligence may require higher costs initially and higher costs after the fact. A party that contested a security interest could nearly always force a court to engage in a fact-laden inquiry about whether the secured party had been diligent.

I want to focus instead, however, on another, less obvious consequence of abandoning a filing system: Secured creditors would lose the substantial benefits it provides them. In fact, benefits to secured creditors may be the primary justification for the present notice-filing system, while the direct benefits to general creditors may be small. Secured creditors benefit from a central file that indicates the existence of a claim in a particular asset belonging to the debtor, and whether that or any subsequent claim would have priority over their claim. By contrast, general creditors rely only in part on the debtor's assets when extending credit. General creditors base their decision to lend on the debtor's general financial health, of which a present or potential encumbrance on the debtor's property is only one factor.

Cases in which general creditors decide to lend because of their mistaken belief that an asset is unencumbered are rare. A security interest should not greatly affect a general creditor's assessment of the riskiness of his loan, because, as a general creditor, he does not look to a particular piece of property to satisfy the debt. Even if he did, he could not effectively prevent the debtor from later encumbering or disposing of the property, because any promises that the debtor makes not to encumber the property are not enforceable against a subsequent good faith purchaser. The general creditor whose debtor falsely indicates that a piece of property is unencumbered is ultimately no worse off than one whose debtor later encumbers the property in violation of an express promise not to.

The unsecured creditor must rely in large part on what his debtor tells him. A filing system might prevent a debtor from misinforming a potential creditor about whether a particular asset is encumbered, but if a debtor would misinform the creditor about whether his property was encumbered, he would be likely to misinform him about other relevant information, such as the extent of the debtor's unsecured obligations, his fixed business costs, and his plans to acquire or dispose of equipment and inventory. The filing system gives notice only of a duty to inquire further. The potential creditor who inquires further must rely on the cooperation of the prospective debtor.

Under a notice-filing system, general creditors can learn only that the debtor might have conveyed some ownership rights to a secured party. For everything else they must rely on the debtor and they must expose themselves to the risk that the debtor will misinform them. If debtor misbehavior is a problem that notice filing is intended to cure, it is a bad rule. Moreover, we should remember that a more elaborate filing system is only one of several possible reforms. If the legal system needs to be changed to give general creditors more protection, additional civil and criminal penalties for debtor misbehavior seem more appropriate than requiring more information in the filing system.

General creditors effectively acquire a lien on the debtor's property the moment a petition in bankruptcy is filed, because the trustee has the status of a hypothetical lien creditor and he represents the interests of the general creditors. But the powers of the trustee after the filing of the petition in bankruptcy do not alter the general creditor's lack of interest in the debtor's property before the filing. With or without a trustee, every general creditor is a potential claimant to the debtor's property. A general creditor brings a lawsuit and reduces his claim to judgment, or he relies on the trustee to act in his behalf. In neither case does the contingent claim against specific assets of the debtor loom large before the fact.

The Code's filing system is of some use to general creditors. Misrepresentations about one's financial health are harder to make when a filing system exists than when it does not. Moreover, trade creditors who might lack access to the debtor's financial records can quickly determine whether any creditor might claim that the goods shipped to the debtor were inventory subject to his security interest. The trade creditor may decide whether to send the goods on open account or to insist upon retaining a purchase money security interest only after checking the filing system. A compulsory public filing system is more accurate than any private system because security interests not properly noted in a public filing system are not enforceable against such competing property claimants as a lien creditor or a trustee in bankruptcy. But although the information in the filing system may be accurate and potentially useful to general creditors, this does not explain why article 9 requires the particular information in the financing statement that it does. That a type of property (which the debtor may not have) may now or in the future be encumbered to an unknown extent is no more important to the general creditor than much other information that he must obtain from the debtor.

In short, the needs of general creditors neither justify the costs of the present filing system nor explain its contours. By contrast, a secured creditor relies on particular assets of the debtor. He needs to know whether a particular piece of property is encumbered. If the property securing his debt is or might become encumbered, the creditor cannot consider the loan secured. The information that the Code provides secured creditors in its filing system is exactly tailored to their need to know whether any claim they make to a particular asset will have priority over any other. The filing system is, in effect, a place where secured creditors stake claims to the debtor's property.

In a study of patent law, Edmund Kitch developed the idea that statutes that require public disclosure of information are like those that govern the acquisition of mineral rights on federal land. Kitch argued that the patent system could be seen as a set of rules that allowed individuals to acquire exclusive rights to develop a known technological opportunity. A miner need detect only some ore before being given exclusive rights to the minerals. Without such rights, he would lack the incentive to invest in further exploration. Similarly, an inventor need claim only that a machine is new, nonobvious, and useful. He need not claim that the machine is far enough developed to be commercially viable. Because he is granted exclusive rights after some showing that he will develop the invention, the inventor has the incentive to invest resources needed to exploit his idea commercially.

Schwartz and Scott have applied Kitch's "prospecting" theory to the Code's notice-filing and first-in-time rules. In their view, these rules together allow a creditor who has discovered a good credit risk (like a miner who has discovered a valuable mineral deposit or an inventor who has hit upon a new idea) to have exclusive rights to the financing opportunity. Little information is included in the filing system so that other creditors do not take advantage of the credit prospect that the first creditor has discovered. This justification of notice filing, however, assumes that subsequent creditors would find the information in a more elaborate filing system useful. As Schwartz and Scott recognize, even comprehensive information about a particular loan transaction might not tell subsequent creditors much about making a different kind of loan at a later time.

The analogy to mineral claims that I draw, however, is a more modest one and makes a simpler point. The notice-filing system is like the law governing mineral claims because it makes the existence of property rights public in a clear and unambiguous way. A prospector in the Old West could explore land, confident that no one else had a claim to it that would be superior to his as long as no markers indicated it belonged to someone else. Similarly, a creditor can lend money to a debtor with confidence because he knows (by looking at the files) that no other existing creditor can claim an interest in the property superior to his own.

The Code's filing system follows from its first-to-file rule. Unlike a potential general creditor, a potential secured creditor needs to know whether an asset is or might become encumbered and whether competing claims will take priority over his claim. Unclear priority rules increase the cost of making secured loans. The Code's priority rules are on the whole clear: The secured party who is first in time wins, and the secured party who is first to file is the first in time.

A rule that dated priority by some other benchmark would be harder to apply. For example, the date the security interest comes into being is not a desirable rule for determining priority, because it depends on a number of facts that are hard to discover. A security interest comes into being (or "attaches," to use the language of article 9) only after the parties have agreed to create a security interest and three conditions are satisfied: (1) the creditor has given value; (2) the debtor has acquired rights in the collateral; and (3) the debtor has signed a written security agreement or the creditor has taken possession of the collateral. A rule that fixed the priority by the date on which any of these three events took place would be unfortunate because it would require potential creditors to rely on the debtor's records.

Moreover, information about the date an agreement was made, value was given, or the rights were acquired is not only in the control of the debtor, but is also less certain than a filing date. For example, "value" does not cover only cash outlays; it also includes any commitment to extend credit in the future. But whether the lender has made a commitment or has reserved the option to cancel the line of credit is sometimes left unclear in revolving credit arrangements. Similarly, a debtor's acquisition of rights in the collateral may be unclear. For example, when does a debtor acquire rights in the collateral if he has a machine built to his order? When the manufacture is completed? When he acquires an article 2 "special property" interest? When the risk of loss passes to him? All of these dates are hard for potential secured creditors to determine. Hence neither they nor the time the security interest itself comes into being seems an appropriate benchmark for determining priority. Not even the date of signing a written security agreement will be clear, because agreements can be amended and loans can involve several written documents, all of which can qualify as security agreements.

By contrast, article 9's notice-filing system meshes perfectly with its first-to-file rule. It clearly establishes the priority of each secured creditor and little else. The notice-filing system is of little use to general creditors who need an overview of the financial condition of their debtors, but it does provide secured creditors with most of the information they need, once one assumes that secured creditors typically do not take multiple security interests in the same property. A creditor cannot safely enter a secured transaction if another creditor already has superior rights to the same asset, unless the senior creditor executes a subordination agreement. Because executing such agreements is costly, article 9's rules rest in some measure on the assumption that most secured parties do not want such junior interests. This assumption seems plausible, however. A piece of equipment is harder to value and less likely to appreciate than land. In practice, creditors do not often take what a real estate lawyer would call a second mortgage. If the legal rule in fact accommodates the needs of the parties rather than vice-versa—that is, if creditors avoid inferior interests in personal property because of the nature of the property, rather than of the legal rules governing it—secured creditors would not need to learn anything from the filing system other than the name of the person who might have a security interest. The benefits of article 9's rules may outweigh the costs they impose on junior secured creditors. Even for those who do seek such interests, a notice-filing system provides the information they need (the name of the secured party and the type of collateral involved) to begin negotiating a subordination agreement.

In offering this explanation of a notice-filing system, I assume that a creditor examines the filing system only after he decides whether to become a secured creditor. If creditors, as a general matter, did all their information gathering before they decided to lend on a secured or unsecured basis, the information in a notice-filing system would be resorted to as often by unsecured creditors as by secured. At the time they decided whether to check the files, creditors would not yet know which they would be. There are, however, two reasons for thinking that a party typically decides on what basis to lend before checking the files. First, many creditors know before they even meet their debtor that they will lend, if at all, on either a secured or unsecured basis. A trade creditor usually does not take a security interest; a finance company like Walter E. Heller invariably does. Indeed, if secured credit brings efficiency gains at all, one would expect the source of these gains to lie in the greater ability or willingness of some creditors to monitor their debtor or to specialize in a transaction of a certain type.

Second, the usefulness of the information in the filing system does not derive from what it tells creditors who are just entering negotiations. At the early stages, creditors can rely on what their debtor tells them. The need to check the files arises when the i's have to be dotted and the t's crossed. The information in the filing system primarily provides reassurance that all is as it appears to be and that the debtor does not have unannounced encumbrances on his assets. That information in the files corresponds to the debtor's representations is a common condition of closing a deal. A lawyer usually does not even have the files checked until the deal is fairly far along, far enough, at any rate, for the decision to have been made whether the loan will be secured. Indeed, if the filing system is checked too early in the negotiations, it will have to be checked again to ensure no intervening interest has arisen.

In short, the Code's notice-filing system addresses principally only one kind of ostensible ownership problem—the one arising from competition between secured creditors. When all security interests were possessory, a secured creditor did not have to worry about other secured creditors, because his security interest was valid as long as he possessed the property. When the secured creditor could create a security interest without acquiring control of the property, he had to account for conflicts with others attempting to do the same. Article 9's notice-filing system largely responds to this need, not to the needs of general creditors.

The rules governing secured transactions try to balance the benefits of secured credit against the costs it imposes on third parties. For four centuries the most significant of these costs has been thought to be the one imposed by the problem of ostensible ownership, the problem that arises when the debtor appears to own property that he possesses, but in which, in fact, another party has a property interest. In this paper, I have argued that article 9 embraced this principle much more narrowly than has been thought. The present filing system serves the useful function of sorting out and protecting the interests of competing property claimants. If this analysis of the notice-filing system is sound, assumptions about when filing should be required and what information the file should contain need to be re-examined. For example, the appropriate analysis of whether descriptions in a financing statement are accurate changes substantially, because the purpose of the description is only to provide information to a narrow class of third parties, those who are property claimants. Similarly, the debate about whether there should be a filing requirement for leases changes significantly if one's identification of the beneficiaries of the filing system changes.

NOTE

According to Baird, "the Code's notice-filing system addresses principally only one kind of ostensible ownership problem—the one arising from competition between secured creditors." This statement overlooks other registry users, in particular non-ordinary course buyers of collateral and execution creditors: see Chapter 5, Part V. The reason for the oversight is, presumably, that the point was not relevant to Baird's main argument; namely, that the registration system is not designed for the benefit of general unsecured creditors and Baird should not be read as implying that only secured creditors benefit from registration. Subject to this caveat, the extract is valuable for explaining why the register is of limited use to general creditors and also for drawing the connection between the notice-filing concept and the first-to-file priority rule for competing secured claims. For further discussion of the notice-filing concept, see Part III.B, below. See also the Jackson and Kronman extract in Chapter 7, Part II.

III. SOME BASIC CONCEPTS

A. Structural Unity of Substantive Personal Property Security Law

As mentioned above, before the enactment of the PPSAs, secured financing was carried out through a range of different types of financing devices that included chattel mortgages, conditional sales contracts, assignments of accounts, and corporate securities. Because of the way in which these devices developed, each came equipped with its own registry. Frequently the technical requirements of one registry were not the same as another. This unsatisfactory state of affairs ended when secured financing law was completely reconfigured in the PPSAs so as to eliminate the traditional security devices and to consolidate all regulation of secured financing in a single regime. The benefits of this transformation were very significant. All registrations are subject to substantially the same requirements. A single search will disclose all consensual charges against the name of the debtor or against a specified item of property.

B. Notice Registration

Before enactment of the PPSAs, most registry statutes required the secured party to file a copy of the security agreement with the registry. Searches involved actual examination of filed agreements or requests for registrar's certificates indicating that no agreements had been filed. Following the Article 9 lead, the PPSAs introduced notice registration as a substitute for document filing (see OPPSA s. 45.) This involves registration of a simple notice (called a "financing statement") containing skeletal information about an existing or potential legal relationship (generally, a security agreement) between the parties. (See OPPSA s. 46(1)-(2) and Minister's Order under the Personal Property Security Act, ss. 2-3.) As the Baird extract above indicates, the financing statement gives the searcher very few details about the secured party's transaction with the debtor. It is designed to do no more than alert the searcher to the possibility that the secured party might have a security interest in one or more specified collateral types. If the searcher wants more information, he must request it from the secured party, and the legislation makes provision for this: OPPSA s. 18.

Notice filing has a number of advantages over document filing. One of the most significant problems under the pre-PPSA registration statutes was the need to store vast numbers of written security agreements. This problem was addressed by requiring secured parties to "renew" the registration periodically. Under this approach, a registration was effective for a specified period of time (usually three or five years), after which it lapsed unless renewed. Notice filing addresses the storage problem and it allows for removal of the registration renewal requirement. The OPPSA allows the secured party to nominate its own registration period in the financing statement, except where the collateral is consumer goods, in which case there is a maximum registration period of five years: s. 51.

A second advantage of notice filing is that it provides a greater measure of confidentiality of business information than is permitted by document filing. The secured party need not release the details of a security agreement with respect to which a financing statement has been registered except upon demand by the debtor or other person specifically authorized to make the demand (OPPSA s. 18). Unless the cooperation of the debtor or of someone else authorized to make the demand is obtained, competitors of the secured party do not have access to these details.

Important features of the PPSA are facilitated by notice registration. Modern financing arrangements require the flexibility that a PPSA system provides. A single financing statement can relate to one or more than one security agreement. Indeed, it is possible that a properly drawn financing statement can meet registration requirements for many security agreements between the same parties entered into over a period of several years (see OPPSA s. 45(4)). A financing statement can be registered before a security agreement is executed between the parties (see OPPSA s. 45(3)). For a discussion of the economic costs and benefits of these rules, see the Jackson and Kronman extract in Chapter 7, Part II.

Notice registration works extremely well in the context of computerized registries, such as those in operation in all common law provinces. Under these systems, a financing statement is a computer screen (referred to under some Acts as an "electronic financing statement") provided to the secured party by the registry software. (See, for example, BC reg. 279/90, s. 1 (definition of "electronic financing statement"), and Ontario *Electronic Registration Act*, SO 1991, c. 44.) The person registering the financing statement simply enters the basic information required by the regulations; this information is then transmitted to the registry database and stored there.

C. Electronic Registration Systems

Originally, personal property security registers were wholly paper-based. Under a paper-based system, the secured party would complete a financing statement and lodge it with the registry office, where registry staff would transcribe the information into the registry database. Correspondingly, the searcher would complete a search application form and lodge it with the registry office, where registry staff would search the register and transcribe the relevant information onto a search certificate. However, in all provinces, including Ontario, the register is now computerized and is accessible electronically. Until recently, the OPPSA gave parties the option of filing and searching either electronically or by paper. However, the legislation was amended in 2006 to eliminate the paper option, and now all financing statements must be in the electronic format approved by the registrar: Minister's Order, s. 2. The registration system in the Atlantic provinces is also fully electronic, but the other provinces and territories continue to offer both electronic and paper registration and search facilities.

One of the advantages of computerization is that it saves transactions costs: it is much quicker and easier for parties to register and search electronically than it is to complete and lodge paper forms, particularly where there is no registry office close by. A second advantage is that, because computerization promotes direct user access to the register, it saves administration costs: if the system is a fully electronic one, there is no need for registry staff to process filing and search applications. A related benefit is that by promoting direct user access, an electronic system avoids time lags between the lodging of a financing statement and registration of the security interest. Time lags reduce the reliability of the register.

For example, assume SP1 lodges a paper financing statement for registration on the morning of June 1. Registry staff process the paperwork and complete the registration on the afternoon of June 2. In the meantime, on the morning of June 2, SP2 searches the register but does not discover SP1's security interest given that it has not yet been entered on the register. There are two main ways the legislation might deal with this problem. The first would be to say that SP1's registration is complete as soon as it lodges the financing statement with the registry office on June 1 (this was the Ontario approach prior to the 2006 reforms).The second would be to say that the registration is not complete until June 2, when it is entered on the register (this is the approach taken in those provinces and territories that still allow paper financing statements: Cuming, Walsh, and Wood, at 240-42). The first approach puts the risk of the delay on SP2 because it means that SP1 has a perfected security interest even though it is unsearchable between the lodgment and entry dates. The second approach puts the risk on SP1 because it means that the security interest is unperfected between the lodgment and entry dates. By contrast, in a fully electronic system lodgment and entry are more or less instantaneous and so the problem does not arise.

In summary, paper-based systems create a time lag problem, and either the registering party or the searcher must bear the risk. Paper-based systems also involve the risk of transcription errors. For example, assume that the debtor's name is XYZ, and SP1 correctly writes the debtor's name as XYZ in a paper financing statement but registry staff incorrectly record the debtor's name as XYY on the register (see, *e.g., Bank of Nova Scotia v. Clinton's Flowers & Gifts Ltd.* (1994), 108 DLR (4th) 448 (Ont. CA)). SP2 searches the register under the debtor's correct name, but, because of the transcription error, the search does not retrieve SP1's entry. In Ontario, prior to the 2006 reforms, the courts took the view that since SP1's registration was complete upon lodgment, the error did not affect the validity of SP1's registration: see *Clinton's Flowers*, above. The implication of this rule is that SP2 bears the risk of transcription errors: SP1 has a perfected security interest, but SP2 is unlikely to discover it because a search under the debtor's correct name will not retrieve the entry. The

212 Chapter 6 Registration

alternative approach would have been for the Act to say that registration does not occur until entry on the register. However, this does not eliminate the risk of transcription errors but merely transfers it to the secured party. OPPSA s. 44 establishes an Assurance Fund to compensate searchers who suffer loss as a consequence of system errors. The effect of this provision is to transfer the risk of transcription errors and the like at least partly to the government. By contrast, a fully electronic system eliminates the transcription function and avoids the problem altogether.

D. Verification Statements and Other Safeguards

When a registration is effected in a personal property registry, the computer automatically prints out a verification statement containing the information that has been entered into the database of the registry relating to that registration. This is immediately sent to the registering party: see Minister's Order, s. 22.

A verification statement permits a registering party to determine whether or not the information contained in the database of the registry relating to its registration is accurate. Errors on the part of the registering party can be immediately identified and corrected.

The Ontario Act contains special provisions designed to protect consumers. See OPPSA s. 45(2) (which precludes effective registration of a security interest in consumer goods before the security agreement is signed by the debtor); s. 45(4) (which requires a separate registration for each security interest in consumer goods); and s. 51(5) (which limits the effectiveness of a registration relating to a security interest in consumer goods to a maximum of five years). See also Minister's Order, ss. 3(1)(i) and (4). The other provincial PPSAs contain no equivalent provisions. What are the policy reasons behind these special provisions? Do you see any difficulties associated with compliance with these rules where the debtor runs a small, unincorporated business?

While there are no equivalent provisions in the other provincial PPSAs, other measures (for the most part, also found in the OPPSA) are available in cases of abuse of the flexibility given to secured parties. The following description includes references to the SPPSA. The secured party is required to deliver a copy of a financing statement or verification statement to the person named as debtor in a registration (s. 43(12)). (See also OPPSA s. 46(6).) Where a registration relates exclusively to a security interest in consumer goods and the obligations associated with the security interest are performed, the secured party is required to register a financing change statement discharging the registration. However, a discharge of the financing statement is not required if the registration automatically lapses within one month of the date the obligations are performed (s. 50(2)). Section 50(3) sets out the circumstances in which a debtor (whether or not a consumer) is entitled to demand that the registration be discharged or amended. In particular, a demand can be made and enforced where (1) a pre-agreement registration has been effected under s. 43(4) but no agreement has been concluded between the "secured party" and the "debtor" (see also OPPSA s. 56(2)); (2) the debtor's obligations under a security agreement have been discharged but the secured party has maintained a registration relating to it (see also OPPSA s. 56(1)); (3) the collateral description in the registration is broader than is warranted by the terms of the security agreement between the parties (see also OPPSA s. 56(2)); or (4) the registration does not distinguish between original collateral and proceeds. A secured party who fails, without reasonable excuse, to comply with a demand under s. 50(3) is liable to the debtor (or the person disclosed as debtor in the registration) for deemed damages under s. 65(4) (see also OPPSA s. 56(2)). Section 50(5) permits a person making a demand to enforce compliance unless a court order is obtained by the secured party. This is accomplished by providing proof to the registrar that the demand was made and that the 15-day period for compliance has passed together with a financing change statement providing for the discharge or amendment of the registration, as the case may be, which the registrar must accept and register. Compare OPPSA s. 56(5), which requires the aggrieved "debtor" to make application to the court to have the registration discharged or partially discharged, as the case may be.

Assume that, at the date a financing statement was registered, the debtor held the collateral as equipment but shortly thereafter began using it as consumer goods. The financing statement provided for a registration period of 15 years. Does the registration become invalid as soon as the use of the collateral changes from equipment to consumer goods? See *Royal Bank v. Wheaton Pontiac Buick Cadillac GMC Ltd.* (1990), 88 Sask. R 151 (QB). The problem is directly addressed in the non-Ontario PPSAs. For example, SPPSA s. 2(3) provides that, "[u]nless otherwise provided in the Act, the determination of whether goods are consumer goods, inventory or equipment is to be made at the time when the security interest in the goods attaches."

E. Debtor Name-Based Registration and Serial Number Registration

1. The Functions of the Two Systems

There are two basic forms a register of personal property security interests might take: security interests might be registrable and searchable against the debtor's name, or they might be registrable and searchable against the collateral's serial number. Of course, serial number registration is only feasible for serial-numbered collateral (for example, motor vehicles, trailers, and aircraft). For other collateral (for example, accounts, crops, and raw materials), debtor's name registration will be the only option.

The Canadian PPSAs combine both systems, although in Ontario the serial number index is limited to motor vehicles, whereas in the other provinces it extends to other kinds of serial-numbered goods as well (for example, tractors, mobile equipment, mobile homes, boats, trailers, and aircraft). The serial number for motor vehicles is the Vehicle Identification Number ("VIN"). Unlike their counterparts in the United States, Canadian provinces never adopted certificate of title systems for motor vehicles. Under the US systems, a security interest in a motor vehicle is recorded on the paper title to the motor vehicle. A third party intending to acquire an interest in the motor vehicle can discover the security interest simply by examining the title. The lack of certificate of title systems in Canada means that security interests in motor vehicles must be registered in public registries if third parties are to be protected.

In Ontario, the legislation provides that if the collateral comprises a motor vehicle that is consumer goods, the financing statement must set out the VIN; on the other hand, if the motor vehicle is equipment or inventory, inclusion of the VIN is optional. The reason is that security interests in present and after-acquired equipment and inventory are common, and the secured party will usually have no way of knowing the VIN of an after-acquired motor

vehicle at the time of preparing the financing statement (on the other hand, the Act prohibits security interests in after-acquired consumer goods: s. 12). Correspondingly, the legislation also provides that a person may search the register using either the debtor's name index
or the VIN index: s. 43. The consequences of omitting or incorrectly stating the VIN if the
vehicle is consumer goods are governed by s. 46(4): the error or omission makes the financing statement materially misleading because it causes the security interest to be unsearchable in the VIN index. A materially misleading error invalidates the financing statement and
this will result in the security interest being unperfected: see further, Part IV, below. The
consequences of omitting or incorrectly stating the VIN if the vehicle is equipment are governed by s. 28(5), also discussed in Part IV, below.

Why does the legislation provide for registration and search against both name and serial
number? The reason is that both systems have their strengths and weaknesses and the aim
is to achieve the best of both worlds from the searcher's perspective. The advantage of a
debtor's name registration system is that a search should retrieve all extant personal property security interests, thereby giving the searcher a reasonably complete picture of the
extent to which the debtor has encumbered its assets. On the other hand, a search in the
debtor's name index will not retrieve a security interest given by a prior owner. For example:
SP1 (A), takes a security interest in collateral belonging to Debtor (B) and registers a financing statement against B's name. B later sells the collateral to Transferee (C) who, in turn, negotiates with SP2 (D) for a loan secured on the same collateral. In these circumstances, a
search by D in the debtor's name index is unlikely to retrieve A's security interest. This is because D will typically search against C's name, whereas A's security interest will be registered
against B's name, not C's. (This is often referred to as the "A-B-C-D" problem.) By contrast,
the pros and cons of a serial number registration system are the reverse: a serial number
search should reveal all extant security interests in the collateral, regardless of who created
them, but what it won't reveal is security interests the debtor may have given in other assets.
The legislation gives searchers the option of searching in either or both indexes, the purpose
being to cater to the various needs of different searchers. Another disadvantage of serial
number registration is that because, *ex hypothesi*, the secured party needs to know the serial
number in order to complete the financing statement, a serial number registration system
cannot accommodate registration of a security interest in after-acquired collateral. This is
why, as noted above, the PPSAs make serial number registration optional if the collateral is
equipment or inventory.

2. The Name Index: Individual Debtors

The Ontario name index comprises an individual debtor name index and a business debtor
name index (OPPSA s. 43(1)) and in the individual debtor name index the searcher has the
option of a specific search or a non-specific search. For a specific search, the searcher must
key in the debtor's first name, middle initial, last name, and date of birth. For a non-specific
search, the searcher must key in only the debtor's first name and last name. A specific search
will retrieve only those entries that match all four search criteria, whereas a non-specific
search will retrieve all entries that match the first and last names the searcher has keyed in,
regardless of middle initials and birth dates. The difference is most likely to matter if the

debtor has a common name, such as John Smith, because in that case a non-specific search is likely to retrieve more entries than a specific search. The searcher will then have to sift through the entries to identify the one she is looking for. To facilitate these search functions, the regulations provide that if the debtor is a natural person, the financing statement must contain the debtor's first name, middle initial, last name, and date of birth: Minister's Order, ss. 3(1) and 16(1). The consequences of failure to comply are governed by OPPSA s. 46(4): see Part IV, below.

Assume that the debtor goes by a name different from the one on her birth certificate. In *Re Haasen* (1992), 92 DLR (4th) 204, at 210 (Ont. Gen. Div.), Farley J concluded that the "correct" name of a debtor for registration purposes is the name found on his or her birth certificate. Killeen J in *CIBC v. Melnitzer* (1994), 6 PPSAC 5 (Ont. Gen. Div.) stated at 42-43:

> The (Ontario) PPSA is somewhat vague on the subject of the correct name of a debtor for registration purposes. Section 46(4) says this about errors in general:
>
>> (4) A financing statement or financing change statement is not invalidated nor is its effect impaired by reason only of an error or omission therein or in its execution or registration unless a reasonable person is likely to be misled materially by the error or omission.
>
> On the other hand, s. 16(1) of O. Reg. 372/89 [now RRO 1990, reg. 912], passed under the PPSA, specifies this:
>
>> 16(1) The name of a debtor who is a natural person shall be set out in the financing statement to show the first given name, followed by the initial of the second given name, if any, followed by the surname.
>
> One might have thought that the *Change of Name Act*, RSO 1990, c. C.7 might be helpful on the question of correct names but it, too, seems wanting in some respects. Section 2 of this Act, reads, in part, this way:
>
>> 2(1) For all purposes of Ontario law,
>>   (a) a person whose birth is registered in Ontario is entitled to be recognized by the name appearing on the person's birth certificate or change of name certificate, unless clause (c) applies;
>>   (b) a person whose birth is not registered in Ontario is entitled to be recognized by,
>>   (i) the name appearing on the person's change of name certificate, if the person's name has been changed under this Act or a predecessor of it, or
>>   (ii) in all other cases, the name recognized in law in the last place with which the person had a real and substantial connection before residing in Ontario.
>
> It might be said that s. 2(1)(a) above provides a useful guide for persons born in Ontario by saying that the name on the Ontario birth certificate is recognized for "all purposes of Ontario law." However, for a person like Melnitzer, born out of Ontario, one is directed to the law of the last place with which the person had a real and substantial connection. This rule is of no real assistance because I have no evidence before me as to Melnitzer's legally recognized name in Quebec, where he resided for many years before coming to Ontario in young adulthood.

Mr. Grace argued, relying on *Re Takhtalian* (1982), 2 PPSAC 90 (Ont. HC), that, for foreign-born citizens, it should be sufficient to use the name of the debtor on his Canadian citizenship certificate.

While, perhaps, a respectable argument can be made for the position that, in the case of foreign-born persons, their original birth certificate name should be used, I think, on balance, that it is practical and rational to opt for the name on a Canadian citizenship certificate, if one exists. The entire subject of correct names on a registration should probably be revisited by the legislature to staunch the flow of cases into the courts.

CCPPSL has approved rules for determining the debtor's correct name for registration purposes and these rules have been adopted in the Atlantic provinces, Alberta, Manitoba, the Northwest Territories, and Nunavut. The rules set out a hierarchy of sources: birth certificate for Canadian born debtors or, where birth is not registered, the name on a current passport, if any, or social insurance card; citizenship documents for Canadians born outside Canada, etc. They also provide that where the law of the jurisdiction where the debtor habitually resides allows a person to use both the name adopted after marriage and the name that person had before marriage, and the debtor uses both names, both the name of the debtor before marriage and the name adopted after marriage must be registered as separate debtor names. In the other non-Ontario jurisdictions, the issue has been left to the courts, "with somewhat mixed results": Cuming, Walsh, and Wood, at 250.

In several of these decisions (most involving trustees in bankruptcy), the courts concluded that the registration was not seriously misleading merely because it was not revealed in a search using the legal name of the debtor as the search criterion. They concluded that there is no requirement that the secured party use as the registration criterion the name of the debtor as it appears on her birth certificate. Regulations are interpreted as allowing the use of a name appearing on other documents such as a driver's licence, credit card, or on the business documents of an incorporated debtor. See, for example, *Re Fraser* (1994), 25 CBR (3d) 58 (BCSC) and *Re Paquette*, [1994] 6 WWR 113 (application for reconsideration refused 19 Alta. LR (3d) 142 (QB)). See *Re Baisley & Richer Air Freight Inc.* (1994), 93 BCLR (2d) 372 (SC). Do you see any difficulties with this approach? Should the searching party be expected to determine and use as search criteria all the possible variations of names used by a debtor?

3. The Name Index: Business Debtors

The regulations do contain rules for determining the debtor's name for registration purposes if the debtor is an artificial body: Minister's Order, s. 16(4), paras. 1-8 and s. 17. For example, if the debtor is a corporation, the financing statement must disclose the debtor's incorporated name. This means that in the case of a numbered company (for example, 123456 Ontario Ltd.) that does business under a trade name (for example, Acme Enterprises), it is the numbered name that must appear in the financing statement and not the trade name. If the corporation has both English and French forms of name, both must be disclosed. There are separate rules for the case where the debtor is a partnership, an unincorporated association, a deceased estate, a trade union, a trust, or a bankruptcy estate. These rules place a premium on the secured party selecting the correct name to include in the financing statement (the consequence of non-compliance will be to invalidate the financing statement: OPPSA s. 46(4)). However, they equally place a premium on the searcher selecting the correct name to search against. If the secured party includes the wrong name in the financing statement, a searcher searching against the correct name as determined by the regulations will not retrieve the entry. Likewise, if the secured party includes the right name, a search will be unsuccessful if the searcher uses a different name.

F. Exact Match and Close Match Retrieval Systems

The Ontario name index register is based on an exact match retrieval system. In other words, a search will not retrieve an entry if there is any deviation at all between the debtor's name as it appears in the financing statement and the name the searcher conducts the search against. So, for example, if the debtor's name appears in the financing statement as John H. Smythe, a search against the name John H. Smyth will be unsuccessful. In the *Clinton's Flowers* case, above, the debtor's correct name was "Clinton's Flowers and Gifts Ltd." The secured party had correctly written the name in the financing statement, but, due to a transcription error by registry staff, the name appeared on the register as "Clinton Flowers and Gifts Ltd." The error caused the registration to be unsearchable. The non-specific search facility in the individual debtor name index is the only concession the legislation makes to imprecision or lack of information on the part of system users.

By contrast, the registers in the other provinces are based on a close similar match system. A close similar match system is forgiving of the kinds of minor errors indicated above. Whereas a search certificate in an exact match system will disclose only entries that exactly match the search criteria the searcher keys in, a search certificate in a close similar match system will disclose all entries that are reasonably close; "reasonable closeness" being a function of programming. This means that the searcher will have to sift through the various entries listed on the search certificate to identify the one she is looking for. In summary, both systems have pros and cons. The main benefit of a close similar match system is the tolerance it allows for user error, but the cost is a potentially noisier search result. It was mainly for this reason that the Canadian Bar Association's Personal Property Securities Law Committee recommended in 1998 against the move to a close similar match system in Ontario: Canadian Bar Association, *Ontario Submission to the Minister of Consumer and Commercial Relations Concerning the Personal Property Security Act* (Toronto: CBAO, 1998), para. 15.

G. Expanded Use of Personal Property Registries

The personal property registries are also made available for the registration of *in rem* interests other than security interests. See, for example, *Repair and Storage Liens Act*, RSO 1990, c. R.25. They are used for the registration of a wide variety of interests ranging from buyers' interests when goods are left in the possession of sellers (see, for example, *Sale of Goods Act*, RSS 1978, c. S-1, s. 26(1)(1.1)), to statutory liens for obligations owing to the Crown (see, for example, *Gasoline Tax Act*, RSO 1990, c. G.5, s. 19.1) or arising from unpaid parking tickets (see the *Summary Convictions Act*, CCSM c. S230 as amended SM 1993, c. 2, adding ss. 23.1-23.4).

IV. ERRORS AND OMISSIONS IN REGISTRATION DATA

Re Lambert
(1994), 20 OR (3d) 108 (CA)

DOHERTY JA:

I. The Issue

When will an error in the contents of a financing statement render the statement invalid and the security interest it represents unperfected as against third parties? The answer depends on the reach of s. 46(4) of the *Personal Property Security Act*, RSO 1990, c. P.10 ("PPSA"), which reads:

> 46(4) A financing statement or financing change statement is not invalidated nor is its effect impaired by reason only of an error or omission therein or in its execution or registration unless a reasonable person is likely to be misled materially by the error or omission.

II. The Facts

Mr. Lambert purchased a motor vehicle under the terms of a conditional sales contract. The vendor sold the contract to the appellant (GMAC). GMAC registered its security interest in the vehicle by filing a financing statement as provided in the PPSA. The financing statement referred to the debtor as Gilles J. Lambert. This was the name used by Mr. Lambert when he signed the conditional sales contract and was also the name used to identify the owner of the vehicle in the records of the Ministry of Transportation and Communication. Unfortunately, it is not Mr. Lambert's proper name. His name, as shown on his birth certificate, is Joseph Phillipe Gilles Lambert. The financing statement correctly identified Mr. Lambert's date of birth and correctly set out the Vehicle Identification Number (the VIN).

Subsequent to the registration, Mr. Lambert made an assignment in bankruptcy and his trustee took possession of the motor vehicle. GMAC filed a proof of claim contending that it was a secured creditor with a security interest in the motor vehicle. At some point subsequent to the assignment in bankruptcy, the trustee acquired a copy of the GMAC financing statement. It identified the vehicle as "consumer goods."

The trustee caused its solicitor to inquire into the claim of GMAC. To do so, she turned to the computerized registration system established under the PPSA. That system made three inquiries available. A searcher could conduct an individual specific debtor name inquiry (a specific debtor inquiry), an individual non-specific debtor name inquiry (a non-specific debtor inquiry) and a vehicle number inquiry (a VIN search). To conduct the specific debtor inquiry, a searcher must enter into the computer the debtor's first name, middle initial, last name and date of birth. This search retrieves only financing statements in which the debtor's first name, middle initial, last name and date of birth as set out in the financing statement exactly match the data entered by the searcher. The non-specific inquiry requires the searcher to enter the debtor's first and last name. It reveals all financing statements where the debtor is described by that first and last name regardless of the middle initial, if any, or the date of birth shown in the financing statement. A VIN search is made by entering the VIN only and retrieves all financing statements in which the collateral is described by the same VIN entered by the searcher regardless of the name of the debtor. The VIN search is available only where the collateral is a motor vehicle. The VIN must be recorded in the financing statement where the motor vehicle is classified as consumer goods. Where the motor vehicle is not so classified, the VIN may be included in the financing statement.

The trustee's solicitor, relying on the name on Lambert's birth certificate, made individual specific inquiries using the names Joseph P. Lambert and Joseph G. Lambert and Lambert's birth date. She also made an individual non-specific search using the name Joseph Lambert. None of these searches revealed the financing statement filed by GMAC since it referred to the debtor as Gilles J. Lambert. The solicitor did not conduct a VIN search, although the trustee had access to that number. A VIN search would have revealed the GMAC financing statement.

The trustee moved for a declaration that the GMAC security interest was not perfected and was, therefore, not effective against the trustee in bankruptcy. The trustee submitted that the errors in the recording of the debtor's name in the financing statement were fatal to the perfection of that interest as against the trustee. GMAC maintained that the errors were cured by s. 46(4) of the PPSA since the trustee should have performed a VIN search and had he done so, he would not have been misled by the errors in the debtor's name. Farley J found in favour of the trustee. His reasons are now reported at (1991), 2 PPSAC (2d) 160, 11 CBR (3d) 165 (Gen. Div.).

III. Analysis

But for s. 46(4), there would be little difficulty applying the terms of the PPSA to this fact situation.

Section 19(b) of the PPSA provides that a security interest is perfected when all steps required for perfection under the PPSA have been completed. Section 23 of the PPSA declares that registration perfects the security interest in all types of collateral. Perfection by registration requires the registering of a financing statement (s. 45). The financing statement must be in the prescribed form (s. 46(2)). The prescribed form is set out in O. Reg. 372/89 (now RRO 1990, Reg. 912). Section 16 of that regulation provides:

> 16(1) The name of a debtor who is a natural person shall be set out in the financing statement to show the first given name, followed by the initial of the second given name, if any, followed by the surname.

Sections 3(7), (8) and (9) of the same regulation are also relevant:

> 3(7) If the collateral includes a motor vehicle and the motor vehicle is classified as consumer goods, the motor vehicle shall be described on line 11 or 12 on the financing statement or in the appropriate place on a motor vehicle schedule.
>
> (8) If the collateral includes a motor vehicle and the motor vehicle is not classified as consumer goods, the motor vehicle may be described on line 11 or 12 on the financing statement or in the appropriate place on a motor vehicle schedule.

(9) The description of the motor vehicle on line 11 or 12 or on a motor vehicle schedule shall include the vehicle identification number, the last two digits of the model year, if any, the model, if any, and the make or the name of the manufacturer.

GMAC's financing statement complied with the relevant parts of s. 3 of the regulation, but did not comply with s. 16 in that it incorrectly stated both Lambert's first name and his middle initial. Accordingly, GMAC's financing statement was not in the prescribed form and but for the possible effect of s. 46(4) of the PPSA, GMAC's security interest in the vehicle was not perfected.

Section 20(1)(b) of the PPSA declares that an unperfected security interest in any collateral is not effective against a trustee in bankruptcy. Again, setting aside s. 46(4) of the PPSA, it would follow that since GMAC's security interest was not registered in accordance with the Act and hence not perfected, it was ineffective as against the trustee in bankruptcy. But for s. 46(4) of the PPSA, the trustee was entitled to the declaration made by Farley J.

Does s. 46(4) of the PPSA alter this result? Two features of s. 46(4) are non-controversial. First, it is potentially applicable to any error in a financing statement: *Re Weber* (1990), 78 CBR (NS) 224 (Ont. SC) at p. 227. Secondly, an error in a financing statement does not *per se* invalidate that statement or impair the security interest claimed by the statement. The validity of the financing statement is unaffected by the error unless the party seeking to invalidate the financing statement demonstrates that "a reasonable person is likely to be misled materially by the error."

Interpreting s. 46(4) becomes more difficult once one ventures beyond these two propositions. Some trial courts in this province have approached s. 46(4) by looking to the effect of the error in the financing statement on the party challenging the security. Cases taking that view include: *Fritz v. Ford Credit Canada Ltd.* (1992), 15 CBR (3d) 311 (Ont. Gen. Div.) at p. 314; *Prenor Rust Co. of Canada v. 652729 Ontario Ltd.* (1992), 4 PPSAC (2d) 139 (Ont. Gen. Div.) at pp. 141-42; *Canamsucco Road House Food Co. v. Lngas Ltd.* (1991), 2 PPSAC (2d) 203 (Ont. Gen. Div.) at p. 208; *General Motors Acceptance Corp. of Canada v. Stetsko* (1992), 8 OR (3d) 537 (Gen. Div.) at pp. 541-42; *Re Rose* (1993), 16 OR (3d) 360, 23 CBR (3d) 58 (Gen. Div.).

In *Fritz, supra,* the debtor's name had been incorrectly spelled on the financing statement, but the VIN was accurately recorded. The trustee performed only a specific debtor inquiry. That inquiry did not retrieve the financing statement. A VIN search would have located the financing statement. The trustee had been told by the debtor that the automobile in question was pledged to the creditor. Chadwick J found that the mistake in the debtor's name constituted an error in the financing statement. He then turned to s. 46(4) of the PPSA. In holding that the creditor had a valid security interest, Chadwick J said at p. 314:

The "reasonable person" that is referred to in considering subs. 46(4) is not an imaginary person but the person who is challenging the validity of the security agreement. In this case, the trustee in bankruptcy had actual notice of the interests of Ford Credit Canada Limited at the time of the assignment in bankruptcy. He was informed by the bankrupt that the 1989 Ford Tempo was fully secured by Ford Canada Limited. The name search under the PPSA by the trustee was only for the purpose of determining whether there were any errors in the registration of the documentation and not for the purpose of a *bona fide* purchaser.

It is obvious from the facts in this case that the trustee was not materially misled as a result of the incorrect registration.

In *Stetsko, supra*, a creditor placed the wrong birth date of the debtor in the financing statement. The trustee was told by the debtor of the creditor's secured interest in the automobile, but he conducted only a specific debtor inquiry. That inquiry did not retrieve the creditor's financing statement because of the error in the birth date. In holding that the creditor's interest remained perfected as against the trustee Maloney J referred, with approval, to the analysis of s. 46(4) found in *Canamsucco*, and said at p. 542:

> [I]n trying to determine whether the "reasonable person" is likely to be misled one can only look to: (1) who that person is, (2) what knowledge he may have had, and (3) how he may be affected by it.

On this view of s. 46(4), the error in the financing statement is of no consequence if the party challenging the statement had knowledge of the security interest, or if that party acting reasonably, given its knowledge, could have located the financing statement using the various searches available under the PPSA. This approach has some attraction, especially in cases where the trustee in bankruptcy is seeking to take advantage of an error in the financing statement. In those cases, the trustee appears more as an opportunist pouncing on a windfall than as a vulnerable prospective creditor or purchaser seeking the protection of reliable registration system: Ziegel, "The New Provincial Chattel Security Law Regimes" (1991), 70 *Can. Bar Rev.* 681 at pp. 715-16. The subjective approach may be said to do "justice" in cases involving the trustee in bankruptcy in that it denies the trustee the windfall.

I cannot, however, agree with this interpretation of s. 46(4). By using the reasonable person standard, the legislature intended that the test provided in s. 46(4) should be an objective one. To limit the inquiry to the effect of the error on the party challenging the security is to impose a personal or subjective test peculiar to that party. Furthermore, this interpretation substitutes a test based on actual prejudice for the reasonable person standard set out in the section. As written, s. 46(4) does not require evidence that the error actually misled any person.

The language of s. 46(4) may be usefully compared to that found in s. 9(2) of the PPSA:

> 9(2) A security agreement is not unenforceable against a third party by reason only of a defect, irregularity, omission or error therein or in the execution thereof unless the third party is actually misled by the defect, irregularity, omission or error.

Section 9(2) expressly declares that a security agreement is not unenforceable by virtue of an error in that agreement unless "the third party is actually misled by the ... error." The language of s. 46(4) which specifically targets financing statements stands in marked contrast to the subjective language of s. 9(2). The approach taken in *Fritz, supra*, *Stetsko, supra*, and similar cases is appropriate to the language of s. 9(2), but not to the very different language found in s. 46(4).

• • •

Support for the conclusion that the reasonable person referred to in s. 46(4) cannot be equated with a person in the position of the party seeking to invalidate the financing statements is found in *Kelln (Trustee of) v. Strasbourg Credit Union Ltd.* (1992), 89 DLR (4th) 427, 9 CBR (3d) 144 (Sask. CA). Section 66(1) of the *Personal Property Security Act,* SS 1979-80, c. P-6.1, provides:

> 66(1) The validity or effectiveness of a document to which this Act applies is not affected by reason of a defect, irregularity, omission or error therein or in the execution or registration thereof unless the defect, irregularity, omission or error is seriously misleading.

This section applies to financing statements registered under the Saskatchewan Act. If anything, the language of s. 66(1), which does not contain any specific reference to the reasonable person, is more susceptible to the subjective actual prejudice approach than in s. 46(4) of the PPSA. Despite that arguable ambiguity, the Saskatchewan Court of Appeal unanimously held that s. 66(1) sets out a purely objective test. The court specifically rejected trial decisions in Saskatchewan which had considered the effect of the error from the vantage point of the party challenging the validity of the financing statement. Bayda CJS at p. 430, speaking only for himself, held that the application of the curative proviso was to be determined by asking:

> … whether a reasonable person using the registration and search systems put in place by the Act is apt by reason of the omission and the circumstances surrounding it to end up believing that something important is so when in fact it is not so.

Vancise JA at p. 442, writing for himself and Wakeling JA, adopted the question posed by Professor Cuming as the appropriate approach:

> Would the defect, irregularity, omission or error be seriously misleading to any reasonable person within the class of person for whose benefit registration or other methods of perfection are required.

> …

I do agree that s. 46(4) sets out an objective test. The inquiry dictated by s. 46(4) cannot focus on a particular party, but must look to the broader class of persons who may have cause to use the search facilities of the registration system. In looking to that broader class of persons, one must determine, not the existence of actual prejudice, but the probability of some member of that class of persons being materially misled by the error. As s. 46(4) lays down an objective test, a party challenging the security on the basis of errors in the financing statement need not demonstrate actual prejudice to that party or anyone else. The trustee in bankruptcy may rely on an error in a financing statement to invalidate a secured interest claimed in that statement if the trustee or other third party can show that the error in the financing statement was likely to materially mislead a reasonable person.

My conclusion that s. 46(4) creates an objective test which requires an assessment of the error's impact on those persons who might use the search facilities of the registration system does not resolve this appeal. It remains to provide a concrete formulation of that test.

I begin with the purpose of s. 46(4). The section is designed to preserve the integrity of the registration system provided by the PPSA. That system has two constituencies: those who register financing statements; and those who search the system for prior registrations. The integrity of the overall system must address the interests of both groups.

Section 46(4) seeks to maintain the system's integrity by distributing the impact of errors, no matter how unavoidable, made in financing statements between the two groups. An interpretation of s. 46(4) which is too forgiving of such errors places too much of the burden on prospective creditors and purchasers (searchers). An interpretation which is too unforgiving of those errors places too much of the burden on creditors (registrants). In either event, the integrity of the registration system suffers. Section 46(4) should be interpreted, to the extent that its language permits, so as to assign the burden of the error system in a manner which best promotes the overall integrity of the system.

I turn next to the context in which s. 46(4) exists. Its reach and limitations can be understood only in the framework of the registration system established under the PPSA and the purposes for which that system is used.

…

In my view, the "reasonable person" in s. 46(4) is a person using the search facilities of the registration system for their intended purpose, that is, to find out whether personal property to be purchased or taken as collateral is subject to prior registered encumbrances. To assess the potential effect of an error in a financing statement one must assume that the property which is the subject of the flawed financing statement is the property targeted by the inquiry made by the prospective purchaser or lender. In this case, therefore, the question becomes—would a potential purchaser of the motor vehicle referred to in the financing statement, or a person considering taking that motor vehicle as security, be materially misled by the error in a previously registered financing statement? This articulation of the test accords with the purpose of the inquiry function of the system, and gives meaning to the requirement that the error be "likely to mislead materially." Unless the effect of the error is addressed in the context of a potential purchase or loan involving the property specified in the financing statement, I am unable to see how an error in that financing statement could be "likely to materially mislead" a prospective purchaser or lender.

In so describing the purpose of the search function of the system, I am not unaware that it has other uses in the commercial world. Some potential creditors may do a PPSA search as part of their inquiry into the credit worthiness of a potential borrower. Those creditors will not be interested in the status of any particular property, but will be looking for any information that may assist in assessing the potential borrower's overall debt situation and credit worthiness. In describing the reasonable person for the purposes of s. 46(4), I would distinguish between a use to which the PPSA system can be put and the purpose for which the system exists. The system was not designed as a credit inquiry service, although it can provide information which will assist in determining credit worthiness. That same incidental use exists with respect to information stored in various other data banks established for a myriad of other purposes.

The preservation of the integrity of the PPSA registration system requires that those who use the system for its intended purpose be protected from errors made by other users where those errors are likely to mislead materially. In my view, the same protection should not be extended to those who put the system to some different use which while commercially beneficial is not the purpose for the system. In my view, the reasonable person in s. 46(4) is not the person using the search facility as part of a general inquiry into a prospective borrower's credit worthiness.

The "reasonable person" using the inquiry function of the registration system for the purpose described above must also be regarded as a person who is familiar with the search facilities provided by the system. That is not to say that the standard is that of the most sophisticated and skilled user. The standard must be that of a reasonably competent user of the system: *Re Millman* (1994), 17 OR (3d) 653, 24 CBR (3d) 190 (Gen. Div.). That reasonable user would be aware of the various searches available in the system and the product produced by each. Furthermore, the reasonable user must be taken to know that potential security interests in motor vehicles may be retrieved through two discrete searches of the system, one using the name of the debtor and the other the motor vehicle's VIN.

Having identified the reasonable person in s. 46(4) as a potential purchaser or lender seeking to locate prior encumbrances on the targeted property, and as a reasonably competent user of the search function of the registration system, I turn now to the information which that reasonable person could be expected to have when making his or her inquiry. No one suggests that the reasonable person would not be able to get the name and birth date of the vendor or borrower through the relevant records. Clearly, he or she would be able to obtain that information.

The reasonable person, as a potential purchaser or lender would not, however, necessarily have access to the names and birth dates of prior owners of the motor vehicle. These prior owners may have encumbered the vehicle. Financing statements giving notice of those encumbrances will be registered under the name of the prior owner and perhaps under the VIN.

In my opinion, the potential purchaser or lender acting reasonably would also obtain the VIN of the motor vehicle. He or she would be in a position to require access to the motor vehicle as a condition of the purchase or loan. Access to the motor vehicle means access to the VIN since it is found on a plate attached to the vehicle's dashboard. Furthermore, a reasonably prudent purchaser or lender familiar with the registration system would appreciate that the VIN could be used to search for prior encumbrances on the vehicle, particularly those registered against prior owners of the vehicle whose identity was unknown to the potential purchaser or lender. Fixed with this knowledge, the reasonable person would realize the importance of the VIN, and would take advantage of his or her position as a purchaser or lender to require access to the VIN.

Would the reasonable person, having access to the seller or borrower's name (and birth date) and the VIN of the motor vehicle, use both sources of information to conduct two searches of the registration system? With respect to the contrary view, I have no doubt that a reasonable person in possession of the information needed to conduct the two searches would in fact conduct both searches. The reasonable person would want to know about any prior encumbrances registered against the motor vehicle and would take all reasonable steps to locate notice of any prior encumbrance in the system. As a reasonable user of the registration system, he or she would know that prior encumbrances for motor vehicles could be registered under the debtor's name, the VIN, or both. A name search might not locate all prior encumbrances. A VIN search might not locate all prior encumbrances if the motor vehicle was not classified as consumer goods for the purposes of a prior transaction. By performing the two searches, the reasonable user would increase the probability of recovering all prior encumbrances. The added protection would come at minimal cost. Any reasonable user would spend the few dollars required for the added information and comfort provided by two independent searches of the registration system.

Those who have held that the reasonable person in s. 46(4) would conduct only a specific debtor name search have emphasized the importance to the registration system of using the debtor's correct name in the financing statement. For example, Donnelly J in *Re Ghilzon* (1993), 21 CBR (30) 71 (Ont. Gen. Div.). "The integrity of the registration system is name-dependent." No doubt this observation is accurate with regard to personal property other than motor vehicles. But where motor vehicles are involved, the integrity of the registration system does not depend only on accurately recording the debtor's name in the financing statement. Indeed, the VIN search function exists specifically because a name-dependent system for motor vehicles would be inadequate and would leave potential purchasers and lenders vulnerable to encumbrances placed on the motor vehicle by prior owners of the motor vehicle. In the case of motor vehicles, the registration system is not name-dependent. Rather, it provides for identification of prior registrations by the combined access to the system afforded by name and VIN searches.

An approach to s. 46(4) which excludes errors in the debtor's name from those which are curable by s. 46(4) harks back to the language of the former curative proviso (s. 47(5)) which declared that only clerical errors or errors in immaterial or non-essential parts of the financing statement were curable under that provision: *Re Weber, supra*, at pp. 228-29. The debtor's name is clearly a material and essential part of the financing statement: *Re Bellini Manufacturing & Importing Ltd.* (1981), 32 OR (2d) 684 at pp. 692-93, 37 CBR (NS) 209 (CA). The present curative proviso does not, however, fix on the part of the financing statement in which the error occurred, but instead looks to the effect of the error on the reasonable person. The present provision may cure any error no matter where it occurs in the financing statement, if that error is not likely to mislead materially a reasonable person. An error may occur in a material part of the financing statement, but may not, in light of additional information, found in the same financing statement and available to the reasonable person, materially mislead that person. Case law under the prior provision identifying the materiality of the debtor's name to the financing statement does not assist in deciding whether the reasonable person referred to in the current section would conduct more than a specific debtor search.

Proponents of the single-search approach also rely on the absence of any requirement in the PPSA that more than one search be done. *Re Weber, supra*, at p. 228. The PPSA does not require that any search be done. A search for prior registered interests is triggered by self-interest, not by any statutory obligation. The nature of the search to be expected from a reasonable person reflects the extent to which a reasonable person would go to protect his or her interests. The absence of any statutory provision requiring one or more searches is of no consequence.

In summary, the reasonable person in s. 46(4) has the following attributes:

- He or she is a reasonably prudent prospective purchaser or lender who looks to the registration system of the PPSA to provide notice of any prior registered claims against the property he or she is proposing to buy or take as collateral for a loan.
- He or she is conversant with the search facilities provided by the registration system and is a reasonably competent user of those facilities.

- Where the property to be bought or taken as collateral is a motor vehicle, the reasonable person will obtain the name and birth date of the seller/borrower as well as the VIN of the motor vehicle.
- Where the property is a motor vehicle, the reasonable person will conduct both a specific debtor name search and a VIN search.

Bearing this reasonable person in mind I move to the final question. Is that reasonable person "likely to be misled materially" by a financing statement which contained an error in the debtor's name, but accurately set out the VIN? The purpose for which the reasonable person uses the search function of the registration system provides the key to determining when it can be said that the reasonable person would be materially misled by an error in a financing statement. The reasonable person uses the system to find prior registered secured interests in the property in question. If the error in the financing statement results in the reasonable person not retrieving that financing statement from the system, then the reasonable person will probably be misled materially. If despite the error, the reasonable person as defined above will still retrieve the flawed financing statement from the system, then the error in the financing statement is not likely to mislead materially.

A reasonable person would not likely be misled materially by an error in a financing statement relating to the debtor's name if that same financing statement accurately set out the VIN. That financing statement would come to the attention of the reasonable person through a VIN search despite the error in the name. The reasonable person would, therefore, be put on notice of the security interest referred to in the financing statement and could proceed accordingly. This conclusion accords with that reached in *Ford Credit Canada Ltd. v. Percival Mercury Sales Ltd. (No. 1)*, [1986] 6 WWR 569, 50 Sask. R 268 (CA).

The result would be very different if the financing statement incorrectly set out the debtor's name and did not contain the VIN, as could be the case if the motor vehicle had not been classified as consumer goods for the purposes of the transaction giving rise to the financing statement. In that situation, the error in the debtor's name would be fatal since the reasonable person conducting both a specific debtor search and a VIN search could not locate the financing statement. That is, however, not this case. This financing statement did include the VIN, and the impact of the error in the debtor's name must be assessed in that light. It supports the purpose behind the registration system to hold that a creditor who includes information in the financing statement which potentially permits a subsequent searcher to locate the financing statement through two independent means is in a better position than a creditor who chooses to limit itself to the bare essentials required by the regulations.

My conclusion would also be different if the VIN was improperly recorded in the financing statement and the debtor's name was accurately set out. In that situation, a reasonable person could well be materially misled by the error in the financing statement. Consider this example. P agrees to purchase a car from V. The car had been previously owned by X who pledged it to Y. Y registered a financing statement correctly identifying X as the debtor, but incorrectly setting out the VIN of the motor vehicle. P, proceeding as I have held a reasonable purchaser would, conducts a specific debtor search in the name of V (his vendor) and a VIN search using the proper VIN. The two searches conducted by P would not reveal Y's financing statement, because of the error made by Y with respect to the VIN. This error would, therefore, probably materially mislead P since it would leave him unaware of Y's claim to a prior security interest in the motor vehicle. My conclusion that an error in the VIN even when coupled with a correct identification of the debtor would not be curable under s. 46(4) is consistent with the result in *Kelln*, *supra*.

Further reference to *Kelln* is necessary. In that case, the VIN was improperly recorded in the relevant financing statement, but the debtor's name was accurately recorded. The court held that the error could not be cured by the Saskatchewan equivalent of s. 46(4) of the PPSA. As indicated above, I agree with that result. Vancise JA went on to hold that an error in the debtor's name where the VIN was properly recorded would be equally fatal. In doing so, he appears to have rejected the same court's holding in *Ford Credit Canada Ltd.*, *supra*. Vancise JA and I part company at this point.

Vancise JA observes at p. 443 that an error in a financing statement is not curable if that error would result in "the failure to properly register or retrieve the information from the register concerning the collateral." I agree with this comment, except I would limit the concern to the proper retrieval of the information.

Vancise JA goes on at pp. 443-44 to hold:

> Thus the conclusion is that the failure to include both of the mandatory registration-search criteria where it is required will result in the registration being seriously misleading and render the security interest unperfected.
>
> As noted, the reason for such objective interpretation is to provide a consistent approach to the registration and perfection of security interests.
>
> The failure to include the debtor's name on a financing statement where there is already a serial number which correctly describes the collateral should render the security interest unperfected. In other words, when there is a requirement for both criteria the failure to include one is seriously misleading and the failure to comply renders the registration invalid. If one or both of the mandatory registration-search criteria contain errors which do not prevent the proper identification or retrieval of the financing statement, the error is not seriously misleading and the security interest should be perfected.

This analysis proceeds on the basis that only a single search need be performed by the prospective purchaser or lender. Consequently, an error in either the name or the VIN which prevented a person conducting either, but not both of those searches from locating the financing statement would be materially misleading.

I reach a different result than Vancise JA because, for the reasons I have already set out, I proceed on the premise that the prospective purchaser or lender would have access to both the seller/borrower's name and the VIN, and would conduct both searches. An error in a financing statement would probably be materially misleading only if the error caused the financing statement to escape the net cast by the combined reach of both searches.

Vancise JA quite properly supports his approach on the basis of the certainty and predictability it achieves. My approach borrows from his, save for the different assessment of the searches a reasonable person would conduct, and achieves the same consistency and predictability. In my estimation, it also more effectively preserves the integrity of the registration system by more fairly balancing the interests of secured creditors and prospective purchasers and lenders. A creditor's secured interest should not fail as against third parties by virtue of an error in the financing statement, if that error would not preclude retrieval of the financing statement by a prospective purchaser or lender taking reasonable steps to protect his or her interest and making reasonable use of the search facilities provided by the registration system.

I would hold that the trustee has not established that the error in the GMAC financing statement would probably have misled materially a reasonable person. The financing statement is therefore not invalidated and GMAC's security interest in the motor vehicle is perfected.

Appeal allowed.

NOTES AND QUESTIONS

1) *Re Lambert* establishes that if the motor vehicle is consumer goods, correct disclosure of the debtor's name in the financing statement will not prevent a VIN error or omission from being a materially misleading one. The reason the court gave was that a reasonable searcher would conduct both a name search and a VIN search, but, even allowing for this, the VIN error is still potentially misleading in an A-B-C-D scenario (as to which, see Part III.E.1, above). See also *Gold Key Pontiac Buick (1984) Ltd. v. 464750 BC Ltd. (Trustee of)* (2000), 2 PPSAC (3d) 206 (BCCA). Other courts have reached the same conclusion, but on the different ground that it is not reasonable to expect a searcher to conduct a search in both the debtor's name index and the serial number index, and a searcher who searches only in the debtor's name index is unlikely to discover the security interest: *Kelln (Trustee of) v. Strasbourg Credit Union Ltd.* (1992), 89 DLR (4th) 427, 9 CBR (3d) 144 (Sask. CA); *Case Power & Equipment v. 366551 Alberta Inc. (Receiver of)* (1994), 23 Alta. LR (3d) 361 (Alta. CA); and *GMAC Leaseco Ltd. v. Moncton Motor Home & Sales Inc. (Trustee of)*, [2003] NBJ No. 140 (NBCA).

2) *Re Lambert* also establishes that if the financing statement incorrectly states the debtor's name, correct disclosure of the VIN will cure the error, on the basis that a reasonable searcher would conduct both a name search and a VIN search and the VIN search would retrieve the entry. See also *Gold Key Pontiac Buick (1984) Ltd. v. 464750 BC Ltd. (Trustee of)*, above. Other courts have taken the opposite view, on the ground that it is not reasonable to expect a searcher to conduct both kinds of search, and, since a search against the debtor's name is unlikely to disclose the security interest, the error is an invalidating one: *Kelln (Trustee of) v. Strasbourg Credit Union Ltd.*, above; *Case Power & Equipment v. 366551 Alberta Inc. (Receiver of)*, above; and *GMAC Leaseco Ltd. v. Moncton Motor Home & Sales Inc. (Trustee of)*, above.

3) The conclusion in *Re Lambert* and *Gold Key* that a registration is not affected by a serious error in the name of the debtor so long as the VIN is correct has been criticized. See Ziegel and Denomme, pp. 403-8. See also R. Wood, "Registration Errors Under the OPPSA: Lambert (Re)" (1995), 24 *CBLJ* 444 and "Registration Errors and Dual Search Criteria: Gold

Key Pontiac Buick (1984) Ltd. v. 46750 BC Ltd." (2001), 35 *CBLJ* 146, and Cuming, Walsh, and Wood, at 274. Here is what Cuming, Walsh, and Wood say:

> [S]erial number searching was intended to be a supplementary mode of searching, not an alternative to debtor-name searching. The ability of a third party to place full confidence in either a debtor name or a serial number search is essential to the integrity of the registry system. Not all searchers will necessarily have ready access to the serial number of particular vehicles of the debtor [prospective execution creditors are a case in point]. Even if access is available, not all searchers are sophisticated enough to appreciate the necessity to search by serial number. Finally, there are situations where the imposition of serial number searching imposes excessive transaction costs on searchers, for example, where the debtor in question holds many pieces of equipment that qualify as serial numbered goods.

These criticisms were endorsed by the New Brunswick Court of Appeal in the *Moncton Motor Home & Sales* case, above. Do you agree?

4) In Ontario, the concern that unsophisticated searchers may not realize the need to conduct a VIN search is ameliorated by the provisions of s. 11.1 of the *Highway Traffic Act*, RSO 1990, c. H.8 and s. 43.1 of the OPPSA (added by SO 1993, c. 13, s. 1), which ensure that, in most cases, the buyer will receive a "used vehicle information package" that contains a registry search based on the VIN of the vehicle being purchased. However, dealers registered under the *Motor Vehicle Dealers Act* are exempt from the requirement to deliver an information package to a buyer. See O. reg. 601/93, s. 2(10) under the *Highway Traffic Act*. Does this represent a major area of exposure for legally unsophisticated buyers of motor vehicles?

5) Section 43(7) of the British Columbia PPSA provides as follows:

> 43(7) Subject to subsection (9), if
>> (a) one or more debtors are required to be disclosed in a financing statement, or
>> (b) collateral is consumer goods that are defined in the regulations as serial numbered goods,
> and there is a seriously misleading defect, irregularity, omission or error in
>> (c) the disclosure of the name of any of the debtors other than a debtor who does not own or have rights in the collateral, or
>> (d) the serial number of the collateral,
> the registration is invalid.

This provision addresses the policy concerns identified in notes 1 to 3, above. There is an equivalent provision in all the non-Ontario PPSAs, although the Saskatchewan version of the provision had not been enacted at the time *Kelln* was decided. In *Gold Key*, above, the British Columbia Court of Appeal, following the Ontario Court of Appeal's decision in *Re Lambert*, concluded that a correctly stated VIN in the financing statement cures a debtor's name error. However, the court overlooked BCPPSA s. 43(7), which clearly points to the opposite conclusion: see *Moncton Motor Home & Sales Inc.*, above, at para. 96. In *Moncton Motor Home & Sales Inc.*, the court declined to follow *Re Lambert* on the grounds first, that the New Brunswick version of s. 43(7) was dispositive of the case and second, that, in any event, the case was wrongly decided for the reasons its critics have given.

6) BCPPSA s. 43(7)(b) makes it clear that a serial number error or omission invalidates the financing statement only if the collateral is consumer goods. The reason is because inclusion of the serial number in the financing statement is mandatory for consumer goods, but optional for equipment and inventory. Given this,

> a third party could never be misled by an erroneous serial number covering equipment or inventory ... because a searcher intent on searching by serial number must act on the premise that the registrant may have elected to omit reference to the serial number and this is why the search failed to disclose [a] match. [Therefore] when dealing with non-consumer goods, an error in the serial number should be treated as the equivalent of an election to omit it. [*Moncton Motor Home & Sales Inc.*, above, at para. 78]

There is no equivalent statutory provision in Ontario, but the considerations that this passage identifies are equally applicable. Consequently, the conclusion in *Re Lambert* that a VIN error or omission will always invalidate a financing statement, even if the debtor's name is correctly stated, should be read as applying only if the collateral is consumer goods.

7) On the other hand, if the collateral is equipment, OPPSA s. 28(5) applies. The section provides as follows:

> 28(5) Where a motor vehicle, as defined in the regulations, is sold other than in the ordinary course of business of the seller and the motor vehicle is classified as equipment of the seller, the buyer takes it free from any security interest therein given by the seller even though it is perfected by registration unless the vehicle identification number of the motor vehicle is set out in the designated place on a registered financing statement or financing change statement or unless the buyer knew that the sale constituted a breach of the security agreement.

The purpose of this provision is to encourage the secured party who knows the VIN at the time of preparing the financing statement to disclose it, even though for registration purposes, the disclosure is optional.

Consider the following case:

> A takes a security interest in B's motor vehicle as equipment and registers a financing statement without the VIN. B later sells the vehicle to C, a dealer, and discloses A's security interest. C in turn sells the motor vehicle to D, fraudulently representing that it is free from encumbrances. B defaults and A claims the motor vehicle from D. Can D rely on OPPSA s. 28(5)?

The answer is "no," because the provision is limited to the case where the security interest is "given by the seller" and, in our example, the seller is C, not B. In other words, the provision overlooks the A-B-C-D problem. This is a fundamental flaw: the main purpose of s. 28(5) is to promote the VIN's inclusion in the financing statement, but the provision does not apply in the very situation that serial number registration was designed to address. The outcome would be different if C purchased the vehicle from B without knowledge of A's security interest. On these facts, C would take the vehicle free from A's security interest by virtue of s. 28(5) and D, in turn, would take clear title from C. Note, though, that while D needs the protection that s. 28(5) offers, C does not because C could discover A's security interest by searching in the debtor's name index.

8) Consider the following variation on the example given in the previous note.

A takes a security interest in B's motor vehicle as consumer goods and registers a financing statement with an incorrect VIN. B later sells the vehicle to C, a dealer, who in turn sells it to D.

In this case, D cannot rely on s. 28(5), which applies only to equipment. However, on the authority of *Re Lambert*, A's VIN error invalidates the registration and so D obtains clear title because the security interest is unperfected: OPPSA s. 20(1)(c).

Now take D out of the picture and assume that C still has the vehicle.

Is A's registration invalid against C? *Re Lambert* is unclear on this point. The court concluded that a VIN error will invalidate the financing statement even if the debtor's name is correctly stated. However, its reasoning presupposed an A-B-C-D scenario. It could be argued that the ruling does not apply to the case under consideration because C (unlike D) could have discovered A's security interest by conducting a name index search. In other words, according to *Re Lambert*, debtor name and VIN are not alternatives when D, a remote party, is a purchaser. Are they alternatives where an immediate party (C) is claiming priority? The answer is probably that they are not. As *Re Lambert* confirms, the s. 46(4) test is an objective one and so it makes no difference whether anyone is actually misled by the error or omission. In other words, the concern is with the potential of the error or omission to mislead, rather than with whether it has in fact done so in the particular case before the court. If the debtor's trustee in bankruptcy can claim the benefit of s. 46(4) on this basis (a point that Doherty JA reluctantly conceded in *Re Lambert*), it should follow that C in our example can do likewise (at least in the absence of fraud on C's part).

9) In a close similar match system, a name or serial number error in the financing statement will not necessarily prevent the security interest from showing up on a search certificate. Whether it will or not depends on the degree of tolerance built into the system. Assume that the security interest does show up on the search certificate. Does it necessarily follow that the error is not an invalidating one? This question is addressed in the following extract.

Coates v. General Motors Acceptance Corp.
(1999), 10 CBR (4th) 116 (BCSC)

GRIST J: This case concerns the validity of the registration of a financing statement filed under an incorrect vehicle serial number.

The respondent, GMAC, registered a financing statement in respect of a Chevrolet dump truck in the Personal Property Registry on January 10, 1996. It listed the vehicle serial number incorrectly. The correct and defective numbers were:

Correct: IG*B*HK34N7SE208052
Defective: IG6HK34N75E208052

The registration showed Alfred Hoelke and Rosella Hoelke as debtors under the security agreement.

On May 27, 1996, Mr. Coates loaned money to Mr. Hoelke. He took security by way of a Promissory Note and a blank signed transfer in respect of the dump truck. The transfer was to be held until the money was paid. Mr. Coates registered the Promissory Note. His registration listed Mr. Hoelke and Rosella Hoelke as debtors.

By October 31, 1997 payments under the Promissory Note were in default. Mr. Coates attended the Government Agent's office and had a clerk search the registry for registrations listing the dump truck serial number. The printed search result showed only the registration of the Promissory Note. Mr. Coates then transferred the truck into his name and tried to take possession of the vehicle.

The dump truck was located on the lot of a local GM dealership. Mr. Coates presented the documentation indicating his ownership of the vehicle. The dealer informed Mr. Coates that GMAC had a prior charge against the vehicle which was effective notwithstanding the faulty registration and refused to give it up. The dealer produced a search conducted using the correct vehicle serial number which showed the registration of the Promissory Note as being the only exact match, but which also showed the GMAC registration as an inexact match or similar registration. The different results of the two searches can be accounted for by the fact that the search in the Government Agent's office was conducted in such a fashion as to reveal only exact matches. Similar registrations were not investigated. The evidence does not indicate whether the clerk did this as a matter of course, in error, or on instruction from Mr. Coates.

The Statute

Section 43 of the Personal Property Security Act, RSBC 1996, c. 359 provides:

43(1) A person who wishes to have a financing statement registered must submit it for registration at an office of the registry. ...

(6) The validity of the registration of a financing statement is not affected by a defect, irregularity, omission or error in the financing statement or in the registration of it unless the defect, irregularity, omission or error is seriously misleading.

(7) Subject to subsection (9), if

(a) one or more debtors are required to be disclosed in a financing statement; or

(b) collateral is consumer goods that are defined in the regulations as serial numbered goods, and there is a seriously misleading defect, irregularity, omission or error in;

(c) the disclosure of the name of any of the debtors other than a debtor who does not own or have rights to the collateral; or

(d) the serial number of the collateral, the registration is invalid.

(8) If it is alleged that a defect, irregularity, omission or error is seriously misleading, it is not necessary to prove that anyone was actually misled by it.

The Case Law

The short question posed by this case is whether the registration of the incorrect serial number was seriously misleading.

···

In *Primus Automotive Financial Services Canada Ltd. v. Kirby (Trustee of)* (1998), 57 Alta. LR (3d) 279 (QB) Master Funduk of the Alberta Court of Queen's Bench dealt with a registration showing a serial number which contained two mistaken characters. The characteristics of the filing and search program in that case did not reveal the registration of the financing statement when a search was done using the correct serial number.

At p. 280 Master Funduk held that the defective serial number was fatal to the registration. He cited Cuming and Wood, *Alberta Personal Property Security Act Handbook*, 3rd ed.:

> An independent assessment of the defective search criterion should be undertaken without regard to whether a search using a different search criterion would have disclosed the registration. *The fact that the party who is actually seeking to invalidate the registration may have conducted such a search (or may have failed to conduct any search at all) is irrelevant. The test is an objective one that can be determined simply by examining the contents of search results.*
> [Cuming and Wood, Alberta Personal Property Security Act Handbook, 3rd ed., p. 369]
> [Emphasis Added].

Master Funduk also held that a typical registration of serial numbered goods listing the two critical search criteria, the name and the serial number, would be seriously misleading if a search under one criteria would not successfully reveal the registration even though a search under the other would.

There has been some dispute as to whether or not the capabilities of the registry computer program should be considered in determining whether or not an error is seriously misleading. In *Re Logan* (1992), 73 BCLR (2d) 377 (SC), Tysoe J dealt with the incorrect registration of the debtor's middle name as Louis rather than the correct middle name which was Louise. The filing and search program employed at that time in respect of name registrations did not reveal the registration when the correct middle name was employed. The user guide for the construction of name searches advised searchers that the regulations to the Act made the registration of middle names optional and, accordingly, a search should list only the first and last names. The search program would then locate all variations which included a middle name or initial. Tysoe J held that the defective registration was not seriously misleading in these circumstances. At pp. 385-386 he commented on cases which suggested that the success of the search alone determined the objective test:

> These cases raise some interesting questions. Collectively, they appear to stand for the proposition that if the PPSA legislation contains a mandatory requirement in connection with the completion of a financing statement, any error or omission in the completion of that requirement will invalidate the security interest corresponding to the statement unless a search on the personal property registry computer using the correct feature (i.e., debtor's name or serial number) will disclose the financing statement containing the error or omission. I have a great deal of difficulty with that proposition. It means that the programming of the computer is determinative of the "objective" test of deciding whether a defect, irregularity, omission or error is seriously misleading. Should an error in the last digit of a serial number be considered to be more seriously misleading than an error in the first digit of the serial number because, unbeknown to the person completing the financing statement, the

computer is programmed to ignore the first digit of the serial number when a search is conducted? Should an error in the spelling of a first name of a debtor that is misleading to no one other than the computer be considered to be seriously misleading, especially when the Law Reform Commission that recommended the curative provision in the Saskatchewan legislation (which is the forerunner of the British Columbia statute) was intending to "repudiate the strict approach" applied to the pre-PPSA statutes? On the other hand, it is difficult to avoid the conclusion that an error in the last name of the debtor or the portion of the serial number that is used as a search criterion by the computer is seriously misleading because the error means that a person searching under the correct last name or the correct serial number would not be able to locate the financing statement. The search criteria utilized by the computer will unavoidably have to be considered in determining whether an error or omission is seriously misleading, but it is my view that the legislature did not intend the programmer of the computer to be the judge of determining what is seriously misleading.

A contrary view is expressed by Cuming and Wood, *British Columbia Personal Property Security Act Handbook* (Scarborough: Carswell, 1996). At pp. 350-352, the authors state:

Judges have sometimes expressed the view that the legislature did not intend that the programmer of the computer should be the judge for determining what is seriously misleading. This confuses the issue. The registry system is required to process and store an enormous quantity of information. This is only feasible through the development of sophisticated search routines. Although an error in a name may appear to be minor, it may be such that the registration is not disclosed. The integrity of the registry would be greatly undermined if such "minor" errors were held not to be seriously misleading. ...

The drafters of Personal Property Security Acts and the designers of personal property registry systems have recognized the prevalence of human fallibility and have attempted to accommodate some deviation from the paradigm by treating some registrations as valid even though they do not comply in every respect with the strict requirements of the Act and Regulations. This, of course, is the purpose of ss. 43(6) to (9). Unfortunately, it has been necessary to state only in the most general of terms the extent to which a secured party may deviate from the perfect registration criterion and still have a valid registration. The test is whether or not the deviation results in the registration being "seriously misleading." The computer program of the registry has been designed so that a search using the perfect search criterion will reveal certain registrations which do not meet the perfect registration criterion. Some or all of these are sufficiently similar to the perfect registration criterion to be treated as inexact matches. ...

Of course, whether or not the hypothetical searching party would or would not be misled by the failure of the registering party to use the perfect registration criterion depends upon the design of the registry program. In order for the registration using other than the perfect registration criterion to be valid (because it is not seriously misleading), the program must disclose the registration to the searching party in such a way that the searching party could reasonably be expected to know or to be suspicious that the debtor disclosed in the registration is the same person whose name the searching party used as his or her search criterion.

I find the latter view to be persuasive. If we are to employ an electronic registry, which can only be searched by a computer program, the crucial fact is whether the incorrect filing prevented a searcher from finding the registration when searching under one of the alternate search criteria. If a search using a correct version of the criteria does not reveal the registration, the registration has failed. It is not a question of whether the filing and search program satisfactorily catches common mistakes, such as transposed numbers, easily mistaken letters and digits, misspellings and the like.

Section 43 offers some forgiveness from error if a filing is wrong but is not seriously misleading. This forgiveness should extend only so far as the capability of the filing and search program to reveal the registration despite the error. If a filing were found not to be seriously misleading on some other basis which forgave a mistake not revealed by the filing and search program, the effect would be to expose the searcher, who is not responsible for the error, to a loss of priority in dealing with the chattel.

...

Summary

The following principles apply in respect of the registration of serial numbered goods:

1. The test of whether a registration is seriously misleading is an objective one, independent of whether anyone was or was not misled by the search, or whether a search was in fact conducted.

2. Total accuracy in registration by name or registration by serial number is not necessary.

3. A seriously misleading description of either the name or the serial number in the registration will defeat the registration.

4. A seriously misleading registration is one that:
   (a) would prevent a reasonable search from disclosing the registration; or
   (b) would cause a reasonable person to conclude that the search was not revealing the same chattel (in the case of a serial number search) or the same debtor (in the case of a name search). The obligation is on the searcher to review the similar registrations to make this determination.

5. Whether a registry filing and search program is reasonable in the sense that its design will reveal simple discrepancies without arbitrary distinction, will not be assessed in determining if a reasonable search would disclose a registration. The only question to be answered is whether a registry search will reveal the incorrect registration.

Conclusion

The Affidavit of Ms. Wybrow, a legal assistant skilled in Personal Property Registry searches, and a review of the registration and search guide published by the Personal Property Registry, indicates that the filing and search program presently employed will reveal similar registrations by focusing on the last six characters of the serial number entered in the search. Registrations which are not an exact match to the serial number used in the search will be:

(1) listed, so long as these last six characters are shown in correct order on the regis-
     tration; and

(2) displayed as similar registrations, notwithstanding:
     (a) the number of characters preceding the last six; or
     (b) the correlation of the first characters to the other characters listed in the
          search.

As an example, if the serial number searched was: ABC012345

Registrations showing serial numbers: XYZ012345, ABCDEF012345 and 012345 will
be displayed as similar registrations.

Registrations showing serial numbers: ABC01234S and ABC012354 will not be
revealed.

Further inspection of similar registrations and any additional information describing
the chattel (i.e., the manufacturer, model year, and the debtor or debtors) should reveal
if the registration is likely a charge meant to encumber the property described in the
search. This system is obviously not specifically designed to track human failings in
identifying or transcribing characters, but as indicated above, this is not the test.

The critical difference in this case as compared to the case before Master Funduk is
the fact that the design of the BC system (or the placing of the errant characters) revealed
the GMAC filing despite the faulty registration. In this case further investigation of the
search result would have revealed that the two debtors listed on the GMAC financing
statement were the same as listed on the filing in respect of the petitioner's Promissory
Note. The type of chattel, the manufacturer and the model year of the vehicle were the
same under each registration. Further, the two mistaken characters were similar to the
actual characters in the correct serial number. All of this in my view would have alerted
a reasonable person to the fact that the GMAC registration was likely in respect of the
same vehicle. Accordingly, the petitioner's application for discharge of the respondent's
registration and delivery up of the vehicle is dismissed.

Adelaide Capital Corp. v. Integrated Transportation Finance Inc.
(1994), 16 OR (3d) 414 (Gen. Div.)

BLAIR J:

Background and Overview

Integrated Transportation Finance Incorporated ("ITFI") and Integrated Transportation
Services Incorporated ("ITS") made voluntary assignments in bankruptcy on April 13,
1993. Prior to their bankruptcies, ITFI and ITS were in the business of leasing truck trailers to various end users in Ontario and elsewhere in Canada.

By orders of this court dated April 5, 1993 and April 14, 1993, Deloitte & Touche Inc.
("Deloitte & Touche") was appointed as interim receiver of the two companies at the instance of certain secured creditors, pursuant to s. 47.1 of the *Bankruptcy and Insolvency
Act*, RSC 1985, c. B-3. Deloitte & Touche is also acting as trustee in bankruptcy of the
defendant companies.

In its capacity as interim receiver, Deloitte & Touche has taken steps to manage and operate the businesses of the companies, to assume possession and control of their assets, and to verify the existence of numerous trailers which are the subject of competing claims by various creditors. By order dated July 14, 1993, Mr. Justice Rosenberg established a procedure by which the various priority disputes that have arisen—and which relate primarily to claims regarding a large number of the truck trailers leased out on long-term and short-term leases by ITFI and ITS—could be determined.

The dispute in question in this proceeding relates to competing claims between Greyvest Leasing Inc. ("Greyvest") and North American Trust Company ("NAT") to 87 such trailers.

Facts

Greyvest seeks the following relief

1) An order directing the interim receiver to deliver up to Greyvest the vans and trailers listed in Schedule "A" to the notice of motion, together with the proceeds of all lease payments or sales proceeds collected by it, as interim receiver, and interest earned thereon;

2) An order authorizing and directing Greyvest to administer and dispose of those assets; and,

3) An order declaring that Greyvest is the owner of the assets in question, or, alternatively, declaring that Greyvest has a first-ranking security interest in the assets in question.

The 87 trailers or vans are the subject of four lease agreements entered into between Greyvest (formerly known as Greyhound Leasing & Financial of Canada Ltd.) and ITFI between December 1986 and August 1990. Financing statements were registered under the *Personal Property Security Act*, RSO 1990, c. R.10 ("PPSA"), and its predecessor.

SECURED CREDITOR	TYPE	DATE OF REGISTRATION	ACT
Greyvest	Lease (50 Units)	Jan. 12 or 20, 1987	PPSA (E, O) and (E, B, D, O)
Greyvest	Lease (25 Units)	Dec. 2 or 16, 1987	PPSA (E, O) and (E, O)
NAT	Debenture (I, E, A, O)	Feb. 1, 1990	PPSA
Greyvest	Lease (10 Units)	June 1, 1990 (I, E, O)	PPSA
Greyvest	Lease (2 Units)	Aug. 13, 1990 (E, O, MV)	PPSA
NAT	—	Nov. 16, 1990	PPSA (I, E, A, O)

There is an initial question to be determined as to whether the leases in question require a registration under the PPSA to preserve Greyvest's claim to priority over the chattels which are their subject matter. Depending on the answer to that question, the dispute between the parties turns, in large part, on the question of priorities based on registration. In that respect, the [foregoing] chart, summarizing the competing transactions as relied on and presented to the court by counsel, may be helpful. In the column entitled "Act" the letters "E," "I," "A," and "O" refer to collateral description "boxes" on a financing statement relating to "equipment," "inventory," "accounts" and "other," respectively.

In terms of the dispute regarding priority by registration, the following additional facts are important to note as well.

As the foregoing table indicates, the financing statements registered by Greyvest in January and December 1987 variously described the collateral in question, in the collateral classification section, as "equipment" (E), "book debts" (BD), and "other" (O). The box in the section for "inventory" (I) was not marked.

It is common ground that the trailers in question were not "equipment," but rather were "inventory" in the hands of ITFI, and there is authority for the proposition that the marking of the category "other" has the effect of *excluding* consumer goods, inventory, equipment or accounts, unless they, themselves, have been marked: *Re Laverty* (1982), 3 PPSAC 1, 47 CBR (NS) 109 (Ont. SC). Greyvest's later registration in June of 1990 (the "June 1990 Greyvest Registration"), did designate "inventory" as well as "equipment," "accounts" and "other" on the collateral classification line of the financing statement.

The February 1990 NAT Registration was for a period of one year, and was allowed to expire from the registry unrenewed. It contained the following description in the optional collateral description segment with respect to the collateral: "50 new Roussy Aluminum 53¢ High Cube Tandem Axle Vans Serial # [50 serial numbers followed]." The November 1990 NAT Registration had all boxes checked off on the collateral classification line, but the optional description lines were not completed.

The Issues

The issues to be determined can be summarized as follows:

1) Are the leases between Greyvest and ITFI the sort of leases which do, or do not, require registration under the PPSA for priority purposes?

2) Can the misclassification of the collateral in the 1987 Greyvest registrations be "cured" by the application of s. 46(4) of the PPSA, such as to preserve Greyvest's priority to the initial 75 trailers?

3) Does the February 1990 NAT Registration prevail, or is it limited in its effect to the "50 Roussy trailers" described in the optional collateral description section of the financial statement, by virtue of s. 46(3) of the PPSA?

4) What is the effect of the expiry without renewal of the February 1990 NAT Registration?

5) Can Greyvest rely upon the June 1990 Greyvest Registration, which did classify the collateral as "inventory," to perfect its earlier security interests in the 1987 leases, by virtue of s. 45(4) of the PPSA which now allows one registration to perfect several security interests?

6) Conversely, if the error in classification of the collateral in the 1987 registrations can be corrected by the operation of s. 46(4) of the PPSA, can Greyvest rely upon those registrations as its "root of title" for all subsequent registrations as well?

7) In any event, does Greyvest have priority with respect to the 12 units covered by the June 1990 and August 1990 Greyvest Registrations?

8) Finally, if NAT has priority by registration on any of the units, is it estopped from asserting that priority because Greyvest relied upon a statement made by Mr. McCleary of NAT to Mr. Micallef of Greyvest to the effect that NAT was not making a claim to any of Greyvest's trailers?

[The court concluded that the leases were "security leases" that required registration.]

...

Misclassification of Collateral

Greyvest registered six financing statements in 1987 which are pertinent to these proceedings. They all precede any registration by NAT.

The first two registrations, dated January 12 and 20—which related to a transaction respecting 50 trailers—classified the collateral variously as "equipment," "book debts" and "other," with no optional general collateral description given.

In December 1987, four financing statements were registered, two on December 2 and two on December 16. These registrations relate to a transaction involving 25 trailers. One of the December 2 registrations classified the collateral as "equipment" and "other" but went on to give the following general collateral description: "Registration made respecting assignment and agreement for lease schedules 13310—1, 2 and 3 assigned by debtor to secured party." One of the December 16 registrations classified the collateral as "equipment," "book debts" and "other," with, in addition, a general collateral description which stated: "Registration made respecting assignment & agreement for lease schedule 13610 assigned by debtor to secured party." The optional collateral descriptions in the latter two cases would appear to relate to that aspect of the overall transaction whereby Greyvest took an assignment of the leases between ITFI and the end users as security for the transaction. The second December 16 registration is identical to the first December 2 registration described above except for the name of "Secured Party."

What is apparent from the foregoing is that the 1987 Greyvest registrations do not mark "inventory" as collateral being secured. It is common ground, and counsel for Greyvest concedes, that the collateral is inventory in the hands of ITFI, and should have been classified as such in the financing statement. Mr. Dunphy submits on behalf of Greyvest, however, that this "error" can and should be cured by the operation of s. 46(4) of the PPSA. Pursuant to that section:

46(4) A financing statement or financing change statement is not invalidated nor is its effect impaired by reason only of an error or omission therein or in its execution or registration unless a reasonable person is likely to be misled materially by the error or omission.

In my view, this argument cannot succeed with respect to the Greyvest registrations in January 1987, or with respect to one of the registrations made on December 2, 1987 (No. 871202 1013 49 5597), or with respect to one of the registrations made on December 16, 1987 (No. 871216 0947 43 9742); but it is entitled to succeed with respect to the first registration on that latter date (No. 871202 1013 49 5596) and with respect to the other registration on December 16, 1987 (No. 871216 0947 9744). My reasons for coming to these conclusions are the following.

The trailers which were the subject matter of the financings that triggered these registrations were inventory in the hands of ITFI and would properly have been classified and described as such in the financing statement. They were not.

The January 1987 registrations variously classify the collateral as "equipment," "book debts" and "other," without anything in the general description section of the financing statement to reflect, refine, expend or limit the type of collateral involved. There is simply nothing in the filing to notify a person doing a search under the PPSA that Greyvest is claiming *any* security interest in the inventory of the debtor. In my opinion, this admitted error is one which is likely to mislead a reasonable person materially and, therefore, is one which invalidates or impairs the effect of the financing statement.

...

For the foregoing reasons, I conclude that the two January 1987 financing statements, the December 2, 1987 financing statement (bearing No. 871202 1013 49 5597), and the December 16, 1987 financing statement (bearing No. 871216 0947 43 9742), are not curable by the operation of s. 46(4) of the PPSA, and are accordingly invalid and ineffective to establish a security interest in the trailers in question, in priority to the claim of NAT.

The same is not the case with respect to the remaining December 1987 financing statements. Neither refers specifically to "inventory," but each contains a general description of the collateral in lines 13 to 15 of the financing statements. A reasonable person doing a search and reading the general description of the collateral provided is not likely to be misled materially, in my view, as to the nature of the collateral in which the security interest is being claimed. In the case of the December 2 financing statement (No. 871202 1013 49 5596), it is those assets listed in the "agreement for lease schedule 13610—1, 2 and 3 assigned by debtor to secured party." In either event, there can be no mistake that Greyvest is claiming a security interest in whatever is listed on those schedules. A subsequent creditor doing a search is thus put on notice to make enquiries in order to clarify precisely what the nature of that security interest is and over precisely what collateral priority is claimed, if it wishes to position itself with regard to that prior security claim.

In August 1990, Greyvest registered a financing statement with respect to a two-trailer transaction. This registration did not classify the collateral as "inventory" in the collateral classification section, but did have a description in the general description section and a reference to vehicle identification numbers. It is therefore effective to protect Greyvest's interest in the two trailers which were the subject matter of that transaction: see *Re*

533812 Ontario Ltd. (1985), 52 OR (2d) 750, 23 DLR (4th) 270, 5 PPSAC 128 *sub nom.*
Touche Ross Ltd. (Trustee in Bankruptcy) v. Ford Credit Canada Ltd., 58 CBR (NS) 49
(SC), affirmed (1987), 7 PPSAC xxxii, 64 CBR (NS) 80*n* (Ont. CA).

This interpretation is consistent with the purpose of the PPSA, which is to give notice
of prior claims to a creditor subsequently providing financing to the debtor, and sufficient information as to the collateral in question to put the creditor on inquiry as to
whether that collateral is the same as the collateral over which it, too, is seeking security.
Professor Richard H. McLaren, in his text *Secured Transactions in Personal Property in
Canada*, 2nd ed. (Toronto: Carswell, 1989), at p. 20-11 of vol. 2, describes the purpose of
the PPSA in these terms:

> The personal property security registration system has a dual purpose. First, it provides the
> necessary mechanism to permit the step required for perfection in s. 19(b) to be accom-
> plished. Secondly, it provides readily available information to prospective credit grantors
> and purchasers of certain forms of collateral. In connection with this latter purpose, the
> registry only contains enough information to enable a person searching the system to know
> who to contact to obtain information regarding the transaction.
>
> ...
>
> The purpose of the Act's registration system is to provide a registration mechanism *and
> information concerning collateral subject to a secured transaction.*

While the system is known as "a notice filing system," and imposes on the credit-
grantor/searcher the obligation to make inquiries to determine the details of the secured
transaction from the parties thereto, certain minimal information must be contained in
the financing statement by statute and regulation. Section 46(2) of the PPSA declares that
"every financing statement ... shall be in the prescribed form" (Form 1). Section 3 of
O. Reg. 372/89 prescribes the contents of financing statements, and includes as a mandatory requirement:

> 3(1) ...
> (f) the classification of the collateral as consumer goods, inventory, equipment, ac-
> counts or that the classification is other than consumer goods, inventory, equipment or
> accounts or any combination thereof;

A general description of the collateral, in lines 13 to 15 of the financing statement, is
optional under the regulations (s. 3(11)).

Where the legislature and the Lieutenant Governor-in-Council have made it a mandatory requirement to classify the collateral, the accurate completion of that exercise can
only be considered a material part of the information to be provided. Therefore, a credit-
or seeking the protection of perfection by registration of a financing statement under the
PPSA is impressed with an obligation to provide at least a sufficient indication of the
collateral in which it is claiming a security interest to alert a subsequent searcher, who is
about to provide credit to the same debtor, that the collateral in which the new credit
grantor is claiming an interest *may* be subject to a prior claim. Where—as in the case of
the January 1987 and December 1987 registrations referred to above—the financing
statements give no indication whatever that "inventory" is covered, and in fact indicate
the contrary by the marking of the "other" category, that information is lacking. Where

the general collateral description is sufficient to direct the searching creditor to the collateral in question, the financing statement is adequate.

The February 1990 NAT Registration

NAT's predecessor, First City Trust Company, provided financing to ITFI, secured by the NAT Debenture dated January 26, 1990. The NAT Debenture contained a fixed charge in respect of various trailers listed (none of which is listed among the Greyvest assets), but also granted a floating charge over all of the assets, property and undertaking of ITFI. A financing statement was registered with respect to this security interest on February 1, 1990.

The financing statement classified the collateral by marking the boxes for all of "inventory," "equipment," "accounts" and "other." It went on, however, to provide the following general description on the collateral secured in the optional section on lines 13 to 15:

> 50 new 1990 Roussy aluminum 53¢ high cube tandem axle vans serial # [the financing statement then went on to list the serial numbers of all 50 trailers].

I think it apparent, from the language of s. 46(3) of the PPSA, that the February 1990 NAT Registration is limited in the priority it provides to the 50 Roussy trailers listed in it. Section 46(3) says:

> 46(3) Except with respect to rights to proceeds, where a financing statement or financing change statement sets out a classification of collateral *and also contains words that* ***appear*** *to limit the scope of the classification*, then, unless otherwise indicated in the financing statement or financing change statement, the secured party may claim a security interest perfected by registration *only in the class as limited*. (Emphasis added.)

Mr. Wigley argued, on behalf of NAT, that completion of the general collateral description portion of the financing statement is an optional, almost gratuitous, exercise, and that by virtue of the check in the "other" box in the classification section, the financing statement "otherwise indicated" that the secured party's interest was not limited to the 50 trailers listed.

I do not agree.

Filling in the general collateral description portion of the financing statement is optional under the PPSA. Having chosen to fill in that portion, however, the secured creditor risks limiting the collateral that is protected by perfection through registration to something less than what may, in fact, be encompassed by the security instrument, if words are used which fail to make it clear that something other than what is described on lines 13 to 15 is also caught by the registration. Here, the general description appears to limit the scope of the registration to the collateral delineated—50 Roussy trailers specifically set out by serial number: see McLaren, *supra*, at p. 20-41 in note 60.

Thus, the February 1990 NAT Registration is valid to perfect NAT's interest in the 50 Roussy trailers only. However, since it is common ground that those trailers do not overlap with the Greyvest assets, it is not valid to perfect a security interest ahead of Greyvest in any of the trailers which are at issue in these proceedings.

Effect of the Expiry of the February 1990 NAT Registration

There was some argument about whether the February 1990 NAT Registration, which expired without renewal on February 1, 1991, could be sustained *for purposes of continuous registration* by the November 1990 NAT Registration.

In view of my conclusion, set out above, that the February 1990 NAT Registration is limited in its scope to the 50 Roussy trailers listed therein, which are not amongst the trailers in dispute in these proceedings, this issue is academic. I would have thought, however, that s. 21 of the PPSA would operate to provide *for continuous perfection.* Mr. Dunphy's attempt to distinguish between "continuous registration" and "continuous perfection" is interesting, but in the end not determinative, because it is *continuous perfection* under the PPSA which counts to preserve a creditor's priority position. The fact that the February 1990 NAT Registration subsequently drops by the wayside because of non-renewal is simply the very kind of situation, I would think, that s. 21 is designed to catch.

The June 1990 Greyvest Registration

Greyvest registered a financing statement on June 1, 1990 as a result of a transaction involving 10 trailers. In this instance, the box for "inventory" in the collateral classification section was checked off, as well as the boxes for "equipment," "accounts" and other." In addition, the general collateral description section was filled in with the words: "Re equipment schedule number 02 to lease agreement number 308700 and the proceeds thereof."

I have come to the following conclusions regarding this registration, having regard to the issues outlined earlier in these reasons:

(i)   the registration is effective to give Greyvest priority over NAT with respect to the trailers listed in the schedule referred to in its general collateral description section (i.e., the 10 trailers which were the subject matter of the immediate transaction), because the February 1990 NAT Registration is not effective to give that priority to NAT, for the reasons outlined above;

(ii)   for those same reasons, the June 1990 Greyvest Registration is limited in its scope to the equipment listed in the schedule referred to;

(iii)   even if I am in error regarding (ii) above, the June 1990 Greyvest Registration, which does classify the collateral as "inventory," cannot operate to perfect Greyvest's security interest in the original 1987 leases through the magic of s. 45(4) of the PPSA.

The June 1990 Greyvest Registration gives priority to the trailers listed …

The first conclusion regarding the June 1990 Greyvest Registration does not require much elaboration. I have already found that the February 1990 NAT Registration does not give NAT priority over any trailers which are part of the disputed assets, but is restricted to the 50 trailers listed therein. Therefore, the June 1990 Greyvest Registration operates to perfect Greyvest's interest in whatever assets are encompassed therein.

Those assets, in my view, are simply the 10 trailers which, I am told, are the assets listed in the schedule to the lease agreement No. 308700 referenced in the general description section.

... but is limited in scope to those trailers listed ...

The same analysis that limited the scope of the February 1990 NAT Registration to the 50 Roussy trailers set out in the general description section of that financing statement limits the scope of the June 1990 Greyvest Registration to the assets listed on "equipment schedule number 02 to lease agreement number 308700 and the proceeds thereof."

A creative argument can be, and was, made by counsel to the effect that the reference to "*equipment* schedule" and "*proceeds thereof*" *otherwise indicate*—in the language of s. 46(3)—that a security interest is perfected in more than meets the eye, i.e., in collateral which is "inventory" or "other" than inventory or equipment. The purpose of the PPSA is to provide notice and information about a priority claim to collateral subject to a secured transaction, however. To my mind, the reasonable person who is searching the index should not be required to be creative and to perform a labyrinthine lawyer-like analysis of the language used by the creditor seeking to preserve its priority. Where the thrust of what meets the eye in the general description of the collateral "*appear[s]* to limit the scope of the classification," as it does here, "the secured party may claim a security interest perfected by registration only in the class as limited": s. 46(3).

...

Order accordingly.

NOTES AND QUESTIONS

1) OPPSA s. 46(3), which, according to Blair J, determined the outcome of the February 1990 NAT registration, was inadvertently repealed in the course of the 2006 PPSA amendments. The repeal anticipates the proposed reforms described in note 3, below, but it is premature for as long as the current collateral description system remains in force. The government plans to put the provision back, pending implementation of the reforms described in note 3, but has not indicated when it will do so.

2) OPPSA s. 45(4) provides that except where the collateral is consumer goods, one financing statement may perfect multiple security interests. In the *Adelaide* case, Blair J held that this provision applies only if the various security agreements are part of the same overall transaction and, further, that the provision does not apply retrospectively. In other words, the secured party cannot rely on s. 45(4) to cure a defect in an earlier registration. This part of his judgment, which is not reproduced in the extract above, calls to mind the concerns expressed in *Coin-O-Matic Service Co. v. Rhode Island Hospital Trust Co.*, 3 UCC Rep. Ser. 1112 (RI Superior Ct. 1966) about the corresponding aspect of Article 9: see Chapter 7, Part V.C. In response to a recommendation by the CBAO Personal Property Security Law Committee, new paragraphs (a) and (b) were added to s. 45(4) in 2000 with the aim of reversing this part of Blair J's judgment.

3) The OPPSA uses a checkbox system for collateral descriptions in the financing state-ment. The *pro forma* financing statement contains five boxes; they are labelled consumer goods, inventory, equipment, accounts, and other. The secured party must check one or more of these boxes to fulfill the collateral description requirement set out in the regulations (Minister's Order s. 3(1)(f)). By contrast, all the other provinces require a collateral descrip-tion "by item or kind," or, in other words, in narrative form. The Ontario Bar Association's Personal Property Security Law Committee recommended in a 2006 submission to the Minister of Government Services that Ontario switch to the item or kind approach. The main reasons were that: (1) the lack of harmonization between Ontario and the other prov-inces is a potential source of confusion among system users; (2) the Ontario system is a his-torical and technological anomaly; and (3) the Ontario system involves unnecessary trans-actions costs because the vagueness of the collateral description results in a high volume of followup inquiries under OPPSA s. 18.

The proposal envisages an amendment to the regulations that would require a collateral description along the following lines:

(1)(a) a description of the collateral by item or kind or as "goods," "chattel paper," secur-ities," "documents of title," "instruments," "money" or "intangibles,"

(b) a statement indicating that a security interest is taken in all of the debtor's present and after-acquired personal property,

(c) a statement indicating that a security interest is taken in all of the debtor's present and after-acquired personal property except specified items or kinds of personal property or except personal property described as "goods," "chattel paper," securities," "documents of title," "instru-ments," "money" or "intangibles," or

(d) a description of the collateral as inventory, but such a description is valid for the pur-poses of this section only while the collateral is held by the debtor as inventory.

(2) A description is inadequate for the purposes of subsection (1) if it describes collateral as consumer goods or equipment without further references to the kind of collateral.

The government has indicated its intention to implement this recommendation, subject to first making the necessary changes to the register computer program. No indication has been given of when this will occur.

V. AMENDMENTS TO REGISTRATION

Heidelberg Canada Graphic Equipment Ltd. v. Arthur Andersen Inc.
(1992), 4 PPSAC (2d) 116 (Ont. Gen. Div.)

[Heidelberg, which had sold equipment to Kennedy Park Ltd., held a registered security interest in "inventory, equipment, accounts and other" of Kennedy Park. When this se-curity interest was assigned to the Chase Manhattan Bank of Canada ("Bank"), the Bank registered a financing change statement. When Kennedy Park got into financial trouble, Rob and Lisa Thomas ("Thomas") loaned the company money and took and registered a security interest in its assets, including its accounts. When further funding was required, Thomas contacted a representative of the Bank and convinced her that the Bank should "remove its registration" with respect to the accounts of Kennedy Park. Apparently, the Bank mistakenly assumed that it did not have a security interest in the accounts. The financing change statement ("FCS#1") that was used for this purpose indicated that it was amending the initial registration. When the Bank realized that it had a security interest in the accounts, it registered another financing change statement—FCS#2—which also provided for an amendment to the initial registration, this time adding back the accounts as collateral.

No interests in the assets of Kennedy Park Ltd. arose between the registration of FCS#1 and FCS#2.

When Kennedy Park made an assignment in bankruptcy, its trustee, acting also as receiver under the Thomas security agreement, attacked the Bank's security interest in the accounts.]

FELDMAN J: At issue in this application is the validity of the security taken by the applicants over the equipment and accounts receivable of the bankrupt, Kennedy Park, and the priority of that security as against the trustee in bankruptcy and two debentures in favour of the two individual respondents. [The main issues are as follows.]

(1) Chase Manhattan Bank of Canada ("Chase") registered (i) a financing change statement ("FCS#1") deleting the reference to "accounts" in order to accommodate subordination of its position to a potential new lender for Kennedy Park, and as a result of an error in its understanding of its security and of the effect of such registration; two days later it registered (ii) another financing change statement ("FCS#2") purporting to restore its registration over accounts.

What was the effect of each of those registrations, and in particular:

(a)   did the first financing change statement discharge or merely unperfect the security interest in accounts;

(b)   did the second financing change statement reinstate or reperfect the security;

(c)   if so, is s. 30(6) of the Personal Property Security Act, RSO 1990, c. P.10 ("PPSA" or "new PPSA") applicable to maintain Chase's priority over the registered debentures of the respondents?

(2) Did the amalgamation of the debtor company, Kennedy Park, require Chase to register a financing change statement?

· · ·

The effect of FCS#1

On its face, FCS#1 does not purport to be a discharge or partial discharge of the security over accounts, but rather a correction of a perceived original error in registration against accounts. It is clear that s. 56(1)(b) contemplates either payment or performance of certain of the obligations under the security agreement before a financing change statement evidencing a partial discharge may be demanded. No payment or performance was made here. This was not a discharge in the sense of a release of security for satisfaction of part of the obligation.

The *Weiss* case, referred to by the respondent, dealt with an interpretation of specific sections of the Bank Act, RSC 1970, c. B-1. In the case of *Re Dante Boutique Shoes Ltd.* (1982), 2 PPSAC 27, 40 CBR (NS) 19, 131 DLR (3d) 243 (Bktcy.), where based on a misunderstanding, the Bank did register a financing change statement in the form of a discharge, Henry J held that the effect under the then PPSA was that the bank's security ceased to be perfected and could only be reperfected if the curative provisions of the Act applied. There was no suggestion that the registration of the discharge had the effect of releasing the security as between the debtor and the secured party. Neither did the registration of FCS#1 have that effect.

The respondents' second argument is that the effect of the first financing change statement was that the registration against accounts "ceased to be effective," using the language of ss. 51 and 52 of the PPSA, and therefore under s. 52(2), Chase could only perfect again by registering a financing statement and not a financing change statement.

In my view, a review of the overall scheme and structure of the PPSA, and in particular Part IV, reveals that the registration system is built on the concept of the registration of a financing statement which may cover more than one type of collateral. Changes can be made to the contents of the financing statement during its life which is its "registration period." However, only a financing statement has a registration period. A financing change statement can only be registered to have effect during the balance of the registration period of the financing statement to which it relates (see, for example, ss. 48(5) and 49), or it may extend or reduce that period (s. 51(2)). The registration period that relates to each category of collateral is the registration period of the financing statement. The financing statement is like a tree, and the financing change statements are like its branches; the branches have no separate lifespan; their lifespan is the lifespan of their tree.

Therefore a financing change statement is not intended under the PPSA to affect the registration period of one of the claimed categories of collateral within the financing statement. I am reinforced in this view by the reference in s. 51(3) to a discharge, but not to a partial discharge, as being one way of ending the registration period of a financing statement. When the PPSA refers in s. 52 to a registration which "has ceased to be effective," it refers to the expiry of the registration period of the financing statement, or its discharge by registration.

Although one argument is that the first financing change statement had no effect because it did not fit within a specific section of the Regulations or of the PPSA, it is clear that Chase intended it to have effect, and anyone doing a search would conclude that Chase was claiming no interest in accounts. It is a case where the security interest in accounts ceased to be perfected. By s. 53 of the PPSA, FCS#1 was effective from the time of its registration.

The effect of FCS#2

The respondents have argued that even if the security of Chase in accounts only became unperfected, it could only be reperfected by registration of a financing statement and not a financing change statement. Section 45(1) mandates as follows:

> 45(1) In order to perfect a security interest by registration under this Act, a financing statement shall be registered.

The respondent also relies on s. 52(2):

> (2) Where a security interest has been perfected by registration and the registration has ceased to be effective, the security interest may be perfected again by the registration of a financing statement.

However, there are specific situations where registration of a financing change statement is used to perfect the security again when it has become unperfected, specifically under s. 48 where the debtor has transferred the collateral or changed its name and a further registration is required to reperfect after the creditor learns of these events.

Again, it follows the form of the registration scheme that where the financing statement remains alive, any changes or amendments are to be done by way of a financing change statement. It is only when the financing statement either does not yet exist or no longer exists, that a new financing statement is required.

Section 49 of the Act is consistent with this structure. It provides two basket categories of circumstances where a financing change statement may be used to modify a financing statement during its life (registration period). I can see no impediment in the Act to using a financing change statement under s. 49 to reperfect a security interest if the circumstances of subss. (a) or (b) exist.

I also note that s. 49 is not a "saving provision" in that it does not confer any priority. Under s. 53, a financing change statement is effective from the time of its registration. It is only in the case where the financing change statement is used to reperfect that s. 30(6) must be considered. So that, for example, if the original financing statement did not include in line 10 an "x" in the collateral designation for inventory, and that was added by a financing change statement at a later date, the secured interest in inventory would only be perfected from the date of registration of the financing change statement, and not from the original registration date of the financing statement.

I am satisfied that s. 49(b) is applicable in this case. The only possible sections within Part IV which may be considered to provide for the same amendment are ss. 45(1) and 52(2). The first of those sections deals with the need for an original registration of a financing statement, and in my view does not mean that individual categories of collateral cannot be perfected later by a financing change statement. Such an interpretation would contradict the specific references in s. 48 to the use of a financing change statement to reperfect where security has become unperfected. Section 52(2) is not applicable because the registration has not ceased to be effective within the meaning of that subsection as discussed above.

The applicability of s. 49(a) depends upon the meaning of the terms "error or omission" as used in that section. The curative section of the PPSA, s. 46(4), also contains the terms "error or omission," and reads as follows:

> (4) A financing statement or financing change statement is not invalidated nor is its effect impaired by reason only of an error or omission therein or in its execution or registration unless a reasonable person is likely to be misled materially by the error or omission.

Under the former PPSA, the curative section (s. 47(5)) limited the errors to clerical errors, and that phrase was narrowly interpreted by the Courts. The new section has deleted that restriction and arguably allows for a broad interpretation of the meaning of "error or omission," within the context of the mechanism of the section.

The section on its face is aimed at the type of error which would have invalidated the financing statement or financing change statement in which it appeared. That would include errors in filling out the form which caused it to be out of conformity with the Regulations, but which, if overlooked, would leave the form with its intended effect. These would include, for example, errors in the spelling of the debtor's name or date of birth.

The section preserves the validity and effectiveness of the registration "unless a reasonable person is likely to be misled materially by the error or omission." In other words, the form is valid in spite of the error, and the court may so declare. However, the section does not provide for correction of an error. Correction is not necessary where the curative provision applies, because the section treats the form as being effective to carry out what it purports to do on its face. (See, however, *Canamsucco Road House Food Co. v. Lngas Ltd.* (1991), 2 PPSAC (2d) 203 (Ont. Gen. Div.), where the section was applied to allow the creditor to correct an error retroactively by filing a financing change statement.)

If the terms "error or omission" in s. 49(a) have the same meaning as in s. 46(4), then the purpose of s. 49(a) would be to provide a mechanism to correct such errors when the secured creditor becomes aware of them, so that there will be no further risk that someone may be materially misled. Again, the correction is only effective from the time of registration of the financing change statement. Before that, the creditor must rely on the curative section.

On the other hand, there are no interpretive constraints contained within s. 49(a) itself, to limit the types of errors or omissions that can be corrected or may be intended to be corrected under that section. From a conceptual point of view, I can see no reason why any error, including errors made deliberately but only recognized as errors afterwards, and including the error of registering the document at all, should not be able to be corrected under this section, when no retroactive priority is accorded by the section.

Because I have held that FCS#2 was properly registered under s. 49(b), I do not need to decide the scope of applicability of s. 49(a) in this case.

Application of s. 30(6)

In my view, s. 30(6) applies to deem the Chase security over accounts to be continuously perfected from the time it was first perfected by the financing statement.

Although it is initially attractive to reason that because the section uses the phrase "becomes unperfected," it was only intended to apply to the situations referred to in s. 48 where that phrase is also used, it is equally arguable that if that limitation had been intended by the Legislature, it would have included that paragraph as a subparagraph of s. 48, or it could have referred to s. 48 within s. 30(6).

Security interests can also become unperfected in other ways, as is demonstrated in this case, and there is no reason to limit the application of s. 30(6), placed as it is within a general list of rules of priority, unless such a limitation is required by the PPSA.

Section 30(6) deems a security interest that was unperfected for a period, to have been continuously perfected from the time of its first perfection except as against persons who "acquired rights in all or part of the collateral" during the period. Chase submits that to give this section any meaning and effect, it cannot be said that a security interest ranking behind the one in question which moves up in priority in respect of the collateral, thereby "acquires rights" in the collateral, because then the section would have no remedial effect.

The argument made by counsel for the respondents is that the sections which it replaces from the prior Act (ss. 53(1)(c) and (d) of the old PPSA), protected from their ambit the rights acquired by any person "by an act or thing done by him during the period," which required a positive act by any such person. However, the language of the new PPSA is passive and therefore can include rights acquired without any positive action by the affected person including just by moving up in priority.

Counsel argues further that the section should be read narrowly, and that it is only intended to cut out a person referred to in s. 30(1) para. 1 who has registered a financing statement during the hiatus period but before its security agreement is signed and therefore before it is perfected, but whose priority would otherwise run from the time of its registration.

Ingenious though this argument is, I cannot give effect to it. I agree with the statement of Montgomery J in *Weber v. Royal Bank* (1984), 4 PPSAC 242 at 246 (Ont. HC), referring to the predecessor section, s. 53(1)(c) of the old PPSA:

> In my view, s. 53(1)(c) is remedial in nature. I give it the broad interpretation that the Legislature intended.

The respondents' interpretation would give a very limited effect to the section and would provide scant remedial effect for secured parties who become unperfected, including by the effect of the PPSA itself in s. 48, while a subsequently secured party may receive a windfall benefit.

The purpose of the section is to preserve the original priority positions when security is reperfected. The section only protects a creditor who acquires some new rights in the collateral during the unperfected period. On the evidence, nothing transpired with respect to the collateral during Chase's unperfected period. Because the respondent debenture holders acquired no new rights in the collateral during the period, nor did any new creditor acquire any such rights, thereby raising the issue of priority as between the three of them. I need not consider further.

· · ·

The Chase security was properly reperfected on February 2, 1990 by the registration of the financing change statement, so that its security is effective against the trustee in bankruptcy. The Chase security also maintains its priority in relation to the subsequent debenture security of the respondents.

The effect of the amalgamation of the debtor

On June 1, 1989 Kennedy Park Print & Litho Ltd., an Ontario company, amalgamated with its parent, B.L. United Enterprises Inc. The parent had no liabilities, and its only assets were shares of Kennedy Park. The name of the amalgamated company is the same as the original debtor, Kennedy Park Print & Litho Ltd.

Two issues are raised with respect to the amalgamation.

(1) Was there a transfer of the collateral from the debtor to the amalgamated company within the meaning of s. 48, requiring the registration of a financing change statement by Chase after it learned of the amalgamation, in order to maintain perfection or to reperfect its security interest? (There was also a factual issue raised as to whether and if so when Chase learned of the amalgamation in order to trigger s. 48.)

(2) More fundamentally, does Chase have any security over accounts receivable generated by the amalgamated company, as its security agreement is only signed by the amalgamating company, the original Kennedy Park, as debtor? Nor did Chase ever register a financing statement against the amalgamated company as debtor.

Both of these issues seek to examine again the nature of the transaction and transformation known as amalgamation, and in particular, whether in any sense and for any purpose, the amalgamated company is considered to be a new or separate entity from the amalgamating companies.

The issue raised by the second question is most conceptually intriguing. Counsel for the respondents argues that the original debtor company can give security over its own future accounts receivable, but it cannot grant security over the future accounts receivable of another company. The clause that makes the agreement binding on successors and assigns of the debtor does not assist; the effect of that clause is that a successor company must abide by the obligations of the debtor contained in the contract—but it does not nor can it create new obligations of a successor company such as pledging that company's future accounts receivable.

Does this analysis also apply in the case of amalgamation? Will an original debtor company bind the future accounts receivable of an amalgamated company of which it becomes one of the amalgamators, by binding its own future accounts receivable?

The effect of the amalgamation of corporations has been considered and determined by the Supreme Court of Canada in *R v. Black & Decker Manufacturing Co.*, [1975] 1 SCR 411, 15 CCC (2d) 193, 13 CPR (2d) 97, 43 DLR (3d) 393, 1 NR 299, and in *Witco Chemical Co. v. Oakville (Town)*, [1975] 1 SCR 273, 43 DLR (3d) 413, 1 NR 453, and its conclusions have been most recently discussed and affirmed in this Court in the decision of Henry J in *Loeb Inc. v. Cooper* (1991), 5 OR (3d) 259, 3 BLR (2d) 8 (Gen. Div.).

Those cases hold that the amalgamating companies do not end their lives with amalgamation, but continue to exist in the amalgamated company. There is no "old" company extinguished or "new" company created. There is no transfer of the assets of the amalgamating companies to the amalgamated company; this is indicated by the use of the term "continues" in the statute together with the statement that the amalgamated company "possesses all the property" of the amalgamating companies. In respect of those two terms Dickson J said the following in *Black & Decker* at p. 417 SCR:

If corporate birth or death were envisaged, one would have expected to find, in the statute, some provision for transfer or conveyance or transmission of assets and not simply the word "possesses," a word which reinforces the concept of continuance ...

(The Canada Corporations Act, RSC 1970, c. C-32 and the Ontario Business Corporations Act, RSO 1990, c. B.16 (the "OBCA") contain the same language; the Canada Business Corporations Act, RSC 1985, c. C-44 contains similar language.)

In the *Loeb* case, Henry J addressed the issue of transfer of assets and liabilities in the context of whether a lease was assigned without consent by an amalgamating company to the amalgamated company upon amalgamation. He found that it was not, applying the Supreme Court of Canada cases referred to and rejecting the contrary analysis of the Saskatchewan Court of Queen's Bench decision in *Crescent Leaseholds Ltd. v. Gerhard Horn Investments Ltd.* (1982), 26 RPR 121, [19831 1 WWR 305, 141 DLR (3d) 679, 19 Sask. R 391 (QB).

In my view, the law is settled that upon amalgamation there is no transfer of assets or liabilities and therefore specifically there is no transfer by the debtor of its interest in the secured collateral upon amalgamation. Consequently s. 48 of the PPSA does not apply.

Although the second question raised by the respondents is not quite so clearly settled, to accede to the argument would be to start the law down the same path from which the Supreme Court diverted it in the two 1975 decisions, because the argument requires a finding that the amalgamated company is a "new" company, not the debtor.

The full reconciliation of the concept behind amalgamation has often been recognized as difficult. As Kelly JA said in *Stanward Corp. v. Denison Mines Ltd.*, [1966] 2 OR 585 at 592, 57 DLR (2d) 674 (CA) [aff'd. [1968] SCR 441, 67 DLR (2d) 743]:

> While it may be difficult to comprehend the exact metamorphosis which takes place, it is within the Legislature's competence to provide that what were hitherto two shall continue as one.

Section 179(b) of the OBCA deals with the status of existing contracts of amalgamating companies: the amalgamated company is "subject to" the *contracts*, liabilities and obligations of each of the amalgamating companies. In my view, the use of the phrase "subject to" is significant. When a corporation is *subject to* a contract, it is not just bound by the contract and bound by its terms, as a successor or assignee of the original debtor; rather it is as a party to the contract, so that the amalgamating company stands in the shoes of the debtor for the purpose of contracts entered into by the debtor. Again, this is consistent with the concept that the original debtor company continues its existence within the amalgamated company, and that the amalgamated company is not a new company.

Therefore the amalgamated company named Kennedy Park is subject to the security agreements signed by the amalgamating company, Kennedy Park, with Heidelberg and which were assigned to Chase. There is no new "debtor." Consequently, the accounts receivable of the amalgamated Kennedy Park constitute part of the collateral over which Chase has a perfected security interest. As well, no new financing statement nor financing change statement need be registered.

In light of the decision on the legal question raised, it is unnecessary to make a finding as to whether and if so when Chase learned of the amalgamation.

···

Conclusion

The attack by Arthur Andersen Inc. as trustee in bankruptcy of Kennedy Park and as receiver on behalf of Lisa Thomas and George Schwartz, on the security of Heidelberg and Chase fails on all grounds.

Application allowed.

NOTES AND QUESTIONS

1) Under the Acts based on the CCPPSL model, the changes in the registration that occurred in this case (deleting and then adding back accounts) would have been treated as amendments to the registration. See, for example, BCPPSA s. 44(3), which provides that "[a]n amendment to a registration, whether the registration is valid or invalid, may be made by registering a financing change statement at any time during the period that the registration is effective and the amendment is effective from the date the financing change statement is registered to the expiry of the registration being amended."

2) Note particularly the comments of the court with respect to the relationship between OPPSA ss. 49(a) and 46(4). Assume that the original registration was "invalid" in that it does not pass the test of s. 46(4) (for example, it does not contain the correct name of the debtor). Can this registration be amended to make it valid, or is it necessary to register a new financing statement containing the correct name of the debtor? See BCPPSA s. 44(3), set out in note 1, above.

3) In *Heidelberg*, the court concluded that s. 30(6) "only protects a creditor who acquires some new rights in the collateral during the unperfected period." This statement must be taken in context; the section is not limited in its effect to rights of creditors. For further discussion, see Chapter 7, Part VI. Assume that, between the dates of the two financing change statements at issue in the *Heidelberg* case, another secured party had taken a security interest in the accounts: who would have had priority? Assume that Kennedy Park had become bankrupt between the dates of the two financing change statements. Would the outcome of the case have been different?

CHAPTER SEVEN

Basic Priority Rules

I. INTRODUCTION

The pre-PPSA priority rules between competing consensual security interests were a complicated amalgam of common law, equitable, and statutory rules. However rational in their historical and doctrinal origins, these rules are difficult to justify in the context of modern financing arrangements. More particularly, the common law placed primary emphasis on the locus of legal title and therefore gave priority to the person who held title unless that person was estopped from denying the authority of the person in possession of the collateral to deal with it or unless he had failed to comply with an applicable registration requirement. The priority of equitable security interests was generally governed by the order of their creation, but this rule was qualified in at least three respects. *First*, an equitable security interest could be defeated by a purchaser for value and without notice of the legal interest (*Joseph v. Lyons* (1884-85), 15 QBD 280 (CA)). *Second*, floating charges were governed by their own priority rules that turned as much on the distinctive character ascribed to the security device by the courts as on its equitable origins. In the *third* place, under the rule in *Dearle v. Hall* (1823), 3 Russ. 1, where there were successive assignments of the same chose in action (and originally such assignments were recognized only in equity), priority went to the assignor who first gave notice of his assignment to the debtor.

The PPSA replaces this disparate set of rules with a much better integrated and functionally oriented regime of rules. This is not to say that they work effortlessly and that their fairness and efficiency will necessarily commend themselves to all. We begin with the basic priority rules in s. 30 of the OPPSA. Although the section describes them as only operating where no other provision applies, it is best to treat them as the starting point for an understanding of the Act's priority structure. The rules in s. 30(1) may be paraphrased as follows:

1. *Rule of first to register.* If the competing security interests have all been perfected by registration, then the order of registration determines the order of priority (s. 30(1), para. 1). The time of attachment or perfection of the interest is not relevant.
2. *Rule of first to register or to perfect by other means.* If one security interest is perfected by registration and the other security interest is perfected by other means, then if registration occurs first, that security interest will take priority. The converse rule applies if the non-registration perfection precedes registration (s. 30(1), para. 2(i)).
3. *Rule of first to perfect.* If both security interests are perfected without registration, then the security interest that is perfected first takes priority (s. 30(1), para. 2(ii)).

4. *Rule of first to attach.* If none of the competing security interests have been perfected, they rank according to the order of attachment (s. 30(1), para. 4).

Section 30.1, which was added to the statute in 2006, enacts special priority rules for security interests in investment property. The key rules are as follows:

1. *Control trumps non-control.* A security interest perfected by control has priority over another security interest perfected otherwise than by control.
2. *Two security interests perfected by control.* If two or more security interests are perfected by control, they rank in priority by first in time to obtain control.
3. *Securities intermediary priority.* Despite the above rules, in the indirect holding system a securities intermediary with a security interest in a security entitlement created by it has priority over other secured parties, unless the intermediary otherwise agrees.

For a more detailed summary, see the Cameron extract in Chapter 5, Part III.

II. JUSTIFICATION FOR THE FIRST-IN-TIME RULE

Thomas H. Jackson and Anthony T. Kronman, "Secured Financing and Priorities Among Creditors"
(1979), 88 *Yale LJ* 1143, at 1161-64 and 1178-82 (footnotes omitted)

To the extent his claim is secured by an interest in specific collateral, a creditor generally enjoys priority over his debtor's unsecured creditors: before the property in question may be appropriated to satisfy their claims, the debt owed to the secured party must be repaid in full. The same principle applies if a debtor has several creditors whose claims are secured by different assets. In this case, each creditor has priority with regard to his own collateral and a subordinate unsecured interest in any asset securing the claim of another creditor.

When two or more creditors claim a security interest in the same item of property, however, an additional problem arises as to how their claims are to be ranked inter se. An ordering principle of some sort is required to establish the relative priorities in this situation. In theory, there are a number of possible solutions. Competing security interests in the same property might be ranked on the basis of size or temporal order, or according to the nature of the transaction out of which they arose; or they might be assigned equal priority. The draftsmen of Article 9 chose a simple timing principle. Section 9-312(5) provides that conflicting security interests are to be ranked "according to priority in time of filing or perfection," with the result that earlier security interests take precedence over later ones. This section codifies a principle—established in the chattel security field long before the enactment of the Code—that may be conveniently expressed by the slogan, "first in time, first in right." In our view, the adoption of such a priority rule, at least as a baseline, is required in order to capture the special efficiencies that secured financing makes possible. Since this is not immediately obvious, a few words of explanation are in order.

Suppose that the law allowed the entire matter of priorities among competing secured parties to be decided by private (but publicly recorded) contractual agreement between the debtor and each of his creditors. To see what priority relationships might be expected to emerge, consider the following case. C1 agrees to make a loan to his debtor ... . [T]he parties conclude that a secured transaction will be to their mutual advantage, and the debtor offers as collateral a single piece of heavy-duty industrial equipment, worth approximately the amount of the contemplated loan. In order to maintain a collateral base for future borrowing, however, the debtor insists that he be allowed to give subsequent creditors a superior interest in the same property—an interest that will override C1's own claim.

C1's response is predictable. If the debtor ever exercises his power to grant later secured creditors priority over C1, C1's claim will be rendered at least partially unsecured. Furthermore, the debtor will have an incentive to exercise this power, since by so doing, he can effectively increase the riskiness of C1's loan without increasing its interest rate. Consequently, it would be irrational in this situation for C1 to treat his credit transaction with the debtor as anything other than an unsecured loan or to charge less than he would if there were no collateral securing it at all.

Therefore, if both parties agree that there is an advantage in making the loan on a secured basis, they will also agree to include a provision in their contract barring the debtor from granting any subsequent creditor a superior interest in the collateral. If a provision of this sort is not or cannot be included, the real savings made possible by a secured transaction will be lost.

This argument applies with equal force to a junior creditor, C2, who intends to make a loan secured by property already encumbered by a prior, superior lien in C1's favor. In setting the interest rate on his loan, C2 will take into account the risk that the property may decline in value, rendering C2's claim partially or entirely unsecured. But the mere existence of a prior claim against the property will not by itself make it irrational for C2 to charge less than he would for lending on an unsecured basis. There is, after all, some probability that the collateral will be worth enough to satisfy both claims in the event of the debtor's insolvency. It would be irrational for C2 to charge less than the unsecured rate, however, if the debtor can encumber the same property a third or fourth time and give subsequent creditors higher priority. Even a junior secured creditor will therefore insist upon an agreement barring the debtor from giving any later lender a priority superior to that which the junior creditor enjoys at the time he makes his loan.

If the priority of competing secured claims were left entirely to private agreement, then we would expect each creditor financing on a secured basis to insist that his claim be preferred to that of any later creditor asserting an interest in the same collateral. The result would be a series of agreements entitling individual creditors to satisfy their claims in the order in which they arose, each claim being subordinated to those that preceded it and superior to those that followed it in time. This is, of course, precisely the result achieved by a first-in-time, first-in-right priority rule. The justification for the rule, then, is that it does what the parties would do for themselves in its absence, and thereby achieves a savings in transaction costs.

···

Article 9 provides that the priority of conflicting security interests "dates from the time a filing is first made covering the collateral or at the time the security interest is first perfected, whichever is earlier." Thus if C1 files a financing statement on May 30, and C2 files a financing statement covering the same collateral on June 30, C1's interest in the property will have priority over C2's, regardless of the order in which they actually make their loans or satisfy the requirements for perfection. Suppose, for example, that C2 discovers on June 30 that C1 has already filed a financing statement and immediately calls the debtor who tells him that he has not yet borrowed a penny from C1. C2 then files a financing statement of his own and simultaneously advances the debtor $1,000 against collateral worth the same amount. As long as C1's financing statement continues to be effective, any loan that C1 makes to the debtor will enjoy priority over C2's $1,000 claim. Knowing this, C2 will do one of three things: look for other, unencumbered collateral, obtain a subordination agreement from C1, or make a loan at the unsecured rate. If C2 lends money to the debtor at the secured rate without obtaining a subordination agreement, the debtor will have an incentive to borrow money against the same property from C1, since by doing so the debtor can unilaterally increase the riskiness of C2's loan without having to pay a higher interest rate.

These results follow from the Code's adoption of a "notice-filing" system that keys priority to the time of filing, rather than to the time of completion of the loan transaction. Such a system appears to be consistent with the general rule that earlier claims should prevail over later ones. In one sense, however, notice-filing tends to subvert this fundamental ordering principle. Under a notice-filing system, unless a junior creditor obtains a subordination agreement, he runs the risk that the claims of senior lenders will be increased, without losing their seniority, after he makes his loan. Functionally, this puts the junior creditor in the same position he would be in if creditor claims were ranked on a last-in-time, first-in-right basis—with the important difference that it would be harder to contract around the risk of subordination in a regime of this sort than it is under a notice-filing system, in which the senior lenders with overriding claims can all be identified, in advance, by the junior creditor.

Because it forces junior creditors either to lend at the unsecured rate or to protect themselves by obtaining costly subordination agreements, a notice-filing system gives senior lenders a competitive advantage in bidding on subsequent loans whenever the collateral in question already belongs to the debtor's estate and so cannot be used to give the junior creditor an overriding purchase money security interest. In some cases, this may work to the debtor's disadvantage by raising his total credit costs. On the other hand, if the parties to a particular credit transaction contemplate a series of loans over a period of time, a notice-filing system permits them to reduce the costs of their transaction by eliminating the need to refile each time an advance is made. Thus, notice-filing "protects" the filing system by "allowing the secured party who has first filed to make subsequent advances without each time having, as a condition of protection, to check for filings later than his."

From the debtor's point of view, a notice-filing system has benefits as well as costs: although it increases the costs of subsequent borrowing from junior creditors, it also reduces the expense of transactions involving the repeated extension of credit from a single senior lender. In some cases—perhaps in most—the advantages of a notice-filing system outweigh its disadvantages. But there are other situations in which this is not true—for example, when the debtor's available collateral is indivisible, and he would like to borrow against it on a secured basis from several different lenders. In such situations, notice-filing may work to the disadvantage of the debtor, and he might, in fact, be better off under a "transactional" filing system similar to those employed by a number of pre-Code chattel security statutes.

As its name implies, a transactional filing system requires each individual credit transaction with the debtor to be separately perfected by filing, and so does not permit filing before credit has actually been extended. Under this system, a junior creditor can determine, merely by inspecting the files, the maximum extent to which his interest can be subordinated to the claims of senior creditors. As a result, it is easier and less costly for a debtor to borrow from junior creditors under a transactional system than under a notice-filing system like that employed by Article 9.

Although Article 9 adopts a notice-filing rule for all security interests perfected by filing rather than by possession, there seems to be nothing in the Code itself to preclude a debtor from contracting into a transactional priority rule if he wishes. A debtor could do this, for example, by expressly noting the effectiveness of a particular filing on the financing statement ("this filing is effective to secure an amount not to exceed $100,000"). Enforcement of such a limitation against the creditor making the loan secured by the filing in question would permit the debtor and his creditor to use a transactional filing system whenever they could benefit by doing so.

Assuming debtors are free to contract around the Code's notice-filing rule, the only remaining question is whether notice-filing provides an appropriate baseline presumption—to be modified by private agreement on an ad hoc basis—for secured transactions of every sort. The presumption seems a sensible one when the collateral involved is either inventory or receivables, and the security interest must therefore take the form of a "floating lien," since a notice-filing system eliminates the need for repeated filings and reduces the parties' transaction costs. On the other hand, the Code's blanket presumption in favor of notice-filing seems less reasonable when the collateral consists of equipment or other large and relatively stable items of property. In such situations, a transactional filing system is likely to be more attractive to the parties, given the reduced need for repeated filings and the debtor's desire to minimize the cost of borrowing against the same collateral from multiple creditors. For secured transactions involving large, stable assets, a presumption that the parties intend a transactional rule to apply—rather than the notice-filing rule presently imposed by the Code—would probably be more efficient. If so, the Code's blanket presumption in favor of notice-filing should be replaced by a pair of presumptions applicable to security transactions of different sorts, reflecting the fact that the costs and benefits of a particular priority rule may vary with the nature of the transaction itself.

III. THE IRRELEVANCE OF KNOWLEDGE

The Robert Simpson Company Ltd. v. Shadlock and Duggan
(1981), 31 OR (2d) 612 (SC)

GRAY J: The issue is whether priority as between competing security interests in the same collateral security is determined under The Personal Property Security Act by whoever perfects or registers first or whether actual notice may defeat a claim to priority based on prior registration or prior perfection.

It was agreed that if priority is determined only by registration or perfection, the Plaintiff has no claim in law but if the doctrine of actual notice prevails, the Defendant cannot succeed on the application to strike out the Plaintiff's Statement of Claim. Between February 18th, 1976 and June 24th, 1976, pursuant to eleven Conditional Sale Contracts, the Plaintiff sold to the debtor certain chattels for installation at a motel property. On or about June 4th, 1976 an employee of the Plaintiff put the Defendants on notice of the Plaintiff's security interest.

On June 14th, 1976 the debtor mortgaged the motel to the Defendants and also on the same date by Chattel Mortgage mortgaged the Chattels and equipment in the motel, including the Plaintiff's Chattels, to the Defendants. The Defendants' Chattel Mortgage was registered under The Personal Property Security Act on June 17th, 1976, but the Plaintiff did not register its Conditional Sales Contracts under that Act until February 7th, 1978.

The relevant sections of The Personal Property Security Act are [ss. 1(k), 1(y), 12(1), 21, 22(1)(a), 25(1), 25(2), 35(1), and 36(3)].

...

The submission made by Counsel for the Defendants in summary form was that the only section of The Personal Property Security Act which applied was Section 35 and this section has provided for a test of priorities with the result that the so-called doctrine of actual notice cannot prevail. It was further argued that the Plaintiff had a purchase-money security interest, that Section 21 defines when a security interest is perfected and that Section 25 covers the question of perfection by registration.

The thrust of this argument was that if no other provision of The Personal Property Security Act is applicable the provisions of Section 35 apply since both security interests were registered with the result that priority would be determined by Section 35(1)(a) by the order of registration if the security interests have been perfected by registration.

The submission made by Counsel for the Plaintiff was that the legislation did not specifically abolish the doctrine of actual notice. My attention was directed to Section 22(1)(a) wherein it is clear that an unperfected security interest is subordinate to the interest of a person who is entitled to a priority under The Personal Property Security Act or any other Act. To decide who is entitled to priority it is necessary to peruse Section 35(1). It was said that subsections (a) and (b) had no application because under (a) both security interests were registered and under (b) both were perfected. In other words Section 35(1)(a) and (b) are of no assistance in resolving the issue in this application because here the contest is between one perfected and one unperfected security interest. The question really involves whether the Defendants are entitled to a priority under Section 22(1) of The Personal Property Security Act. The conclusion I was invited to reach was that the only purpose of requiring registration was to give notice to third parties and that if in fact a third party has acquired knowledge of the security interest then the underlying requirement has been met.

I reserved judgment on this application because the legislation is relatively new and the academic writers have indicated that there are conflicting policy arguments with an unresolved problem.

It was said that there is an omission in Section 35(1) which could easily have been rectified by the legislative draftsman so that the case at bar could have been covered. It was also said, with some force, that the doctrine of actual notice is deeply rooted in our law and that one of the well known rules of statutory interpretation is that the provisions of the common law cannot be changed without an express statutory provision to that effect.

I have considered the following cases:

Re Jung and Montgomery, [1955] 5 DLR 287.
Pitcher v. Shoebottom, [1971] 1 OR 106.
Re Dominion Stores Ltd. and United Trust Co. (1973), 42 DLR (3d) 523.
United Trust Company v. Dominion Stores, [1973] 2 SCR 915.

These cases generally stand for the proposition in cases involving The Land Titles Act, RSO 1970, c. 234 as amended that "the doctrine of actual notice as to all contractual relations and particularly the law of real property has been firmly based in law since the beginning of equity. Such a cardinal principle of property law cannot be considered abrogated unless the legislative enactment is in the clearest and most unequivocal of terms." This latter phrase was used by Spence J in delivering the majority decision in the Supreme Court of Canada in *United Trust Company v. Dominion Stores (supra)*.

I have come to the conclusion that this application should succeed. The provisions of The Personal Property Security Act to some extent flow from the earlier provisions of the US Uniform Commercial Code. Although the language is different it is interesting to compare Section 9-312 of the UCC with Section 35 of The Personal Property Security Act. The language is similar and notice makes no difference [*Bloom v. Hilty* (1967), 234 A2d 860].

In my view nothing in Section 35 says anything about lack of knowledge being a prerequisite for its operation.

In an action in The County Court of the Judicial District of Ottawa-Carleton between *The Bank of Nova Scotia Plaintiff and Dilauri Chevrolet Oldsmobile Ltd. and Craig Edward Schwartz, Defendants*, the plaintiff bank with prior registration succeeded even though it had notice. Judge E.E. Smith made the following statement:

> It is argued that as between the two claimants in this case, the Bank of Nova Scotia and Dilauri Chevrolet Oldsmobile Ltd., a subsequent registration by the Bank ought not to be allowed to prevail where there was actual notice. It is conceded that Dilauri's failure to comply with the Act was innocent and in no way misled the Bank.
>
> If I were to accede to the argument, it seems to me that I would be reading into this rather comprehensive piece of legislation something which was (deliberately—the concept of actual notice being well known to the drafters) omitted and in the process thwarting many of the obvious purposes of the legislation.

In the present case I adopt that reasoning and that language.

I would also adopt the language of Lord Cozens-Hardy MR in *Re Monolithic Building Company; Tacon v. The Company*, [1915] 1 Ch. 643, at 556-66 [who,] quoting James LJ in an earlier case, said:

> I think it would be dangerous to engraft an equitable exception upon a modern Act of Parliament.

and at 666:

> Both parties stood on their legal rights—neither of them was misleading the other. It is not consistent with the policy of the Legislature to import fine equitable distinctions into these cases, and I am therefore of opinion that the argument founded on the knowledge of the judgment creditor cannot prevail.

I have likewise reviewed Sections 36 and 37 [new Act, ss. 34-35] and have concluded that the special priority rules thereunder have no connection with this application. The Plaintiff's submission depends on looking to see a fixed time for registration but there is nothing in The Personal Property Security Act that fixes the time when the Court looks to see if there has been registration. This is a new statute which should be dealt with upon its own merits rather than some considerations which might apply to The Land Titles Act. Sections 22 and 36(3) contemplate knowledge but it is my view that this appears in The Personal Security Act for two situations and I draw the inference that the actual notice principal doesn't therefore apply elsewhere in the Act.

Prof. R.H. McLaren in his textbook *Secured Transactions in Personal Property in Canada*, Vol. 1, 1979, at 6-2 states the general or residual rule [of] Section 35 thus: "The general rule of priority is built around the key concepts of attachment and perfection. No other statute has ever attempted to state even a single priority rule let alone one of such general application as s. 35. If no special priority rule governs then the rules of subs. (1) are used to resolve competing claims in the same collateral. ... The three rules of s. 35 disregard the pre-Act law and its reverence for legal title to the collateral and application of the equitable principle of good faith and notice."

I adopt the foregoing and am reinforced in my view by the judgment of Laskin CJ in *United Trust v. Dominion Stores (supra)* albeit a dissenting judgment.

Judgment for defendant.

NOTE

For a judgment to the same effect, see *National Trailer Convoy of Can. Ltd. v. Bank of Montreal* (1980), 1 PPSAC 87 (Ont. HC) and other cases cited in Ziegel and Denomme, at p. 251, n. 7. The policy considerations are discussed in the following extract.

Douglas G. Baird and Thomas H. Jackson, "Information, Uncertainty and the Transfer of Property"
(1984), 13 *Journal of Legal Studies* 299, at 312-16 (footnotes omitted)

Filing systems work because the legal rules provide not only a benefit to a person who desires to acquire a property right but also a corresponding responsibility. One is obliged to stake one's claim in the filing system so that future parties will be able to find it. If the files do not properly reflect the existing claim of a creditor to a debtor's sea shell because, for example, that creditor failed to file or filed improperly, or because his filing has become improper through some change in the world, the files cannot be said to impart notice of his interest.

A later claimant, however, may have actual knowledge of the interest of that creditor, obtained from some other source. If that person then acquires a property interest in the shell, should he be able to claim that his actual knowledge does not defeat his priority over the other creditor, because of the absence of notice from the filing system? This inquiry we shall call the question of *knowledge*, and it asks whether the legal system should treat knowledge as equivalent, for purposes of ordering claims of interests in an asset, to the constructive notice that comes from an interest properly noted in the files.

A second question is whether subsequent parties can point to defects in an earlier party's filing or to the absence of a filing altogether, even if they never checked the filing system and never relied on the absence of proper notice. This inquiry we shall call the question of *reliance*, and it asks, as between a creditor who fails to file properly and a subsequent creditor who fails to examine the files, if there remains any reason for continuing to prefer the subsequent creditor.

Neither of these questions looms large in litigation surrounding real property, for the most part because the transactions are sufficiently large and the rituals sufficiently well known that defective filings are the rare exception rather than the rule. Defective filings, however, are an everyday affair when at issue are security interests in personal property, and thus the question is far from being merely of theoretical interest.

···

The main difference among the various filing systems in use today turns on the role of actual knowledge. The three principal recording systems, both in real property law and in pre-Code chattel security law, are "notice," "race-notice," and "race" statutes. Under a notice statute, only a subsequent purchaser with neither record notice nor actual or constructive knowledge of an existing property claim at the time of his purchase transaction prevails over a prior purchaser holding such existing property claim. Under such a system, however, the subsequent purchaser without knowledge or notice of an earlier party's interest will prevail over that party regardless of whether either ever files.

Under a race-notice statute, a subsequent purchaser, if he has neither actual nor constructive knowledge of the claim of a prior purchaser at the time he enters into a purchase transaction, will prevail if, but only if, he records his claim first. Notice and race-notice schemes differ only in the post-transaction period: while the notice statute treats events occurring after that transaction as irrelevant for purposes of determining the priority between these two purchasers, the race-notice statute imposes an additional race requirement in that post-transaction period before priority is ultimately determined.

Under a race statute, knowledge gained outside the filing system (or from possession) is irrelevant. The first party to file—and hence the first party to give record notice—wins. The race system, while it is the purest system in regarding as exclusive the information in the files, exists in very few states with respect to real property. And while article 9 of the Uniform Commercial Code has, with a few exceptions, adopted a race system for security interests in personal property, this itself is a deviation from most pre-Code chattel mortgage systems. Indeed, prior to the 1956 revisions of article 9, courts usually read a knowledge requirement into statutes that were otherwise silent.

Two considerations, however, lead us to conclude that the knowledge of the claims of those not in possession, who have failed to record or who have recorded improperly should be irrelevant. First, even if there are advantages from insisting that subsequent purchasers meet the traditional requirement of being without knowledge, these advantages seem to pale beside the costs they impose. Any inquiry into knowledge is likely to be expensive and time consuming. It is simply much easier to live in a world in which everyone knows that he must comply with a few simple formalities or lose than to live in a world in which the validity of someone's property rights turns on whether certain individuals had knowledge at some particular time in the past. Those who are required to make appropriate filings, in the main, either are professionals or engage the services of professionals. We think it likely that everyone is ultimately better off with a clear rule than with a legal regime that is somewhat more finely tuned but much more expensive to operate. Ferreting out those who took with knowledge despite a defective filing generally is not worth the uncertainty and the litigation it generates.

Second, and less obvious but perhaps even more important, the virtues of punishing those with knowledge are more apparent than real. We think there are few advantages to be gained by incorporating a knowledge requirement, even apart from a consideration of its costs. Acting with knowledge, without more, is not the same as acting in bad faith. We deny thieves the right to convey any title at all to third parties, because we want to discourage theft. We refuse to recognize the rights of those who lie or are otherwise acting in bad faith, because we want to discourage fraud. We should not, however, penalize those with knowledge just for having knowledge. Other things being equal, we want to encourage people to gather information, while we do not want to encourage people to steal or lie. Because making rights turn on knowledge is always costly and because having knowledge is generally good, those who want to justify the common-law rule bear a heavy burden.

We can think of two arguments that might be advanced to justify a knowledge requirement. First, one could argue that penalizing the subsequent party with knowledge is desirable because it takes away any benefit the subsequent party might receive from failing to disclose the information. Thus, he is more likely to correct the files himself or tell the errant filer about his mistake. The rule, in other words, is desirable because it ultimately works to improve the information in the filing system, and, hence, increases the value of property. Second, one can argue that the rule is justified because it deprives the subsequent party *only* of an opportunity to take advantage of someone else's mistake. Both arguments, however, ultimately fail.

Someone with knowledge has no incentive to disclose in a notice or race-notice regime. Furthermore, someone with knowledge enjoys no special advantage in a pure-race regime. The relevant focus should not be on the relative rights of the prior and subsequent purchasers, but rather on the relative rights of the two possible kinds of subsequent purchasers—those with knowledge and those without it. In a system in which only subsequent parties with knowledge lose to prior interests that are not properly filed, those with knowledge will not bid as much for an asset as those without the knowledge. A potential subsequent purchaser with knowledge could, of course, compete with the other purchasers by providing them with the knowledge as well, either by telling them directly, or by incorporating it in the files, where it would become a part of the filing system's notice. But gaining this parity by incorporating the knowledge into the filing system imposes on this purchaser some costs, such as the costs of notification, that the other creditors do not bear. And, after taking such steps, this purchaser then must compete with the owner's other potential purchasers only on an equal and now second priority basis.

Implementing a notice recording system, at best, penalizes only a party who actually *makes* a loan or other purchase. The rule may be more likely to drive away any party with knowledge than it is to result in having that knowledge incorporated into the transfer system. At the margin, such a rule may discourage people from gathering information about property in the first instance. Nothing under the present "notice" systems encourages anyone *except* a subsequent purchaser from imparting the knowledge he has to the filing system. Where there is a well-organized market for the particular type of property in question, this result may tend to drive away the person with information. The earlier party will still lose the priority contest with the subsequent purchaser. The only difference is that the subsequent purchaser is simply someone else who is more ignorant.

Introducing knowledge into the ordering of priorities, moreover, creates insoluble circular priority problems when more than two parties are involved, one has knowledge of a prior interest, and another does not. For example, imagine that A, B, and C acquire interests in Blackacre in that order. A fails to file, while both B and C file properly. B acquired his interest with actual knowledge of A's unrecorded interest; C knew nothing about it. A circular priority arises under either a notice or a race-notice system, and it is impossible to determine who, among A, B, and C, should have priority. A prevails against B, because B's interest arose later in time and B had actual knowledge. B prevails against C, because C's interest arose later in time and C was on constructive notice of B's interest, because of the proper filing. C prevails against A, because, although his interest arose later in time, he had neither notice nor actual knowledge of A's interest. A beats B, B beats C, and C beats A.

Certain categories of legal rules, such as those banning insider trading, act to prohibit persons with knowledge from taking advantage of that knowledge. Whatever the justifications of those rules, however, they do not apply here. An insider with knowledge can enjoy profits from selling long or short that those without the knowledge cannot. He, therefore, has an incentive to use such information to gain such profit. A potential subsequent property claimant with knowledge of a defective filing by an earlier claimant enjoys no such advantages. Even with a pure-race rule, he is no better off than someone who knows nothing about the prior interest: he must pay the market price for the property.

IV. PRIOR LENDER'S COMPETITIVE ADVANTAGE

James Talcott, Inc. v. Franklin National Bank of Minneapolis
194 NW 2d 775 (S. Ct. Minn. 1972)

RONALD E. HACHEY JUSTICE: This is an appeal taken from a summary judgment in favor of defendant, Franklin National Bank of Minneapolis. The action was commenced for the recovery of possession of several motor vehicles, or their value, in which plaintiff, James Talcott, Inc., claimed a superior security interest.

The case was heard on stipulated facts. On February 20, 1968, Noyes Paving Company, hereinafter referred to as "debtor," entered into a conditional sales contract with Northern Contracting Company, as seller, covering the purchase, on an installment basis, of two dump trucks and other construction equipment. On that same day, the seller assigned, without recourse, the conditional sales contract to plaintiff, together with all sums payable thereunder and all right, title, and interest in and to the equipment covered by the contract. On February 21, 1968, a financing statement was filed with the secretary of state naming Noyes Paving Company as debtor, Northern Contracting Company as secured party, and James Talcott, Inc., as assignee of the secured party. The financing statement covered the following items of property: "Construction Equipment, Motor Vehicles."

On May 1, debtor entered into an equipment lease with defendant bank covering one dump truck; and on May 31, a similar lease agreement was entered into between the same parties covering two additional dump trucks and other equipment. Each lease provided that debtor, if not in default, could purchase the leased goods at the end of the lease term for the sum of $1. Defendant did not at that time file a financing statement regarding the equipment described in the two lease agreements.

During the latter part of the year 1968, debtor experienced difficulty in making payments on the conditional sales contract. On January 30, 1969, debtor and plaintiff entered into an agreement extending the time for payment. In consideration of the extension granted, debtor gave plaintiff a security interest "in all goods (as defined in Article 9 of the Uniform Commercial Code) whether now owned or hereafter acquired." An attached schedule merely repeated in substantially identical form the list of goods attached to the original conditional sales agreement. The new agreement went on to provide that the security interest was granted to secure the payment of all loans, advances, debts, liabilities, obligations, covenants, and duties owing by debtor to plaintiff, including, without limitation, any debt, liability, or obligation owing from debtor to others which plaintiff may have obtained by assignment or otherwise. No additional financing statement was filed in connection with the extension agreement of January 30. At that time, plaintiff did not know of the existence of the motor vehicles and other equipment listed in defendant's two equipment leases and did not rely upon their existence in entering into the extension agreement.

Following the date of the extension agreement, debtor ran into more financial difficulty and defaulted in payments with respect to both the conditional sales contract and the equipment leases. On May 21, 1970, copies of the leases were filed by defendant bank as financing statements with the secretary of state. Sometime during May 1970, defendant repossessed the equipment in question and this action ensued. The precise date on which defendant made the repossession is not clear from the record. The parties agreed that it took place during the month of May 1970. All of the equipment was located with exception of one item. By agreement between plaintiff and defendant, the equipment was sold, and the proceeds were placed in a special account pending the outcome of this case.

The issues on appeal are: (1) Whether an equipment lease which gives the lessee the right to acquire title to the equipment for $1 upon compliance with the lease terms is a "security agreement" within the meaning of Article 9 of the Uniform Commercial Code (Minn. St. 336.9-101, et seq.); (2) whether debtor had sufficient ownership of the leased equipment so that it became secured property under the extension agreement with plaintiff; (3) whether the description of the secured property, as it appeared in the extension agreement, was sufficient to meet the requirements of Article 9 of the Uniform Commercial Code; (4) whether the financing statement filed at the same time the first security agreement was assigned to plaintiff was sufficient to protect a security interest in the property covered by the extension agreement; and (5) which security interest was entitled to priority.

[Hachey J answered questions 1 to 3 in the affirmative and continued:]

4. Was the financing statement, filed at the time the first security agreement was assigned to plaintiff, sufficient to reflect a security interest in the property covered by the extension agreement?

Defendant argues that plaintiff did not perfect its security interest in the equipment covered by the second security agreement (the extension agreement of January 30, 1969) because of the failure to file an amendment to the financing statement. The trial court also followed this line of reasoning in arriving at its decision that plaintiff had not perfected its security interest.

Section 336.9-402(1) provides that "[a] financing statement may be filed before a security agreement is made or a security interest otherwise attaches." This is what happened in the instant case. The financing statement filed February 21, 1968, met all requirements of the code since it described by type ("Construction Equipment, Motor Vehicles") not only the property covered by the original sales agreement which was assigned to plaintiff but also the property, which likewise consisted of motor vehicles and constructional equipment, financed by defendant. The code does not require a reference in the financing statement to after-acquired property. Section 336.9-402(4) states:

> The term "financing statement" as used in this article means the original financing statement and any amendments but if any amendment adds collateral, it is effective as to the added collateral only from the filing date of the amendment.

A careful reading of that section does not compel a finding that the financing statement must be amended when the security agreement is altered.

Section 336.9-204(3) specifically approves the inclusion of after-acquired property in the security agreement. It states:

> ... [A] security agreement *may* provide that collateral, whenever acquired, shall secure all obligations covered by the security agreement. (Italics supplied.)

That section permits the inclusion of after-acquired property in a security agreement, but it does not require such inclusion in all cases where subsequent collateral is to be added. When §§336.9-402(1) and 336.9-204(3) are read together, it is clear they sanction the essential elements of the transaction in the instant case. The financing statement was filed February 21, 1968, and described the type of goods covered as "Construction Equipment, Motor Vehicles." It was sufficient to give notice of the security agreement entered into on February 20, 1968, and was also sufficient to give notice of the second security agreement of January 30, 1969. As pointed out herein, §336.9-402(1) specifically permits the filing of a financing statement in advance of the making of the security agreement itself.

The whole purpose of notice filing would be nullified if a financing statement had to be filed whenever a new transaction took place between a secured party and a debtor. Once a financing statement is on file describing property by type, the entire world is warned, not only that the secured party may already have a security interest in the property of that type (as did plaintiff in the property originally financed), but that it may later acquire a perfected security interest in property of the same type acquired by the debtor in the future. When the debtor does acquire more property of the type referred to in the financing statement already on file, and when a security interest attaches to that property, the perfection is instantaneous and automatic. §336.9-303(1).

Different fact situations may arise resulting in different arrangements between the secured party and the debtor, all within the contemplation of the code. For instance, in their initial dealings they may contemplate either a number of financing transactions, all secured by the property to which the security interest originally attaches, or they may create a single obligation from the debtor to the secured party, to be secured by property the debtor then owns and additional property that he will later acquire. Furthermore, a transaction between the parties may involve a combination of both of these. Even where the parties originally contemplate a single debt, secured by a single item of property or a single group of items, the secured party and the debtor may enter into further transactions whereby the debtor obtains additional credit and the secured party is granted more security. The validity of such arrangements as against creditors, trustees in bankruptcy, and other secured parties has been widely recognized by many courts. See, *DuBay v. Williams*, 417 F2d 1277 (9 Cir. 1969); *Grain Merchants of Indiana, Inc. v. Union Bank & Sav. Co.*, 408 F2d 209 (7 Cir.), certiorari denied sub nom. *France v. Union Bank & Sav. Co.*, 396 US 827, 90 S. Ct. 75, 24 L. Ed. 2d 78 (1969); *Rosenberg v. Rudnick*, 262 F. Supp. 635 (D. Mass. 1967).

Using future-advance clauses and using after-acquired property clauses in the original security agreement are not the only means by which perfected security interests can be obtained in subsequently contracted obligations or in goods the debtor may later come to own. There is nothing exclusive about §336.9-204(3, 5). Parties may use future-advance and after-acquired clauses, and they are a great convenience. But, if they are not used, there is nothing in the code which prevents the parties from accomplishing the same result by entering into one or more additional security agreements.

Upon a review of decision law in other jurisdictions it would appear that there is a difference of opinion as to perfection and priority of a later advance where it was not made pursuant to the original security agreement but pursuant to a later agreement which may or may not have satisfied the requirements of the code as to security agreements. The better view holds that, where originally a security agreement is executed, an indebtedness created, and a financing statement describing the collateral filed, followed at a later date by another advance made pursuant to a subsequent security agreement covering the same collateral, the lender has a perfected security interest in the collateral not only for the original debt but also for the later advance. The instant matter involves a parallel situation. See, *In re Rivet*, 299 F. Supp. 374 (ED Mich. 1969).

The error of the trial court in the instant matter was apparently prompted by its reliance on §336.9-402(4), which provides that any amendment adding collateral to a financing statement is effective as to the added collateral only from the filing date of the amendment. As has been pointed out, however, the financing statement originally filed was broad enough to cover the after-acquired collateral. If, for instance, the equipment leases between debtor and defendant had included items which did not fall within the description "Construction Equipment, Motor Vehicles" (for example, machine tools), then it would have been necessary, in order for the plaintiff to perfect its security interest in such different goods, to file either a new financing statement or an amendment to the original one. In either event, the effective date would have been the date of filing.

5. Priority

As has been pointed out, the record is not clear as to what date defendant repossessed the equipment. The exact date the conflict arose would be helpful in determining which portion of §336.9-312 should be applied in determining priorities.

From an examination of the record, it is clear that §336.9-312(4) is inapplicable inasmuch as defendant's security was not perfected within the allotted time thereunder—that is, no financing statement had been filed at the time that the debtor received the equipment or within 10 days thereafter. Had a financing statement covering the equipment leases been filed at the time the transaction between debtor and defendant took place or within 10 days thereafter, defendant would have had priority under this section of the code. Unfortunate as it may be for defendant, this did not take place; hence, §336.9-312(4) does not govern despite the bank's later filing.

Turning our attention to §336.9-312(5), we must determine whether paragraph (a) or paragraph (b) governs. Again, the date that the dispute arose is not clear. The parties have agreed that it arose sometime during the month of May 1970. Hence, whether the filing of the financing statement (equipment leases) by defendant was prior to or subsequent to the repossession date is not established. It then follows that §336.9-312(5)(a) may or may not be applicable. That section provides in part:

> (5) In all cases not governed by other rules stated in this section … , priority between conflicting security interests in the same collateral shall be determined as follows:
> (a) In the order of filing if both are perfected by filing, regardless of which security interest attached first … and whether it attached before or after filing.

With certain exceptions not applicable in the case at bar, a security interest is perfected when a financing statement is filed. Therefore, a reading of paragraph (a) leads us to the conclusion that, if a dispute arises over priority of perfected security interests (both having been perfected by filing before the dispute arose), then the order of filing of the financing statement governs. We are aware of the date that defendant filed its financing statement (May 21, 1970), but, again, the record is not clear as to the date that the dispute arose (i.e., the date of repossession). Defendant might have filed first and then repossessed, or it might have repossessed first and, upon being confronted with a dispute over priorities, decided to file forthwith. As we have said, if defendant filed first and then repossessed, §336.9-312(5)(a) governs.

Conversely, if the dispute arose first and thereafter the bank filed, then paragraph (a) of §336.9-312(5) is inapplicable, and we direct our attention to paragraph (b), which gives the following alternative method of determining priorities under this subsection:

> In the order of perfection unless both are perfected by filing, regardless of which security interest attached first under section 336.9-204(1) and, in the case of the filed security interest, whether it attached before or after filing.

Defendant's security interest did attach first, but (assuming it was filed after repossession) it was not perfected. Plaintiff's security interest attached later—actually after its filing had occurred. But neither of these factors is material in the application of the first-to-perfect rule. Accordingly, when the conflict arose (still assuming it was before defendant had filed) plaintiff was entitled to priority. Once plaintiff's priority had been acquired, no subsequent filing by defendant (more than 10 days after debtor received possession) could alter the situation. Moreover, even if §336.9-312(5)(a) should apply, plaintiff would still have priority under the first-to-file rule as its filing preceded defendant's by many months.

In passing, it could be said that plaintiff is to receive an unearned windfall, being the beneficiary of a security interest in property of which it wasn't even aware. Unquestionably, defendant bank, through misunderstanding of the applicable provisions of the code, will suffer a substantial loss. By its own failure to conform to and comply with very simple and obvious provisions of the code, it has found itself entangled in other provisions which are admittedly more complex but which are absolutely essential to the whole concept of notice filing. The fundamental purpose of Article 9 of the code is to make the process of perfecting a security interest easy, simple, and certain. It was intended to be a complete reversal of prior chattel security law and to rid the unaware of the traps of requirement of specific types of acknowledgments, technical affidavits of consideration, selection of specific proper forms, and other pitfalls that were not uncommon. The code very simply and briefly provides for a notice-filing procedure with a minimum of information required to be publicized in a filed financing statement. All that is required is a minimal description, and it may be by type or kind. The statement need not necessarily contain detail as to collateral, nor any statement of quantity, size, description or specifications, or serial numbers. No preciseness is required with respect to whether the collateral exists at the time of filing or is to be acquired thereafter, and no statement of charges, payment schedule, or maturity date need be included in the statement. The first to file shall prevail. Although there are a few exceptions, they are very clearly and definitely stated. To affirm here would amount to a limitation upon the efficacy of the first-to-file rule, which is basic and essential to the certainty that Article 9 seeks to achieve. Moreover, to hold that plaintiff was required to file an additional financing statement to cover the extension agreement of January 30, 1969, would have a disastrous effect upon financing transactions.

Reversed and remanded for further proceedings.

NOTES

1) Consider the following case:

SP1 and D are negotiating a security agreement. On January 1, SP1 registers a financing statement. The collateral description is inventory. On February 1, D approaches SP2 for a secured loan. SP2 does a register search and discovers SP1's registration. SP2 asks for details pursuant to OPPSA s. 18. SP1 replies saying that there is no security agreement between the parties and that negotiations are presently suspended. On February 15, SP2 enters into a security agreement with D and registers a financing statement. The collateral description is inventory. On March 1, SP1 and D resume negotiations, resulting in a security agreement covering all D's present and after-acquired inventory. D defaults against SP1 and SP2. Who has priority?

This is a variation on the hypothetical case discussed in the second half of the Jackson and Kronman extract in Part II, above. OPPSA s. 30(1), para. 1, in common with Article 9 and the other provincial PPSAs, provides that priority turns on the order of registration, rather than the order of perfection, and s. 45(3) allows for registration of a financing statement in advance of the security agreement (see Chapter 6, Part III.B). The result is that SP1 has priority. What could SP2 have done to protect itself? For a critical analysis, see the Jackson and Kronman extract in Part II, above.

2) Now consider the following case:

SP1 and D are negotiating a security agreement. On January 1, SP1 registers a financing statement. The collateral description is inventory. SP1 and D conclude a security agreement on January 15. The security agreement describes the collateral as all present and after-acquired blue widgets. On February 1, D approaches SP2 for a secured loan, offering to put up all present and after-acquired green widgets as collateral. SP2's register search discloses SP1's registration. SP1 informs SP2 that its security agreement covers blue widgets only. On February 15, SP2 and D enter into a security agreement. The security agreement describes the collateral as present and after-acquired green widgets. SP2 registers a financing statement. The collateral description is inventory. On May 1, SP1 and D enter into a second security agreement for a new loan, this one covering present and after-acquired green widgets. D defaults. SP1 and SP2 both claim the green widgets. Who has priority?

This is a variation on the facts of the *James Talcott* case and the outcome under the Canadian PPSAs is the same as under Article 9: OPPSA s. 45(4) provides that one financing statement may perfect one or more security interests created or provided for by one or more security agreements (see Chapter 6). This provision, in combination with s. 30(1), para. 1, leads to the conclusion that SP1 has priority. The lesson is that ss. 45(3) and (4), read in combination with s. 30 (1), rule 1, have similar effects and Jackson and Kronman's analysis is equally relevant in this second context.

3) Note that in the *James Talcott* case, the Franklin National Bank had a purchase-money security interest. This means it would have had priority over Talcott if it had registered a financing statement within 10 days after delivering the equipment to the debtor. The governing provision in Ontario is PPSA s. 33(2) (see Chapter 8). This would have been the simplest way of protecting itself. However, having allowed the 10-day grace period to elapse, the bank forfeited its super-priority entitlement and became subject to the basic first-in-time priority rule. In these circumstances, what could the bank have done to protect itself? (See the Jackson and Kronman extract in Part II, above.)

V. SECURITY FOR FUTURE ADVANCES

A. Introduction

Consider the following example:

On June 1, SP1 opens a line of credit in D's favour secured by a security interest in D's inventory. On the same date, SP1 registers a financing statement and D draws down $60. On July 1, SP2 and D enter into a security agreement, giving SP2 a security interest in the same inventory. SP2 registers a financing statement and makes D a loan of $30. On August 1, D draws an additional $50 on its line of credit with SP1. On September 1, D defaults against SP1 and SP2 and, on that date, the value of D's inventory is $100. SP1 claims the inventory for its June 1 and August 1 advances. SP2 argues that its claim to the inventory in relation to SP2's July 1 advance has priority over SP1's claim to the inventory in relation to SP1's August advance.

B. The Law

Prior to the enactment of the PPSAs, the type of dispute described above was governed by the equitable doctrine of "tacking." The rule was that SP1 had priority over SP2 for the August 1 advance, but not if SP1 had notice of SP2's July 1 loan: *Hopkinson v. Rolt* (1861), 9 HLC 514, 11 ER 829; the rule applied whether or not SP1 was under a commitment to make the August 1 advance: *West v. Williams*, [1899] 1 Ch. 132 (CA). "Notice" meant actual knowledge of SP2's security interest, as opposed to constructive notice deriving from SP2's registration.

The PPSAs replace the tacking doctrine with a set of statutory rules. In Ontario, the governing provisions are OPPSA s. 13 read in conjunction with s. 30(3). Section 13 provides that a security agreement may secure future advances, while s. 30(3) provides that, where future advances are made while a security interest is perfected, the security interest has the same priority with respect to each future advance as it has with respect to the first advance. Note that SP1's state of knowledge is irrelevant. Why?

Section 1(1) defines "future advance" to mean "the advance of money, credit, or other value secured by a security agreement *whether or not such advance is given pursuant to commitment.*" In the above example there is nothing to suggest that SP1 has a discretion to refuse the August 1 advance. On this basis, the loan is given pursuant to commitment, it is a "future advance," and so ss. 13 and 30(3) apply. Suppose that the agreement between SP1 and D had expressly given SP1 the option of declining to provide further credit at any time unless satisfied that it was sufficiently secured. This case is covered by the closing part of the definition: SP1's August 1 advance is still a "future advance" and ss. 13 and 30(3) still apply.

C. Policy Considerations

The above example is a variation on the hypothetical case discussed in the second part of the Jackson and Kronman extract in Part II, above. Note that, as in Jackson and Kronman's hypothetical case, the effect of the statute is to give SP1 a competitive advantage over SP2 and to force SP2 to negotiate a subordination agreement with SP1 if SP2 wants to be sure of its priority position in relation to the July 1 loan; functionally, the statute puts SP2 in the same position as if creditor claims were ranked on a last-in-time, rather than a first-in-time, basis. As Jackson and Kronman suggest, the policy justification for giving SP1 priority over SP2 for its August 1 advance, despite these consequences, is that it saves transactions costs by allowing SP1 to make subsequent advances "without each time having, as a condition of protection, to check for filings later than his." From D's point of view, while it is true that the statute increases the costs of subsequent borrowings from junior creditors, "it also reduces the expenses of transactions involving the repeated extension of credit from a single senior lender." Particularly in fact situations like the one in the example, which involve revolving credit arrangements, it is probably safe to assume that the benefits to D exceed the costs.

There is another relevant consideration. Consider the following variation on the above example:

> On June 1, SP1 agrees to lend D $110, on the basis that D will receive $60 immediately and the remaining $50 on August 1. D gives SP1 a security interest in its inventory to se- cure repayment and SP1 registers a financing statement. All other facts in the original problem remain the same.

The contract between SP1 and D is in substance a single contract for the loan of $110, payable in installments. If SP1 had paid D the $110 in full right at the outset, SP1 would clearly have had priority over SP2 for the whole amount. In principle, it should make no difference that SP1 paid D in installments, because it is the substance of the transaction, not its form, that should govern.

This analysis holds only if SP1 is under a commitment to make the August 1 payment. If SP1 has a discretion, then the transaction between SP1 and D is the same in substance as if SP1 had made two separate loans to D. Assume that this is in fact what happens:

> On June 1, SP1 agrees to lend D $60. D gives SP1 a security interest in its inventory to secure repayment and SP1 registers a financing statement. On August 1, SP1 agrees to lend D a further $50 and takes a security interest in D's inventory. All other facts in the original problem remain the same.

On these facts, SP1's August 1 payment is not a "future advance" because it is subject to a separate security agreement. Therefore, ss. 13 and 30(3) do not apply. However, that is not the end of the story: by virtue of OPPSA s. 45(4), SP1's June 1 registration is sufficient to perfect both its June 1 and August 1 security interests and, since priority between SP1 and SP2 turns on the order of registration (s. 30(1), para. 1), SP1 still has priority over SP2 for the August 1 advance (see the *James Talcott* case extracted in Part IV, above, but contrast the *Coin-O-Matic* case, extracted below). In principle, the outcome should be the same in the analogous case where SP1 and D's June 1 security agreement contemplates future advances but without any commitment on SP1's part. To treat the two cases differently would be to elevate form over substance. Recall that Jackson and Kronman, among others, express reservations about these priority outcomes. The point for present purposes, though, is simply that, whatever the priority rule, it should be the same for both transactions.

Another reason for having the OPPSA s. 30(3) priority rule apply whether or not SP1 was under a commitment to make the August 1 payment is to save litigation costs by avoiding case-by-case inquiries into whether SP1 was subject to a commitment or not. The following passage illustrates the nature of the issue:

> The distinction between advances under commitment and optional advances no doubt must arise out of the nature of the conditions which will and will not excuse the lender's performance. Clearly, a lender's commitment to make a future advance which excuses performance if he dislikes the way the debtor has parted his hair on the day the latter asks for the advance is not a real commitment. It is quite a different matter, however, if the lender's commitment to make an advance is excused only if the debtor's balance sheet, audited by an independent accountant, shows that the debtor's net current asset-debt ratio has fallen below an agreed-upon, reasonable standard. [P.F. Coogan, "The New UCC Article 9" (1972-73), 86 *Harv. L Rev.* 477, at 505-7]

Coin-O-Matic Service Co. v. Rhode Island Hospital Trust Co.
3 UCC Rep. Ser. 1112 (RI Superior Ct. 1966)

LICHT J: This matter is before the court on an agreed statement of facts. The following is a summary of the facts which will help place the case in proper perspective.

On July 11, 1963, Munroe Doroff purchased a motor vehicle from Warwick Motors, Inc., on a time payment basis (Exhibit "A"). The security agreement representing the purchase was assigned to the Rhode Island Hospital Trust Company. The security agreement did not have any provision for after-acquired property or future advances. It described the collateral as one Chevrolet Station Wagon Greenbrier 1963. The financing statement filed July 16, 1963 contained a reference to the same Chevrolet Greenbrier Station Wagon (Exhibit "B").

On October 2, 1964 Doroff became indebted to Coin-O-Matic Service Company in the sum of $5,600.00 represented by a promissory note and secured by a security agreement (Exhibits "C" and "D"). A financing agreement was filed October 23, 1964 (Exhibit "E"). On November 13, 1964, Doroff owed the Hospital Trust Company $302.77 on the security agreement of July 11, 1963 and on that date Rhode Island Hospital Trust Company loaned Doroff the sum of $1,000.00 from which sum he paid to Rhode Island Hospital Trust Company $302.77 in full satisfaction of his July 11, 1963 obligation. Rhode

Island Hospital Trust Company thereupon cancelled the old agreement. Doroff executed a new promissory note secured by a security agreement (Exhibit "F"). A new financing statement was filed on November 17, 1964 (Exhibit "G"). On December 7, 1964 Doroff went into bankruptcy. It was stipulated that the value of the motor vehicle at the time it came into Rhode Island Hospital Trust Company's possession was $1,200.00. It was further stipulated that the automobile was used in Doroff's business and there is no question that the automobile was part of the collateral given to Coin-O-Matic Service Company, the plaintiff.

...

The defendant contends that its original financing statement was sufficient not only to protect the original conditional sales agreement but the subsequent agreement despite the fact that there intervened a security agreement between Doroff and Coin-O-Matic and a filed financing statement in connection therewith.

The issues raised require a consideration of the Uniform Commercial Code. There is no dispute that the word "equipment" used in the security agreement between Doroff and Coin-O-Matic was within Section 6A-9-109(2).

Section 6A-9-312 provides in part:

(5) In all cases not governed by other rules stated in this section (including cases of purchase money security interests which do not qualify for the special priorities set forth in subsections (3) and (4) of this section), priority between conflicting security interests in the same collateral shall be determined as follows:

(a) in the order of filing if both are perfected by filing, regardless of which security interest attached first under §6A-9-204(1) and whether it attached before or after filing;

The defendant relies wholly upon what it considers the compelling literal meaning of the language of the section. That is to say, that having entered into a security transaction which covered the 1963 Chevrolet Greenbrier Station Wagon and having filed a financing statement it comes ahead of the plaintiff who had a security interest in the same collateral but whose filing of a financing statement was subsequent in time to the original filing and ahead of defendant's second filing. Obviously with respect to the original transaction there is no dispute that the prior filing of the financial statement would govern. But the defendant carries its argument a step further and contends that the original financing statement is an umbrella which gives the defendant a priority with respect to its second security transaction notwithstanding that the plaintiff's security interest was established in point of time prior to defendant's second security transaction.

The defendant contends that as long as there is a financing statement on file the whole world is given notice that the debtor is obligated; that there is a security interest in the particular collateral and that the debtor may at any time after the original transaction become further indebted and enter into an additional security agreement with respect to the collateral. In support of this position the defendant cites a colloquy between Peter Coogan, a member of the Permanent Editorial Board of the Uniform Commercial Code, and a member of the bar at a panel discussion conducted under the auspices of the American Bar Association in August of 1963. The following is the colloquy which is of such interest that the court in order to place the matter in its proper perspective sets it forth as follows:

Mr. Kripke: Before you go on, let us take a hard case. Let us suppose you had this original mortgage for a dollar and then you have another intervening contractual chattel mortgage, and Sydney has no future advance clause but takes a third mortgage instrument for the half million dollars on the same property and there has already been an intervening filing with respect to it. Now where does Sydney rank?

Mr. Coogan: Let's see if I follow you—

Mr. Kripke: You have an original chattel mortgage for a dollar, perfected by a notice which says "industrial equipment." You have an intervening chattel mortgage for another lender on the same equipment for a hundred thousand dollars, let us say. Then Sydney takes a third piece of paper, a chattel mortgage on the same piece of equipment—one never in the original contemplation of the parties. Where do their parties rank?

Mr. Coogan: Sydney comes ahead of everybody. This is an illustration of the first-to-file rule. Where two security interests have both been perfected through filing, and no specific priority rule applies the priorities date from the time of the filing.

Mr. Kripke: You mean the original notice determines priorities as of its date even for a transaction that was not contemplated at the time?

Mr. Coogan: That is correct.

Mr. Kripke: It would cover an advance which was not even covered by a future advance clause?

Mr. Coogan: That is correct. (19 *Bus. Law* 20, 52 (1963))

It will be observed as already noted that the original conditional sales agreement between Doroff and Warwick Motors, Inc. which was assigned to the defendant has no provision for future advances.

Section 6A-204, subsection (5) provides:

Obligations covered by a security agreement may include future advances or other value whether or not the advances or value are given pursuant to commitment.

Defendant contends that this provision merely permits a lender to include a provision for future advances in the original security agreement and that when this is so provided it obviates the necessity of executing subsequent security agreements with respect to future advances as long as the financing statement covering the collateral in question is prior in time and additional security agreements are obtained with each new loan. This is, according to the defendant, the thrust of Mr. Coogan's remarks to which reference has already been made. If this is so, it places a lender in an unusually strong position vis-à-vis the debtor and any subsequent lenders. In fact, it gives the lender a throttle hold on the debtor. For example, a debtor borrows $25,000.00 from a lender to be paid over a three-year period without any right of anticipation. The security is the equipment of the debtor. No provision is made for future advances. The financing statement is filed. The debtor reduces the obligation to $12,500.00 and now seeks to borrow an additional $5,000.00. The original lender is not interested in making a second loan. The debtor is in no position to pay off the loan without borrowing from another lender. The original lender does not desire to liquidate the obligation except in strict accordance with the agreement. Under the theory advanced by the defendant the original debtor cannot borrow from the second lender because no second lender can safely advance the money as long as there is a possibility that a future advance by the original lender would have priority in the collateral over the second lender. The interpretation contended for by the defendant does not appear to this court to be necessary for the protection of lenders nor does it seem necessary for facilitating commercial transactions. Defendant's counsel does not deny that this is so but contends that it makes no difference because Section 6A-9-312(5)(a) gives the original lender such protection. Counsel for the defendant concedes a difference in a case in which the lender is paid off, the balance on the original transaction is reduced to zero and in which the financing statement is not terminated by a termination agreement as provided in Section 6A-9-404 but it distinguishes the instant case from such a situation. The termination statement section provides in part as follows:

> Termination Statement.—(1) Whenever there is no outstanding secured obligations and no commitment to make advances, incur obligations or otherwise give value, the secured party must on written demand by the debtor send the debtor a statement that he no longer claims a security interest under the financing statement, which shall be identified by file number. ...

It seems, however, that the defendant, notwithstanding his recognition of a difference in the illustration put forth, should nevertheless take the position that as long as the financing statement is not terminated the lender is protected even when the original balance is liquidated, provided that additional funds are loaned and a new security agreement is entered into between the original lender and debtor. In such a case the original lender would come ahead of an intervening security transaction in which a financing statement had been filed for the same collateral. But why should the law be so interpreted to produce such a result? In all of these cases a lender can protect himself against the situation involved herein by providing in the original security agreement for future advances. In other words, the conclusion urged upon this court by the defendant is not required in the interest of facilitating commercial transactions particularly in the light of the fact that the Code provides for future advances in Section 6A-9-204(5). Comment 8, under this section, is as follows:

> 8. Under subsection (5) collateral may secure future as well as present advances when the security agreement so provides. At common law and under chattel mortgage statutes there seems to have been a vaguely articulated prejudice against future advance agreements comparable to the prejudice against after-acquired property interests. Although only a very few jurisdictions went to the length of invalidating interests claimed by virtue of future advances, judicial limitations severely restricted the usefulness of such arrangements. A common limitation was that an interest claimed in collateral existing at the time the security transaction was entered into for advances made thereafter was good only to the extent that the original security agreement specified the amount of such later advances and even the times at which they should be made. In line with the policy of this Article (Chapter) toward after-acquired property interests this subsection validates the future advance interest, provided only that the obligation be covered by the security agreement. This is a special case of the more general provision of subsection (3).

And Example 4 under 6A-9-312 is as follows:

Example 4. On February 1 A makes an advance against machinery in the debtor's possession and files his financing statement. On March 1 B makes an advance against the same machinery and files his financing statement. On April 1 A makes a further advance, under the original security agreement, against the same machinery (which is covered by the original financing statement and thus perfected when made). A has priority over B both as to the February 1 and as to the April 1 advance and it makes no difference whether or not A knows of B's intervening advance when he makes his second advance.

The case falls under subsection (5)(a), since both interests are perfected by filing. A wins, as to the April 1 advance, because he first filed even though B's interest attached, and indeed was perfected, first. Section 9-204(5) and the Comment thereto should be consulted for the validation of future advances. Section 9-313 provides for cases involving fixtures.

It will be observed that under this example the advance is made pursuant to the original security agreement, meaning thereby that the original security agreement contains a future advance provision. The author directs attention to §9-313 in order to protect a lender in the case of future advances.

This is a case of first impression. No case has been cited to this court but counsel informed the court that there is no decided case involving the precise issue presented herein.

···

The provisions of the Code with respect to notice is, in the judgment of this court, helpful in the matter of interpreting §9-312(5).

Section 9-402 [OPPSA s. 45] provides for the financing statement and the filing.

Section 9-208 [OPPSA s. 18] provides that a debtor may request information from the lender as to the amount due on the obligation and the collateral covered by the security agreement. If the secured party, without reasonable excuse, fails to comply with the request he is liable for any loss caused to the debtor thereby and if the debtor has properly included in his request a good faith statement of the obligation or a list of the collateral or both, the secured party may claim a security interest only as shown in the statement against persons misled by his failure to comply.

If the Code gives the lender an interest in the collateral for future advances even though no provision is made for such future advances, then the information secured by the debtor and given to a subsequent lender is of little value because the second creditor surely could not rely upon the information. If the defendant's interpretation of the Code is correct, there seems to be hardly any substantive reason why the original lender should be bound to comply with the borrower's request for information concerning a correct statement of the outstanding balance and the collateral covered under the security agreement.

It should be observed that the defendant and the original debtor believed that the original conditional sales transaction was a single transaction and did not provide for future advances by virtue of the original financing statement. This is clear from an examination of the agreed statement and the exhibits attached thereto. When, on November 15th, Doroff's balance with the Hospital Trust was $302.77 on the security agreement of July 11, 1963, and when, on that date, the defendant loaned Doroff $1,000.00 which paid off the original balance and the old agreement was cancelled, Doroff executed a new promissory note secured by a new security agreement and a new financing statement was filed with the Secretary of State on November 17, 1964.

It would seem to this court that without a consideration of the meaning of §9-312(5) this case might properly be decided on what the parties themselves did and what the parties themselves intended. Insofar as Doroff and the Rhode Island Hospital Trust Company were concerned these parties intended an entirely new transaction when the additional loan was made and they considered the original transaction as terminated. They did not intend to affect an intervening creditor. Certainly Doroff, although he subsequently went into bankruptcy, might well have not agreed to a new transaction if such new transaction was to have the effect of cutting out the intervening creditor. What these parties intended was a completely separate transaction and the claim now that the defendant is entitled to the protection of the original financing statement comes, in the judgment of this court, as an after-thought.

It is the considered judgment of the court after a careful consideration of the agreed statement of facts and the applicable provisions of the Commercial Code that particularly in this case the defendant is not entitled to rely upon the original financing statement in order to bring its subsequent loan ahead of that of the intervening creditor. This is said not because of the application of the principles of estoppel or waiver but because the parties surely are not prohibited under the Code from treating their transactions as separate and unrelated transactions. See 6A-1-102(2) and 6A-1-201(3).

Section 6A-9-312(5) deals with priority between conflicting security interests in the same collateral and gives a priority in the order of the filing but that obviously does not relate to separate and distinct security transactions. Moreover, a careful examination of 6A-9-312 and the other applicable provisions of the Code lead to the conclusion that the reasonable interpretation of 6A-9-312 is that a security agreement which does not provide for future advances is a single transaction and in the case of subsequent security agreements there is required a new financing statement. That is to say, a single financing statement in connection with a security agreement when no provision is made for future advances is not an umbrella for future advances based upon new security agreements, notwithstanding the fact that involved is the same collateral.

Judgment for plaintiff.

NOTES AND QUESTIONS

1) Was *Coin-O-Matic* a future advances case? Is Judge Licht's interpretation of the Code provisions consistent with the Supreme Court of Minnesota's decision in *James Talcott, Inc. v. Franklin National Bank of Minneapolis*, in Part IV, above?

2) Do you agree with the court's conclusion that Article 9, s. 9-312(5) (Revised Article 9, s. 9-322(a)(1)) should be qualified by reference to the parties' intentions at the time of the second transaction (or the first transaction)? Is there a contrary policy argument? *Coin-O-Matic* was not followed in subsequent US decisions and was strongly criticized by commentators.

3) How would a case like *Coin-O-Matic* be decided under the OPPSA? Note that in the *Adelaide Capital Corp.* case, extracted in Chapter 6, Part IV, Blair J expressed similar concerns about the operation of s. 45(4) and read down the provision accordingly, but this part of his judgment was reversed by statutory amendment in 2000.

VI. PRIORITY OF REPERFECTED SECURITY INTERESTS

Consider the following example:

> On January 1, SP1 takes a security interest in D's pickup truck and registers a financing statement. On February 1, SP2 takes a security interest in the same pickup truck and registers a financing statement. On November 1, SP1's security interest becomes unperfected. On December 1, SP1 reperfects its security interest by registering a new financing statement. On December 15, D defaults. SP1 and SP2 both claim the truck.

How might C's security interest have become unperfected? There are various possibilities, for example:

- If D's name changes and SP1 fails to register a financing change statement within the s. 48(3) grace period, SP1 will be unperfected from the end of the grace period until it does register a financing change statement.
- If D transfers its interest in the collateral to T and SP1 fails to register a financing change statement within the s. 48(2) grace period, SP1 will be unperfected from the end of the grace period until it does register a financing change statement.
- If SP1's registration is for, say, a five-year period and SP1 fails to register a financing change statement before the five years is up, SP1 will be unperfected from the end of its registration period until it registers a new financing statement pursuant to s. 51(2).

The provision relevant to our hypothetical case is OPPSA s. 30(6), which provides as follows:

> 30(6) Where a security interest that is perfected by registration becomes unperfected and is again perfected by registration, the security interest shall be deemed to have been continuously perfected from the time of first perfection except that if a person acquired rights in all or part of the collateral during the period when the security interest was unperfected, the registration shall not be effective as against the person who acquired the rights during such period.

The purpose of the provision is to prevent a later secured party gaining a windfall because an earlier secured party has failed to reperfect a security interest after the original registration lapsed for some reason. Applying the first part of the provision to our hypothetical case, the result is that SP1 has priority over SP2.

Let us change the facts in the hypothetical slightly so that SP2's dealing with D takes place on November 15, rather than on February 1. All other facts remain the same. Since SP2 acquired rights during the period that SP1 was unperfected, the second part of s. 30(6) applies and SP2 has priority over SP1. Here, in contrast to the first version of the hypothetical, SP1's security interest was unsearchable at the time of SP2's dealing with D and the purpose of the provision is to avoid prejudice to SP2.

For an actual example of s. 30(6) in operation, see the *Heidelberg Canada Graphic Equipment* case, extracted in Chapter 6, Part V. In *Heidelberg*, the court concluded that s. 30(6) "only protects a creditor who acquires some new rights in the collateral during the unperfected period." This statement must be taken in context; the section is not limited in its effect to rights of creditors. Would a trustee in bankruptcy qualify? (See *1231640 Ontario Inc. (Re)*, extracted in Chapter 5, Part V.) Are the categories of the "persons" referred to in the section broader and more numerous than the persons mentioned in s. 20 who have priority over an unperfected security interest? What if the person acquiring an interest during the period of unperfection is a buyer of the collateral who was aware at the time of the purchase that the collateral was subject to the unperfected security interest? Do the categories of persons referred to in s. 30(6) include a secured party holding a security interest that prior to the period of unperfection was subordinate, and who (with or without knowledge of the unperfected security interest) makes an additional advance to the debtor during the period of unperfection? What is the position of a subsequent secured party who registers a financing statement during the period of unperfection, but who does not take a security interest in the debtor's property until after the prior security interest has been perfected? Note that there is no limit on the period of time between discharge or lapse and reperfection.

Other questions are as follows (for a detailed discussion, see Ziegel and Denomme, §30.5, at pp. 257-60):

1. Does s. 30(6) apply where the security interest was originally perfected by possession and, if not, why should a distinction be drawn between a security interest perfected by registration and a security interest perfected by other means?
2. Does s. 30(6) apply where the original registration occurred outside Ontario and there was a gap in re-registration after the collateral was brought into Ontario? (See Chapter 14 on conflict of laws questions.)
3. Does s. 30(6) apply where the secured party reperfects by taking possession of the collateral and does not file an amended financing statement?
4. Must the secured party reperfect within a given time? Should there be a time limit?
5. Finally, and not least, given the importance that the Act elsewhere attaches to continuous perfection, what is the justification for making an exception to the policy in this case?

Note the differences between OPPSA s. 30(6) and the corresponding provision in the other provincial PPSAs, of which Saskatchewan PPSA s. 35(7) is representative.

35(7) Where:
    (a) registration of a security interest:
        (i) lapses as a result of a failure to renew the registration; or
        (ii) is discharged without authorization or in error; and
    (b) the secured party registers the security interest not later than 30 days after the lapse or discharge;
the lapse or discharge does not affect the priority status of the security interest in relation to a competing perfected security interest that, immediately prior to the lapse or discharge, had a subordinate priority position, except to the extent that the competing security interest secures advances made or contracted for after the lapse or discharge and prior to the re-registration.

VII. SUBORDINATION AGREEMENTS

Subordination agreements, and subordination clauses in security agreements, are very common. A *subordination agreement* occurs when a senior secured party agrees to subordinate its security interest to the security interest of a junior secured party. In doing this, the senior secured party is not acting out of a spirit of altruism; rather, it is in the senior creditor's interest not to foreclose the debtor's access to other sources of credit. A subordination agreement may also be reached when the secured parties are not sure about their priority positions vis-à-vis each other (for example, an accounts receivable financer and an inventory financer) or are concerned about an overlap in the collateral covered by their respective agreements. A *subordination clause* differs from a subordination agreement in that it appears in the security agreement between the secured party and the debtor; other secured parties are not privy to it although they are expected to benefit from the clause. Subordination clauses are common in "all asset" type agreements and in medium- and long-term secured debentures.

OPPSA s. 38 provides that a secured party may, in the security agreement or otherwise, subordinate the secured party's security interest to any other security interest and such subordination is effective according to its terms. The provision reinforces the point that the PPSA priority rules are default rules and that the parties can contract for a different priority order if they want to.

Section 38 provides that the subordination may be "in the security agreement or otherwise." It follows that SP1 and SP2 may deal directly, via a subordination agreement or, indirectly, via a subordination clause in the security agreement between SP1 and D. In the latter case, SP2 is typically not a party to the contract and so at common law it may not be able to enforce it. However, in *Euroclean Canada Inc. v. Forest Glade Investments Ltd.* (1985), 16 DLR (4th) 289, the Ontario Court of Appeal held that OPPSA s. 38 creates an exception to the privity doctrine. The corresponding provision in the other provinces makes the point explicitly: for example, SPPSA s. 40(1) provides that the subordination provision may be enforced by a third party "if the third party is the person ... for whose benefit the subordination was intended."

Section 38 provides that a subordination agreement or provision "is effective according to its terms." This aspect of the provision has generated a body of case law focused on the question of whether a negative pledge clause in the security agreement between SP1 and D, by which D promises not to create equal or prior ranking security interests, with the exception of purchase-money security interests (PMSIs), amounts to a subordination agreement in favour of, and enforceable by, the holder of a later purchase-money security interest (SP2) or whether it is simply a covenant enforceable by SP1 against D. These cases concern the interaction between the subordination provision in s. 38 and the PMSI super-priority rules in OPPSA s. 33 (see Chapter 8).

Euroclean settled the point that the beneficiary of a subordination clause is not required to perfect its security interest before it can invoke the clause, but it does not settle another issue that troubled US lawyers in the 1960s. This was whether a subordination clause or subordination agreement creates a security interest given by the senior creditor in favour of a junior creditor and must therefore be perfected under Article 9. To ensure that the courts would not reach this conclusion, UCC 1-209 (now s. 1-310) was added in 1966, making it clear that a subordination clause does not create a security interest: see Ziegel and Denomme, §38.6. The OPPSA does not contain a similar provision, so in Canada the point is still arguable.

The answer may depend on the nature of the subordination agreement. One common type is the so-called "turnover agreement." In a turnover agreement, SP1 promises that if it enforces its security interest, it will pay the proceeds to SP2 up to the value of the collateral. For example, assume the value of the collateral is $100. Debtor owes SP1 $70 and it owes SP2 $40. Under a turnover agreement, SP1 promises to pay SP2 the first $40 out of the collateral sale proceeds. It might be argued that this kind of transaction involves the assignment of an account, or at least part of an account. The account is the payment obligation Debtor owes SP1 and by agreeing to hand over the collection proceeds, in effect SP1 is acknowledging a transfer of the entitlement. If this analysis is right, the transaction is a deemed security agreement by virtue of OPPSA s. 2(b), and so SP2 should register a financing statement. Otherwise, it will be at risk if SP1 becomes bankrupt because then the trustee can invoke s. 20(1)(b) and the assignment will be ineffective. On the other hand, if SP2 does perfect, it can enforce the agreement and this means it will be paid in full ahead of SP1's unsecured creditors.

The alternative possibility is that SP1's promise is simply a personal one: in other words, SP1's promise is to make a payment to SP2 when and if SP1 enforces its security interest against Debtor, but not to transfer SP1's claim. If this analysis is right, the PPSA does not apply and there is nothing for SP2 to register. Assume that SP1 becomes bankrupt and the trustee refuses to honour the subordination agreement. SP2 will have a claim for damages against the trustee, which it will have to prove for in the bankruptcy proceedings. The end result is that it may get some sort of pro rata payment, but it will not be paid in full. Which of these competing views is the correct one is a question of interpretation and it can only be answered on a case-by-case basis. To reduce the uncertainty, some of the provincial PPSAs, following the Article 9 lead (see above), have a provision creating a presumption that a subordination agreement does not create a security interest: see, for example, Saskatchewan PPSA s. 40(2).

Assuming that a subordination agreement does not create a security interest, there is no need for SP2 to register a financing statement. Nor is there any requirement to register a financing change statement to record the subordination. The reason is that the subordination agreement does not affect the searchability of either SP1's or SP2's security interest: a search against D's name should reveal both security interests, assuming they were properly registered in the first place, and a s. 18 inquiry should lead to discovery of the subordination agreement. Moreover, at least in the case of a subordination agreement *simpliciter*, the agreement only affects priorities between SP1 and SP2 and, since it does not affect third parties, there is no need for publicity. However, although there is no requirement in the Act for registration of a financing change statement to record a subordination agreement, s. 50 makes a financing change statement for this purpose permissible. The main reason for taking advantage of this facility is to make SP2 the party of record in place of SP1, requiring searchers in future to direct their s. 18 inquiries to SP2.

VIII. CIRCULAR PRIORITIES

Royal Bank of Canada v. General Motors Acceptance Corporation of Canada Ltd.
(2006), 274 DLR (4th) 372 (NLCA)

ROWE JA:

Facts

[1] At issue is priority among secured creditors of Hickman Equipment Limited (HEL) to the proceeds of sale ($884,500) from eight units of heavy equipment (three backhoes, three excavators and two loaders) that were owned by HEL.

[2] HEL is bankrupt. It had been in the business of selling or leasing heavy equipment, primarily for road construction and forestry.

[3] In large measure, the facts are not in dispute; rather, the dispute centres on the legal effect of a subordination agreement between the Appellant, Royal Bank of Canada (RBC), and Canadian Imperial Bank of Commerce (CIBC), and how (if at all) this affects priority as between RBC and the Respondent, General Motors Acceptance Corporation (GMAC), to the proceeds of sale of the eight units.

[4] RBC's "Concise Statement of Facts" was largely accepted by GMAC. Accordingly, I reproduce it below, noting an area of difference raised by GMAC.

By a Receiving Order made on the 13th day of March, 2002, pursuant to the provisions of the *Bankruptcy and Insolvency Act* ("BIA") and filed with the Supreme Court of Newfoundland and Labrador in Bankruptcy on the 14th of March, 2002, Hickman Equipment (1985) Limited ("HEL") was adjudged bankrupt and PricewaterhouseCoopers Inc. ("PWC") was appointed Trustee of the bankrupt estate (the "Trustee"). By a further Order of the Court granted on the 13th of March, 2002, and filed with the Court on the 14th of March, 2002, it was ordered that PWC be appointed Receiver ("Receiver") of HEL (the "Receivership Order"). The Receivership Order gave PWC the overall mandate of developing a plan and procedural structure for the liquidation of the assets of HEL, as defined in paragraph 6 of the Receivership Order, and also a plan for the determination of the rights of all creditors and claimants. In that regard, a Claims Plan was approved by [the Trial Division] by an Order dated May 14, 2002, and filed May 17, 2002 (the "Claims Plan"). Paragraph 14 of the Claims Plan required the Trustee to issue a Final Determination either allowing a claim as a valid secured claim under s. 135(4) of the BIA, or disallowing it as a valid secured claim. Paragraph 15 of the Claims Plan provided that claims disallowed by the Trustee under this process were afforded a 30-day right of appeal under the BIA. The Trustee was not required under the Claims Plan to make findings as to the priorities between the security interests in the assets of HEL as claimed by competing secured creditors.

Royal Bank of Canada ("RBC") presented its security interest claim to the Trustee and the Trustee issued its Final Determination of the RBC Claim and allowed the RBC Claim as a valid secured claim. Canadian Imperial Bank of Commerce ("CIBC") presented its security interest claim to the Trustee and the Trustee issued its Final Determination of the CIBC Claim and allowed the CIBC Claim in part as a valid secured claim. General Motors Acceptance Corporation ("GMAC") presented its security interest claim to the Trustee and the Trustee issued its Final Determination of the GMAC Claim and allowed the GMAC Claim as a valid secured claim.

The Trustee, in the Final Determinations of the CIBC Claim, the GMAC Claim and the RBC Claim, made the following determinations, which were not been (sic) appealed to the [Trial Division]:

(a) The CIBC security interests in the RBC Collateral were created by two security agreements, namely:

(i) A Debenture dated January 7, [1985] and Supplemental Debentures dated February 19, 1990; April 17, 1997; August 7, 1997 and July 9, 1998 (collectively the "Debenture and Supplemental Debentures");

(ii) A General Security Agreement dated January 25, 2000 (the "GSA").

(b) The GMAC security interest in the RBC Collateral was created by a Security Agreement (Leasing) between GMAC and HEL dated July 25, 2000.

(c) The RBC security interest in the RBC Collateral was created by secured transactions between RBC and HEL in the form of equipment leases dated March 14, 2001, April 4, 2001 and May 3, 2001.

(d) The perfection dates for determining the priority of the CIBC security interest created by the Debenture and Supplemental Debentures are January 29, 1985 (the Debenture), February 22, 1990 (First Supplemental Debenture), April 30, 1997 (Second Supplemental Debenture) August 29, 1997 (Third Supplemental Debenture) and July 15, 1998 (Fourth Supplemental Debenture).

(e) The perfection date for determining the priority of the GMAC security interest is December 13, 1999.

(f) The perfection date for determining the priority of the CIBC security interest created by the GSA is January 25, 2000.

(g) The perfection dates for determining the priority of the RBC security interest are March 14, 2001; April 2, 2001; and May 3, 2001 depending on the particular RBC Collateral.

By Order of the [Trial Division] dated May 14, 2002, the Trustee commenced and completed liquidation of substantially all the assets of HEL by auction.

. . .

Paragraph 20 of the Claims Plan provided that the order of priority of claims to the proceeds arising from the sale of the assets of HEL be determined using the priority rules established by the *Personal Property Security Act*, SNL 1998, c. P-7.1 (the "PPSA") and other applicable law. Paragraph 21 of the Claims Plan provided that issues of priority and entitlement to collateral between secured claimants may, upon application, be brought before [the Trial Division] for determination; pursuant to the provisions of s. 68 of the PPSA.

RBC applied to the Court pursuant to the Claims Plan and s. 68 of the PPSA for (i) a determination of the priority entitlement of RBC vis-à-vis other claimants, to the proceeds of the sale of the RBC Collateral, and (ii) an Order that the Trustee pay the proceeds from the sale thereof to RBC. Each of CIBC and GMAC filed an objection to the priority claim of RBC.

. . .

RBC claimed priority and entitlement to the proceeds arising from the sale of the [eight units] of the RBC Collateral ($884,500.00) by virtue of a specific subordination agreement between CIBC and RBC contained [in] letters dated April 3, 2001 and May 2, 2001 (the "Priority Agreements"). GMAC was not requested by RBC to execute similar priority agreements.

On the basis of the residual priority rules under s. 36 of the PPSA, the competing security interests in the RBC Collateral had the following priority rankings:

(a) The CIBC security interest created by the Debenture and Supplemental Debentures;

(b) The GMAC security interest;

(c) The CIBC security interest created by the GSA; and

(d) The RBC security interest.

[In its Factum, GMAC stated that the foregoing priorities are not "facts," but rather are RBC's position; the foregoing priorities accord with the findings of fact of the Trial Judge ... .]

. . .

In the [Trial Division], CIBC did not seek to enforce its security interests in [the eight units] of the RBC Collateral, and CIBC withdrew its objection to RBC's claim to the proceeds arising from the sale of [the eight units]. In the decision appealed from, the [Trial Division] granted GMAC priority over RBC to the proceeds arising from the sale of [the eight units] of the RBC Collateral. ... .

. . .

Issues

[7] It is not in issue that CIBC subordinated its security interests in the eight units to RBC's security interest in them. Rather, what is in issue is whether by virtue of that subordination: (a) RBC moves up to stand in the place of CIBC and thereby gains priority over GMAC; or (b) while CIBC ranks in priority behind RBC, nonetheless GMAC retains its priority over RBC.

. . .

Analysis

. . .

[15] RBC's security interests were perfected in March, April and May, 2001. In April, 2001 and May, 2001, CIBC subordinated its security interests in the eight units to RBC's. What impact, if any, does that have on the priority of RBC's and GMAC's security interests? RBC says the subordination agreements with CIBC have the effect of giving RBC the priority that CIBC has, i.e. ahead of GMAC. GMAC denies this and says that while the subordination agreements may govern priority as between CIBC and RBC, they do not affect GMAC's security interest, which has priority over RBC's (having been perfected before RBC's).

[16] The issue thus crystallizes into whether or not the CIBC-RBC subordination agreements have the effect of advancing RBC's priority to the rank of CIBC's, thus gain-

ing priority over GMAC's. If they have this effect, RBC ranks ahead of GMAC; if not, GMAC ranks ahead of RBC.

[17] The analysis that follows must be considered in light of s. 41 of the PPSA:

> 41(1) A secured party may subordinate, in a security agreement or otherwise, the secured party's security interest to any other interest.
>
> (2) A subordination is effective according to its terms between the parties and may be enforced by a third party if the third party is the person or one of the class of persons for whose benefit the subordination was intended.

[18] At para. 22-23 of his Factum, counsel for RBC sets out the central proposition in his case:

> A subordination does not extinguish the subordinated creditor's security interest in the collateral [here, CIBC's security interest]. The subordinated security interest continues to have full force and effect. The benefiting creditor [here, RBC] obtains the benefit of the subordinated security interest and acquires priority over the subordinated creditor [here, CIBC] and any intervening creditor [here, GMAC] over whom the subordinated creditor has priority by virtue of the subordinated security interest. In this regard, a subordination is used to change the effect of the residual priority rules that would otherwise prevail under the PPSA. ...
>
> Where a subordination is enforced by the benefiting creditor [RBC] for its benefit, the amount secured by the subordinated security interest simply goes toward satisfying in whole or in part two claims as opposed to one: the benefiting creditor's claim [RBC's] and the subordinated creditor's claim [CIBC's]. The benefiting creditor shall receive payment in full of its claim, before the subordinated creditor receives any payment on the subordinated debt. Where there is an intervening security interest [GMAC], the result is equitable, because the intervening creditor will receive what it expected to receive, the fund less the amount secured by the higher ranking subordinated security interest. Otherwise, the intervening creditor receives a windfall and the statutory rights bestowed on the subordinating creditor to subordinate its security interest and the benefiting creditor to enforce the subordination for its benefit are thwarted.

[19] If RBC can show the foregoing is sound in law, then as outlined above RBC will gain priority over GMAC by virtue of RBC's subordination agreements with CIBC

[20] In his Factum (at para. 24), counsel for RBC sets out the authorities upon which he relies. I reproduce portions that relate to Canadian cases and texts ... :

> R.C. Cuming and R.J. Wood, *Alberta Personal Property Security Act Handbook*, [4th ed. (Toronto: Carswell, 1995)], pages 381-382:
>
> > A situation may arise where an intervening security interest ranks between the security interest of the subordinating creditor and the claim of the party in favour of whom the subordination is made. This is displayed in the following scenario:
> >
> > > A debtor (D) grants a security interest to SP1 covering all of D's present and after-acquired personal property. The security agreement secures $200,000. D grants a security interest in all present and after-acquired personal property to SP2 to secure a loan in the sum of $100,000. D then grants SP3 a security interest in all present and

after-acquired personal property to secure an advance of $150,000. SP1 and SP3 enter into a subordination agreement under which SP1 agrees to postpone his claim until SP3's claim is fully satisfied. The collateral is sold and $225,000 is realized. The proceeds of realization are insufficient to satisfy all the secured claimants.

The priority competition is resolved as follows:

> The amount of SP1's claim ($200,000) would be set aside and SP3's claim would be satisfied out of this fund. The remainder ($50,000) would be allocated to SP1. SP2's claim would then be satisfied out of the remainder of the fund ($25,000). The ultimate distribution therefore would be SP1: $50,000; SP2: $25,000; SP3: $150,000. In essence, the ranking of the claims and distribution of proceeds is determined apart from the operation of the subordination agreement. The subordination agreement is then applied to permit SP3 to satisfy her claim out of SP1's share of the proceeds.

Rico Enterprises Ltd. (Re), [1994] BCJ No. 414 (BCSC), at [paras. 36-37]:

> ... If one creditor subordinates its claim to the claim of another party without subordinating to other claims ranking in priority to the claim of the other party, it is my view that a distribution of the assets of the bankrupt debtor should be made as if there was no subordination except to the extent that the share of the distribution to which the subordinating creditor would otherwise be entitled should be paid to the party in whose favour the subordination was granted ...
>
> It is not appropriate to simply take the subordinating creditor out of the class to which it belongs and put it in the class ranking immediately behind the holder of the subordination right. I say this for two reasons. First, the creditors in the same class as the subordinating creditor should not receive the benefit of a subordination agreement to which they are not a party and on which they are not entitled to rely. They would receive a windfall benefit by the removal of the subordinating creditor from their class in the event that there were insufficient monies to fully pay their class because the total indebtedness of the class would be reduced and the *pro rata* distribution would be increased. Second, if the parties to the subordination agreement turned their minds to it, they would inevitably agree that the subordinating creditor should receive its normal share of the distribution and give it to the party in whose favour the subordination was granted. The party receiving the subordination would agree because it would be paid a portion of a distribution to a higher class of creditor that it would not otherwise receive and the subordinating creditor would agree because it would not receive the money in either event.

Bank of Montreal v. Dynex Petroleum Ltd., [1997] AJ No. 341 QL Systems (Albt. CQB) [per Rooke J] at [paras. 86 and 88]:

> An apparent circularity problem does arise, in that the trustee in bankruptcy has priority over the unregistered interest of Odessa and Meridian; Odessa and Meridian have priority over the [B of M] by virtue of the [B of M's] subordination; and the [B of M] has priority over the trustee in bankruptcy by virtue of its security. However, the solution to the apparent circularity has long been recognized in similar situations occurring in bankruptcy proceedings.

...

The concept of the subordinated creditor holding in trust the accounting to the senior creditor was also discussed by [R.M.] Goode, [Legal Problems of Credit and Security, 2d. (London: Sweet & Maxwell, 1988)] at 23-24, where he said:

> ... if the subordinated creditor enforces his security he holds what he receives on trust for the senior creditor up to the amount due to the latter or any lower sum fixed by the subordination agreement—but that in other respects each of the two [interest holders] retains exactly the same interest as he held before. ...

Grove Packaging Inc. (Re), [2001] OJ No. 5502 (Ont. SCJ), at [para. 4]:

> It appears to me that the reasoning of Rooke, J in Bank of Montreal v. Dynex Petroleum Ltd., (1997), 46 CBR (3d) 36 (Alta. QB) satisfactorily deals with the apparent circularity. ... While it is true that this decision was overturned by the Court of Appeal 1999 ABCA 363 (CanLII), (1999), 15 CBR (4th) 5 (Alta. CA), that appeal decision ... did not deal or comment upon the bankruptcy issue [i.e. that referred to above].

[21] I reproduce the American text on which counsel for RBC relies only because I read it as being consistent with Canadian authorities set out above and because of its exceptional clarity.

Grant Gilmore, *Security Interests and Personal Property*, Vol. II (Boston: Little, Brown and Company, 1965) at:

At p. 1020:
> §39.1 Types of circularities. What should be done when an inadequate fund is to be distributed among competing claimants and under applicable rules of law A is entitled to priority over B, who is entitled to priority over C, who is entitled to priority over A?

At p. 1021:

> •••
>
> The simplest of the three situations, which may be dismissed as not involving a "true circularity," arises from a contractual subordination or waiver. To start with, A, B and C have claims against debtor X or his property which are entitled to priority in alphabetical order: the classical example is that of first, second and third mortgages on Blackacre. A subordinates his claim to C's. Blackacre is sold and the resulting fund is insufficient to satisfy all three claims. There is a comforting unanimity, among courts and commentators, on the proper distribution of the fund.
>
> 1. Set aside from the fund the amount of A's claim.
> 2. Pay the amount so set aside to:
>   (a) C, to the amount of his claim;
>   (b) A, to the extent of any balance remaining after C's claim is satisfied.
> 3. Pay to B the amount of the fund remaining after A's claim has been set aside.
> 4. If any balance remains in the fund after A's claim has been set aside and B's claim has been satisfied, distribute the balance to
>   (a) C,
>   (b) A.
>
> Thus C, by virtue of the subordination agreement, is paid first, but only to the amount of A's claim, to which B was in any event junior. B receives what he had expected

to receive [from] the fund less A's prior claim. If A's claim is smaller than C's, C will collect the balance of his claim, in his own right, only after B has been paid in full. A, the subordinator, receives nothing until B and C have been paid except to the extent that his claim, entitled to first priority, exceeds the amount of C's claim, which, under his agreement, is to be first paid.

At p. 1032:

§39.3 Circularity litigation since 1940. ... The most popular solution has been to apply the rule used in cases of apparent circularity resulting from a subordination agreement. In the subordination case A, B and C have liens which rank in that order; A then subordinates his claim to C's. The solution is to set aside from the fund the amount of A's claim; pay that to C and the balance, if any, going to A and B in that order. In a true subordination case, it is assumed that there is no difficulty in establishing the normal order of priority which would have settled the distribution (A first, then B, then C) except for A's subordination to C.

[22] While U.S. and English authorities cited by RBC also support its position, I omit them and place reliance only on Canadian authorities.

•••

[25] The argument set out for RBC is persuasive. I adopt the above reasoning, notably as set out in the excerpts from R.C. Cuming and R.J. Wood, *Alberta Personal Property Security Act Handbook, supra,* and Grant Gilmore, *Security Interests and Personal Property, supra.* Accordingly, I would allow the appeal and give judgment in favour of RBC.

•••

Wells CJNL and Welsh JA concurred.

NOTES

1) Philip Wood identifies two main types of subordination, which he calls "turnover subordinations" and "contractual subordinations": *The Law of Subordinated Debt* (London: Sweet & Maxwell, 1990), paras. 2.3-2.5. "In the case of a turnover subordination, on the insolvency of the debtor, the junior creditor agrees to turn over to the senior creditor all recoveries received by the junior creditor in respect of the junior debt."* In the case of a contractual subordination, "the junior creditor agrees with the debtor that, so long as the senior debt is outstanding, the junior debt is not payable unless and until the senior debt has been

---

* There is a subsidiary question as to the nature of C's entitlement under a turnover subordination. There are various possibilities: (1) C may have merely a personal right of action against A for recovery of its entitlement; (2) A may hold C's entitlement on trust for C; (3) C may have a lien on A's entitlement for the amount of C's entitlement; or (4) there may be an equitable assignment of A's claim to C. The proper characterization of C's position depends on the construction of A's and C's agreement. The characterization matters in A's bankruptcy. If C has only a personal claim, it will rank for payment with A's other unsecured creditors, but if C has a proprietary interest—as in Cases 2 to 4, above—it may be entitled to priority. However, at least in Cases 3 and 4 and possibly also in Case 2, C may need to register a financing statement: see Part VII, above. UCC 1-310 is noteworthy in this connection. It provides that "subordination does not create a security interest as against either the common debtor or a subordinated creditor." For criticism of the thinking behind this provision, and more generally, see Gilmore, vol. II, chapter 37.

paid in full." Contractual subordinations are sometimes referred to as "step aside" or "stand back" agreements.

2) Gilmore's solution to the circular priorities problem, which the court endorsed in the *RBC* case, presupposes a turnover subordination. This is apparent from Cuming and Wood's example: SP1 is entitled to $200,000 before SP2 gets anything and SP1 agrees to turn over $150,000 of its entitlement to SP3. One consequence of Gilmore's solution is to give SP3 (C in Gilmore's terminology) priority over SP2 [B]. At first glance, this may seem strange because SP2 [B] was not a party to SP1 [A] and SP3's [C's] agreement. However, on closer inspection the outcome makes sense all round. In the first place, SP2 [B] was never going to get the first $200,000 of collateral value anyway, given SP1's [A's] priority, and SP2 [B] should be indifferent whether this money goes to SP1 [A] or SP3 [C]. In the second place, Gilmore's solution meets SP1's [A's] and SP3's [C's] expectations by giving effect to the turn-over arrangement between them.

3) In the case of a contractual subordination, SP1 [A] renounces its claim until SP3 [C] is paid in full. Since SP3 [C] is subordinate to SP2 [B] independently of SP1's [A's] and SP3's [C's] agreement, the agreement in effect subordinates SP1 [A], not only to SP3 [C], but to SP2 [B] as well. This means that SP2 [B] and SP3 [C] should be paid in full before SP1 [A] gets anything. Using Cuming and Wood's figures, SP2 [B] gets $100,000, SP3 [C] gets $125,000, and SP1 [A] gets nothing.

4) The agreement at issue in the *RBC* case was a turnover subordination agreement, and so the court was correct in applying Gilmore's solution. However, while turnover subordinations are more common that contractual subordinations, it is important to keep in mind that Gilmore's solution is not appropriate for contractual subordinations. The court's first step should always be to construe the subordination agreement to determine its type. Only then will it be in a position to decide on the appropriate solution to the circular priorities problem.

5) SP1 [A] and SP2 [C] may attempt to head off circular priorities problems by express provision in the subordination agreement. There are various types of provision in use.* One type provides that if the agreement triggers a circular priorities problem, the agreement does not apply to the extent of the circular priority. The intended result, apparently, is to make the subordination agreement contingent on the absence of any SP2 [B] and, concomi-tantly, to give SP3 [C] an incentive to locate SP2 [B] and negotiate a separate subordination agreement with him. A second type of provision states that SP1's [A's] and SP3's [C's] agree-ment is ineffective to the extent that SP3 [C] does not obtain a similar subordination from any SP2 [B]. This formulation seems to be the same in substance as the previous one. A third approach is to say that SP1's [A's] and SP3's [C's] agreement shall not be interpreted so as to benefit any third party. The objective, presumably, is to make it clear that SP1 [A] and SP3 [C] intend a turnover subordination, not a contractual one.

6) Subordination agreements are not the only cause of circular priority problems. For example, the problem can also surface if a perfected security interest becomes unperfected and is later reperfected. In Ontario, the governing provision is OPPSA s. 30(6): see Part VI, above. Consider the following modified version of Cuming and Wood's example.

---

* We are grateful to David Denomme for this information.

A debtor (D) grants SP1 [A] a security interest covering all of D's present and after-acquired personal property. The security agreement secures $200,000. D grants SP2 [B] a security interest in all present and after-acquired personal property to secure a loan in the sum of $100,000 and SP2 [B] registers a financing statement. SP1's [A's] security interest is perfected by registration at the time of D's contract with SP2 [B], but it subsequently becomes unperfected. While SP1's [A's] security interest is unperfected, D grants SP3 [C] a security interest in all present and after-acquired personal property to secure an advance of $150,000, and SP3 [C] registers a financing statement. SP1 [A] subsequently reperfects its security interest. Ultimately the collateral is sold and $225,000 is realized. The proceeds of realization are insufficient to satisfy all secured claimants.

SP1 [A] has priority over SP2 [B] under the first part of the rule in s. 30(6), regardless of when SP1 [A] reperfects, SP2 [B] has priority over SP3 [C] under the first-to-register rule in s. 30(1), and SP3 [C] has priority over SP1 [A] under the second part of the rule in s. 30(6). What solution should the court use for the circular priorities problem in this case? According to Gilmore (at p. 1032), in the United States the most popular solution for circular priority problems arising other than in the context of subordination agreements

> has been to apply the rule used in cases of apparent circularity resulting from a subordination agreement. In the subordination case, A, B and C have liens which rank in that order; A then subordinates his claim to C's. The solution is to set aside from the fund the amount of A's claim; pay that to C and the balance, if any, going to A and B in that order.

The court in the *RBC* case quoted this passage with approval, and so the case is at least persuasive authority for the conclusion that the same solution applies in Canada. Ziegel and Denomme also support this view at §30.7.

7) In the case of a circular priorities problem arising in the context of a subordination agreement, the justification for giving SP3 [C] priority over SP1 [A] is that this distribution gives effect to their subordination agreement. According to Ziegel and Denomme, the justification for preferring SP3 [C] over SP1 [A] in the present context is a little different. The purpose is "to appropriately [penalize] SP1 [A] for its failure to perfect its security interest" and "to protect SP3's [C's] reliance interest triggered by the absence of a prior perfected security interest." However, in the example in note 6, above, SP2 [B] was earlier in time than SP3 [C] and so, regardless of SP1's [A's] lapse of perfection, SP3 [C] could never have expected to take priority over SP2 [B]. Therefore, if the objective is to protect SP3's [C's] reliance interest, SP3 [C] should receive only $125,000 (the difference between the value of the collateral ($225,000) and the amount of SP2's [B's] claim ($100,000)). In other words, for cases of this type, Step 2a of Gilmore's formula (see the *RBC* case at para. 21) should be modified to read "[pay] C the amount of his claim up to the difference between the value of the collateral and the amount of B's claim," or words to that effect. This approach was favoured by Dixon J in *Hoag v. Sayre*, 33 NJ Eq. 552 (1881), and in the United States it is known as the "Dixon approach."

8) The following two examples further illustrate the Dixon approach. Assume that SP3's [C's] claim is for $250,000 instead of $150,000 and all other facts remain the same. Here the amount of SP3's [C's] claim exceeds the amount in the reserve fund ($200,000). Gilmore's Step 2a says to "pay the amount so set aside to C, to the amount of his claim," but this as-

sumes that there is enough in the fund to satisfy SP3's [C's] claim. If there is not, as in the case under discussion, one solution would be to say that SP3 [C] is entitled to the amount of his claim or the amount of the fund, whichever is less. On this basis, SP3 [C] would get $200,000, SP1 [A] would get nothing, and SP2 [B] would get $25,000. The other solution would be to say, as suggested above, that SP3 [C] is entitled to the amount of his claim up to the difference between the value of the collateral and the amount of SP2's [B']s claim. On this basis, the distribution would be the same as in the original example: SP3 [C] gets $125,000, SP1 [A] gets $75,000, and SP2 [B] gets $25,000. The justification for the latter outcome is that, as in the original example, SP3 [C] should never have expected to receive more than $125,000 and so the former outcome gives him a windfall.

Now assume that SP2's [B's] claim is for $250,000 and all other facts remain the same. Here the amount of SP2's [B's] claim exceeds the value of the collateral ($225,000). On these facts, SP3 [C] should get nothing because it should have known about SP2's [B's] priority and it had the means of knowing that SP2's [B's] claim would exhaust the collateral. If SP3 [C] gets nothing, SP1 [A] would get $200,000 and SP2 [B], as before, would get $25,000. However, according to Gilmore's solution, SP3 [C] would still get $150,000, SP1 [A] would get $50,000, and SP2 [B] again would get $25,000. The former outcome is preferable because it prevents SP3's [C's] windfall.

9) Consider the following case:

SP1 [A] has priority over SP2 [B], SP2 [B] has priority over SP3 [C], and SP3 [C] has priority over SP1 [A]. Each has a claim for $100 and the collateral value is $100.

On the Dixon approach, SP1 [A] recovers $100, while SP2 [B] and SP3 [C] recover nothing. Applying Gilmore's solution, SP3 [C] recovers $100 while SP1 [A] and SP2 [B] recover nothing. This example brings into sharp relief the relative advantages and disadvantages of the two approaches: the Dixon approach avoids a windfall to SP3 [C] but, by the same token, it delivers the whole fund to SP1 [A] even though SP1 [A] was the party at fault. Gilmore's solution has the reverse effect: it appropriately penalizes SP1 [A], but gives SP3 [C] a windfall. On the other hand, the example perhaps overstates the relative disadvantage of the Dixon approach because, in any case where the value of the collateral exceeds the amount of SP2 [B]'s claim, SP3 [C] will recover something at SP1 [A]'s expense and so SP1 [A] is penalized, at least to some extent: cf. *Kingsberry Mortgage Co. v. Maddox*, 233 NE 2d 887 (Ohio Com. Pl., 1968).

10) There is a third context in which circular priorities problems may surface, and which Gilmore (at p. 1023) exemplifies as follows. Federal law gives the government a lien over a taxpayer's assets as security for unpaid taxes and it gives the lien priority over any competing lien created by State law in favour of local taxing authorities. State law gives a local taxing authority a lien as security for unpaid taxes and it gives the lien priority over prior and subsequent consensual security interests. However, a prior security interest retains priority over the federal tax lien.

This case is different from the two cases previously discussed because here none of the competing claimants is responsible for the problem: the circularity arises because inconsistent rules of priority have been established by statute for different interests. Here is another example of the same phenomenon, this time with a Canadian spin.*

---

*We are grateful to Rod Wood for this example and also for the example above in Note 9.

Bank obtains a security interest pursuant to s. 427 of the *Bank Act*, SC 1991, c. 46 (see Chapter 15); Financer later obtains a security interest in all the debtor's present and after-acquired personal property and registers a PPSA financing statement; later still, Seller supplies the debtor with inventory pursuant to a conditional sale agreement. Seller registers a PPSA financing statement, but fails to notify Bank or Financer of its purchase-money security interest before giving the debtor possession of the inventory (cf. OPPSA s. 33(1)). The priorities are as follows: Bank has priority over Financer by virtue of *Bank Act* s. 427(2), Financer has priority over Seller under the PPSA first-to-register priority rule (the purchase-money super-priority rule being inapplicable in the circumstances), and Seller has priority over Bank through the operation of *Bank Act* s. 427(2). What is the appropriate solution for this kind of case?

According to Gilmore (pp. 1032-46), courts in the United States, by and large, have applied the subordination rule discussed above, disregarding arguments that the present type of case calls for a different solution. The difficulty with this approach is that, since none of the competing claimants caused the problem, there is no objective way of assigning the A, B, and C roles among them. As Gilmore says, in relation to the tax claims case (at p. 1033):

> We may state the case thus: the city lien has priority over the mortgage, which has priority over the federal lien, ... which has priority, etc. Or thus: the federal lien has priority over the city lien, which has priority, etc. Which of the three claimants is A, which B, which C? Until we know, there is no way in which we can distribute the fund according to the subordination rule.

Furthermore, unless there is an obvious place to break the circle, "the results which the rule produces may appear to be whimsical and arbitrary":

> B, who gets nothing when A's claim equals or exceeds the fund, is progressively better off as A's claim decreases (since B takes the balance). C is in the reverse position: the larger A's claim (which C takes), the better C fares. Whether or not A takes anything depends on the size of C's claim; whenever it equals or exceeds his own, A takes nothing until B and C have been paid in full; the smaller C's claim, the more A gets. [at p. 1043]

So far as we are aware, there is no Canadian case law on this type of circular priorities problem. Nor is it addressed in any of the leading PPSA texts. However, the *RBC* case provides at least some support for the prediction that, if a dispute of this type were to emerge, the court would apply the subordination rule, relying as much "on instinct [as on] reason" in deciding where to break the circle (Gilmore, p. 1033).

CHAPTER EIGHT

Purchase-Money Security Interests

I. INTRODUCTION

Purchase-money security interests (PMSIs) are an important exception to the priority rules in s. 30. Broadly speaking, a purchase-money security interest is a security interest given to facilitate purchase by the debtor of the collateral to which the security interest relates. The simplest example is where SP sells an item to Debtor on conditional sale terms. A variation on the same theme is where SP lends Debtor money to purchase an item from Seller and takes a security interest in the item to secure repayment of the loan. "Purchase-money security interest" is defined in OPPSA s. 1(1): see the Notes following the Jackson and Kronman extract, reproduced below.

Sections 33(1) and (2) of the OPPSA provide, respectively, that a PMSI in inventory or its proceeds and a PMSI in other types of collateral or its proceeds has priority over any other security interest in the same collateral. (The Act distinguishes between inventory and non-inventory collateral because of the nature of inventory financing and its particular requirements.) The economic reason usually given for according priority to the purchase-money financer is that the financer is making it possible for the debtor to add to her stock of assets and that the financer therefore deserves to be preferred. A more sophisticated explanation is given in the Jackson and Kronman extract below.

Consider the following case:

SP1, a bank, holds a security interest perfected by registration in all Debtor's present and after-acquired personal property. SP2 sells Debtor a pickup truck pursuant to a conditional sale agreement. Debtor gets into financial difficulty and SP1 and SP2 both claim the pickup truck. At common law, the likely outcome of a dispute like this is that SP2 would have priority on the formal ground that, since title to the truck was at all relevant times with SP2, the truck was never Debtor's property and so it never became subject to SP1's security interest. The influence of the common law position can be seen in PPSA PMSI rules. On the other hand, the legislation differs from the common law in a number of important respects, not the least of which is that the statutory outcomes are explicitly driven by commercial policy considerations rather than by the formalism that characterized the common law's approach.

295

II. THEORY OF PMSI PRIORITY

Thomas H. Jackson and Anthony T. Kronman,
"Secured Financing and Priorities Among Creditors"
(1979), 88 *Yale LJ* 1143, at 1165-75 (footnotes omitted)

Two general characteristics of the purchase money priority should be noted at the outset. First, the special priority for purchase money lenders is linked logically to the recognition of security interests in after-acquired property. This follows from the definition of a purchase money security interest. To qualify as a purchase money lender, a creditor must make an "enabling" loan—a loan that makes it possible for his debtor to acquire rights in property that he did not previously have. If a debtor already owns a particular asset, he may of course use it to secure any number of loans, but no creditor making an advance against the property will be eligible for purchase money status.

Since, by definition, a debtor cannot own the property securing a purchase money loan before the loan itself is made, a prior creditor can only claim an interest in such property through an "after-acquired property clause" in his security agreement, which extends his security interest to assets that subsequently become part of the debtor's estate. It is therefore not surprising that in the chattel security field the idea of a special priority for purchase money lenders did not emerge until courts had finally accepted the notion that a debtor can validly encumber property he does not yet own.

A second striking characteristic of the purchase money priority is its limitation to loans that can be traced to identifiable, discrete items of property. Loans made for unrestricted purposes such as general use in the course of the debtor's business have never been accorded purchase money status, even if the loan can be shown to have increased the value of the debtor's estate or, more particularly, the value of the collateral securing a prior creditor's claim. Before a creditor can assert the rights of a purchase money lender, he must demonstrate that his loan has been used by the debtor to acquire a specific and identifiable asset. This limitation, which historically has been incorporated in the definition of a purchase money security interest, is today embodied in the tracing requirement of section 9-107.

These introductory remarks suggest three related issues that we shall address in the following sections in a way that builds upon and is consistent with the general theory already developed. The close link between purchase money priority and security interests in after-acquired property makes it logical to begin by considering why a debtor and his creditor would ever agree to include an after-acquired property clause in their contract. We then discuss the special difficulties created by an after-acquired property clause, difficulties that might explain the establishment of an overriding priority for purchase money lenders. Finally, we attempt to explain the limitation of purchase money status to those creditors who can trace their loans to identifiable items of property.

2. The After-Acquired Property Clause

It is sometimes assumed that the principal function of an after-acquired property clause is to decrease the riskiness of a particular claim by expanding the pool of collateral that secures it. If this were the only advantage of such a clause, however, it is hard to see what incentive the parties to a credit transaction would have to include an after-acquired property clause in their contract. For while the clause makes one creditor's claim less risky, it simultaneously increases the riskiness of loans made by the debtor's other creditors. In fact, in the absence of transaction costs, we would expect these effects to exactly offset one another, leaving the total cost of credit to the debtor unchanged; what the debtor gained by having the interest rate on one loan reduced, he would lose in increased payments to his remaining creditors.

When transaction costs are taken into account, however, both the advantages of an after-acquired property clause and a basis for predicting when such a clause will be used emerge more clearly. If the collateral securing a loan is a type of property, such as inventory or receivables, that is turned over rapidly in the ordinary course of the debtor's business, both the debtor and his creditor are likely to view an after-acquired property clause as a cost-saving device. In a case of this sort, the clause saves the parties the expense of writing a new contract, or rewriting their original one, whenever individual items of collateral are liquidated and replaced by new items of the same kind. Because it allows transaction cost savings, a legal regime that recognizes the validity of after-acquired property clauses is more efficient than one that does not.

3. Situational Monopoly and the Purchase Money Priority

Although the after-acquired property clause saves costs, it also creates what economists call a "situational monopoly," in that a creditor with a security interest in after-acquired property enjoys a special competitive advantage over other lenders in all his subsequent dealings with the debtor. In our view, the purchase money priority is best thought of as a device for alleviating the situational monopoly created by an after-acquired property clause. Therefore, when a debtor and his creditor have an incentive to include such a clause in their contract, they are also likely to favor the inclusion of a provision empowering the debtor to create an overriding purchase money priority in subsequently acquired assets. These principles may be illustrated by a hypothetical case.

...

Despite the transaction costs savings it offers, then, the after-acquired property clause gives a competitive advantage to the creditor in whose favor it is written. It also works to the disadvantage of the debtor by raising the cost of future credit above what it would be in the absence of the clause, because the advantaged creditor can exploit his monopoly power at any time after the clause is written. Consequently, if we assume that the debtor cannot override an after-acquired property clause by giving later lenders a purchase money security interest, we can expect him to insist upon and, if the credit market is competitive, to obtain a reduction in the interest rate on C1's original loan sufficient to offset the expected increase in the cost of subsequent credit attributable to C1's situational monopoly. The magnitude of this reduction will depend upon how large a premium the parties think the creditor making the original loan will be able to extract in future transactions as a result of the after-acquired property clause. Their estimates regarding the size of this premium will depend, in turn, on the frequency with which they expect the debtor to require additional extensions of credit and, most importantly, on their predictions concerning the bargaining power each party is likely to exert in negotiations over the price term in any subsequent credit transaction.

Suppose now that the parties are free to include a provision in their contract empowering the debtor to override an after-acquired property clause by giving later lenders purchase money priority. By including this provision, the parties can often blunt the situational monopoly created by an after-acquired property clause. In the absence of such a clause, a purchase money provision would of course be superfluous. But when an after-acquired property clause has been included in the contract, the purchase money provision often ensures that the debtor will be able to obtain future loans on nearly competitive terms—whether from the original lender or from some other supplier of credit. To return to the hypothetical case, if the debtor can give C2 a purchase money security interest in the new inventory, the monitoring costs associated with the $1,000 loan will be the same for both creditors, just as they would be the same if C1's original contract with the debtor did not contain an after-acquired property clause in the first place.

Although a purchase money provision blunts the situational monopoly that would otherwise be created by an after-acquired property clause, it does not annul the savings in transaction costs that a clause of this sort makes possible. The debtor and C1 are still relieved of the need to rewrite their contract whenever one item of collateral is replaced by another. This explains why the parties to a credit transaction might prefer a contract that contained both sorts of provisions to one that contained neither. But when coupled with an after-acquired property clause, a purchase money provision weakens the situational monopoly that the creditor would enjoy in its absence, and we would therefore expect the price of a contract with both terms to be higher than one that contained only an after-acquired property clause.

One might think that the parties would be indifferent between a contract that contained an after-acquired property clause together with a purchase money provision and a contract that contained only an after-acquired property clause but also had a lower price term. The second package, however, is almost certain to be more costly to negotiate since it requires the parties to determine how much the price term must be reduced to compensate the debtor for the adverse effects of the creditor's situational monopoly—a determination that cannot be made without assessing a host of future contingencies and evaluating the relative bargaining strength of the parties themselves. Since both parties have an interest in avoiding protracted and expensive negotiations, they will agree to include a purchase money provision in their contract whenever they have independently decided to include an after-acquired property clause in order to reduce transaction costs. Inclusion of a purchase money provision leaves the parties in the same position they would have been in if they had simply reduced the contract price to reflect the cost to the debtor of the situational monopoly created by an after-acquired property clause, without involving the additional negotiation expenses that a price reduction would entail. The purchase money provision in Article 9 merely legislates a standard contract term that the parties would be likely to adopt in its absence.

For the sake of clarity, the foregoing argument ignores a number of complicating factors. There is, however, one factor that is sufficiently important to mention at this point. In developing a rationale for the purchase money priority, we have stressed the competitive advantage created by an after-acquired property clause, and have suggested that the special priority afforded purchase money lenders may be viewed as a device for blunting this advantage. Even if his contract with the debtor does not contain an after-acquired property clause, however, a prior lender may nevertheless enjoy an advantage over his competitors. The very fact that he has made a previous loan to the debtor and is already engaged in monitoring the debtor's behavior is likely to give the prior lender, C1, an informational advantage over later lenders such as C2. The cost of initially acquiring certain basic information about the debtor may be viewed as a start-up cost that every creditor will have to incur. Having already incurred this cost, C1 can extend credit to the debtor on more advantageous terms than can a creditor who is dealing with the debtor for the first time. This undoubtedly explains, at least in part, why debtors engage in "repeat" transactions with particular creditors rather than shifting frequently from one supplier of credit to another.

If C1 enjoys an informational advantage of this sort, however, it is due to his pre-existing relationship with the debtor and not to the presence of an after-acquired property clause in their credit agreement. Furthermore, it is difficult to see how this informational advantage could be eliminated at reasonable cost, or why the parties would want to prevent C1 from acquiring such an advantage in the first place. Although it is true that the information C1 acquires in the course of his dealings with the debtor may give him a competitive advantage over other creditors in bidding for subsequent loans, the debtor is not likely to view this as a detriment at all. He is more likely to think of C1's information as a capital asset that both parties can potentially exploit to their mutual advantage.

NOTES

1) The definition of purchase-money security interest (PMSI) in OPPSA s. 1(1) is critically important, particularly where it is a lender who is claiming a PMSI status. The lender's claim will be defeated if the lender fails to satisfy the definitional requirements *as well as* the requirements in ss. 33(1) and (2). Antecedent competing secured parties have a strong incentive to challenge a PMSI claim so as to protect their ranking under s. 30(1). (For a detailed examination of the definition, see Ziegel and Denomme, at pp. 26-36.)

Paragraph (a) of the definition is straightforward and essentially reproduces the familiar proposition that a seller selling on credit can retain a PMSI to secure payment of the price. For example, assume SP sells goods to Debtor pursuant to a conditional sale agreement: SP has a PMSI within the meaning of para. (a) of the definition.

Paragraph (b) applies to lenders and entitles a lender to claim PMSI status provided it can show:

1. that its value was given for the purpose of enabling the debtor to acquire rights in or to the collateral; and
2. that the value was in fact so applied.

For example, assume SP lends Debtor money to buy goods from Seller and takes a security interest in the goods to secure repayment of the loan. Provided Debtor actually does use the money to make the purchase, SP has a PMSI within the meaning of para. (b) of the definition.

2) Paragraph (c), which was added as part of the 2006 OPPSA amendments, refers to the interest of a lessor of goods under a lease for a term of more than one year. Recall that the Act applies to a lease for a term of more than one year whether or not the lease in substance secures payment or performance of an obligation: see Chapter 2, Part V.A. If the lease does secure payment or performance of an obligation, then it is in substance the same as a conditional sale agreement and, to this extent, para. (c) of the PMSI definition overlaps with para. (a) and the justification is the same (see the Jackson and Kronman extract, above). However, para. (c) also applies to a lease that does not secure payment or performance of an obligation. Consider the following case:

> Debtor is in the road construction business. SP1, a bank, has a security interest perfected by registration in all Debtor's present and after-acquired personal property. SP2 sells and rents industrial equipment. Debtor is about to start work on a new project and rents a piece of earthmoving equipment from SP2 for two years, the expected duration of the project. SP2 registers a financing statement before delivering the equipment to Debtor. Subsequently, Debtor gets into financial difficulty and SP1 claims Debtor's assets, including the leased equipment.

But for para. (c) of the PMSI definition, the dispute between SP1 and SP2 would be governed by the general priority rules in OPPSA s. 30 and, since SP1's financing statement was registered before SP2's, SP1 would have priority. This outcome is contrary to the parties' likely *ex ante* preferences because it increases the risk to SP2 of carrying on its business, so making it harder and more expensive for customers like Debtor to rent equipment. Since it is in SP1's interests to facilitate, rather than obstruct, Debtor's new projects, *ex ante* SP1 would probably want SP2 to have priority in the circumstances under consideration. Paragraph (c) of the definition achieves this result by deeming SP2's interest to be a PMSI, so qualifying SP2 for super-priority status, provided SP2 perfects within the period that s. 33(2) prescribes.

3) As originally drafted, the definition closed with the words "but does not include a transaction of sale by and lease back to the seller." However, these words were inadvertently deleted by the 2006 OPPSA amendments. The government has indicated its intention to put the words back, but it has not said when it will do so.

The exception relates to the following kind of case:

> Debtor owns a machine. It sells the machine to SP for $100 and SP leases the machine back to Debtor for a three-year term.

SP has a security interest for the purposes of the Act (see Note 2, above), but it should not have PMSI status. The reason is straightforward. The transaction does not bring in any new assets to offset the new debt: the case is in substance the same as if Debtor had borrowed $100 from SP and given SP a security interest in the machine—which Debtor already owns—to secure repayment.

III. SCOPE OF PMSI PRIORITY

Agricultural Credit Corp. of Saskatchewan v. Pettyjohn
[1991] 3 WWR 689 (Sask. CA)

[In 1981, Mr. and Mrs. Pettyjohn applied for a loan from ACCS to buy cattle, and these were to serve as security for the loan. The loan was approved, subject to the stipulation that the Pettyjohns were not to sell any of the cattle without the previous written consent of ACCS. In fact, ACCS made the loan monies available only after the Pettyjohns had purchased the cattle.

The Pettyjohns purchased additional cattle and irrigation equipment in 1984, after receiving approval for a further loan agreement from ACCS. Since there was again a delay in ACCS making the monies available, the Pettyjohns borrowed the money with which to pay for these items from the Bank of Montreal. When the Pettyjohns received the ACCS funds, they used them to pay off the Bank of Montreal loan.

In 1986 and 1987, the Pettyjohns sold all of the cattle derived from the two ACCS loans and invested the proceeds in a new breed of cattle (Watusi cattle). The sales took place without the knowledge or consent of ACCS. Since the debtors were in default with their payments, ACCS sought to repossess the Watusi cattle, claiming they represented the proceeds from the sale of the earlier cattle financed by ACCS. Under the Saskatchewan Farm Security Act, the Watusi cattle were exempt from seizure unless ACCS had a PMSI in them.

There were therefore two principle issues before the Saskatchewan Court of Appeal: (1) whether ACCS had a PMSI in the 1984 cattle; and (2) assuming they did, whether the Watusi cattle represented the proceeds from the sale of the earlier cattle. The following extract only deals with the first issue.]

SHERSTOBITOFF JA (Vancise JA, concurring):

Procedural history

The Pettyjohns made the required payments on their various loans with the ACCS until December 1987. Upon default, ACCS attempted to realize on its security. The Pettyjohns then declared bankruptcy, and claimed that their present Watusi cattle were exempt from seizure under the Saskatchewan Farm Security Act, SS 1988-89, c. S-17.1 ["SFSA"]. Under the SFSA, both parties acknowledge that the Watusi cattle are exempt from seizure unless ACCS had a PMSI in those cattle.

On March 13, 1990 Geatros J directed a trial to determine the issue of whether ACCS had a PMSI in the Watusi cattle. The trial took place on May 8 and 9, 1990 before Barclay J. On August 27, 1990 Barclay J issued reasons including that ACCS did not have a PMSI in the Watusi cattle.

With reference to 1981 and 1984 loans and cattle purchases, the trial judge found as a fact that the cattle purchases took place before funds were advanced. He then concluded, as a matter of law, that a PMSI was not created in these circumstances.

As a result, I am convinced that ACC did not truly advance moneys to the respondents for them to purchase cattle, as the cattle had already been purchased by the respondents prior to the advance of the loan funds. Therefore, it has not been established that ACCS has a purchase money security interest claim in that it has not been shown that "value was applied to acquire such rights" as enunciated by Gerein J in *Royal Bank v. Pioneer Property Mgmt. Ltd.*, [1987] 2 WWR 445, 53 Sask. R 228 (QB).

The test under s. 2(gg)(ii) for a PMSI can be conveniently broken down into three requirements. The first requirement is that the lender has taken a security interest in the property. The second is that the lender has given value for the purpose of enabling the debtor to acquire rights in the property. The third requirement is that the value has in fact been used to acquire those rights.

Although the trial judge did not make any finding of fact with respect to the first requirement, that of a security interest, it is clear on the evidence that ACCS did take a security interest in the 1981 and 1984 cattle.

In dealing with the second and third requirements, the trial judge focused on the advance of the loan moneys as being the value in question. In doing so, the trial judge defined value too narrowly. The PPSA defines value in broad terms:

> 2. In this Act:
>
> (gg) "value" means any consideration sufficient to support a simple contract and includes an antecedent debt or liability.

ACCS contends that the final loan approval letter which was sent to the Pettyjohns can be treated as a unilateral contract and a binding commitment to advance credit, so that it was itself value given to the Pettyjohns satisfying the second and third requirements.

A number of American cases have considered the issue of what constitutes value in similar, though not identical, legislative schemes. These cases have concluded that value is given where a lender makes a binding commitment to extend credit, notwithstanding the fact that the loan advances occur later. For instance, in *Thet Mah & Assoc. Inc. v. First Bank of North Dakota (NA), Minot*, 336 NW 2d 134, 36 UCC Reporting Service 649 (North Dakota SC, 1983), the court makes the following comments with respect to "value" under the uniform commercial code (at p. 653):

> For purposes of the uniform commercial code, a person gives value for rights if he acquires them in return for a binding commitment to extend credit, and generally for any considerations sufficient to support a simple contract.

It is notable that the language used by the court is very similar to the language in our PPSA.

A similar conclusion was reached in *US v. Cahall Bros.*, 674 F2d 578 (CA 6th Circ., 1982). However the statutory language in that case was more specific than is our PPSA: see also *Honea v. Laco Auto Leasing Inc.*, 454 P2d 782 (CA, 1969), and *State Bank & Trust Co. of Beeville v. First Nat. Bank of Beeville*, 635 SW 2d 807, 33 UCC Reporting Service 1775 (Texas CA, 1982).

Although, in some cases, the American "binding commitment" test is based on more specific statutory language than is contained in the PPSA, the test itself is entirely congruent with the language of the PPSA. A binding commitment is, by definition, consideration sufficient to support a simple contract. It is, therefore, value in the eyes of the PPSA.

It is not entirely clear whether the loan approval letters issued in 1981 and 1984 themselves create a binding commitment, and it is not in the end necessary to decide that.

...

The final loan approval and letter of eligibility between them make it clear that the Pettyjohns were invited to rely on the letter of final loan approval. Thus, at least at the point when the Pettyjohns, in essence, accepted this offer by relying on the final loan approval in making their purchases on credit and/or with the aid of interim financing, ACCS became subject to a binding commitment to extend credit. This represents value given by ACCS to the Pettyjohns. The trial judge ought, therefore, to have approached the second and third requirements for a PMSI with this form of value in mind. Since the trial judge did not approach it on this basis, we must now make our own findings of fact in relation to these requirements.

The purpose for which ACCS gave value in the form of a binding commitment to extend credit to the Pettyjohns is easily ascertained, since it is set out in the letter of final approval itself. It is clear that the purpose of the value given was to enable the Pettyjohns to acquire rights in the property in question.

It is equally clear that the Pettyjohns did, in fact, use this value in order to obtain those rights. In one case, the Pettyjohns bought the cattle on credit, and then used the loan advances to pay off the credit. In another case, the Pettyjohns obtained interim financing from the Bank of Montreal in order to purchase cattle, and used the loan advances from ACCS to pay back the Bank of Montreal. In both cases, the whole course of the transaction indicates unequivocally that the Pettyjohns used the binding commitment from ACCS to supply credit as the ultimate source of value with which to acquire their rights in the 1981 and 1984 cattle.

On this basis, the claim of the ACCS to a PMSI in the 1981 and 1984 cattle is established.

Even on the basis that the value given by ACCS was the advance of the loan moneys, rather than the final loan approval, the claim of ACCS to a PMSI could be established.

The purpose of the PPSA as a whole is to simplify commercial transactions and to make the law governing them accord with practical commercial realities. Analyzed in this light, the second requirement for a PMSI, whether value was given for the purpose of enabling the debtor to acquire rights in the chattels, does not present a problem. The whole series of events leading up to the 1981 and 1984 loans and purchases leads inexorably to the conclusion that the purpose of ACCS in giving value to the Pettyjohns was to enable them to acquire rights in the 1981 and 1984 cattle. This is how the loan application and approval were structured, and was the understanding under which both ACCS and the Pettyjohns operated. The fact that value was given after the purchase does not lead inevitably to the conclusion that its purpose was not to enable the purchase, and looking at the entire series of transactions it is clear that this was in fact its purpose.

The third requirement, that the value have been used to acquire such rights, presents greater difficulties. How can it be said that the moneys advanced were used to acquire rights when the purchase had already taken place and the rights already acquired? It is, however, commercially unreasonable to divide the transactions so minutely. The Petty-johns used the value given to them to pay off interim financing, but the interim financing had not been obtained as a separate transaction, but always with the view that it would be repaid through the moneys advanced by ACCS. The Pettyjohns used the value given as part of a larger, commercially reasonable transaction to acquire rights in the 1981 and 1984 cattle. The fact that the use of the value given was, due to the nature of the trans-action, after the acquisition of rights does not alter the conclusion that the value given was used to acquire those rights.

For all these reasons, the trial judge was mistaken in concluding that ACCS did not acquire a PMSI in the 1981 and 1984 cattle, whether one focuses upon the binding com-mitment or the actual advances as the value given.

NOTES

1) Compare *Pettyjohn* with the Nebraska Supreme Court decision in *North Platte State Bank v. Production Credit Ass'n*, below, in Part VI. Are the two cases distinguishable? Would the Saskatchewan Court of Appeal have decided the issue differently if there had been a pri-ority contest between the ACCS and an earlier secured party with an interest in the collat-eral? Did ACCS's commitment to make funds available to the Pettyjohns actually enable them to acquire the cattle? If so, from whom?

2) Presumably, the Bank of Montreal (BOM) held a PMSI for its advances before it was paid off. Prior to this date, did the BOM and the ACCS both have a PMSI in the cattle? If ACCS had obtained an assignment of the bank's security interest, would this have given it PMSI status? Even if there was no assignment, could ACCS have claimed to be subrogated in equity to the BOM's security interest? Would this be consistent with the structure and policies of the OPPSA?

3) Meaning of "collateral" for the purposes of the definition:

"Collateral" is very broadly defined in s. 1(1) of the Act but US courts have given it a narrow reading for the purpose of satisfying the definition of a purchase money security interest. In *Northwestern National Bank S.W. v. Lectro System, Inc.*, [262 NW 3d 678, 22 UCC Rep. 199 (1977)] it was held that an advance made to enable the debtor to complete a contract and which was secured against payments due under the contract did not confer a purchase money security interest on the financer. The court reasoned that loaned funds must be intended and actually used for the acquisition of an identifiable asset, and the "performance of a contract" is not an asset. White and Summers note that if the plaintiff's argument had succeeded in *Lectro*, all business loans would qualify as purchase money loans.

The Saskatchewan Court of Appeal came close to sanctioning this result in *Battlefords Credit Union Ltd. v. Ilnicki* [(1991), 82 DLR (4th) 69]. In this case, the credit union made various loans to the defendant farmer over a period of years. Some of the loans were for the purchase of farm equipment; the purpose of the other loans was not clear. The defendant also obtained purchase money loans from other lenders. In 1984, the credit union refinanced all these loans under a consolidation loan which was secured by all of the defendant's machinery and equipment. The Court of Appeal held, approving two lower court decisions to the same effect, that the consoli-dation loan was a purchase money loan since it enabled the debtor to pay off prior security interests and to increase his own bundle of rights in the collateral. The court did not refer to the contrary American authorities nor did the judgments draw a distinction between a consolidation loan made by a lender holding a PMSI and a consolidation loan made to pay off a purchase money loan made by another lender.

Of even greater concern is that Cameron and Vancise JJA's expansive view of a purchase money security interest is not consistent with the history and object of the concept and that it will undermine still further the value of a general security interest held by a prior financer. The *Ilnicki* approach is also inconsistent with the structure of ss. 33(1) and (2) of the Ontario Act, which clearly envisage that the creation of the PMSI's will coincide with the debtor's acquisition of the collateral. In our view, therefore, *Ilnicki* should not be followed in Ontario, at any rate not where the conflict involves two competing secured parties.

(Ziegel and Denomme, at pp. 30-31.) Do you share the authors' concerns?

Unisource Canada Inc. v. Laurentian Bank of Canada
(2000), 47 OR (3d) 616 (CA)

WEILER JA: [1] Laurentian Bank of Canada ("Laurentian") and Unisource Canada Inc. ("Unisource") disagree as to which of them has priority to realize on a security interest under the Personal Property Security Act, RSO 1990, c. P.10 (the "Act"). The issue in this appeal is whether the motions judge erred in holding that the general security agreement held by Unisource had priority. Laurentian appeals on the basis that it had a purchase-money security interest ("PMSI") and that the motions judge erred in holding that it did not. The reasons of the motions judge are reported at (1999), 14 PPSAC (2d) 206 (Gen. Div.).

[2] Section 1 of the Act defines a "purchase-money security interest" in part as "a security interest taken by a person who gives value for the purpose of enabling the debtor to acquire rights in or to collateral to the extent that the value is applied to acquire the rights."

[3] Pursuant to s. 33(2) of the Act, "a purchase-money security interest in collateral or its proceeds has priority over any other security interest in the same collateral given by the same debtor" provided that certain conditions are met. There is no dispute that, if the security interest held by Laurentian meets the definition of being a PMSI, the conditions of s. 33(2) were fulfilled and Laurentian's security interest has priority over that of Unisource.

[4] The background facts to the appeal are not in dispute. Printer's Group acquired a Mitsubishi printing press, sold it to the Royal Bank, and then entered into a lease of the printing press from the Royal Bank for a period of five years with an option to buy the press at the end of the term. The Royal Bank registered and perfected a security interest in the printing press on August 30, 1995. Printer's Group also owed money to Unisource for the supply of paper. Printer's Group gave Unisource a general security agreement over its assets that was perfected by registration on February 7, 1996. The Royal Bank's security interest, registered first in time, was first in priority while that of Unisource was second.

[5] Laurentian subsequently agreed with Printer's Group to refinance the printing press. If, as part of the refinancing, Laurentian had taken an assignment of the Royal Bank's first security interest, there would be no dispute that Laurentian's interest would have priority over that of Unisource. Instead, Laurentian paid to the Royal Bank the amount outstanding on the printing press and registered a general security agreement. After receiving the money from Laurentian, the Royal Bank's security interest was discharged on April 15, 1997 and legal title of the press passed to Printer's Group. Printer's Group went bankrupt in May 1997. Laurentian claimed a priority interest in the printing press on the basis that it held a PMSI.

[6] Unisource brought a motion for a summary judgment that its security interest had priority over Laurentian's. The position of Unisource was that the security interest of Laurentian was not a PMSI because, in paying the Royal Bank, Laurentian did not enable "the debtor to acquire rights in or to collateral."

[7] The motions judge held:

> The Laurentian refinancing did not alter or improve the debtor's [Printer's Group] position with respect to the press in any material way. The debtor did not add to its pool of assets or otherwise enhance its financial position by acquiring something it did not have previously. The effect of the Laurentian refinancing was merely to substitute one financing technique or vehicle for another. As a result of the refinancing, it is true that the debtor did, for a brief time, acquire legal title to the press, but it quickly reconveyed that title to Laurentian under the terms of its general security agreement which provided that the debtor:
>
> > ... grants, sells, assigns, conveys, transfers, mortgages, pledges and charges as in by way of fixed and specific mortgage and charge to and in favour of the bank and grants to the bank a security interest in all personal property of every nature and kind whatsoever and wheresoever situate.
>
> The debtor's right to retain possession and use of the press was still contingent upon it making the payments required under its loan, now to Laurentian, for an amount that included the price of the press. In my view, neither the acquisition of legal title, nor the change in the arrangements for the financing of the press, satisfy the statutory definition for a PMSI. Laurentian's financing merely altered the manner in which the debtor financed the acquisition or retention of the press and did not result in any new assets being added to the debtor's pool of assets. It follows that the purpose of the PMSI exception has not been met.

[8] The appellant asks that the judgment be set aside and replaced with a judgment declaring that Laurentian has a PMSI in the printing press.

[9] For the reasons that follow I would respectfully disagree with the conclusion of the motions judge that the acquisition of legal title by Printer's Group did not satisfy the statutory definition of a PMSI. Laurentian's financing did not merely alter the manner in which the debtor financed the press. It enabled Printer's Group to acquire further rights in the press that it previously did not have. In so doing, Laurentian met the statutory definition for a PMSI.

[10] The purpose of giving priority to a PMSI is to enable the person who has advanced funds for the acquisition of a particular asset to have the first priority over creditors who hold general security over all of the assets: see *Re 1151162 Ontario Ltd.* (1997),

13 PPSAC (2d) 16 (Ont. Gen. Div.) at p. 18; *Royal Bank v. Tisdale Credit Union* (1992), 4 PPSAC (2d) 44, [1993] 1 WWR 439 (Sask. QB). In this case, Laurentian advanced the funds that enabled Printer's Group to acquire title to the press. The motions judge was of the opinion that, given the existing lease/option to purchase arrangement with the Royal Bank, the acquisition of title by Printer's Group amounted to a distinction without a difference. Under the Royal Bank lease/option to purchase financing, however, the equitable interest of Printer's Group was a contingent one, the contingency being the election by the debtor to exercise the option to purchase. Printer's Group might never acquire title. Notably, the definition of a PMSI excludes "a transaction of sale by and lease back to the seller." Under the Laurentian financing, the interest of Printer's Group was not contingent. There was certainty of title.

[11] The motions judge appears to have been of the opinion that where the debtor has already taken possession of an asset a refinancing does nothing to improve the debtor's position and a PMSI cannot be created. In support of his opinion, the motions judge cited the following extract from the reasons of Gotlib J in *Greyvest Leasing Inc. v. Canadian Imperial Bank of Commerce* (1991), 1 PPSAC (2d) 264 at p. 269 (Ont. Gen. Div.):

> If a creditor could obtain a PMSI merely by helping a debtor to pay for something of which the debtor had already taken possession then all lenders to debtors who had not fully paid for all property in their possession could obtain PMSI's and take priority over earlier general creditors. That cannot have been the legislator's intention.

In her reasons, however, Gotlib J recognized that the mere possession of equipment by a debtor prior to entering into a security agreement did not exclude it from a PMSI provided that further legal rights were acquired. At p. 269 she stated:

> Because a debtor has some rights in an item of collateral does not mean that it cannot obtain further rights. By giving value to the debtor after the debtor has acquired rights in the collateral the creditor has not enabled the debtor to acquire those rights but the creditor may have enabled the debtor to acquire other subsequent rights in the collateral. Only where the debtor has acquired "all possible rights" in the collateral (*North Platte State Bank v. Production Credit Association of N. Platte*, 200 NW 2d 1 S. Ctr. Nebraska. (1972)) does it follow that a subsequent giving of value by the creditor could not have enabled the debtor to acquire rights in the collateral.

[12] On the facts of the case before her, Gotlib J concluded that the giving of value did not enable the debtor to acquire further rights. As I have indicated, that is not the situation here because title to the printing press was acquired.

[13] The interpretation I propose is consonant with sound commercial policy. If a difference between a lease/option arrangement and the acquisition of title is recognized, it will be easier for the debtor to enter into a new financing arrangement to acquire further rights in collateral without the co-operation of the original lender being required. The debtor and its business will benefit. The proposed interpretation also accords with the original expectations of the parties in this case that the security interest granted to Unisource would rank second in priority. It would be unfair for Unisource to have added to the pool of its security the printing press purchased with funds from Laurentian. To hold as the motions judge did results in Unisource receiving a windfall.

[14] I would therefore hold that the motions judge erred in his conclusion that there was no significant difference between the two types of transactions. By enabling Printer's Group to acquire title, the transaction with Laurentian did enable Printer's Group "to acquire rights in or to collateral."

...

Appeal allowed.

NOTE

For a critical discussion of the Ontario Court of Appeal's judgment, see A.J. Duggan, "Hard Cases, Equity and the PPSA" (2000), 34 *CBLJ* 129.

PMSI status and subrogational rights. Neither *Battlefords Credit Union Ltd. v. Ilnicki* (1991), 82 DLR (4th) 69 nor *Unisource Canada* considered the possibility of the refinancing lender being entitled to claim PMSI status, not because it satisfied the statutory test but because of the operation of equitable rules of subrogation.

It is well-settled mortgage law that if a person pays off a senior mortgage at the request of the debtor, the lender will be entitled to be subrogated to the position of the mortgagee and will enjoy the same seniority as the mortgagee. In general, this equitable principle should also apply to PPSA security interests, and has been so applied in US cases under Article 9. What remains unclear is how the equitable principle meshes with the PMSI requirements under the OPPSA and the integrity of the registry system, and (a) whether a refinancer is entitled to step into the shoes of the original PMSI financer even though the original financing statement has been discharged, and (b) whether as a matter of sound policy the refinancer should be obliged to give prompt notice of its subrogational claim to any prior secured party of record to prevent that party being misled about its status. Depending on how these questions are answered, it may well turn out that the anxious debates in *Ilnicki* and *Unisource Canada* were unnecessary and that the refinancing lender is entitled to claim priority simply on the strength of its subrogational right provided that it can prove that the secured party whose claim was paid off held a perfected PMSI.

See Ziegel and Denomme, p. 33. See also *N'Amerix Logistix Inc. (Re)* (2001), 57 OR (3d) 248 (SC).

IV. THE INVENTORY PMSI

Clark Equipment of Canada Ltd. v. Bank of Montreal
(1984), 4 PPSAC 38 (Man. CA)

MATAS JA: Clark Equipment of Canada Ltd. (Clark) and Clark Equipment Credit of Canada Ltd. (Credit) have appealed from an order of Deniset J declaring that the appellants' interest in three pieces of equipment was subordinate to the interest of the Bank of Montreal (Montreal).

The question of priority is determinable under the Personal Property Security Act, SM 1973, c. 5 (also CCSM, c. P35) (the Act) which came into force on September 1, 1978.

Clark is a manufacturer and vendor of equipment. Credit is the financing arm of Clark. Maneco Equipment Co. Ltd. (Maneco) was a distributor of Clark's products. It sold and leased equipment. For the purposes of this litigation the two appellants are treated as one.

In 1977 Montreal made a loan to Maneco. As security, Montreal obtained a demand debenture which was duly registered. Under the terms of the debenture the bank had a floating charge on the assets of Maneco, then owned and after-acquired. The security was continued in force by operation of law (s. 65(2) [am. 1977, c. 28, s. 13] of the Act).

On September 7, 1978, Clark and Credit sent a notice to the bank, pursuant to s. 34(2) [am. 1973, c. 102, s. 7] of the Act, to notify the bank that they had or expected to have a purchase-money security interest in the then owned or after-acquired inventory of Maneco. The appellants filed financing statements in the personal property registry on September 20, 1978, indicating that they held a purchase-money security interest in inventory of Maneco. Maneco and the appellants entered into a new security agreement dated September 26, 1978 (replacing an earlier agreement).

In September 1979, August 1980 and April 1981, respectively, Maneco acquired three pieces of new equipment from Clark that had been manufactured by Clark. Montreal did not advance any funds to Maneco to finance the purchase.

In June 1981, Montreal placed Maneco in receivership. Clarkson Company Limited was appointed the receiver (Clarkson). Clarkson seized the three pieces of equipment in August 1981 and sold them. The sale proceeds are being held pending resolution of the question of priority between Montreal and the appellants.

At the first hearing of the appeal, Montreal contended that the appellants had been doing business with Maneco by way of consolidated accounting and that the appellants had not maintained specific individual accounts for each piece of equipment. The hearing was adjourned.

Before resumption of argument on the adjourned hearing, the appellants filed additional information to provide more detail about the particulars of the transactions between the appellants and Maneco. The additional material shows the purchase price for each piece of equipment, the course of dealing with the equipment, and how the balances due for each item was determined. Counsel for the appellants confirmed that their claim would be limited to the amount owing for each piece of equipment. Counsel for Montreal agreed that separate accounts had been kept by the appellants.

The learned Chambers Judge held that the appellants had not complied with s. 34(2) of the Act, they did not have a purchase-money security interest, the "first to register rule" prescribed in s. 35 applied, and that Montreal, as the first to register, was entitled to priority.

It will be necessary to examine the provisions of the Act and the security agreement in some detail. We have been greatly assisted in that undertaking by counsel having provided us with a careful exposition of Canadian and American cases and commentaries.

The case for the appellants is founded on their claim that they hold a purchase-money security interest in collateral (i.e., the equipment) and that they are entitled to the special priority prescribed in s. 34(2) of the Act.

One of two kinds of purchase-money security interest defined in the Act is a security interest taken or reserved by a seller to secure payment of the purchase price. The classic example is a conditional sale agreement. (The second kind of security interest is not applicable in this case.) The term "collateral" means property that is subject to a security interest: ss. 1(d), (u) and (aa). [See] Catzman, *Personal Property Security Law in Ontario* (1976), at 28; McLaren, *Secured Transactions in Personal Property in Canada*, vol. 1, §§1.02[1][b], 1.02[1][c].

> 1. In this Act, ...
>
> (d) "collateral" means property that is subject to a security interest; ...
>
> (u) "purchase-money security interest" means a security interest that is
>
> (i) taken or reserved by the seller of the collateral to secure payment of all or part of its price, or
>
> (ii) taken by a person who gives value that enables the debtor to acquire rights in or use of the collateral, if that value is applied to acquire those rights; ...
>
> (aa) "security interest" means
>
> (i) an interest in goods, fixtures, documents of title, instruments, securities, chattel papers or intangibles that secures payment or performance of an obligation, ...

Unless the special priority rules of s. 34 apply, recourse would be made to the general rules set out in s. 35. I adopt McLaren's summary of the effect of s. 35, ibid., §6.01[2][a]:

> ... The priority is to be determined by the:
>
> (i) order of registration; (known as the first to register rule)
>
> (ii) order of perfection; (known as the first to perfect rule)
>
> (iii) order of attachment; (known as the first to attach rule).

And see *Nat. Trailer Convoy of Canada Ltd. v. Bank of Montreal* (1980), 1 PPSAC 87, 10 BLR 196 (Ont. HC); *Simpson (Robert) Co. v. Shadlock* (1981), 31 OR (2d) 612, 1 PPSAC 272 (HC); and *Roynat Inc. v. United Rescue Services Ltd.*, [1982] 3 WWR 512, 23 Man. R (2d) 290, 2 PPSAC 49 (CA).

In the case at Bar, Montreal registered first and would have priority under s. 35 unless the appellants are entitled to a special priority granted by s. 34(2).

Section 34(2) is designed to permit the purchase of goods and the obtaining of financing from the seller without running counter to the rights of an existing security interest which includes an after-acquired property clause (as Montreal had in this case). McLaren, ibid., §§1.02[1][b], 6.01[3][a]; Clark, Barkley, *The Law of Secured Transactions under the Uniform Commercial Code* (1980), Warren, Gorham and Lamont, at 3-55.

In order to qualify for the special priority granted by s. 34(2), the creditor must establish first of all that it has a purchase-money security interest in inventory. A purchase-money security interest in inventory will be entitled to special priority if three conditions are met:

(a) Perfection of the purchase-money security interest at the time the debtor (Maneco) received possession of the collateral;

(b) Notification to a prior security interest holder (Montreal) about the purchase-money security interest before the debtor received possession of the collateral; and

(c) The notification must inform the prior holder that the seller (the appellants) had or expected to acquire a purchase-money security interest in inventory describing the inventory by item or type.

Section 34(2) reads in part [see OPPSA s. 33(1)]: ...

And note s. 10 on enforceability of a secured interest. The section reads [see OPPSA s. 11(1)]: ...

Clause 1 of the security agreement, headed "Statement of Purpose," says that the parties will have a continuing relationship and, to avoid the need of further documentation, Maneco would grant a security interest in all products, parts, rental contracts and certain chattel paper to secure all liability of Maneco to Clark and Credit.

In cl. 2, the definition section, "products" are said to include "all new equipment and machinery manufactured or offered for sale by CLARK, and used equipment and machinery of the same general type whether or not manufactured or offered for sale by CLARK." "Liability" is defined as "any and all obligations of BORROWER [Maneco] to CLARK or to CREDIT of every kind and description, now existing or hereafter arising, whether arising under this Agreement or otherwise. ..." "Collateral" is defined as "Chattel Paper for which value is given by CLARK or CREDIT and any and all Products, Parts and Rental Contracts."

After-acquired property is included in cl. 3, headed "Grant of Security Interest." The clause reads: "To secure payment of Liability, BORROWER hereby grants to CLARK and CREDIT, a security interest in Collateral in the proceeds of each, whether such Collateral is now owned or hereafter acquired by BORROWER."

Clause 5, headed "Request for Loans," authorizes future advances for purchase of Clark products and for other purposes.

Clause 6, "Statements of Account," stipulates that Credit will provide Maneco a separate accounting regularly in respect of acquisition of collateral which has been financed by Credit.

Phraseology consistent with the terms of the security agreement is used in the schedule of collateral attached to the financing statements and in the notification letter referred to, *supra* (at 42-43).

The financing statements identified the type of instrument as a purchase-money security interest. So identifying it is not determinative, just as the omission of the phrase in the security agreement is not determinative. The real question, as always, is the substance of the agreement; not what the parties happened to call it.

Inventory is defined in the Act as goods that are held by a person for sale or lease (s. 1(p)). The three pieces of equipment in question were manufactured by Clark, were purchased by Maneco on credit from Clark, and were financed by Credit. The equipment is "inventory."

Montreal argued that the intent of the security agreement entered into between the appellants and Maneco was

to give the Appellants for want of a better expression, a "floating charge" over all of the inventory of Maneco then owned or thereafter acquired whether or not such inventory was manufactured or distributed by Clark and whether or not the purchase of such equipment was financed by Credit. ...

It was also argued by Montreal that the appellants must be denied the status of holder of a purchase-money security interest because they encompassed too wide a field in their security agreements ("add-on" or "cross collateral" clauses, in American terminology).

Counsel for Montreal referred us to several American decisions which are consistent with this position. He also referred us to decisions which were not in agreement. (See, e.g., *Re Manuel*, 507 F2d 990 (1975); *Re Simpson*, 4 UCC Reporting Service 243 (1966); and *cf. Re Conn*, 33 UCC Reporting Service 701 (1982).)

It may be helpful in understanding the Act and agreements made pursuant to its provisions to relate concepts in the Act to more familiar forms of commercial instruments, e.g., conditional sale agreements, or chattel mortgages or floating charges. But it is essential that the principles underlying the use of older forms should not be used to attenuate the principles expressed in the Act.

The Act envisages provisions for future acquisition and for future advances in a security agreement. Section 13 says that a security agreement may cover after-acquired property (with a proviso in s. 14 [re-en. SM 1977, c. 28, s. 2] in respect of consumer goods which is not applicable here). Section 15 permits the securing of future advances. The sections read:

> 13 Except as provided in section 14, a security agreement may cover after acquired property.
>
> 15 A security agreement may secure future advances or other value [*sic*] whether or not the advances or other values are given pursuant to commitment.

Inclusion of the provisions with regard to the "after acquired" goods and "future advances" does not convert the security agreement into a floating charge and does not adversely affect the appellants' claim to a security interest in the equipment. The Act is designed to permit this kind of commercial relationship without the imposition of a need to prepare and file a separate agreement every time a piece of equipment is purchased for inventory on credit.

In several comments gleaned from the American experience reference is made to the problems arising where the Court is expected to unravel the complexity of a melange of accounting records and lists of collateral. That is not the situation before us. Here, the amount owing on each piece of equipment is clear-cut. The proper groundwork is laid for a purchase-money security interest.

The agreement expresses an intention on the part of Clark and Credit to take or reserve a security interest in some equipment, within the ambit of the meaning of "purchase-money security interest" (s. 1(u)(i) of the Act). Other kinds of interests are also included in the agreement. Does the mixture of a purchase-money security interest with other security interests preclude the appellants from claiming a purchase-money security interest in the three pieces of equipment?

The question of severability of a security document was considered by the Supreme Court of Canada in *Rosen v. Anglin*, [1957] SCR 755, 10 DLR (2d) 113. In *Rosen*, the defendant had taken a chattel mortgage covering substantially the whole of the mortgagors' property. The amount of the mortgage was $5,700, but only $3,800 was advanced in cash. The balance covered an antecedent debt. The same goods had been previously mortgaged to the plaintiffs. The defendant had been honestly ignorant of the plaintiffs' mortgage and did not have constructive notice. Cartwright J, at 763 [SCR], (for the majority, Locke J dissenting) applied the principle expressed by Gwynne J in *Campbell v. Patterson; Mad-*

der v. S.F. McKinnon & Co. (1892), 21 SCR 645 and by the Appellate Division of the Supreme Court of Ontario in *Hunt v. Long* (1916), 35 OLR 502, 27 DLR 337, and held that the part of the transaction relating to the $3,800 was severable. Priority was granted to that portion of the chattel mortgage.

...

The question of severability was referred to but was not decided in the only Canadian case cited to us on this point under the Act (*Nat. Trailer Convoy, supra*). In that case, a vendor of a tractor-trailer unit and a bank which had advanced the down payment for the purchase claimed a security interest in the unit under the Act. At the time of making the arrangement with the bank the purchaser was in debt to the bank. The bank loaned him the amount required for the down payment and reconstituted the loan to include the existing debt plus the new loan. The bank's security interest covered both amounts. The bank filed before the vendor did. Saunders J applied s. 35(1)(a) of the Act and granted priority to the bank. Saunders J held that it was unnecessary to decide whether the interest of the bank was in whole or in part a purchase-money security interest.

I do not find anything in the Act which inevitably precludes the existence of more than one kind of security agreement. In the case at Bar, it is my view that the purchase-money security interest aspect of the agreement can exist with other kinds of security interests and can be effective. I would apply what was said in *Rosen, supra*, and would hold that the preliminary requirement of s. 34(2) (i.e., existence of a purchase-money security interest in inventory) has been established.

The appellants have met the requirements of the Act with respect to perfection, i.e., the security interest attached and all steps required for perfection under the provisions of the Act have been completed (s. 21). The interest had been perfected prior to Maneco receiving possession of the collateral. The provisions of s. 12, with regard to attachment, have been complied with. Under the security agreement the parties intended a security interest to attach upon acquisition of equipment by Maneco from the appellants. Value was given by the sale on credit. Maneco obtained rights to the collateral when it acquired the equipment. The appellants complied with s. 25(1)(b) by registering financing statements on September 20, 1978. The relevant sections read:

...

The requisite notice sent by the appellants to the bank on September 7, 1978 (*supra*, at 41) reads as follows:

This is to notify you, pursuant to Section 34(2) of the Manitoba Personal Property Security Act, that the undersigned, jointly and severally, have or expect to acquire a purchase money security interest in the now owned or hereafter acquired inventory of subject business consisting of:

Inventory now owned or hereafter acquired consisting of all new products manufactured or distributed by Clark Equipment of Canada Ltd., including but not limited to (1) industrial lift trucks, industrial tractors, backhoes and loaders, power hand trucks, straddle carriers, industrial material handling vehicles; (2) front end loaders, dozers, scrapers, backhoes, skidders, power cranes and shovels, excavators, crushing plants, conveyors, asphalt plants, and pavers, screening and washing equipment, graders, rollers, tampers and other construction, material handling, road building, earth moving, farm, log handling, compaction and mining equipment; (3) all used products of the same general type as those described in (1) and (2) whether or not manufactured or distributed by Clark Equipment of Canada Ltd.; and (4) all parts, accessories and attachments for any of the foregoing products; and chattel paper arising from the sale, rental or other disposition of any of the foregoing. Proceeds of the collateral are also covered.

Montreal acknowledged having received the notice but argued that the notice was deficient in the way it described the collateral.

Section 10 of the Act requires a description to be sufficient to enable the collateral to be identified. Section 34(2)(c) is more specific and calls for description of inventory by item or type. Two American cases were cited by counsel for the appellants. In *Fedders Financial Corp. v. Amer. Bank & Trust Co. of Pennsylvania*, 9 UCC Reporting Service 894 (1971), it was held that a description of inventory as "air conditioners," etc., was sufficient compliance with the statutory requirements for notification. And in *GAC Credit Corp. v. Small Business Administration*, 8 UCC Reporting Service 952 (1971), it was held that the description "RCA merchandise" was sufficient. The description in the case at Bar goes considerably beyond those general categories. Montreal should not have been in doubt about the kind of collateral. If there were doubts they could have been resolved by a request for further information (s. 20 of the Act). I would hold the notification complies with the Act.

In its factum, Montreal acknowledges that if the appellants could satisfy the requirements of s. 34(2) of the Act, the appellants would be entitled to priority over Montreal. This is in accord with the policy of the Act referred to by McLaren, *supra*. At §6.01[3][a], the learned author says:

> The Act will give a purchase-money security party who complies with its requirements, a priority over any person who may claim an interest in the collateral by operation of an after-acquired property clause. The policy behind the rule is one of ensuring that the debtor is always able to obtain credit from a new financier if he wishes to make additional purchases of property. The purchase-money financier is adding to the debtor's pool of assets in which the earlier secured parties have an interest by their agreements. However, they were at the time of their loan satisfied with the security base without the inclusion of any after-acquired (new) collateral. Thus, the new financier is given priority in recognition of the fact that it is his money which has enabled the debtor to increase his pool of assets. The special rule then enables the financier to look to the collateral which he has financed as security for his loan before anyone else's claim to that collateral.

I have concluded that the appellants have complied with all the statutory requirements entitling them to special priority prescribed by s. 34(2) of the Act.

Appeal allowed.

NOTES

1) *Clark Equipment* was decided under the Manitoba equivalent of old Ontario s. 34(2). Would the case have been decided differently under s. 33(1) of the current Act?

2) Note that under s. 33(1), the inventory financer must both perfect its security interest and notify any prior secured party of record of his proposed PMSI in order to secure priority. What is the purpose of the notification requirement? Consider the following case.

SP1 holds a perfected security interest in D's present and after-acquired inventory, which secures a line of credit in D's favour. SP1's practice is to run an inventory check before every advance to make sure there is enough collateral value to cover D's commitment. D negotiates with SP2, a trade supplier, for the supply on credit of green widget inventory secured by a PMSI.

In the absence of a notice requirement, SP2 would have priority over SP1 in relation to the green widget inventory, provided it perfects its security interest before D takes delivery. SP2's super-priority may affect SP1's decision to make further advances. How will SP1 learn about D's PMSI in the green widget inventory when it runs its next and subsequent inventory checks? The only sure way is by doing a register search before each new advance. However, this may be impractical, particularly if D is making frequent drawings. The notice requirement provides a low-cost solution: it gives SP1 warning of SP2's prior claim on the green widget inventory so that SP1 can make an informed decision about further advances.

3) Contrast s. 33(2), which applies where the collateral is personal property other than inventory or its proceeds. Here there is no notice requirement and SP2 has up to 10 days after delivery of the collateral to the Debtor to perfect its security interest. For discussion, see the Note following the *North Platte State Bank* extract in Part VI, below.

Re Chrysler Credit Can. Ltd. and Royal Bank of Canada
(1986), 30 DLR (4th) 616 (Sask. CA)

CAMERON JA: This is an appeal [5 PPSAC 64] from an unsuccessful application made by Chrysler Credit Canada Ltd. pursuant to s. 63 of the *Personal Property Security Act*, 1979-80 (Sask.), c. P-6.1, for an order declaring that, as an inventory financier, it had priority over the Royal Bank of Canada, a general financier, to the used-car inventory of an automobile dealer in receivership.

Before the *Personal Property Security Act* came into force on May 1, 1981, the dealer, White Plymouth Chrysler Ltd. of Moose Jaw, operated with a Royal Bank line of credit secured by a general debenture and an assignment of book debts. Both were subordinated, however, to other conventional security held by Chrysler Credit who financed the dealer's purchase of new cars from the manufacturer, Chrysler Canada Ltd.

After the Act came into force both the bank and the finance company were granted new forms of security. A "General Security Agreement" entered into between the bank and White to secure a $200,000 line of credit gave the bank an interest in the entire undertaking of White, and on April 8, 1983, the bank registered a financing statement disclosing an interest in collateral described as (i) "all goods now or hereafter owned or acquired by the debtor, including without limitation, all equipment … and vehicles," and (ii) "all proceeds, including but not limited to trade-ins … ."

Chrysler Credit, to secure its revolving line of credit for the wholesale purchase of new cars, entered into an "Inventory and Lease Financing Security Agreement" with White, in which White conveyed to Chrysler Credit an interest in all inventory supplied by the manufacturer, Chrysler Canada Ltd., as well as in the proceeds from the sale of that inventory. Later, on April 13, 1983, five days after the bank had registered in relation to its security, Chrysler Credit registered a financing statement disclosing a purchase-money security interest in (i) "all inventory whether now owned or … hereafter acquired by the dealer supplied by Chrysler Canada Ltd. to the dealer, including but not limited to … new and used motor vehicles," and (ii) in "all proceeds … including but not limited to trade-[ins]. …"

Following the registration of its financing statement Chrysler Credit served a notice on the bank informing it of the purchase-money security interest being claimed by Chrysler Credit in both the automobile inventory of White and the proceeds to be derived from the sale of that inventory, including trade-ins.

It was White's practice to purchase new cars from the manufacturer by way of conditional sales contract, with Chrysler Credit advancing the wholesale purchase price. Each time the manufacturer shipped a new car to the dealer, the manufacturer would invoice Chrysler Credit for the wholesale price of the car. Chrysler Credit would then pay the invoice, take an assignment of the conditional sales contract, and enter the transaction on a "Wholesale Inventory Sheet." The total indebtedness of White to Chrysler Credit at any given time was recorded on the "Sheet," as was the amount owing from time to time in relation to each transaction.

In late 1983 White encountered financial trouble, and in December of that year was placed into receivership by the bank. On taking over the business the receiver immediately turned over to Chrysler Credit all of the new cars in White's automobile inventory, but declined to part with the used vehicles, not knowing whether Chrysler Credit or the Royal Bank were entitled to them. The sum of the dealers' indebtedness to the bank and to the finance company exceeded the value of the used car inventory, with Chrysler Credit, alone, being owed $155,000 on new cars whose wholesale purchase by White had been financed by loans from Chrysler Credit.

There were 44 second-hand vehicles in stock when the receiver assumed control of the business. Their origins fell into one of three categories:

1. Four were identified as first trades on the sale of new cars—the loans for whose wholesale purchase by White had not been repaid to Chrysler Credit.
2. Thirty-one were first or later trades traceable to the sale of new cars—the loans for whose wholesale purchase by the dealer had been repaid to Chrysler Credit.
3. Nine were incapable of being linked, either directly or indirectly, to the sale of new cars.

By arrangement between the parties, the vehicles were sold and the proceeds of sale deposited in trust with the receiver to await the outcome of these proceedings.

···

By virtue of s. 34(2) of the Act a purchase-money security interest in inventory or its proceeds has priority over any other security interest in the same collateral given by the same debtor, provided the purchase-money security interest is perfected when the debtor receives possession of the goods, and that notice, as required by the subsection, is served upon others having a registered security interest in that type or kind of collateral.

Section 30(b) of the Act provides that a buyer of goods sold in the ordinary course of business of the seller takes free of any security interest therein (except in limited circumstances which are of no concern here). And under s. 28 where collateral is dealt away with the approval of a secured party, the security interest in the collateral extends to the proceeds, and is deemed to be a continuously perfected security interest in all cases where the security interest in the original collateral was perfected by the registration of a prescribed financing statement.

…

It is common ground:

(i)   that each of the bank and Chrysler Canada had a perfected security interest in the inventory of the dealer;

(ii)   that Chrysler Credit had a purchase-money security interest therein; and

(iii) that having served a s. 34(2) notice upon the bank, Chrysler Credit's interest generally ranked ahead of the bank's.

The issue, then, is the extent of Chrysler Credit's priority: to which of the three categories of used vehicles did it extend?

To begin with, every time White sold a new car to the ordinary course of its business, Chrysler Credit ceased to have any security interest in that car (s. 30(1)). It did, however, have a security interest in such trade as might have been taken in by the dealer—either on the footing the trade formed part of the collateral included in the security agreement (it covered both new and used inventory), or that the trade constituted "proceeds" derived from the sale of the original collateral (s. 28(1)(b)). At the moment it was taken in by the dealer, a trade linked to the sale of a new car (whose wholesale purchase by the dealer had been financed by Chrysler Credit) constituted "proceeds," and at that moment Chrysler Credit clearly enjoyed the same purchase-money security priority in relation to that trade as it enjoyed in respect of the original collateral (s. 34).

That being the case, and there being no exceptions applicable to the facts before us, Chrysler Credit undoubtedly had priority to the first of the three categories of used vehicles.

The second category differs from the first only to the extent that, in each case, the specific advance enabling the dealer to purchase the new car to which the trade was traceable had been repaid. In light of that the bank contended Chrysler Credit had ceased to have a purchase-money security interest in each of these vehicles—it continued to have interest but not a purchase-money security interest—hence its claim no longer enjoyed priority. The bank had registered first.

Similarly, the bank submitted that since none of the vehicles in the third category could be traced, directly or indirectly, to the sale of new or used cars whose purchase by the dealer had been made possible by loans from the finance company, Chrysler Credit did not have a purchase-money security interest in any of the vehicles; it had only an ordinary security interest therein, and, since the bank was first in time, it had priority. Having regard for the definition of "purchase-money security interest" in s. 2(gg) of the Act, I believe the bank is right about this. The real dispute, then, is over the second category of used car inventory.

Clauses 1 to 3 of the "Inventory and Lease Financing Security Agreement" entered into between Chrysler Credit and White are of particular significance. To the extent they bear upon the issue, they read thus (with those portions having the most direct bearing being italicized):

AGREEMENT

1. In consideration of Chrysler Credit extending credit or continuing to extend credit on motor vehicles and related equipment and accessories sold by Chrysler Canada Ltd. to the Dealer or otherwise acquired by the Dealer, (the continuation of such extension of credit to be nevertheless in the sole discretion of Chrysler Credit) and also *to secure the performance and payment of any and all present and future obligations of the Dealer to Chrysler Credit, the Dealer does hereby* grant, bargain, sell, mortgage and *convey a purchase-money security interest to Chrysler Credit in and to the Collateral referred to in paragraph 3 hereof together with all proceeds as* hereinafter defined of any disposition thereof. The security interest created hereby constitutes a first lien on the Collateral and the Dealer shall keep the Collateral free from any other line, encumbrance or security interest other than the interest of a lessee from the Dealer. The Dealer shall keep and maintain such insurance upon the Collateral in such amounts and manner as Chrysler Credit may require, with loss, if any, under such insurance payable to Chrysler Credit or its assignee and the Dealer as their respective interests may appear.

2.(a) The Dealer has requested and *Chrysler Credit hereby grants to the Dealer a revocable, revolving line of credit* for loans (i) to finance its purchases of new motor vehicles ... built in whole or in part by Chrysler Canada Ltd. and of used motor vehicles (all of which are hereinafter collectively called the "Vehicles") ...

(b) Each loan to be made to Dealer hereunder and the related Vehicle or Vehicles in which a security interest is created hereby shall be evidenced by (i) in the case of a Vehicle purchased from Chrysler Canada Ltd., a CHRYSLER CANADA LTD., VEHICLE INVOICE and such loan shall be in the amount set out in said invoice opposite the words "INVOICE TOTAL"; and (ii) in the case of any other Vehicle, such form of document, including a chattel mortgage, approved by Chrysler Credit from time to time and setting forth the amount of the loan ... The Dealer shall from time to time at the request of Chrysler Credit deliver to Chrysler Credit all chattel paper created through the sale or lease of a vehicle or Vehicles, such chattel paper including but not limited to all leases so created. The provisions of this agreement shall apply to each Vehicle and the loan related thereto separately.

SECURITY INTEREST AND COLLATERAL

3.(a) The security interest in the Collateral is granted to secure the performance and payment *of all obligations and indebtedness* of the Dealer to Chrysler Credit arising out of (i) the financing by Chrysler Credit of the purchase by Dealer of Vehicles for lease or sale to other persons or for use as demonstrators of service vehicles by Dealer, and (ii) the financing by Chrysler Credit of the lease of Vehicles by Dealer to other persons, whether now existing or hereafter incurred, and *of every kind and character, direct or indirect, and whether such indebtedness is from time to time reduced and thereafter increased or entirely extinguished and thereafter re-incurred* including without limitation any sums advanced by Chrysler Credit for taxes, assessments and other charges shall not be discharged or impaired by reason only that such Vehicles are refinanced by Chrysler Credit upon the leasing thereon by Dealer to other persons.

(b) The collateral covered by this agreement is as follows: all inventory, whether now owned or now in the possession of the Dealer or hereafter acquired by the Dealer, supplied by Chrysler Canada Ltd. to the Dealer including but not limited to the following types or kinds of property: new and used motor vehicles and related accessories, and all additions and accessions thereto, and substitutions and parts therefore, and all proceeds of every type or kind of such property, including but not limited to trade-in machinery and equipment, cash, notes, chattel paper, goods, contract rights, accounts and any other property or obligations directly or indirectly received when such collateral or proceeds are sold, exchanged, collected, damaged, destroyed, disposed of or otherwise dealt with.

The importance of the instrument creating the security interest is evident on reference to s. 9 of the Act which reads thus:

> 9. Except as otherwise provided in this or any other Act, a security agreement is effective according to its terms.

Having regards generally for the breadth of the security agreement in issue, and more specifically to the highlighted portions of it, I believe that the parties to the agreement intended Chrysler Credit's security interest to attach to the whole of the new and used car inventory, as well as to the component parts thereof. In other words they intended, I think, to have the whole of the inventory answerable for the whole of the debt, so that as long as any part of the indebtedness remained owing, the inventory remained liable to satisfy it. As between Chrysler Credit and White, then, each of the trades in the second category secured not only one advance—the one relating to the new car to which that trade was traceable—but all of the advances, or in other words, the whole of the indebtedness from time to time outstanding. The trades must be seen as forming part of a class of property, namely, inventory; and it was that class which was used to secure the grant of credit on an ongoing or revolving basis.

This, too, is consistent, I think, with the Act. Before any of the provinces adopted personal property security legislation of the kind now in effect in several Canadian jurisdictions—patterned after that in the United States—Professor Ziegel, in an article entitled "The Legal Problems of Wholesale Financing of Durable Goods in Canada," 41 *Can. Bar Rev.* 54 (1963), made these comments [at 55]:

...

Having thus identified the problems, Professor Ziegel went on to recommend the following solutions at 56:

> *First*, the financer must be freed from the necessity of having to record every agreement securing an advance made by him. This introduces us to the concept of "notice filing."
>
> *Secondly*, the recording law must accept one underlying, or master, agreement as sufficient written evidence of the financer's security interest in the goods acquired through his

advances. The need for separate instruments evidencing each transaction must be dispensed with.

Thirdly, the agreement must provide, and the law should recognize, the financer's rights to a "cross-over" security, that is to say, all of the trader's stock-in-trade, or at least that part of it which is financed by the financer, both present and future, must secure both present and future advances. Here we enter the realm of the "floating" lien or charge.

Fourthly, the agreement must provide that the financer shall have a security interest in *the proceeds of any sale* to the extent of *any* outstanding advances. The function of a model law here is to ensure that the financer's claim to the proceeds will not come into conflict with any other recording law, such as a bills of sale act, an assignment of book debts act, and so forth.

(Emphasis added.)

In its Report to the Attorney General: Proposals for a Saskatchewan Personal Property Security Act: July 1977, the Law Reform Commission of Saskatchewan suggested that existing law was no longer adequate to accommodate modern commercial practices, and that a new regime, recognizing functional rather than formal differences between security agreements, was required. More specifically it referred to the problems associated with inventory financing and the need for changes in this respect (at XV):

> 3. THE PROPOSED ACT EMPLOYS NEW CONCEPTS WHICH FACILITATE INVENTORY FINANCING.
>
> Because of the lack of a common conceptual basis for security arrangements, modern forms of secured financing must be designed so as to fit into one of the traditional categories of security devices. However, many of these devices were developed at a time when methods of financing and the circumstances in which the need for security arrangements existed were quite different from what they are at the present time. In other words, the existing system lacks flexibility and fails to recognize techniques and concepts which are required by the business community.
>
> With some notable exceptions, existing chattel security law was developed to facilitate short-term, single-transaction agreements involving fixed security. However, modern stock-in-trade financing frequently involves shifting collateral and open-ended credit arrangements. This type of secured financing requires not only much more flexibility than that permitted by present law, but it also requires the use of concepts which are not now recognized by Saskatchewan law. For example, when a financer gives credit to a merchant on the security of his stock-in-trade, he will want a security interest in present and future-acquired stock ... In addition, he will want a security interest in the proceeds of the stock-in-trade because the stock will eventually be sold to a buyer in the ordinary course of business who will get clear title. The proceeds may be cash, items traded in or accounts arising from the sale of the stock. Since existing law does not recognize the concept of a security interest in proceeds as a form of collateral itself, the only way the financer would be able to get any measure of protection is to use several types of security agreements, with each agreement covering a specific form of collateral that the proceeds may take. In addition, he may have to comply with two or more registry statutes.
>
> The proposed Act frees the parties to a secured transaction from the conceptual straight-jackets of existing law by permitting them maximum freedom to employ agreements with

form and content most suitable to their circumstances (see section 9). This does not mean that total freedom is contemplated. Some limitations are required if structure is to exist. However, the limitations prescribed by the Act are based on functional or social policy considerations only.

In order to permit needed flexibility in secured wholesale financing, the proposed Act employs the concept of a continuing general lien (see section 12). While this concept is presently the central feature of equitable security devices such as the equitable chattel mortgage, the floating charge and the assignment of future accounts, its full potential has not been realized under existing law. The proposed Act removes the impediments which, until now, have limited the usefulness of the concept. The continuing general lien, unlike the equitable floating charge, is a fixed security interest. Further, a security interest in after-acquired property is given a status fully equivalent to a "legal" interest without the need for specific appropriation by the debtor (see section 13).

The second major feature of modern inventory financing, future advance agreements, is recognized in section 14. The proposed Act (see section 35(5)) rejects the troublesome rule set down in the case of *Hopkinson v. Rolt* (1861), 9 HLC 514, under which a secured party could never safely make advances pursuant to a prior agreement on the assumption that he was fully secured by a mortgage taken on the debtor's assets.

(Emphasis added.)

The commission went on to describe as "one of the most innovative features" of the proposed Act, its notions of proceeds and their treatment, concluding with the observation that under the proposed Act an inventory financier could readily obtain a perfected security interest in the proceeds of his primary collateral, a thing he could do only with great trouble, if at all, under the law as it then stood.

There are two things here which I think merit particular emphasis. The first is the primacy, under the new regime proposed by the commission, of function over form—a purchase-money security interest, whether or not it arises out of conventional forms of contract (conditional sale, chattel mortgage, or whatever) enjoys special priority status. The second is the nature of the security interest in property such as inventory: the secured party enjoys a continuing general lien, fixed rather than floating. Both are consistent with Professor Ziegel's earlier recommendations. And while the Act, either as proposed or enacted, is not altogether explicit about this, I believe, having regard for its wording, for the policy underlying it, and for the commercial necessities alluded to by Professor Ziegel, that the Act recognizes the inventory financier's right to "cross-over" security: all of the dealer's inventory financed by the financier secures all of the advances which enabled the dealer to acquire it. And, of course, that is, as we have seen, what was contemplated in the security agreement in issue in this instance.

This view of the Act appears to be shared by McLaren & de Jong, who in their text *Secured Transactions in Personal Property in Canada, supra,* suggest that should the parties concerned in these transactions desire more refined arrangements than those contemplated by the statute, they may bring them about through subordination agreements (s. 47). The authors say this (at 12-22.2):

... secured parties will frequently desire to make refinements in their priority positions beyond which might be achieved through the Act. The typical situation, as mentioned, will arise between a purchase money financier and a general financier, both securing equipment or inventory. From an accounting or financial perspective the respective financiers may take the view that the unpaid purchase money vendor's collateral is secured by the supplier but the paid-for collateral is security of the general financier. The priority provisions of the Act do not work in such a fashion.

The priority of s. 34(2) and (3) is as a class of collateral contained in a security interest superior to the general financier's claim until full payment of purchase money vendor's accounts owing. The parties may wish to achieve a refinement of the priority by providing that the purchase money financier is to have priority for all collateral which is unpaid. Priority for collateral which is partly paid for is to be divided in the ratio of paid or unpaid collateral. Finally, the paid for collateral will secure the general financier's security interest.

On this view of the Act and the security agreement in issue, Chrysler Credit enjoyed priority over the bank to the second category of used car inventory, as well as to the first.

Accordingly, I would allow the appeal to the extent of declaring that Chrysler Credit enjoyed priority in relation to the first and second categories of used car inventory. The bank's claim in relation to the third category ranked ahead of that of Chrysler Credit.

Appeal allowed in part.

NOTE ON REVOLVING PMSIs AND *UNISOURCE CANADA INC. v. HONGKONG BANK OF CANADA*

In *Unisource Canada Inc. v. Hongkong Bank of Canada* (1998), 43 BLR (2d) 226 (Ont. SC), aff'd. (2000), 13 OAC 24 (CA), Unisource, a major Canadian manufacturer of fine paper, agreed to provide JG, a printing company, with supplies of its products. Subsequently, JG executed a general security agreement and a wholesale security agreement in Unisource's favour. Both agreements were duly perfected. The wholesale security agreement was intended to create a PMSI in Unisource's favour and Unisource gave notice of its PMSI to HKBC, which held a prior registered general security interest against JG's assets. It was conceded at trial that Unisource held a valid PMSI with respect to the paper it had supplied to JG and the proceeds thereof.

JG became bankrupt, owing large amounts of money to Unisource and HKBC, as well as to shareholders of JG, who also held a general security interest in JG's assets. At the time of its bankruptcy, JG still held some of the paper supplied by Unisource in its original form; most of the other supplies, however, for which Unisource had not been paid, had been converted by JG into brochures and other printed products. A key issue before Reilly J, for the purpose of determining Unisource's share of the proceeds from the disposition of the printed products, was whether Unisource held a *cumulative* PMSI in the printed products with respect to all monies owing to it or whether its priority was limited to the paper content in each batch of printed products for which it had not been paid. Reilly J held that the second answer was the correct one.

In an article critical of Reilly J's decision, Professor McLaren has argued that the court should have recognized Unisource's revolving PMSI in the inventory in JG's hands, even though the composite inventory could not be traced to specific orders. He reasons that in the case of smaller items and fungible goods it is often impractical to expect the supplier to keep track of how much has been paid with respect to each delivery. The supplier should, therefore, have the benefit of a cross-over purchase-money priority: "PMSI and Commingled Goods—*Unisource v. Hongkong Bank of Canada*" (2000), 15 *BFLR* 319. The suggestion is a reasonable one, but it is not consistent with the existing definition of a purchase-money security interest in the Ontario and other PPSAs. To accomplish this objective, the PPSAs would have to adopt a revised definition comparable to the definition in Revised Article 9, s. 103(b). This definition provides that:

A security interest in goods is a purchase-money security interest:

(1) to the extent that the goods are purchase-money collateral with respect to that security interest;

(2) if the security interest is in inventory that is or was purchase-money collateral, also to the extent that the security interest secures a purchase-money obligation incurred with respect to other inventory in which the secured party holds or held a purchase-money security interest; and

(3) also to the extent that the security interest secures a purchase-money obligation incurred with respect to software in which the secured party holds or held a purchase-money security interest.

The suggested change has the support of the Uniform Law Conference of Canada's PPSA Committee.

V. THE PMSI PRIORITY IN PROCEEDS

Massey-Ferguson Industries Ltd. v. Melfort Credit Union Ltd.
(1986), 6 PPSAC 120 (Sask. QB)

WALKER J: This is an application for:

1. An order, pursuant to s. 63(e) of the Personal Property Security Act, SS 1979-80, c. P-6.1 ("PPSA"), declaring that the applicant (herein called "Massey") has a valid purchase-money security interest in the parts inventory of the respondent North East Implements Ltd. (herein called "the dealer") which has been seized by the respondent Melfort Credit Union Limited (herein called "the Credit Union").

2. A further order that the Credit Union release to Massey all of the parts inventory which it has seized.

3. A further order pursuant to s. 63(d) of the Act staying the enforcement by the Credit Union of any rights provided in Part V of the Act until such time as the right of the Credit Union to seize and sell the property has been determined.

This is a contest between the applicant inventory financer and the respondent receivables financer—a contest between "goods-credit or supplier credit," on the one hand, and "money-credit or bank credit," on the other.

Massey's "security agreement—inventory" with the dealer is dated March 18, 1981. Its financing statement claiming a purchase-money security interest was registered, in the Personal Property Registry, May 1, 1981 against this collateral:

> Existing or to be acquired new Massey Ferguson goods including farm and industrial machinery, Massey Ferguson repair parts and Massey Ferguson used machinery of similar type and all proceeds.

Massey sent a notice dated July 8, 1982, to the Credit Union advising it of its purchase-money security interest in the inventory of the dealer.

The dealer agreement between the dealer and Massey was terminated effective November 18, 1985. November 19, 1985, the dealer gave Massey a list of its parts inventory as of termination of a value of approximately $100,000. As of December 6, 1985, $106,281.25 was due and owing to Massey from the dealer with respect to the parts inventory supplied by Massey to the dealer. From August 31, 1982 on, Massey supplied parts inventory to the dealer of the total value of $585,742.

On June 18, 1980, the dealer executed a floating and specific charge debenture in favour of the Credit Union. On March 7, 1981, the dealer entered into a line of credit agreement with the Credit Union. The debenture was registered under the Corporation Securities Registration Act June 19, 1980 [superseded by the PPSA]. The debenture later on found its way on to Personal Property Registry under the Act, the registration date being June 19, 1980. The Credit Union says it did not at any time subordinate its interest in the inventory in favour of Massey. The supplementary affidavit has exhibited the financial statements of the dealer for the year ending October 31, 1982, for the purpose of proving "new value."

It is to be noted that the relief asked by Massey and the counterrelief asked by the Credit Union relate only to the inventory as such. It is to be noted also that the Credit Union's opposition to the application is based solely on the position that s. 34(4) not s. 34(2) should govern. There is no reliance on the failure of Massey to meet the conditions of operation of s. 34(2).

Section 34 [of the PPSA] reads:

> 34(1) Subject to section 28, a purchase-money security interest in:
>   (a) collateral or its proceeds, other than intangibles or inventory, that is perfected within fifteen days after the day the debtor obtains possession of the collateral; or
>   (b) an intangible or its proceeds that is perfected within fifteen days after the day the security interest in the intangible attaches;
> has priority over any other security interest in the same collateral or its proceeds given by the same debtor.
>
> (2) Subject to section 28 and subsection (4) of this section, a purchase-money security interest in inventory or its proceeds has priority over any other security interest in the same collateral given by the same debtor if:
>
> (3) The notice required in subsection (2) shall: ...
>
> (4) No purchase-money security interest in proceeds of inventory has priority over a security interest in accounts given for new value where a financing statement relating thereto is registered before the purchase-money security interest is perfected or a financing statement relating thereto is registered.

(5) A non-proceeds purchase-money security interest has priority over a purchase-money security interest in proceeds under subsections (1) and (2) in the same collateral if the non-proceeds purchase-money security interest is perfected at the time the debtor obtains possession of the collateral or within fifteen days thereafter.

Massey relies on s. 34(2). The Credit Union relies on s. 34(4), saying that new value was given and that its registration was first in time. Section 34(2) is subject to s. 34(4) on its own terms if s. 34(4) has application.

The Credit Union relied on this extract. R.C.C. Cuming, in ["Second Generation Personal Property Security Legislation in Canada"], 46 *Sask. Law Review* 5, has this to say of accounts financing [at 38]:

> ... However, there is no uniformity among the three Acts [Ontario and its western counterparts] when the priority dispute is between an inventory financer claiming a purchase money security interest in accounts as proceeds of his inventory and an accounts financer claiming priority on the basis of a prior registration. All three Acts allow an inventory financer to assert a purchase money security interest in proceeds of inventory collateral in which he has a perfected purchase money security interest. [s. 34(2)] Since generally purchase money security interests have priority over any other security interests in the same collateral, [s. 34(2)] an inventory financer with a purchase money security interest and claiming accounts as proceeds will defeat an accounts financer claiming accounts as primary collateral unless the purchase money priority rule is modified in favour of the accounts financer. Such a modification is contained in the Saskatchewan and Manitoba Acts, which provide that a purchase money security interest in proceeds of inventory does not have priority over a security interest in accounts given for new value where a financing statement relating to the latter is registered before the purchase money security interest is perfected or a financing statement relating thereto is registered. [s. 34(4)] ...
>
> The result is that an accounts financer is given priority over an inventory financer claiming accounts as proceeds if as between the two the accounts financer has registered first.

This extract seems not to favour the Credit Union in present circumstances.

...

Massey relies on *Elmcrest Furniture Manufacturing Ltd. v. Price Waterhouse Ltd.* (1985), 5 PPSAC 22, 41 Sask. R 125 (Sask. QB). That case was decided under s. 34(2). In that case the Court held that the holder of a purchase-money security interest had priority over the bank's security interest. The purchase-money security interest holder's priority dated from the time he gave notice to the bank. Section 34(4) did not fall to be considered. The applicant also relies on *Re Fosters Service (81) Ltd.: Terra Power Tractor Co. v. Touche Ross Ltd.* (1985), 5 PPSAC 192, 42 Sask. R 102 (Sask. QB). Section 34(4) did not fall to be considered there. Section 34(2) deals with "a purchase-money security interest in inventory or its proceeds," and its priority over "any other security interest in the same collateral given by the same debtor." Section 34(2) is the general rule. Section 34(4) is a narrow exception to it. Section 34(5) is a special rule involving two purchase-money security interests upon which the Credit Union did not rely and which has no application. Does s. 34(4), an exception to the general rule in s. 34(2), apply?

The s. 34(4) exception to the general rule in s. 34(2) is very narrow. This inventory has not been sold. There has been no sale by the dealer of the inventory generating a receivable. There are no proceeds. There are no accounts. Massey is claiming not the proceeds, but the inventory as such. So is the Credit Union. Section 34(4) has no application. There may be other reasons for the non-application of s. 34(4) but I do not find it necessary to go beyond the question of proceeds. This is consistent with *Elmcrest*.

Section 34(4) has no application. Section 34(2) governs. The date of delivery of the first inventory by Massey to the dealer is not clear beyond peradventure. The inference is possible that there was no delivery prior to the notice from Massey to the Credit Union, from the fact that there was inventory in value of $585,742 delivered subsequent to the notice and there is now inventory in value of approximately $100,000, and an account of $106,281.25. The Credit Union did not argue this point in any way. In fact, the Credit Union rested solely on the applicability of s. 34(4) and non-applicability of s. 34(2), in effect conceding that the application was to be decided on which subsection applied with the conditions of those sections being considered to have been met. In result, there will be an order that Massey has a valid purchase-money security interest in all parts inventory delivered subsequent to its notice to the Credit Union of July 8, 1982. The Credit Union is ordered to release to Massey that part of the inventory. If the parties cannot agree in this area, the matter may be referred back for further direction.

Order accordingly.

NOTES

1) What is the appropriate priority rule for a competition between an inventory financer claiming accounts receivable as proceeds of inventory and an accounts financer claiming the same accounts as original collateral? The policy issues were debated extensively in the United States during the 1960s. Some leading US articles are: Kripke, "Suggestions for Clarifying Article 9: Intangibles, Proceeds and Priorities" (1966), 41 *New York University L Rev.* 687; Weiss, "Original Collateral and Proceeds: A Code Puzzle" (1967), 42 *New York University L Rev.* 785; and Coogan and Gordon, "The Effect of the UCC Upon Receivables Financing—Some Answers and Some Unresolved Problems" (1963), 76 *Harvard L Rev.* 1529. A leading Canadian contribution is Cuming, "Second Generation Personal Property Security Legislation in Canada" (1981-1982), 46 *Saskatchewan L Rev.* 5 at 38-39.

2) There are at least three possible approaches:

1. the first to register gets priority;
2. the inventory financer gets priority under the PMSI provision, regardless of the order of registration, and without the need for prior notice to the accounts financer; and
3. the inventory financer gets priority under the PMSI provision, regardless of the order of registration, but subject to giving the accounts financer prior notice.

3) The United States has chosen Option (1): Revised Article 9, UCC 9-324(b). The Official Comment explains the thinking behind this provision as follows:

As a general matter ... the purchase-money priority does *not* carry over into proceeds consisting of accounts or chattel paper. Many parties financing inventory are quite content to protect their first-priority security interest in the inventory itself. They realize that, when the inventory is sold, someone else will be financing the resulting receivables (accounts or chattel paper) and the priority for inventory will not run forward to the receivables constituting the proceeds. Indeed, the cash supplied by the receivables financer often will be used to pay the inventory financer. In some situations, the party financing the inventory on a purchase-money basis makes contractual arrangements that the proceeds of receivables financing by another be devoted to paying off the inventory security interest.

4) Most of the Canadian PPSAs have also chosen Option (1). Cuming explains the thinking as follows:

It is impossible to justify [Option (1)] on the grounds that accounts financers are more important to the business community than are inventory financers. However, it is possible to justify it on the grounds that it is sensible from both a commercial and equitable point of view. If a secured party is approached by a potential customer seeking inventory financing, he will conduct a search of the registry to determine whether or not any priority claims to the potential customer's accounts have been registered. If the search reveals a prior claim, the inventory financer must decide whether or not he would be adequately secured without having as collateral the accounts which are proceeds of his inventory. The decision that the accounts are necessary may, but need not, lead to the conclusion that the potential customer must be turned away. The accounts financer may be prepared to execute a subordination agreement giving the inventory financer priority to the accounts which are proceeds of his inventory. In any event, if priority is given to the accounts financer, the inventory financer is in a position to take measures to avoid loss to anyone simply by refusing to deal with the person seeking further credit. [at pp. 38-39]

5) Option (2) represented the position in Ontario until the 2006 PPSA amendments. Cuming describes the problem with Option (2) as follows:

Every accounts financer who has registered a financing statement and has loaned money to a debtor in Ontario faces the risk of loss of his security to subsequent inventory financers claiming purchase money security interests in the debtor's accounts. There are no measures an accounts financer can take to protect himself. The result is that accounts financers must make sure that any advances they make are fully secured by existing accounts which cannot be traced as the proceeds of sale of a debtor's inventory. [at p. 39]

6) Option (3) has been adopted in the Canadian Atlantic provinces and Ontario switched to Option (3), effective August 1, 2007. Kripke explains the thinking behind Option (3) as follows:

[It recognizes] that when an accounts financer is first to file, he should be entitled to rely on his first filing. He should not have to search the records continually to guard against the arrival of another financer claiming a priority based on lending at an earlier stage in the chain of production. Similarly, it is suggested in the present context that the inventory financer who asserts a prior claim to accounts as proceeds should have to notify the first filer as to accounts and that, having done so, he should be entitled to priority. [at p. 717]

However, he goes on to identify the drawback to Option (3) as follows:

Consider where [Option (3)] would leave the accounts financer who was first to file. Unless and until he had been notified of the inventory claimant, he would, of course, be entitled to rely on his own first-filed position. Suppose, however, that [Option (3)] were to be adopted ... [The account financer's] only recourse would be to break off his accounts financing [and he may suffer loss as a consequence]. In the first place, he might have been relying on accounts subsequently arising to restore a collateral ratio which he had temporarily allowed to go below standard, *e.g.*, a temporary over-advance to enable the debtor to buy peak inventory. Worse than that, until liquidation of his accounts collateral acquired before the notice, he would find himself in a daytime version of the account financer's worst nightmare—split financing of accounts on an indirect collection basis. The debtor would have to transfer some collections to one financer, with Solomon-like decisions as to which financer was entitled to collections where part of a single running account of an account debtor had been assigned in one direction and part in the other direction. Finally, the financer would have to forego the profits from financing on a contract which he might have entered into originally with considerable risk, only to find it now "creamed off" by another financer who stepped in after the credit stability of the debtor has been improved. [at p. 718]

7) Consider the following case:

SP1 has a security interest in Debtor's present and after-acquired inventory, perfected by registration. Debtor subsequently assigns its present and after-acquired accounts to SP2 and SP2 registers a financing statement. Later still, Debtor sells an item out of inventory to Customer on 90-day terms. SP1 and SP2 both claim the account.

On these facts, SP1 has priority under all of Options (1), (2), and (3).

Contrast the following case:

SP1 has a security interest in Debtor's present and after-acquired inventory, perfected by registration. Debtor subsequently assigns its present and after-acquired chattel paper to SP2. Later still, Debtor sells an item out of inventory to Customer pursuant to a conditional sale agreement and delivers the chattel paper to SP2. SP1 and SP2 both claim the chattel paper.

The governing provision is OPPSA s. 28(3)(b), which provides that SP2 has priority despite SP1's prior registration and even if SP2 knows about SP1's security interest. See further, Chapter 11, Part III.

Why does the statute discriminate between accounts and chattel paper in this way? According to Kripke, the explanation is as follows:

[T]he drafting in the present Code was consciously predicated on the view that accounts as such did not have the same status and importance in commerce as chattel paper, another species of receivables flowing out of inventory. In the case of chattel paper, [Article 9] provides that, even though there is known to be a claim to the chattel paper as proceeds of inventory, a person purchasing the chattel paper for value and taking delivery thereof has priority over the person claiming the account "merely as proceeds." In the writer's recollection, this provision represented a definite policy conclusion that chattel paper was an important item of commerce so competitively sought for that the Code should not give the inventory-secured party a preemptive position to the resulting chattel paper through a claim thereto as proceeds, even if he were the first to file. In contrast, as a deliberate decision, a comparable rule for accounts was omitted, on the theory that they were more intimately inter-related with and less able to be separated from inventory financing, and that there was no pressing public policy in favour of making the accounts available to a competing financer as against the first-filed inventory financer. Thus, if the inventory financer filed first, it was expected that he would have a proceeds claim to accounts (in contrast to chattel paper) which was impregnable. On the other hand, if he did not file first, he was to receive no special protection. [at p. 715]

Note that Kripke's focus is on US law. In Canada, the PPSA drafters simply copied the US priority rules for chattel paper without inquiry into whether the same commercial considerations applied in Canada. As it happens, taking possession of chattel paper as a method of perfection did not reflect *pre*-PPSA law or industry practice in Canada, and it has never been demonstrated that chattel paper is more important than accounts in Canada or that there are public policy reasons in Canada for discriminating in favour of chattel paper. Is there a case, then, for repealing the special chattel paper priority rules and treating chattel paper on the same footing as accounts? Caution may be advisable here. It is possible that industry practice in Canada has evolved *post*-PPSA, in response to the special chattel paper priority rules, and, if that is the case, repealing them now might cause significant dislocation. The bottom line is that it may be necessary to find out more about current industry practice in Canada before making recommendations for reform of the law on this topic.

VI. THE NON-INVENTORY PMSI

North Platte State Bank v. Production Credit Ass'n
200 NW 2d 1 (Neb. S. Ct. 1972)

WHITE Chief Justice: ... This case deals with the priority of secured creditors, each having a perfected security interest in the same collateral. For convenience, the plaintiff-appellant, North Platte State Bank, is hereinafter referred to as Bank, and the defendant-appellee, Production Credit Association of North Platte, is hereinafter referred to as PCA.

In August 1967, Gerald S. Tucker received an "operating loan" from PCA, the loan being subject to annual renewal in the month of December. A contemporaneously executed security contained an after-acquired property clause which applied PCA's security interest to, inter alia, "all livestock now owned or hereafter acquired by debtor, whether by purchase, natural increase or otherwise." PCA perfected its security interest by properly filing a financing statement which covered all of the Debtor's livestock, and all subsequent transactions between PCA and Tucker. No other financing statement was filed by PCA.

From November 1967 through January 1968 PCA advanced approximately $70,000 to Tucker, primarily for periodic purchases of cattle. In February 1968, a second security agreement was entered into by Tucker and PCA to cover newly purchased cattle. PCA inspected the Tucker ranch in March and September of 1968 to count the number of head of cattle that had been added by purchase and by natural increase. Still another security agreement was executed by the parties in September to cover the increase in calves.

In October or November of 1968, Tucker approached D.M. Mann, hereinafter referred to as Seller, to purchase certain Angus heifers in the Seller's possession. It should be mentioned that the Seller was merely an agent acting for the true owner of the cattle but this fact has no bearing on a determination in this case. Tucker agreed to purchase as many of the 100 head of cattle as tested pregnant, and the price was $225 per head. The Seller and Tucker agreed that Tucker *was to take delivery of the cattle before January 1, 1969,* but payment and transfer of a bill of sale were to take place after that date. Sometime in November and again in December of 1968, Tucker went to the Bank to discuss opening a line of credit but there was no discussion of a specific loan for any particular purpose.

On November 30, 1968, a trucking company hired by Tucker took 79 head of impregnated Angus heifers from the Seller's ranch and hauled them to the Tucker ranch. PCA had inspected the Tucker ranch earlier in November, and then in December 1968, PCA made a routine search of the security interest filing records in several counties pursuant to a loan renewal scheduled for December but not formally executed until March 24, 1969. PCA did not see any Angus cattle on the Tucker ranch when it inspected in November, and the December search of the records revealed that only the PCA financing statement of August 1967 was on file.

On January 13, 1969, approximately *a month and a half after he took possession of the cattle,* Tucker drew a check on the Bank for $17,775, the total purchase price for the 79 head of cattle. The Seller, payee of the check, mailed the check to the Bank for deposit. The check was returned for lack of funds, but upon the Seller's inquiry, the Bank acknowledge that a loan to Tucker had been discussed and that if Tucker would come in to complete the necessary papers, the loan would be granted and the check would be honored. Because of weather conditions, Tucker was unable to reach the Bank until January 30, 1969. A note advancing $20,000 to Tucker and a security agreement were executed that day and the next day the Bank honored the check presented by the Seller. Near this point in time, the bill of sale dated January 12, 1969, to the cattle was given to Tucker. On February 5, 1969, the Bank filed a financing statement, thus perfecting a security interest in the 79 head of cattle.

PCA became aware of the presence of the Angus cattle on the Tucker ranch sometime in February 1969. Tucker told PCA that the Angus cattle were purchased with the proceeds of a sale of several calves of another breed. Having checked the records in December 1968, and receiving this explanation for the presence of the Angus cattle, PCA saw to it that a loan renewal note was signed by Tucker and a security agreement including, specifically, the 79 Angus cattle, was executed on March 24, 1969.

In December 1969, unable to locate all of Tucker's cattle in which it had a security interest, PCA checked the filing records and found the Bank's financing statement of February 5, 1969. Late in December 1969, after Tucker defaulted on the PCA note of March 24, 1969, PCA took possession of all the cattle on Tucker's ranch, including the 79 head of Angus cattle. After the Bank claimed priority to the Angus heifers, PCA and the Bank agreed to sell the cattle and to hold the proceeds in escrow pending a determination as to the priority of their respective security interests.

...

There are two basic questions presented in this case. As we see it, the resolution of either one of these questions will be decisive in the case. The first question is whether the Bank did in fact under the pertinent provisions of the Code have a purchase money security interest in the collateral? The second question is that, if it did have a purchase money security interest in the collateral, did it acquire priority under section 9-312(4), UCC?

Did the Bank have a purchase money security interest?

A purchase money security interest is defined in section 9-107, UCC. It states:

· · ·

Tucker and the Seller (agent for Long) made an oral contract for sale sometime in November 1968. Later when the 79 pregnant cows were identified, they were finally delivered to Tucker on November 30, 1968. It is apparent, therefore, that the actual goods contracted for were delivered to the buyer under the previous contract for sale; that Tucker physically received them; and that they were therefore in his legal possession. The ordinary understanding of the term "possession" means that a person has possession when he has physical control of the property. *Boyd v. Travelers Fire Ins. Co.*, 147 Neb. 237, 22 NW 2d 700. The only further question to be determined here is whether the actual physical delivery of the cows and their acceptance by Tucker, the buyer, was affected by the fact that the payment of the price and the delivery of the bill of sale were postponed. It is true that delivery by a seller under a contract for sale can take place prior to the receipt of the goods by the buyer. Receipt is defined by section 2-103(1)(c), UCC, as taking physical possession. It is clear that the tender of delivery by the Seller for Long took place here under section 2-503(1), UCC, and the buyer received and accepted the goods on arrival at his ranch. It is not argued and, indeed, it could not be argued, that the postponement of payment and the later delivery of the bill of sale had any effect upon the time that Tucker received legal possession of the goods. The buyer had received the goods under the precise terms of the Code and this receipt was evidenced by his taking of the actual physical possession. It seems quite obvious that when the cows were delivered to Tucker under the contract for sale and were actually physically received by him, they were in his legal possession and we so hold.

We turn now to the question of whether Tucker on November 30, 1968, acquired more rights in the cows than their possession. It appears from the evidence in this case that Tucker acquired title to the cows as well on November 30, 1968. There is considerable colloquy about the understanding of the parties and particularly about the testimony of the Seller, Long's agent, about what he relied upon in delivering the cows, and what he would have done had the cows not been paid for. What is important is that the Seller said Tucker's word was good enough for him. All of the indications of the oral testimony are that the Seller was relying on Tucker's willingness and ability to make payment of the price and that he was making a sale on open credit. Neither Seller nor Long made any effort to reclaim the goods under section 2-702, UCC, granting an unpaid seller on open account the right to reclaim the goods if he discovers his buyer's insolvency. This right must be exercised within 10 days, it was not so exercised, nor did the Seller nor Long know until long after November 30, 1968, that Tucker had become insolvent.

Whatever the parties may have thought, the provisions of the Uniform Commercial Code govern, and it is clear that title to the cows actually passed to Tucker when they reached his ranch and he received the actual physical possession of them. Section 2-401(2), UCC, says that unless otherwise *explicitly* agreed, title passes to the buyer at the time and place at which the seller completes his performance with reference to the physical delivery of the goods, despite any reservation of a security interest. There is no evidence that the sales agreement, either expressly or impliedly, contained an *explicit* provision or term reserving the title until payment had actually been accomplished. We therefore come to the conclusion that after November 30, 1968, once the cattle reached Tucker's ranch and came into his physical possession, under the completely oral transaction the Seller had no enforceable security interest in them and no other interest of any kind. Title and possession were merged in Tucker, it was an unsecured credit transaction, and no cause of action existed against Tucker except one for the agreed price of the cattle under the terms of the agreement.

What, then, was the nature of the Bank's security interest? We pause to observe that at the moment the cattle reached Tucker's ranch, PCA's perfected security interest immediately attached to the 79 cows. All of the conditions necessary had been met, there was a written security agreement with an after-acquired property clause containing a description sufficiently broad to include the cows, value had been given in the form of the original loan, and subsequent extensions of credit which had been renewed a number of times. As we have seen, Tucker had acquired both possession and title to the cows. At the time of delivery and possession of title to Tucker, on November 30, 1968, the financing statement of PCA was the only financing statement on file.

As we have pointed out, section 9-107(b), UCC, provides that a security interest cannot become a purchase money security interest unless it is taken by a person who by making advances or incurring an obligation gives value to enable the debtor *to acquire rights in or the use of collateral* if such value is in fact so used. Clearly, the Bank could not qualify as the seller of the 79 cows. Obviously, by advancing the $20,000 and taking the mortgage it did not acquire a security interest in the cows. The distinction is vital to the disposition of this case. The money advanced by the Bank enabled Tucker to pay the price to Seller for the cows. But it was not used by Tucker to acquire any rights in the cows because he already had all the possible rights in the cows he could have with both possession and title.

There is a further and even more fundamental reason why the Bank may not succeed in establishing any priority over PCA in the enforcement of its security interest. This is because although it filed its statement within 10 days after it made its loan, the filing occurred almost 2 months after the cows had been delivered and the title had passed to Tucker. At the risk of repetition, we will repeat the basic portion of section 9-312(4), UCC, which states: "... if the purchase money security interest is perfected at the time the *debtor* receives possession of the collateral or within ten days thereafter." (Emphasis supplied.) The application of this plain, simple, and forceful language to the facts in the case at bar seem so obvious as not to require any further argument. However, the Bank argues at length and persistently that Tucker did not become a "debtor" within the meaning of section 9-312(4), UCC, until the money was loaned by the Bank and that, therefore, "debtor" Tucker never had full "possession of the collateral" in the section 9-312(4), UCC, sense until the loan was made by the Bank and the security agreement signed. Therefore, the Bank argues that since it filed a financing statement within 10 days after the execution of the security agreement with Tucker, it qualifies for the special priority of section 9-312(4), UCC.

Manifestly, on January 30, 1969, when the Bank executed the loan, Tucker was a "debtor" of both the Bank and PCA. Section 9-105(1)(d), UCC, provides that unless the context otherwise requires a "debtor" is "the person who owes payment or other performance of the obligations secured, whether or not he owns or has rights in the collateral … ." Tucker did not or could not receive possession from the Bank and it is uncontrovertible that he became a "debtor" to the Seller on November 30, 1968. While Tucker may not have been the Bank's "debtor" until January 30, 1969, it is inescapable in the context of the Code that he was the "debtor" in the section 9-312(4), UCC, sense when he became a "debtor" to PCA. On November 30, 1968, the time and the only time that he "received" possession, Tucker was a "debtor" of PCA and Seller only. To hold otherwise renders the language of the statute meaningless, and purports a construction wholly unrelated to setting up an ascertainable time standard by which priorities may be established so that a subsequent lender can achieve priority over the first to file. This interpretation is well stated in 2 Coogan, Hogan & Vagts, *Secured Transactions Under the Uniform Commercial Code*, section 19.02(3)(a), at 1979, wherein it is stated: "The time at which the debtor receives possession starts the running of the ten-day grace period for perfection. Problems will undoubtedly arise as to when the debtor 'receives possession' of the collateral. The Code does not offer a specific definition of the term, but there are indications that actual delivery to the buyer or a third party is crucial. *It is important to realize that this priority rule turns on the more easily ascertained time of receipt of possession and not upon the time the debtor obtains 'rights' in the collateral.*" (Emphasis supplied.)

The very purpose of the 10-day grace period was to relieve from the rigidity of a requirement of a loan first and acquisition second or simultaneousness of receipt of possession and execution of the loan. At the same time the integrity of the transaction had to be guaranteed by an ascertainable standard related to the receipt of possession, and the retroactive granting of priority over the first to file and the first to advance funds. See II Gilmore, Security Interests in Personal Property, s. 29.2, at 782.

···

The Bank relies almost completely on the decision of the Court of Appeals in *Brodie Hotel Supply, Inc. v. United States*, 431 F2d 1316 (9th Cir., 1970). There are two answers to this contention, besides the analysis and the decision we have reached on the merits. In the first place, the *Brodie* case is inapposite on the facts. The court reached the correct decision in the *Brodie* case because the purchase money security holder in fact perfected his filing within 10 days after Lyon, the purchaser, obtained possession of the equipment and thereby achieved priority over the lender. The language and the reasoning of the *Brodie* case, however, relied upon by the Bank have been seriously criticized. For a full discussion of this case, see 27 *The Business Lawyer*, Kennedy, *Secured Transactions*, 755 at 768 (1972); and Comment, 49 *NCL Rev.* 849 (1971).

···

We therefore hold in this case that the Bank failed to comply with the requirements of section 9-312(4), UCC, because it did not file a financing statement until more than 10 days had passed from the time the cattle came into the "debtor" Tucker's possession.

Therefore, the first to file rule of section 9-312(5)(a), UCC, applies, and the original priority of PCA controls.

Judgment affirmed.

NOTE

In Ontario, the provision governing non-inventory PMSIs is s. 33(2). In contrast to s. 33(1), there is no notice requirement in s. 33(2) and SP2 has up to 10 days after delivery of the collateral to the Debtor to perfect its security interest. Section 33(2) typically applies where the collateral is equipment. The purpose of the 10-day grace period is to accommodate retailing practice. For example: assume Debtor is a farmer. SP, a dealer, sells Debtor a truck pursuant to a conditional sale agreement. The grace period allows SP to give Debtor immediate delivery without having to wait until registration of a financing statement. The concession was perhaps more important in the days of paper-based registration because the preparation and lodging of a paper financing statement might take some time, whereas under an electronic system SP can register a financing statement more or less instantaneously.

Brodie Hotel Supply, Inc. v. US
431 F2d 1316 (CCA 9 1970)

HAMLEY Circuit Judge: Brodie Hotel Supply, Inc. (Brodie) brought this action against the United States to determine which of the parties had priority, under their respective chattel mortgages, to the proceeds of the sale of certain restaurant equipment. The facts were stipulated and the property was sold and proceeds impounded by agreement. The district court granted summary judgment for Brodie and the United States appeals.

In 1959, Brodie sold the restaurant equipment to Standard Management Company, Inc., for use in a restaurant at Anchorage, Alaska. Standard Management went bankrupt. Brodie repossessed the equipment but left it in the restaurant. With the consent of Brodie, James Lyon took possession of the restaurant and began operating it on June 1, 1964. Throughout the summer of 1964, Brodie and Lyon negotiated over the price and terms under which Lyon was to purchase the equipment.

On November 2, 1964, Lyon borrowed seventeen thousand dollars from the National Bank of Alaska and, as security for the loan, which was evidenced by a promissory note, executed a chattel mortgage covering the restaurant equipment. This equipment consisted of 159 separate types of items, including a refrigerator, a dishwasher, an ice cream cabinet, spoons, forks, cups, ladles, pots, pans, and assorted glassware and chinaware. The bank assigned its mortgage to the Small Business Administration (SBA), represented in this action by the United States. On November 4, 1964, the bank filed a financing statement, showing the SBA as assignee.

On November 12, Brodie delivered to Lyon a bill of sale covering the equipment. On the same day Lyon executed a chattel mortgage on the equipment, naming Brodie as mortgagee. This mortgage was given to secure the unpaid purchase price of the equipment. Brodie filed a financing statement on November 23, 1964.

Alaska has adopted the Uniform Commercial Code (Code). Under section 9-312(5)(a) of the Code (Alaska Statutes [AS] 45.05.754(e)(1)), the general rule of priority, if both interests are perfected by filing, is that the secured party who first files a financing statement (in this case SBA as assignee of the bank) prevails, regardless of when his security interest attached. However, there is a special exception for purchase-money security interests in collateral other than inventory. Brodie had such an interest. Under this exception, the purchase-money security interest prevails over conflicting interests in non-inventory collateral if "the purchase money security interest is perfected [i.e., here it was perfected by filing a financing statement] at the time the debtor receives possession of the collateral or within 10 days after the debtor receives possession." AS 45.05.754(d) (Code, 9-312(4)).

On the basis of these stipulated facts, Brodie moved for summary judgment. Brodie contended that although Lyon received possession of the restaurant equipment on June 1, 1964, over five months before Brodie's financing statement was filed, Lyon did not become a "debtor," and the equipment did not become "collateral" until November 12, 1964, when Lyon received the bill of sale and executed Brodie's chattel mortgage. Accordingly, Brodie contended, it was not until November 12, that "the debtor [Lyon] receive[d] possession of the collateral" within the meaning of the statute referred to above. As already indicated, Brodie's financing statement was filed within ten days of that date. The district court agreed with this analysis in granting summary judgment for Brodie.

If, in AS 45.05.754(d), the term "debtor" is given the meaning ascribed to it in AS 45.05.698(a)(4), Brodie was entitled to priority. It was not until November 12, 1964, that Lyon purchased the equipment and became obligated to pay the purchase price. Until that obligation came into being, Lyon was not Brodie's debtor with power to mortgage the restaurant equipment as collateral for the unpaid purchase price.

But the United States argues that in the context of this case the priority statute, AS 45.05.745(d), is ambiguous as to whether "debtor" is used in the sense defined in AS 45.05.698(a)(4), or whether it is used merely to identify an individual in possession, who ultimately becomes indebted to the purchase-money mortgagee. In contending that this "ambiguity" should be resolved in favor of the latter construction, the United States refers to the history and underlying purposes and policies of the Code, the assertedly different language of the prior Uniform Conditional Sales Act, and the fact that, under AS 45.05.770(a) (Code, §9-402(1)) a financing statement may be filed before a security agreement is made or a security interest otherwise attaches, notwithstanding the fact that this section refers to "debtor," "secured party," and "security interest."

We are not persuaded that either recourse to the history or consideration of the underlying purposes of the Code supports the Government's position. In our view, the term "debtor" as it is used in this particular priority statute, AS 45.05.754(d) (Code, §9-312(4)), means "the person who owes payment or other performance of the obligation secured." AS 45.05.698(a)(4) (Code, §9-105(d)). Although Lyon might have been liable for the reasonable rental of the equipment or for its return to Brodie, he did not owe performance of an "obligation secured" by the collateral in question until November 12, 1964, and therefore was not a "debtor" for purposes of AS 45.05.754(d) (Code, §9-312(4)). Brodie's filing was therefore within the ten-day period and Brodie has priority over the conflicting security interest held by SBA.

The Government has urged us to look at the policy and the purposes of the Code to resolve what it considers to be the ambiguous meaning of "debtor." The Code has granted a specially favored position to the holder of a purchase-money security interest in non-inventory collateral. The holder of such an interest need not follow the notice procedures which are prescribed for the holders of purchase-money interests in inventory. AS 45.05.754(c) (Code, §9-312(3)). Such a holder is also given a special priority position. His interest, perfected second, but within the ten-day grace period, will prevail over any previously perfected security interest. This priority exists even though the framers of the Code knew that the holder of the conflicting security interest would be relying on the possession of the collateral and upon the absence of a prior filing. Similarly, the holder of a purchase-money security interest in non-inventory collateral will have priority over a previously perfected security interest which includes the collateral by virtue of an after-acquired property clause. Code, §9-312(4), Official Comment 3. Such a holder therefore is not required to search the files to determine the existence of such a conflicting interest in order to be sure of his priority.

The protection which the Code confers upon a purchase-money interest in non-inventory collateral is not unduly extended by a decision giving priority to Brodie's interest. Although it is true that Brodie could have filed a financing statement as soon as Lyon went into possession and thus protected itself, it is also true that the bank, SBA's assignor, could have protected itself by inquiring into Lyon's interest in the equipment before accepting his chattel mortgage. Due to the favored status given by the Code to the holder of a purchase-money interest in non-inventory collateral, we are not convinced that the trial court erred in refusing to impose this burden on Brodie.

Affirmed.

NOTES

1) Do you agree with the criticism of *Brodie Hotel Supply* referred to in *North Platte State Bank*? Did White CJ not indirectly endorse the 9th CCA's construction of the meaning of "debtor" in UCC 9-312(4) when he justified the court's decision on the ground that the vendor had filed its financing statement within 10 days after Lyon obtained possession of the equipment? Had the US government not argued that the 10 days should be calculated from the time Lyon started to operate the restaurant business and not from the date (November 12, 1964) on which he agreed to buy the equipment?

OPPSA s. 33(2)(a)(i) adopts the reasoning in *Brodie* by requiring the PMSI to be perfected "before or within ten days after (i) the debtor obtained possession of the collateral *as a debtor* ..." (emphasis added). (See *Air Products Canada Ltd. v. Farini Corp.* (2000), 16 CBR (4th) 18 (Ont. SCJ).)

2) In light of the decision in *North Platte*, should the PMSI definition be expanded to include the security interest of a lender whose loan enables the debtor to pay off the seller, whether or not the buyer has already acquired title to the goods?

3) Can there be a PMSI in an intangible? If yes, how does s. 33(2) apply to it? Cf. *Re Berman* (1979), 24 OR (2d) 79 (rev'd. on other grounds (1979), 26 OR (2d) 389 (SCJ)) and the discussion of the case by Ziegel in (1979-80), 4 *CBLJ* 54, at 69-75. OPPSA s. 32(4)(b)

now recognizes that there may be a PMSI in an intangible and provides for its priority. The recognition is also extended in s. 20(3).

4) The PPSAs do not indicate what evidence is admissible to allow a lender to prove that his loan was used by a debtor to enable him to acquire new collateral. In *Dube v. Bank of Montreal* (1986), 5 PPSAC 269 (Sask. CA), Vancise JA held, *inter alia*, that extrinsic evidence was not admissible to prove the purpose of the loan where the loan agreement itself made no mention of it. Is this a proper application of the parol evidence rule? Is the decision consistent with the purpose of the purchase-money priority? (The court in *Dube* subsequently withdrew the judgment in 5 PPSAC 269 and replaced it with a new judgment omitting any reference to the evidentiary issue.)

5) Can there be more than one PMSI in the same collateral and, if there can, how do the claimants rank in relation to each other? In *Polano v. Bank of Nova Scotia* (1979), 96 DLR (3d) 510 (Ont. Div. Ct.), the purchasers of a mobile home obtained loans from two different lenders to enable them to pay for it and gave each lender a chattel mortgage on the home. Both financing statements were registered within 10 days of the execution of the security agreement. Loukidelis DCJ held that each lender held a PMSI, but he refused to apply s. 34(3) [now s. 30(2)] to determine the ranking of the security interests. In his view, s. 34(3) did not apply to such a situation. (Do you agree?) Instead, he applied the first-to-register rule in s. 35(1)(a) [now s. 30(1)1], thus giving priority to the lender whose financing statement was registered first.

Is this an appropriate solution? Would it be fairer to prorate the two loans in the ratio that each loan bears to the sum of the two loans? Cf. s. 37 of the OPPSA, which applies such a solution to security interests held in commingled goods. Should this solution also be applied where the conflict arises between a seller of the collateral and a lender? See the discussion by Ziegel in (1979-80), 4 *CBLJ* 54, at 75-78. The current Act adopts the position that the seller's security interest should be given priority. Section 33(3) provides:

> (3) Where more than one purchase-money security interest is given priority by subsections (1) and (2), the purchase-money security interest, if any, of the seller has priority over any other purchase-money security interest given by the same debtor.

Is this a reasonable priority rule?

VII. SUBORDINATION AGREEMENTS

OPPSA s. 38 provides that a subordination agreement or provision "is effective according to its terms": see Chapter 7, Part VII. In *Euroclean Canada Inc. v. Forest Glade Investments Ltd.* (1985), 16 DLR (4th) 289 (Ont. CA), SP1 and D entered into a general security agreement covering all D's assets. The agreement contained the following provision:

> The Corporation [D] shall not, without the consent in writing of the Holder [SP1], create any mortgage, hypothec, charge, lien or other encumbrance upon the mortgaged property or any part thereof, ranking or purporting to rank in priority to or pari passu with the charge created by this debenture, except that the Corporation may give mortgages or liens in connection with the acquisition of property after the date hereof or may acquire property subject to any mortgage, lien or other encumbrance thereon existing at the time of such acquisition *and any*

such mortgage, lien or other encumbrance shall rank in priority to the charge hereby created.
[Emphasis added.]

SP1 registered a financing statement and, some time later, SP2 supplied D with goods pursuant to a conditional sale agreement. SP2 failed to register a financing statement. D defaulted and a priority dispute arose between SP1 and SP2 over the goods that SP2 had supplied to D.

SP2 held a PMSI and so, if it had registered in time, it would have had priority over SP1 pursuant to what is now OPPSA s. 33. Correspondingly, its failure to register in time meant that it did not have super-priority under old s. 34 (now s. 33). However, the court held that SP2 had priority because of the express provision in the security agreement. In other words, the agreement displaced the statutory rule.

In *Chiips Inc. v. Skyview Hotels Ltd.* (1994), 116 DLR (4th) 385 (Alta. CA), the facts were similar to those in the *Euroclean* case. As in the *Euroclean* case, there was a provision in SP1 and D's security agreement prohibiting D from creating any prior ranking security interest in the collateral, and the provision was subject to the following proviso:

> [P]rovided, however, that this covenant shall not apply to, nor operate to prevent, and there shall be permitted:
>> the assuming or giving of purchase money mortgages or other purchase money liens on property acquired by the Company [D] or the giving of mortgages or liens in connection with the acquisition or purchase of such property or the acquiring of property subject to any mortgage, lien or encumbrance thereon existing at the time of such acquisition; provided that such purchase money mortgages or purchase money loans shall be secured only by the property being acquired by the Company [D] and no other property of the Company.

This provision is similar to the one in *Euroclean*, except it does not explicitly state that PMSIs have priority. However, the court held that the statement was implicit and it gave SP2 priority on that basis. For a critical discussion of *Chiips*, see K. Morlock, "Floating Charges, Negative Pledges, the PPSA and Subordination: Chiips Inc. v. Skyview Hotels Limited" (1994-1995), 10 *BFLR* 405.

Contrast *Sperry Inc. v. Canadian Imperial Bank of Commerce* (1985), 17 DLR (4th) 236 (Ont. CA), where the relevant provision read as follows:

> the undersigned [D] represents and warrants that, except for the security interest created hereby and except for purchase money obligations, the undersigned [D] is, or with respect to collateral acquired after the date hereof will be, the owner of collateral free from any mortgage, lien, charge, security interest or encumbrance.

This is different from the provision in *Chiips* because it does not explicitly give D permission to create PMSIs. The court held that the provision was no more than a warranty of title and it did not amount to a subordination agreement. *Kubota Canada Ltd. v. Case Credit Ltd.* (2005), 253 DLR (4th) 171 (Alta. CA) is a similar case. Following *Sperry*, the court held that the provision was not a subordination agreement.

In *Engel Canada Inc. v. TCE Capital Corp.* (2002), 34 CBR (4th) 169 (Ont. SCJ), the warranty provision read as follows:

[D warrants that] the collateral is genuine and owned by [D] free of all security interests, mortgages, liens, claims, charges, licences, leases, infringements by third parties or other encumbrances (hereinafter collectively called "Encumbrances"), save for [SP's] security interest and those encumbrances shown on Schedule A hereto or hereafter approved in writing, prior to their creation or assumption by [SP] hereinafter called "permitted encumbrances").

Schedule A listed various forms of PMSI: purchase-money liens, conditional sale agreements, etc. The court (Wilson J) held that these provisions explicitly permitted and anticipated PMSIs and that, when read together, they were more like the *Chiips* provision than the *Sperry* provision.

In the *Kubota* case, SP1 argued that "commercial reality dictates that whenever a PMSI is granted, that PMSI should, perfected or not, have implied priority over any general security." The court responded as follows (para. 22):

> [C]ommercial reality stops short of requiring that these PMSIs should have priority in all circumstances. There is no commercial reality which would dictate against requiring the subsequent PMSIs to be registered or otherwise perfected for the priority to arise or continue.

The logical implication is that PMSIs should not have priority at all unless they comply with s. 33. The problem with this conclusion is that it disregards the statement in s. 38 that a subordination agreement is "effective according to its terms."

Contrast Wilson J's statement in *Engel* (at para. 53):

> Allowing the purchase of specified encumbered assets without granting priority in the encumbrance appears to be a hollow right that does not make commercial sense unless subordination is implicit.

The logical implication is that if SP1 allows D to create PMSIs, the PMSI should always have priority whether it complies with s. 33 or not. The problem with this conclusion is that it undermines the notice and timely registration requirements in s. 33.

The courts so far have steered a middle course between the two extremes, aiming to balance s. 33 and s. 38 by dealing with the issue on a case-by-case basis. The problem with the case-by-case approach is that it creates uncertainty: the cases turn on fine distinctions, so that a minor difference in drafting may affect the outcome. Uncertainty leads to more litigation because parties have no way of being sure what the court will say until it says it. Do you think an amendment is called for to solve the problem? If so, what form should the amendment take?

In *Euroclean*, Houlden JA referred to the view expressed by Peter Maddaugh in the Law Society of Upper Canada *Special Lectures 1982*, at pp. 361-62, that there is nothing in the Ontario Act to prohibit a generalized subordination given in advance and that mere use of the term "floating charge" in describing the security interest in the security agreement may implicitly carry with it a generalized subordination—"that is, the consent of the secured party to the debtor to deal with the charged collateral in the ordinary course of his business free of, or subordinate to, the lien represented by that charge."

Do you agree? Is this construction consistent with the explicit language of s. 11(2) of the Act? (Mr. Maddaugh was writing before the adoption of the 1989 Act, which added s. 11(2).)

See the discussion of s. 11(2) in Chapter 4, and the case law there cited. Granting that float-ing charge language in a security agreement must at least impute some sort of licence to the debtor to carry on the business, is it the same as saying that the secured party agrees to postpone its security interest *in its entirety* to a future crystallizing event? Would this not restore the common law position that s. 11(2) was at pains to reverse? Mr. Maddaugh was prescient, however, in anticipating that some Canadian courts would construe the debtor's licence to carry on business as implicitly subordinating the licensor's security interest to non-consensual security interests arising by operation of law during the debtor's business activity. See, for example, *Royal Bank of Canada v. Sparrow Electric Corp.*, [1997] 1 SCR 411, extracted in Chapter 4, Part IV.C.

CHAPTER NINE

Fixtures, Accessions, and Commingled Goods

I. INTRODUCTION

This chapter continues with the topic of priority rules dealt with in the previous chapter. Its focus is the conflict that arises when the collateral is deemed to have changed its character because of a transforming event. In the case of fixtures, the change has come about because the goods have been affixed to land. In that event, a dispute may arise between a person who has or acquires a security interest in the goods or fixture and a person who has or acquires an interest in the land to which the goods are affixed. There are various permutations, but here is one example:

> SP holds a security interest in D's machine. D fixes the machine to her factory floor. T holds a mortgage over the factory premises. D defaults against SP and T and they both claim the machine.

OPPSA s. 34 contains a series of priority rules aimed at this kind of dispute. The rules vary depending on whether: (1) the security interest attaches before or after the goods become a fixture; and (2) the competing party acquired its interest in the land before or after the goods became a fixture. For example, if the security interest attached before the goods became a fixture and the competing party had already acquired its interest in the land before the goods became a fixture, as in our example, the security interest has priority. The rationale is that otherwise the competing party would get a windfall at the secured party's expense because the competing party would not have had the fixture in mind at the time it acquired its interest in the land. On the other hand, if the goods become a fixture before the competing party acquires its interest in the land and the security interest has already attached at that point, the competing party has priority unless the secured party filed a notice of its interest in the Land Registry Office before the competing party's acquisition. The rationale is that, in the absence of notice, the competing party is likely to assume that its acquisition includes the fixture. Note that in this case, the secured party's priority depends on registration, not in the PPS register, but in the Land Registry Office. This is the place where a prospective purchaser of the land is most likely to search, and it avoids the need for prospective land purchasers to search twice.

In the case of accessions, a component (the "accessory") has been added to a larger item (the "principal goods") so as to become part of the whole. In that event, a dispute may arise between a person who has or acquires a security interest in the accessory and a person who has or acquires an interest in the principal goods. For example:

> SP1 holds a security interest in D's truck. SP1 supplies D with new tires pursuant to a conditional sale agreement and D fits the tires to the truck. D defaults against both SP1 and SP2. SP1 claims the tires on the basis that they have become part of the truck and SP2 claims them relying on its rights under the conditional sale agreement.

This is analogous to the fixtures example given above, and OPPSA s. 35 contains a set of rules, paralleling the fixtures rules in s. 34, for the resolution of disputes involving accessions.

The commingling of goods involves goods from different sources that lose their separate identities when they are mixed together or when they are used as components or ingredients in the manufacture or production of an entirely new product or mass. For example:

> SP1 supplies D with flour pursuant to a conditional sale agreement and SP2 supplies D with eggs, also pursuant to a conditional sale agreement. D uses the flour and eggs to make pancakes and subsequently defaults against both SP1 and SP2, who both claim the pancakes.

OPPSA s. 37 contains rules aimed at this and related kinds of dispute.

II. FIXTURES

A. Introduction

Goods are frequently bought and then, while they are still subject to a security interest, attached to land. (By "land" we include of course any attachment to a structure or building that is itself treated as having become part of the land.) Alternatively, after the goods have become fixtures, their owner may wish to pledge them separately from the land either because the fixture owner does not own the land or because the fixture owner wishes to use the fixture (for example, a machine cemented to the floor) as collateral together with other equipment and machinery that have not become attached to the land. The term "fixture" is often used indiscriminately to describe (a) goods that have become attached to land but have retained their separate identity, and (b) goods that have become an integral part of the land or a building on the land: for example, bricks in a wall. For the purpose of analyzing the statutory provisions and the case law referred to in this section, it will be helpful to distinguish between the following three categories of goods: (1) goods that are on the land to be used for the better enjoyment of the land but have never become physically attached to it; (2) goods that have become attached to the land but are not an integral part of it (true fixtures); and (3) goods that have become an integral part of the land.

Nineteenth-century Anglo-Canadian law generally favoured realty interests and readily found that goods attached to land had become part of the realty and had lost their separate identity as goods. See, for example, Blackburn J's judgment in *Holland v. Hodgson* (1872), LR 7 CP 328. This meant that those who had claims to the land (landlords, realty mortgagees, etc.) could also claim the fixtures. There were some exceptions to the rule, of which a tenant's right to remove household or trade fixtures on or before the termination of the tenancy was one of the best known. However, the exceptions were not significant enough to allay the misgivings of conditional sellers in the 19th century who realistically anticipated that the goods sold by them would or might become fixtures.

Their response was to include a clause in the security agreement providing that the goods were to remain chattels even if they were affixed to land; surprisingly, early Ontario and Manitoba courts upheld the effectiveness of such clauses. However, the English Court of Appeal rejected such sleights of hand in *Hobson v. Gorringe*, [1897] 1 Ch. 182, and the House of Lords did the same shortly afterward in *Reynolds v. Ashby*, [1904] AC 466. (Does this suggest that English courts were more realty oriented than Canadian courts?)

Hobson v. Gorringe sufficiently disturbed the burgeoning installment sales industry in Ontario that they were able to persuade the Ontario legislature to adopt a neutralizing amendment almost as soon as news of the English Court of Appeal's decision reached Canada's shores: see Stat. Ont., 60 Vict., c. 3, s. 3 and c. 14, s. 80. This provided that:

> (1) Where any goods or chattels subject to the provisions of this Act are affixed to any realty without the consent in writing of the owner of the goods or chattels, such goods and chattels shall notwithstanding remain so subject, but the owner of such realty, or any purchaser, or any mortgagee, or other incumbrancer on such realty, shall have the right as against the manufacturer, bailor or vendor of such goods or chattels, or any person claiming through or under them, to retain the said goods and chattels upon payment of the amount due and owing thereon.

The same provision was reproduced (but without any reference to the seller's consent not having been obtained to the affixation of the goods) in the *Uniform Conditional Sales Act* adopted by the Canadian Uniformity Commissioners in 1922.

In *Hoppe v. Manners*, [1931] 2 DLR 253, the Ontario Court of Appeal unexpectedly held that, the statutory provision notwithstanding, goods subject to a security interest became part of the realty on their affixation to the land, and that conditional sellers would have to comply with the registration requirements under the Registry Acts if they wished to protect their interests against the claims of subsequent realty interests in the land. This decision led both Ontario and the Uniformity Commissioners to modify substantially their respective provisions. In both cases, the conditional seller was now required to register a copy of the conditional sale agreement in the appropriate land registry office *as well as* in the conditional sales registry. It was also made clear that the seller's right to remove the goods on default did not apply to "building materials" or to fixtures that could not be removed without substantial injury to the land. On all the above, see further Goode and Ziegel, *Hire-Purchase and Conditional Sale: A Comparative Survey of Commonwealth and American Law* (London: British Institute of International and Comparative Law, 1965), at 173-78; and W.J. Tremeear, *A Treatise on the Canadian Law of Conditional Sales of Chattels and of Chattel Liens* (Toronto: Canada Law Book, 1899), at 116-19.

The PPS legislation in Canada has introduced some important changes to the treatment of security interests in fixtures. Section 34 of the OPPSA is based on the 1962 version of UCC 9-313 and reproduces s. 36 of the old Act with only minor amendments. Note in particular the following features: (1) s. 34 distinguishes between security interests in the chattels created *after* as well as before the chattels became fixtures (the pre-PPSA conditional sales Acts only covered pre-affixation security interests); (2) a similar distinction is drawn between interests in real property created before and after affixation of the chattels to the land; (3) if the security interest in the chattel is created *before* affixation, it prevails over the claim of any person with an interest in the real property; (4) if the security interest in the chattel is created *after* affixation, it is subject to existing interests in the real property; (5) in situations (2) and (3), a security interest in the fixture is subordinated to the interests of subsequent purchasers and mortgagees of the real property without knowledge of the security interest. Section 54 provides for the filing of a notice in prescribed form in the Land Registry Office, and also provides that such notice constitutes deemed knowledge of the security interest for the purpose of s. 34(2) of the Act; (6) if the secured party wishes to seize and remove the fixture, it must reimburse any encumbrancer or owner of the real property for the cost of repairing "any physical injury" caused by the removal but excluding any diminution in the value of the real property caused by the removal of the chattel; and (7) a person with an interest in the real property may retain the fixture on paying the balance owing under the security agreement.

B. Meaning of "Fixture"

Cormier v. Federal Business Development Bank
(1983), 3 PPSAC 161 (Ont. Co. Ct.)

SALHANY Co. Ct. J: At issue in this application is who is entitled to possession of five items of machinery and equipment which are situate on the premises owned by the applicants and which had been leased to Country Squire Auto Body Limited under an oral lease which expired on February 17, 1983, when Country Squire made an assignment in bankruptcy. The Federal Business Development Bank claims priority under a chattel mortgage dated September 11, 1979, on four of those items. The Continental Bank claims priority and seeks to recover the fifth, namely, a Black Hawk Power-Cage Serial No. BHYPC 35, which it sold to Country Squire pursuant to a conditional sales contract dated the 2nd of July 1980. On July 15, 1982, a chattel mortgage in writing was given to the Toronto-Dominion Bank on all five items of equipment. However, the Toronto-Dominion Bank has not entered an appearance in this application or taken any position with respect to its entitlement to recover any of the items covered by its security.

The facts are not in dispute and have been settled by an agreed statement prepared by the parties. They may be summarized as follows:

1. The applicants are the owners in joint tenancy of the lands and premises at 6 Forwell Road in Kitchener pursuant to a deed registered on March 8, 1968. Located on that property is a commercial building containing 16,000 square feet.

2. In 1977, the applicants rented the premises to Country Squire Auto Body Limited to operate an automobile and truck body repair business. No written lease was ever executed by the parties. Initially, only part of the premises was rented but later Country Squire expanded its business to occupy the entire building for the annual rental of $5,900.

3. Apparently the principals of Country Squire, Thomas and Barbara Stoliker, had expressed to the applicants a desire to purchase the premises at some time in the future. On May 15, 1981, this intention was formalized by a deed registered on that day conveying the property to Thomas and Barbara Stoliker. The purchaser price was $543,500 payable $7,500 by way of cash, the assumption of a first mortgage of $96,500 and the balance of $439,500 secured by way of a second mortgage given by the Stolikers to the applicants. Country Squire continued to rent the premises from the Stolikers upon the same terms.

4. In February of 1983 the second mortgage went into default. As a result, the Stolikers gave a quitclaim of the property to the applicants by a deed which was registered on February 17, 1983. At the same time, the lease to Country Squire was terminated by mutual agreement.

5. During the period that Country Squire was a tenant of the premises, the machinery and equipment which are the subject-matter of this application were installed on the premises. Those items are as follows:

    (a) an Ingersoll Rand Temprite Air Make Up unit;
    (b) a Bearcat frame straightener;
    (c) a Binks spray booth;
    (d) a Bee Line Optoflex alignment machine; and
    (e) a Black Hawk Power-Cage Serial No. BHYPC 35.

6. The Ingersoll Rand Temprite Air Make Up unit was installed by Country Squire with the knowledge and consent of the applicants prior to October 1977. The unit consists of two parts. The first performs a heating function and consists of a propane furnace mounted to the outside of the roof of the building, together with ducts leading from the furnace into the spray area. The second performs an exhaust function and consists of vents about 3½ feet in diameter leading from the floor to the roof.

7. The Bearcat frame straightener was installed on the premises by Country Squire with the knowledge and consent of the applicants in November 1978. It is a machine 25 feet long, 12 feet wide and weighs approximately five tons. Its purpose is to straighten the frame on small and medium sized vehicles. To install the machine it was necessary to remove an area of the original poured concrete floor and a new floor of 6-inch thick concrete was installed. This machine is fastened to the floor by 4 one-half-inch diameter lag bolts. Concrete pedestals were added at the contact points and a pit was constructed underneath the machine in order to enable a man to stand while working beneath the machine. The cost of installation was approximately $28,000 paid entirely by Country Squire. There was no discussion of any future restoration of the premises.

8. The Binks spray booth was installed on the premises by Country Squire with the knowledge and consent of the applicants in November of 1979. It measures 33 feet long by 14 feet in width and is secured to the floor by sixty-five 5/16-inch diameter lag bolts. A cement block pedestal was also added to the floor to

accommodate the spray booth. Exhaust fumes from the booth are vented to the outside of the building through a vent measuring 3½ feet in diameter, extending from the booth through the roof of the building.

9. The Bee Line Optoflex alignment machine was installed by Country Squire with the knowledge and consent of the applicants on November 23, 1979, and is used to align the wheels of automobiles and trucks. It consists of two parts: a machine upon which the vehicles are driven measuring 15 feet by 12 feet and a screen measuring 16 feet by 5 feet upon which the alignment of a vehicle's wheels may be measured. It weighs approximately two tons. To install it, it was necessary to remove an area of the original poured concrete floor measuring 17 feet by 18 feet and then lower the floor 2 feet below the original floor level and install a new floor of 6-inch thick reinforced concrete. The machine and screen are fastened to the floor each by four ¾-inch lag bolts. A pit deep enough to permit a man to stand while working was also constructed beneath the machine. The cost of installing the machine, including the price, was approximately $55,000 which was paid entirely by Country Squire. Country Squire never discussed future restoration of the premises with the applicants.

10. The Black Hawk Power Cage was installed by Country Squire with the knowledge and consent of the applicants over a two-week period in June of 1980. The machine is 36 feet in length, 12 feet in width, and weighs approximately five tons. It is used to straighten frames on large vehicles, trucks, buses and trailers. To install the machine, it was necessary to remove an area of the existing concrete floor measuring 20 feet by 43 feet. The floor was then lowered two feet below the original floor level and a new floor of 6-inch thick reinforced concrete was installed. Extensive renovations were then carried out to the building to accommodate the machine. This involved removing 11 wood trusses from the roof and replacing them with seven steel girders above the area of the machine. Two steel runners were also added to the ceiling to permit pulleys to be used along each side of the machine. Six steel I-beams were mounted on concrete pillars and placed around the area to support the weight of the roof. The purpose of this construction was to install various pulleys which are not essential to the operation of the cage. The cage itself is fastened to six 1-inch diameter lag bolts. Additional changes were also made to an overhead door and furnace duct work and electrical systems to accommodate the machine. The cost of installation, exclusive of the price of the machine, was approximately $29,000 which was paid by Country Squire. There was no discussion between Country Squire and the applicants about the future restoration of the premises. In addition to the construction work carried out to accommodate the machinery, Country Squire also constructed a concrete block room in a corner of a bay housing the Bearcat, Optoflex and Black Hawk machines in order to house an air compressor necessary to run the machinery. The compressor itself is secured to the floor by four bolts.

11. On September 24, 1979, the Federal Business Development Bank filed a financing statement under the Personal Property Security Act pertaining to their chattel

mortgage dated September 11, 1979. It covered, *inter alia*, the first four items which are the subject-matter of this application. That registration was amended on March 6, 1981, to record a change of the debtor's name and was renewed on August 26, 1982. The chattel mortgage was to secure the principal sum of $55,000.

12. On July 24, 1980, the Continental Bank of Canada filed a financing statement under the Personal Property Security Act pertaining to their conditional sale contract dated July 2, 1980, on the Black Hawk Power-Cage. That financing statement was to secure the sum of $113,266 made up of the principal amount of $78,115 and financing charges of $35,151.

13. Following the quitclaim deed, the Federal Business Development Bank made an arrangement to pay the applicants' occupation rent of $1,058 per month pending the resolution of the dispute as to entitlement to the machinery. Rent has been paid since March of 1983 to date.

It was argued on behalf of the applicants that all of the machinery and equipment had been affixed to the realty in such a manner that it should be considered part of the realty. Since there was no agreement to the contrary, the respondents, who were claiming through the tenant, had no right to remove these fixtures unless they could establish that they had priority under the Personal Property Security Act, RSO 1980, c. 375 (PPSA).

The respondents' position, on the other hand, was that this machinery and equipment was never really affixed to the realty except for the purpose of steadying the equipment and permitting it to be used properly. It was further argued that, even if it was found to be affixed to the realty and became part of the freehold, nevertheless it could be severed because it was for the purpose of carrying on a trade, in which case it ceased to be "fixtures." Upon resuming its character as chattels, it could be removed by the respondents provided that such removal could be effected without serious injury to the freehold and before the expiration of the term, unless the time for removal was extended by agreement. It was further submitted that even if the machinery and equipment constituted fixtures within the meaning of the PPSA, then their security interest on the machinery and equipment gave them a claim in priority to that of the applicants under the Act.

The general rule at common law was that whatever was affixed to the freehold became part of it and subject to the laws governing the freehold. Over the years a number of exceptions arose to alleviate the harsh results of this inflexible doctrine. These exceptions were in relation to chattels which were used for the purpose of carrying on a trade or of domestic convenience or ornament. Such chattels, though affixed to the realty, could still be severed in which case they ceased to be "fixtures" and resumed their character as chattels. In such instance, they could be removed by the tenant or his assigns provided that such removal could be effected without serious injury to the freehold and provided that the tenant removed them before the expiration of the tenancy or before any time for removal which had been extended by agreement between the parties: see Canadian Law of Landlord and Tenant by Williams and Rhodes (5th ed.), at 3-10, 13-30; Canadian Law of Real Property by Anger and Honsberger (1959), at 463-65, 485; and Report of the Ontario Law Reform Commission on "Landlord and Tenant Law" (1976), c. XIV.

In the course of their argument, counsel referred to a number of authorities supporting their contention that the machinery and equipment in question were or were not fixtures. It is apparent from a review of these decisions that often the decision reached by the Court depended on the particular facts before it. In *Stack v. T. Eaton Co.* (1902), 4 OLR 335 (CA), the leading case in Ontario, five rules were laid down to assist the Court in determining what constituted a fixture:

1. Articles not otherwise attached to the land than by their own weight are not to be considered as part of the land, unless the circumstances are such as to show that they were intended to be part of the land;

2. Articles affixed to the land, even slightly, are to be considered part of the land unless circumstances are such as to show that they were intended to continue to be chattels;

3. The circumstances necessary to be shown to alter the *prima facie* character of the articles are circumstances which show the degree of annexation and the object of such annexation, which are patent for all to see;

4. The intention of the parties affixing the article to the soil is material only so far as it can be presumed from the degree and object of the annexation; and

5. Even in the case of tenant's fixtures put in for the purpose of trade, they form part of the freehold, with the right, however, to the tenant, as between him and his landlord, to bring them back to the state of chattels again by severing them from the soil, and they pass by a conveyance of the land as part of it subject to this right of the tenant.

In *Argles v. McMath* (1894), 26 OR 224 (HC), affirmed, 23 OAR 44, Armour CJ stressed the distinction that had to be drawn between fixtures which he described as fixtures in the primary sense and were irremovable and fixtures in the secondary sense of the term which were removable. Fixtures in the secondary sense of the term included fixtures affixed to the freehold for the purpose of trade or of domestic convenience or ornament and gave to the tenant qualified property rights in them. See also *Carscallen v. Moodie* (1858), 15 UCQB 304 (CA).

I am satisfied on the material before me that the five pieces of machinery and equipment which are the subject matter of this application were for the purpose of carrying on a trade. Even if it can be said that these articles were "affixed to the land even slightly" and thus were "to be considered part of the land" within Rule 2, I am of the view that the tenant or the assignee of the tenant was entitled "to bring them back to the state of chattels again by severing them from the soil" (Rule 5).

Counsel for the respondents submitted that, when Country Squire went into default on the security agreements held by the respondents, this enabled them to step into the shoes of Country Squire as assignees (*Devine v. Callery* (1917), 40 OLR 505, 38 DLR 542 (CA)) or as successors in interest (*Gillett v. Lawrence's Ltd.*, [1922] 2 WWR 584, 14 Sask. LR 438 (CA)) and to sever the fixtures from the land and to remove them as chattels. Thus, it was argued that this enabled the respondents to sever and remove the machinery and equipment in the same way that Country Squire would have been able to do had they not given up their lease to the applicant.

In my view, the fact that there has been a default under a chattel mortgage or conditional sales agreement does not automatically make a secured creditor an assignee or a successor in interest of the debtor in the absence of some agreement in writing or otherwise transferring the debtor's interest to the creditor. This submission also ignores the fact that the PPSA and its predecessor statutes such as the Conditional Sales Act, RSO 1970, c. 76 (but not the Chattel Mortgages Act) have sought to settle the competing interests of landlords and secured creditors to fixtures. Accordingly, it is important to consider the provisions of the PPSA to determine whether the priority rules in that Act resolve the competing interests to the parties in this application.

Section 2(a) of the PPSA makes the Act apply:

(a) to every transaction without regard to its form and without regard to the person who has title to the collateral that in substance creates a security interest, including, without limiting the foregoing.

(i) a chattel mortgage, conditional sale, equipment trust, floating charge, pledge, trust deed or trust receipt, and ...

Section 36 [now s. 34] of the Act provides:

36(1) Subject to subsection (3) of this section and notwithstanding subsection 34(3), a security interest that attached to goods before they became fixtures has priority as to the goods over the claim of any person who has an interest in the real property.

(2) Subject to subsection (3), a security interest that attached to goods after they became fixtures has priority over the claim of any person who subsequently acquired an interest in the real property, but not over any person who had a registered interest in the real property at the time the security interest attached to the goods and who has not consented in writing to the security interest or disclaimed an interest in the goods as fixtures.

(3) The security interest referred to in subsections (1) and (3) are subordinate to the interest of,

(a) a subsequent purchaser or mortgagee for value of an interest in the real property;

(b) a creditor with a lien on the real property subsequently obtained as a result of judicial process; or

(c) a creditor with a prior encumbrance of record on the real property in respect of subsequent advances,

if the subsequent purchase or mortgage was made or the lien was obtained or the subsequent advance under the prior encumbrance was made or contracted for, as the case may be, without actual notice of the security interest.

(4) If a secured party, by virtue of subsection (1) or (2) and subsection (3), has priority over the claim of a person having an interest in the real property, he may on default, subject to the provisions of this Act respecting default, remove his collateral from the real property if, unless otherwise agreed, he reimburses any encumbrancer or owner of the real property who is not the debtor for the cost of repairing any physical injury excluding diminution in the value of the real property caused by the absence of the goods removed or by the necessity for replacement, but a person so entitled to reimbursement may refuse permission to

remove until the secured party has given adequate security for any reimbursement arising under this subsection.

(5) A person having an interest in real property that is subordinate to a security interest by virtue of subsection (1) or (2) and subsection (3) may, before the collateral has been removed from the real property by the secured party in accordance with subsection (4), retain the collateral upon payment to the secured party of the amount owing under the security interest having priority over his claim.

Subsection 34(3) [now s. 33(2)] referred to in s. 36(1) provides that:

(3) A purchase-money security interest in collateral or its proceeds, other than inventory, has priority over any other security interest in the same collateral if the purchase-money security interest was perfected at the time the debtor obtained possession of the collateral or within ten days thereafter.

...

Unfortunately, the term "fixture" is not defined in the Act. Thus no distinction is made between a fixture "in the primary sense" which may not be severed from the freehold and a fixture "in the secondary sense" which may be severed if it is for the purpose of carrying on a trade or of a domestic convenience or ornament. If the term "fixture" as used in the Act is intended to cover all fixtures, even ones which may be severed and removed by the tenant, then the provisions of s. 36 would apply insofar as the rights of the parties are concerned. On the other hand, if the term "fixtures" was restricted to only those which cannot be severed, then the provisions of the PPSA would not apply and the competing claims of the parties would have to be settled by the common law.

In my view, the word "fixtures" was intended to cover all chattels attached to the land by the tenant whether they are removable or not. Since the common law has always regarded trade, domestic or ornamental fixtures as "fixtures" until the tenant exercised his right of severance and removal, it seems to me that it must have been the intention of the Legislature to include all chattels attached to the land even if they are subject to severance. I find support in that view from the inclusion of s. 36(4) of the Act. It is incomprehensible to me that the Legislature would give to a secured creditor a right to remove fixtures not generally severable from the freehold beyond the term of the tenancy and not that same right to fixtures which are severable. That was the view reached by the Ontario Court of Appeal in *Hoppe v. Manners*, 66 OLR 587, [1931] 2 DLR 253, dealing with the meaning of fixtures under the Conditional Sales Act and supports the conclusions which I have reached.

Turning now to the claim of the respondents, the agreed statement of facts indicates that the Ingersoll Rand Temprite Air Make Up unit and the Bearcat frame straightener were affixed to the property prior to the chattel mortgage, and the Binks spray booth and the Bee Line Optoflex alignment machine subsequent thereto. Applying the conditions set out in s. 12 defining the time of attachment, I find that attachment occurred on September 11, 1979, when the chattel mortgage was executed at which time the principal funds were advanced to the tenant. Thus s. 36(1) gives the Federal Business Development Bank priority with respect to the last two items over the claim of any person who has an interest in the property and who is not a person mentioned in subs. (3). At that time the applicants were the owners of the property and therefore their claim to those two items is subordinate to the claim of the Federal Business Development Bank by s. 36(1). Nor does s. 36(3) assist the applicants. Even if they did become the registered owners after the receipt of the quitclaim deed, it can be hardly said that they were a subsequent purchaser for value without actual notice of the security interest. On the other hand, because the applicants were the registered owners of the property when the first two items became fixtures, I am of the view that s. 36(2) gives them a claim in priority to that of the Federal Business Development Bank unless they "consented in writing to the security interest or disclaimed an interest in the goods as fixtures." Since there has been no such consent or disclaimer, I find that the applicants are entitled to retain these two items.

The Black Hawk Power-Cage was installed and became a fixture in June of 1980 prior to the execution of the conditional sales agreement on July 2, 1980. However, I am of the view that the date of the execution of a conditional sale contract is not necessarily determinative of when attachment occurred under s. 12. As was noted by Arnup JA in *Rogerson Lbr. Co. v. Four Seasons Chalet Ltd.* (1980), 29 OR (2d) 193, 1 PPSAC 160, 12 BLR 93, 36 CBR (NS) 141, 113 DLR (3d) 671 (CA), the provision for retention of title in the vendor is not invalidated by the PPSA unless there is an agreement in writing and registered pursuant to the Act as there was under s. 10(b) of the Conditional Sales Act, RSO 1970, c. 76.

As indicated earlier, s. 12 [now s. 11(2)] requires three conditions to exist before attachment occurs:

1. the parties must intend it to attach;

2. value must be given; and

3. the debtor has rights in the collateral.

I am prepared to concede that the validity of a conditional sales agreement is not dependent upon there being an agreement in writing. Thus, there may be instances when the parties may agree orally that a security interest will attach immediately even though the agreement is subsequently formalized by a document in writing. However, there is no indication in the agreed statement of facts that Country Squire had any meeting with the Continental Bank prior to June of 1980 from which it can be inferred that it was intended that the security interest was to attach at that time. Nor is there any indication when the sum of $2,000 was paid by Country Squire as a down payment which would enable me to find that value was given before installation of the Black Hawk Power-Cage. I am simply asked to infer that such arrangements took place prior to installation; otherwise Country Squire would not have been in a position to purchase the equipment. It is equally consistent, however, that the arrangements for financing were made immediately after installation, that is, when the contract was signed. In the absence of any such evidence, the only conclusion that I can come to on the evidence is that the security interest attached when the conditional sales agreement was signed on July 2, 1980. Since the Black Hawk Power-Cage became a fixture prior to that time, s. 36(2) gives the applicant a prior claim over that of the Continental Bank.

In view of the foregoing reasons, the applicants are entitled to the Ingersoll Rand Temprite Air Make Up unit, the Bearcat frame straightener, and the Black Hawk Power-Cage serial No. BHYPC 35. The respondent, Federal Business Development Bank, is entitled to receive the Binks Spray Booth and the Bee Line Optoflex alignment machine upon payment of the costs of removal pursuant to s. 36(4).

Counsel may speak to me to arrange a time to present their submissions on the cost of removal at which time the issue of costs may also be spoken to.

Addendum

SALHANY Co. Ct. J: Mr. Earnshaw has applied pursuant to Rr. 528 and 529 requesting that I reconsider my findings as to who is entitled to recover the Black Hawk Power-Cage. In my reasons delivered October 25, 1983, I determined that as between the plaintiffs and the Continental Bank of Canada, the plaintiffs had priority under the Personal Property Security Act.

Mr. Earnshaw, on behalf of the Federal Business Development Bank, points out that there must have been a misunderstanding because his notice of motion specifically seeks a determination as to his client's entitlement to the Black Hawk Power-Cage even though the agreed statement of facts may not clearly set out that such a claim has been asserted.

Mr. Bumstead agreed that this was his understanding but says that this matter should be more properly dealt with by way of appeal. However, he concedes that he was contacted the day following the release of my judgment and advised that he intended to have this issue clarified when the matter resumed for determination of the remaining issues raised in the notice of motion. I am satisfied that no prejudice will result to the plaintiffs by a determination of this issue at this stage of the proceedings, and I will proceed to do so.

On p. 171 of my earlier decision, I held that s. 36(1) of the Personal Property Security Act gave the Federal Business Development Bank priority with respect to any chattel installed on the property after attachment occurred on September 11, 1979, over the claim of any person who had an interest in the property and who was not a person in s. 36(3) of the Act. I also held that since the applicants were the owners of the property at the time of attachment their claim was subordinate with respect to any chattels attaching after that time. Thus, it follows that although the applicants have a claim in priority over the Continental Bank of Canada to the Black Hawk Power-Cage, that claim is subordinate to the claim of the Federal Business Development Bank. Accordingly, the Federal Business Development Bank will also be entitled to recover the Black Hawk Power-Cage.

Order accordingly.

NOTES AND QUESTIONS

1) Note that the priority rule in OPPSA s. 34(1)(a) does not depend on perfection of the security interest in the fixture. Can you see why?

2) In *Cormier*, the court held that the disputed equipment was tenant's (or trade) fixtures. As the judgment makes clear, the distinguishing characteristic of tenant's fixtures is that the tenant retains a right of removal and, upon removal, they lose their connection with the land and go back to being goods pure and simple. In *Cormier*, the landlords' claim depended on the fact that Country Squire (the debtor/tenant) had not removed the equipment because otherwise the landlords would have had no claim to them by virtue of owning the premises. As an alternative to the fixtures argument, the landlords might have claimed a

right of distress over the equipment. This is conceptually the reverse of the fixtures argument: the fixtures argument depends on characterizing the equipment as realty, whereas the distress argument depends on characterizing it as personalty (since the landlord's right of distress is limited to goods on the leased premises). Does the landlord's right of distress extend to tenant's fixtures? See *859587 Ontario Ltd. v. Starmark Property Management Ltd.* (1998), 40 OR (3d) 481 (CA), extracted below.

3) The court's treatment in *Cormier* of the Black Hawk Power Cage raises some tricky questions. The court concluded that the bank had priority over the landlords by virtue of OPPSA s. [34(1)(a)], that the bank also had priority over Continental by virtue of OPPSA s. [30(1)], and that the landlords had priority over Continental by virtue of OPPSA s. [34(1)(b)]. Therefore, the final priority ranking was: (1) FBDB; (2) the landlords; and (3) Continental. This conclusion is questionable in several respects. First, it overlooks the fact that FBDB's security interest did not attach to the cage until after it had become a fixture because the cage was installed on the land before the conclusion of Continental's security agreement with the debtor. On this basis, the court should have applied [s. 34(1)(b)], not [s. 34(1)(a)] and, under the second part of [s. 34(1)(b)], the landlords were entitled to priority. Second, the court's conclusion that FBDB had priority over Continental appears to overlook the fact that Continental held a PMSI in the cage so that Continental may have had priority by virtue of [s. 33(2)]. On this basis, it seems that the correct priority ranking should have been: (1) the landlords; (2) Continental; and (3) FBDB.

4) The OPPSA s. 34 fixtures provisions potentially raise circular priorities problems in their interaction with other priority rules. For example:

A has a security interest in all of D's equipment. Some of the equipment has become fixtures in D's plant. On February 1, A registered a financing statement in the chattel security registry but failed to file a notice pursuant to OPPSA s. 54. B also acquired a security interest in the same fixtures and properly filed its financing statement and s. 54 notice, both on April 15. On April 30, D gave C a mortgage on its land that was duly registered in the Land Registry Office.

With regard to circular priorities generally, see Chapter 7, Part VIII. For an actual case involving a circular priorities dispute between a fixture security interest and two competing realty interests, see *GMS Securities and Appraisals Limited v. Rich-Wood Kitchens Limited* (1995), 21 OR (3d) 761 (CA), criticized in Ronald C.C. Cuming, Catherine Walsh, and Roderick J. Wood, *Personal Property Security Law* (Toronto: Irwin Law, 2005), at pp. 494-96.

C. Fixtures and Landlord's Right of Distress

859587 Ontario Ltd. v. Starmark Property Management Ltd.
(1998), 40 OR (3d) 481 (CA)

DOHERTY JA: This is an appeal from the judgment of Dambrot J declaring that the appellant's (Starmark Property Management Limited) distraint and sale of a spray paint booth located on property leased by Starmark to a tenant was unlawful. Dambrot J further held that the respondent, Atlantic International Equipment Sales, the vendor of the booth under the terms of a conditional sales contract, was entitled to reacquire possession of it upon compliance with s. 34(4) and (5) of the Personal Property Security Act, RSO 1990, c. P.10 (PPSA).

The essential facts are these:

- In February 1996, H.K. Auto Centre rented certain premises from Starmark.

- Under the terms of the lease, all improvements, except trade fixtures, became the property of Starmark when the lease expired. The tenant was required to remove trade fixtures at its own expense at the expiration of the lease. The lease gave the tenant very limited rights to remove and replace trade fixtures during the term of the lease. That limited right was not available if the tenant was in default under the lease.

- In March 1996, Atlantic sold the spray booth to H.K. Auto Centre for $27,659. Under the terms of the agreement, ownership of the booth remained with Atlantic until all payments had been made. Atlantic did not register its agreement under the PPSA.

- The booth was installed in the leased premises in March 1996.

- The booth was 28 feet by 14 feet and weighed some 3,500 pounds. It was attached to the floor by numerous small nails which could be easily removed and was connected by various pipes to the electrical, water and air systems within the leased premises. Exhaust fumes from the booth were expelled through a vent which exited the building through a hole in the roof. The vent was bolted to the roof.

- In September 1996, H.K. Auto Centre owed rent arrears of about $12,000. Starmark levied a distress on the leased premises and took possession of the spray booth. The booth remained on the rented premises in the same condition it was in prior to the distraint.

- At the time of the distraint, H.K. Auto Centre had paid about $11,000 toward the purchase of the spray booth and owed Atlantic about $17,000.

- Starmark sold the spray booth to a third party who had agreed to lease the space formerly leased by H.K. Auto Centre.

- Atlantic became aware of the purported sale, registered its conditional sales agreement under the PPSA and commenced these proceedings.

Starmark claims that it was entitled to sell the spray booth and apply the proceeds to pay the rent arrears either because the booth was a fixture and became part of the property which it owned, or because the spray booth was a chattel, and although owned by Atlantic, was subject to distraint under s. 31(2) of the Landlord and Tenant Act, RSO 1990, c. L.7. Atlantic takes the position that the spray booth was not subject to distraint as it was a fixture and that under the terms of s. 34 of the PPSA, its interest had priority over Starmark's interest.

Dambrot J made a careful and detailed analysis of the evidence and the issues. His reasons are reported (1997), 34 OR (3d) 43, 10 RPR (3d) 238, and as I am in substantial agreement with them, I need not repeat much of what appears in those reasons.

Dambrot J found that the spray booth was a trade or tenant's fixture. That finding involved the application of long-established legal principles to largely uncontested facts. As Dambrot J neither misapprehended the evidence, nor the applicable law, his finding must stand unless it is unreasonable. Given the manner in which the equipment was attached to the land, the terms of the lease, and the purpose of the attachment (i.e., to improve the functioning of the machinery and not to improve the property), I think the characterization of the spray booth as a fixture and not as a chattel was a close call. I cannot say, however, that Dambrot J's characterization was unreasonable. The case must be approached on the basis that the spray booth was a trade fixture.

Can a landlord distrain against a trade fixture? If the answer is yes, then when Starmark distrained against the spray booth it acquired a lien over that property: *Commercial Credit Corp. v. Harry D. Shields Ltd.* (1981), 32 OR (2d) 703, 122 DLR (3d) 736 (CA), affirming (1980), 29 OR (2d) 106, 112 DLR (3d) 153 (HCJ). Under the terms of s. 4(1)(a) and s. 20(1)(a)(i) of the PPSA, that lien would have priority over the security interest of Atlantic which was unperfected when the distraint occurred and the lien arose: *Leavere v. Port Colborne (City)* (1995), 22 OR (3d) 44 at pp. 49-50, 122 DLR (4th) 200 (CA).

As Dambrot J observed, a landlord's right to distrain against trade fixtures is a matter of some controversy in the case law. Most of those cases come from the last century and make difficult reading for those unschooled in the intricacies and idiosyncrasies of the common law of real property. As I understand the old cases, they describe two situations in which things placed on the leased premises by the tenant for the purpose of carrying out the tenant's business could not be distrained by the landlord. First, if the thing had become fixed to the property so as to become part of it, it could not be distrained. Second, even if the thing had not become affixed to the property so as to become part of it, it could not be distrained if, upon payment of the arrears, it could not be returned to the tenant in the same condition it was in before the distraint. This second qualification on the landlord's power to distrain developed when distraint required the actual removal of the goods from the leased premises to a pound. If that removal would damage the property so as to render restitution in the same condition impossible, then the property could not be distrained: *Hellawell v. Eastwood* (1851), 6 Exch. 295, 155 ER 554 at p. 295, 561 …

As indicated above, Dambrot J found that the spray booth was a trade fixture. A trade fixture is a thing which has become part of the property, is used by the tenant in the tenant's business and is removable at the instance of the tenant: *Deloitte & Touche Inc. v. 1035839 Ontario Inc.* (1996), 28 OR (3d) 139 at p. 150 (Gen. Div.), affirmed without reference to this point, June 23, 1998 (CA) [now reported 39 OR (3d) 607n]. The status of trade fixtures while they are attached to and are part of the property was explained by Meredith CJ in *Stack v. T. Eaton Co.* (1902), 4 OLR 335 at p. 338 (Div. Ct.):

> That, even in the case of tenants' fixtures put in for the purposes of trade, they form part of the freehold, with the right, however, to the tenant, as between him and his landlord, to bring them back to the state of chattels again by severing them from the soil, and that they pass by a conveyance of the land as part of it, subject to this right of the tenant.

A trade fixture is as much a part of the freehold as any immovable fixture as long as the trade fixture has not been severed from the freehold by the tenant at the time of the distraint. As distraint runs against the tenant's property found on the land and not against the land itself, it follows that trade fixtures which are part of the land at the time of the purported distraint cannot be subject to distraint: *Crossley Brothers Ltd. v. Lee*, [[1908] 1 KB 86] at p. 90; *Provincial Bill Posting Co. v. Low Moor Iron Co.*, [1909] 2 KB 344 at p. 349, 78 LJKB 702 (CA); *Bailey v. Miller*, [1932] 3 WWR 260 at p. 263 (Sask. CA); *Bruce v. Smith*, [1923] 3 DLR 887 at p. 889, 19 Alta. LR 523 (CA); *Cashman Holdings Ltd. v. Canada Trustco Mortgage Co.* (1990), 1 CBR (3d) 80 at p. 85 (BCSC).

...

It has long been established that immovable fixtures are not distrainable at common law. Trade fixtures are different from immovable fixtures in that they can be restored to the status of chattels at the option of the tenant. Despite that difference, trade fixtures have been treated, certainly in this province, as true fixtures as long as they are attached to and part of the land. The strong weight of authority supports the position that as long as trade fixtures are fixtures, they are no more subject to distraint than immovable fixtures. The complaint that this position makes the landlord's right to distrain depend, in some cases, on matters as inconsequential as a few screws or nails has validity, but is not a new complaint: see *Crossley Brothers Ltd. v. Lee*, supra. Although the landlord and tenant relationship is now closely regulated by statute, the Legislature has not seen fit to abandon the common law distinction between fixtures and other goods and chattels of the tenant for the purpose of determining the landlord's right of distraint. Nor has the Legislature altered the common law definition of fixture applicable to the law of distraint. As long as the common law prevails, the manner in which the property is attached to the land will be a significant consideration when deciding whether property is subject to distraint.

In the absence of any legislative initiative, I do not think it would be wise for the judiciary to strike out on a different course and formulate a new approach to the determination of the landlord's rights to distrain property on a leased premise. The present law as to the nature of trade fixtures has been settled in this province for over 90 years. I am not convinced that a different approach would yield benefits that would offset the inevitable uncertainty that a new approach would engender.

Having determined that Dambrot J correctly held that the tenant had no right of distraint against the spray booth and hence no lien, I move to s. 34 of the PPSA. That section settles priorities between those who have a security interest in a fixture and those who have an interest in the property to which the fixture is attached. ... The scheme created by s. 34 constitutes a legislative determination that the annexation of secured goods to realty should not result in the loss of a security interest which had attached but had not been perfected prior to the goods becoming part of the land: *Surrey Metro Savings Credit Union v. Chestnut Hill Homes Inc.* (1997), 29 BLR (2d) 43 at pp. 50-51, 30 BCLR (3d) 92 (SC).

It was argued that s. 34 applies only to immovable fixtures and not to trade fixtures. The case law reviewed above denies the validity of that distinction. Nor does s. 34 qualify the use of the word "fixture." Indeed, s. 34(3), which gives the secured interest holder a qualified right to remove the secured goods from the property, strongly supports the conclusion that s. 34 applies to trade fixtures. I would align myself with those authorities which have so held: *Deloitte & Touche v. 1035839 Ontario Inc.*, supra; *Cormier v. Federal*

Business Development Bank (1984), 25 BLR 194 at p. 205 (Ont. Co. Ct.). Section 34 of the PPSA applies to this case.

Section 34(1)(a) is the applicable subsection. Even though Atlantic did not perfect its security interest until after distraint proceedings, it had, under the terms of s. 11 of the PPSA, an attached security interest at the time the spray booth was installed on Starmark's property. Starmark had no interest in the spray booth before it became a fixture. Under the terms of s. 34(1)(a), Atlantic's attached secured interest had priority over Starmark's claim which arose out of its interest in the real property. Atlantic was entitled to reacquire the property under s. 34.

Appeal dismissed.

NOTES

1) As Doherty JA remarks in the *Starmark* case, the rule that a landlord cannot distrain against trade fixtures is a "matter of some controversy in the case law" and can give rise to fine distinctions ("a few screws or nails"). However, he declined the opportunity to reconsider the law, on the ground that a new approach would engender "inevitable uncertainty." Do you agree? How should judges balance the need for certainty in the law with the need for legal change? For a discussion of some of the issues, see "Panel Discussion on the Supreme Court's Final Note Decision" (2001), 36 *CBLJ* 89.

2) "Fixture" is not defined in s. 36 of the old Act or s. 34 of the new Act. Does this mean that it retains its common law meaning or should the courts be willing to find even more readily than they were before that a chattel has become a fixture? How relevant is it for this purpose (a) that the secured party is given a broad right under s. 34(3) to remove the fixture subject only to making good any physical damage, and (b) that s. 34 requires him, as the holder of a security interest in a fixture, to register his claim in the Land Registry Office? It will be noted that in *Cormier's Case* (approved by the Court of Appeal in *Starmark*), Salhany Co. Ct. J applied the common law test of a fixture.

3) The definition of "personal property" in OPPSA s. 1(1) expressly excludes "building materials that have been affixed to the realty." This exclusion also appeared in the Ontario *Conditional Sales Act* and in the *Uniform Conditional Sales Act*. "Building materials" is not defined, but a frequently cited exposition of the meaning is that by O.E. Lennox, Assistant Master, in *Alexander v. McGillivray* (1931), 41 OWN 407-8:

> When the term "building materials" is used [in the Act], the ordinary ingredients such as lumber, mortar, brick and stone are the first to suggest themselves as logical illustrations. But on further consideration there are a great many other things that go into the construction of a building which do not come under these headings, which nevertheless are integral parts of the whole construction, as compared with other articles which are mere adjuncts or appendages. In determining what is building material it is necessary to consider the entire construction. Certain equipment that by itself would appear to come under the classification of a chattel, may in the general construction of a building become so closely interlinked and identified with other materials generally described as building material, that they must for all practical purposes be considered as building materials, within the meaning of s. 8. It would seem that, in

determining this question, similar principles must be applied as in dealing with the question of fixtures. The degree and the object of the annexation must be considered. No doubt the distinction here should not be so finely drawn as in the case of fixtures, but the underlying principle is the same.

Not surprisingly, courts have reached different conclusions in applying his test. Thermal windows in a building (*Rockett Lbr. Building Supplies Ltd. v. Papageorgiou* (1979), 30 CBR (NS) 183 (Ont. Co. Ct.)) and an electric motor truck scale to be used in a seed mill (*Chas. A. Hare Ltd. v. Payn* (1982), 2 PPSAC 93 (Ont. SC)) have been characterized as building materials for the purposes of s. 36; on the other hand, a furnace (*Collis v. Carew Lbr. Co.*, [1930] 4 DLR 996 (Ont. CA)) and even an elevator installed in an apartment building (*Montreal Trust Co. v. Goldaire Rentals Ltd.*, [1967] 1 OR 40 (HCJ)) were not so regarded under the earlier legislation. In *Manning v. Furnasman Heating Ltd.* (1985-86), 5 PPSAC 67 (Man. CA), Sullivan JA, at 77-78, also appears to have been influenced in his conclusion that a furnace had become part of the structure by the fact that the supplier could have filed a lien under the *Builders' Liens Act*, SM 1980-81, c. 7, s. 35. Why should this affect a secured party's rights under the OPPSA? What are the advantages to the secured party claiming under the PPSA rather than under a construction lien Act?

III. ACCESSIONS

The accessions rules in OPPSA s. 35 (corresponding to those in UCC 9-314 (9-335 in Revised Article 9)) are intended to mirror the fixtures rules in OPPSA s. 34. Are the situations in fact identical? Consider the following example:

D Co. buys an airplane for cash. Subsequently, D Co. decides to install an improved radio communications system in the aircraft. D Co. finances the acquisition of the equipment by giving SP a purchase-money security interest in it. SP duly registers a financing statement. Still later, D Co. sells the aircraft to T, but fails to disclose the outstanding security interest in SP's favour. T made a search in the PPS registry but found no financing statement involving the aircraft.* T made no other searches.

Should T have anticipated that there might be financing statements involving accessories in the aircraft? Suppose T subsequently sold the aircraft to U believing it had clear title to it. Should SP be entitled to assert its security interest against U even though U knew nothing about it and would not have discovered it by searching the registry under T's name? The example involves the familiar A-B-C-D problem discussed in Chapter 6, Parts III.E.1 and IV, but it is made more complicated here by the possibility that separate security interests exist against discrete parts of a larger chattel.

The common law rules on security interests in accessions were unsettled, as is shown by the conflicting views expressed in the case that follows.

---

* There have been discussions between federal and provincial officials and agreement in principle was reached in 1985 on the desirability of establishing a national registry for security interests in aircraft coupled with uniform provincial legislation. To date, however, these plans have not matured into legislative action. See Joel Cuperfain, "A Canadian Central Registry for Security Interests in Aircraft: A Good Idea but Will It Fly?" (1991), 17 *CBLJ* 380. On relevant international developments, see Chapter 15, Part V, below.

Industrial Acceptance Corp. v. Firestone Tire & Rubber Co.
(1968), 8 DLR (3d) 770 (Alta. AD), rev'd. on appeal
(1971), 17 DLR (3d) 229 (SCC)

SMITH CJA: The appellant appeals from the judgment of Cullen DCJ, who held that the respondent was entitled to maintain its security on tires on a truck purchased under a conditional sale agreement which was assigned by the vendor to the appellant.

One Vanderlinden purchased the truck under conditional sale agreement and the vendor assigned its interest in that agreement to the appellant. Vanderlinden, according to the concession of both counsel, replaced the tires on the vehicle with tires purchased by him from the respondent under conditional sale agreements. Upon Vanderlinden making default under the agreement providing for the sale of the truck, the truck was seized by the appellant. Thereupon the respondent claimed the tires under its conditional sale agreements.

The dispute was heard and determined by the trial Judge in a summary way upon an agreed statement of facts.

The facts are clear and the point at issue is a narrow one: does the doctrine of accession apply so as to cause the tires to have become part of the truck and thus available as part of the security of the appellant?

This is an ancient principle which apparently comes to us from Roman law. Interesting articles on the subject are found in 9 *Aust. LJ* 50, 27 *Mod. LR* 505, at 507, Crossley Vaines, *Personal Property*, 4th ed., at 383, 39 *Aust. LJ* 408 and 5 *University of Western Aust. L Rev.*, at 496 *et seq.*

The principle has been applied to materials and equipment worked into ships as well as to parts and tires which have been built in or attached to motor cars.

Crossley Vaines summarizes the legal position at 385 as follows:

To this and similar problems a more precise answer may be found in the many Commonwealth and American decisions which deal with accession in relation to motor vehicles. The right of accession gives the property in the whole to the owner of the principal chattel, which is probably that which is the greater in value, and the degree of annexation sufficient to constitute an accession may be decided in the light of various tests: (1) that of "injurious removal"—can there be a separation of the original chattels without destroying or seriously injuring the whole?; (2) that of "separate existence"—has the incorporated chattel ceased to exist as a separate chattel?; or again, (3) would the removal of the incorporated chattel destroy the utility of the principal chattel? Yet another test has been suggested as one particularly suited to English law because of its flexibility and by virtue of its association with realty, namely the test of the degree and purpose of annexation.

So far as a ship is concerned I refer to *Seath & Co. v. Moore* (1886), 11 App. Cas. 350, and the statements of Lord Watson at 380-81, as follows:

The English decisions to which I have referred appear to me to establish the principle that, where it appears to be the intention, or in other words the agreement, of the parties to a contract for building a ship, that at a particular stage of its construction, the vessel, so far as then finished, shall be appropriated to the contract of sale, the property of the vessel as soon as it has reached that stage of completion will pass to the purchaser, and subsequent additions made to the chattel thus vested in the purchaser will, accessione, become his property.

There is another principle which appears to me to be deducible from these authorities and to be in itself sound, and that is, that materials provided by the builder and portions of the fabric, whether wholly or partially finished, although intended to be used in the execution of the contract, cannot be regarded as appropriated to the contract, or as "sold," unless they have been affixed to or in a reasonable sense made part of the corpus. That appears to me to have been matter of direct decision by the Court of Exchequer Chamber in *Wood v. Bell*, 6 E & B 355. In *Woods v. Russell*, 5 B & Al. 942 the property of a rudder and some cordage which the builder had bought for the ship was held to have passed in property to the purchaser as an accessory of the vessel; but that decision was questioned by Lord Chief Justice Jervis, delivering the judgment of the Court in *Wood v. Bell*, 6 E & B 355, who stated the real question to be "what is the ship, not what is meant for the ship," and that only the things can pass with the ship "which have been fitted to the ship and have once formed part of her, although afterwards removed for convenience." I assent to that rule, which appears to me to be in accordance with the decision of the Court of Exchequer in *Tripp v. Armitage*, 4 M & W 687.

Cases in which parties in the position of the respondent have succeeded as against the party holding security on the vehicle are: *Lewis v. Andrews & Rowley Pty. Ltd.* (1956), 56 SR (NSW) 439; *Bergougnan v. British Motors Ltd.* (1930), 30 SR (NSW) 61; *Goodrich Silvertown Stores v. McGuire Motors Ltd.*, [1936] 4 DLR 519; *Dawson v. Floyd Dunford Ltd.*, [1961] OWN 225, and *Rendell v. Associated Finance Pty. Ltd.*, [1957] VR 604.

An opposite conclusion was reached by the Court of Appeal of Saskatchewan in *Regina Chevrolet Sales Ltd. v. Riddell*, [1942] 3 DLR 159, [1942] 2 WWR 357. The view of that Court, as stated in the [DLR] headnote, was that: "Tires are an integral part of a truck necessary to its proper working, and as such when used to equip a truck become by accession the property of the person who has the property in the truck." In that case the rival claimants were the vendor of the truck under a conditional sale agreement and the chattel mortgagee of the tires on the truck which were not the original tires and which had been sold by the mortgagee to the purchaser of the truck.

After consideration of the general nature of the doctrine of accession, *Seath v. Moore*, *supra*, and *Goodrich Silvertown Stores v. McGuire Motors Ltd.*, *supra*, Macdonald JA, delivering the judgment of the Court, said at 162-63:

> In this case the tires were in my opinion practically available for the purpose for which they were manufactured, only as parts of the truck; for it seems to me that the truck must be regarded not as a mere aggregation of separate parts, but as a working unit into which the several parts have been integrated and harmonized.
>
> Learned counsel for the defence referred to *Goodrich Silvertown Stores v. McGuire Motors Ltd.*, [1936] 4 DLR 519, where there are references to a number of American decisions supporting his contention that the tires did not pass to the plaintiff, though they were on the truck which was the property of the plaintiff. The ground on which these decisions are based seems to be that tires can be detached from a truck without injury to it, are not integral and permanent parts of a truck but merely temporary and separable attachments.

With all due respect it seems to me that the ground on which the decisions are based is too narrow. Even the engine could easily be removed without doing damage to the rest of the car. I am of opinion that the question is whether tires are necessary parts of the truck as a machine capable of operating as intended. This I would answer in the affirmative. ...

I agree with the reasoning and conclusion of the Saskatchewan Court of Appeal and in the language used by Crossley Vaines that the "utility of the principal chattel" would be destroyed by the removal of the tires and that this is a sound reason for coming to the conclusion in the circumstances of this case that the tires have become subject to the security of the appellant.

[On appeal to the Supreme Court of Canada ...]

LASKIN J: The issue in this appeal is whether the assignee of the conditional seller of a truck, which it repossessed upon the buyer's default, may retain the tires then mounted on the truck as against the claim of the unpaid conditional seller of the tires to priority.

Nothing turns on either registration or non-registration of the respective conditional sale contracts, nor on notice of them apart from registration. There is nothing unusual about the relevant facts. The conditional buyer of the truck, which was a used truck when he bought it under a conditional sale contract, subsequently purchased other tires for it from the appellant, again under a conditional sale contract. Eight months after the truck was purchased, it was seized by the respondent for default in payments thereon. As a result of interpleader proceedings, an adjudication on the competing claims of the appellant and the respondent was made in favour of the appellant by Cullen DCJ. His determination was reversed by the Appellate Division of the Supreme Court of Alberta, which relied mainly on a utility conception of the doctrine of accession, which it held to be applicable, and on the exposition of that doctrine by the Saskatchewan Court of Appeal in *Regina Chevrolet Sales Ltd. v. Riddell*, [1942] 3 DLR 159, [1942] 2 WWR 357.

It is common ground that the tires are removable without physical injury to the body of the truck or to any of its constituent parts. The appellant urges this factor as the governing principle in the application of the doctrine of accession between competing security claimants. The respondent contends for a principle of integral convenience or utility in invoking the same doctrine. The authorities cited by opposing counsel reveal that the doctrine of accession has yielded different results in the same fact situations. This has been because of the attempt, on the one hand, to give it a consistent meaning, regardless of the purpose for which it is invoked or of the relationship of the litigating parties; and because of the attempt, on the other hand, to give it a functional direction to take account of the purpose to be served and of the character of the claims for which its support is sought. I can make a compendious reference to these authorities, Canadian, Australian and American, by noting an article by A.G. Guest, "Accession and Confusion in the Law of Hire Purchase," 27 *Mod. L Rev.* 505 (1964).

The present case is unembarrassed by any suggestion that the accessory chattels have lost their identity. Nor are we concerned with an accession to the title of the purchaser of a fabricated product, be it a ship or other chattel, by the maker thereof. Again, we are not concerned with the enhancement of a security holder's position in some way. In my opinion, whatever be the rationale of the doctrine of accession in taking effect in the foregoing situations, it ought not to be applied to the present case where removable and identifiable accessory chattels are claimed by the holder of an original title thereto, retained as security for their value, against the prior security title holder of the principal chattel.

There is no justification for a conclusion in this case that would give the respondent a windfall against a third party who has reserved title. I know of no policy of commercial dealing in chattels of the kind in question here that would warrant subordination of the claim of their title holder to that of another who has given no value for them. The respondent is not a subsequent purchaser of the principal chattel, and it cannot even urge here that as such a purchaser for value and without notice of the security claim to the tires it is entitled to retain them as accessories to its purchase.

It was submitted on behalf of the respondent that a decision adverse to its claim of accession would mean that numerous searches for possible conditional sale agreements, covering separable automobile parts, would become necessary, and thus hamper commercial dealing in the sale and purchase of automobiles. This might be so in the case of dealings with private sellers. It is hardly likely if business is done with reputable retailers.

The result I would reach here is consistent with the apparent factual situation in *Regina Chevrolet Sales Ltd. v. Riddell, supra*, albeit the exposition of the law there may have gone further than was necessary on the facts. In that case, the conditional buyer of a truck purchased other tires for it, which he obtained on credit without the seller reserving a security title. Some months later, the seller of the tires was given a chattel mortgage on them by the buyer. In subsequent litigation between the conditional seller of the truck and the chattel mortgagee of the tires, the former prevailed. This is easily explicable on the ground that title to the tires mounted on the truck had passed to the buyer upon purchase, and they thereupon came under the security title of the conditional seller of the truck. The buyer could only mortgage them thereafter subject to that conditional seller's prior claim. Counsel for the respondent conceded that under the exposition of the law in the Saskatchewan case, which he supported, the buyer of the tires, although liable for their price, could resist their seizure by their conditional seller for default in payment. I cannot agree with a view of the doctrine of accession that would produce such a result.

Appeal allowed.

NOTES

1) The PPSA definition of "accession" is much broader than the common law test: the only question is whether the goods have been installed or affixed to other goods. It makes no difference whether the disputed goods can be removed without damaging the principal goods, or whether removing them would destroy the utility of the principal goods. By the same token, the common law priority rule turns solely on whether or not the disputed goods are accessions: if so, they become part of the principal goods and so they belong to whoever is entitled to the principal goods; if not, the owner has no claim to them. By con-

trast, the statute requires a two-stage inquiry. The first question is whether the disputed goods are accessions in the statutory sense. The second question is, if so, which of the variables in OPPSA s. 35 does the case exhibit?

2) How would *Firestone* have been decided under the OPPSA?

3) The following case deals with the relationship between OPPSA s. 35 and the *Repair and Storage Liens Act*, RSO 1990, c. R.25 (RSLA). The RSLA gives a person who repairs goods a possessory and non-possessory lien over the goods to secure payment of the repair bill. As a general rule, the RSLA lien has priority over all other interests in the goods. The RSLA is described more fully in the extract below and in Chapter 10, Part II. Is the fitting of a car radio a "repair" within the meaning of the RSLA? If so, then the fitter can claim an RSLA lien *in the car* with priority over a perfected PPSA security interest. If not, the fitter can protect itself by taking a PPSA security interest *in the radio*. OPPSA s. 35 will then apply to determine priority between the fitter's security interest in the radio and a competing security interest in the car itself.

GMAC Leaseco Ltd. v. Tomax Credit Corp.
[2001] OJ No. 2927 (SC)

CAMERON J: GMAC Leaseco Limited ("GMAC") owned a vehicle which it leased under a true lease to its lessee. GMAC filed a financing statement under the Personal Property Security Act ("PPSA"). The lessee arranged for the supply and installation in the vehicle by an electronics company of a radio and speakers and an electronic door locking and security system, which constituted about 31.5% of the total cost of $2,600 plus tax of $390.00. The transaction was financed under a conditional sales agreement between the lessee and Tomax Credit Corporation ("Tomax") for $5,988 repayable over 36 months including interest at 2.5% per month and administration charges. The installer electronics company assigned to Tomax a purported lien under s. 3 of the Repair and Storage Lien Act ("RSLA") which Tomax registered under RSLA s. 10. The lessee defaulted under the lease and removed the radio and speakers which she put in her house. The lessee filed a consumer proposal. GMAC seized the vehicle, from which the radio had been removed. Tomax claimed a non-possessory lien in the vehicle in priority to the rights of the owner GMAC for the full amount owing under the conditional sales contract under RSLA s. 7(1). GMAC paid $7,200 of the proceeds of sale of the vehicle into court to secure the Tomax lien in substitution for the vehicle.

GMAC asserts a priority to the vehicle under PPSA s. 35(1) as the radio and speakers are an "accession" under the PPSA.

Does the Tomax lien under the RSLA attach to the vehicle and the proceeds of its sale for the full amount owing under the conditional sales contract?

The lien in s. 3(1) of the RSLA is restricted to the amount agreed to be paid for, or the fair value of, the repair. "Repair" is defined in s. 1(1) of the RSLA to mean:

> an expenditure of money on, or the application of labour, skill or materials to, an article for the purpose of altering, improving or restoring its properties or maintaining its condition ...

The lien assigned by the electronics company includes not only its charges for goods and services to repair but also the interest and administration charges agreed by the lessee in the conditional sales contract with Tomax: *General Motors Acceptance Corp. of Canada v. Tomax Corp.*, [1999] OJ No. 2801.

In view of the paramountcy of the PPSA under s. 73 of that Act, the definition of "repair" in the RSLA must be read so as to give reasonable meaning to the definition of an "accession" in the PPSA and the priorities provided under s. 35(1) of the PPSA.

"Accession" is defined in s. 1(1) of the PPSA to mean "goods that are installed in or are affixed to other goods."

A radio is not an integral part of a vehicle. Many new vehicles do not contain a radio. A radio installed in a vehicle is not a repair under the RSLA. It does not alter, improve or restore the properties of the vehicle. It is different from tires, windows, brakes, transmission, exhaust system, dented fenders, scraped paint, etc. A vehicle continues to operate as a vehicle, a safe, efficient and presentable means of transportation when the radio is removed. A radio merely increases the user's pleasure while occupying the vehicle. A radio can exist and operate separate from the vehicle. It is an addition to the vehicle, not an alteration, improvement or restoration of the properties of the vehicle.

Failure to make this distinction deprives the PPSA application to accessions of any practical effect.

On the other hand I find the electronic door locking system and security system to be an improvement to the properties of the vehicle. A locking system is a part of every new vehicle and is useless except as part of a vehicle. These costs are secured by the RSLA lien in priority to GMAC's claim: *VFC Inc. v. Tomax Corp.*, [1998] OJ No. 5100. I find this amount, including GST and PST, to be 31.5% of the total conditional sales amount of $5,988.52 or $1,886.00.

As a matter of commercial expediency, vehicle owners benefit from repairs. However they cannot protect their interests from the addition and removal of accessions. Those who deal in accessions and seek a non-possessory security interest therein must accept the priorities of PPSA s. 35 or search title and security interests to ensure they obtain the priority they seek in the asset to which the accession is attached.

IV. COMMINGLED GOODS

What the marginal note to OPPSA s. 37 describes as a section concerned with "commingled goods" in fact covers substantially more. The section equally applies "if the goods are so manufactured, processed, assembled, or commingled that their identity is lost in the product or mass." It therefore applies to such familiar examples as flour, sugar, and eggs that are combined to make a cake, iron ore that is converted into steel, and components that are assembled into a machine. See UCC 9-315, Official Comment, s. 3 (Revised Article 9, UCC 9-336). As the following case shows, a claim to proceeds (OPPSA s. 25, discussed in Chapter 12) and a claim under s. 37 can easily coincide. Whether or not they do, s. 37 raises difficult problems of construction and application.

In the Matter of San Juan Packers, Inc.
696 F2d 707 (CCA 9 1983)

PER CURIAM: This is a dispute between a secured creditor of a bankrupt food processor and a secured creditor of farmers from whom the food processor bought vegetables. The food processor, San Juan Packers, Inc., bought cans on credit from a can manufacturer, National Can Corporation, and granted the can manufacturer a floating lien on all of its inventory. In late summer, 1976, the food processor bought vegetables from many farmers, including the three involved in this litigation. These three farmers had obtained financing from Peoples State Bank and had granted the bank a security interest in their crops and the "proceeds" thereof.

The food processor filed a petition in bankruptcy after it had received the farmers' vegetables and processed and sold a portion of them, but before it had finished paying all purchase price installments due the farmers. Not having been paid by the food processor, the farmers did not pay the bank. The bank brought this adversary proceeding in bankruptcy court against all of the food processor's secured creditors to establish the priority of the bank's security interest in the farmers' vegetables and in the cash proceeds thereof. The parties agreed to the sale of all vegetables in the food processor's possession and creation of a fund from the proceeds to satisfy any judgment that might arise from this action.

The bankruptcy court found for the bank, and the can manufacturer appealed to the district court, which affirmed. The can manufacturer appeals to this court, advancing three contentions.

I.

The can manufacturer first contends that money received by the food processor for the farmers' vegetables is not "proceeds" to which the bank's security interest attached under its security agreements with the farmers.

The Uniform Commercial Code (UCC) provides that "[p]roceeds includes whatever is received when collateral or proceeds is sold, exchanged, collected or otherwise disposed of." Section 9-306(1). Under this definition, the money the food processor received for the farmers' vegetables is "proceeds" unless the vegetables ceased to be collateral when purchased by the food processor.

"'Collateral' means the property subject to a security interest ..." Section 9-105(1)(c). "Except where ... Article [9] otherwise provides, a security interest continues in collateral notwithstanding sale ... by the debtor unless his action was authorized by the secured party ..." Section 9-306(2). Since the can manufacturer does not dispute the bankruptcy court's finding that the bank did not authorize the sale free of its security interest, and Article 9 does not otherwise provide, it would appear that the bank's security interest continued in the vegetables after their sale to the food processor, that the vegetables remained "collateral," and that whatever was received by the food processor when the vegetables were sold is "proceeds."

The can manufacturer points out that section 9-306(2) provides that a security interest continues, "notwithstanding sale ... *by the debtor* and ... in any identifiable proceeds including collections *received by the debtor*" (emphasis supplied), and argues that the bank's security interest was not saved by section 9-306(2) when the vegetables were sold and cash received by the food processor rather than by the farmers because the farmers and not the food processor were the "debtors." But under §9-105(1)(d), the food processor *is* the "debtor":

> (1) In this article, unless the context otherwise requires:
>
> (d) "Debtor" means the person who owes payment or other performance of the obligation secured, whether or not he owns or has rights in the collateral ... *Where the debtor and the owner of the collateral are not the same person, the term "debtor" means the owner of the collateral in any provision of the Article dealing with the collateral,* the obligor in any provision dealing with the obligation, and may include both where the context so requires.

(emphasis supplied).

Official Comment 2 to section 9-105 makes it clear that an owner of the collateral is a "debtor" whether he acquired his rights in the collateral at the time the security interest was created or at a later date:

> In all but a few cases the person who owes the debt and the person whose property secures the debt will be the same. Occasionally, one person furnishes security for another's debt, and *sometimes property is transferred subject to a secured debt of the transferor which the transferee does not assume*; in such cases, under the second sentence of the definition, the term "debtor" may, depending on the context, include either or both such persons.

(emphasis supplied).

The can manufacturer protests that under this view the bank could follow these vegetables into the hands of the ultimate consumer. But this is precisely what the plain language of the UCC requires. *See* B. Clark, The Law of Secured Transactions under the Uniform Commercial Code ¶8.4[3][a], at 8-22 to -23 (1980); R. Henson, Secured Transactions under the Uniform Commercial Code 143-44 (1979); *cf. Garden City Production Credit Ass'n. v. Lannan*, 186 Neb. 668, 186 NW 2d 99 (1971) (plaintiff's security interest in livestock continued through unauthorized sale by farmer and resale by farmer's transferee). As a practical matter, of course, it would be difficult for the secured party to identify its collateral far down a chain of purchasers.

Cases relied upon by the can manufacturer did not consider section 9-105(1)(d). *See Get It Kwik of America, Inc. v. First Alabama Bank*, 361 So. 2d 568 (Ala. Civ. App. 1978); *Beneficial Finance Co. v. Colonial Trading Co.*, 4 UCC Rep. Serv. (Callaghan) 672 (Pa. Ct. of Common Pleas 1967).

II.

The can manufacturer's second argument is that by the terms of section 9-306(2) the bank's security interest continued only in "identifiable proceeds" and was lost because the food processor mixed together vegetables purchased from various farmers making it impossible to identify vegetables, or proceeds from the sale of vegetables remaining in the food processor's possession, as attributable to any particular farmer.

Section 9-315 of the UCC requires rejection of this argument. The bank had a perfected security interest in the farmers' vegetables, and those vegetables became part of a mass of vegetables in the hands of the food processor, so commingled that their identity became lost in the mass. By the express terms of section 9-315(1), where collateral loses its identity by commingling or processing, the security interest continues in the mass or product—and it is not disputed that the proceeds in the fund established in this case can be traced to commingled vegetables in the hands of the food processor.

Cases relied upon by the can manufacturer involved nonfungible goods that did not lose their identity when commingled with other goods. *See Howarth v. Universal C.I.T. Credit Corporation*, 203 F. Supp. 279 (WO Pa. 1962); *Chrysler Credit Corporation v. Bank of Wiggins*, 358 So. 2d 714 (Miss. 1978).

III.

Finally, the can manufacturer argues that if section 9-315 is applied, the can manufacturer was entitled to share in the fund since the can manufacturer had a security interest in the vegetables in the food processor's possession grown by farmers other than the three in whose crops the bank had a security interest, and by the terms of section 9-315 each party whose collateral is commingled in the mass is entitled to a ratable share of the proceeds of the sale of the mass.

The bank resists application of section 9-315 on the ground, relied upon by the district court, that section 9-315(1) "requires the attachment of two security interests to the product or mass." The attachment of two security interests to the product or mass is an explicit condition only to the operation of section 9-315(2), not section 9-315(1). Moreover, this condition to the application of section 9-315(2) was satisfied because both the bank's interest in the vegetables of the three farmers with whom the bank had its security arrangement and the can manufacturer's security interest in the other vegetables in the food processor's inventory attached to the mass of each variety of vegetables when the vegetables of the same variety purchased from various farmers were commingled.

The bank contends further that section 9-315 does not apply because the vegetables were not sufficiently processed. The statute, however, refers to processing *and* commingling, both in the caption of the section and in section 9-315(1)(a). "Commingled" is not a term of art in this context; it simply means "to mix together," *Webster's Third New International Dictionary* 457 (1961), or "[t]o put together in one mass." *Black's Law Dictionary* 246 (5th ed., 1979). As the bank points out, Official Comment 3 to section 9-315 refers to commingling flour, sugar and eggs into cake mix, a process involving more than mere mixing, but there is no indication that the drafters meant to exclude simple mixing of fungible goods.

Application of section 9-315(2) does not, however, completely resolve this case. It is not clear from the record whether vegetables of the bank's three farmers were sold between the time these vegetables were delivered to the food processor and the time the food processor filed a bankruptcy petition. If such sales occurred and proceeds were not dissipated before bankruptcy, they are available to the secured parties subject to the provisions of section 9-306(4). Proceeds of sales made under the supervision of the bankruptcy court are, of course, not subject to section 9-306(4). Furthermore, there may be more than one section 9-315(2) ratio for each mass of vegetables because additional deliveries from farmers other than the three having security arrangements with the bank were subject to the can manufacturer's security interest; when such deliveries were added to the various masses of corn, peas, and carrots, the proportion of the security interest in each mass to which the can manufacturer was entitled increased.

The judgment appealed from is therefore vacated, and the case is remanded for further proceedings:

(1) to determine what proportion of each mass of the various vegetables was sold by the food processor prior to its bankruptcy;

(2) to apportion the available proceeds, if any, from such sales between the bank and the can manufacturer in accordance with sections 9-315(2) and 9-306(4); and

(3) to apportion the proceeds of sales made under the bankruptcy court's supervision between the bank and the can manufacturer in accordance with section 9-315(2).

NOTE

In *Unisource Canada Inc. v. Hongkong Bank of Canada* (1998), 43 BLR (2d) 226, aff'd. (2000), 13 OAC 24 (CA), one question the court had to determine was whether paper used in the production of printed matter qualified as "commingled goods" within the meaning of OPPSA s. 37. Reilly J held as follows (at 272):

I conclude first that the paper supplied by Unisource to Johanns did indeed become "part of a product" (commingled goods). In my view, the goods were "so processed ... that their identity was lost in the product." I come to this conclusion as a matter of common sense. Unisource supplied blank paper to Johanns. Putting aside any "change" in identity as a result of cutting, Johanns then "processed" the paper by printing on it, adding graphics, et cetera, and then binding it into an advertising brochure, a pamphlet, or whatever. It had lost its identity as blank paper stock. If one holds up a magazine and asks a friend, "What is this?," the answer will be, "It's a magazine," or, on a close inspection, "It's a copy of *Macleans*." The answer will *not* be, "It's a number of blank pages of paper on which words and pictures have been printed and then the pages were stapled together." Such an answer would be completely ridiculous, because the original identity (blank paper) has been lost forever (subject to recycling).

Do you agree?

Grant Gilmore, *Security Interests in Personal Property*, Vol. II
(Boston: Little, Brown, 1965), at 851-53 (footnotes omitted)

Section 9-315(2) establishes the priorities when, under subsection (1), "more than one security interest attaches to the product or mass." We may assume that (with one exception) it will be a rare case in which two or more secured parties deliberately and with malice aforethought put themselves into a §9-315(2) situation. The subsection (2) priority rule will apply principally to cases where the debtor has without authority processed or commingled collateral belonging to different secured parties; in view of the overlap between §9-314 and §9-315, the rule could conceivably be exploited by the supplier of parts or accessories who found his rights under §9-315 more attractive than his rights under §9-314. Finally (this is the exception previously referred to) the rule will become relevant in cases of conflicting purchase-money and after-acquired (or non-purchase-money) interests in manufacturing inventory.

The subsection (2) rule is that security interests which attach to a product or mass "rank equally according to the ratio that the cost of the goods to which each interest originally attached bears to the cost of the total product or mass."

Since subsection (1) allows only previously perfected interests to "continue" in the product or mass, only such interests share under subsection (2). Nowhere in the Article is any light shed on the meaning of "rank equally": presumably any interest entitled to share would have the rights given to a secured party on default by Part 5; if one such secured party repossessed and sold the product, he would no doubt be under a duty to account for the proceeds to his fellows. Perhaps wisely, the draftsmen made no attempt to explore the complications of "rank equally"; the courts will have to do it for them.

The secured parties who rank equally do not of course share equally: they share, as the Comment puts it, "ratably." How they share depends on the meaning of the subsection (2) formula, which is notably obscure. The formula is geared not to value or obligation but to "cost," and cost seems to mean "cost to the debtor" (not how much the secured party has advanced but how much the debtor has invested). The formula requires that two different costs be ascertained. The first is the "cost of the goods to which each interest originally attached"; presumably this means their purchase price. The second is "the cost of the total product or mass"; presumably this means (in the case of a product) the cost of raw materials plus labor and overhead. When we have ascertained these costs, the formula tells us that the secured parties share "according to the ratio" between the costs. We may inquire into the meaning of "according to the ratio" by working out an example.

Assume the case of the debtor who manufactures candy from sugar and chocolate. Secured party A has financed the acquisition of the sugar by advancing the entire purchase price; secured party B has done likewise for the chocolate. For simplicity's sake assume the following figures:

Cost of sugar (A)	3
Cost of chocolate (B)	5
Labor and overhead	2
Cost of candy	10

If there is a foreclosure sale of the candy, the formula tells us that A and B will share in the proceeds "according to the ratio" of $3/10$ to $5/10$. If the candy sells for 10, this works out properly: A gets 3; B gets 5; since both A and B have been paid in full, the residue goes either to the debtor or his trustee in bankruptcy. Suppose, however, that the candy sells for less than 8—to make the arithmetic simple, say that it sells for 5. If the formula means that A gets $3/10$ of 5 and B gets $5/10$ of 5, the result is that A gets 1½ and B gets 2½, with the residue (1) going as before to debtor or trustee in bankruptcy. This result seems wrong, since neither A nor B has been paid in full and, until they have been, nothing should go back to the debtor or over to his unsecured creditors through the trustee. (The foregoing comment assumes that a secured party who has financed raw materials and claims a security interest in the product is entitled, up to the amount of his advance, to the full value of the product.) The correct result, if the candy sells for 5, is for A and B to divide the proceeds in the proportion of 3-to-5: A should get ⅜ of 5 (or 1⅞); B should get ⅝ of 5 (or 3⅛); there is no residue and there should be none unless the candy sells for more than enough to pay both A and B in full. It would be clear that this is the result contemplated by §9-315(2) if the formula read: according to the ratio that the cost of the goods to which each interest originally attached bears to the sum of the costs of all goods which have become part of the product and which were originally subject to security interests entitled to rank equally in the product under this subsection. Or if it read: according to the ratio that the cost of the goods to which each security interest to the ratio that the cost of the goods to which each security interest originally attached bears to the cost of the total product or mass (excluding, however, from the total cost any costs which represent labor, overhead or the cost of goods not subject to security interests entitled to equal rank under this subsection).

Another weakness in the formula becomes apparent if we vary our hypothetical case by assuming (at whatever damage to the quality of the candy) that A made an advance of 3, which represented 50 per cent of the cost of the sugar, and B made an advance of 5, which represented 100 per cent of the cost of the chocolate. If the candy is sold and A and B are to share ratably in the proceeds, it would seem that they ought to share in a 3-to-5 ratio. However, since the formula is geared to cost of goods, the apparent result is that they will share in a 6 (for A) to 5 (for B) ratio. A, who has advanced less than B, gets a greater share of the proceeds. If cost means the purchase price to the debtor, the formula leads to an inequitable result whenever the advances made by the secured parties represent different percentages of the costs to the debtor.

NOTES

1) Revised Article 9 addresses the problem that Gilmore identifies. The new commingled goods provision is UCC 9-336, which reads in part as follows:

> (f) If more than one security interest attaches to the product or mass under subsection (c), the following rules determine priority:
>
> (1) A security interest that is perfected under subsection (d) has priority over a security interest that is unperfected at the time the collateral becomes commingled goods.
>
> (2) If more than one security interest is perfected under subsection (d), the security interests rank equally *in proportion to the value of the collateral* at the time it became commingled goods. [Emphasis added.]

(Subsection (c) says that, if collateral becomes commingled goods, a security interest attaches to the product or mass, and subsection (d) says that if a security interest is perfected before the collateral becomes commingled goods, the security interest that attaches to the product or mass under subsection (c) is perfected.)

2) In *Borden (UK) Ltd. v. Scottish Timber Products Ltd.*, [1981] Ch. 25 (CA), the plaintiff company sold large quantities of chipboard resin to the defendant company. The sales contract contained a reservation of title clause in the plaintiff's favour. The resin supplied was used by the defendant in its manufacturing process, in conjunction with other ingredients,

to form a "glue mix." The glue mix was then blended with various grades of wood chippings and pressed together to form the end product, chipboard.

The defendant became bankrupt and, at the time of bankruptcy, was indebted to the plaintiff for a very large sum of money arising out of the supply of resin. Because it had retained title to the resin until it was paid for, the plaintiff claimed to be entitled to trace the resin into the chipboard and to have a charge on the chipboard for the amount of the outstanding indebtedness. The trial judge allowed the claim; the English Court of Appeal reversed his order.

Bridge LJ, who delivered the main judgment in the Court of Appeal, gave three principal reasons. The first was that the plaintiff was not entitled to a tracing remedy in equity because there was no fiduciary relationship between the parties. The plaintiff had supplied the resin knowing and intending that the defendant would use it in the manufacture of chipboard. The defendant was not acting as the plaintiff's agent in conducting its manufacturing operations. Second, the earlier decision of the Court of Appeal in the *Romalpa* case (*Aluminium Industrie Vaassen BV v. Romalpa Aluminium Ltd.*, [1976] 1 WLR 686) was distinguishable because there the buyer had expressly agreed to hold the aluminum foil and the proceeds from the sale thereof as bailee for the seller. Moreover, the foil retained its identity and had never become admixed with goods of a different character.

The third reason given by Bridge LJ was that the tracing remedy was in any event not available under the rule in *Re Hallett's Estate* (1880), 13 Ch. D 696, where there is "a mixture of heterogeneous goods in a manufacturing process wherein the original goods lose their character and what emerges is a wholly new product." He continued at 683-84:

> Some extreme examples were canvassed in argument. Suppose cattle cake is sold to a farmer, or fuel to a steel manufacturer, in each case with a reservation of title clause, but on terms which permit the farmer to feed the cattle cake to his herd and the steelmaker to fuel his furnaces, before paying the purchase price. Mr. Mowbray concedes that in these cases the seller cannot trace into the cattle or the steel. He says that the difference is that the goods have been consumed. But once this concession is made, I find it impossible to draw an intelligible line of distinction in principle which would give the plaintiffs a right to trace the resin into the chipboard in the instant case. What has happened in the manufacturing process is much more akin to the process of consumption than to any simple process of admixture of goods. To put the point in another way, if the contribution that the resin has made to the chipboard gives rise to a tracing remedy, I find it difficult to see any good reason why, in the steelmaking example, the essential contribution made by the fuel to the steel manufacturing process should not do likewise.
>
> These are the principal considerations which have led me to the conclusion that the plaintiffs are not entitled to the tracing remedy which they claim. But I am fortified in that conclusion by the further consideration that if the remedy were available in such cases, a most intractable problem could, and in many cases would, arise in quantifying the proportion of the value of the manufactured product which the tracer could claim as properly attributable to his ingredient. In the instant case, a breakdown of the actual costings of chipboard over a period of seven months to July 29, 1977, has been agreed, attributing 17 per cent of the total cost to the cost of resin, subject to a reservation with respect to wastage and over-usage. But one can well see that in many cases where the cost of materials and labour involved in a particular production process were constantly fluctuating, it might be quite impossible to assign a proportion of the total cost properly attributable to one particular ingredient with any certainty at all. ...

3) How would *Scottish Timber Products* be decided under s. 37 of the OPPSA? The United Kingdom has no registration requirements for conditional sale or hire-purchase agreements and, before the decision in the *Romalpa* case discussed in Bridge LJ's judgment, supra, it was not customary for inventory to be sold in the United Kingdom subject to conditional sale terms with a proceeds clause. The implications of *Romalpa* are explored in a wider setting by Professor Goode in "The Right To Trace and Its Impact in Commercial Transactions" (1976), 92 *LQ Rev.* 360 and 528 (pts. I and II). See also Michael G. Bridge, *The Sale of Goods* (Oxford: Clarendon Press, 1997), at 104-10.

CHAPTER TEN

Liens Arising by Statute or Rule of Law

I. INTRODUCTION

In addition to having to consider its position vis-à-vis other consensually secured creditors, a secured party must also take into account another critically important source of competition—the claims of creditors whose liens or similar *in rem* claims arise by statute or operation of law and not as the result of any agreement with the debtor. Broadly speaking, such creditors fall into two groups. The first group comprises creditors who are given a possessory (and, increasingly, non-possessory) lien on the debtor's chattels at common law or by statute for services rendered or materials supplied to the debtor. The second group comprises liens and deemed trusts, almost invariably created by statute, in favour of federal and provincial government departments, agencies, and commissions for monies owing to them by the debtor.

II. LIENS IN FAVOUR OF PRIVATE CREDITORS

Well-known examples of these are a repairer's lien for work and materials, an innkeeper's lien for a guest's unpaid bill, and a warehouse person's lien for stored goods. For examples of statutory recognition and regulation of such liens, see the *Repair and Storage Liens Act*, RSO 1990, c. R.25 (for details, see the Ziegel and Denomme extract, below); the *Innkeeper's Act*, RSO 1990, c. I.7, ss. 2-3; and the *Mining Act*, RSO 1990, c. M.14, s. 106. See, generally, R.A. Wood and M.I. Wylie, "Non-Consensual Security Interests in Personal Property" (1992), 30 *Alta. L Rev.* 1056, esp. at pp. 1066-71. Technically speaking, a landlord's right to levy distress on its tenant's goods is not regarded as a lien, although it becomes a lien once the right is exercised: see *Commercial Credit Corp. Ltd. v. Harry Shields Ltd.* (1981), 32 OR 703 (CA), extracted in Chapter 2.

The general common law rule is that a lienor can acquire no greater rights in the chattel than the lienee itself has. This rule is, or was, subject to several exceptions: (1) where the debtor has implied or express authority to contract for the services giving rise to the lien rights: see *Gen. Securities Ltd. v. Brett's Ltd.* (1956), 19 WWR 385 (BC) for a review of the earlier authorities and, generally, Goode and Ziegel at pp. 180-85; (2) in the case of an innkeeper, his lien extended to all chattels in his guest's possession, whether or not the guest owned them, the reason being that the law "compelled an innkeeper to receive the guest and the goods and, regardless of their ownership, the innkeeper was given little opportunity to inquire as to title": *Bank of Montreal v. 414031 Ontario Ltd.* (1983), 2 PPSAC 248, at 250 (Ont.); and (3) at common law, the landlord's right of distress likewise extended to any goods in the tenant's possession, whether or not they belonged to the tenant.

In many of the provinces, the landlord's right has been modified by statute. In Ontario, for example, s. 31(2) of the *Commercial Tenancies Act*, RSO 1990, c. L.7; SO 1999, c. 6, limits the landlord's right of distress to the tenant's goods and chattels, but exempts from this restriction the claim of a person "whose title is derived by purchase, gift, transfer or assignment from the tenant … or by way of mortgage or otherwise, [and also] the interest of the tenant in any goods or chattels on the premises … under a contract for purchase, or by which he may or is to become the owner thereof upon performance of any condition … ." The Saskatchewan *Landlord and Tenant Act*, RSS 1978, c. L-6, s. 25, as am., contains a similar provision, but *excludes* from the landlord's reach a "purchase-money security interest" (PMSI) defined in the same way as in the SPPSA. See *Dube v. Bank of Montreal* (1986), 5 PPSAC 269 (Sask. CA).

The difference between the Ontario and Saskatchewan approaches is that Ontario s. 31(2) only excludes one type of PMSI, that represented by the common law-style conditional sale agreement, whereas the Saskatchewan provision applies to all PMSIs. Efforts to persuade the Ontario government to update s. 31(2) by extending it to all PMSIs have so far proven unsuccessful. It remains to be seen whether Ontario courts will be willing to make the change judicially by a creative reading of s. 31(2) in light of the reconceptualization of security interests under the OPPSA.

The common law did not give employees a lien on their employer's assets for unpaid wages or other benefits (can you guess why not?), but this omission is now repaired in the employment standards and other legislation, federal and provincial. For Ontario, see the *Employment Standards Act*, RSO 1990, c. E.14, the *Pension Benefits Act*, RSO 1990, c. P.8, and the OPPSA ss. 30(7) and (8). Section 427(7) of the *Bank Act* also confers a priority in favour of employees for unpaid wages over a bank's s. 427 security interest, although the priority only applies where the employer has gone bankrupt. Section 81.3 of the *Bankruptcy and Insolvency Act* (BIA), RSC 1985, c. B-3, incorporated by amendments enacted in 2007, gives the employees of a bankrupt employer a claim of up to $2,000 for unpaid wages and the like earned during the six months before the bankruptcy secured by a lien on all the employer's current assets.

At common law and under the provincial sale of goods Acts, unpaid sellers have a possessory lien and a (largely theoretical) right of stoppage of the goods while in transit (see Ziegel and Duggan, *Commercial and Consumer Sales Transactions*, 4th ed. (Toronto: Emond Montgomery, 2002), c. 15), but these rights come to an end once the goods reach the buyer. Thereafter, the seller is limited to suing for the price of the goods unless it has retained a consensual security interest. Here again the federal Parliament has intervened to assist unpaid suppliers who are perceived not to be capable of adequately protecting their own interests. See *Bank Act* s. 427(7)(b) (growers and producers of agricultural products), and BIA ss. 81.1 and 81.2. The BIA amendments were added in 1992.

Section 4(1)(a) of the OPPSA provides that the Act does not apply "to a lien given by statute or rule of law, except as provided in subclause 20(1)(a)(i) or section 31." Recall that in *859587 Ontario Ltd. v. Starmark Property Management Ltd.* (1998), 40 OR (3d) 481 (CA), extracted in Chapter 9, Part II.C, the debtor ran a car repair business. It leased workshop premises from Starmark. The debtor purchased a piece of equipment from Atlantic pursuant to a conditional sale agreement and fixed it to its work premises. Starmark attempted to levy distress against the equipment and Atlantic also claimed the equipment, relying on its unperfected security interest. The court held that the landlord's right of distress does not apply to trade fixtures, but it did mention in passing what the outcome would have been otherwise: the landlord's right of distress, once exercised, is a lien given by statute or rule of law within the meaning of OPPSA ss. 4(1)(a) and 20(1)(a)(i) and so, since Atlantic's security interest was unperfected, Starmark would have had priority. Section 20(1)(a)(i) provides that an unperfected security interest is subordinate to the interest of a person who has a lien given under any other Act or by a rule of law. Does this mean that, by implication, a perfected security interest has priority over a competing non-consensual lien? See *Leavere v. Port Colborne (City)*, extracted below.

Section 31, which is based on UCC 9-310, confers priority over a perfected security interest in favour of the lien of a person who, in the ordinary course of business, furnishes materials or services with respect to the goods in his possession "unless the lien is given by an Act that provides that the lien does not have such priority." In other words, the presumption is that the lien has priority over any consensual security interest, including a PMSI. The common law position was not quite as favourable to the lienholder, but the practical results were or are about the same under either regime. See Ziegel and Denomme, §§31.2-3.

There has been no significant litigation on s. 31 and the courts have experienced little difficulty in giving it its intended meaning: see, for example, *Algoma Truck & Tractor Sales Ltd. v. Blais* (1981), 1 PPSAC 319 (Ont. Dist. Ct.). *General Electric Capital Equipment Finance Inc. v. Transland Tire Sales & Service Ltd.*, extracted below, deals with the interaction between OPPSA s. 31 and the *Repair and Storage Liens Act*. What is the rationale of s. 31? Is it based on the premise that a secured party should not be enriched at the expense of a repairer who has increased the value of the collateral? Is the increase in value necessarily the same as the amount of the lien claimant's bill?

There has been some discussion about the significance of s. 4(1)(a) being limited to liens. Professor McLaren has suggested, for example, that if a right of seizure or detention of the debtor's assets does not technically amount to a lien (he uses the landlord's right of distraint as an example), then "it may be" subject to PPS legislation. See McLaren, (1986), vol. 1, para. 6.03[2][a][iii]. Is this correct? Are not all non-consensual claims implicitly excluded by the terms of s. 2? What does it mean to say that a right of distraint may be subject to the OPPSA?

**Jacob S. Ziegel and David L. Denomme, *The Ontario Personal
Property Security Act: Commentary and Analysis*, 2d ed.**
(Markham, ON: Butterworths, 2000) §§31.4-31.4.3 (footnotes omitted)

Repair and Storage Liens Act. There is no comfortable fit between the RSLA and s. 31 of
the OPPSA. It seems the RSLA drafters intended the RSLA to supersede s. 31 although
the RSLA does not say so explicitly and the drafters appear to have overlooked the effect
of s. 73 of the OPPSA dealing with conflicts between the OPPSA and other Acts. For the
purposes of the following summary, it will be assumed that there is no difficulty in maintaining the supremacy of the RSLA in the unlikely event that a conflict is found between
the RSLA and the OPPSA.

Scope of RSLA. The Act applies to a repairer and storer of an article. "Repairer," "storer," and "article" are each broadly defined. There is no requirement that a repairer or
storer must be acting in the course of its business when providing the services (a condition, as we have seen, of the lienholder acquiring priority under s. 31 of the OPPSA) or
that the repair or storage will enhance the value of the article.

Possessory and non-possessory liens. Both repairers and storers are given possessory
and non-possessory lien rights in respect of their claims. There is, however, an important
difference between the priorities conferred on repairers' and storers' liens. If the other
requirements discussed below are satisfied, a repairer's possessory lien has priority over
the interests of all other persons. A storer's lien on the other hand is limited to the unpaid
amount owing in respect of the 60-day period calculated from the date the article was
received under the following circumstances. The circumstances are (1) that the storer
knows or has reason to believe that possession of the article was received from a person
other than its owner or a person having the owner's authority, and (2) that within 60 days
of receiving the article the storer has failed to give notice of the lien to every person
whom the storer knows or has reason to believe is the owner or has an interest in the
article.

A possessory lien comes to an end, and cannot be revived, if possession of the article
is surrendered to or lawfully comes into the possession of the owner or other eligible
person. The possessory lien is then replaced by a non-possessory lien for the unpaid
amount, which, it is clear, arises automatically on surrender of possession.

Priority of possessory and non-possessory liens and conditions of enforceability. There
are also important differences in the priority accorded to possessory and non-possessory
liens. A possessory lien, as previously noted, has priority over the interests of "all" other
persons in the article. This language is broad enough to subordinate a secured party's interest not only where the debtor is in possession with the secured party's consent but
equally so where a transferee from the debtor gave the goods for storage or repair and
even where the goods were stolen from the debtor. It remains to be seen whether the
courts will seek to avoid such extravagant results, as they have in other areas raising similar issues.

A non-possessory lien too has priority over the interest in the article of other persons,
but is subordinated to: (1) the holder of a possessory lien even where the non-possessory
lien has been registered; and (2) a buyer from a person selling the article in ordinary
course of business where the repair or storage services giving rise to the non-possessory

lien were rendered at the request of the seller or its agent unless the buyer signs an acknowledgment of indebtedness in the lienholder's favour. The first exception appears to be based on the premise that a repairer with a possessory lien would not be willing to render its services unless it could be assured of first priority where there are competing liens. The second exception is obviously based on the analogy of s. 28(1) of the OPPSA entitling a buyer in ordinary course to take free of a security interest given by a dealer.

So far as priorities among competing non possessory liens are concerned, this is governed by the combined effect of ss. 7(3) and 16(1)(e) and leads to the following sequence where the article has been sold by a lien claimant with a non-possessory lien under Part II of the RSLA: the proceeds are used, first, to satisfy the claim of the lien claimant making the sale and, second, in satisfaction of the claims of other non-possessory lien claimants with registered liens who have given timely notice to the enforcing lien claimant and *in reverse order* to the order in which the lien claimants gave up possession. The "reverse order" priority rule is the exact opposite of the first to register or to perfect rule adopted in s. 30 of the OPPSA and appears to rest on the reasoning that the priority given to lien claimant with possession should also be given to lien claimants releasing possession since otherwise there would be a strong disincentive to release the article to the person authorizing the work or the storage. The priority given to the non-possessory lien claimant making the sale is less easy to explain and presumably is intended as a form of bonus, though it may have perverse economic effects.

A non-possessory lien is only enforceable if it satisfies the following requirements. (1) The lien claimant must obtain a signed acknowledgment of indebtedness from the debtor but there is no requirement that the acknowledgment must occur before the goods are released. This requirement apparently ensures for the benefit of all persons, including the lien debtor. (2) The lienholder must register a claim for lien. This condition only ensures for the benefit of "third parties," an expression that is not defined but presumably covers all persons other than the person requesting the repair or the service. The perfection requirement is comparable to s. 20 of the OPPSA, but there are important differences in consequences. An unperfected lien claim under the RSLA is only subordinated to the rights of those persons who have acquired a right against the article *after* the non-possessory lien has arisen.

The contents of the claim for lien form are prescribed by regulation. ... Suffice it to say ... that they differ in important respects from the requirements for financing statements. Several other features concerning non-possessory liens also need to be noted. A claim for lien ("CFL") may relate to more than one article," but a CFL cannot cover more than one lien and cannot be registered before the lien debtor has signed an acknowledgment of indebtedness. In short, the CFL registration does not function as a notice filing system and differs, in this as in other important respects, from the OPPSA structure. Given these shortcomings, repairers and storers should consider the desirability of opting for a contractual security interest where they anticipate regular dealings with a commercial customer. There is nothing in the RSLA precluding the parties from signing a security agreement and nothing, it would seem, to preclude a repairer or storer from invoking its contractual as well as statutory rights, assuming that the signing of a security agreement is not treated as a waiver of statutory rights. If a repairer or storer does opt for a security agreement, it must of course consider the disadvantages as well as its benefits.

General Electric Capital Equipment Finance Inc. v.
Transland Tire Sales & Service Ltd.
(1991), 6 OR (3d) 131 (Gen. Div.)

LANGDON J: This is a contest for priority over personal property between a lender, GECEF Inc., and a repairer, Transland Ltd.

The lender claims under a conditional sales contract (security agreement), validly registered under the Personal Property Security Act, 1989, SO 1989, c. 16 (PPSA), June 22, 1990. The repairer asserts a non-possessory repairer's lien under the Repair and Storage Liens Act, 1989, SO 1989, c. 17 (RSLA) claimed by it to have been validly registered November 22, 1990.

The RSLA addresses itself both to enforceability of non-possessory liens against third parties (s. 10(1) of the RSLA), and to priority of interest of non-possessory liens over the interest of any person (other than one who claims a possessory lien (s. 7(3) of the RSLA).

I have concluded that the repairer must first demonstrate that his non-possessory lien is enforceable against third parties. Only if it is first enforceable, does the question of priority arise.

The Facts

On May 1, 1990 the lender sold a number of trailers, including the one at issue (the article) to Amber Freight Systems Inc. (Amber or the owner).

Amber Freight Systems Inc. is an Ontario business corporation. It was originally incorporated May 18, 1989 as 840203 Ontario Ltd. (the numbered company). By articles of amendment effective October 5, 1989, the corporate name was changed to Amber Freight Systems Inc.

In the conditional sales agreement by which Amber bought the article on May 1, 1990, it was described by its correct incorporated name.

However, on May 3, 1990, when Amber registered the article under the Highway Traffic Act, RSO 1980, c. 198, it did so in its former corporate name (the numbered company). The registration (plate) number was therefore assigned to the numbered company in the records kept by the Ministry of Transportation and Communication (MTC).

The repairer, in the ordinary course of its business, performed repairs on the article on seven occasions, each documented by a work order/invoice, between May 9, 1990 and October 14, 1990. Each work order/invoice contained a signed acknowledgement of the indebtedness. Following each repair, the repairer gave up possession of the article to the owner. The owner has never paid for those repairs, the value of all of which totals about $1,500.

On September 1, 1990 the owner defaulted under the security agreement; the lender then became entitled, under the agreement, to accelerate the balance due and to repossess the trailer(s).

On October 15, 1990 the repairer made a plate number search of MTC records which disclosed that the article's owner was the numbered company.

On November 22, 1990 the repairer registered a claim for its non-possessory lien under the RSLA against the numbered company and Amber Transport, the latter being the name inscribed on five of the seven work orders/invoices.

On November 28, 1990, six days after registration of the repairer's lien claim, the lender repossessed the trailer.

On December 20, 1990 and January 7, 1991 the solicitors for the repairer and lender exchanged perfunctory letters respectively asserting and denying the repairer's claim for lien.

On May 27, 1991 the repairer seized the trailer from the lender's possession.

On August 1, 1991 the repairer issued to the lender a notice of sale. That notice claimed the $1,500 for repairs and the following:

Bailiff's fees for seizure:	$ 1,800.00
Storage May 27th–August 28th, 1990 @ $65.00 per day	$ 6,110.00
GST on seizure & storage	$ 553.70
Interest on lien claim at 24%	$ 467.35
TOTAL	$10,500.05

On September 5, 1991 the lender, on payment into court of $10,335.27, obtained an order from Morrissey J granting possession of the article to the lender and restraining both from selling it pending determination of this application.

This is obviously a "test case." No one asserts that the 1979 Fruehauf trailer could be worth this amount of money or aggravation, but the parties wish a determination of this dispute in order to resolve this and other pending and potential disputes.

The Issues

Issue 1

Can the repairer enforce its non-possessory lien against the lender?

[Langdon J found that the repairer's lien had not been properly registered, and continued:]

Issue 2

Assuming registration were valid, would the repairer have priority over the lender?

In making its argument for priority the repairer sought to rely on s. 10(1) of the RSLA. For reasons which I will develop, I think he was looking in the wrong place. Section 10(1) in its entirety is as follows:

> 10(1) A non-possessory lien is enforceable against third parties only if a claim for lien has been registered, and, where a person acquires a right against an article after a non-possessory lien arises, the right of the person has priority over the non-possessory lien to the lien claimant if a claim for lien was not registered before the person acquired the right.

Assuming that registration had been valid, the substance of the section as it applies to the present case is as follows: if the lender acquires a right against an article after a non-possessory lien arises, the lender has priority over the non-possessory lien if his rights were acquired before the lien was registered.

To apply this section requires the determination of the following issues: (1) When was the non-possessory lien registered? (2) When did the non-possessory lien arise? (3) When did the lender "acquire a right against the article?"

1. When was the non-possessory lien registered?

In this case, assuming that registration had been valid, that registration was made November 22, 1990.

2. When did the non-possessory lien arise?

Section 7(2) provides:

> (2) A non-possessory lien arises and takes effect when the lien claimant gives up possession of the article.

The lender's work orders disclose that he performed work on the article May 9, May 23, May 28, October 5, October 9, and October 14, 1990. Possession of the article was surrendered to the owner after most, if not all, of those repairs. It was argued that the non-possessory lien arose as early as May 9, 1990 and as late as October 14, 1990.

Under s. 3(2) of the RSLA a repairer's possessory "lien arises and takes effect when the repair is commenced." Under s. 5 of the RSLA that lien "is discharged and cannot be revived as an interest in the article if possession ... is surrendered to ... the owner." Under s. 7(2) the non-possessory "lien arises and takes effect when the lien claimant gives up possession of the article."

Subsections 26(1) and (2) of the RSLA state:

> 26(1) A separate lien arises under this Act each time an article is repaired ...
>
> (2) A lien under the Act cannot be tacked onto another lien under this Act.

A separate non-possessory lien arose each time the repairer surrendered possession of the article to the owner. In the light of the prohibition against tacking, it seems unlikely that the single claim for the aggregate amount of the seven separate liens would be valid. This is particularly so because, as McLaren, [*Secured Transactions in Personal Property in Canada*, 2d ed. (Toronto: Carswell, 1989)], at para. 11.03(2) states:

> Under s. 16(d) of the RSLA, priority as between competing non-possessory liens is to be determined in reverse order to the order in which the lien claimants gave up possession. Therefore, the last lien claimant who made a repair ... will have first priority, provided the lien has been registered ...

If registration of a series of non-possessory lien claims were permitted simply by stating the cumulative total of the aggregate claims, it would become impossible to determine priorities between different claimants. At the very least, therefore, the statute requires that such a claim clearly identify the separate liens, the amount of each and the date on which each arose. More likely, the statute requires separate registration of each claim. I conclude therefore that this claim, as filed, would be considered invalid even if the name had been correct. On the basis of the claim as filed one could not determine when the non-possessory lien arose.

3. When did the lender "acquire a right against the article"?

The repairer argues that the purpose of the RSLA is to provide a mechanism whereby the repairer can part with possession and still both retain his lien and assert it against third parties. He says that if I interpret s. 10 of the RSLA in such a way as to deprive the repairer of priority in favour of the prior conditional sales agreement, then the very purpose of the RSLA will be defeated. Therefore, he argues that I should rule on the facts of this case that the lender acquired its rights against the article, i.e., its right to repossess the article when the default occurred under the conditional sales agreement, i.e., September 1, 1990. On this interpretation, he asserts that at least the liens which arose before September 1 could have priority over the lender's rights.

This argument fails for two reasons. First, it confuses enforceability and priority. Second, it incorrectly characterizes the rights which the lender acquired under the conditional sales agreement.

The purpose of s. 10 of the RSLA is to enable the repairer who has validly registered his non-possessory lien to enforce that lien against the rights of any secured lender under any conditional sales agreement except only one which occurs in a very specific "window" of time, namely, after the non-possessory lien arises and before registration of the non-possessory lien.

The lender acquired his rights against the article when the agreement was signed on May 1, 1990. Those rights became enforceable by the lender against third parties upon perfection of his security interest by registration on June 22, 1990. Those rights are properly characterized as "the right to repossess the article upon default by the owner." The right was acquired when the agreement was signed, not when default occurred. Default was the event which triggered the exercise (not the acquisition) of the right.

This interpretation does not defeat the stated object of the statute, i.e., to permit the non-possessory lien claimant to part with possession and still both retain his lien and assert it against third parties. To make his lien enforceable he must perfect it by registration. Once he has done so, s. 31 of the PPSA provides:

> 31. Where a person in the ordinary course of business furnishes materials or services with respect to goods that are subject to a security interest, any lien that the person has in respect of the materials or services has priority over a perfected security interest unless the lien is given by an Act that provides that the lien does not have such priority. ...

The Act which gives the non-possessory lien, the RSLA, clearly provides in s. 7(3) that such a lien "has priority over the interest in the article of any other person" except one who claims a possessory lien, i.e., one who is in possession and has never given it up: see s. 5 of the RSLA.

Therefore, assuming that the claimant registers validity and thereby acquires enforceability, the statutes combine to grant to him priority over any already perfected security interest (s. 20(1)(a) of the PPSA grants the same priority over an unperfected security interest).

The answer to Issue 2 is, therefore, that the repairer's claim fails by virtue only of lack of enforceability resulting from defective registration. If registration had been valid, the repairer's claim would have been entitled to priority over the previously perfected security interest NOT because of anything contained in s. 10(1) of the RSLA, but because of the combined effect of s. 31 of the PPSA and s. 7(3) of the RSLA.

•••

Application granted.

III. GOVERNMENTAL LIENS

There are a large number of such liens and they have given rise to a very large body of complex litigation and much non-curial discussion and debate. See, *inter alia*, Law Reform Commission of British Columbia, *Report on the Crown as Creditor: Priorities and Privileges* (1982); Baird, "Priority of Non-PPSA Secured Creditors," in D.E. Baird and F. Bennett, *Handbook on the Personal Property Security Act* (1982), c. 5; *Study Committee on Bankruptcy and Insolvency Legislation* (1970), at 122 et seq.; Canada, *Report of the Advisory Committee on Bankruptcy and Insolvency* (Ottawa: Queen's Printer, 1986), at 77-79; W.A. Bogart, "Statutory Claims and Personal Property Security Legislation: A Proposal" (1983), 8 *CBLJ* 129; Anne E. Hardy, *Crown Priority in Insolvency* (Toronto: Carswell, 1986); and Francis L. Lamer, *Priority of Crown Claims in Insolvency* (Toronto: Carswell, 1996).

There is no consistency in the statutory language conferring a preferred status on the governmental claim. Often it is described as a lien on the debtor's assets, in which case it may be a "first lien," a "special lien," a "lien and charge," or a "lien ... payable in priority over all liens, charges or mortgages." Bogart, op. cit., at 134-35. Where a debtor is required to make deductions from a payroll (for example, pursuant to income tax or employment insurance requirements) or to collect taxes from a third party (for example, with respect to sales taxes) and to remit them to the government, a popular statutory device is to create a "deemed" trust with respect to amounts that should have been remitted but were not. See, for example, *Income Tax Act* (ITA), SC 1970-71-72, c. 63, s. 227(4) as am., *Canada Pension Plan Act*, RSC 1985, c. C-8, ss. 23(3)-(4) as am., and *Employment Insurance Act*, SC 1996, c. 23, s. 86.

Another feature of the ITA, which has caused secured creditors much anguish (and greatly incensed the members of the Alberta Court of Appeal), is s. 224(1.2) entitling the Crown to attach monies owing to the debtor by a third party where the debtor has failed to remit deductions to the Canada Revenue Agency. Such an attachment overrides any prior perfected security interest given by the debtor.

Further complications arise because the status of such preferential claims may vary depending on whether the issue arises (1) before, or (2) after the debtor's bankruptcy. If before bankruptcy, then the claim will be governed by the applicable provincial or federal law. If after, then the *Bankruptcy and Insolvency Act* (BIA), RSC 1985, c. B-3, as amended, will have the final word. Before the 1992 amendments, s. 136(1) of the BIA established the order of priority of claims, other than those by secured creditors, and, in s. 136(1)(j) (formerly s. 107(1)(j)) conferred priority on claims of the Crown. The Supreme Court of Canada held that s. 136(1)(j) reduced a governmental lien, even one that is registered, to the status of a preferred creditor. See *Deputy Minister of Revenue v. Rainville*, [1980] 1 SCR 35. There was, however, much uncertainty about the status of deemed trusts, which was only put to rest by the Supreme Court in 1989 in *British Columbia v. Henfrey Samson Belair Ltd.*, [1989] 2 SCR 24. The 1992 amendments made important changes to the status of deemed trusts in bankruptcy and the ranking of Crown claims: see Note 2 following the *DaimlerChrysler* extract, below.

The following is a very limited sampling of recent case law interpreting the scope of non-consensual statutory liens outside bankruptcy and their ranking vis-à-vis consensual security interests.

Leavere v. Port Colborne (City)
(1995), 22 OR (3d) 44 (CA)

The judgment of the court was delivered by GALLIGAN JA: These appeals, which were argued together, raise the same issue. It is whether a municipality distraining a taxpayer's chattels for arrears of business taxes is entitled to those chattels as against a creditor of the taxpayer who has a registered perfected security interest in those same chattels.

The specific facts of the two cases are different but for the purposes of the appeals there is no material distinction between them. Each of the appellants loaned money to the taxpayers and took back security agreements giving them security interests in the taxpayers' chattels. The appellants perfected their security interests by proper registration pursuant to the provisions of the *Personal Property Security Act*, RSO 1990, c. P.10 (the "PPSA"). Later, when the taxpayers fell into arrears in the payment of business taxes, each municipality, acting pursuant to s. 400(2) of the *Municipal Act*, RSO 1990, c. M.45, levied the unpaid taxes by distress upon the taxpayer's chattels by taking possession of them. They were the same chattels to which the appellants' perfected security interests related.

It is the position of the appellants that, because their security interests were perfected by registration before the municipalities levied by distress, the provisions of the PPSA give them priority over the municipalities' claims for arrears of business taxes. It is the contention of the respondent municipalities that the PPSA does not apply to these circumstances and that their levies by distress entitle them to recover their claims for arrears of business taxes out of the chattels. Both judges in motions court, from whose decisions these appeals are taken, decided the issue in the municipalities' favour.

The appeals raise two main issues. The first is whether the PPSA applies to the municipalities' claims. The second is the determination of priorities if the PPSA does not apply. I will deal with the issues separately.

A. The Applicability of the PPSA to the Municipalities' Claims for Arrears of Business Taxes

The resolution of this issue requires a consideration of three statutory provisions. They are s. 400(2)(a) of the *Municipal Act*, and ss. 4(1) and 20(1)(a)(i) of the PPSA. Those provisions are as follows:

The Municipal Act

400(2) Subject to section 399, in case of taxes that are not a lien on land remaining unpaid for twenty-one days after demand or notice made or given under section 392, 395 or 399 or, where a longer period has been authorized under subsection 399(6) such taxes remain unpaid at the expiry of that period, the collector or, where there is no collector, the treasurer may alone or by an agent, subject to the exemptions provided for in subsection (4), levy them with costs by distress,

(a) upon the goods and chattels of the person taxed wherever found within the county in which the municipality lies for judicial purposes.

The Personal Property Security Act

4(1) This Act does not apply,

(a) to a lien given by statute or rule of law, except as provided in subclause 20(1)(a)(i) or section 31. ...

20(1) Except as provided in subsection (3), until perfected, a security interest,

(a) in collateral is subordinate to the interest of,

(i) a person who has a perfected security interest in the same collateral or who has a lien given under any other Act or by a rule of law or who has a priority under any other Act. ...

As s. 4(1) states, the PPSA does not apply to a lien given by statute or by a rule of law except as provided in the two provisions named therein. It is common ground that unpaid business taxes fall within the provisions of s. 400(2) of the *Municipal Act*. Section 400(2)(a) authorizes the municipality to levy unpaid business taxes "by distress" upon the goods and chattels of the person taxed.

There are two issues which must be decided in order to determine whether the PPSA applies to a municipality's levy of unpaid taxes by distress against a taxpayer's chattels:

1. Does a levy by distress by unpaid business taxes result in a lien upon the chattels either under a statute or by a rule of law?

2. If so, is such a lien excepted by one of the statutory exceptions contained in s. 4(1)(a) of the PPSA?

I will deal with the two issues in that order.

1. *Does a levy by distress of unpaid business taxes result in a lien upon the chattels either under a statute or by a rule of law?*

[See *Commercial Credit Corp. Ltd. v. Harry Shields Ltd.* in Chapter 2.]

2. *Is the lien upon the taxpayer's chattels, resulting from the exercise of the right of distress, excepted by the provisions of s. 4(1)(a)?*

The exceptions referred to in s. 4(1) are s. 20(1)(a)(i) and s. 31. It is common ground that s. 31 has no application to these appeals. The provision of the PPSA with which the courts were concerned in *Commercial Credit*, s. 3(1)(a), did not have an exception similar to that contained in s. 20(1)(a)(i) of the present Act. The result in *Commercial Credit* was that, because the lien was one given by a rule of law, the PPSA did not apply to it. The lienholder, the landlord, succeeded notwithstanding the prior perfected security interests registered under the PPSA. Therefore, unless the exception in s. 20(1)(a)(i) has the effect of making all of the PPSA applicable to these liens, that case is decisive. I will, therefore, examine whether the exception applies to these cases.

Before considering s. 20(1)(a)(i) I note that s. 20(3) does not apply to these cases. To facilitate the understanding of s. 20(1)(a)(i) I delete the words referring to s. 20(3) and rewrite the provision so that it reads as follows:

> Until perfected, a security interest in collateral is subordinate to the interest of
> (a) a person who has a perfected security interest in the same collateral;
> (b) a person who has a lien given under any Act in the same collateral;
> (c) a person who has a lien given by a rule of law; and
> (d) a person who has a priority in the collateral under any other Act.

In order to simplify even more the reading of the provision I will make reference only to the lien given by a rule of law because it is the only one of those interests which is relevant to these appeals. The provision then reads that, until perfected, a security interest in collateral is subordinate to the interest of a person who has a lien given by a rule of law.

It was Mr. Swartz's neat submission that when the legislature used the words "until perfected" it meant that once it was "perfected" the security interest would have priority over the interest of the person with the lien. He said that, because his client's security interest was perfected, the PPSA applied to the extent of giving it priority over the municipality's lien.

I am unable to read the provision in that fashion. Reading s. 20(1)(a)(i) with s. 4(1)(a) leads me to conclude that the legislature intended the Act to apply only to the extent of specifically determining what would happen in the event of a contest between an unperfected security interest and a lien given by a rule of law. At common law priorities were determined in accordance with the chronological order of the encumbrances. Authority for the common law rule is found in *Spence on Equitable Jurisdiction of the Court of Chancery* (1850), vol. 2 at p. 727, where the following appears:

> It has already been stated that the general rule, though not without exceptions as will presently appear, is, that statutes, judgments, and recognizances, at law and in equity, and equitable charges of every kind, in equity, all rank according to their dates: therefore, in the absence of particular circumstances, the successive periods of their execution or attainment constitute the order in which they will be directed to be satisfied.

(Footnote omitted.)

Accordingly, if there were no s. 20(1)(a)(i), in the event that an unperfected security interest predated the exercise of a right of distress it could be argued that the unperfected security interest would have priority over the lien given by rule of law. I read the exception provided for in s. 4(1)(a) as an expression of legislative intent that in all cases an unperfected security interest is to be subordinate to the interest of a person who has a lien given by a rule of law. It is my view that the exception was enacted to deal specifically with the problem of a competition between such a lien and an unperfected security interest. I cannot read the provision as going any further than that.

I conclude, therefore, that the exception provided for in s. 20(1)(a)(i) is simply inapplicable in the circumstances of these two cases. The opening words of s. 4(1)(a) are applicable and the PPSA does not apply to the liens which the municipalities have on the taxpayers' chattels in these cases. Since the exception in s. 20(1)(a)(i) is not applicable, it is my opinion that this issue is determined by the decision in *Commercial Credit*. In that case this court held at pp. 703-04 that the landlord's lien need not be registered in accordance with the PPSA. Because the PPSA does not apply to liens given by a rule of law, that Act does not apply to give the holders of perfected security interests priority over the liens of these municipalities which are liens given by a rule of law.

The appellants also contend that there is a conflict between the provisions of s. 400(2) of the *Municipal Act* and the provisions of the PPSA and rely upon s. 73 of the PPSA. Section 73 of the PPSA provides that when there is a conflict between one of its provisions and a provision of any general or special Act (other than the *Consumer Protection Act*) the provisions of the PPSA prevail. This argument can be answered shortly. Section 73 of the PPSA is identical with the provisions of s. 68 which were in force at the time *Commercial Credit* was decided. In that case this court held that, because the PPSA did not apply to the lien given by a rule of law, s. 68 had no application to the case. That is the precise situation in these cases. Section 73 being a part of the PPSA cannot apply because the PPSA itself does not apply to these cases. That contention cannot succeed.

During argument counsel for the respondents argued that the PPSA did not apply for another reason. Section 2 provides that the PPSA applies to "every transaction ... that ... creates a security interest." It was contended that a lien given by a rule of law was not a "transaction" and therefore the PPSA could not apply to it. In view of the fact that I have concluded on other grounds that the PPSA does not apply, I do not think it necessary to address that interesting argument.

For the reasons set out above, it is my opinion that the provisions of the PPSA do not apply to the municipalities' liens in these cases.

B. The Priorities Between the Appellants and the Municipalities in the Absence of the PPSA

Because I have concluded that the provisions of the PPSA do not apply to the municipalities' liens in these cases it is necessary to determine the priorities in the absence of that Act.

It appears to have been accepted in *Commercial Credit, supra*, that, if the PPSA did not apply, the lien given by a rule of law had priority over the chattel mortgage. The applicability of that assumption to this case is challenged because the appellants contend that if the PPSA does not apply then the common law rule, that encumbrances rank in the order of their coming into existence, must be applied. They say that the application of that rule in these cases requires that their security agreements be given priority over the municipalities' liens for the simple reason that they came into existence before the liens were created. So far as I can tell a similar argument does not appear to have been made in *Commercial Credit*. In my view, therefore, it is appropriate that the issue now be addressed.

I think that the issue can be dealt with fairly shortly. In the earlier part of these reasons I noted that the rule at common law, to which there were exceptions, was that priorities were determined in accordance with the chronological order of the encumbrances. For the purposes of this discussion I will assume that a lien given by a rule of law is an encumbrance upon the property to which it attaches, so that if the common law rule is applicable it would apply to a conflict between such a lien and a security agreement which is obviously an encumbrance upon the property subject to it.

There is no need for any detailed examination of the exceptions to the rule which existed at common law. What has always been recognized is that the common law rule could be displaced by the provisions of a statute. It often is. There is, in my opinion, a statutory provision the effect of which is to give the municipalities' liens priority over the appellants' security interests. It is s. 400(2)(c)(ii) of the *Municipal Act*:

> 400(2) Subject to section 399, in case of taxes that are not a lien on land remaining unpaid for twenty-one days after demand or notice made or given under section 392, 395 or 399 or, where a longer period has been authorized under subsection 399(6) such taxes remain unpaid at the expiry of that period, the collector or, where there is no collector, the treasurer may alone or by an agent, subject to the exemptions provided for in subsection (4), levy them with costs by distress,
>
>   (c) upon any goods and chattels in the possession of the person taxed where title to them is claimed,
>
>   (i) by virtue of an execution against the person taxed,
>
>   (ii) by purchase, gift, transfer or assignment from the person taxed, whether absolute or in trust, or by way of mortgage or otherwise.

An analysis of that provision shows that a municipality may levy by distress upon the chattels in the possession of the person taxed where title is claimed by someone who has obtained title from the person taxed "by way of mortgage or otherwise." The appellants' claims to the chattels in question are based upon their security agreements. The security agreements between the appellants and the persons taxed, upon which the appellants' claims to the chattels are founded, are not called mortgages. Strictly speaking it could be said that the appellants' security agreements with the persons taxed are not "mortgages" within the meaning of s. 400(2)(c)(ii). The reason that they are not called mortgages is that the PPSA does not speak of mortgages but of security agreements and these documents were prepared with the intention of complying with the provisions of the PPSA. The definition of security agreements in the PPSA is wide enough to include mortgages and these security agreements are so similar to mortgages in purpose and effect that I think they must be included in the word "otherwise" found in the provision. It follows that the statute authorized the levy by distress against the chattels covered by the appellants' security agreements. I am unable to read s. 400(2)(c)(ii) in any fashion other than clearly expressing a legislative intent that municipalities are entitled to levy by distress upon chattels in the possession of a person taxed even though the chattels are subject to security agreements.

As I pointed out in the earlier section of these reasons the statute itself does not create a lien. The municipalities' liens arose when the municipalities took possession of the chattels in the exercise of their statutory power to distrain. Because the statute authorizes distress upon chattels subject to security agreements I am constrained to conclude that the lien which arises upon the exercise of that right must take priority over the security agreements. It would, in my view, amount to an absurdity if the statute authorized distress upon chattels covered by security agreements but did not intend as well that the lien created by the exercise of the right of distress was to have priority over the security agreement. The power to distrain upon chattels subject to security agreements would be rendered nugatory if the security agreements were not required to rank behind the liens which had arisen by rule of law. The legislature cannot have intended that the statutory right, which it granted, to distrain on such chattels was to be without effect.

It is my opinion, therefore, that s. 400(2)(c)(ii) should be read as giving the municipalities' liens priority over the appellants' security agreements. Thus the common law rule cannot apply to give the appellants' security agreements priority over the municipalities' liens.

...

Appeals dismissed.

NOTES

1) The Court of Appeal's willingness to read s. 400(2) so broadly to accommodate municipalities is surprising on two grounds. The first is that the Supreme Court held in *Board of Industrial Relations v. Avco Financial Services*, [1979] 2 SCR 699 that, in the absence of very clear language to the contrary, a provision conferring priority on a statutory tax lien is deemed only to be prospective in its effect and is not to be read as overriding existing interests. Galligan JA does not refer to this well-established canon of construction. The second reason is that conferring retroactive priority on a tax lien undermines the carefully conceived priority structure of the OPPSA and makes it very difficult for secured parties to predict how their security will fare in practice.

Municipalities (like other government agencies claiming a super-priority lien) will no doubt respond that a tax lien is the only effective weapon at their disposal to ensure collection of what is owing to them and that it would not be fair to give preferred treatment to consensually secured creditors at the expense of other taxpayers.

For an oft-cited article supporting the Crown's position along these lines, see M. Shanker, "The Worthier Creditors (and a Cheer for the King)" (1975-76), 1 *CBLJ* 340. Are you persuaded by this reasoning? Should a distinction be drawn between different types of Crown lien claims—for example, a simple claim for unpaid taxes as compared with a claim for sales taxes collected by a taxpayer and not remitted to the Crown?

2) In *Leavere*, the court was able to identify a priority rule in the statute that created the lien. What would the position have been otherwise? *Royal Bank of Canada v. Sparrow Electric Corp.*, [1997] 1 SCR 411, extracted in Chapter 4, Part IV.C, is a case in point. Recall that the case involved a dispute between the bank and the Crown in relation to money that the debtor's receiver had paid into a trust account. The bank held a perfected security interest

in the debtor's present and after-acquired inventory and it claimed the money as proceeds of inventory. The Crown claimed the money, relying on the deemed trust provision in s. 227(5) of the *Income Tax Act*. The court held unanimously that, in the absence of a priority rule in the ITA, the common law applied. The common law rule is "first in time" and the court concluded, again unanimously, that the bank was first in time because its security agreements predated the Crown's deemed trust. Recall that the bank's security agreements gave the debtor an implied licence to sell its inventory in the ordinary course of business and use the proceeds to pay its general operating expenses and the court divided on whether the implied licence displaced the bank's priority. Note that the court treated the date of the bank's security agreements as the relevant one for the purposes of the first-in-time rule. Why did it do this rather than relying on the respective dates of attachment? See Kevin Davis, Comment (1998), 29 *CBLJ* 145.

3) In the wake of *Sparrow*, the government amended the ITA. New s. 227(4.1) provides that "where at any time an amount deemed by subsection 227(4) to be held in trust for Her Majesty is not paid to Her Majesty in the manner and at the time provided under this Act, property of the person and property held by any secured creditor ... that but for a security interest would be property of the person, equal to the amount so deemed to be held ... in trust is deemed to be held in trust for her Majesty whether or not the property is subject to a security interest ... and is property beneficially owned by Her Majesty notwithstanding any security interest in such property and in the proceeds thereof, and the proceeds of such property shall be paid to the Receiver-General in priority to all such security interests." The application of these amendments was at issue in the *DaimlerChrysler* case, extracted below.

DaimlerChrysler Financial Services (Debis) Canada Inc. v. Mega Pets Ltd.
[2002] BCJ No. 808 (CA)

NEWBURY JA: [1] This appeal is about the application and interpretation of one of the so-called "super-priority" provisions of the Income Tax Act, RSC 1985, c. 1. (5th Supp.). The provisions in question, s. 227(4) and (4.1), deem a trust for Her Majesty to exist wherever a person deducts or withholds an amount required under the Act. In very general terms, if the person fails to pay such an amount to the Crown as required, then notwithstanding any other enactment (including the Bankruptcy and Insolvency Act), property of the person and "property held by any secured creditor ... that but for a security interest" would be property of the person, up to the amount deemed to be held in trust, is deemed not to form part of the person's property but to be beneficially owned by Her Majesty.

[2] The trial judge in this case ruled that the s. 227 super-priority applied to entitle Her Majesty to the entire proceeds of sale of a motor vehicle that was the subject of an earlier conditional sale agreement between the appellant finance company (herein called "DaimlerChrysler") as the assignee of a conditional seller, and two conditional co-purchasers, the defendants Mega Pets Ltd. ("Mega Pets") and Mr. Kenal, the father of Mega Pets' principal shareholder. Mega Pets had failed to remit approximately $46,000 in deductions made under the Act, to Her Majesty. DaimlerChrysler appeals the trial judge's ruling, which is reproduced at (2000) 11 BLR (3d) 121.

Facts

[3] The facts of the case may be briefly stated. Mega Pets is a British Columbia company whose principal was Mr. Brett Kenal. The company needed a vehicle for its business and proposed to buy one through a Chrysler dealer and sought financing for the purchase. The seller would agree to the financing, to be carried out through a conditional sales contract, only if Mr. Kenal, Sr. would become a joint owner of the vehicle and a joint obligor under the contract. Mr. Kenal, Sr. agreed, and on January 29, 1998, he and Mega Pets signed a conditional sale agreement for the purchase of a 1998 Plymouth Voyageur. The terms of the agreement were not remarkable—for our purposes it is sufficient to note that title to the vehicle was to remain in the seller until all payments had been made under the agreement, and that the two purchasers were "jointly and severally liable" to the seller for all obligations under the contract. The purchasers were required to make 48 monthly payments (including interest) of $563.23, for a total of $27,035.04.

[4] The contract was immediately assigned by the seller to DaimlerChrysler, which perfected a purchase money security interest by the filing of a financing statement as required by the Personal Property Security Act, RSBC 1996, c. 359 ("PPSA"). For Motor Vehicle Act purposes, the vehicle was registered in the name of Mega Pets. Nevertheless, Mr. Kenal deposes that he had keys to the vehicle, and that although Mega Pets had "primary possession," he used the van "quite a bit and basically any time on request." He frequently washed it and filled the tank with gas. The licensing and insurance on the vehicle were paid for by Mega Pets.

[5] Unfortunately, Mega Pets' business encountered financial difficulties. Evidently, it failed to remit to the Crown some $45,955 in deductions made by it from employees' wages for income tax, CPP and EI. On October 26, 1999, the respondent Canada Customs & Revenue Agency ("CCRA") had the vehicle seized under a writ of seizure issued under the Excise Tax Act. Ultimately, CCRA instructed the bailiff to sell the van. A total of $15,300 was realized on the sale in November 1999. From the time of seizure, no monthly payments were made under the conditional sale agreement. The proceeds of sale of the vehicle are being held in trust pending the resolution of priorities as between DaimlerChrysler (which is still owed $15,770 under the conditional sale agreement), CCRA and Mr. Kenal, Sr. He pleaded that CCRA had wrongly converted the vehicle, and that he "would seek" indemnity or contribution to set-off any liability due to DaimlerChrysler by any amount paid by CCRA to the finance company.

The Issues

[6] The relevant portions of s. 224 and s. 227 of the Income Tax Act provide as follows:

[224] (1.3) In subsection 224(1.2),

"secured creditor" means a person who has a security interest in the property of another person or who acts for or on behalf of that person with respect to the security interest and includes a trustee appointed under a trust deed relating to a security interest, a receiver or receiver-manager appointed by a secured creditor or by a court on the application of a secured creditor, a sequestrator or any other person performing a similar function;

"security interest" means any interest in property that secures payment or performance of an obligation and includes an interest created by or arising out of a debenture, mortgage, lien, pledge, charge, deemed or actual trust, assignment or encumbrance of any kind whatever, however or whenever arising, created, deemed to arise or otherwise provided for; ...

[227] (4) Every person who deducts or withholds an amount under this Act is deemed, notwithstanding any security interest (as defined in subsection 224(1.3)) in the amount so deducted or withheld, to hold the amount separate and apart from the property of the person and from property held by any secured creditor (as defined in subsection 224(1.3)) of that person that but for the security interest would be property of the person, in trust for Her Majesty and for payment to Her Majesty in the manner and at the time provided under this Act.

(4.1) Notwithstanding any other provision of this Act, the Bankruptcy and Insolvency Act (except sections 81.1 and 81.2 of that Act), any other enactment of Canada, any enactment of a province or any other law, where at any time an amount deemed by subsection 227(4) to be held by a person in trust for Her Majesty is not paid to Her Majesty in the manner and at the time provided under this Act, property of the person and property held by any secured creditor (as defined in subsection 224(1.3)) of that person that but for a security interest (as defined in subsection 224(1.3)) would be property of the person, equal in value to the amount so deemed to be held in trust is deemed

(a) to be held, from the time the amount was deducted or withheld by the person, separate and apart from the property of the person, in trust for Her Majesty whether or not the property is subject to such a security interest, and

(b) to form no part of the estate or property of the person from the time the amount was so deducted or withheld, whether or not the property has in fact been kept separate and apart from the estate or property of the person and whether or not the property is subject to such a security interest

and is property beneficially owned by Her Majesty notwithstanding any security interest in such property and in the proceeds thereof, and the proceeds of such property shall be paid to the Receiver General in priority to all such security interests.

(4.2) For the purposes of subsections 227(4) and 227(4.1), a security interest does not include a prescribed security interest.

[7] In CCRA's argument, certain parts of the Personal Property Security Act are also relevant. They state:

1(1) In this Act: ...
"security interest" means
(a) an interest in goods, ... that secures payment or performance of an obligation, ... and
(b) the interest of
(i) a transferee arising from the transfer of an account or a transfer of chattel paper,
(ii) a person who delivers goods to another person under a commercial consignment, and
(iii) a lessor under a lease for a term of more than one year,
whether or not the interest secures payment or performance of an obligation; ...

2(1) Subject to section 4, this Act applies

    (a) to every transaction that in substance creates a security interest, without regard to its form and without regard to the person who has title to the collateral, and

    (b) without limiting paragraph (a), to a chattel mortgage, a conditional sale, a floating charge, a pledge, a trust indenture, a trust receipt, an assignment, a consignment, a lease, a trust, and a transfer of chattel paper if they secure payment or performance of an obligation.

It will be noted that prima facie at least, the term "security interest" has a broader meaning in the PPSA than it does in the Income Tax Act.

[8] There is no doubt that the purpose of the PPSA was to simplify the thicket of statutory and common law rules that previously governed various forms of chattel security, including chattel mortgages, leases, debentures and conditional sale agreements.

•••

[9] In the court below and on appeal, counsels' arguments proceeded largely on the basis that the "property" in issue was the vehicle itself. CCRA relied heavily on what it called the "substance, not form" principle enshrined in s. 2(1) of the PPSA, which it said should also apply to the interpretation of s. 227 of the Income Tax Act. It took the position that the vehicle had "in substance" been sold to Mega Pets, that the conditional sale agreement was a security agreement that created a "security interest" within the meaning of s. 224(1.3), and that the "'but for' test" imported by s. 227(4.1) was met. In the words of the trial judge below:

> [CCRA] argues that the "but for" test is met because but for the granting of security, Mega Pets would have title to the vehicle. It submits that this interpretation is consistent with a purposive approach to the interpretation of the legislation. The purpose is to protect unremitted payroll deduction through the device of a statutory deemed trust. [at para. 7; ... .]

[10] The argument of DaimlerChrysler was diametrically opposed to that of the Crown. It contended that the vehicle was the property of DaimlerChrysler, not of Mega Pets and/or Mr. Kenal; that common law principles rather than the PPSA should be looked to determine the nature of its interest; and that the "but for" test was not met in any event because if the conditional sale agreement had not been entered into, the property (i.e., the vehicle) would be property of DaimlerChrysler rather than of either conditional purchaser. It also relied on a "purposive approach" to the interpretation of the Income Tax Act. As the trial judge noted, DaimlerChrysler argued that it could not be the purpose of the legislation to enable the Crown:

> ... to require an innocent third party to be responsible for the tax debt of another taxpayer. This is particularly so where, in a vendor financed conditional sales contract, the vendor will lose the vehicle of which it remained legal owner and which constituted the sole collateral for the debt. This, it argues, is expropriation without compensation. [para. 10]

[11] In the alternative, DaimlerChrysler submitted that even if it were found to be a "secured creditor" having a "security interest" within the meaning of the Income Tax Act, the fact that Mr. Kenal was a joint owner of the vehicle meant that the "but for" test was not met. In other words, even if CCRA were correct as to the application of the test, the

vehicle would be the property of both Mega Pets and Mr. Kenal rather than of Mega Pets alone. This argument was supported by Mr. Kenal.

The Trial Judgment

[12] The trial judge began her analysis by referring to the decision of the Supreme Court of Canada in *Royal Bank of Canada v. Sparrow Electric Corp.*, [1997] 1 SCR 411. It was decided before the enactment of what is now s. 227. The primary issue dealt with by the Court was whether the deemed trust created by what was then s. 227(4) of the Income Tax Act had priority over Bank Act security and debenture security registered under the Alberta PPSA. The majority of the Court, per Iacobucci J, held that the deemed trust did not take priority notwithstanding the "licence to sell" given to the borrower under the debenture.

[13] The trial judge in the case at bar observed that the Court in Sparrow Electric did not limit the kind of interest that could be "trumped" by a deemed trust. (para. 18) With respect to the "purposive" approach to the interpretation of the Income Tax Act advocated by DaimlerChrysler, she stated that the purpose of the current provisions was still to "[protect] unremitted payroll deductions through the device of a statutory deemed trust," citing para. 36 of Sparrow Electric. She did not refer directly to the majority's agreement with the general statement of the minority, per Gonthier J, that in interpreting the Income Tax Act, courts must apply the "plain meaning" rule. Gonthier J stated the applicable approach as follows:

> The principle that the plain meaning of the relevant sections of the Income Tax Act is to prevail unless the transaction is a sham has recently been affirmed by this Court in *Canada v. Antosko*, [1994] 2 SCR 312. Iacobucci J, writing for the court held at pp. 326-27 that:
>
>> While it is true that the courts must view discrete sections of the Income Tax Act in light of the other provisions of the Act and of the purpose of the legislation, and that they must analyze a given transaction in the context of economic and commercial reality, such techniques cannot alter the result where the words of the statute are clear and plain and where the legal and practical effect of the transaction is undisputed. ...
>
> I accept the following comments on the Antosko case in P.W. Hogg and J.E. McGee, *Principles of Canadian Income Tax Law* (1995), Section 22.3(c) "Strict and purposive interpretation," at pp. 453-54:
>
>> It would introduce intolerable uncertainty under the Income Tax Act if clear language and a detailed provision of the Act were to be qualified by unexpressed exceptions derived from a court's view of the object and purpose of the provision. ... (The *Antosko* case) is simply a recognition that "object and purpose" can play only a limited role in the interpretation of a statute that is as precise and detailed as the Income Tax Act. When a provision is couched in specific language that admits of no doubt or ambiguity in its application to the facts, then the provision must be applied regardless of its object and purpose. Only when the statutory language admits of some doubt or ambiguity in its application to the facts is it useful to resort to the object and purpose of the provision.

The majority also expressed the other side of the coin in *Sparrow Electric* as follows:

Finally, I wish to emphasize that it is open to Parliament to step in and assign absolute priority to the deemed trust. A clear illustration of how this might be done is afforded by s. 224(1.2) ITA, which vests certain moneys in the Crown "notwithstanding any security interest in those moneys" and provides that they "shall be paid to the Receiver General in priority to any such security interest." All that is needed to effect the desired result is clear language of that kind. In the absence of such clear language, judicial innovation is undesirable, both because the issue is policy charged and because a legislative mandate is apt to be clearer than a rule whose precise bounds will become fixed only as a result of expensive and lengthy litigation.

[14] The trial judge in the case at bar also cited a judgment of this Court, *Royal Bank of Canada v. Tuxedo Transport Ltd.* (2000) 190 DLR (4th) 139, which was decided after the enactment of s. 227(4.1) and concerned a priority contest between a receiver under a general security agreement ("GSA") and the Crown under the deemed trust provision in the Income Tax Act. This court reversed the trial judge, holding on appeal that the new language of the Act met the "required degree of clarity to give priority of the fund to the Crown," and rejecting the taxpayer's argument that after-acquired assets were not caught by the language of the statute. Thus Parliament had fulfilled the prediction of Iacobucci J in *Sparrow Electric*, having used sufficiently clear language to "overtake a fixed and specific charge" created by a GSA.

· · ·

[16] Last, the trial judge in the case at bar noted the decision of Tysoe J in *Re United Used Auto & Truck Parts Ltd.* (2000) 83 BCLR (3d) 191 (BCSC), which revolved around the "requirement to pay" provision at s. 224(1.2) of the Income Tax Act. This provision includes a "but for" test somewhat similar to that in the present s. 227. The Court held that CCRA was entitled to enforce the payment to it of payments due from the debtor to a finance company under a purchase money security agreement, commenting:

> The second submission on behalf of Mr. Mott [the creditor] is that his security agreement provides that the proceeds from the sale of the charged vehicle parts are to be held by United in trust for him and that, therefore, the Requirement to Pay did not attach to the funds. The answer to this submission is that the definition of "security interest" in s. 224(1.3) specifically includes trusts. If it were not for Mr. Mott's security interest, which includes the trust provision as well as the charge against the vehicles and their parts, the funds would be payable to United. Clause (b) of 224(1.2) is engaged, with the result that the funds become the property of Her Majesty and must be paid to the Receiver General in priority to Mr. Mott's security agreement, including the trust as well as the charge.

[17] Having cited these cases, the learned trial judge said that nothing in the language of s. 227(4) or 227(4.1) of the Income Tax Act required the property in question first to have been in the hands of the tax debtor and then to have been transferred to a secured creditor. In her view, the real question was "whether DaimlerChrysler is a secured creditor, holding a security interest for security purposes." After recounting DaimlerChrysler's argument and the effect of the PPSA on the interpretation of s. 227 of the Income Tax Act, she concluded she could look to the PPSA to characterize DaimlerChrysler's interest in the vehicle for Income Tax Act purposes. She relied in particular on

para. 54 of *Sparrow Electric*, where the minority observed that the PPSA had "fundamentally changed the characterization of security interests" and that as a result, what would previously have been a floating charge now attached immediately upon execution of a security agreement. Thus, said the trial judge, "whatever the common law principles may be, they cannot be taken to alter the effect of the PPSA on the characterization of security interests." The PPSA was, she noted, applicable by its terms to every transaction that in substance creates a security interest, and specifically, to conditional sale agreements (see s. 2(1) of the PPSA, quoted supra, at para. 7) and there was "no meaningful difference" between a GSA and a conditional sale contract in competition with the Crown's deemed trust. In her words:

> In both cases title is with the secured creditor. In *Sparrow Electric* the Bank's security gave it a fixed and specific charge which gives it title, subject to the equitable right of redemption.
>
> Therefore DaimlerChrysler holds a security interest as defined in the ITA. The "but for" test found in s. 227 of the ITA is satisfied. But for the granting of security, Mega Pets would have had title to the vehicle.
>
> This conclusion is supported by cases where the courts have found that conditional sales contracts are security agreements notwithstanding arguments by conditional sales vendors that title or property remains with the vendor and ought to be insulated from claims of other creditors: *Haibeck v. No. 40 Taurus Ventures Ltd.* (1991), 59 BCLR (2d) 229 (BCSC); *Euroclean Canada Inc. v. Forest Glade Investments Ltd. et al.* (1985), 49 OR (2d) 769 (Ont. CA).

(The latter cases cited by the trial judge involved priority contests between security interests registered under the PPSA.)

[18] The trial judge turned next to the second argument raised by DaimlerChrysler—the fact that Mr. Kenal had appeared in the conditional sale agreement as a joint owner of the vehicle.

...

On Appeal

[20] DaimlerChrysler appeals both conclusions of the trial judge—i.e., the ruling that s. 227(4.1) of the Income Tax Act applied to the conditional sale agreement to give Her Majesty the beneficial owner of the proceeds of sale of the vehicle; and the ruling that Mega Pets was the "sole owner" thereof. In my opinion, DaimlerChrysler must succeed on both grounds.

Joint Ownership

[21] I will deal first with the second and less difficult ground of appeal—the nature of Mr. Kenal's involvement in the conditional sale transaction.

...

[Newbury JA found that Mega Pets and Mr. Kenal were joint tenants and not tenants in common, and, therefore, until the joint tenancy was severed, it could not be said that the vehicle itself was the "property of" Mega Pets within the meaning of ITA 227(4.1) at the time the CCRA purported to seize and sell it.]

The Effect of Section 227

[31] In my respectful opinion, the trial judge also erred on two related points that led her to conclude incorrectly that for purposes of the Income Tax Act provisions, the conditional sale agreement was indistinguishable from a debenture, mortgage, pledge or other charge. First, as a matter of statutory interpretation, there is no basis for construing the term "security interest" as defined in s. 224(1.3) of the Income Tax Act, with reference to the PPSA of British Columbia. The definitions in s. 224 purport to be free-standing and do not incorporate or refer to any other statute. Although the term "security interest" has now entered common legal parlance and is often understood to refer to interests covered by the PPSA of whatever province one is considering, the definition contained in the Income Tax Act is the only one properly considered in determining the meaning of the term for purposes of s. 227. In this regard, I note the proposition adopted by Gonthier J in *Husky Oil Operations Ltd. v. Minister of National Revenue*, [[1995] 3 SCR 453], that terms such as "secured creditor," when used in a federal statute (in that case the Bankruptcy Act) must be interpreted "as defined by the federal Parliament, not by the provincial legislatures." (para. 32) Similarly, the definition of "security interest" for purposes of the Income Tax Act cannot be determined by provincial legislation such as the PPSA. (See also *Schwab*, infra, at para. 38, per Dovell J) I do not read *Sparrow Electric* as casting any doubt on this proposition, and indeed I note Gonthier J's observation at para. 54 that the PPSA did not govern the priority contest between the statutory trust created by the Income Tax Act and a security interest under the provincial PPSA. Thus whereas the trial judge in the case at bar stated that "whatever the common law principles may be, they cannot be taken to alter the effect of the PPSA on the characterization of security interests," the correct proposition was that whatever the PPSA may provide, it cannot be taken to alter the effect of the Income Tax Act on common law principles.

[32] For convenience, I set out the definition of "security interest" as it appears in s. 224 of the Income Tax Act:

> "security interest" means any interest in property that secures payment or performance of an obligation and includes an interest created by or arising out of a debenture, mortgage, lien, pledge, charge, deemed or actual trust, assignment or encumbrance of any kind whatever, however or whenever arising, created, deemed to arise or otherwise provided for;

It will be noted that in contrast to the PPSA (see above at para. 7), conditional sale agreements are not included in the list of security interests. This omission seems strange if (as CCRA argued) Parliament intended to include such agreements, since they are a widely-known form of chattel security. Although it is arguable in a colloquial sense that a conditional sale agreement creates an interest in property that secures the performance of an obligation, the fact that all the instruments specifically listed involve the borrower's transferring to, or "charging" the property in favour of, the creditor, must at least give one pause. I would not have thought that, apart from the PPSA, one would speak of a conditional vendor or lessor as having an interest that "secures payment." Rather, title is retained to secure payment. It is the conditional purchaser who acquires a property interest in the chattel over time, reflecting his or her increasing "equity." That interest does not secure payment of an obligation.

[33] The absence of conditional sale agreements from the list in the statutory definition of "security interest" was noted in a recent decision of the Saskatchewan Court of Queen's Bench, *Canada (Deputy Attorney General) v. Schwab Construction Ltd.* (2001), 25 CBR (4th) 289, aff'd at [2002] SJ No. 16 (Sask. CA). *Schwab* was a priority contest between Her Majesty (relying on the deemed trust provisions of ss. 227(4) and (4.1) of the Income Tax Act) and in one instance, a lessor of chattels, and in another instance, a conditional seller. As in the case at bar, CCRA submitted in *Schwab* that the leases and conditional sale agreement in question came within the definition of "security interest."

[Newbury JA considered the trial and appellate judgments in *Schwab* as well as *Bank of Nova Scotia v. Turyders Trucking Ltd.* (2001), 32 CBR (4th) 14 (Ont. SCJ), and continued:]

[38] Both *Schwab* and *Turyders*, then, may be taken to support the view that the vehicle in issue here was not property subject to a "security interest" within the meaning of s. 227(4.1) because in the absence of clear language the courts will not construe a statute so as to "expropriate" a third party's property. To this I would add that for the reasons set out above at para. 32, neither a conditional sale agreement nor a lease with option to purchase creates a "security interest" in the creditor, as seems to be intended by the Income Tax Act (and in particular by the "but for" test).

The "But For" Test

[39] This in turn leads to a closely related point of statutory construction—the question of whether it can be said that "but for" the "interest," the vehicle would have been property of Mega Pets. For convenience I reproduce s. 227(4.1) of the Income Tax Act again below:

> (4.1) Notwithstanding any other provision of this Act, the Bankruptcy and Insolvency Act (except sections 81.1 and 81.2 of that Act), any other enactment of Canada, any enactment of a province or any other law, where at any time an amount deemed by subsection 227(4) to be held by a person in trust for Her Majesty is not paid to Her Majesty in the manner and at the time provided under this Act, property of the person and property held by any secured creditor (as defined in subsection 224(1.3)) of that person that but for a security interest (as defined in subsection 224(1.3)) would be property of the person, equal in value to the amount so deemed to be held in trust is deemed
>
> (a) to be held, from the time the amount was deducted or withheld by the person, separate and apart from the property of the person, in trust for Her Majesty whether or not the property is subject to such a security interest, and
>
> (b) to form no part of the estate or property of the person from the time the amount was so deducted or withheld, whether or not the property has in fact been kept separate and apart from the estate or property of the person and whether or not the property is subject to such a security interest
>
> and is property beneficially owned by Her Majesty notwithstanding any security interest in such property and in the proceeds thereof, and the proceeds of such property shall be paid to the Receiver General in priority to all such security interests.

[40] Assuming for the moment that the "property" being referred to is the vehicle it-self, can it be said that "but for" DaimlerChrysler's security interest, the vehicle "would be property of" Mega Pets or of the co-purchasers? In my view it cannot. Unlike the situation where a debenture, mortgage or other charge is granted to a creditor, the vehicle here never was and never did become "property of" Mega Pets or its co-owner. "But for" the security interest, the vehicle would be the property of the seller (or in this case its assignee DaimlerChrysler), not of the co-purchasers, who were required to pay all amounts owing under the agreement before title to the vehicle would pass.

[41] Of course, the distinction between conditional sale agreements and other forms of chattel security was effectively eliminated for purposes of the PPSA—as Cuming and Wood noted in their handbook, ... one of the goals of the legislation was to ensure that the "juridical nature of the security interest" was secondary to the registration regime. This is the lesson of the cases cited by the trial judge at para. 33 of her Reasons: *Haibeck v. No. 40 Taurus Ventures Ltd.*, supra, *Euroclean Canada Inc. v. Forest Glade Investments Ltd.*, supra, and *Re Ottaway* (1980) 110 DLR (3d) 231 (BCCA). But as Cuming and Wood also note, the same approach cannot be used outside the PPSA regime. The particular terms of the agreement in question, such as that reserving title in the conditional seller, remain valid and must be considered in applying the wording of the Income Tax Act.

...

Appeal allowed.

NOTES

1) *DaimlerChrysler* is a good example of a court's willingness to torture quite clear statutory language because of the court's hostility to what it perceives to be confiscatory language. Is this a proper exercise of the court's role or should it be left to Parliament to correct defects in taxation legislation? For a critical discussion of *DaimlerChrysler*, see J.S. Ziegel, "Conditional Sales and Superpriority Crown Claims Under ITA s. 227" (2003), 38 CBR (4th) 161.

2) There have been a variety of proposals over the years to resolve the conflict between Crown liens and consensual security interests. One solution, much favoured by secured creditors, is simply to abolish preferred status altogether for Crown claims. This is in effect what BIA s. 86, added in 1992, does in the bankruptcy context. Another approach, put forward by Professor Bogart ((1983), 8 *CBLJ* 129), is to require all Crown liens to be registered in the PPS registry and to give them the priority accorded to consensual security interests, and no more. How workable is this solution? So far it has made no apparent impression on provincial authorities, but it did influence the drafters of s. 87 of the 1992 amendments to the BIA. This provides in substance that a Crown lien created under federal or provincial legislation has no effect unless it is registered in a provincial PPS registry and that, when registered, it shall rank after all previously perfected security interests. For several years now there have been discussions, as part of future amendments to the BIA, of the desirability of Parliament enacting a *Crown Priorities Act* that would deal comprehensively with federal and provincial tax lien claims and establish a priorities regime that the private sector can also live with.

CHAPTER ELEVEN

Protection of Transferees in Ordinary Course

I. INTRODUCTION

In previous chapters we have examined the interaction between secured parties and general creditors and their representatives, and among secured parties themselves. In this chapter we focus on the following issue: under what circumstances is the debtor authorized or able under the PPSA to pass good title to the collateral to a third party free of the security interest? For example:

SP has a security interest in D's truck. D sells the truck to T. Does D take the truck free of SP's security interest?

The general rules are in OPPSA ss. 20(1)(c), and 20(1)(d), and 25(1)(a). Section 20(1)(c) provides that an unperfected security interest in chattel paper, documents of title, securities, instruments, or goods is not effective against a transferee thereof who takes under a transfer that does not secure payment or performance of an obligation and who gives value and receives delivery thereof without knowledge of the security interest. Section 20(1)(d) enacts a parallel rule for accounts. Section 25(1)(a) provides that where collateral gives rise to proceeds, the security interest therein continues as to the collateral, unless the secured party expressly or impliedly authorized the dealing with the collateral free of the security interest. Read together, these provisions enact three general rules:

1. If the security interest is unperfected, the transferee gets clear title provided the transferee gave value, took delivery, and had no knowledge of the security interest (if the collateral is accounts, there is no delivery requirement).
2. If the security interest is perfected and SP expressly or impliedly authorized the transfer, the transferee gets clear title. The typical case is where the collateral is inventory. D must have the right to sell inventory in the ordinary course of business because otherwise her business will not be viable. An inventory security agreement may include a provision stating expressly that D has the right to sell inventory in the ordinary course of business. But even if the agreement is silent, the court is likely to imply a provision along these lines.
3. If the security interest is perfected and SP did not expressly or impliedly authorize the transfer, the transferee takes subject to SP's security interest.

OPPSA s. 28 carves out some exceptions to general rule 3. If a s. 28 exception applies, then T gets clear title even if SP has perfected its security interest and whether or not SP has authorized the dealing. Part II, below, deals with s. 28(1) (the "buyer in ordinary course" provision). Part III deals with s. 28(3) (transfer of chattel paper). Part IV deals with s. 28(4) (transfer of instruments and documents of title). Part V deals with ss. 28(6) to 28(10) and 28.1 (transfer of securities) and related provisions in the *Securities Transfer Act, 2006*.

II. SALE OF GOODS IN ORDINARY COURSE

A. Introduction

OPPSA s. 28(1) provides:

> 28(1) A buyer of goods from a seller who sells the goods in the ordinary course of business takes them free from any security interest therein given by the seller even though it is perfected and the buyer knows of it, unless the buyer also knew that the sale constituted a breach of the security agreement.

This is mainly, but not exclusively, a consumer protection provision. For example, consider the following case:

> D is a furniture retailer. SP has a perfected security interest in D's inventory. The security agreement authorizes D to sell inventory in the ordinary course of business, and it goes on to say that SP may withdraw authority by serving notice on D. SP serves a notice on D and shortly afterward D sells an armchair to T, a retail customer. Does T get clear title?

If general rule 3 applied, the answer would be "no": SP's security interest is perfected and SP has not authorized D's dealing with T. However, s. 28(1) displaces general rule 3: T gets clear title unless T knew the sale was in breach of the security agreement. The purpose is to avoid retail customers being at risk of unpublicized restrictions on D's right to sell its inventory. What steps might SP take to prevent D from selling inventory in breach of the notice?

B. Buyer

OPPSA s. 28(1) applies only if T is a "buyer." Section 28 draws a distinction between "buyers" and "purchasers." For example:

> D is a furniture retailer and SP1 has a security interest in D's inventory. D gives SP2 a security interest in one of its sofas.

SP2 is a "purchaser" within the meaning of the Act: s. 1(1) defines "purchase" to include "taking by sale, lease, negotiation, mortgage, pledge, lien, gift or any other consensual transaction creating an interest in personal property." However, SP2 is not a "buyer," and so s. 28(1) does not apply. Instead, in the event of a priority dispute between SP1 and SP2, the governing provision is s. 30 if SP2's security interest is perfected, or s. 20(1)(a)(i) if it is not perfected.

Assume that T is a retail customer and she rents a sofa from D. Section 28(1) does not apply, because T is not a buyer. Section 28(2) applies instead. Section 28(2) is a parallel provision for leases. It provides that T holds the goods, to the extent of her rights under the lease, free from SP's security interest. In other words, SP cannot interfere with T's possession of the sofa during the term of the lease.

C. Security Interest Given by Seller

OPPSA s. 28(1) applies only if the security interest is "given by the seller." For example:

D is an accountant. SP has a perfected security interest in D's office furniture as equipment. D sells the furniture to X, a secondhand dealer. X resells the furniture to T. X takes the furniture subject to SP's security interest.

Section 28(1) does not apply because the sale to X was not in the ordinary course of D's business (see further, Part II.D, below). T also takes the furniture subject to SP's security interest. Section 28(1) does not apply because T bought the furniture from X, whereas SP's security interest was given by D.

Could T have protected herself by searching the register before buying the furniture? In the first place, it may not occur to T that there is any need for a search, given that she is buying the goods from a retailer in the ordinary course of business. But even if T does search, she is likely to search under X's name, not D's and a search under X's name will not disclose SP's security interest. This is the A-B-C-D problem again (see Chapter 6, Part III.E.1). In the other provinces, there is a special provision for low-value transactions which provides that a buyer of goods that are acquired as consumer goods takes the goods free of any security interest if the value of the goods did not exceed $2,000 at the time the security interest attached, provided the buyer gave value and did not know about the security interest. This provision gives a measure of protection to buyers like T in our example, subject to the value of the goods. However, there is no corresponding provision in Ontario.

The buyer is somewhat better protected, though, if the collateral is a motor vehicle. Consider the following example:

D is an accountant. SP has a perfected security interest in D's car as equipment. D sells the car to T.

In these circumstances, in Ontario D will have to supply T with a "used vehicle information package" (UVIP): see Chapter 6, Part IV. The UVIP will include a PPS register search against the car's VIN. Assuming the VIN is correctly recorded in SP's financing statement, the search will alert T to SP's security interest. On the other hand, if SP's financing statement omits the VIN or incorrectly records it, s. 28(5) applies and T will obtain clear title. Now consider the following variation on the above example:

D is an accountant. SP has a perfected security interest in D's car as equipment. D sells the car to X, a dealer who, in turn, sells it to T.

Note that the UVIP requirement does not apply to dealers. This means that T will only discover SP's security interest if: (1) she realizes the need for a register search; and (2) SP has correctly recorded the VIN in the financing statement. Assuming SP has not done so, does s. 28(5) apply? See note 7 following the *Re Lambert* extract in Chapter 6, Part IV.

D. Ordinary Course of Business

Camco Inc. v. Olson Realty (1979) Ltd.
(1986), 50 Sask. R 161 (CA)

[The issue in this case was whether buyers of household appliances, who purchased them with their condominium units, obtained good title under the Saskatchewan equivalent of OPPSA ss. 28(1) and (2). Section 30(1) of the Saskatchewan Act reads:

> 30(1) A buyer or lessee of goods sold or leased in the ordinary course of business of the seller or lessor takes free of any perfected or unperfected security interest therein given by or reserved against the seller or lessor or arising under section 29, whether or not the buyer or lessee knows of it, unless the secured party proves that the buyer or lessee also knows that the sale or lease constitutes a breach of the security agreement.

Muxlow was a real estate developer and manager in Saskatchewan. It developed a condominium project in Regina (the "Cedar Meadows" project) comprising 171 units, which were expected to be sold as a tax shelter. Each unit came equipped with four kitchen appliances, i.e., washer, dryer, refrigerator and stove. All 171 units were sold to individual buyers under a purchase and sale agreement.

The appliances were purchased by Muxlow from Camco, an appliance manufacturer, on conditional sale terms, Camco did not know that Muxlow intended to resell the appliances. Conditions 3 and 4 of the conditional sale agreement provided:

> 3. The purchaser warrants that as of the date hereof the purchaser is not purchasing the equipment for the purpose of reselling same or any part thereof except that the same be sold with the building in which it is a chattel and then only after the Vendor has been paid in full hereunder.
>
> 4. The property in and title to the equipment shall not pass to the purchaser, but shall remain in the vendor until the total unpaid purchase price and any other amounts payable to the vendor by the purchaser have been paid and the purchaser has performed all his obligations pursuant to the Agreement.

Camco duly perfected its security interest by registration under the Saskatchewan PPSA. The individual buyers of the condominium units were not aware that the appliances were subject to a conditional sale agreement. Most unit buyers did not retain their own solicitors but used the legal services provided by Muxlow, which were included in the unit price.

The trial judge, applying s. 30(1), found in favour of the unit buyers. On appeal Camco argued (i) that there were no sales of the appliances to the unit buyers, and (ii) that the sales were not made in the ordinary course of Muxlow's business.]

TALLIS JA (for the Court): I first turn to the appellant's contention that the respondents were not "buyers" of the appliances from Muxlow. As a starting point I observe that the Act does not define "buyer" or "sale." Whether the respondents are "buyers" within the intendment of s. 30(1) is essentially a question of fact for the trial court and that court's determination of the issue should not be disturbed unless the standards of appellate review mandate such intervention.

The appellant asserts that the Condominium Purchase and Construction Agreement with each of the respondent unit purchasers creates the relationship of principal and agent with respect to the appliances. While paragraph 3 of the agreement does appoint Muxlow as agent for certain purposes, the stipulated facts do not support the contention that Muxlow acquired the appliances for the respondents as their agent with the result that no actual sale of the appliances by Muxlow to the respondent unit purchasers took place. Paragraph 5 stipulates that the appliances are included in the purchase price. Muxlow purchased the appliances from the appellant in 1982 and thereafter sold the appliances to the respondent purchasers as and when sales of the condominium units were made.

In this case we have the passing of title to the appliances from the seller (Muxlow) to each of the respondents for a stipulated price. Furthermore, the appliances were delivered to the respondent buyers prior to Muxlow's default under the agreement with the appellant. Accordingly I do not find it necessary or desirable to address technical passage-of-title rules in the factual context of this case. Whether one should look to passage-of-title provisions in other legislation such as the Sale of Goods Act, RSS 1978, c. S-1, when dealing with issues under s. 30(1) of the Act is left open for future consideration.

The conclusion of the learned trial judge on this issue comports with commercial reality and is fully supported by the evidence. I therefore reject this ground of appeal.

Buyer of Goods Sold in the Ordinary Course of Business of the Seller

I now consider the question whether the respondent buyers attained the status of buyers of goods sold in the ordinary course of business of the seller (Muxlow)—a question which involves the application of s. 30(1) and its effect on the appellant's perfected security. For convenience I again recite s. 30(1) of the Act: [see above].

...

Speaking generally in the context of this case, this provision is an exception to the priority rules under the Act. It protects such a buyer from a security interest *created by his seller* even though the security interest is perfected and the buyer knows of its existence, unless the buyer also knows that the sale was in violation of the security agreement. Thus, the protective value of "perfection" of a security interest is subject to an important qualification: the security interest remains good against the debtor himself and various third party claimants but not good against certain bona fide purchasers—the buyer of goods sold in the ordinary course of business of the seller. In this case the respondent buyers were not aware of the appellant's security interest. As their good faith is not in issue, I do not need to consider the scope of any such limitation. Furthermore, this case is limited to a consideration of a perfected security interest.

In my opinion s. 30(1) represents an outgrowth of the notion that a "buyer in the ordinary course of trade" should take free of a security interest. In our commercial law the holder in due course of negotiable instruments, the bona fide purchaser of negotiable instruments, the bona fide purchaser of investment securities and various other bona fide purchasers have been accorded privileges—with the result that they sometimes acquire rights better than the rights of some kinds of claimants who did not authorize or approve of the sale or transfer. Thus a special kind of bona fide purchaser of goods is described in s. 30(1)—he must buy goods sold in the ordinary course of business of the seller. Under such circumstances the secured party has no claim against the buyer: he must look to the seller only for satisfaction. The statutory protection extended to such a buyer undoubtedly rests on principles of justice and commercial utility. In many cases the collateral involved is of such a kind that the debtor's ability to dispose of it in the usual course of business may be important so that he can continue his business as a going concern and thereby pay his indebtedness to the secured party. Such a consideration would apply with equal force to authorized sales. But even if this is not so—the security agreement may stipulate to the contrary—the secured party who permits a businessman to have possession of the goods, runs the risk that the buyer taking from the businessman may qualify as a "buyer of goods sold in the ordinary course of business of the seller."

Furthermore one can discern a public policy consideration in the legislation which favours the safeguarding of sales transactions over the safeguarding of secured transactions in such a case. In most cases the seller will pay the secured party but whether he does or does not is of no concern to a person with the status of buyer under s. 30(1). This result is desirable where the buyer is an uninformed consumer buyer.

Learned counsel for the parties appearing on this appeal accordingly focused primary attention on the question who is a "buyer of goods sold in the ordinary course of business of the seller." The Act does not define such a buyer. (This may be contrasted with s. 1-201(9) of the *Uniform Commercial Code* which provides in the relevant part:

> "Buyer in ordinary course of business" means a person who in good faith and without knowledge that the sale to him is in violation of the ownership rights or security interest of a third party in the goods buys in ordinary course from a person in the business of selling goods of that kind but does not include a pawnbroker.)

So in considering this issue one must consider the express words of the statute in the context of the functional design and legislative intent of the Act. Since considerable argument centered on the point, I first consider an ancillary issue of law—whether s. 30(1) applies only to security interests in inventory.

•••

While this section is primarily applicable to inventory, I am of the opinion that it is not so limited. It is true that s. 30(1) requires that the buyer buy goods "in the ordinary course of business of the seller" and that such goods would often be inventory of the seller. But there is no explicit language in this section that limits it only to security interests in inventory. Furthermore, I do not find any such intent by implication. In each case the critical question is not whether the appliances are classifiable as inventory but whether the buyer is a buyer of goods sold "in the ordinary course of business of the seller." On this branch of the case I refer to *Hempstead Bank v. Andy's Car Rental System Inc.*, 312

NYS (2d) 317, at 321, where Martuscello J, speaking for the Supreme Court, Appellate Division, said:

> Similarly, while the Official Comment to section 9-307 indicates that that section applies primarily to sales from "inventory," it does not indicate that every sale from inventory is protected thereby. Indeed, section 9-307 itself does not even employ the word "inventory." The major consequences of the classification of Andy's cars as inventory is the manner in which any security interest therein is required to be perfected (see UCC ss. 9-302 to 9-305). It would seem, therefore, that the critical question here is not whether the cars are classifiable as inventory, but whether Andy's was "in the business of selling goods of that kind."

I also observe that s. 9-307(1) of the *Uniform Commercial Code* provides:

> "A buyer in ordinary course of business" (subsection (9) of section 1-201) other than a person buying farm products from a person engaged in farming operations takes free of a security interest created by his seller even though the security interest is perfected and even though the buyer knows of its existence.

Until 1956, this subsection read as follows:

> In the case of inventory, and in the case of goods as to which the secured party files a financing statement in which he claims interest in proceeds, a buyer in ordinary course of business takes free of a security interest even though perfected and even though the buyer knows of the terms of the security agreement.

Having concluded that s. 30(1) is not limited only to security interests in inventory, I now turn to the appellant's attack on the trial judge's finding that the respondents are buyers under s. 30(1) of the Act. First the appellant submits that the court should take judicial notice of the ordinary manner in which the appliances in question are normally sold. Learned counsel submitted that such appliances are normally sold in retail outlets that deal with such types of chattel. This branch of the argument involved a consideration of security interests in inventory which I have previously discussed. As a further point, the appellant submits that generally a purchaser of realty does not purchase major appliances with realty for a global consideration. Conversely the seller of realty does not normally sell appliances with the realty. Under such circumstances the appellant contends that one who purchases appliances in such an abnormal manner is not a buyer within the intendment of s. 30(1). Consequently such a buyer bears the responsibility of first checking the registry of liens against personal property and if he fails to do so, then he must bear any consequent loss.

The appellant, in asking this court to overturn the trial court's conclusion, asserts that s. 30(1) contemplates an inquiry as to the normal manner in which goods of this type are sold. This suggested approach is probably an outgrowth of the language used in s. 30(1) of the Ontario Personal Property Security Act which provides:

...

In discussing this Ontario subsection, the learned author of McLaren, *Personal Transactions in Personal Property in Canada* (1979), states at pages 10-31:

> A seller will be considered to be dealing in the ordinary course of business if he normally deals in the class of items in which the goods fall and the terms of sale are the same as

usually found in that type of business. General commercial practice appears to be the guiding criterion. Factors such as whether or not the transaction is one that is normally entered into by people in the seller's business, where the transaction is executed, the nature of the buyer, the quantity of goods sold, and the price obtained, are proper considerations in determining whether a sale complies with the requirements of s. 30(1).

This approach was also discussed in Catzman et al., *Personal Property Security Law in Ontario* (1976), where the learned authors state at pages 144-145:

The person whose conduct is claimed to come under the description must be engaged in carrying on a business, that business must involve as subjects of traffic things of the class in which the item dealt in falls, and the basis of dealing must be on the normal terms of dealing with that class of items in that type of business. General commercial practice rather than the dealer's particular operating methods is the criterion.

Purchasers

All three subsections speak only of purchasers in the ordinary course of business. Such transactions as mortgages or pledges, even though in ordinary course of business, are not included. The USUCC which speaks of "buying" (the [Sask.] Act substitutes "purchasing") in ordinary course of business specifies that it "may be for cash or by exchange of other property or on secured or unsecured credit and includes receiving under a pre-existing contract for sale, but does not include a transfer in bulk or as security for or in total or partial satisfaction of a money claim."

As to goods, a purchaser's protection under this section arises when the seller sells within the meaning indicated by the foregoing quotation. As to chattel paper or a non-negotiable instrument, there must be such a sale (since the provisions apply only as to purchasers) and additionally the purchaser must take possession. Thus, for goods title passage suffices but for chattel paper and non-negotiable instruments it must be supplemented by a transfer of possession.

Aside from goods, chattel paper, and non-negotiable instruments, there are no special rules about purchasers in ordinary course of business. Thus, for example, dealings in documents of title or securities are not affected by this section.

Whose Course of Business

For goods, the inquiry is whether the seller sells in the ordinary course of business. For chattel paper and instruments, only a purchaser taking possession in the ordinary course of his business receives the protection.

The market for chattel paper and instruments is financial institutions. To be entitled to extraordinary protection, they can fairly be required to show that they were following accepted business practices of such institutions.

The market for goods is the public at large buying for a variety of purposes, non-business as well as business, and a buyer should not be called on to show more than that he bought in the same way as the seller's customers generally.

This question was also canvassed by Linden J, in *Fairline Boats Ltd. v. Leger et al.* (1980), 1 PPSAC 218, at 222:

Thus in deciding whether a transaction is one that is in the ordinary course of business, the courts must consider all of the circumstances of the sale. Whether it was a sale in the ordinary course of business is a question of fact. ... The usual, or regular type of transaction that people in the seller's business engage in must be evaluated. If the transaction is one that is not normally entered into by people in the seller's business, then it is not in the ordinary course of business. If those in the seller's business ordinarily do enter into such agreements, then, even though it may not be the most common type of contract, it may still be one in the ordinary course of business.

Linden J then went on to articulate the relevant factors in determining the question (at 222 and 223):

... where the agreement is made. If it is at the business premises of the seller it is more likely to be in the ordinary course of business. If it is away from the business premises of the seller, in suspicious circumstances for example, a court may hold that it is not in the ordinary course of business.

The parties to the sale may also be significant, although certainly not controlling. If the buyer is an ordinary, everyday consumer, the likelihood of his being involved in a sale in the ordinary course of business is greater. If the buyer is not an ordinary consumer, but a dealer or financial institution, then the court may take this out of the ordinary course of business, but not necessarily so because dealers and others too may, in proper circumstances, receive the benefit of the provision.

The quantity of the goods sold must also be considered, although this too is not definitive. If there is only one or a few articles sold in the ordinary way, the court is more likely to hold this to be a sale in the ordinary course of business. On the other hand, if a large quantity of items are sold, many more than are sold in the ordinary course of business, and perhaps forming a substantial proportion of the stock of the seller, then the court is less likely to consider it to be in the ordinary course of business.

The price charged for the goods must also be examined, thus if the price charged is in the range of the usual market price, courts are more likely to consider the sale in the ordinary course of business, whereas if the price is unduly low, the courts may hold that this is not a transaction in the ordinary course of business.

In my opinion, these authorities from Ontario, while helpful, must be read with caution. The Ontario Provision is materially different from the Saskatchewan one because of the addition in the Saskatchewan provision of the words "*of the seller.*" These words in our legislation must be considered with the usual regard for rules of statutory interpretation. Accordingly, I would not fasten on such authorities as *Fairline* for a conclusive definition or approach in our jurisdiction. In my opinion, the trial court in deciding this issue in Saskatchewan, must consider the business of the particular seller rather than limit the inquiry to the ordinary course of business in the trade or industry as a whole.

Since the question whether a buyer is a buyer under s. 30(1) is a question of fact, I would not attempt to articulate an all inclusive definition of what is a sale of "goods in the ordinary course of business of the seller." I do however hold that the trier of fact should consider whether the person was a person in the business of selling goods of that kind and whether the transaction(s) took place in the ordinary course of that business. And in my opinion the court should give a generally liberal interpretation to the phrase "buyer of goods sold in the ordinary course of business of the seller," in order to carry out the purpose of s. 30(1)—to protect the buying public in cases where the secured party furnishes goods which are sold to the public by the debtor in the regular course of the debtor's business. This comports with the underlying philosophy of the provision to protect the security interest so long as it does not interfere with the normal flow of commerce.

In my opinion, the conclusion of the learned trial judge on this issue is fully supported by the evidence. In this case the seller was involved in an economic enterprise—he was selling condominium units on a systematic basis—and this fact was known to the appellant as evidenced by the project report. The trial court was not here concerned with an isolated transaction. The mere fact that the seller was engaged in the selling of appliances as an incident to his primary business of selling condominium units does not preclude the operation of s. 30(1).

I accordingly reject the appellant's second ground of appeal.

...

Appeal dismissed.

NOTES

1) The main purpose of OPPSA s. 28(1) is to protect T against unpublicized restrictions on D's authority to sell inventory. However, according to *Camco*, the section is not limited to inventory. In *Camco*, the appliances were presumably either inventory or equipment, depending on whether Muxlow intended to sell them at the time Camco's security interest attached. In clause 3 of the conditional sale agreement, Muxlow warranted that it was not purchasing the appliances for resale and this is possibly conclusive evidence of Muxlow's intention at the relevant time. In any event, the judgment proceeds on the assumption that the appliances were not inventory and that, presumably, they were equipment. On this basis, Muxlow had no authority to sell the appliances, but the unit buyers had no easy way of discovering this. It is true that they might have searched the register, but it is unlikely that it would have occurred to them to do so; to all outward appearances, the appliances were inventory and so the buyers could reasonably have expected to obtain clear title regardless of any security interest. In any event, would a register search necessarily reveal the debtor's lack of authority to sell? It is worth noting that, according to the agreed statement of facts, most buyers did not retain their own solicitors because legal services were provided by Muxlow and were included as part of the purchase price. Should this matter?

2) The court in *Camco* stressed the fact that Muxlow was selling condominium units on a "systematic basis." This suggests that if the sale is part of a pattern, the court will probably conclude that it is in the ordinary course of business. What if the seller is just starting up in business so that there is no previous pattern of sales? This is more or less what happened in *Agricultural Commodity Corp. v. Schaus Feedlots Inc.*, [2001] OJ No. 2908 (SCJ). There, the court made two main points: first, that "the frequency and number of sales is not determinative"; and second, that the question must be addressed from the buyer's perspective (is there anything to warn the buyer that this sale is out of the ordinary course of business?). If there is a prior pattern of sales, that will usually conclude the matter. But even if there is no previous pattern, the sale may still be in the ordinary course of business if that is what a rea-

sonable buyer would think. This is consistent with the decision in *Camco*: the court there proceeded on the basis that the appliances were equipment rather than inventory, but its conclusion that the sales were in the ordinary course of Muxlow's business is tantamount to a finding that a reasonable buyer would be likely to have assumed that the appliances were inventory that Muxlow was free to sell.

3) Consider the following case:

D is an accountant. SP has a perfected security interest in D's office furniture as equipment. D sells the furniture to T. Does T get clear title?

If s. 28(1) was limited to inventory, the answer would be "no." However, *Camco* establishes that the provision is not so limited and that it may apply to a sale of equipment in appropriate circumstances. If D's sale is a one-off, the answer is reasonably clear: s. 28(1) does not apply. But if D has a practice of selling off its office furniture, the question is less straightforward. According to Cuming, Walsh and Wood:

> While there is no easy way to determine where the sale of equipment becomes a sale in the ordinary course of business ... , there are two factors that must be brought into the determination. These are the frequency with which the sales take place and the circumstances in which they occur. Simply because a debtor is engaged in business activity, it does not follow that any sale by the debtor of its equipment is in the ordinary course of its business. However, if as a regular part of carrying on its business, the debtor sells goods that to that point were being used as equipment under circumstances in which goods of that kind are generally sold, the sales are in the ordinary course of its business. [*Personal Property Security Law* (Toronto: Irwin Law, 2005), 293]

4) The court in *Camco* appears to have overlooked the possibility that the appliances may have been fixtures. If they were, then the court should have applied the Saskatchewan equivalent of OPPSA s. 34. What would the outcome of the case have been if this provision had applied?

5) OPSSA s. 28(1) is limited to sales in the ordinary course of business. Contrast s. 28(5), which applies to the sale of motor vehicles outside the ordinary course of business: see Part II.C, above, and Chapter 6, Part IV, Note 7, following the *Lambert* extract. As noted above, the purpose of s. 28(1) is to protect the buyer against undiscoverable restrictions on the debtor's authority to sell. Note, though, that the provision's failure to address the A-B-C-D problem means that the protection it gives to buyers is incomplete: see Part II.C, above.

Tanbro Fabrics Corp. v. Deering Milliken Inc.
39 NY 2d 623 (CA 1976)

BREITEL Chief Judge: In an action for the tortious conversion of unfinished textile fabrics (greige goods), plaintiff Tanbro sought damages from Deering Milliken, a textile manufacturer. Tanbro, known in the trade as a "converter," finishes textile into dyed and patterned fabrics. The goods in question had been manufactured by Deering, and sold on a "bill and hold" basis to Mill Fabrics, also a converter, now insolvent. Mill Fabrics resold the goods, while still in Deering's warehouse, also on a bill and hold basis, to Tanbro.

Deering refused to deliver the goods to Tanbro on Tanbro's instruction because, although these goods had been paid for, there was an open account balance due Deering from Mill Fabrics. Deering under its sales agreements with Mill Fabrics claimed a perfected security interest in the goods.

At Supreme Court, Tanbro recovered a verdict and judgment of $87,451.68 for compensatory and $25,000 for punitive damages. The Appellate Division, by a divided court, modified to strike the recovery for punitive damages, and otherwise affirmed. Both parties appeal.

The issue is whether Tanbro's purchase of the goods was in the ordinary course of Mill Fabrics' business, and hence free of Deering's perfected security interest.

There should be an affirmance. Mill Fabrics' sale to Tanbro was in the ordinary course of business, even though its predominant business purpose was, like Tanbro's, the converting of greige goods into finished fabrics. All the Uniform Commercial Code requires is that the sale be in ordinary course associated with the seller's business (§9-307, subd. [1]). The record established that converters buy greige goods in propitious markets and often in excess of their requirements as they eventuate. On the occasion of excess purchases, converters at times enter the market to sell the excess through brokers to other converters, and converters buy such goods if the price is satisfactory or the particular goods are not available from manufacturers. Both conditions obtained here.

Tanbro and Mill Fabrics were customers of Deering for many years. Goods would be purchased in scale on a "bill and hold" basis, that is, the goods would be paid for and delivered as the buyers instructed. When the goods were needed, they were delivered directly where they were to be converted, at the buyers' plants or the plants of others if that would be appropriate. Pending instructions, the sold and paid for goods were stored in the warehouses of the manufacturer, both because the buyers lacked warehousing space and retransportation of the goods to be processed would be minimized.

Mill Fabrics, like many converters, purchased greige goods from Deering on credit as well as on short-term payment. Under the sales notes or agreements, all the goods on hand in the seller's warehouse stood as security for the balance owed on the account. Tanbro was familiar with this practice. It was immaterial whether or not particular goods had been paid for. If the goods were resold by Deering's customers, Deering obtained for a period a perfected security interest in the proceeds of resale for the indebtedness on the open account (Uniform Commercial Code, §9-306, subds. [2], [3]).

Deering's sales executives advised Tanbro's that it had discontinued production of a certain blended fabric. Upon Tanbro's inquiry, the Deering sales executives recommended to Tanbro that it try purchasing the blended fabric from Mill Fabrics, which Deering knew had an excess supply. Ultimately, Tanbro purchased from Mill Fabrics through a broker 267,000 yards at 26 cents per yard. Tanbro paid Mill Fabrics in full.

During October and November of 1969, approximately 57,000 yards of the blended fabric was released by Deering on Mill Fabrics' instructions and delivered to a Tanbro affiliate. There remained some 203,376 yards at the Deering warehouse.

In early January of 1970, Tanbro ordered the remaining fabric delivered to meet its own contractual obligation to deliver the blended fabric in finished state at 60 cents per yard. Deering refused.

By this time Mill Fabrics was in financial trouble and its account debit balance with Deering at an unprecedented high. In mid-January of 1970, a meeting of its creditors was called and its insolvency confirmed.

As noted earlier, under the terms of the Deering sales agreements with Mill Fabrics, Deering retained a security interest in Mill Fabrics' "property" on a bill and hold basis, whether paid for or not. This security interest was perfected by Deering's continued possession of the goods (Uniform Commercial Code, §1-201, subd. [37]; §9-305). Tanbro argued that if it had title by purchase its goods were excluded from the security arrangement which was literally restricted to the "property of the buyer," that is Mill Fabrics. In any event, unless prevented by other provisions of the code, or the sale was not unauthorized, Tanbro took title subject to Deering's security interest.

Under the code (§9-307, subd. [1]) a buyer in the ordinary course of the seller's business takes goods free of even a known security interest so long as the buyer does not know that the purchase violates the terms of the security agreement. As defined in the code (§1-201, subd. [9]) "a buyer in ordinary course" is "a person who in good faith and without knowledge that the sale to him is in violation of the ownership rights or security interest of a third party in the goods buys in ordinary course from a person in the business of selling goods of that kind but does not include a pawnbroker. 'Buying' may be for cash or by exchange of other property or on secured or unsecured credit and includes receiving goods or documents of title under a preexisting contract for sale but does not include a transfer in bulk or as security for or in total or partial satisfaction of a money debt." Critical to Tanbro's claim is that it purchased the goods in the ordinary course of Mill Fabrics' business and that it did not purchase the goods in knowing violation of Deering's security interest.

Under the code whether a purchase was made from a person in the business of selling goods of that kind turns primarily on whether that person holds the goods for sale. Such goods are a person's selling inventory. (Uniform Commercial Code, §1-201, subd. [9]; §9-307, subd. [1]; Official Comment, at par. 2.) Note, however, that not all purchases of goods held as inventory qualify as purchases from a person in the business of selling goods of that kind. The purpose of section 9-307 is more limited. As indicated in the Practice Commentary to that section, the purpose is to permit buyers "to buy goods from a dealer in such goods without having to protect himself against a possible security interest on the inventory" (Kripke, Practice Commentary, McKinney's Cons. Laws of NY, Book 62½, Uniform Commercial Code, §9-307, p. 491, par. 1). Hence, a qualifying purchase is one made from a seller who is a dealer in such goods.

A former Mill Fabrics' employee testified that there were times when Mill Fabrics, like all converters, found itself with excess goods. When it was to their business advantage, they sold the excess fabrics to other converters. Although these sales were relatively infrequent they were nevertheless part of and in the ordinary course of Mill Fabrics' business, even if only incidental to the predominant business purpose. Examples of a nonqualifying sale might be a bulk sale, a sale in distress at an obvious loss price, a sale in liquidation, a sale of a commodity never dealt with before by the seller and wholly unlike its usual inventory, or the like (see *National Bank of Commerce v. First Nat. Bank & Trust Co. [Tulsa]*, 446 P2d 277, 282 [Okl.]; cf. *Sternberg v. Rubenstein*, 305 NY 235, 239, 112 NE 2d 210, 211; *Whitmire v. Keylon*, 12 UCC Rept. Serv. 1203, 1206-1207 [Tenn.]).

The combination of stored, paid for goods, on a hold basis, and the retention of a security interest by Deering makes commercial sense. Mill Fabrics' capacity to discharge its obligation to Deering was in part made possible because it sold off or converted the goods held at the Deering warehouse. Mill Fabrics, as an honest customer, was supposed to remit the proceeds from resale or conversion to Deering and thus reduce, and eventually discharge its responsibility to Deering. Thus, so long as it was customary for Mill Fabrics, and in the trade for converters, to sell off excess goods, the sale was in the ordinary course of business. Moreover, on an alternative analysis, such a sale by Mill Fabrics was therefore impliedly authorized under the code if its indebtedness to Deering was to be liquidated (see Official Comment to §9-307, par. 2; *Draper v. Minneapolis Moline*, 100 Ill. App. 2d 324, 329, 241 NE 2d 342).

All subdivision (1) of section 9-307 requires is that the sale be of the variety reasonably to be expected in the regular course of an on-going business (see *Newton-Waltham Bank & Trust Co. v. Bergen Motors*, 68 Misc. 2d 228, 230, 327 NYS 2d 77, 81, affd., 75 Misc. 2d 103, 347 NYS 2d 568; *cf. First Nat. Bank, Martinsville v. Crone*, 301 NE 2d 378, 381 [Ind. App.]). This was such a case.

…

Order of Appellate Division affirmed.

NOTES

1) *Tanbro Fabrics* triggered a lively debate between those who thought it was wrongly decided and those who defended it as correctly interpreting the intent of UCC 9-307(1). Professor Kripke falls into the first category. See Kripke, "Should Section 9-307(1) of the Uniform Commercial Code Apply Against a Secured Party in Possession?" (1977), 33 *Bus. Lawyer* 153.

Professor Kripke accepts the fact that the buyer need not obtain possession of the goods in order to secure the protection of UCC 9-307(1), but he argues that 9-307(1) was never intended to apply to a case where the secured party has retained possession of the goods as security for the debtor's obligation. He reasons as follows (ibid., at 159-60):

> The difference between a possessory security interest perfected by virtue of the possession and a non-possessory security interest perfected by filing is more than a difference between alternate methods of perfecting the security interest, which methods Article 9 treats equally, in general. The fact of possession in the secured party, the pledge relationship, means that the secured party has taken the goods out of the hands of the debtor (or withheld them from the debtor) and thus has made it impossible for the debtor to take any advantage from his apparent ownership of the goods as evidenced by possession or to exhibit them or to deliver them upon sale. Until this case I believe that it was always assumed that possession of the secured party protected him from being surprised by a sudden devastation of his security through sales by the debtor to buyers in the ordinary course of business. For this reason, even though the Code facilitated perfection by filing of security interests on shifting inventories, some secured parties demanded warehouse arrangements through field warehousemen, thus exerting a physical control over the goods. Until this case, I believe it was thought that this precluded the debtor from selling the goods out to a buyer in ordinary course of business, thus leaving the secured

party to try to recoup from the proceeds if he could find and obtain them from a debtor to whom the secured party had refrained from entrusting them. Field warehousing arrangements are widely used even though the lenders frequently perfect the security interests by filing. The possession of the goods by field warehousemen is not just a means of perfection, which can be accomplished by filing, but it adds something else. Or at least it was thought to do so until now.

It is, of course, true that when a buyer in ordinary course of business buys goods "from a person in the business of selling goods of that kind" (section 1-201(9)), the buyer's entitlement to the protection of section 9-307(1) cannot be precluded—so long as the debtor is in possession of the goods by the secured party and debtor contracting, or purporting to contract, that the debtor does not have liberty of sale. It does not follow that the same result should apply when possession of the goods has been withheld from the debtor (and apparent ownership denied to him) for the very purpose of protecting the seller's normal right to payment before he surrenders the goods, sections 2-507, 2-511. ...

Are you persuaded by this reasoning or do you agree with Mr. Birnbaum's reply that Professor Kripke is confusing the position of a buyer who knows there is an outstanding security interest with the position of a buyer who knows the seller is selling *in violation* of the inventory financer's interest? See Birnbaum, "Section 9-307(1) of the Uniform Commercial Code Versus Possessory Security Interest—A Reply to Professor Homer Kripke" (1978), 33 *Bus. Lawyer* 2607.

2) Professor Kripke's concession that UCC 9-307(1) does not require the buyer to take possession of the goods is not made by other scholars. Professor Braucher's recollection was that Karl Llewellyn thought it obvious that there could be no "buying" without the buyer receiving delivery of the goods. See Baird and Jackson, *Cases, Problems and Materials on Security Interests in Personal Property* (Mineola, NY: Foundation Press, 1984), at 767. Professor Skilton, on the other hand ((1974), *Wis. L Rev.* 1, at 20), thought that the omission in UCC 1-201(9) to the need for delivery of the goods was deliberate. See also "Comment" (1981), 60 *Neb. L Rev.* 848 and cf. the provisions in Ontario SGA s. 25(2) and *Factors Act* s. 2(1), both of which require transfer of possession. Is the secured party prejudiced by the buyer's not taking possession of the goods?

3) Revised Article 9, UCC 9-320 has now resolved the controversy in the secured party's favour in the following provisions:

(a) [*Buyer in ordinary course of business.*] Except as otherwise provided in subsection (e), a buyer in ordinary course of business, other than a person buying farm products from a person engaged in farming operations, takes free of a security interest created by the buyer's seller, even if the security interest is perfected and the buyer knows of its existence.

(b) [*Buyer of consumer goods.*] Except as otherwise provided in subsection (e), a buyer of goods from a person who used or bought the goods for use primarily for personal, family, or household purposes takes free of a security interest, even if perfected, if the buyer buys:

(1) without knowledge of the security interest;
(2) for value;
(3) primarily for the buyer's personal, family, or household purposes; and
(4) before the filing of a financing statement covering the goods.

(c) [*Effectiveness of filing for subsection (b).*] To the extent that it affects the priority of a security interest over a buyer of goods under subsection (b), the period of effectiveness of a filing made in the jurisdiction in which the seller is located is governed by Section 9-316(a) and (b).

(d) [*Buyer in ordinary course of business at wellhead or minehead.*] A buyer in ordinary course of business buying oil, gas, or other minerals at the wellhead or minehead or after extraction takes free of an interest arising out of an encumbrance.

(e) [*Possessory security interest not affected.*] Subsections (a) and (b) do not affect a security interest in goods in the possession of the secured party under Section 9-313.

Contrast OPPSA s. 28(1.1)(a) and (b), inserted by the 2006 amendments. These provisions take the opposite tack from Article 9: they say that s. 28(1) applies whether or not the buyer takes possession of the goods and whether or not the seller was in possession. The new provisions are based on recommendations made by the Ontario Bar Association's Personal Property Security Law Committee in 1998. However, the Committee also recommended the following additional provision with a view to following the Article 9 lead on the *Tanbro* issue:

Despite s. (1.1)(a), subsection (1) does not apply where ... the security interest given by the seller was perfected by possession and the buyer did not take possession of the goods.

This provision was not included in the amendments.

E. Sale and Agreement to Sell

Royal Bank of Canada v. 216200 Alberta Ltd.
(1987), 51 Sask. R 147 (CA)

VANCISE JA: The issue on this appeal is whether a perfected security interest under the Personal Property Security Act, SS 1979-1980, c. P-6.1, covering all present and after-acquired inventory of a retail vendor, takes priority over the claims of persons who, in the ordinary course of business, have placed a deposit or made a partial payment on goods in the possession of the vendor or prepaid all or a portion of the purchase price of goods not in the possession of the vendor.

I

The respondent 216200 Alberta Ltd. owned and operated The Sofa Factory and The Waterbed General Store in both Saskatoon and Prince Albert, and carried on business as a furniture retailer. In July of 1982, it granted a debenture to the appellant, securing all its present and future assets. The debenture was registered pursuant to the provisions of the Personal Property Security Act, SS 1979-80, c. P-6.1, creating a security interest in all present and after-acquired property of 216200 Alberta Ltd.

The respondent, 216200 Alberta Ltd. defaulted under the debenture and on April 22, 1983, Sirois J made an order appointing Price-Waterhouse Ltd. as receiver and manager (the receiver) of all property and operations of 216200 Alberta Ltd.

Prior to the appointment of the receiver, a number of people had paid all or a portion of the purchase price on furniture they intended to purchase from 216200 Alberta Ltd. In some instances the furniture was in the possession of the vendor, and in others it had been ordered but had not arrived on the date of the appointment of the receiver. Subsequent to receivership, Mr. Justice W.R. Matheson, on May 5, 1983, ordered that the receiver be permitted to deliver to customers personal property in the possession of the receiver for which they had paid the full purchase price.

The appellant brought an application in chambers pursuant to s. 56 of the Personal Property Security Act to obtain a declaration in connection with the following four classes of transactions:

Class One
The status of the claims of persons who have paid the full purchase price for personal property, but the personal property is not in the possession of the defendant.

Class Two
The status of the claims of persons who have paid part of the purchase price for personal property in the possession of the defendant.

Class Three
The status of the claim of persons who have paid part of the purchase price for personal property not in the possession of the defendant.

Class Four
The status of claims of persons to whom cash refunds are owed by the defendant.

The learned chambers judge found that with respect to classes one and three, persons who paid the whole or part of the purchase price to 216200 Alberta Ltd. for goods not in its possession, had paid the money in trust, and with respect to class four, the refunds or rebates were to be held in trust for the purchasers and accordingly all such moneys, paid or due, took priority over the security interest of the appellant. She also found that purchasers under class two who had paid a deposit on goods which were in the possession of the vendor were entitled to priority over the interests of the appellant because they purchased the goods in the ordinary course of business pursuant to the provisions of s. 30(1) of the Act.

II

Priority of a buyer of goods sold in the ordinary course of business pursuant to s. 30(1):

As a general rule, the holder of a perfected security interest has an interest in the secured property and the proceeds from the sale in priority to the interests of unsecured creditors of the debtor, and subsequent purchasers of property take subject to the security agreement. A principal exception to this rule is contained in s. 30(1) which provides as follows:

[See *Camco Inc. v. Olson Realty (1979) Ltd.* in Part II.D above for terms of s. 30(1).]

...

In order to determine whether or not the exception applies to the second class of transaction, one must determine whether the purchaser is a "buyer" of goods sold in the ordinary course of business. If the person who paid a portion of the purchase price or placed a deposit on goods in the possession of 216200 Alberta Ltd. is not a buyer in the ordinary course of business, the person does not take priority over the secured party but is merely an unsecured creditor whose interest is subordinate to that of the appellants who had a perfected security interest.

The Act does not define "sale" or define "buyer in the ordinary course of business." The Act adopts a generic and functional approach to personal property and is a complete code for granting of security in consensual commercial transactions. Title is not relevant for the purpose of determining whether or not an agreement is a security agreement under the Act. That is, however, a different question from determining whether or not someone is a buyer of goods sold in the ordinary course of business. The appellant contends that before any security can be obtained by a buyer in the ordinary course of business, there must be a sale as contemplated by the provisions of the Sale of Goods Act, RSS 1978, c. S-1. It contends that the priority extends only to "buyers of goods sold in the ordinary course of business," that the word "sold" encompasses the concept of a completed sale, and that to determine whether or not there has been a sale one must have reference to the provisions of the Sale of Goods Act. It contends that title must pass before there can be a sale as contemplated by the section. The alternate approach is that title need not pass, in the strict legal sense, but that the "sale" or "contract to buy" must be made in the ordinary course of business. If "the sale" passes that test, then priority extends to the buyer of the goods. The determination of that issue does not appear to have been dealt with in Canada. There are two approaches which have been taken in the US. One is represented by *Herman v. First Farmers' State Bank of Minier*, 392 NE 2d 344 (1979); 26 UCCR 1350 (Illinois Appellate Court). In that case, the Court considered the application of paragraph 9-307(1) of the Uniform Commercial Code which is equivalent to s. 30(1) of the Personal Property Security Act. That article reads as follows:

...

The Code in para. 2-402(b) states that if a contract of sale provides for the delivery by the seller to the buyer, title does not pass until delivery has been made. Notwithstanding that proviso, the Court held that "technical passage of title rules" should not be used to defeat the claim of a buyer in the ordinary course of business. The Court preferred to rely on the ordinary course of business requirement as determining the exception, rather than the question of title. The Court held that whether a person was a buyer in the ordinary course of business is not determined by title, but rather by whether there has been a completed sale in the ordinary way. Transference of title was found to be irrelevant for the purpose of determining whether the sale was ordinary or typical of the trade. It should be noted, however, that there is a difference between s. 30(1) of the Act and para. 9-307(1) of the Code. Section 30(1) speaks of a buyer of goods "sold in the ordinary course of business," while para. 9-307(1) refers only to "a buyer in the ordinary course of business." The question arises as to whether or not the addition of the phrase, "goods sold in the ordinary course of business," imports a further element into the question of the determination of priority under the Act. The code defines "buyer" as "a person who buys or contracts to buy goods." It would appear that it is not necessary, having regard to that definition, for one to actually complete a sale, or for title to pass, before one could be a "buyer" in the ordinary course of business under the Code.

The second line of cases in the US contemplates the actual passage of title before one is entitled to the exemption provided under para. 9-307(1). The case of *Chrysler Corp. v. Adamatic, Inc.*, 208 NW 2d 97 (1973) (Wisconsin Supreme Court) is an example of that approach. There, the question posed by the Court was whether one can be a buyer in the ordinary course of business before a sale has occurred. They concluded that a contract to sell and a contract of sale are not synonymous, and because title had not passed to the buyer he was not a "buyer" in the ordinary course of business. They took the position that a completed sale was necessary before one could become a buyer, notwithstanding that certain inequities might result.

I am of the opinion that before a buyer can take property free of the security interest of the appellant, he must establish that there has been a sale and that he is a buyer in the ordinary course of business. The application of the provisions of the Sale of Goods Act, while not being specifically referred to in s. 30, must be referred to determine whether or not there has been a sale. Section 3(4) of the Sale of Goods Act [Ontario SGA s. 2(3)] defines "sale" as follows:

> 3(4) Where under a contract of sale the property in the goods is transferred from the seller to the buyer the contract is called a sale; but where the transfer of the property in the goods is to take place at a future time or is subject to some condition thereafter to be fulfilled the contract is called an agreement to sell.

Goods are sold when title passes to the buyer and sections 18, 19 and 20 are relevant for the determination of that issue. The import of those sections is that no title passes to the buyer in unascertained goods until the goods are ascertained and appropriated to the sale. When there is a sale of specific or ascertained goods, title passes when the parties intend it to pass. Unless a different intention appears from the documentation, s. 20 sets out the rules for ascertaining the intention of the parties as to the time at which the property or the goods is to pass to a buyer. Rule 1 covers a situation where there is an unconditional sale of a specific item in a deliverable state. Title passes at the time of the making of the contract. Where there was a sale of a specific item of furniture in the possession of 216200 Alberta Ltd., which was in a deliverable state and identified in some fashion as being the goods purchased, title passed on the making of the contract, notwithstanding that the full amount of the purchase price had not been paid. The purchaser, in those circumstances, is entitled to priority over the appellant's security agreement. He is entitled to either the goods, on the payment of the balance of the purchase price, or the return of that portion of the purchase price paid, if the sale was made in the ordinary course of business.

In those cases where there was furniture of the type described in the contract of sale but which was not identified as belonging to the buyer, there has been no appropriation of the goods of this sale as contemplated by s. 19. Title did not pass, the buyer is an unsecured creditor, and the security interest of the appellant takes priority.

The second element which must be satisfied before the buyer obtains the goods free of the security interest of the appellant is whether the sale was "one in the ordinary course of business."

...

In my opinion, a sale, in the ordinary course of business, includes a sale to the public at large, of the type normally made by the vendor in a particular business where the basic business dealings between buyer and seller are carried out under normal terms and consistent with general commercial practice. It does not include private sales between individual buyers.

Here the sales of goods of the kind normally sold by the vendor were made at its premises, to members of the public at large, under normal terms and conditions of sale of retail merchants. The sales were clearly sales to buyers in the ordinary course of business.

The two indicia for sale in the ordinary course of business have therefore been met. Those persons who paid part of the purchase price for goods in the possession of the vendor which were in a deliverable state, and identified in some fashion as being the goods purchased, have priority over the security interests of the appellant. Those persons are entitled to the goods, on payment of the balance of the purchase price, or if the goods have been sold, to a return of the amount paid.

Before turning to the remaining classes of transaction, there is one specific case which was argued on the appeal by the respondent John Beattie that must be dealt with, because it does not fit within the four classes of transaction outlined in the notice of motion. Mr. Beattie was given leave to file additional material particularizing his claim on the hearing of this appeal. Briefly stated, on March 11, 1983, he purchased a Simmons hide-a-bed from 216200 Alberta Ltd., on condition that the vendor could supply a matching sofa. The hide-a-bed was in stock, identified and appropriated to the sale. Mr. Beattie gave a salesman of 216200 Alberta Ltd. a cheque for the full amount of the purchase price of the Simmons hide-a-bed. The cheque was marked "not to be cashed until instructed." The invoice bore the notation "if unsuitable will cancel." Notwithstanding these instructions, the cheque delivered to 216200 Alberta Ltd. by Mr. Beattie was negotiated. He was ultimately advised that the manufacturer no longer had fabric to match the hide-a-bed and requested the return of his money. He was promised a refund but did not receive it before 216200 Alberta Ltd. was put into receivership. The appellant claims priority over the claim of Mr. Beattie by reason that the sale was conditional and had not been completed prior to receivership. It contends that all he is entitled to is a refund and as such is an unsecured creditor. I do not agree with that position. The sale of the sofa was completed. Title to the property passed to Mr. Beattie and at the time of receivership the goods were still being held for him by reason that he had not received the refund. As between the appellant as holder of a security interest and Mr. Beattie, a bona fide purchaser for value pursuant to s. 30(1) of goods ascertained and appropriated, he must be taken to have priority.

III

The priority between the appellant and those persons in classes one, three and four are the most difficult to reconcile. It is necessary, in my opinion, to separate classes one and three from class four. The persons in class four are persons entitled to receive a rebate or refund. 216200 Alberta Ltd. was simply indebted to them. They have no perfected interests in the property of 216200 Alberta Ltd., and as between themselves and the appellant are unsecured creditors. It follows that the appellant must in those circumstances take priority.

The persons in classes one and three claim a priority on the basis of a trust relationship which, they contend, gives them a priority over the perfected security interests of the appellant. Shortly stated, they contend that the money paid to 216200 Alberta Ltd. was paid in trust on condition that it be applied on the purchase price on goods to be ordered. None of the goods had arrived or were in the possession of 216200 Alberta Ltd. at the date of receivership. They contend that the money did not become the property of 216200 Alberta Ltd., and as such could not form part of the assets which were covered by the security interest of the appellant. Batten CJQB found:

> The moneys so paid over were not intended to become the property of the defendant. The defendant was given the money to ensure that the money would be available as consideration for an agreement for sale should such an agreement be entered into at a later date— when the required merchandise was acquired and made available to the purchaser and approved by the purchaser at which time an agreement to purchase would be entered into. The purchaser would, at that time, pay over the purchase moneys and probably authorize the defendant to retain the deposit as part of the purchase price.

The fundamental question which must be answered is whether the security interest of the appellant to personal property in the possession of the vendor which was perfected under the provisions of the Act can be defeated by an unregistered interest in trusts. That question involves both a legal and policy decision.

The policy of the Act can be divined from the comments made by the Saskatchewan Law Reform Commission in Tentative Proposals for the Saskatchewan Personal Property Security Act at 7:

> Any modern personal property security legislation must embody a system designed to protect innocent third parties who might otherwise suffer loss as a result of dealing with a person who has given a security interest in his property. The Commission has concluded that a system which avoids deception in cases where security transactions are involved can be employed with equal effectiveness in cases where certain types of non-security agreements create the same type of deception. It is totally unrealistic to attempt to bring within the scope of the Act every kind of transaction in which deception results from a separation of interest and appearance of interest. However, it is realistic to include in the perfection system of the Act certain types of transactions which because of their commercial importance are likely to continue to produce significant disruption if left out.

The scheme of the Act is to register the security interest as to both goods and proceeds. Any scheme which permits trust classes or devices outside the Act will cause commercial uncertainty and produce disruption in commercial transactions. Here, such facts as are contained in the material are relatively straightforward. The buyers paid all or a portion of the purchase price for furniture which 216200 Alberta Ltd. was to order for them. After the money was paid but before the goods were appropriated to the sale, 216200 Alberta Ltd. was placed in receivership by the appellant. The appellant claims to be entitled to all the personal property of 216200 Alberta Ltd. in priority to the persons who paid all or a portion of the purchase price of goods to be ordered. The contract of sale was made in the ordinary course of business as previously defined, but was for future goods.

How does one categorize the transaction here? Is it one where the purchasers paid a deposit, or part-payment of the purchase price, or a transaction where the purchaser paid money to the vendor in trust not to be applied or used until the happening of certain events, or is it an implied or constructive trust because of the unjust enrichment of the vendor?

The money was paid to 216200 Alberta Ltd. in the ordinary course of business and it became the property of the vendor. In order to determine whether it is impressed with a trust, one must examine the intention of the parties advancing the money. Here there was no evidence that they intended the money to be held in trust. It was not impressed with an express trust and it was not to be kept separate and apart from other funds of 216200 Alberta Ltd. It is possible for the funds to be categorized as a trust in some other way, as for example a constructive trust where the money, the title to which is in 216200 Alberta Ltd., in reality is the property of the purchasers. The constructive trust has been utilized as a remedy for injured parties when there has been an unjust enrichment. There is no evidence that that was the situation here. The sale was one made in the ordinary course of business, utilizing an accepted commercial mode of sale.

In my opinion, the money was paid as a deposit or a partial payment for the purchase price of future goods. The purchaser, in the ordinary course, would be entitled to return of the amount paid to 216200 Alberta Ltd. in the event of default. It is a payment made to secure the transaction and is a debt due from 216200 Alberta Ltd. to the proposed purchasers in the event of default. As between the appellant, as the holder of a perfected security interest, and the persons in the class of transaction described in one and three, the appellant takes priority.

The suggestion has been made that the depositors ought to have protection and take priority over a commercial lender such as the appellant, because the commercial lender is far better able to protect itself from loss and to absorb the loss should one occur. That may be true, but in the circumstances of this case, if such protection is to be provided it is for the legislators to provide and not the courts. It would be relatively easy for the legislature to provide that moneys paid in the circumstances described here would be deemed to be held in trust for the purchaser so as to give it priority over a security interest. The device of a deemed trust and charge has been utilized by the legislature in the Education and Health Tax Act, RSS 1978, c. E-3, to ensure just such a priority.

In the result, the appellant will have priority with respect to those classes of transaction described as one, three and four, but not over the transaction described in two or over the Beattie transaction.

Appeal allowed in part.

NOTES

1) *Royal Bank v. 216200 Alberta Ltd.* should be read in conjunction with the materials in Ziegel and Duggan, *Commercial and Consumer Sales Transactions*, 4th ed. (Toronto: Emond Montgomery, 2002), c. 13, on the sales rules for the transfer of title. As will be noted, the underlying issue in the present case was to what extent the Saskatchewan counterpart to s. 28(1) of the Ontario Act can or should be used to protect prepaying buyers.

2) The decision in the *Royal Bank* case seems to be a very technical one. Why should the buyer's entitlement to the goods turn on the legal meaning of "sells" and not the colloquial meaning? In policy terms, one argument against the decision is that the buyers were involuntary creditors. In other words, the buyers arguably did not accept the risk of the debtor's insolvency when they made their prepayments. It probably does not even occur to most consumers that there may be a risk in these circumstances and that they should take steps to protect themselves. As it happens, various suggestions have been made over the years for protecting prepaying buyers who do not receive the goods they have paid for. In 1987, the BC Law Reform Commission recommended the adoption of a statutory lien in favour of *consumer buyers* (LRC 93, 1987) and this recommendation was given effect to in 1993 by the addition of Part 9 to the BC *Sale of Goods Act*. For details, see Ziegel and Duggan, op. cit., at 493 et seq. and Arthur Close, QC, "The British Columbia Buyer's Lien—A New Consumer Remedy" (1995), 25 *CBLJ* 127. The Part 9 lien covers monies held by the seller in an account with a "savings institution" as well as inventory in the seller's possession that corresponds in description with the goods for which the buyer has prepaid.

3) Whatever the merits of the BC solution, OPPSA s. 28(1) is arguably not an effective mechanism for protecting the prepaying buyer. Assume that the court in the *Royal Bank* case had reached the opposite conclusion and held that the section applied. The consequence would be to defeat the secured party's claim, but the buyers might still lose out. For example, assume that the debtor goes into bankruptcy before the dispute is resolved and the debtor's trustee in bankruptcy claims the goods as property of the estate: *Bankruptcy and Insolvency Act*, RSC 1985, c. B-3, s. 71. OPPSA s. 28(1) does not assist the buyer in this context because it is limited to the buyer's claim against the secured party. The buyer's claim against the debtor and, by extension, the debtor's trustee in bankruptcy, depends on whether or not property in the goods has passed to the buyer pursuant to the sale of goods legislation and, on the facts under consideration, it has not.

Incidentally, the trustee in bankruptcy has a choice on facts like these: she may elect either to complete the sale and collect the balance of the purchase price for the estate or, alternatively, she may reject the contract and keep the goods. The receiver in the *Royal Bank* case probably had a similar choice. Of course, if the trustee or receiver elects to perform the contract, the buyer suffers no loss. The trouble is that the higher the buyer's prepayment, the more attractive it will be for the trustee or receiver to reject the contract. Can you see why?

4) There is another, related argument in favour of the *Royal Bank* decision. OPPSA s. 28(1) presupposes that, but for the security interest, the buyer would be entitled to the goods. Consider the following variation on the *Royal Bank* facts:

Debtor is a furniture retailer. SP holds a perfected security interest in Debtor's inventory. Buyer orders a sofa from Debtor and pays a 20 percent deposit. Debtor agrees to deliver the sofa to Buyer in two weeks time. In the meantime, SP appoints a receiver. At the date of the receivership, there are three sofas in Debtor's storeroom that are identical to the one Debtor has ordered, none of them subject to other outstanding orders. Which sofa belongs to Debtor?

OPPSA s. 28(1) does not address this question and the answer depends on the sale of goods legislation. Applying the sale of goods legislation, Buyer has no claim to any of the sofas because none of them has been appropriated to the contract. To make the illustration even sharper, assume that there are three sofas in the warehouse and three other customers in the same position as Buyer. Which three customers do the sofas belong to? Again, the answer lies in the *Sale of Goods Act*, not OPPSA s. 28(1), and applying the sale of goods legislation, the answer is "none." This rule provides a brutally simple solution to the problem of choosing between multiple equally deserving claimants. A better solution might be to give each customer a pro rata share in the sofas, but that would require an amendment to the sale of goods legislation and it has nothing to do with the PPSA. In any event, the point for present purposes is that it does Buyer no good for OPPSA s. 28(1) to extinguish SP's security interest if Buyer has no title to the sofa anyway.

5) OPPSA s. 28(1.1)(c) provides that subsection (1) applies whether or not title to the goods passed to the buyer. Section 28(1.2) provides that despite subsection (1.1), subsection (1) does not apply if the goods were not identified to the contract of sale, and s. 28(1.3) provides that goods are identified to the contract when they are (a) identified and agreed upon by the parties at the time the contract is made, or (b) marked or designated to the contract by the seller or by the buyer, with the seller's consent or authorization. These provisions were enacted as part of the 2006 amendments. They are based on a recommendation of the Ontario Bar Association's Personal Property Security Committee. The aim was to clarify the law as stated in the *Royal Bank* case, and as considered in *Spittlehouse v. Northshore Marine Inc. (Receiver of)*, which is reproduced below. How helpful do you think the new provisions are?

Spittlehouse v. Northshore Marine Inc. (Receiver of)
[1994] 18 OR (3d) 60 (CA)

GRANGE JA: This is an appeal from the order of Keenan J declaring the plaintiffs to be the owners of a certain boat manufactured in Singapore and transported to New Jersey and apparently now in Ontario awaiting the result of this appeal.

The plaintiffs entered into a contract with the defendant Northshore Marine for a Grand Banks 46-foot classic boat for the selling price of $555,000. They have paid 90% of the purchase price and are more than willing to pay the balance upon delivery of the boat as provided in the contract of sale "in the water at Port Credit, Ontario."

The difficulty is two-fold. First, the defendant Transamerica Commercial Finance Corporation has a perfected security interest in all the assets of Northshore including this boat and secondly, the contract of sale provided that "title to the above described equipment shall be transferred to the buyer when the buyer has made payment in full for the equipment."

At some time in the course of delivery of the boat, an official of Northshore Marine advised Transamerica of certain defalcations on its (Northshore's) part including its failure to pass on trust moneys. As a result of this information and a general default on payments by Northshore to Transamerica, the latter perfected its security, appointed the Receiver and through it seized the boat in question. This action resulted.

The claim of the defendants is simply stated. Transamerica has a perfected security against the boat. The plaintiffs have no title to the boat having a contractual not a property interest and can rank only as unsecured creditors against the estate of Northshore. It is conceded that there will be little recovery for those unsecured creditors.

The judge of first instance recognized that the result claimed by the defendants would "produce a result that is manifestly unjust." He accepted "with great reluctance" that the *Sale of Goods Act* rules for ascertaining the passing of title could not be invoked in the plaintiffs' favour but found the plaintiffs to have an equitable interest in the boat which was not defeated by the reservation of title. He considered but felt he did not have to decide whether the plaintiffs were the beneficiaries of a resulting trust of the boat.

In my view, the whole issue is readily resolved by the provisions of s. 28(1) of the *Personal Property Securities Act*, SO 1989 which provides as follows:

> 28(1) A buyer of goods from a seller who sells the goods in the ordinary course of business takes them free from any security interest therein given by the seller even though it is perfected and the buyer knows of it, unless the buyer also knew that the sale constituted a breach of the security agreement.

There is no question that in the contract between the plaintiffs and Northshore the latter was acting in the ordinary course of business. It was a dealer in boats and its business was to sell them. The plaintiffs were seeking to buy a boat, indeed the very boat that was the subject of the contract. They had no knowledge of the security agreement between Northshore and Transamerica much less of any breach of that agreement (if indeed there was a breach). The only possible problems are whether the plaintiffs were buyers of the boat and Northshore was the seller. In my opinion they indubitably were.

There is no definition of "buyer" or "seller" in the *Personal Property Security Act* but the transaction between the plaintiffs and Northshore was in common parlance clearly a sale. It is what used to be called a conditional sale and was governed by what was called the *Conditional Sales Act* replaced by the *Personal Property Security Act of 1976* the forerunner of the present Act. The Act is replete with reference to "sales," "purchasers" and "sellers" in reference to the transaction between the conditional vendor and the conditional purchaser. This transaction is a sale with title withheld until the purchase price is fully paid. It is a device to protect the seller until full payment is made and no more. It is valid to the extent that the purchasers cannot demand the transfer of title until all of the purchase price is paid.

This conclusion might seem contrary to that reached by the Saskatchewan Court of Appeal in *Royal Bank of Canada v. 216200 Alberta Ltd.*, 33 DLR (4th) 80, the only Canadian case on the subject I can find. The Court was concerned with the priorities between a secured interest holder and certain customers of an insolvent furniture dealer. Saskatchewan had a section of their PPSA almost identical with ours. When dealing with the status of the claims of persons who have paid part of the purchase price for personal property in the possession of the seller, the court stated:

> I am of the opinion that before a buyer can take property free of the security interest of the appellant, he must establish that there has been a sale and that he is a buyer in the ordinary course of business. The application of the provisions of the Sale of Goods Act, while not being specifically referred to in s. 30, must be referred to to determine whether or not there has been a sale. Section 3(4) of the Sale of Goods Act defines "sale" as follows:
>
> > 3(4) Where under a contract of sale the property in the goods is transferred from the seller to the buyer the contract is called a sale; but where the transfer of the property in

the goods is to take place at a future time or is subject to some condition thereafter to be fulfilled the contract is called an agreement to sell.

Goods are sold when title passes to the buyer and ss. 18, 19 and 20 are relevant for the determination of that issue. The import of those sections is that no title passes to the buyer in unascertained goods until the goods are ascertained and appropriated to the sale.

The court reached its conclusion after examining two lines of cases in the United States under Article 9.307(1) of the *Uniform Commercial Code* (similar to our s. 28(1) of the PPSA and s. 30 of the Saskatchewan Act) and specifically approved the case of *Chrysler Corp. v. Adamatic, Inc.* (1973), 208 NW 2d 97, a decision of the Wisconsin Supreme Court which held that a "buyer" was not a "buyer" within the meaning of the Code until title had passed. That decision was in effect reversed by the very court that pronounced it in *Daniel v. Bank of Hayward* (1988), 425 NW 2d 416 in which it was said at pp. 420-21 in words equally appropriate, in my view, to the case at bar:

> ... The cases and commentaries that have considered the issue since *Chrysler* have generally been critical of the reasoning the court employed in *Chrysler*. ... We conclude that we erred in relying on the date of transfer of title as the date on which a purchaser becomes a buyer in ordinary course of business. Reliance on the concept of title is contrary to the thrust of the *Uniform Commercial Code* and the commentary. The drafters of the *Uniform Commercial Code* tried to avoid giving technical rules of title a central role in furthering the policies of the *Uniform Commercial Code* [cite omitted]. Although title issues may be of significance in determining some issues under the Code, we conclude that reliance on title to interpret s. 409.307(1) is an unduly narrow and technical interpretation.

In my opinion, the *Sale of Goods Act* is not relevant or material to the resolution of our problem. Here, there was a sale with a seller and a purchaser who between them agreed that title in the goods would not pass until all purchase money was paid. The agreement between them states "the dealer agrees to sell and the buyer agrees to purchase" and refers "to the equipment being purchased" and that such equipment "is being sold." It cannot be regarded as anything but a sale. The *Sale of Goods Act* may affect the time when property in the goods passes but it cannot change what is clearly a sale in another Act into something it is not.

For these reasons, I would not follow the *Royal Bank* case. The plaintiff may take advantage of s. 28(1) of our Act upon tendering the balance of the purchase price and I would dismiss the appeal accordingly.

Appeal dismissed.

NOTES

1) Grange JA's reasoning in *Spittlehouse* is criticized in a comment by Professor Ziegel, although he supports the actual result. See Comment (1995), 24 *CBLJ* 457 where Professor Ziegel makes the following points, among others: (1) Justice Grange was mistaken in ignoring the definitions of "contract of sale," "buyer," and "seller" in the Ontario *Sale of*

Goods Act since the SGA is a basic component of Ontario's commercial law and there is no other source to provide a meaning for these terms where they appear in the OPPSA or in other contexts; (2) the American decisions on old UCC 9-307(1) (Article 9's counterpart to OPPSA s. 28(1)) have to be handled with great circumspection since the property provisions in Article 2 of the Code are not the same as in the SGA. In particular, UCC 2-501 recognizes a special property interest in the buyer's favour on identification of the property to the contract and before full title has been transferred to the buyer; and (3) there is no reason to believe that preference for the line of American cases represented by *Chrysler Corp. v. Adamatic, Inc.* was an essential part of the decision in *Royal Bank*.

2) Professor Ziegel concludes, however, that the decision in *Spittlehouse* could have been justified on other grounds. First, a conditional sale agreement is treated as a security agreement under the OPPSA (s. 2(1)), so it is clear that a buyer under such an agreement is treated as the beneficial owner of the goods and should be so treated for the purposes of OPPSA s. 28(1). Second, UCC 1-201(9), in defining "buyer in ordinary course of business," explains that "buying" may be for cash or on secured or unsecured credit. This again makes it clear that a buyer is protected under s. 28(1) against the inventory financer's claim even though the seller is retaining a security interest in the goods. This result is also fair since the inventory financer will be able to claim the proceeds from the sale in the seller's hands (OPPSA s. 25).

3) OPPSA ss. 28(1.1)(c) and (d), enacted as part of the 2006 amendments, provide that s. 28(1) applies whether or not title to the goods passed to the buyer and whether or not the seller took a security interest in the goods. Again, these provisions derive from a recommendation by the Ontario Bar Association's Personal Property Security Law Committee. The purpose is to confirm the actual result in *Spittlehouse* while at the same time preserving the general thrust of the *Royal Bank* case.

F. Priorities with Respect to Repossessed or Returned Goods

OPPSA s. 27 deals with the competing interests that may arise where goods subject to a security interest are sold in ordinary course by the debtor and then are repossessed by the debtor or are returned to him by the buyer—for example, because the goods are defective or of the wrong kind or because the buyer cannot afford or does not wish to keep them. The competing interests that may arise are: (a) between the debtor and a prior secured party; (b) between the debtor and the transferee of chattel paper or an account generated under the prior sale; and (c) between the prior secured party and a transferee of chattel paper or an account.

Section 27(1) regulates the rights to the returned/repossessed goods between the debtor and the prior secured party; s. 27(3) does the same with respect to the rights of the transferee of chattel paper or an account. Section 27(5) states when the transferee of an account is deemed to have acquired a perfected security interest in the goods for the purpose of resolving priority disputes, and implicitly refers the reader to the basic priority rules in OPPSA ss. 30 and 33 to determine an actual contest. (Assuming the contest is with a prior inventory financer of the debtor, whose security interest will have priority?)

Finally, OPPSA s. 27(6)(a) regulates contests between the inventory financer and the transferee of chattel paper in terms of the priority rules applying to the chattel paper itself (as to which, see s. 28(3)). Section 27(6)(b) deals with priority conflicts between the transferee and other secured parties claiming an interest in the goods.

Note that OPPSA s. 27 has nothing to say about the rights of a transferee of an instrument. Presumably this is due to an oversight. What rules should be applied? Section 27 also does not answer the question whether the buyer who has returned the goods is discharged from further liability to the transferee of the account or chattel paper. To what extent does OPPSA s. 40 answer the question? How would the common law answer it?

III. TRANSFER OF CHATTEL PAPER

"Chattel paper" is defined in OPPSA s. 1(1) as meaning "one or more than one writing that evidences both a monetary obligation and a security interest in or a lease of specific goods." Typical examples of chattel paper are conditional sales and chattel mortgages that are generated when goods are sold on credit by a retailer and the seller retains a security interest in the goods. The Uniform Commercial Code explains commercial practices with respect to such paper:

> ... Such paper has become an important class of collateral in financing arrangements, which may—as in the automobile and some other fields—follow an earlier financing arrangement covering inventory or which may begin with the chattel paper itself.
>
> Arrangements where the chattel paper is delivered to the secured party who then makes collections, as well as arrangements where the debtor, whether or not he is left in possession of the paper, makes the collections, are both widely used, and are known respectively as notification (or "direct collection") and non-notification (or "indirect collection") arrangements. In the automobile field, for example, when a car is sold to a consumer buyer under an installment purchase agreement and the resulting chattel paper is assigned, the assignee usually takes possession, the obligor is notified of the assignment and is directed to make payments to the assignee. In the furniture field, for an example on the other hand, the chattel paper may be left in the dealer's hands or delivered to the assignee; in either case the obligor may not be notified, and payments are made to the dealer-assignor who receives them under a duty to remit to his assignee. The widespread use of both methods of dealing with chattel paper is recognized by the provisions of this Article, which permit perfection of a chattel paper security interest either by filing or by taking possession. [old UCC 9-308, Official Comment, para. 1]

The common law does not recognize chattel paper as a separate category of specialty; instead, it insists on disaggregating such paper into its component parts of an interest in goods (the seller's retention of title) and a chose in action (the buyer's debt), and applying separate rules to the transfer of each. See, for example, *Re George Inglefield*, [1933] 1 Ch. 1 and *Olds Discount Co. Ltd. v. John Playfair Ltd.*, [1938] 3 All ER 275. See further, Ziegel, "Wholesale Financing of Durable Goods ..." (1963), 41 *Can. Bar Rev.* 54, at 110-14. (Recall the similar problems with respect to realty mortgages discussed in Chapter 2, Part VI.C.) The original UCC and OPPSA definitions of chattel paper applied only to security agreements, including security leases of goods; they did not apply to non-security leases, even though dealings in such paper are as common as dealings in paper embodying security leases. This created significant practical problems since it meant that purchasers of such paper would have to perfect their security interest in the reversionary interest in the chattel by filing a financing statement in the place where the chattel was located. See *In the Matter of Leasing Consultants, Inc.*, 486 F2d 367 (CCA 2 1973). Because of this difficulty, the UCC and OPPSA definitions were amended to include specifically a lease of goods.

OPPSA s. 28(3)(a) provides:

> 28(3) A purchaser of chattel paper who takes possession of it in the ordinary course of business and gives new value has priority over any security interest in it,
>
> (a) that was perfected by registration if the purchaser did not know at the time of taking possession that the chattel paper was subject to a security interest; ... .

For example:

D is a dealer. SP1 has a security interest in D's present and after-acquired personal property, perfected by registration. D sells X goods under a conditional sale agreement. D discounts the chattel paper to SP2, who is in the discounting business, and SP2 takes possession of the chattel paper. D defaults against SP1 and SP1 and SP2 both claim the chattel paper.

Section 28(3)(a) applies and the outcome is that SP2 has priority, even though SP1's security interest was perfected by registration, provided SP2 had no knowledge of SP1's security interest at the time of taking possession. SP1 could have avoided this outcome either by taking possession of the chattel paper itself or, alternatively, by marking the chattel paper to notify SP2 and others of its interest.

The reference in s. 28(3) is to the *purchaser's* (that is, SP2's) ordinary course of business. Contrast s. 28(1), where the reference is to the *seller's* (that is, D's) ordinary course of business. Assume that SP2 is not in the discounting business after all and that this is a one-off transaction for him. Now s. 28(3)(a) does not apply and the general or default rules in s. 30 apply instead. The analysis runs as follows: SP1 has a security interest perfected by registration. SP2 has a deemed security interest in the chattel paper (s. 2(b)) and its security interest is perfected by possession. Section 30(1), rule 2 provides that as between a security interest perfected by registration and a security interest perfected by possession, priority turns on the order of events. Since SP1 registered before SP2 took possession, SP1 has priority over SP2.

Returning to our original example, assume that, instead of selling the chattel paper outright, D gives SP2 a security interest in the chattel paper to secure repayment of a loan and SP2 perfects its security interest by taking possession of the chattel paper. Whereas s. 28(1) is limited to buyers, s. 28(3) applies to purchasers and "purchase" is defined expansively in s. 1(1) to include, among other things, the taking of a security interest. This means that s. 28(3) applies not only to the case where SP2 buys the chattel paper outright from D, but also where D uses the chattel paper as collateral for a loan from SP2.

The policy behind the provision is to facilitate chattel paper financing. Section 28(3) is copied from Article 9 and chattel paper financing was in its infancy when Article 9 was enacted. Giving the dedicated chattel paper financer priority was a way of boosting the new industry. As pointed out in the notes following the *Massey-Ferguson* extract in Chapter 8, Part V, the special chattel paper priority rules were imported into the Canadian PPSAs apparently without detailed analysis and it is not clear that public policy or industry developments in the United States are a sufficient justification for the rules in Canada. A second possible argument in favour of the chattel paper priority rules is that they help to break the monopoly advantage the statute gives to the first-in-time general lender (see Chapter 7, Part IV). In this respect, they are similar to the PMSI super-priority rules in s. 33 (see Chapter 8, Part II). Is this a sufficient justification?

Section 28(3)(b) provides:

> 28(3) A purchaser of chattel paper who takes possession of it in the ordinary course of business and gives new value has priority over any security interest in it,
>
> • • •
>
>   (b) that has attached to proceeds of inventory under section 25, whatever the extent of the purchaser's knowledge.

For example:

SP1 has a security interest in D's inventory, perfected by registration. D sells goods to X under a conditional sale agreement. Subsequently, D borrows money from SP2, a financer, and gives SP2 a security interest in the chattel paper to secure repayment. SP2 takes possession of the chattel paper with knowledge of SP1's security interest. D defaults against SP1 and SP2 and they both claim the chattel paper.

Section 28(3)(b) applies and the outcome is that SP2 has priority despite SP1's prior registration and SP2's knowledge of SP1's security interest.

Note that this outcome depends on SP1's being a dedicated inventory financer. Assume instead that SP1 is D's general financer and has a security interest in all D's present and after-acquired personal property. Section 28(3)(b) does not apply because now SP1's claim is to the chattel paper as original collateral rather than as proceeds. Instead, the governing provision is s. 28(3)(a). Section 28(3)(b), like para. (a), was borrowed directly from Article 9 and, as the above illustration suggests, the purpose was to give the dedicated chattel paper financer an advantage over the dedicated inventory financer, with a view to providing support for chattel paper financing. Contrast the special treatment that s. 28(3)(b) gives the chattel paper financer relative to the inventory financer claiming the chattel paper as proceeds with the more limited concessions that s. 33 makes in favour of the accounts financer relative to the inventory financer claiming the accounts as proceeds. The difference reflects an empirical judgment made by the drafters of Article 9 about the relative importance of the different methods of financing, but it appears that Canadian lawmakers imported the provision into the PPSAs without asking whether Canadian public policy and market conditions justified the same approach: see the notes following the *Massey-Ferguson* case extract in Chapter 8, Part V.

Revised Article 9, UCC 9-330 is the current US counterpart of OPPSA s. 28(3). However, there is a significant difference in that the American provision extends to electronic chattel paper, a term defined in UCC 9-102 to mean "chattel paper evidenced by a record or records consisting of information stored in an electronic medium." Both limbs of UCC 9-330 apply where the purchaser takes possession of tangible chattel paper or obtains control of electronic chattel paper, and UCC 9-105 defines control of chattel paper as follows:

> A secured party has control of electronic chattel paper if the record or records comprising the chattel paper are created, stored, and assigned in such a manner that:
>
>   (1) a single authoritative copy of the record or records exists which is unique, identifiable and, except as otherwise provided in paragraphs (4), (5) and (6), unalterable;
>
>   (2) the authoritative copy identifies the secured party as the assignee of the record or records;
>
>   (3) the authoritative copy is communicated to and maintained by the secured party or its designated custodian;
>
>   (4) copies or revisions that add or change an identified assignee of the authoritative copy can be made only with the participation of the secured party;
>
>   (5) each copy of the authoritative copy and any copy of a copy is readily identifiable as a copy that is not the authoritative copy; and
>
>   (6) any revision of the authoritative copy is readily identifiable as an authorized or unauthorized revision.

The question whether the Canadian PPSAs should be amended along similar lines is still under debate. Proponents of the reform argue that it is necessary in order to bring the law up to date with technological developments and to facilitate the spread of electronic chattel paper. Opponents argue that given the uncertain policy basis of the rules as they currently stand in Canada, it makes no sense to extend their application without first determining whether they are commercially justifiable.

Chattel paper has a dual aspect in that there is the potential for priority disputes over the chattel paper itself or the goods to which the chattel paper relates. Consider the following case:

> SP1, a dealer, sells D a truck pursuant to a conditional sale agreement and registers a financing statement. SP1 later assigns the chattel paper to SP2. Still later, SP1 assigns the chattel paper a second time to SP3, without SP2's consent. Meanwhile, D sells the truck to T without anyone's consent. SP2, SP3, and T all claim the truck.

The resolution of this dispute involves a two-tier inquiry: (1) As between SP2 and SP3, who has priority in relation to the chattel paper? (2) As between the winner of this dispute and T, who has priority in relation to the truck? With regard to the first question, OPPSA s. 28(3)(a) may apply, depending on the facts. Otherwise, one or other of the general priority rules will apply. With regard to the second question, on the assumption that the truck is equipment in D's hands, the answer depends on whether SP1 included the VIN in the financing statement. If not, s. 28(5) may apply and, if so, T will obtain clear title.

IV. TRANSFER OF INSTRUMENTS AND DOCUMENTS OF TITLE

Jacob S. Ziegel, "Perfection by Registration, Instruments, Securities, Documents of Title, and the Personal Property Security Act 1989"
(1989), 15 *CBLJ* 242, at 246-48 and 250-51 (footnotes omitted)

[Section 28(4)] reads:

> (4) A purchaser of collateral that is an instrument or negotiable document of title has priority over any security interest therein perfected by registration or temporarily perfected under section 23 or 24 if the purchaser,
>> (a) gave value for the interest purchased;
>> (b) purchased the collateral without knowledge that it was subject to a security interest; and
>> (c) has taken possession of the collateral.

... The rationale of subsec. (4) is that a purchaser of negotiable or quasi-negotiable paper should not be obliged to search the PPS registry before consummating a transaction because that would defeat the essential qualities of these types of collateral. If the secured party does not have sufficient confidence in the integrity and solvency of the debtor then it should not leave the collateral in the debtor's possession.

Subsection (4) has a substantial number of technical components. "Purchaser" and "purchase" are defined in s. 1. The important point to note is that they have much broader meaning than the layperson's understanding of the terms. In particular, "purchaser" includes a secured party. In other words, a lender making a secured loan to the debtor can override a prior perfected non-possessory security interest in an instrument or negotiable document, provided the lender takes possession of the collateral and satisfies the other requirements of subsec. (4).

"Instrument" is defined in s. 1 and again has a wider meaning than might at first be supposed. It covers not only negotiable money obligations under the federal Bills of Exchange Act but also "any other writing that evidences a right to the payment of money and is of a type that in the ordinary course of business is transferred by delivery with any necessary endorsement or assignment." A debenture made payable to order or to bearer is a good example, assuming it does not fall within the definition of "security" in s. 1. "Document of title" is defined in s. 1 but not "negotiable document of title." Ontario does not have a documents of title Act corresponding to Article 7 of the Uniform Commercial Code but some guidance may be derived from the definition of "negotiable receipt" in s. 1(e) of the Warehouse Receipts Act and from the other provisions in the Act dealing with the negotiation of warehouse receipts.

A transferee under s. 28(4) must satisfy three requirements to override the prior security interest. First, he must have given value. "Value" is defined in s. 1 as any consideration sufficient to support a simple contract. Unlike UCC 9-308 and s. 28(3) of the Ontario Act, subsec. (4) does not require the giving of *new* value. The second requirement is that the transferee must have purchased the collateral "without knowledge" that it was subject to a security interest. "Knowledge" is defined in s. 69 of the Act. In practice s. 69(c) is likely to be the applicable paragraph. It provides that, in the case of a corporation, the knowledge must have come to the attention of a senior employee of the corporation with responsibility for matters to which the information relates "under circumstances in which a reasonable person would take cognizance of it." To translate this test into a concrete situation, the fact that counsel in the lender's legal department knows that the debtor has given a prior general security interest to Financial Institution X will not defeat the lender's specific loan to the debtor against the possessory security of a negotiable bill of lading or warehouse receipt if the loan manager was not aware of the prior security interested. It is *his* state of knowledge, not counsel's, that is relevant if only the loan manager was involved in making the loan decision and completing the transaction.

Finally, s. 28(4)(c) requires that the purchaser must have taken possession of the collateral. The Act does not define what constitutes possession but s. 22 makes it clear, for purposes of perfecting a security interest, that possession must be by the secured party or on its behalf "by a person other than the debtor or the debtor's agent." It seems safe to assume that possession will be given at least this much meaning in s. 28(4).

· · ·

Section 29 provides *inter alia* that the rights of a holder in due course of a bill, note or exchange under the BOE "are to be determined without regard to this Act." ... "Holder in due course" is defined in part in [s. 55(1) of the *Bills of Exchange Act*, RSC 1985, c. B-4 (BOE Act)] as a holder who took the bill in good faith and for value and without notice, at the time the bill was negotiated, of any defect in title of the person who negotiated the bill to him. "Defect in title" is not defined in the Act and, curiously, the leading Canadian text on bills of exchange does not indicate whether a subsisting security interest amounts to a defect in title.

Even if astonishingly it were not so, it would surely be held that the debtor's negotiation of a bill in violation of the express or implied terms of the security agreement would be bad faith negotiation under [BOE Act, s. 55(2)], and notice of it would deny the transferee the status of a holder in due course. It is a thoroughly well established proposition of bills of exchange law that notice under [s. 55] means actual notice of the debilitating facts or wanton disregard of such circumstances as would have enabled the transferee to learn the true facts. Constructive notice or negligent behaviour is not sufficient.

Section 29 does not provide, as did s. 31(2) of the old Act, that registration under the Ontario Act is not such notice as to affect the rights of persons mentioned in subsec. (2). Subsection (2) was deleted because the drafters felt it was redundant, and it was redundant because the new Act has not retained the constructive notice provision in old s. 53. (The provision did not apply in any case to instruments, letters of credit, advices of credit, or negotiable documents of title.) Even if the provision had been retained, it is unlikely that it could have changed the meaning of "notice" in a federal Act.

NOTES

1) Consider the following example:

SP has a perfected security interest in D's present and after-acquired inventory. D sells an item of inventory to X, a customer, in the ordinary course of business and X pays D by cheque. D buys a widget from T and signs over ("negotiates") the cheque in payment. Does T get clear title to the cheque?

If the general PPSA rules applied, the answer would be "no" because SP has a perfected security interest in the cheque as proceeds of the inventory: OPPSA s. 20(1)(c). However, s. 28(4) displaces this outcome, assuming that T had no knowledge of SP's security interest at the relevant time. Section 28(4) applies because s. 1(1) defines "purchase" to include taking by negotiation. In this connection, note s. 46(5)(a), which provides that the registration of a financing statement does not constitute constructive notice or knowledge of its existence or contents.

2) As the above extract suggests, the rationale for OPPSA s. 28(4) is to preserve the negotiability of cheques and other instruments. The main characteristic of a negotiable instrument is that it can be freely transferred in the market place. To this end, the transferee must be sure of getting clear title. Otherwise she may not be prepared to accept the instrument, and if transferees become reluctant to accept instruments, they lose their negotiability. A second and related reason for s. 28(4) is to maintain consistency with the federal *Bills of Exchange Act*, RSC 1985, c. B-4 (BOE Act). The BOE Act provides that a person who takes a negotiable instrument for value in good faith and without notice of any defect in the transferor's title gets clear title (the "holder in due course rule").

3) OPPSA s. 29(a) repeats the point in different language: it provides that the rights of a holder in due course of a bill, note, or cheque are to be determined without regard to this Act (that is, the OPPSA). Even without OPPSA ss. 28(4) and 29(a), the holder in due course rule would still apply by virtue of the paramountcy doctrine. Section 29(b) is a parallel provision for money: it provides that the rights of a person who is a transferee from the debtor of money are to be determined without regard to this Act.

4) The Saskatchewan PPSA equivalent of OPPSA s. 28(4) was in issue in *Flexi-Coil Ltd. v. Kindersley District Credit Union Ltd.* (1993), 107 DLR (4th) 129 (Sask. CA). The case is extracted in Chapter 12, but the following is a short summary of the parts that are presently relevant. SP held a security interest perfected by registration in D's inventory. D made sales to various customers, who paid by cheque. D deposited the cheques into its account at K Credit Union. The account was in overdraft and K reduced the amount of the overdraft as soon as it received the cheques and before it sent off the cheques for clearance. One of the issues was whether the deposit extinguished SP's security interest in the cheques as proceeds of the inventory and the court held that it did, by virtue of s. [28(4)], reasoning as follows.

Whether a bank is a purchaser for the purposes of s. [28(4)] depends on whether it receives the cheque in the capacity of: (1) a collecting bank; or (2) a discounting bank. If it is simply a collecting bank, it does not acquire property in the cheque, but if it is a discounting bank, it does. A bank becomes a discounting bank if it allows the customer to draw on the cheque prior to final clearance and, in that case, it receives payment of the clearance funds on its own account. A bank also becomes a discounting bank if it reduces an existing overdraft by the amount of the cheque before sending it for clearance. On this basis, K was a discounting bank in relation to the cheques and this meant that it acquired a sufficient interest in the cheques to make it a purchaser in the PPSA sense. K gave value for its interest *via* the revolving credit arrangement that the overdraft represented: the crediting of the cheques to the overdrawn account reduced the amount owing and *pro tanto* restored D's right to draw down further funds. In short, all the requirements of s. [28(4)] were satisfied.

5) The decision in *Flexi-Coil* turned on the court's finding that K was a discounting bank in relation to the cheques. What is the position where the bank is a collecting bank? In that

case, s. [28(4)] does not apply because the bank is not a "purchaser." The cheque remains D's property during the clearance process and SP's security interest in the cheque continues. This means that the bank may become liable to SP in conversion when it collects the cheque. However, the bank will normally have a defence under s. 175 of the BOE Act: "[w]here a bank, in good faith and without negligence, receives for a customer payment of a cheque crossed generally or specially to itself and the customer has no title or a defective title thereto, the bank does not incur any liability to the true owner of the cheque by reason only of having received that payment."

V. TRANSFER OF SECURITIES

John Cameron, "Secured Transactions Under Ontario's Securities Transfer Act, 2006"
(2007), 22 *BFLR* 309, at 326-35 and 340-42 (footnotes omitted)

The Direct Holding System

(a) *Protected Purchasers*

Prior to January 1, 2007, section 28(6) of the PPSA and section 69(2) of the *Business Corporations Act* contained "good faith purchaser" rules which protected certain secured creditors and buyers of securities. Those rules were repealed as of January 1, 2007 when the STA and related PPSA amendments came into force. Those rules were replaced by the "protected purchaser" rules. "Protected purchaser" is defined in section 1(1) of the STA, as follows:

> "protected purchaser" means a purchaser of a certificated or uncertificated security, or of an interest in the security, who,
> (a) gives value,
> (b) does not have notice of any adverse claim to the security, and
> (c) obtains control of the security.

[T]he broad definition of "purchase" includes the creation of a security interest. There are three requirements conditions for a secured creditor to qualify as a protected purchaser. First, the secured creditor must give "value," which is defined [in s. 1(1) of the STA] to mean "any consideration sufficient to support a simple contract and includes an antecedent debt or liability." This requirement will be satisfied whenever a debtor creates a security interest by contract, securing a debt or liability. Any executory consideration should suffice, if it would suffice as consideration to support a simple contract. This interpretation is consistent with UCC §1-204, which defines value for the purposes of (among other things) Articles 8 and 9 as follows:

> Except as otherwise provided in Articles 3, 4, [and] 5, [and 6], a person gives value for rights if the person acquires them:
> (1) in return for a binding commitment to extend credit or for the extension of immediately available credit, whether or not drawn upon and whether or not a charge-back is provided for in the event of difficulties in collection;

(2) as security for, or in total or partial satisfaction of, a preexisting claim;

(3) by accepting delivery under a preexisting contract for purchase; or

(4) in return for any consideration sufficient to support a simple contract.

As a result of the broad definition of value, a binding commitment to extend credit would clearly qualify as value, even before the commitment is drawn upon.

Second, the secured party must not have notice of any adverse claim to the security. "Adverse claim" is defined [in s. 1(1) of the STA] to mean a claim that a claimant has a property interest in the security and it is a violation of the claimant's rights for another person to hold, transfer or deal with that security. This narrow definition means that awareness that someone other than the debtor may have a property interest in the secur-ity is not, by itself, sufficient notice of an adverse claim. The definition also requires that the secured party know that the creation of the security interest violates a third party's rights. As well, this narrow definition excludes claims which are merely contractual, without involving any property claim based on equity or otherwise. Sections 18 to 22 of the STA contain rules dealing with notice of an adverse claim. In particular, section 18 provides that:

A person has notice of an adverse claim if,

(a) the person knows of the adverse claim;

(b) the person is aware of facts sufficient to indicate that there is a significant probability that the adverse claim exists and deliberately avoids information that would establish the existence of the adverse claim; or

(c) the person has a duty, imposed by statute or regulation, to investigate whether an adverse claim exists and the investigation, if carried out, would establish the existence of the adverse claim.

The definition of "notice" in section 3 of the STA is not applicable in this context. "Knowledge" is defined [in s. 1(1) of the STA] to mean "actual knowledge." The test in section 18(b) addresses willful blindness. In the case of a secured party which is an or-ganization, sections 3(4) to 3(6) of the STA provide guidance as to whose knowledge is relevant, focusing only on the knowledge of the individual conducting the transaction, provided the organization maintains "reasonable routines" for communicating signifi-cant information to the individual conducting the transaction and there is "reasonable compliance" with those routines. As to the test in section 18(c), according to the Com-ment, in Canada there are no statutory or regulatory requirements to investigate whether an adverse claim exists. Section 22 of the STA states that registration of a financing state-ment under the PPSA is not notice of an adverse claim.

Third, the secured party must obtain control of the security [see Chapter 5, Perfec-tion]. As the Comment notes, "[t]o qualify as a protected purchaser there must be a time at which all of the requirements are satisfied. Thus if a purchaser obtains notice of an ad-verse claim before giving value or satisfying the requirements for control, the purchaser cannot be a protected purchaser." A secured party is only a protected purchaser if it does not have notice of *any* adverse claim. If the secured party has notice of A's adverse claim but not B's, the purchaser is subject to the claims of both A and B, unless it can take ad-vantage of the "shelter" principle (described below).

Unlike the definition of "good faith purchaser," the definition of "protected purchaser" does not employ the phrase "good faith." The rule about willful blindness (summarized above) displaces the requirement of good faith, and is designed to more precisely define the circumstances in which a person can acquire the status of a protected purchaser. The statutory obligation of good faith in the performance or enforcement of a contract, and the definition of "good faith," set forth in section 4 of the STA have no application to determine whether a secured party has acquired the status of a protected purchaser.

Section 70 of the STA states that "[a] protected purchaser, in addition to acquiring the rights of a purchaser, also acquires the purchaser's interest in the security free of any adverse claim." Section 28.1(2) of the PPSA states that "[t]he interest of a protected purchaser of a security under the *Securities Transfer Act, 2006* takes priority over an earlier security interest, even if perfected, to the extent provided in that Act." Therefore, nothing in the PPSA limits the rights that a protected purchaser of a security has under the STA: PPSA, s. 28.1(1).

The "shelter" principle embodied in section 69 of the STA allows a purchaser (including a secured party) to take a security free of any adverse claims, even if that purchaser is not a protected purchaser, so long as the person transferring the security to the purchaser is a protected purchaser. Section 69(1) provides that "[e]xcept as otherwise provided in subsections (2) and (3), a purchaser of a certificated or uncertificated security acquires all rights in the security that the transferor had or had power to transfer." For example, Debtor creates a security interest in securities in favour of Secured Party, who perfects by registration of a financing statement. Debtor then sells the securities to Buyer without Secured Party's consent, in circumstances where Buyer does not have notice of Secured Party's claim and therefore is a protected purchaser. Buyer then transfers the securities to Transferee who knows of Secured Party's claim. Despite that notice, Transferee will take the securities free of Secured Party's claim. Secured Party could have protected itself by taking control of the securities. An exception to the "shelter" principle precludes a purchaser of a certificated security who as a previous holder had notice of an adverse claim from improving that purchaser's position by virtue of taking from a protected purchaser [STA s. 69(3)].

The interplay between the protected purchaser rules in the STA and the priority rules in section 30.1 of the PPSA merits further comment. According to section 30.1, a secured party (SP2) which obtains control of investment property (including securities) has priority over another secured party (SP1) which does not have control. SP2 does not need to rely on the protected purchaser rules in these circumstances, and SP2 will obtain priority even if SP2 knew of SP1's security interest and that the creation of SP2's security interest violated a security agreement in favour of SP1. Where applicable, the protected purchaser rules operate to protect SP2 from other adverse claims—for example, a claim that the debtor does not beneficially own the securities.

However, section 28.1 of the PPSA raises some potential confusion about the interplay between these rules. Section 28.1 attempts to address that interplay as follows:

> (1) This Act does not limit the rights that a protected purchaser of a security has under the *Securities Transfer Act, 2006.*

(2) The interest of a protected purchaser of a security under the *Securities Transfer Act, 2006* takes priority over an earlier security interest, even if perfected, to the extent provided in that Act.

(3) This Act does not limit the rights of or impose liability on a person to the extent that the person is protected against the assertion of a claim under the *Securities Transfer Act, 2006*.

Some lawyers believe that section 28.1 is unnecessary. The Report of the Working Group 2002-2003 to the Uniform Law Conference of Canada recognizes this belief, and suggests that the primary purpose of section 28.1 is to clarify that a purchaser (including a buyer) that is unable to rely on the rules in sections 28(6) to 28(10) of the PPSA, may still have resort to the protected purchaser rules in the STA. That Report describes the purpose of section 28.1 as follows:

> Section 28.1 overlaps with sections 28(6)-(9/10). The Group was not able to reach a final conclusion as to the need for this section. However, the [Uniform Securities Transfer Act Task Force of the Canadian Securities Administrators] suggested its inclusion on the basis that users of the legislation [who] do not have a perfect understanding of the USTA may otherwise have difficulty appreciating the interface between the PPSA cut-off rules and the USTA protected purchaser provisions. ...

In this context, does section 28.1 of the PPSA allow a secured party to use the protected purchaser rules to subvert the priority rules in section 30.1 of the PPSA? For the reasons that follow, I think not. Before setting forth those reasons, it is worth noting that this question can arise in only very narrow circumstances, where the collateral consists of uncertificated securities and two or more secured parties have each perfected by the use of control agreements. This question does not arise where the collateral consists of a certificated security, because a secured party qualifying as a protected purchaser will necessarily be the only person with control of that security. Similarly, this question does not arise where the collateral consists of an uncertificated security, and the secured party has obtained control by becoming the registered owner of the security, because a secured party qualifying as a protected purchaser will necessarily be the only person with control of that security. In these cases, there is no potential for conflict between section 28.1 and section 30.1 because both rules grant priority to the secured party which has control of the security. Finally, this question does not arise in relation to a security entitlement under the indirect holding system (discussed below) because the protected purchaser rule does not apply to a security entitlement.

As mentioned above, this question can only arise where the collateral consists of an uncertificated security and two or more secured parties have each perfected their security interests by separate control agreements with the issuer of that security. In that hypothetical situation, the question is as follows: Can a secured party (SP2) which obtains a control agreement second in time, without knowing of an earlier control agreement in favour of an another secured party (SP1), rely on the protected purchaser rule to obtain priority over SP1 despite the clear priority rule in section 30.1(4) which gives priority to SP1? The answer is no. Section 30.1(1) states that "[t]he rules in this section govern priority among conflicting security interests in the same investment property," making the priority rules in section 30.1 paramount over the protected purchaser rules. This interpretation is consistent with the purpose of the priority rules in section 30.1. Although not addressing this question, the Official Comment to the corresponding provisions in Rev. §9-328 underscores the need for simple rules to determine priority between secured parties, which do not require an examination of the knowledge of each other's security interest for the purpose of determining priority, stating in part, that:

> A principal objective of the 1994 revision of Article 8 and the provisions of Article 9 governing investment property was to ensure that secured financing transactions can be implemented on a simple, timely, and certain basis. One of the circumstances that led to the revision was the concern that uncertainty in the application of the rules on secured transactions involving securities and other financial assets could contribute to systemic risk by impairing the ability of financial institutions to provide liquidity to the markets in times of stress. The control priority rule is designed to provide a clear and certain rule to ensure that lenders who have taken the necessary steps to establish control do not face a risk of subordination to other lenders who have not done so.
>
> *The control priority rule does not turn on an inquiry into the state of a secured party's awareness of potential conflicting claims because a rule under which a person's rights depended on that sort of after-the-fact inquiry could introduce an unacceptable measure of uncertainty. If an inquiry into awareness could provide a complete and satisfactory resolution of the problem in all cases, the priority rules of this section would have incorporated that test.* The fact that they do not necessarily means that resort to other law based solely on that factor is precluded, though the question whether a control secured party induced or encouraged its financing arrangement with actual knowledge that the debtor would be violating the rights of another secured party may, in some circumstances, appropriately be treated as a factor in determining whether the control party's action is the kind of egregious conduct for which resort to other law is appropriate. [Emphasis added.]

Paragraph 3 of the Official Comment to Rev. §9-328 addresses the equivalent of section 30.1(4) of the PPSA, and does not mention the possibility that a secured creditor which obtains control second in time might obtain priority over a secured creditor which obtained control first in time; in fact, it states the opposite by asserting that the rules do not require any examination of the knowledge of the secured parties. Nothing in the Official Comment to Rev. §9-331, which corresponds to section 28.1, addresses the type of situation described above.

This interpretation of sections 28.1 and 30.1 gives full effect to the policy underlying section 30.1. At the same time, this interpretation still leaves room for the rules in section 28.1 to operate. For example, section 28.1 clarifies that a purchaser which is not also a secured party (*e.g.*, a buyer) is entitled to rely on the protected purchaser rules in the STA even if that purchaser does not qualify under any of the cut-off rules in the PPSA. In summary, this interpretation of section 28.1 does not permit a secured party to rely on the protected purchaser rule to undermine the priority enjoyed by another secured party with control, as provided in section 30.1.

(b) Cut-off Rule for Buyers of Securities

Prior to January 1, 2007, section 28(7) of the PPSA provided a cut-off rule for the protection of securities dealers and others who purchased a security in the ordinary course of business and took possession of it, affording those purchasers priority over any security interest perfected by registration or temporarily perfected under the PPSA, even though the purchaser knows of the security interest, as long as the purchaser did not know the purchase constituted a breach of the security agreement. This special cut-off rule was designed to facilitate the marketability of securities. There was no counterpart in Article 8 of the Uniform Commercial Code because, until recently, a security interest in a certificated security could only be obtained through possession of the security, and registration of a financing statement under the Uniform Commercial Code did not perfect a security interest in securities.

As of January 1, 2007, sections 28(6) and (7) of the revised PPSA retain this cut-off rule in a slightly different form. The new cut-off rule is available only to a buyer of a security (and not available to a secured party) who obtains control and does not know that the acquisition by it of the security breaches a security agreement. It is implicit in this rule that a buyer may know of a security interest, but takes free of that security interest as long as the buyer does not know that the transfer breaches a security agreement. The old requirement for a purchase in the ordinary course of business is eliminated. Section 28(6) now provides as follows:

> (6) A purchaser of a security, other than a secured party, who,
>> (a) gives value;
>> (b) does not know that the transaction constitutes a breach of a security agreement granting a security interest in the security to a secured party that does not have control of the security; and
>> (c) obtains control of the security,
> acquires the security free from the security interest.

Section 28(7) clarifies that a buyer relying on the cut-off rule in section 28(6) is not required to determine whether a security interest has been granted, nor whether the transaction breaches a security agreement. Section 28(7) provides as follows:

> (7) A purchaser referred to in subsection (6) is not required to determine whether a security interest has been granted in the security or whether the transaction constitutes a breach of a security agreement.

To state the obvious, sections 28(6) and 28(7) allow the buyer to acquire the security *free* from the prior security interest. These rules are not merely rules of priority. They offer the buyer more protection than is available to a secured party which obtains control and is relying on section 30.1(2) of the PPSA.

In addition, sections 28(6) to 28(7) provide some additional protection for a buyer as compared with the protected purchaser rule in section 70 of the STA. Clause 28(6)(b) requires that the buyer does not *know* the transaction constitutes a breach of a security agreement; and section 28(7) disclaims any obligation for the buyer to make enquiries. In contrast, the definition of protected purchaser would require that a buyer not have notice of any adverse claim—a standard defined by the STA to preclude a buyer's willful blindness. It is probably easier for a buyer to satisfy the test under sections 28(6) and (7) of the PPSA, than the test in the definition of protected purchaser. While the differences between these tests are subtle, at least some members of the PPSA Working Group of the Uniform Law Conference of Canada (with whom the Canadian Securities Administrators' *Uniform Securities Transfer Act* Task Force consulted in 2003) considered that it would be useful to, in effect, clarify that a buyer of securities was never obligated to carry out due diligence, even where the buyer knew a financing statement registered under the PPSA against the seller was broad enough to perfect a security interest in securities, as long as the buyer did not know that the transfer to it would breach a security agreement.

Whatever view one takes about the relative protection offered to a buyer under sections 28(6) and 28(7) of the PPSA as compared with the protected purchaser rule in section 70 of the STA, the PPSA cannot derogate from the buyer's rights under section 70 or otherwise. Hammering home this theme in three different ways, sections 28.1(1) to 28.1(3) of the PPSA provide:

> (1) This Act does not limit the rights that a protected purchaser of a security has under the *Securities Transfer Act, 2006.*
>
> (2) The interest of a protected purchaser of a security under the *Securities Transfer Act, 2006* takes priority over an earlier security interest, even if perfected, to the extent provided in that Act.
>
> (3) This Act does not limit the rights of or impose liability on a person to the extent that the person is protected against the assertion of a claim under the *Securities Transfer Act, 2006.*

...

The Indirect Holding System

(a) Cutting-off claims by third parties who are not entitlement holders

An entitlement holder is protected against any adverse claim to a financial asset if the entitlement holder acquired its security entitlement for value and without notice of the adverse claim [STA s. 96]. The meaning of "value" and "notice of an adverse claim" discussed above ... apply equally in this context; but the relevant notice in this instance is "*the* adverse claim"—not "*any* adverse claim"—which has the effect of narrowing the number of adverse claims which can be asserted against an entitlement holder. Unlike the rule for protected purchasers in the direct holding system (which states that a protected purchaser "acquires" the security free of any adverse claim), this cut-off rule in the indirect holding system merely states that an action based on an adverse claim "may not be asserted" against the protected entitlement holder. In the words of leading US commentators:

> This apparently minor difference in phrasing actually reflects two important structural differences of the indirect holding system. First, ... the property rights associated with every security entitlement are potentially subject to diminution at the hands of other entitlement holders, not as a result of judicial process but as the result of the securities intermediary's creating additional security entitlements without acquiring additional corresponding financial assets. And second, ... when a security entitlement is created, the entitlement holder does not "acquire" it from a prior holder in the same sense that a buyer in the direct holding system does, because each security entitlement is created for its entitlement holder.

This rule does not preclude a secured party (among others) from acquiring a superior claim to a financial asset based on other provisions in the STA, such as section 105(2) in the case of a secured party who acquires control of the financial asset.

(b) Cutting off other claims

Persons who purchase (including a secured party) an interest in a security entitlement, without becoming an entitlement holder, are also protected from adverse claims to a financial asset or security entitlement, if the purchaser acquires the interest for value and without notice of the adverse claim, and obtains control of the security entitlement [STA s. 104(1)]. A "shelter" principle also protects a purchaser of an interest in a security entitlement, regardless of value, notice of an adverse claim, or control, if the entitlement holder from whom the interest is derived would be protected [STA s. 104(2)]. If two secured parties acquire a security interest in a security entitlement, the priority rules in the PPSA apply ... ; but if two purchasers acquire an interest and one is not a secured party, then the priority rules in the STA apply [STA s. 104(3)], and these rules operate in a similar way as the PPSA priority rules ... . In any case, a securities intermediary as purchaser has priority over a conflicting purchaser with control unless otherwise agreed by the securities intermediary [STA s. 104(4)].

While an entitlement holder has a property interest in a financial asset in his securities account, an entitlement holder cannot sell or redeem a financial asset. When an entitlement holder wishes to sell or redeem a financial asset, it must instruct the securities intermediary to do so. When the securities intermediary sells or redeems the financial asset on the instructions of the entitlement holder, in practice the securities intermediary will extinguish the related security entitlement. If the financial asset is sold to someone else in the indirect holding system, the buyer acquires a new security entitlement for itself—it does not obtain a transfer of the seller's security entitlement.

If a financial asset held by a securities intermediary is registered in the name of a customer of that securities intermediary, or payable to the order of or specially endorsed to that customer, and has not been endorsed to the securities intermediary or endorsed in blank, then the STA considers that financial asset to be held directly by the customer and not to be part of a security entitlement [STA s. 95(3)].

CHAPTER TWELVE

Proceeds

I. INTRODUCTION

One of the PPSA's many innovative features is that it spells out clearly the secured party's right to follow the proceeds where the debtor has disposed of the collateral, with or without the secured party's consent. This is important in the inventory financing context where, as we have seen, the debtor will usually be able to pass good title to the collateral to a third party if the goods are sold in the ordinary course of the debtor's business pursuant to ss. 28(1) and 28(2). However, proceeds claims also arise in many other contexts, such as where the debtor has disposed of collateral that can no longer be traced (or perhaps is not worth reclaiming) and the secured party wants to be able to assert a claim against the proceeds instead. Another example arises where the collateral has been destroyed or damaged and the secured party wants to be subrogated to the debtor's claim under an insurance policy or to bring a claim against a third party that may have caused the loss or damage to the collateral.

The common law and equitable rules concerning the secured party's right to follow the proceeds were both complex and uncertain, and depended, in part, on the terms of the security agreement and, in part, on the identifiability of the proceeds. Unhappily, as we will see, not all of these difficulties have been resolved in OPPSA s. 25 or its counterparts in the other PPSAs.

This chapter deals with three key aspects of s. 25: (1) the nature and source of the secured party's claim to proceeds; (2) what the secured party must do to perfect its security interest in the proceeds; and (3) the extent to which the proceeds can be followed by the secured party.

II. NATURE AND SOURCE OF THE CLAIM TO PROCEEDS

The following decision of the Supreme Court of Canada, although decided under s. 88 (now s. 427) of the *Bank Act*, is still important in illuminating and clarifying the conceptual significance of the right to trace in s. 25.

Flintoft v. Royal Bank of Canada
[1964] SCR 631

JUDSON J: The contest in this litigation is between a bank holding security under s. 88(1)(b) of the *Bank Act*, RSC 1952, c. 12, substituted 1953-54, c. 48, and a trustee in bankruptcy of the bank's customer concerning the ownership of certain uncollected debts owing to the customer at the date of bankruptcy. These debts arose from the sale by the customer of goods covered by the bank's security. The trustee says that he is entitled to collect these debts for administration under the *Bankruptcy Act*, RSC 1952, c. 14, because an assignment of book debts held by the bank was void for lack of timely registration. The bank says that the fact that these debts arose from the sale of the goods covered by the bank's security gives them to the bank notwithstanding the failure of the assignment of book debts. There is no dispute about the facts. It is admitted that the bank's security under s. 88(1)(b) was a valid security and that the assignment of book debts held by the bank is void for want of timely registration.

The judge of first instance declared that the trustee in bankruptcy was entitled to all book debts of the bankrupt unpaid at the date of bankruptcy. The Manitoba Court of Appeal held that to the extent that the book debts of the customer outstanding at the time of the bankruptcy represented debts owing to the customer for goods sold and covered by the bank's s. 88 security, these accounts went to the bank. Freedman JA dissented and would have held that the proceeds of these sales must come under the assignment of book debts, that the bank could only claim in its capacity as holder of this assignment and that, therefore, its claim failed.

My opinion is that the majority judgment is correct. By agreement in writing between bank and customer an express trust of these accounts was created in favour of the bank in the following terms:

> The proceeds of all sales by the Customer of the property or any part thereof, including, without limiting the generality of the foregoing, cash debts arising from such sales or otherwise, evidences of title, instruments, documents and securities, which the Customer may receive or be entitled to receive in respect thereof, are hereby assigned to the Bank and shall be paid or transferred to the Bank forthwith, and until so paid or transferred shall be held by the Customer in trust for the Bank. Execution by the Customer and acceptance by the Bank of an assignment of book debts or any additional assignment of any of such proceeds shall be deemed to be in furtherance hereof and not an acknowledgment by the Bank of any right or title on the part of the Customer to such book debts or proceeds.

In addition to the creation of the trust, the agreement rejects in advance any suggestion that the bank's right to these accounts will depend upon a valid assignment of book debts. This agreement does no more than set out the terms upon which a bank as holder of s. 88 security permits a customer to sell the property of the bank in the ordinary course of business.

The property rights of the bank are defined by ss. 88(2) and 86(2) of the Bank Act. Under s. 88(2) the bank gets the same rights and powers as if it had acquired a warehouse receipt or bill of lading in which the property was described. Under s. 86(2) it acquires all the rights and title of the customer.

...

Section 88 is a unique form of security. I know of no other jurisdiction where it exists. It permits certain classes of persons not of a custodier character, in this case a manufacturer, to give security on their own goods with the consequences above defined. Notwithstanding this, with the consent of the bank, the one who gives the security sells in the ordinary course of business and gives a good title to purchasers from him. But this does not mean that he owns the book debts when he has sold the goods. To me the fallacy in the dissenting reasons is the assumption that there is ownership of the book debts in the bank's customer once the goods have been sold and that the bank can only recover these book debts if it is the assignee of them.

We are not concerned here with the rights of a purchaser for value without notice of the proceeds of the sale of the bank's security. It is true that s. 63 of the *Bankruptcy Act* avoids in favour of the trustee the assignee of book debts held by the bank because of defective registration. Subject to this, the trustee has no higher rights than the bankrupt and he takes the property of the bankrupt merely as a successor in interest and not as an innocent purchaser for value without notice. He takes the property of the bankrupt subject to the express trust created by the agreement noted above, which, in my opinion, cannot be characterized as an assignment of book debts in another form. When these debts, the proceeds of the sale of the s. 88 security, come into existence they are subject to the agreement between bank and customer. As between these two the customer has nothing to assign to the bank. The actual assignment of book debts which was signed does no more than facilitate collection. Any other assignment, whether general or specific, of these debts by the customer to a third party would fail unless the third party was an innocent purchaser for value without notice.

In *Union Bank of Halifax v. Spinney and Churchill* [(1907), 38 SCR 187], the proceeds of the sale of the bank's security came into the hands of Spinney, a third party, who was a guarantor of the customer's account with the bank. The proceeds were in the form of drafts drawn in favour of the guarantor instead of the bank, as they should have been. Spinney took with knowledge that the drafts were in payment for meal, ground from corn, on which the bank held security and he was held liable to account. I can find in the report no mention of any written agreement similar to the one in existence in the present case but it is clear that the oral understanding between bank and customer was to the same effect. Any other understanding would be inconceivable in commercial dealings. Why would any lender who lends for the purpose of enabling another to acquire and manufacture goods, permit the sale of goods on which he holds security except on terms that the borrower must bring in the proceeds of the sale of those goods?

Re Goodfallow, Traders' Bank v. Goodfallow [(1890), 19 OR 299] is a similar case. The contest there was between the bank and the administrator of the deceased customer. The customer was a miller who had given a warehouse receipt to the bank. At the date of his death there was found to be a shortage of wheat which had commenced shortly after the warehouse receipt had been given. During the period of shortage some of the wheat had been converted into flour and sold. The proceeds were paid to the administrator, who was compelled to pay the money to the bank. The ratio of the judgment of Boyd C is contained in the following short extract from his reasons: "As long as the 'product' of this wheat can be traced, whether it be in flour or in money, it is recoverable by the bank as against the deceased and his administrator."

Again, I can find in the report no mention of any agreement in writing, but even in its absence the principle is plainly to be spelled out that if you sell my goods with my consent, it is on terms that you bring me the money in place of the goods. Although the bank's customer does not sell as agent for the bank, he does not sell free of the bank's claim to the proceeds. There is an analogy with the case where goods are consigned to a factor to be sold by him and reduced to money. There has never been any doubt of the right of the owner to trace the money or any other form of property into which the money has been converted. (Underhill's Law of Trusts and Trustees, 11th ed., p. 561.)

The only other case to which I wish to refer is *Banque Canadienne Nationale v. Lefaivre et al.* [[1951] Que. KB 83, 32 CBR 1], where the Quebec Court of Appeal, on facts which cannot be distinguished from those of the present case, anticipated the judgment of the Manitoba Court of Appeal. In the Quebec case the bank and customer had executed an agreement in the following terms:

> Art. 5: dans le cas de vente par le client des effets, en tout ou en partie, le produit de cette vente y compris les espéces, les effets de commerce, les billets ... ordre, titres et valeurs qui en seront la considération de même que les créances contre les acheteurs, appartiendront ... la banque ... qui ils devront être immédiatement versés ou remis, et jusqu' ... ce versement ou cette remise le client ne les détriendra qu'en fidéicommis pour la banque. L'exécution par le client et l'acceptation par la banque des transports de dettes de livres seront censés résulter de la présente convention et ne constitueront pas une reconnaissance de la part de la banque que le client a des droits ou un titre quelconque ... ces dettes de livres.

The contest was between the bank and the trustee in bankruptcy of the customer. The trustee contended that the accounts of the customer representing the proceeds of the sale of the s. 88 security were part of the assets of the bankrupt estate because they had not been validly transferred to the bank in accordance with Art. 1571 of the *Civil Code*. It was held that the use of the words "en fidéicommis" was merely an attempt to translate the English expression "in trust." The majority judgment is founded squarely on the ground that the claims against the buyers of the goods became the property of the bank by virtue of its s. 88 security and never were the property of the customer so as to be affected by the assignment in bankruptcy.

Appeal dismissed.

NOTES

1) As will be noted, Judson J in *Flintoft* takes the position that the inventory financer's right to the proceeds arises from the nature of inventory financing even if the agreement itself is silent on the subject. As he says, above, "even in its absence [that is, of a proceeds clause in the security agreement] the principle is plainly to be spelled out that if you sell my goods with my consent, it is on terms that you bring me the money in place of the goods." This proposition is now codified in OPPSA s. 25(1). Consider the following example:

> D is a horse trader. SP has a security interest in D's present and after-acquired inventory, perfected by registration. D sells T a horse in the ordinary course of business. T writes D a cheque for $1,000. Does SP have any claim against: (1) T for the horse; or (2) D for the cheque?

Applying s. 25(1)(a), SP's security interest does not continue in the horse because SP expressly or impliedly authorized the dealing, assuming D's sale to T was in the ordinary course of business and there were no relevant restrictions in the security agreement on D's authority to sell. But applying s. 25(1)(b), SP's security interest extends to the proceeds, regardless of whether the security agreement says anything expressly about SP's right to the proceeds.

2) Assume that, in our example, D banks T's cheque and the proceeds become mixed with other funds in D's bank account. Can SP trace the proceeds of the cheque into the bank account? In *General Motors Acceptance Corp. v. Bank of Nova Scotia* (1986), 55 OR (2d) 438, the Ontario Court of Appeal suggested that, in the absence of a provision in the security agreement to the effect that the debtor holds any proceeds on trust for the secured party, the secured party cannot trace. The court appears to have had in mind the former rule of equity that the right to trace depends on proof of a trust or fiduciary relationship between the parties. If the decision is right, it would represent a significant limitation on the position as stated in *Flintoft* and OPPSA s. 25(1): a proceeds clause in the security agreement may not be necessary to establish SP's basic claim to proceeds, but it will be necessary if SP wants tracing rights. However, the old rule of equity is probably no longer good law in Canada. In any event, in *Flexi-Coil Ltd. v. Kindersley District Credit Union Ltd.* (extracted below in Part IV.B), the Saskatchewan Court of Appeal held that "the secured party's right to trace proceeds is a statutory right [under the PPSA] not dependent on finding a fiduciary relationship between the debtor and the secured party claiming proceeds." See Part IV, below, for further discussion of tracing.

3) Consider the following variation on our earlier example:

SP has a security interest in D's racehorse (as equipment), perfected by registration. D owes SP $5,000. D sells the horse to T without SP's authority. The then current value of the horse is $2,700. T pays D $1,000. Six months later, SP locates the horse. Now it is worth $2,000. D banks the $1,000 as soon as he receives it from T and the money is still in D's account. There are no other funds in the account. Does SP have any claim against: (1) T for the horse; or (2) D for the money in the bank account?

Applying OPPSA s. 25(1)(a), SP's security interest continues in the horse because SP did not authorize the sale to T. And applying s. 25(1)(b), SP's security interest extends to the bank deposit as proceeds. It appears that these rights are cumulative and so there is the prospect of a windfall to SP: SP turns out to be secured for $3,000, whereas if D had not sold the horse to T in the first place, SP would only have been secured for $2,700. The non-Ontario PPSAs address this problem by providing in their equivalent to s. 25 that SP cannot claim in total more than the value of the original collateral at the time D sold it to T. In our example, this would mean that SP has rights to both the horse and the money, but only up to $2,700. The same limitation is implicit in the OPPSA.

4) Consider the following case:

SP holds a perfected security interest in Debtor's computer. Debtor wrongfully sells the computer to Trader. Trader, in turn, sells the computer to Buyer who, in part-payment also provides Trader with a printer as trade-in. Can SP claim the cash and trade-in received by Dealer as proceeds from the disposition of the computer?

In Ontario, the answer appears to be "yes," because the OPPSA does not require the proceeds to have been received by the debtor: see Ziegel and Denomme, at 197. Under the Saskatchewan Act the answer would be "no," because the definition of proceeds in s. 2(1) is restricted to personal property, etc., "in which the debtor acquires an interest." The restrictive language does not appear in the OPPSA or in UCC Revised Article 9. All the other provinces and territories, except the Yukon, are in line with the Saskatchewan model.

The rationale for the Saskatchewan approach is two-fold: (1) to avoid "the risk of the geometric multiplication of proceeds claims that could otherwise arise"; and (2) to prevent the potential prejudice to third parties who may have no reason to suspect that they are dealing with proceeds and may have no means of discovering SP's security interest: see Ronald C.C. Cuming, Catherine Walsh, and Roderick J. Wood, *Personal Property Security Law* (Toronto: Irwin Law, 2005), at 462-64. For a contrary view and arguments in support of the Ontario position, see Ziegel and Denomme, at 198.

III. PERFECTION OF SECURITY INTEREST IN PROCEEDS

The governing provisions are OPPSA ss. 25(2), 25(3), and 30(5). Sections 25(2) and 25(3) provide that if SP had a perfected security interest in the original collateral, it is also perfected as to the proceeds. Section 30(5) provides that for the purposes of the priority rules in s. 30(1), SP's original registration date is also the date that counts for proceeds.

Consider the following example:

> D is a furniture retailer. SP1 has a security interest in D's inventory perfected by registration on June 1. D sells furniture to O, a retail customer, in the ordinary course of business. D uses the sale proceeds to buy a delivery truck from X. On December 1, SP2 lends D money. SP2 takes a security interest in the truck and registers a financing statement. D defaults. Who has priority?

SP1's security interest extends to the truck as proceeds of inventory, and by virtue of ss. 25(2) and 25(3) its security interest in the proceeds is continuously perfected. Applying s. 30(5), SP1's registration date for the truck is the same as its registration date for the inventory; that is, June 1. Since SP2 did not register until December 1, SP1 has priority.

This outcome is hard on SP2 because it had no way of knowing that SP1's perfected security interest extended to the truck: SP1's financing statement disclosed a security interest in inventory, but not equipment. Contrast the position under the non-Ontario PPSAs. Sections 28(2) and 28(3) of the Saskatchewan PPSA are as follows:

> 28(2) A security interest in proceeds is a continuously perfected security interest if the interest in the original collateral is perfected by registration of a financing statement that:
>
> (a) contains a description of the proceeds that would be sufficient to perfect a security interest in original collateral of the same kind;
>
> (b) covers the original collateral, if the proceeds are of a kind that are within the description of the original collateral; or
>
> (c) covers the original collateral, if the proceeds consist of money, cheques or deposit accounts in banks or similar institutions.

(3) Where the security interest in the original collateral is perfected in a manner other than a manner described in subsection (2), the security interest in the proceeds is a continuously perfected security interest, but becomes unperfected on the expiration of 15 days after the security interest in the original collateral attaches to the proceeds unless the security interest in the proceeds is otherwise perfected by any of the methods and under the circumstances specified in this Act for original collateral of the same kind.

In our example, if these provisions applied, SP1 would have a 15-day grace period after D bought the truck to register a financing statement or a financing change statement to cover the truck. After that, SP1 would be unperfected as to the truck.

The only concession the OPPSA makes to the problem is s. 25(5):

25(5) Where a motor vehicle, as defined in the regulations, is proceeds, a person who buys or leases the vehicle as consumer goods in good faith takes it free of any security interest therein that extends to it under [s. 25(1)(b)] even though it is perfected under [s. 25(2)] unless the secured party has registered a financing change statement that sets out the vehicle identification number in the designated place.

For example:

D is a furniture retailer. SP has a security interest in D's inventory perfected by registration. D sells furniture to O, a retail customer in the ordinary course of business. D uses the sale proceeds to buy a car from X. D later sells the car to T without SP's authority. T buys the car for personal use.

Section 25(5) applies because the car is proceeds of the inventory, T bought the car as consumer goods, and SP had not registered a financing change statement that set out the VIN.

The Ontario position appears to have been influenced by the fact that the Ontario regulations only require the secured party to check off a box in the financing statement identifying the *class* of collateral (*viz.* "consumer goods," "inventory," "equipment," "book debts," and "other"), and that a searching party would be no wiser if the secured party were required to check off a new box entitled "proceeds." Does this prove the need for better descriptive requirements than presently obtain under the Ontario regulations? Recall that the Ontario government has committed to replacing the "check box" collateral description system with the "same item or kind" approach that the other provinces use, but it has not indicated when it will make the change: see Chapter 6, Part IV.

PROBLEM

D buys a car on conditional sale from SP in Winnipeg. SP duly perfects its security interest in Manitoba. Subsequently, D brings the vehicle to Hamilton and uses it as a trade-in on the purchase of a new car. SP becomes aware of D's actions only after the trade-in has occurred. Can SP claim a security interest in the new vehicle? What must SP do in order to perfect the security interest in Ontario?

IV. TRACING

A. Introduction

Consider the following case:

> SP has a security interest in D's racehorse as equipment. D sells the racehorse to T without SP's authority. T pays D $1,000. D spends the money on a week of riotous living. D defaults against SP. D's only remaining asset is a speedboat. The horse is lamed in a training accident and T has it put down. Can SP claim the speedboat as proceeds?

The answer depends on the common law and equitable rules about tracing. These are imported into the OPPSA by the definition of "proceeds" in s. 1(1), which provides that "proceeds" means "identifiable or traceable personal property in any form derived directly or indirectly from any dealing with collateral." The words "derived directly or indirectly" imply that there has to be some connection between the original collateral and the asset that SP is claiming.

This is confirmed by *Agricultural Credit Corp. of Saskatchewan v. Pettyjohn*, extracted below, where the Saskatchewan Court of Appeal said:

> Tracing at common law and equity is a proprietary remedy. It involves following an item of property either as it is transformed into other items of property, or as it passes into other hands, so that the rights of a person in the original property may extend to the new property. In establishing that one piece of property may be traced into another, it is necessary to establish a close and substantial connection between the two pieces of property, so that it is appropriate to allow the rights in the original property to flow through to the new property.

In our example, there is no connection between the horse and the speedboat, and so SP has no claim to the speedboat.

Now assume that instead of frittering the money away, D deposits the money in his bank account. There are no other funds in the account. This is a simple example going the other way: the bank deposit is traceable personal property derived from D's dealing with the horse, and so it is proceeds of the horse.

B. Tracing Into an Overdrawn Account

Assume that in our previous example D's account is overdrawn when he banks the money. This was the position in *Flexi-Coil Ltd. v. Kindersley District Credit Union Ltd.*, extracted below. There, SP had a security interest in D's present and after-acquired inventory. Some of D's retail customers paid by cheque and D deposited the cheques into its account with K Bank. The account was overdrawn and one of the questions the court had to decide was whether SP's security interest extended to the bank deposits as proceeds of the cheques.

As the court explains, the answer depends on the nature of the banker–customer relationship. If the customer's account is in credit, the relationship is debtor–creditor. The customer is the creditor and the bank is the debtor. Each deposit increases the amount of the bank's debt and each withdrawal reduces it. A bank account with a credit balance is property belonging to the customer: in PPSA terminology, it is an "account."

Assume that in *Flexi-Coil*, D had been in credit with K Bank. On these facts, when D deposits the cheques, the deposit is an "account" in PPSA terms and SP acquires a security interest in it as proceeds of the cheque. Contrast the position if D is overdrawn. The relationship between D and the bank is still debtor–creditor, but now D is the debtor and the bank is the creditor. Each deposit reduces the amount of D's debt and each withdrawal increases it (subject to any provision in the banker–customer agreement to the contrary). The bank account is still property, but the property belongs to the bank, not D. When D makes a deposit, this reduces his obligation to the bank, but it does not create any property rights in D.

Returning to our example, assume that six months after depositing the cheque into his overdrawn account, D draws on the account to buy a speedboat. Does SP have any claim to the speedboat? The foregoing analysis suggests that the answer is "no": D dissipates the fund when he deposits the cheque into his overdrawn account and so there is no connection between the racehorse and the speedboat.

Note the order of events here: (1) D sells the horse; (2) he pays the sale proceeds into his overdrawn bank account; (3) some time later, he draws on the account to buy the speedboat. Now change the sequence: (1) D buys the speedboat, drawing on his overdraft to pay for it; (2) he sells the horse; and (3) straight away he pays the sale proceeds into his overdrawn bank account. Is this case any different? *Agricultural Credit Corp. of Saskatchewan v. Pettyjohn*, extracted below, suggests that it might be. The facts in *Pettyjohn* were like our example, except that the transactions involved a new herd of cattle and an old herd of cattle rather than a speedboat and a horse. The court held that the new herd was proceeds of the old herd. The reasoning went like this: (1) If D had sold the old herd and used the sale proceeds to buy the new herd, the new herd would clearly have been proceeds of the old herd; (2) in substance, this is what D did: D's aim was to swap the herds over and he only used the overdraft as an interim financing measure; (3) since what D did was in substance the same as a direct swap, the same rules should apply.

Agricultural Credit Corp. of Saskatchewan v. Pettyjohn
(1991), 79 DLR (4th) 22 (Sask. CA)

[For the facts of this case, see Chapter 8. The following extract from the majority judgment deals only with the plaintiff's right to follow the proceeds from the disposition of the cattle into the defendant's hand.]

SHERSTOBITOFF JA: This conclusion leads to the second issue, whether the present cattle holdings of the Pettyjohns constitute proceeds of the 1981 and 1984 cattle, so that ACCS may claim a PMSI in the present Watusi cattle as well.

Section 28(1) of the PPSA provides that a security interest in the collateral extends to any proceeds of that collateral.

> 28(1) Subject to the other provisions of this Act, where collateral is dealt with or otherwise gives rise to proceeds, the security interest therein:
>> (a) continues as to the collateral unless the secured party expressly or impliedly authorizes such dealing; and
>> (b) extends to the proceeds.

The PPSA defines "proceeds" as identifiable or traceable personal property derived directly or indirectly from any dealing with the collateral or proceeds therefrom.

> 2. In this Act: ...
>
> (ee) "proceeds" means identifiable or traceable personal property in any form or fixtures derived directly or indirectly from any dealing with the collateral or proceeds therefrom, and includes insurance payments or any other payments as indemnity or compensation for loss of or damage to the collateral or proceeds therefrom, or any right to such payment, and any payment made in total or partial discharge of an intangible, chattel paper, instrument or security; and money, cheques and deposit accounts in banks, credit unions, trust companies or similar institutions are cash proceeds and all other proceeds are non-cash proceeds;

The question is, therefore, whether one can trace from the 1981 and 1984 cattle to the present Watusi cattle owned by the Pettyjohns.

The PPSA does not contain any definition of "tracing" or "traceable." Accordingly, in defining the notion of tracing under the PPSA, we must have reference to the notion of tracing in the common law and equity. However, certain changes in the concept of tracing will be required in the context of the PPSA. Indeed, as Vancise JA said in *Transamerica Commercial Finance Corp., Canada v. Royal Bank of Canada* (1990), 70 DLR (4th) 627, 79 CBR (NS) 127, 84 Sask. R 81 (CA), it is the "appropriate features" of the law of tracing which must be incorporated into the PPSA.

Tracing at common law and equity is a proprietary remedy. It involves following an item of property either as it is transformed into other forms of property, or as it passes into other hands, so that the rights of a person in the original property may extend to the new property. In establishing that one piece of property may be traced into another, it is necessary to establish a close and substantial connection between the two pieces of property, so that it is appropriate to allow the rights in the original property to flow through to the new property. The question has most often arisen in the context of a trust, when the trustee has improperly disposed of the trust assets.

Ignoring for the moment features of the law of tracing which protect innocent third parties, in establishing this close and substantial connection, the common law and equity have focused upon the form of the various transactions taking place. Thus, if a person sells an item of property, and uses the money thereby gained in order to purchase a second item of property, the first may be traced into the second. Because of its focus on the form of transactions, the common law and equity have run into problems when the proceeds of a transaction are mixed with other proceeds. This occurs most frequently in the case of money and bank accounts. The common law and equity have established presumptions and rules which govern various kinds of cases.

In the present case, the form of the transactions involving the 1981 and 1984 cattle, and the new Watusi cattle, is set out in the table annexed. Two things should be noted about this table. First, the defendant does not concede that all of the sale proceeds referred to were sales of the 1981 and 1984 cattle. As has been said, the Pettyjohns owned a large number of cattle, in only some of which ACCS had a PMSI. Second, the bank account was not the only source of funds for the purchase of the Watusi cattle, though it was the predominant source.

If one attempts to apply the traditional tracing principles of equity to these trans-actions, the following result emerges. The sale proceeds were deposited into the account, but were then immediately used to pay down the overdraft. The overdraft had been incurred partially to purchase the new Watusi cattle, and partially for other purposes. Therefore, the first problem in tracing from the old cattle to the new cattle is that the proceeds from the 1981 and 1984 cattle were used to pay debts. It has been the traditional view of equity that where proceeds are used to pay debts, they have been dissipated and are gone, and can no longer be traced. Professor Waters puts it in this way in *Law of Trusts in Canada*, 2nd ed. (Toronto: Carswell, 1984), at pp. 1041-2:

> On the other hand when the funds are used to pay the debts of the original wrongdoer or any subsequent holder of the funds the fund has gone. The creditor is a bona fide purchaser for value, so the fund cannot be traced into his hands, and, if the trust beneficiary were to be subrogated to the rights of the creditor against the debtor, this can only be because the debtor ought not to have employed the trust funds to which the beneficiary had a better title. It cannot be a tracing action, because the debtor no longer has the trust funds.

However, the matter is not quite that simple, as Professor Waters goes on in a footnote to qualify this statement:

> They [the funds] may still be traceable if the donee spent the loan on the acquisition of an asset which he still has, but in this case the trust funds would effectively have been convert-ed into the asset in question.

This qualification could apply to the present situation, as ACCS contends that the debts which were repaid from the funds were debts incurred in purchasing the Watusi cattle.

The authors of *Snell's Principles of Equity*, 28th ed. (London: Sweet & Maxwell, 1982), come to an equally ambivalent conclusion, at p. 300:

> Even if the recipient has used the trust money to pay off secured or unsecured loans or other identifiable debts, there can be no tracing; for the payment purchases no asset but merely extinguishes the debt, and there is no equity to revive it or create a new debt in its place.

Yet they add, also in a footnote:

> But possibly there would be a claim by subrogation if an identifiable asset had been pur-chased with the money lent.

The authors of *Hanburg and Maudsley Modern Equity*, 13th ed. (Stevens & Sons, 1989), also suggest, at pp. 642-3, that subrogation could be appropriately applied in such a situation.

In order to apply the doctrine of tracing by subrogation in this situation, a number of things would have to be established. First, the payment of funds into the account from the cattle sales would have to be matched with the debts which had been created by the Watusi purchases. That is, since there were a number of sources of funds both into and out of the account, in order to apply the doctrine of tracing by subrogation we must con-nect the payments in with the appropriate payments out, using an appropriate principle of tracing. The principle which would cover the situation best is the rule in *Clayton's Case* (1816), 1 Mer. 572, 35 ER 767, which held that in the case of a continuing account a payment shall be taken to apply to the oldest non-statute-barred debt then in existence. Thus, the first debt would be paid by the first payment, and so on. If one applies this doctrine to the present case, some of the debts incurred in purchasing the Watusi cattle can be connected to the proceeds of the 1981 and 1984 cattle, while others cannot.

The second matter which would have to be settled in order to adopt this approach would be what rights ACCS could obtain by subrogation. It is not clear whether the debts which were paid were secured or not. The commentators also do not make it clear whether this matters or not.

Finally, in order to adopt this approach, the factual question of whether the proceeds listed in the table as resulting from the sale of the 1961 and 1984 cattle did result from the sale of those cattle would also have to be settled.

However, in light of the view we take of the tracing remedy under the PPSA, it will not be necessary to settle any of these questions. It is possible that the tracing by subrogation approach would be appropriate in some cases as a method of establishing the close and substantial connection between old and new property which is necessary for the tracing remedy under the PPSA. However, the connection which this approach establishes is essentially an arbitrary one, focusing upon the form rather than the substance of the relevant transactions. Of course, it will often be appropriate for tracing to be arbitrary. If, for instance, the cattle had been sold, and the moneys been used to purchase a motor home, the connection between the cattle and the motor home would be arbitrary, but it would be close and substantial, making it an appropriate case for tracing. However, the connection in the present case between the old cattle and the new cattle is anything but arbitrary. The Pettyjohns sold their old cattle, and replaced them with the new cattle. The close and substantial connection between the old cattle and the new cattle has nothing to do with the form of the transactions which led from one to the other, but rather has everything to do with the nature of the property, and its function in the affairs of the Pettyjohns, which is that the new cattle replaced the old.

To hold that a close and substantial connection established through the substance of a series of transactions through which one set of chattels replaces another of the same kind can be sufficient to found a tracing remedy irrespective of the form in which the transactions take place is to extend the equitable concept of tracing for the purposes of the PPSA. However, this is an appropriate extension, in keeping with the spirit of both the PPSA and the equitable tracing remedy. In *Canadian Imperial Bank of Commerce v. Marathon Realty Co.* (1987), 40 DLR (4th) 326 at p. 338, [1987] 5 WWR 236, 57 Sask. R 88 (CA), Tallis JA characterized the purpose of the PPSA as being "to simplify the law governing commercial transactions and also to bring it up to date with commercial practices." Indeed, s. 64(1) of the PPSA sets out commercially reasonable behaviour as the standard expected of parties under the PPSA:

> 64(1) All rights, duties or obligations arising under a security agreement, under this Act or under any other applicable law, shall be exercised or discharged in good faith and in a commercially reasonable manner.

To examine the substantive nature of the transactions in question to establish a close and substantial connection between the old and new property is consistent with this focus upon commercial realities.

The notion of a close and substantial connection is also consistent with the traditional principles of tracing in equity. While the rules of tracing in equity were formal, their only purpose could be to establish that there was a connection between old and new properties such that the rights held by a person to one should carry over to the other.

We hold, therefore, that ACCS may trace from the 1981 and 1984 cattle to the new Watusi cattle, not by reason of the form of the transactions which led from one to the other, but instead because the new Watusi cattle replaced the 1981 and 1984 cattle in the farming operations of the Pettyjohns as a matter of commercial reality.

The appropriate principle of tracing in such a case is that where a set of chattels is replaced by another of like function in the affairs of the debtor, it shall be open to the court to find that the proceeds from the first were used to acquire the second, whatever the formalities of the transactions in question. It should be noted in passing that the formalities of the transactions will have some bearing, however, on whether the transactions can be characterized as a "replacement." There is no doubt in this case that the Watusi cattle did replace the previous cattle of the Pettyjohns.

This approach to the tracing remedy is in keeping with the comments of Tallis JA. In *Canadian Imperial Bank of Commerce v. Marathon Realty Co.*, supra, at pp. 338-9, concerning the tracing of proceeds when inventory is sold and new inventory is purchased:

> Under the Personal Property Security Act a security interest continues in "proceeds" as inventory is sold. Generally speaking, an interest continues in whatever is received upon disposition of the proceeds; in this way a continuous, perfected security interest is provided—inventory, proceeds, inventory again, more proceeds, and so on. In short, to hold that a debtor and secured party legally need not engage in a continuing turnover, pay-over arrangement to have a perfected non-attackable transaction comports with commercial reality. Why require needless acts of no benefit to other creditors when the financier and borrower can accomplish by a simple means what they could unquestionably do by a more elaborate and time consuming arrangement?

While the question of whether tracing can be a matter of substance as well as a matter of form did not arise in that case, emphasis was placed on the fact that inventory was substantially replacing inventory, with money from sales as an intermediate element, rather than upon the formal details of the transactions, such as into what accounts moneys were deposited or from what accounts moneys were paid.

Having found that ACCS may trace from the 1981 and 1984 cattle to the present Watusi cattle, it remains only to determine in what proportion of the present herd ACCS holds a PMSI. Before replacement of the herd in 1986/87, the Pettyjohns owned a herd of cattle whose exact numbers is not known because of the offspring involved. The Pettyjohns, in their factum, concede that if ACCS had a PMSI, it extended to 47% of them. The Pettyjohns entirely replaced the herd with 66 Watusi cattle. The herd was not merely replaced—it was significantly reduced in size as well. Since ACCS held a PMSI in only 47% of the original cattle, it may only trace its PMSI into 47% of the present Watusi cattle. For the purpose of clarity, we will round this figure to 50%, that is, one half. This leaves some of the proceeds generated from the sale of the 1981 and 1984 cattle unaccounted for, but ACCS did not identify any other items to which these proceeds might be traced.

The alternative approach, which would give ACCS a PMSI in the entire herd up to the limit of the remaining debt, is not in keeping with the basic character of the tracing remedy. This approach is initially attractive, in that it seems intuitively unfair that the Pettyjohns should gain some advantage through their sale of the 1981 and 1984 cattle which was, after all, in breach of contract. However, the tracing remedy is not concerned with fairness as between the debtor and any particular creditor. Being a proprietary remedy, the tracing remedy never arises unless there are insufficient assets in the hands of the debtor to repay all of the creditors. The tracing remedy is therefore concerned not with fairness as between debtor and creditors, but rather is concerned with fairness as amongst creditors.

More specifically, the tracing remedy must balance the claim of the security holder whose security has been improperly disposed of, with the claims of the unsecured creditors who are interested in any residue remaining after secured interests are paid. In balancing these two claimants, it may initially seem obvious that the security holder in the original item improperly disposed of ought to retain priority over any unsecured creditors. After all, having taken no security, an unsecured creditor can expect no more. However, in the context of the tracing remedy fairness is not such a simple matter. For the unsecured creditor had no notice that some property of the debtor which seemed unencumbered was actually the proceeds of a secured item and will be subject to a tracing claim. The unsecured creditor extends credit upon its analysis of the financial viability of the debtor, and in doing so expects that items which do not appear to be subject to a security interest are not, in fact, subject to such an interest The tracing remedy upsets this expectation ex post facto, for the sake of preserving the interest of the secured creditor in the original security. As such, there is a sense in which the tracing remedy is itself unfair to the unsecured creditors. However, where there is a close and substantial connection between the original security and its proceeds, the balance of fairness swings in favour of the prior security holder.

Fairness to the unsecured creditors at least demands, however, that this close and substantial connection be between secured property and its proceeds. In a case where 50% of the original property was available to unsecured creditors, so that unsecured creditors will have extended credit on that understanding, and 50% was subject to a security interest, and the whole of the property is dealt with in such a way as to give rise to proceeds, fairness as between secured and unsecured creditors in the context of a tracing remedy demands that the proportion of the proceeds available to secured and unsecured creditors remain the same as it had been with regard to the original property. To extend the secured proportion further would be to allow the secured creditor to claim security on assets that unsecured creditors would legitimately have looked to for repayment of their debts.

This case, of course, does not quite follow this pattern in that the dispute over tracing does not arise in the context of disputes among creditors, but instead arises in the context of a claim by the Pettyjohns that certain assets are exempt from seizure by ACCS, a claim which is defeated to the extent that ACCS holds a PMSI in the present cattle. However, we must be able to apply the principles of tracing established in this case to other, more usual, cases in which tracing will arise. Furthermore, it remains true in this context that fairness as between the debtor and creditor is not relevant. For the very existence of the exemption from seizure is itself unfair to the creditor. By virtue of the security agreements entered into by the Pettyjohns, ACCS has a security interest in all of the cattle owned by the Pettyjohns, including the 1981 and 1984 cattle in which ACCS also had a PMSI, but also including all the other cattle the Pettyjohns disposed of, and indeed the present Watusi cattle. ACCS is, however, prevented from realizing upon its security by the exemption provisions of the SFSA [*Saskatchewan Farm Security Act*, SS 1988-89, c. S-17.1], except to the extent that they hold a PMSI. This is most unfair to ACCS, but the legislature has decided that as a matter of public policy it is more important for farmers to retain the assets required to engage in farming than for lenders to be able to realize on security, except where a PMSI exists.

Thus, in a case where 50% of the original herd was subject to a PMSI, while 50% was not, and was therefore exempt from seizure, and the whole herd is dealt with in such a way as to give rise to proceeds, we should approach the question of the proportion of the proceeds to which a PMSI may be traced, and thus seized, not on the basis of what is fair as between the debtor and creditor, but instead on the basis of what will best achieve the public policy embodied in the legislative determination that the ability of the farmer to continue farming is more important than simple security, but not more important than a PMSI. When approached in this manner, it is clear that the proportion between the exempt and non-exempt portions of the original property should remain the same when it is indivisibly converted to other property also required in the farming operations of the debtor.

This conclusion might be different had the sales by the Pettyjohns been a deliberate fraud, in the sense that the transactions were carried out for the purpose of defeating the security of ACCS by way of an anticipated exemption claim. However, there is no evidence to suggest that this was so. While the sale of the 1981 and 1984 cattle was wrongful, it was not a deliberate fraud.

The trial judge dealt with the question of the onus of proof in dealing with exemption claims involving PMSIs. Because of the view which we have taken of the applicable law, there are no factual disputes which require that we speak to this issue.

In the result, therefore, the appeal must be allowed to the extent that ACCS holds a PMSI in 50% of the present Watusi cattle of the Pettyjohns, whatever their present numbers may be, including any offspring. The parties should have no difficulty in determining this number, but leave is given to apply for directions should this prove necessary.

Appeal allowed.

[Wakeling JA dissented from the majority's ruling that ACCS was only entitled to a 50 percent PMSI in the Watusi cattle on the ground that the ruling was inconsistent both with precedent and with the basis on which the majority had established the plaintiff's right to follow the proceeds of sale into the purchase of the Watusi cattle.]

Flexi-Coil Ltd. v. Kindersley District Credit Union Ltd.
(1993), 107 DLR (4th) 129 (Sask. CA)

JACKSON JA:

Introduction

This judgment concerns a secured transactions priority dispute between a lender and an inventory supplier following the bankruptcy of their mutual customer: a retail farm equipment dealer. The lender and the supplier both claim priority to cheques deposited by the customer to a revolving account in negative balance and to funds deposited by electronic transfer to the same account. After a trial, the learned judge held that the lender took priority over the inventory supplier. I agree with the trial judge's conclusion, but respectfully disagree with his reasons.

Facts

Churchill Farm Equipment Ltd. was a farm equipment dealer. The owners of Churchill tried to transfer control of their successful business to their son. Several disastrous business decisions later, Churchill declared bankruptcy. Flexi-Coil Ltd. was a long-time Churchill supplier and the Kindersley District Credit Union was Churchill's banker. The dispute in this case is between Flexi-Coil and the credit union over $86,659 which had been deposited in Churchill's account and applied to the line of credit supporting the account. Following deposit of this amount, Churchill wrote cheques to other creditors completely drawing on the line of credit.

The legal relationship between Flexi-Coil and Churchill was governed by a standard security agreement executed October 30, 1981. The security agreement covered the inventory supplied by Flexi-Coil plus any proceeds generated from the sale of the inventory. Flexi-Coil's security interest was duly registered in the personal property registry.

Churchill opened a bank account with the credit union early in 1984. The account was created with an operating line of credit of $150,000 payable on demand, which was increased in March, 1984, to $175,000. A loan agreement in this amount was executed and secured by a security interest on land and all stock and equipment. Churchill did not grant a security interest to the credit union with respect to any of the collateral or proceeds claimed by Flexi-Coil. As will be apparent, the competition in this case is between Flexi-Coil as a proceeds-secured creditor and the credit union as an unsecured creditor.

Operations between Flexi-Coil, Churchill and the credit union worked this way. As Churchill sold Flexi-Coil's machinery, it would deposit the cheques in its credit union account. (In some cases the funds were electronically transferred *via* another deposit-taking institution.) In due course, Churchill would pay Flexi-Coil the amount owed by cheques drawn on the same account. Flexi-Coil was aware of this practice. Credit union personnel testified it knew nothing of the secured relationship between Flexi-Coil and Churchill; it was not their policy to conduct searches at the personal property registry even when registering their own security interests at the personal property registry.

Churchill began to have severe financial problems in the fall of 1984. From October 31, 1984 to January 28, 1985, $249,276.16 was deposited or transferred into Churchill's credit union account. Of this amount, sales of Flexi-Coil's equipment accounted for $86,659, of which approximately $28,249 was deposited by electronic transfer. During this time, the credit union honoured cheques written by Churchill in the total amount of $225,524.88 and, in so doing, Churchill used its line of credit which had been credited, in part, as a result of cheques received from the sale of Flexi-Coil's inventory, *i.e.*, Churchill paid other creditors rather than paying Flexi-Coil. On January 8, 1985, Churchill attempted to pay Flexi-Coil $102,054.43 by writing cheques on its account in the usual way. These cheques were returned by the credit union for non-sufficient funds. Subsequently, Churchill made an assignment in bankruptcy.

Flexi-Coil sued the credit union for $86,659 which represented the amounts deposited with the credit union that Flexi-Coil claimed belonged to it. It claimed that amount as "identifiable or traceable proceeds" under the *Personal Property Security Act*, SS 1979-80, c. P-6.1 (the "PPSA") arising from Churchill's sale of Flexi-Coil's inventory.

Decision of the trial judge [98 Sask. R 124, 30 ACWS (3d) 1069]

The trial judge found for the credit union on two alternative grounds: (i) the security agreement did not extend to the moneys Churchill deposited with the credit union because Flexi-Coil allowed Churchill to deposit such moneys in the ordinary course of business; and (ii) Flexi-Coil implicitly subordinated its interest by its actions and, therefore, s. 39 of the PPSA conferred a higher priority on the credit union. In my respectful opinion, the trial judge's decision cannot be sustained on these grounds.

It was not open to the trial judge to conclude the security agreement did not extend to the moneys deposited with the credit union simply because Flexi-Coil allowed Churchill to deposit such moneys in its current account. Section 28(1)(a) of the PPSA provides that, where collateral is dealt with or otherwise gives rise to proceeds, the interest in the collateral is extinguished by an authorized dealing. No such words qualify the secured party's right to the proceeds: s. 28(1)(b) states that, where collateral gives rise to proceeds, the security interest in the collateral "extends to the proceeds." The purpose of s. 28(1)(b) is to ensure, in such circumstances, the security interest continues in such proceeds. To hold otherwise would be contrary to the fundamental basis of *Transamerica Commercial Finance Corp., Canada v. Royal Bank of Canada* (1990), 70 DLR (4th) 627, 79 CBR (NS) 127, 84 Sask. R 81 (CA), which gave priority to the proceeds-secured party over a lender with respect to funds deposited into a current account with the lender.

On the issue of whether Flexi-Coil subordinated its interest in the proceeds to that of the credit union, one begins by reviewing s. 39 of the PPSA:

39. A secured party may, in the security agreement or otherwise, subordinate his security interest to any other security interest.

To support his conclusion, the trial judge referred to a clause in the security agreement which allowed the debtor to use the collateral in its possession in any manner not inconsistent with the agreement. He found that, by allowing Churchill to deposit the cheques with the credit union, Flexi-Coil had [at p. 128] "implicitly subordinated its interest in the proceeds to the interest of Kindersley as banker for Churchill, and as *otherwise* allowed for in s. 39."

In deciding this issue, the trial judge relied on *Euroclean Canada Inc. v. Forest Glade Investments Ltd.* (1985), 16 DLR (4th) 289, 54 CBR 65, 4 PPSAC 271 (Ont. CA). *Euroclean* involved a competition between a perfected floating charge debenture holder and a subsequent unperfected conditional sales vendor. A clause in the floating charge allowed the debtor to "give mortgages or liens in connection with the acquisition of property" after the execution of the floating charge. The Ontario Court of Appeal held that this was an agreement to subordinate the interest of the debenture holder to the interest of those in the position of the conditional sales vendor.

With all due respect to the trial judge, *Euroclean* does not apply to the case at bar. The purpose of s. 39 is to give a third party, who is not party to a subordination agreement, the right to rely on such an agreement as its intended beneficiary. There was no agreement between Churchill and Flexi-Coil to the effect that Flexi-Coil would subordinate its interest in proceeds to others. Clause 4 of the security agreement between Flexi-Coil and Churchill provided that Churchill could "use the collateral in any manner not inconsistent with this agreement," but it would have been inconsistent with the security agreement for Churchill to have "used" the proceeds so that the security interest in the proceeds would be lost.

Whether it is even possible for a secured party to subordinate its security interest by a course of conduct is doubtful, but need not be decided in this case as the course of conduct was insufficient to give rise to such an inference. Flexi-Coil was not aware Churchill was applying the proceeds from the sale of Flexi-Coil equipment as payment on a line of credit, nor did Flexi-Coil acquiesce in Churchill paying the proceeds from the sale of its inventory to another creditor. The terms of the consignment or sale agreements between Churchill and Flexi-Coil required payment by the 10th of the month, or immediately if it was a sale out of existing inventory or a special order. It was simply easier for Churchill to deposit the cheques written to it (which represented the full purchase price) and to write new cheques to Flexi-Coil for Flexi-Coil's portion of the purchase price. One cannot infer Flexi-Coil had subordinated its interest in the proceeds by acquiescing in this practice. To infer an implicit subordination would seriously affect inventory suppliers.

As part of his reasoning, the trial judge pointed to s. 51 of the PPSA which provides that registration of a security interest in the personal property registry is not constructive notice or knowledge of its contents to third parties. It is unclear what the trial judge meant by this reference. At this point, it is sufficient to say the purpose of s. 51 was to remove the possibility of registration being held to constitute constructive notice in priority competitions. Where knowledge is a factor in determining priority under the PPSA, only actual knowledge is relevant: see, *e.g.*, ss. 21 and 67(3) of the PPSA.

Arguments on appeal

Although the trial judge's decision cannot be supported on the grounds listed above, the credit union argued the result could be sustained on other grounds. The credit union agreed the cheques and electronically transferred funds were proceeds of Flexi-Coil's inventory but argued, first, it took the cheques free and clear of Flexi-Coil's security interest as: (i) a *bona fide* purchaser for value; (ii) a purchaser under s. 31(3) of the *Personal Property Security Act* [OPPSA s. 29]; or (iii) a holder in due course under ss. 73 and 165(3) of the *Bills of Exchange Act*, RSC 1985, c. B-4. Secondly, the credit union argued the deposit of the cheques did not create second-generation proceeds because, when the cheques were deposited, the account was in negative balance. It argued that electronically transferred funds should be treated in the same way as cheques. Following initial argument, the credit union put forward two additional arguments, namely: (i) if second-generation proceeds were created, they were set off against the money owed to the credit union on the line of credit; and (ii) the doctrine of change of position protected the credit union when funds were readvanced on the line of credit.

Flexi-Coil advanced that the credit union took the cheques subject to Flexi-Coil's interest, but fundamentally, when the cheques and funds were deposited, there existed a right to payment as the proceeds of its collateral. In other words, Flexi-Coil would have us find that when the credit union advanced further funds on the line of the credit, it advanced its own funds and not the proceeds belonging to Flexi-Coil.

Operation of the account

The credit union's and Flexi-Coil's arguments are dependent on an analysis of the process at the credit union when the cheques and electronically transferred funds were deposited. Credit union personnel testified as to the operation of Churchill's account: when cheques were presented for payment, they were accompanied by a deposit slip, initialled or signed by Churchill, directing the credit union to "credit" the current account; when the funds were electronically transferred, a similar document was prepared by the credit union. An official with the credit union testified the credit union's system was on-line, and, when cheques were deposited, the account would be credited automatically. If the account was in a debit balance, *i.e.*, any of the $175,000 drawn down, the crediting of the account reduced the amount owing on the line of credit and Churchill was immediately given the right to reborrow that amount. If the account was in a credit balance, *i.e.*, none of the $175,000 drawn down, the amount paid in would augment the account. This latter state of affairs never occurred with Churchill. Throughout the life of the account, the line of credit was always significantly drawn down. The automatic process was conditional on the cheques ultimately being honoured by the drawee banks. If a deposited cheque was not honoured for some reason, the previous debit balance would be increased by the amount of the dishonoured cheque the next working day. It was possible for cheques written by Churchill on the account to be honoured before deposits cleared since credit was "immediately" given when cheques were deposited.

There were no agreements showing how the operating account worked. There was a "Loan Agreement" and a "Line of Credit Agreement" but these did not specifically address the revolving nature of the account. Credit union personnel testified the revolving account operated on the basis of custom for such accounts.

One exhibit at trial was a document entitled "Member's Statement of Accounts" which was introduced in evidence to show, by example, how the account operated. This document, produced by the credit union's computerized system, showed the state of

Churchill's current account in relation to the line of credit for a one-month period. As of the beginning of the month, the "Balance" column showed a negative balance as it did throughout the account's existence. When a deposit was made, it would be shown in a column headed "Credits/Principal" and the "Balance" column would be reduced by such amount. This indicated that the deposit and the negative balance were in essence "netted" to display a lower negative balance as of the moment the cheques or funds were deposited.

Issue: Whether the cheques were taken by the credit union free of Flexi-Coil's interest

(a) Bona fide purchaser for value

I turn then to the credit union's first argument: that the interest of Flexi-Coil was defeated when the cheques were deposited into Churchill's bank account because the credit union was a *bona fide* purchaser for value without notice. The basis of this claim is that Flexi-Coil must be able to trace its proceeds into the hands of the credit union, and to do so, it is argued, Flexi-Coil must rely on the equitable rules of tracing. At equity, a person seeking to trace property would not be successful if the property came into the hands of a *bona fide* purchaser for value. It has been said this rule did not form part of the common law rules of tracing, which permitted a plaintiff to follow money as long as the funds were not mingled in a bank account. In Fridman's *Restitution* (1992), at p. 417, the author stated:

> The distinction between legal and equitable titles and between tracing at common law and in equity is of considerable importance. One reason for this is that a common law proprietary claim may not be defeated by the fact that the defendant acquired the property in good faith and for value; he may still not be able to assert a title that is superior to that of the original legal owner. Only if the common law recognizes a situation in which title may be lost involuntarily, for example, through estoppel or under the provisions of a Factors Act, will the owner at law lose his proprietary rights. In contrast, if the plaintiff's claim is based on equitable title, he may be defeated should the defendant be a *bona fide* purchaser for value without notice of that title.

Clearly, this bar to tracing in equity extends to situations where it is not goods, but money or its equivalent which is transferred to the third party for value without notice. As stated by Denning J in *Nelson v. Larholt*, [1947] 2 All ER 751 (KB), at p. 752:

> The relevant legal principles have been much developed in the last 35 years. A man's money is property which is protected by law. It may exist in various forms, such as coins, Treasury notes, cash at bank, cheques, or bills of exchange, but, whatever its form, it is protected according to one uniform principle. If it is taken from the rightful owner, or, indeed, from the beneficial owner, without his authority, he can recover the amount from any person into whose hands it can be traced unless and *until it reaches one who receives it in good faith and for value and without notice of the want of authority.*

(Emphasis added.) See also, *Re Cohen & Lyons*, [1927] 1 DLR 577 at pp. 581-2, 8 CBR 23, [1927] 1 WWR 162 (Alta. CA).

Section 28(1)(b) of the PPSA [OPPSA s. 25(1)] provides: "Subject to the other provisions of this Act, where collateral is dealt with or otherwise gives rise to proceeds, the security interest therein ... (b) extends to the proceeds." Section 2(ee) [OPPSA s. 1(1)] of the PPSA defines "proceeds" to mean "identifiable or traceable personal property in any form ... derived directly or indirectly from any dealing with the collateral or proceeds therefrom." The PPSA provides no further guidance for determining when an asset is identifiable or traceable so as to be proceeds, but this court has interpreted this clause on several occasions. A sampling of such cases is: *Canadian Imperial Bank of Commerce v. Marathon Realty Co.* (1987), 40 DLR (4th) 326, [1987] 5 WWR 236, 57 Sask. R 88; *Transamerica, supra; Agricultural Credit Corp. of Saskatchewan v. Pettyjohn* (1991), 79 DLR (4th) 22, 1 PPSAC (2d) 273, [1991] 3 WWR 689; and *Indian Head Credit Union v. Andrew* (1992), 97 DLR (4th) 462, 7 BLR (2d) 196, [1993] 1 WWR 673.

Vancise JA in *Transamerica*, at pp. 633-4, accepted Professor Donovan Waters' analysis of what constitutes identifiable and traceable proceeds as taken from "Trusts in the Setting of Business, Commerce, and Bankruptcy" (1983), 21 Alta. Law Rev. 395 at pp. 431-4. Based on this article, Vancise JA concluded: "... 'identifiable' refers to the ability to point to the particular property obtained by the debtor as a result of the dealing with the collateral, while 'traceable' refers to the situation where the collateral is commingled with other property so that its identity is lost." In *Transamerica*, cheques were deposited into a bank account in positive balance. The bank had applied the credit to an existing indebtedness without the debtor's authorization. The proceeds-secured party was permitted to trace into the account to defeat the bank's claim. Vancise JA held the right to trace under the PPSA was not limited by equity's requirement of a fiduciary relationship between the debtor and the secured party: see p. 634.

In *Indian Head Credit Union*, this court gave priority to the credit union as the proceeds-secured party over the Royal Bank. The collateral claimed as proceeds was a term deposit purchased with the proceeds of a cheque made payable to the debtor as compensation for the destruction of cattle, the original collateral covered by the credit union's security interest. The cheque was deposited by the debtor into his account at the bank. He subsequently purchased a term deposit with the amount on deposit and used the term deposit as security for a new loan from the bank. The case turned essentially on the finding that the bank knew the cheque was proceeds of the cattle, but the credit union was able to trace its security interest to the term deposit and defeat the bank which claimed the term deposit as its security.

In *Pettyjohn*, the issue was whether certain cattle were traceable as proceeds of other cattle. The debtor, under a security agreement with the Agricultural Credit Corp. of Saskatchewan, argued that when he paid down his debt on a revolving line of credit at his bank with proceeds from the sale of the first herd of cattle, ACCS lost its purchase-money security interest. Subsequently, the debtor purchased other cattle (using the same bank account) which ACCS now claimed as proceeds of the first cattle. There had been numerous deposits and withdrawals to the account, rendering it difficult to identify, with certainty, a direct link between the paying down of the debt and the withdrawal of funds to purchase the second herd. The court, however, developed a fundamental equivalency test based on a close and substantial connection to find the second herd proceeds of the first.

From these cases, one concludes that the secured party's right to trace proceeds is a statutory right not dependent on finding a fiduciary relationship between the debtor and the secured party claiming proceeds. Furthermore, the mingling of funds in a bank account with other funds does not prevent a successful proceeds claim; the funds remain traceable. When one reads these cases with *Re Diplock*, [1948] 1 Ch. 465 (CA); affirmed [1951] AC 251 *sub nom. Ministry of Health v. Simpson* (HL), the leading case on tracing in equity, it is clear this court has not simply adopted the common law or equitable rules of tracing to determine when a secured party can trace under the PPSA, but rather, has developed rules based on the PPSA which are uniquely designed to achieve the flexibility and certainty required by the PPSA. To such an end, the courts, in resolving disputes which invoke the right to trace, should use the common law and equitable rules as their base but, as far as possible, seek to found solutions on the statute and its underlying policy. It is especially important to look to the PPSA to determine whether the statute provides a rule in this case where the right to follow, at common law, may not be restricted by the purchase for value of the cheques, but at equity the right to trace would be. Clearly, it is open to the credit union to make additional arguments based on equitable principles as contemplated by s. 64(5) of the PPSA which reads as follows:

> 64(5) The principles of the common law, equity and the law merchant, except insofar as they are inconsistent with the express provisions of this Act, supplement this Act and continue to apply.

However, where the issue is addressed almost conclusively by the statute, it is preferable to look to the applicable priority rule in the PPSA which is s. 31(3). This eliminates, on this point at least, the necessity of determining whether the common law or equitable rules would allow tracing in these circumstances: see R.M. Goode, "The Right to Trace and its Impact in Commercial Transactions—I" (1976), 92 Law Q Rev. 360.

(b) Purchaser under s. 31(3)

Section 31(3) of the PPSA [OPPSA s. 28(4)] provides in relevant part as follows:

> 31(3) A purchaser of an instrument ... has priority over any security interest in the instrument ... perfected under section 25 [the registration section] ... if the purchaser:
>> (a) gave value for his interest;
>> (b) acquired the instrument ... without notice that it was subject to a security interest; and
>> (c) took possession of the instrument ...

The cheques deposited to the credit union were instruments (see s. 2(u) of the PPSA), Flexi-Coil's interest was perfected by registration under s. 25 of the PPSA and the credit union took possession without notice of Flexi-Coil's prior security interest. "Purchaser" is defined by s. 2(hh) of the PPSA as "a person who takes by purchase." "Purchase" is defined by s. 2(ff) of the PPSA to include "taking by sale, lease, discount, negotiation, mortgage, pledge, lien, issue or reissue, gift or any other voluntary transaction creating an interest in personal property." Section 2(qq) defines "value" as "any consideration sufficient to support a simple contract and includes an antecedent debt or liability." Thus, the issues remaining are, when the cheques were deposited: (i) was the credit union a purchaser; and (ii) did it give value?

To determine whether the credit union was a "purchaser" requires some consideration of its status when it took the cheques. Crawford and Falconbridge, *Banking and Bills of Exchange*, 8th ed. (Toronto: Canada Law Book Inc., 1986), at pp. 1041-3 and Ogilvie, *Canadian Banking Law*, at pp. 584-5 discuss the status of a "collecting bank." Whether a deposit-taking institution acts as principal or agent, they conclude, is a question of fact. Ogilvie at pp. 584-5 said:

> ... it is necessary to establish the legal status enjoyed by a bank when it collects a cheque, both at common law and pursuant to section 165(3) of the *Bills of Exchange Act* ...
>
> At one time it was fundamental to determine whether the bank was acting as a collecting bank or a discounting bank. When it was simply a collecting bank, it did not acquire property in the cheque but where it was a discounting bank, it permitted the customer to draw against the funds in the cheque prior to final clearance and received payment of the funds on its own account. A bank also became a discounting bank where it reduced an existing overdraft by the amount of the cheque before sending it for clearance ...

Thus Ogilvie would conclude that, when a cheque is deposited to a revolving account in negative balance, the collecting bank acts as a discounting bank in relation to the cheque.

Both texts acknowledge that a collecting bank which receives notice a cheque has been dishonoured is entitled to reverse provisional credit. But if the customer has already drawn upon the account (such that the reversal does not fully compensate the bank), the bank retains rights in the cheque even if partial recovery from the account has been made. The collector is entitled to proceed against the drawer of the cheque, its own customer or the payee: see Ogilvie, at p. 589 and Crawford and Falconbridge, at pp. 1056-7. This right exists whether the collector is a principal or agent by virtue of s. 165(3) of the *Bills of Exchange Act*, and arises simply by reducing an overdraft: see Crawford and Falconbridge, at p. 1756.

I note also that Crawford and Falconbridge at pp. 1443-51 and Baxter's *The Law of Banking*, 3rd ed., at p. 73, would accord the credit union the status of a holder for value.

It is not necessary to determine the credit union's exact status as a holder or collecting bank. It is only necessary to determine whether it acquired an interest to bring it within s. 2 (ff) and (hh) of the PPSA. When Churchill presented a cheque, accompanied by a deposit slip, to the credit union, one must infer Churchill gave the cheque to the credit union in order to reduce the balance: see *Kimmel v. Bean*, 75 P. 1118 (SC Kan., 1904) at p. 1121; and *Agard v. Peoples Nat. Bank of Shakopee*, 211 NW 825 (SC Minn., 1927). Conceptually, it cannot be otherwise. The value of a cheque could not create a positive balance in the account as the credit union waited for some further direction, from Churchill, to credit the account while at the same time interest continued to accrue on the outstanding balance on the line of credit. After reducing the overdraft, immediate credit was given. That the credit could be reversed is irrelevant. Based on the above statements which describe a collecting bank's rights and status, the credit union's reduction of Churchill's debt and the grant of further credit gave the credit union a sufficient interest in each cheque to make it a purchaser for the purpose of s. 31(3).

As indicated, when the cheques were deposited, the account was immediately credited and Churchill was able to write cheques on the account equivalent to the amount of the cheques deposited, subject to the $175,000 limit. Based on the definition of value, value was given in exchange for the cheques when the amount owing on the line of credit was reduced and, of course, when the right to draw additional funds was made available. Thus, the credit union took the cheques free and clear of the interest of Flexi-Coil when the cheques were deposited by virtue of s. 31(3).

Having reached this conclusion, it is unnecessary to consider the credit union's third argument on this point.

Issue: Whether second-generation proceeds were created

In considering this issue, it is helpful to return again to the definition of "proceeds" in s. 2(e) of the PPSA. From this definition, one concludes proceeds must have the following characteristics: (i) the proceeds must be personal property; (ii) the proceeds must be identifiable or traceable; and (iii) the proceeds, which must arise from a commercial dealing, can be derived either from a dealing with the original collateral or other proceeds. It is this third feature which makes it necessary to ask whether a dealing with the cheques resulted in another "generation" of proceeds to which Flexi-Coil's interest attached.

It is possible to describe a fourth feature of proceeds under the PPSA: the debtor must have an interest in the personal property *claimed as proceeds*. Versions of the PPSA, more recent than Saskatchewan's, contain an express statement to that effect in the proceeds definition: see, *e.g.*, the *Personal Property Security Act*, SBC 1989, c. 36, s. 1(1), definition "proceeds." The absence of an express statement does not permit a secured party to claim, as proceeds, collateral in which the debtor has no interest. On this point, see R.C.C. Cuming, "Protecting Security Interests in Proceeds: Equity and the Canadian Personal Property Security Acts" (a paper prepared for the Second International Symposium on Trusts, Equity and Fiduciary Relationships, University of Victoria, British Columbia, January 20-23, 1993), at pp. 6 and 15:

> A security interest, whether in original or proceeds, collateral can attach only to personal property in which the debtor has a proprietary interest. Quite apart from the conceptual consistency which the limitation preserves, there is an important public policy reason for it. One of the more difficult policy issues endemic to the Personal Property Security Acts is the position of remote third parties who cannot protect themselves through a search of the registry. The problems associated with the use of the debtor name as the appropriate registration-search criterion would be multiplied if the Acts were to recognize that a security interest extends to personal property in which the debtor did not acquire an interest. ...
>
> ... statutory tracing is more limited than tracing in Equity in that it applies only where the debtor has acquired rights in the personal property that is claimed as proceeds.

Flexi-Coil claimed: (i) the deposit of the cheques created a right to payment which was an account or an intangible belonging to Churchill which was attached by its interest; or, in the alternative, (ii) when the cheques passed through the clearing process, the funds generated belonged to Churchill and were at that time applied to reduce the debt. This argument is based on Professor Goode's article referred to above at pp. 379-80:

If T [Churchill] receives a cheque to which O [Flexi-Coil] is entitled to possession and, though accountable to O at common law, gives the cheque for collection to his own bank to be credited to his account, the right to follow has to be looked at in relation not to one asset but to three.

The three assets referred to are: (i) the cheque; (ii) the chose in action, namely, the claim which the customer acquires against his or her bank when the account is credited; and (iii) the money representing the proceeds of the cheque. The credit union argued that no proceeds within the meaning of the PPSA were created after the cheques were deposited. In advancing its position, the credit union relied heavily on the account's status as a revolving one in negative balance.

(a) Proceeds in the form of an account or an intangible

To assess whether an account or an intangible was created when the cheques were deposited, it is necessary to compare the relationship between a banker and a depositor when an account is in overdraft to that relationship when an account is in positive balance. With respect to the former relationship, Ogilvie, *Canadian Banking Law*, said at p. 464:

> As long as an account is in funds, the customer is the creditor of the banker. However, once an account has a negative balance or a deficit, the relationship is reversed and the banker becomes the creditor of the customer. An account in overdraft is legally characterized as a loan which is granted to the customer.

As to what happens when a deposit is made to an account in overdraft, reference may also be made to *M'Lean v. Clydesdale Banking Company* (1883), 9 App. Cas. 95 (HL). In this case, a drawer of a cheque stopped payment on a cheque already deposited to an overdrawn account. When the cheque was credited to the payee's account, the court found the deposit of the cheque extinguished the sum overdrawn, to that extent therefore giving the bank priority.

This is to be contrasted with the situation when a cheque is deposited to an account in positive balance. Again, taking from Ogilvie at p. 463:

> The indebtedness of the bank created when a deposit is made would appear to come into existence at the time of the deposit being made. Where a deposit is made in cash, the time when the indebtedness of the bank would appear to arise is when the customer's account is credited either by a passbook entry or by inputting through a computer terminal to a computerized account record where the account does not carry a passbook. This is so whether the deposit is made in person or through a banking machine. Where the deposit is made by negotiable instrument, the position is less clear since an entry either in a passbook or a computerized record is provisional until the instrument is cleared. It is arguable that the indebtedness arises when the instrument is paid in by the customer and a provisional credit is made because in most cases the provisional credit will be cleared and in the event that is not the case other legal remedies are available to permit a bank to recover funds drawn by the customer against the uncleared deposit.

Thus, when a cheque is deposited with a deposit-taking institution when an account is in positive balance, the debtor-creditor relationship between the institution and the depositor gives rise to a monetary obligation on behalf of the bank. Under s. 2(b) of the PPSA a "monetary obligation not evidenced by chattel paper, an instrument or a security" is an account. The account which comes into existence when a cheque is deposited to an account in positive balance is the proceeds of a dealing with the cheque. This is the basis upon which the proceeds-secured party was able to trace the proceeds of the cheques into the deposit account in *Transamerica*. Similarly, in *Indian Head Credit Union*, the bank argued it was entitled to priority because, when it sold the term deposit to Mr. Andrew, it was a holder of money under s. 31(1) of the PPSA and, therefore, knowledge of the credit union's interest was irrelevant. Madam Justice Gerwing said this at p. 477:

> The Bank in seeking to protect itself by s. 31(1), that is, as a holder of money, overlooks the two stages in the transaction. The Bank in taking the cheque from Andrew clearly received an instrument. His account was then credited with the amount of the cheque. This placed Andrew and the bank in a debtor-creditor relationship. The Bank did not acquire "money" from Andrew, within the definition of that term in s. 2, and not having "acquired the money" is not within s. 31(1). It acquired an instrument which may have been subsequently converted. The Bank cannot, by purporting to ignore the sequential legal steps in the deposit of the cheque and the crediting of the account, place itself within a section which was not designed to cover this situation.

Counsel for Flexi-Coil argued the "Member's Statement of Accounts," referred to above, was evidence the deposit of the cheques gave rise to an "account" within the meaning of the PPSA. It was argued that, based on *Transamerica* and *Indian Head*, the deposit of the cheques gave rise to a monetary obligation on the part of the credit union in favour of Churchill, thus giving rise to a debtor-creditor relationship sufficient to be personal property. The significant difference between the two cases above and the case before us is, in this case, there never was a point at which Churchill could have called for the proceeds of the cheque to be paid to him. The account was never in positive balance. Churchill had directed his account be credited. Since it was in negative balance, the result was a netting of the two amounts. When an account is in overdraft, based on Ogilvie's analysis, no property right arises. The customer is the debtor of the deposit-taking institution.

I accept the credit union's argument that the reference to "Credit" in the "Member's Statement of Accounts" was not a "credit" in the sense it represented an amount available to Churchill or proceeds available to Flexi-Coil. Rather it was merely a form of bookkeeping. The credit union was required to deposit the amount to that account by Churchill's direction on the deposit slip, and since the account was in negative balance, it was required to apply the funds to the amount owing. It never existed as a positive amount in the account for even a fraction of time. Churchill's right to the amount represented by the cheque was dependent on the credit union honouring its agreement to readvance the equivalent amount under the line of credit. Once Churchill directed the credit union to credit the account, when in negative balance, there were no proceeds of the cheque to which Churchill was entitled or to which Flexi-Coil's security interest could attach.

When the cheques were deposited, the credit union's only obligation to Churchill was to credit the overdraft and then make further credit available up to the $175,000 limit, provided the line of credit agreement was not otherwise in default. Following the making of a deposit, Churchill could not have sued the credit union and recovered the deposit. The credit union's obligation to credit the account is not an intangible to which a security interest can attach to permit recovery by forcing a payment from the credit union to Flexi-Coil. Churchill's only right after making the deposit was to have the account balance credited. If Flexi-Coil attached this right, it could be in no better position than Churchill.

(b) Proceeds in the form of funds from the clearing process

That brings us to Flexi-Coil's second argument on second-generation proceeds: the funds generated through the clearing process were collected for Churchill's account and were applied at that time to reduce its indebtedness. Flexi-Coil's counsel argued that, when the cheques were honoured by the payee banks, the funds which came to the credit union were Flexi-Coil's proceeds converted by the credit union. This argument, too, must fail. When the cheques were deposited, Churchill's debt was reduced. It is true this process was subject to reversal if a cheque was dishonoured, but if a cheque was honoured, the funds were collected for the credit union's account and not for Churchill: see the above quote taken from pp. 584-5 of Ogilvie. Value had already been given to Churchill in exchange for the cheques when the outstanding balance was reduced.

Clearly, the funds need not be in existence to sustain a proceeds claim. In *Transamerica* and *Indian Head Credit Union*, there were no proceeds left as such because the lenders had applied the funds to their customers' debts. In *Transamerica*, cheques were deposited and subsequently applied to reduce the indebtedness to the bank, and, yet, a third party was allowed to trace into the account and subsequently pursue the bank for the equivalent of the amount that had been in the account. Similarly, in *Indian Head Credit Union*, a cheque was deposited with the bank and the proceeds were used to purchase a term deposit and subsequently claimed by the bank as its security. But, in those cases there had been proceeds in which the debtor, and therefore the proceeds-secured party, had an interest and those proceeds had been appropriated by the lender. Here, the credit union took the first-generation proceeds, *i.e.*, the cheques, free and clear of the interest of Flexi-Coil. Churchill received value for those cheques. After the cheques passed through the cheque-clearing process, there were no proceeds in which Churchill, and therefore Flexi-Coil, had an interest.

In passing I should refer to the only case directly on point which is *C & H Farm Service Co. of Iowa v. Farmers Savings Bank*, 449 NW 2d 866 (Iowa SC, 1989). This case concerned a competition between a proceeds-secured party and a bank. The proceeds-secured party, C & H, had taken a security interest in the Schellhorns' crops. Some grain was sold and the cheques deposited to the Schellhorns' chequing account at the bank. At all material times, the account was in negative balance. The bank continued to honour the overdraft which was credited by the deposit of further cheques. The Iowa District Court found for the bank on the basis that the proceeds were not identifiable because the account was in negative balance. That court reasoned that, if the account had always been in positive balance, the Schellhorns could have always paid other creditors and no claim would lie against the bank for converting the proceeds. The Iowa Supreme Court reversed the District Court's decision and found for the proceeds-secured party. The Supreme Court found the Schellhorns' overdrafts were not paid from identifiable cash proceeds deposited to the Schellhorns' account, but from the bank's own funds. The Supreme Court said this at p. 876:

> Rather, various creditors of the customer presented cheques to the bank for payment from an account which had an overdrawn, or debit balance. *The bank paid these cheques out of its own funds.* In effect, the bank loaned Schellhorns enough money to cover the amount of the grain for deposit and applied those proceeds to reduce the debit balance of Schellhorns' account, it was simply satisfying Schellhorns' antecedent debt to it with proceeds in which C & H had a security interest ... the bank paid cheques to other creditors of its customer with its own funds and then paid itself with proceeds in which a secured party, C & H, had a security interest.

(Emphasis added in original.) The Supreme Court said, when the bank paid Schellhorns' cheques in overdraft, the bank became Schellhorns' creditor and accepted the risk of an unsecured loan. It concluded that, when cheques were deposited, the bank set off what it owed the Schellhorns against that which the Schellhorns owed the bank on the overdraft. The Supreme Court said the bank could not do this, and went on to say at pp. 876-7, that the bank could not loan money to Schellhorns by paying Schellhorns' overdrafts and then expect to "jump over" C & H's priority to identifiable proceeds of C & H's collateral.

Another case dealing with a somewhat similar fact situation is *General Motors Acceptance Corp. of Canada Ltd. v. Bank of Nova Scotia* (1986), 6 PPSAC 53, 55 OR (2d) 438 (CA). In this case, which also involved a revolving line of credit and a proceeds-secured party seeking to trace, the court found for the bank largely because the payments were made in the ordinary course of business. This case may very well be confined to its own facts. I note, in this regard, the analysis by J.S. Ziegel, "Tracing of Proceeds under the Ontario Personal Property Security Act: *General Motors Acceptance Corp. of Canada, Ltd. v. Bank of Nova Scotia*" (1987-88), 13 *CBLJ* 177.

Counsel for the credit union is to be commended for drawing the court's attention to the *C & H Farm Service* case as it appears to be adverse in interest, but I find the case to be distinguishable. On a review of the facts, it appears the bank decided on its own to create the overdraft. There is also a suggestion of knowledge of the proceeds-secured party's interest. The language used in the case is strong, but it does not address the facts in the case before us: (i) the credit union had no knowledge of Flexi-Coil's interest; and (ii) the deposit was made to a revolving account in negative balance. In so far as it addresses this case, I prefer the analysis of the lower court.

Finally, it is worth noting that, if counsel for Flexi-Coil were correct, a deposit-taking institution would stand as its customers' guarantor with respect to customers' obligations to proceeds-secured parties. For example, in the *Pettyjohn* case, *supra*, the Pettyjohns banked with the Bank of Montreal. Their deposit account interacted with a line of credit. Whenever the balance of the account went below zero, funds in multiples of $5,000 were automatically borrowed, by agreement, against the line of credit and deposited into the account. Whenever the account balance rose above $5,000, funds in multiples of $5,000 were automatically withdrawn to make payments on the line of credit. As Sherstobitoff JA found at p. 32, the chequing account was itself only a conduit leading to the line of credit. In the case at bar, the credit union stands in the same position as the Bank of Montreal in the *Pettyjohn* case. If Flexi-Coil is correct in its position, ACCS could have also sued the Bank of Montreal in *Pettyjohn* to recover the money applied to the line of credit but which were the proceeds of the sale of cattle in which ACCS had an interest. This cannot have been the intention of the legislature.

Having concluded that no second-generation proceeds were created, it is not necessary to consider the credit union's arguments with respect to set-off and change of position.

Electronic transfer of funds

Counsel for Flexi-Coil pointed out that s. 31 of the PPSA does not deal with electronic transfers of funds and therefore, whatever decision is reached in relation to the cheques, Flexi-Coil must succeed in relation to the credit transfers. These transfers occurred without the use of money or an instrument as defined in the PPSA or the *Bills of Exchange Act*: see Falconbridge and Crawford, *op. cit.*, at pp. 1011-27. Counsel for the credit union argued it would be inconsistent as a matter of policy, to accord a different legal status to credit transfers than that given to money or cheques. It was submitted that a medium of payment such as electronic transfers, accepted by the banking system as a substitute or equivalent for money or cheques, should receive the same treatment at law.

When the PPSA was drafted, credit transfers were relatively new and therefore they are not referred to in the PPSA. What then should be the result? The credit union's proposal is entirely consistent with s. 31(1), (2) and (3) of the PPSA. There is a great deal of merit to the credit union's position. Arguably, these sections, in so far as they deal with matters in federal jurisdiction, were not needed and merely restate the federal law. The goal of these sections is to leave money and cheques largely free from security interests to preserve the integrity of the payment system in Canada which now includes credit transfers. Churchill initiated these credit transfers, in the ordinary course of business, and they were treated by the credit union in the same way as the cheques. When a credit transfer was made, it was immediately applied to reduce the account balance. After the transfer occurred, no second-generation proceeds were created. Accordingly, it is my opinion the credit transfers and the cheques should be treated alike judicially and priority given to the credit union with respect to the credit transfers as well.

Miscellaneous points

There are two miscellaneous matters which require comment. The first is the effect of this decision on secured parties who finance inventory. On this point, different public policy objectives of the PPSA collide. One goal of the PPSA is to provide security for those who finance inventory. It is expected inventory will be sold and proceeds will be generated. Prior to the enactment of the PPSA, the status and security of proceeds claims were beset with problems. These are documented in J.S. Ziegel and R.C.C. Cuming, "The Modernization of Canadian Personal Property Security Law" (1981), 31 *UTLJ* 249. The PPSA significantly addresses these problems. In this case, it may appear as a matter of policy Flexi-Coil, the inventory supplier, should win. However, there are two policy reasons which support a resolution of this case to the contrary. The first is the need to maintain certainty within the banking system. Clearly, s. 31(3) of the PPSA is designed to achieve that end. It, like the other subsections in s. 31, is an exception to the general priority provisions of the PPSA. The second is the need to preserve the debtor's right to pay its creditors. The PPSA recognizes this need in s. 31(1) and (2). As a matter of practical analysis, what Churchill did here was direct a payment to its creditor. At the end of the day it is the latter two policy considerations which govern in this case.

As an extension of this point, it was urged upon us that a result in favour of the credit union would significantly affect the priority given to inventory suppliers; that lending institutions would simply require their customers to deposit all retail cheques to accounts in negative balance to avoid the claims of inventory suppliers. This was of concern to the court, but since the court did not have before it any evidence of such dealings, this issue is best left to another day without further comment.

The second miscellaneous matter concerns the "Loan Agreement" and the "Line of Credit Agreement" between the credit union and Churchill referred to earlier. Under the loan agreement, the credit union granted a loan to be paid in full on March 23, 1985, or on demand. The agreement provided that the deposit account could be charged with payments as they matured. The line of credit agreement provided that Churchill granted to the credit union "a lien against any monies on deposit." If Churchill defaulted in any payment due under the line of credit agreement, the credit union had the authority to exercise its lien on the deposit account. Following the initial hearing of the appeal, the court requested further submissions as to the effect of this clause on the operation of the revolving credit account. After reviewing these submissions, I accept that this clause in the line of credit agreement merely reflects s. 34 of the *Credit Union Act*, 1985, SS 1984-85-86, c. C-45.1. The intention of the clause was to grant a lien on sums in positive balance and is not pertinent.

Appeal dismissed.

C. Tracing Into a Mixed Fund

Anthony Duggan, "Tracing Canadian Style:
Re Graphicshoppe and Other Recent Cases"
(2006), 43 *CBLJ* 292, at 292-300

1. Introduction

Consider the following cases.

Case 1

T misappropriates $1,000 from funds T holds on trust for B and deposits the money in T's personal bank account. The account already contains $500 of T's own money. There are no further movements in the account. T becomes bankrupt. Can B claim recovery of the misappropriated trust funds?

The answer is straightforward. Equity facilitates the tracing of trust property into a mixed fund by giving the beneficiary a charge over the fund to the extent of the beneficiary's entitlement. The charge gives the beneficiary's claim priority over the trustee's unsecured creditors: D.W.M. Waters, Mark Gillen and Lionel Smith, *Waters' Law of Trusts in Canada*, 3rd ed. (Toronto: Thomson Carswell, 2005), p. 273.

Case 2

The facts are the same as in Case 1, except that the day after the deposit, T withdraws $400 leaving $1,100 in the account. There are no further movements in the account. T becomes bankrupt. Can B claim recovery of the misappropriated trust funds?

Again, the answer is straightforward. According to the rule in *Re Hallett's Estate*, the court will presume T's $400 withdrawal to have been made against his own share of the mixed fund (*Re Hallett's Estate; Knatchbull v. Hallett* (1880), 13 ChD 696 (CA)). This means that B and T share the $1,100 remaining in the account in the proportions 1,000:100 and, as in Case 1, B is entitled to a charge over the entire fund to secure payment of her claim. The rule in *Re Hallett's Estate*, in contrast to the rule in *Clayton's* case (*Devaynes v. Noble, Clayton's* case (1816), 1 Mer. 529 at 572; 35 ER 767, at 781 (Rolls Ct.)), does not depend on the order of deposits and withdrawals. For example, assume that T's account balance is zero immediately before he deposits the trust money. The following day he deposits $500 of his own money into the account and the day after that he withdraws $400, leaving $1,100 in the account. Under the rule in *Clayton's* case the $400 withdrawal is debited against the earlier deposit (the $1,000 trust money) and so the closing account balance comprises $600 trust money and $500 of T's own money. By contrast, under the rule in *Re Hallett's Estate*, the outcome is the same as in Case 2.

Case 3

The facts are the same as in Case 2 except that the $500 which is in the account at the outset is not T's own money, but trust funds belonging to C. What are B and C's respective rights in relation to the $1,100 still in the account?

The rule in *Re Hallett's Estate* has no application here because it is limited to cases where the contest is between the wrongdoer (the defaulting trustee) and the wrongdoer's victim (the beneficiary). In the present case, the contest is between two innocent victims. Under the rule in *Clayton's* case, the $400 withdrawal would be debited against C's money so that B and C share the $1,100 remaining in the account in the proportions 1,000:100. This is an arbitrary outcome because it depends entirely on the timing of the deposits. If the deposit of B's $1,000 had preceded the deposit of C's $500, then under the rule in *Clayton's* case, B and C would share the $1,100 remaining in the account in the proportions 600:500: in other words, in the one case, C bears the whole loss and in the other case B bears the whole loss. In *Ontario (Securities Commission) v. Greymac Credit Corporation* (1986), 55 OR (2d) 673, 30 DLR (4th) 1, aff'd. [1988] 2 SCR 172, the Ontario Court of Appeal held that the rule in *Clayton's* case was inappropriate where the contest is between innocent victims and it opted for a *pro rata* sharing rule instead. On this basis, B and C share the remaining money in the proportions 2:1.

Case 4

The facts are the same as in Case 2, except that there are two further movements in the account. The day after making the $400 withdrawal T withdraws another $200, leaving $900 in the account. The day after that, he deposits $800 of his own money so that there is $1,700 in the account when T becomes bankrupt.

This case concerns the application of the "lowest intermediate balance rule." In *Law Society of Upper Canada v. Toronto-Dominion Bank* (1998), 169 DLR (4th) 353 (Ont. CA) (the *LSUC* case), Blair JA stated the lowest intermediate balance rule as follows (at para. 14):

> [A] claimant to a mixed fund cannot assert a proprietary interest in that fund in excess of the smallest balance in the fund during the interval between the original contribution and the time when a claim with respect to that contribution is being made against the fund.

Applying the rule to the facts of Case 4, B's claim is limited to $900, which was the lowest intermediate balance between the date T deposited B's money in the account and the date of B's claim.

The lowest intermediate balance rule derives from *James Roscoe (Bolton) Ltd. v. Winder*, [1915] 1 Ch. 62. In the *LSUC* case, Blair JA described the rationale for the rule as follows (at para. 17):

> [the] concept is grounded, ultimately, on the premise that tracing rights are predicated upon the model of property rights. [The lowest intermediate balance rule] seeks to recognize that, at some point in time, because of earlier misappropriations, an earlier beneficiary's money has unquestionably left the fund and therefore cannot physically still be in the fund. Accordingly, it cannot be "traced" to any subsequent versions of the fund that have been swollen by the contributions of others, beyond the lowest intermediate balance in the fund.

Assume that T had not made the final $800 deposit, but instead had left the cash in a drawer at home. Would B have had a claim to the $800 cash in the drawer? The answer is clearly not and there is no reason why B should suddenly acquire a claim to the money just because T deposits it in the bank account: Lionel Smith, "Tracing in Bank Accounts: The Lowest Intermediate Balance Rule on Trial" (2000), 33 *Canadian Business Law Journal* 75, at 79-81.

Case 5

The facts are the same as in Case 4, except that now the final $800 deposit is not T's money, but trust funds T has misappropriated from C.

In principle, the analysis should be the same as for Case 4. If T had not deposited C's $800 into the account, B would have had no claim to it and it is hard to see how B could acquire a claim simply by virtue of the deposit. C's claim should be subject to the same limitation. For example, assume that following the deposit of C's $800, T withdraws $1,500 reducing the account balance to $200 and then deposits $2,000 of his own money so that the closing balance is $2,200. Applying the lowest intermediate balance rule, B and C's claims are limited to $200 to be shared *pro rata* between them (see Case 3) and the remaining $2,000 goes to T's estate. In the *LSUC* case, however, the Ontario Court of Appeal rejected this analysis: see further, Part 2, below.

2. *Some recent Canadian cases*

In the *LSUC* case, a solicitor over time misappropriated more than $900,000 he was holding for clients in a trust account with the Toronto-Dominion Bank. The final misappropriation, on September 24, 1991, left a balance of $66,242.68. On September 25, 1991, the bank deposited $173,000 into the account. The money was intended as a mortgage loan for one of the solicitor's clients. The account was frozen before the transaction could be completed. On October 2, 1991, the bank unilaterally withdrew the $173,000 and paid it over to another solicitor to complete the transaction. The Law Society applied to the court for directions. The bank's withdrawal was arguably improper, but to avoid litigation on the issue the bank agreed that the case should be determined on the basis least favourable to it, namely that the withdrawn funds were still in the account. The question for the court was what claims did the bank and the solicitor's defrauded clients have to the money in the account on the date the account was frozen?

The facts are similar to Case 5, above. If the court had applied the lowest intermediate balance rule, the defrauded clients' claims would have been limited to $66,242.68 and the remainder would have gone to the bank. However, the trial judge refused to apply the lowest intermediate balance rule and the Court of Appeal upheld his decision. Blair JA delivered the Court of Appeal's judgment.

According to Blair JA, while the lowest intermediate balance rule may be appropriate in the case of a dispute between the defaulting trustee and the trustee's victims, where the dispute is between the trustee's victims themselves, different considerations apply:

> in the latter type of situation, everyone is a victim of the wrongdoer. Presumptions about what the wrongdoer may or may not have intended—in terms of replenishing the fund with subsequent contributions, or in terms of being honest and using his or her own funds first—are of little assistance (at para. 26).

Partly for this reason and partly because he thought the lowest intermediate balance rule is too difficult to apply in cases where there are numerous competing claimants, Blair JA opted for what he called a "*pari passu ex post facto*" solution instead. By this he meant that the remaining funds should be shared between the bank and the clients in proportion to their various contributions and without regard to any intervening state of the mixed fund.

As the analysis of Cases 4 and 5, above suggests, Blair JA's assertion that different considerations apply in the case of a contest between the trust claimants themselves is questionable. Lionel Smith has criticized the decision for this reason and also on the grounds that: (1) it is contrary to earlier Canadian authorities upholding the lowest intermediate balance rule; (2) Blair JA overstated the complexity of the calculations the lowest intermediate balance rule requires; and (3) even if the calculations were as complex as Blair JA supposed, that is not a sufficient reason to take money away from another claimant whose case is easier to prove ("The Lowest Intermediate Balance Rule on Trial," *supra*). These points seem irrefutable but, as later developments demonstrate, the court, having let the genie out of the bottle, has not yet succeeded in getting it back in.

In *Re Graphicshoppe Ltd.*, [2004] OJ No. 5169, a company, Graphicshoppe, deposited trust money totaling $93,000 or thereabouts into its general operating account where it became mixed with other funds. At some point, the account balance dropped to zero or below. Graphicshoppe discounted accounts receivable to another company, Textron, and Textron paid $145,000 into Graphicshoppe's account. Graphicshoppe went into bankruptcy soon afterwards. The issue in the case was what claim, if any, did the trust beneficiaries have to the money in Graphicshoppe's account? If the lowest intermediate balance rule applied, the answer would be none because the account balance was at zero or lower for some of the time before the date of the beneficiaries' claim.

However, Lax J, relying on the *LSUC* case, held that she was not required to apply the lowest intermediate balance rule but was "bound to search for the method of allocating the loss which is the more just, convenient and equitable in the circumstances" (at para. 34). In the present case, the contest was between the wronged trust beneficiaries whose property had been taken and Graphicshoppe's unsecured creditors. "It would be unjust and inequitable to apply the [lowest intermediate balance rule] in these circumstances to deprive [the beneficiaries] of their own property and correspondingly benefit the creditors of the bankrupt's estate at their expense" (*ibid.*). Therefore, the beneficiaries were entitled to payment of their claims in full out of the money in the account.

Assume Graphicshoppe had not been bankrupt. Presumably Lax J would still have found in favour of the trust beneficiaries: if there are just and equitable grounds for preferring the beneficiaries' claims over the claims of the wrongdoer's innocent creditors, *a fortiori*, justice and equity should favour the beneficiaries over the wrongdoer itself. Lax J's decision rests on the assumption that the closing balance was, as to $93,000, the beneficiaries' "own property." This is questionable, as the analysis of Case 4, above, demonstrates. Moreover, she fails to explain why, given that the contest was between the beneficiaries and the wrongdoer's creditors rather than the wrongdoer itself, considerations of justice and equity should favour one group of innocent claimants over another. A possible answer is that "creditors should not expect to benefit from their borrower's dishonest dealings with trust beneficiaries": *Re Graphicshoppe Ltd.*, [2005] OJ No. 5184 at para 111 *per* R.G. Juriansz JA. However, this simply begs the question.

Lax J's decision took the *LSUC* case one step further. The *LSUC* case suggests that the lowest intermediate balance rule should not be applied in a case like Case 5, above. Lax J's reasoning implies that the rule should not be applied even in cases like Case 4: that is to say, she implies that the rule should be abandoned altogether. Contrast Smith:

> [t]he lowest intermediate balance rule is imposed by logic. To reject it is to detach the exercise of tracing in bank accounts from the central idea underlying the concept of tracing, which is the finding of transactional links between one asset and another. A court can only dispense with the rule if it is willing to discard a fundamental part of the Western legal tradition, namely that your losses are yours and my assets are mine. *Any court that takes that step must stand ready to articulate the principles according to which it will redistribute the assets of litigants (op. cit. 91)* (emphasis added).

The case went on appeal to the Ontario Court of Appeal which, by a majority (Moldaver JA and R.P. Armstrong JA, J.G. Juriansz JA dissenting) reversed Lax J: *Re Graphicshoppe Ltd.*, [2005] OJ No. 5184. Moldaver JA, for the majority, held that the *LSUC* case was distinguishable. It involved a Case 5 scenario, whereas the present case involved a

Case 4 scenario: "in LSUC, all of the funds in issue were trust funds. Even though the defalcating lawyer had made an assignment into bankruptcy, there was no issue about whether the funds in question formed part of the estate divisible among his creditors; they did not. Rather, in LSUC, the court was concerned solely with how best to allocate the funds remaining in the mixed trust account between competing beneficiaries." The "reasons in support of the pari passu ex post facto approach have no application in a case where the concern is not how to allocate the shortfall of funds remaining in a mixed trust account between competing beneficiaries but is rather how to determine if funds in the hands of a bankrupt at the date of bankruptcy are, actually, in whole or in part, trust funds" and so not property divisible among creditors in bankruptcy (paras. 125 and 128). In summary, the lowest intermediate balance rule does still apply in a Case 4 scenario, but it does not apply in Case 5.

Moldaver JA went on to say that Blair JA's reasoning "ought not to apply here, because I cannot accept that, at the date of the bankruptcy, the bankrupt's bank account in this case was, in fact, a 'mixed' fund. Since it is clear on the evidence that the [trust monies] were totally dissipated before the monies from Textron were deposited into the bankrupt's bank account, as a matter of fact, there is no mixture here" (at para. 129). This statement is true of Case 4, but it is equally true of Case 5, as the above analysis demonstrates, and so it tells against Moldaver JA's claim that the facts of *Re Graphicshoppe* and the *LSUC* case were distinguishable.

3. The wider commercial implications

The *LSUC* case and *Re Graphicshoppe* concerned the tracing of misappropriated trust funds. However, both decisions have wider commercial implications. For example, the provincial personal property security statutes provide that where collateral gives rise to proceeds, the security interest extends to the proceeds: *e.g.*, Personal Property Security Act, RSO 1990, c. P-10, s. 25(1)(b). If a debtor sells collateral and deposits the sale proceeds into its general account, a Case 4 scenario may arise. If the debtor sells a second secured creditor's collateral and deposits the sale proceeds into the same general account, a Case 5 scenario may arise.

In *Port Alice Specialty Cellulose Inc. (Trustee of) v. Conoco Phillips Co.*, [2005] BCJ No. 1205 (BCCA) (the *PASC* case), Conoco delivered 23,000 barrels of fuel oil to PASC. The "new oil" was placed in a storage tank where it became mixed with 18,000 or so barrels of "old oil" that was already in the tank. Between October 6, 2004 and November 24, 2004, PASC withdrew approximately 30,000 barrels of oil from the tank. PASC went into bankruptcy. Conoco claimed possession of the remaining oil pursuant to s. 81.1 of the Bankruptcy and Insolvency Act, RSC 1985, c. B-3. This provision gives an unpaid supplier the right to reclaim goods supplied to a debtor within 30 days before the debtor became bankrupt or a receiver was appointed. For the section to apply, the goods must be identifiable as the supplier's goods, they must be in the same state as they were before delivery and they must not have been resold. The issue in the case was whether Conoco's oil (the new oil) remained identifiable for the purposes of s. 81.1, following its mixture with the old oil. Conoco argued that, applying the rule in *Clayton's* case, all the remaining oil in the tank was identifiable as its oil. The rule in *Re Hallett's Estate* would have led to the same conclusion on the facts of the case: see Case 2, above, but this point seems to have been overlooked in argument. In any event, the chambers judge held that some, but not all, the remaining oil was identifiable as Conoco's. Relying on the *Greymac* case, the judge held that the rule in *Clayton's* case is not appropriate in the case of a contest between two or more innocent claimants. The present case fell into this category because the contest was between Conoco and PASC's unsecured creditors. The solution in such a case is to divide the fund between the competing claimants on a *pro rata* basis. The Court of Appeal upheld the chambers judge.

The decision is open to question. Consider the following variation on the facts. Conoco holds a perfected security interest in the 23,000 barrels of oil and when PASC goes into bankruptcy, Conoco claims the 11,000 barrels remaining in the tank as proceeds of its original collateral. The *PASC* case suggests that Conoco would be entitled to only a *pro rata* share of the remaining oil. Assume now that PASC is not bankrupt so that the contest over the remaining oil is between Conoco and PASC itself. On these facts, the rule in *Re Hallett's Estate* applies: see Case 2, above and Conoco is entitled to all the remaining oil. In summary, the *PASC* case implies that Conoco's rights may vary depending on whether or not PASC is bankrupt. This is inconsistent with a basic principle of bankruptcy law, namely that the trustee in bankruptcy succeeds to whatever property the debtor owns at the date of the bankruptcy and no more. The principle is enshrined in s. 71 of the Bankruptcy and Insolvency Act, RSC 1985, c. B-3 and the reason for it is that otherwise creditors may behave opportunistically. In a case like *PASC*, for example, the unsecured creditors might put the debtor into bankruptcy solely as a way of getting at the oil. The court in *PASC* treated the case as being like Case 3, above on the basis that Conoco and the other creditors were all innocent claimants. However, it should probably have treated the case as being like Case 2, for the reason just given.

The *PASC* case was like either Case 3, above (on the court's view of the matter) or Case 2 (the better view). However, it might have been like either Case 4 or Case 5 if PASC had put more oil in the tank between the date of the last withdrawal and the bankruptcy date. Then the court would have been squarely faced with the question whether the lowest intermediate balance rule applied. The sooner the application of the rule is settled the better, for both the law of trusts and commercial law at large.

CHAPTER THIRTEEN

Enforcement of the Security Interest

I. INTRODUCTION

The enforcement of security interests is dealt with in Part V of the PPSA. The provisions of this part govern four stages in the enforcement regime: (1) the events triggering the debtor's default; (2) the secured party's entitlement to take possession of tangible collateral if not already in its possession; (3) retention or disposition of the collateral by the secured party, or its redemption by the debtor; and (4) the post-disposition relationship between the parties (*viz.* the debtor's right to any surplus and the creditor's right to claim for any deficiency).

As was true of other aspects of pre-PPSA chattel security law in Canada, creditors' remedies if the debtor defaulted turned in part on the terms of the agreement and, still more importantly, on the characterization of the agreement. Thus, conditional sales, chattel mortgages, accounts receivable, and the fixed and floating charge each had its own common law or equitable enforcement rules, sometimes (but not always) supplemented by statutory rules of greater or lesser intrusiveness: see Chapter 1, Part III. A primary purpose of all the PPSAs is to replace the multiplicity of pre-PPSA rules with a single enforcement regime, and to adopt rules that are functional in character and seek to strike a reasonable balance between the competing interests of creditors and debtors when the debtor is in default.

However, it is important to note that, whatever the aspirations of the drafters may have been, Part V of the PPSA is not self-sufficient. Depending on the circumstances, the parties will often have to consider the impact of the following additional sources of law.

(a) *Consumer protection legislation.* This exists at both the federal and provincial levels, although, with respect to the enforcement of PPS creditor rights, the provincial provisions are more important than the federal provisions. Some of the restrictions appeared in the early conditional sales acts (for example, with respect to the circumstances under which the seller was entitled to recover a deficiency after repossession and sale of the collateral), and were then substantially augmented during the Depression era with strongly pro-debtor provisions, notably the "seize or sue" option imposed on repossessing secured parties of chattels.

(b) *Receivership law.* Before the PPSAs, where a secured party held a fixed and floating charge against the debtor's assets, it was common for the security agreement to authorize the secured party to appoint a receiver-manager (a privately-appointed receiver) to take control of the debtor's business and to dispose of it if the debtor was in default. Alternatively, the secured party could apply to the court to appoint a receiver-manager (a court-appointed receiver), in which case the receiver was deemed to be an officer of the court and had to follow the court's directions with respect to the management and disposition of the debtor's business. Although fixed and floating charges have been abolished by the PPSAs, the system of privately and court-appointed managers and receivers has been retained and is expressly recognized in the legislation (see, for example, OPPSA s. 60). Consequently, where a receiver or receiver-manager has been appointed, it is the court order appointing the receiver or the terms of the agreement authorizing his appointment that will determine the receiver's rights and duties.

(c) *Canadian bankruptcy law.* If the debtor is bankrupt or insolvent at the time of the enforcement of the security interest, the creditor's enforcement rights will be qualified in the following respects: (i) if the secured party wishes to enforce a security interest in all or substantially all of the debtor's inventory, accounts receivable, or property, the secured party must first give the debtor ten days' notice of the secured party's intention (BIA s. 244(1))—the purpose of the notice is to give the debtor an opportunity to secure an alternative source of financing or, alternatively and more likely, to initiate proposal proceedings under Part III, Division 1 of the BIA or to seek creditor protection under the *Companies' Creditors Arrangement Act* (CCAA), RSC 1985, c. C-36, as am.; and (ii) if the debtor has preempted the creditor's enforcement strike by first giving notice of his intention to make a commercial proposal to the debtor's creditors under Part III.1 of the BIA, the creditor's hands will be stayed under BIA ss. 69(1) and 69.1(1) and the creditor will not be able to proceed without a court order. Similarly, if the debtor has opted for protection under the CCAA, the court's "first day" order under s. 11(3) will also almost certainly include a stay of enforcement proceedings by the secured creditor.

II. PROCEDURAL AND SUBSTANTIVE LIMITS ON ENFORCEMENT RIGHTS

Waldron v. Royal Bank
(1991), 4 WWR 289 (BCCA)

ANDERSON JA: This appeal concerns two major issues:

(1) Was it necessary for the Royal Bank of Canada (the "Bank") to give the plaintiffs a reasonable time for payment prior to the enforcement of collateral security given in accordance with s. 178(1)(b) of the Bank Act, RSC 1985, c. B-1, to secure payment of a demand loan?

(2) [...]

The plaintiffs, Mr. and Mrs. Waldron (appellants), live in Crescent Spur, BC, which is approximately 100 miles southeast of Prince George. Mr. Waldron is a contractor and heavy equipment operator engaged in logging and road building. In 1984, Mrs. Waldron began to operate a ceramics business in Prince George under the name "The Blue Unicorn." Financing was obtained from the Bank (respondent). In 1985, as the business grew, more financing was necessary and some security was given. The business continued to grow, its indebtedness mounted, and in April 1986 the Bank agreed to refinance the indebtedness. The plaintiffs signed a demand note for the amount owing and gave security, including an assignment under s. 178 of the Bank Act.

On 26th May 1986 Mrs. Waldron was admitted to hospital in McBride, British Columbia. ... On 12th June 1986 Mr. Waldron caused to be placed in the local Prince George newspaper an advertisement for a "Moving Out Sale" for the Blue Unicorn. ... Mr. Waldron asked Mr. Karpes to oversee the financial operation of the business. He authorized him to receive some of the receipts of sales from the business for the purposes of paying certain business expenses through Mr. Karpes' trust account.

· · ·

On 17th June 1986 the management of the Royal Bank decided to act. It wrote a letter dated 17th June 1986 addressed to Ron Waldron Contracting operating as the Blue Unicorn, at the address on 3rd Avenue in Prince George. The letter was marked for the attention of Ron Waldron and Peg Waldron. A copy of the letter was sent to Mr. Waldron's accountant, Karpes & Company.

The Bank gave the letter to the defendant Classic Bailiffs Ltd. with instructions to deliver the letter to the business address of the Blue Unicorn in Prince George. The Bank also instructed the bailiff to seize all of the assets of the business by having the locks on the premises changed.

The letter of 17th June reads, in part, as follows:

> We hereby make formal demand for payment of the entire amount due and owing by you, which sum is to be paid upon presentation of this letter. ...
>
> Under Section 178 of the Bank Act, should payment not be made upon demand, the Bank will take such action as necessary to protect its security.

Mr. Bohn and another employee of the defendant Classic Bailiffs Ltd., Eileen Milliken, attended at the business premises of the Blue Unicorn on the afternoon of 17th June.

The Bank's letter addressed to Mr. Waldron and the Blue Unicorn was handed to an employee of the business, Mrs. Mary Armella. Mr. Bohn then read the contents of the letter to her. The landlord and a locksmith attended at the business premises. The locks on the door were changed. Both keys to the door were given to Mr. Bohn.

The defendant relies upon the terms of the demand promissory note, and upon para. 6 of the loan agreement [which provided that "in the event of failure by the Customer to make due payment to the Bank of any debt or liability or part therefore" the Bank could without demand realize on its security "in such manner and upon such terms and conditions as the Bank deems best"].

· · ·

In my view, for the reasons which follow, the judgment of Estey J in [*Ronald Elwyn Lister Ltd. v. Dunlop Can. Ltd.*, [1982] 1 SCR 726] applies to the facts of the case on appeal and should have been followed by the learned trial judge.

The judgment of Estey J in *Lister v. Dunlop* reads in part as follows, at pp. 288-9, CBR:

> The principal difference between the courts below was on the right of the company and the Listers to reasonable notice from Dunlop when enforcing its claims under the note, the

debenture and the guaranties. Both courts below agreed that the debtor had the right to reasonable notice but, as quoted above, the majority of the Court of Appeal found that the debtor must ask for time to make the payment claimed to be due and none was asked for by the plaintiff-appellants. The facts of the demand have been set out. The debenture and note signed and delivered by the company provide for payment "on demand." By its terms the debenture further provides that the principal and interest shall "forthwith become due and payable" on the happening of any of 19 specified events such as a default in payment of interest and principal by the company. The security thereby constituted by the debenture likewise becomes enforceable at the same time. The guaranty by the Listers is performable upon "notice in writing" delivered personally or by mail.

The rule has long been that enunciated in *Massey v. Sladen* (1868), LR 4 Ex. 13 at 19, 38 LJ Ex. 34: the debtor must be given "some notice on which he might reasonably expect to be able to act." The application of this simple proposition will depend upon all the facts and circumstances in each case. Failure to give such reasonable notice places the debtor under economic, but nonetheless real duress, often as real as physical duress to the person, and no doubt explains the eagerness of the courts to construe debt-evidencing or creating documents as including in all cases the requirement of reasonable notice for payment.

• • •

LAMBERT JA: ... Mr. Justice Anderson has dealt with the appeal comprehensively and I propose to deal only with those points on which my opinion about the applicability of the principle in *Lister v. Dunlop* to this case particularly rests.

• • •

The principle in *Lister v. Dunlop* is that a person from whom a seizure is being made under a security instrument is entitled to receive such notice of the proposed seizure as is reasonable in the circumstances. The principle may also apply to other seizures but it is not necessary in this case to determine whether that is so.

It is possible for the principle in *Lister v. Dunlop*, [1982] 1 SCR 726 to be limited, modified or eliminated by constitutionally enacted legislation. Subject to that, it is my opinion that the principle applies to the realization of all security interests where a person's property is being taken away by the security holder.

I turn first to the general language in which the principle has been expressed. In *Lister v. Dunlop* itself Mr. Justice Estey, for the Supreme Court of Canada, referred, at p. 746, to the application of the principle in relation to "debt-evidencing or creating documents." In *Canadian Imperial Bank of Commerce v. Prosser* (1982), 41 NBR (2d) 656 (NBCA), Mr. Justice Stratton said, at p. 661, that the principle was applicable to "instruments creating a debt." In *Whonnock Industries Ltd. v. National Bank of Canada* (1987), 16 BCLR (2d) 320, Mr. Justice Seaton, for this Court, said, at p. 323, that the *Lister* case "established the Canadian law on the question of the reasonable time for payment of a demand loan."

The *Lister* case has been applied to a number of different types of security instruments. In the *Lister* case itself the security interest was created by a demand debenture. In *Jim Landry Pontiac Buick v. CIBC* (1987), 40 DLR (4th) 343 (NSSC), Chief Justice Glube treated the principle as applicable to a conditional sale agreement and to a chattel mortgage. *West City Motors Ltd. v. Delta Acceptance Corp. Ltd.* (1963), 40 DLR 818;

[1963] 2 OR 683 (Aylen J, Ont. HC) and *Camway Trucking Ltd. v. Toronto Dominion Bank* (11 March, 1988; Nos. 13227A/82, 7579/82, 1488/87) (Holland J, Ont. HC) were cases where the security interest was a chattel mortgage. In *Barclay Construction Corporation v. Bank of Montreal* (1989), 41 BCLR (2d) 239 (BCCA) and in *Bank of British Columbia v. Rivard* (CA005333; 11 March, 1987) (BCCA), this Court treated the principle as applicable, within its scope, to assignments of book accounts. In *Proud v. National Bank of Canada* (1985), 57 Nfld. and PEIR 14 (PEICA), the principle was applied to a seizure under a pledge agreement.

In my opinion the *Lister* principle applies, in accordance with its scope, subject only to contrary legislation, to all security interests where a person's property may be taken away by the security holder.

The *Lister* principle is a principle about giving reasonable notice before a seizure. The mischief which the principle was designed to remedy, from its earliest origins, was the possibility that a person might suffer serious harm from an unanticipated seizure that was not necessary.

The *Lister* principle is not a principle about the law of negotiable instruments or about whether presentment or demand must precede an action on a bill or note; nor is it a principle about the steps that must be taken to make a debt become due or become payable. There is no need for any requirement of reasonable notice in those areas of the law. It is the realization of security, collateral or otherwise, which raises the call for fairness to which the law has responded.

...

Since I have decided that the *Lister* principle is a principle in relation to seizures and not a principle about the interpretation of security instruments, and since I have decided that it applies to securities under paras. 178(1)(a) and 178(1)(b) of the Bank Act, it is my opinion that the *Lister* principle was applicable in this case to this seizure and that the Bank should be considered to have acted in violation of that principle if it seized the property of the plaintiffs without reasonable notice to them. Whether it did so must be determined by the trial judge when the remaining issues are tried.

Appeal allowed.

NOTES

1) The BCPPSA was not the applicable law in *Waldron*. Part V of the PPSA becomes operative upon default by the debtor (OPPSA s. 59). Default is defined as "the failure to pay or otherwise perform the obligation secured when due or the occurrence of any event whereupon under the terms of the security agreement the security becomes enforceable" (OPPSA s. 1(1)). Apparently, the parties to a security agreement are free to define what amounts to default so long as the standards (such as those of OPPSA s. 59(4)) are met. The Act provides that "upon default the secured party may take possession of the collateral" (OPPSA s. 62). Does the *Lister* principle apply in a case where the security agreement provides that the debtor is "in default" upon the happening of some specific event identified in the agreement? Is there not a conflict between the *Lister* principle and the PPSAs?

2) Section 58(2) of the Saskatchewan PPSA makes the right to take possession of the collateral upon default subject "to any rule of law regaining prior notice." All Acts based on the CCPPSL model require that, when exercising rights under Part V, a secured party must act "in good faith and in a commercially reasonable manner." See, for example, SPPSA s. 65(3). Perhaps this type of provision can be seen as embodying the *Lister v. Dunlop* principle. However, there is no equivalent provision in the OPPSA. Are these standards implicitly included in the Act?

3) As previously mentioned, under ss. 244(1) and 244(2) of the *Bankruptcy and Insolvency Act*, RSC 1985, c. B-3, a secured creditor (broadly defined in s. 2 of the Act) who intends to enforce security in all or substantially all of the inventory, accounts, or other property of an insolvent debtor (also broadly defined) acquired by the debtor for use in a business, must give a notice of its intention. A period of at least 10 days must elapse between the date the notice is sent and the date of enforcement of the security interest. The section applies to secured parties who use receivers to enforce security agreements. Commentators are divided over the question whether the notice provision in the BIA was intended to codify the rule in *Lister v. Dunlop*. The argument has been made that the purpose of the 10-day pre-seizure notice is to give the debtor an opportunity to file a notice of intention to make a commercial proposal under s. 50.4 of the Act and not to dispense with the *Lister v. Dunlop* requirements. Does this reasoning make sense, and would it not reintroduce all the uncertainties that the 10-day notice requirement in s. 244(1) was intended to dispel?

4) *Acceleration clauses.* The PPSAs permit security agreements to include an acceleration clause whereby, on default in payment of any part of the obligation secured, the entire amount becomes due immediately. Note, however, that if the contractual right to accelerate the maturity of the entire obligation arises whenever the secured party is or deems itself to be insecure, the right is exercisable "only if the secured party in good faith believes and has commercially reasonable grounds to believe that" the prospect of payment or performance is impaired (OPPSA s. 16). Does an election to accelerate involve a demand for payment, thereby invoking the *Lister* principle?

5) *Rights of Reinstatement and Redemption.* Do the Part V right of reinstatement (which is permitted by the Acts based on the CCPPSL model) and the right of redemption, examined later in this chapter, provide an acceptable statutory substitute for the protection provided by the *Lister* principle? What "mischief" was the *Lister* principle designed to address?

6) The PPSA may not be the only source of statutory regulation of rights and obligations associated with enforcement of security interests. In some jurisdictions, the defaulting debtor can invoke judicial intervention to prevent seizure of the collateral. See, for example, the *Unconscionable Transactions Relief Act*, RSO 1990, c. U.2, s. 2(d), which, however, has a very limited reach.

7) Section 25(1) of the Ontario *Consumer Protection Act*, SO 2002, c. 30, provides:

> 25(1) Where a consumer under a future performance agreement has paid two-thirds or more of his or her payment obligation as fixed by the agreement, any provision in the agreement, or in any security agreement incidental to the agreement, under which the supplier may retake possession of or resell the goods or services upon default in payment by the consumer is not enforceable except by leave obtained from the Superior Court of Justice.

What is the policy of this section? (It was inspired by a provision in earlier British hire-purchase legislation restricting the owner's right of repossession where the hirer had paid one-third or more of the hire-purchase price.) How often is a buyer likely to default after she has paid two-thirds of the purchase price? Why does the section apply only to secured installment sales contracts and not to secured loan transactions? Note that the equivalent provision in the BCPPSA (ss. 58(3) to 58(5)) applies to both secured sales and secured loan transactions.

III. SEIZURE OF COLLATERAL

The PPSA gives the secured party upon default by the debtor under the security agreement, "unless otherwise agreed, the right to take possession of the collateral by any method permitted by law" (OPPSA s. 62(a)). The section appears to incorporate any limitation on seizure of collateral prescribed by federal law or provincial law.

R v. Doucette
(1960), 25 DLR (2d) 380, [1960] OR 407 (CA)

SCHROEDER JA (for the court): … The respondents were duly licensed as bailiffs by the Municipality of Metropolitan Toronto after having received a certificate of qualification in accordance with the provisions of the Bailiffs Act, RSO 1950, c. 30. Under the terms of such licence they were entitled to engage in the business or calling of bailiffs but they were not clothed with any official status as peace officers or as duly authorized officers of any Court. Persons so licensed are frequently engaged by merchants or finance companies to repossess merchandise sold under the terms of conditional sales agreements and when thus engaged they are acting in a private and unofficial capacity as the authorized agents of the vendor of the goods in question or of his assignee.

The facts giving rise to the indictment laid against the respondents arose out of a seizure made by them on the afternoon of November 6, 1959, at or about the hour of 4.30 p.m. at the apartment of one John Chappell contained in a building known and described for municipal purposes as No. 2110 Dundas St. West. Chappell occupied a small second storey apartment at that address with his wife and five young children. The respondents had driven to the premises in a station wagon for the purpose of repossessing a television set which had been purchased by Chappell under the terms of a conditional sales contract. The purchaser, Chappell, stated in evidence that the vendor had accepted an old television set in part payment of the purchase-price and that he had paid approximately $15 in cash. A copy of the contract which has been filed does not indicate that any allowance was made for a used television set, but it is not disputed that at the time of the seizure the payments due under the agreement were in arrears.

Only Doucette and McNutt entered the premises in the first instance. The front door leading to the ground floor hall was opened to them by Chappell's 11-year-old-son who called to his father to advise him that some men wished to see him. The visitors did not wait for an invitation to enter Chappell's apartment but immediately proceeded to ascend the stairs. Chappell's evidence is that there was a small gate stretched across the hall entrance to his apartment and placed at the head of the stairs. He stated that the two respondents, while still standing on the stairway, advised him of the purposes of their visit; that they had not at that time passed the gate to enter the upstairs hallway. He then advised them that he would not permit them to take the television set until a policeman could be summoned. He stated that one of the two men then unfastened the gate and pushed him back across the upstairs hall into the living room where the television set was kept. There is a conflict in the evidence upon this point, both Doucette and McNutt having testified that they had not observed the gate referred to; that they did not see Chappell until they entered the living room of the apartment; and that when they announced their intention of repossessing the television set, Chappell stated plainly and emphatically that he objected to their doing so, and when no favourable reaction occurred he attempted to push Doucette out of the room. It is not disputed that Chappell at that time requested his wife to go out to telephone the police and at the same time ordered these two men, Doucette and McNutt, to leave his premises and to remain downstairs until the arrival of the police. They, however, refused to comply with this request and persisted in remaining in the apartment. A fight then occurred between Chappell and Doucette in which McNutt endeavoured to intervene. At this point the third respondent, Dongen, a sturdy man about 6 ft. in height and weighing 240 lbs. entered the room, unbidden by anyone, and his mere presence apparently sufficed to terminate the fighting. One thing that emerges clearly from the evidence is the fact that Chappell had made it abundantly clear that he protested against the presence of these men on his premises; that he objected to the removal of the television set of which he was at the time in peaceable possession under a claim of right, and that he made it very plain that if they attempted to remove it before the arrival of the police he would resist their efforts. In all the circumstances Chappell's suggestion that they desist from carrying out the seizure until the police were called, emanating from a man who had serious doubts as to his legal rights in this affair, was not unreasonable. Notwithstanding this one of the three accused men scoffingly declared that they would be gone before the police arrived. Then, while Chappell was leaning on the television set, Doucette disconnected the electric plug and Dongen seized the instrument and carried it towards the stairs, followed by Doucette and McNutt. The latter acting as a rear guard, walked backwards with his fists raised in order to hold off Chappell, who was apparently following the trio in a threatening manner. McNutt then pushed forward past Doucette who was on the upper steps, and assisted Dongen in carrying the television set down the remaining steps. Doucette who was then last in line, believing that Chappell was about to strike him, directed a hard blow at Chappell's mouth which felled him to the floor. The three bailiffs left the premises carrying the television set with them before the police could arrive on the scene.

The learned trial Judge made no express findings of fact and disposed of the case in these few words:

> With respect to the charge of assault in the second indictment, I am satisfied there that the complainant was the author of his own misfortune and that also will be dismissed.

It is not easy to discern precisely what the learned Judge meant by these words. ... I cannot think that the learned trial Judge gave proper consideration to the legal rights and obligations of the respondents in attempting to carry out their object and to the corresponding rights and obligations of the complainant, Chappell. Since there appears to be a popular misconception in the minds of many people, particularly in the minds of persons engaged in the business or calling of licensed bailiffs as to the extent of their rights and privileges, it may serve a useful purpose to review the law bearing upon the issues directly involved in this case.

It should be made clear at the outset that the recaption or resumption of possession of goods by the act of the owner through an agent or bailiff acting under his written authority, is not a lawful execution of any process against lands or goods, or is not the making of a lawful distress or seizure within the meaning of s. 110(c) of the Cr. Code which is directed against resistance to or wilful obstruction of any person engaged in the performance of such acts. This is placed beyond question by the decision of the Court of Appeal in *R v. Shand* (1904), 8 Can. CC 45, 7 OLR 190.

The limitations upon the right of an owner to repossess his goods without process of law are stated clearly and succinctly in 3 *Blackstone's Commentaries* at 4-5, from which I quote:

> Recaption or *reprisal* is another species of remedy by the mere act of the party injured. This happens when any one hath deprived another of his property in goods or chattels personal ... in which case the owner of the goods ... may lawfully claim and retake them wherever he happens to find them, so it be not in a riotous manner, or attended with a breach of the peace. The reason for this is obvious; since it may frequently happen that the owner may have this only opportunity of doing himself justice: his goods may be afterwards conveyed away or destroyed; ... if he had no speedier remedy than the ordinary process of law. If therefore he can so contrive it as to gain possession of his property again without force or terror, the law favors and will justify his proceeding. But as the public peace is a superior consideration to any one man's private property; and as, if individuals were once allowed to use private force as a remedy for private injuries, all social justice must cease, the strong would give law to the weak, and every man would revert to a state of nature; for these reasons it is provided that this natural right of recaption shall never be exerted where such exertion must occasion strife and bodily contention, or endanger the peace of society.
>
> ...

It is very clear that whatever rights the vendor or his assignee or their authorized agent might have had under the terms of the conditional sales contract (the purchase-money being in arrear and unpaid) to enter upon Chappell's premises to resume possession of the goods in question, it would be illegal for them to take such possession by force. *Traders Bank of Canada v. G & J Brown Mfg. Co.* (1889), 18 OR 430, cited by counsel for the respondents is authority for this proposition. In *Re Nu-Way Meat Market Ltd. & Grobstein & Commercial Acceptance Corp.* (1940), 22 CBR 46, 46 Rev. de Jur. 418, it was held that the liquidator might claim possession of a truck sold to a debtor under suspensive conditions of property, where the vendor had taken possession of it by force and deceit since the winding-up, and had neglected to furnish the liquidator with the detailed account of what was still owed by the debtor; whatever the terms of the deed, no one had the right to take the law into one's own hands.

Reference may also be made on this point to *Devoe v. Long*, [1951] 1 DLR 203, at 225-26, 26 MPR 357, a judgment of the Appeal Division of the Supreme Court of New Brunswick.

The right to resort to self-help was again discountenanced in *Nilan v. McAndless* (1912), 8 DLR 169, where at 171, Macdonald J stated:

> He was not justified, however in taking the law in his own hands when he found that he could not get peaceable possession. His proper course was to obtain possession by legal means.

There must be reasonable limits imposed upon the right of self-help assumed and asserted by private individuals in order to preserve peace and tranquility and to avoid the evil consequences which are bound to flow from insistence upon a right to use private force. Under s. 39 of the Cr. Code, the peaceable possessor of movable property under a claim of right is protected from criminal responsibility (although not from civil responsibility) for resisting its taking even by the person legally entitled.

The principle which must govern in cases of this kind was stated in clear and unmistakable terms by Osler JA, in *R v. Shand*, 8 Can. CC at 52-53, 7 OLR, at 196-97, from which I quote the following excerpt:

> The law is the same where goods are improperly detained by one in defiance of his agreement to yield them up to the owner with or without demand. If the owner can acquire possession peacably he may do so. If he attempts to take it forcibly and in a riotous manner as was done in the case before us, he becomes himself a breaker of the law, as much so as one who attempts to take possession of real property by a forcible entry, contrary to 5 Rich. II., stat. 1, ch. 8, even when it has been agreed that he was to re-enter; *Edwick v. Hawkes* (1881), 18 Ch. D 199; and see *Beddall v. Maitland* (1881), 17 Ch. D 174. If resistance is offered or possession refused he should have recourse to his action, and the code, sec. 144, would then have its full force in making unlawful any resistance to seizure made in due course of law. That is what is meant by a lawful seizure. It was never intended to enlarge the civil rights or powers of individuals, or to convert a breach of contract or resistance to private force into a criminal offence.
>
> ...

It follows logically that if a person enters premises lawfully in the first instance for the purpose of resuming possession of his movable property and subsequently abuses his authority, he becomes in law a trespasser. It is rather singular that three bailiffs had to descend upon the complainant to repossess a chattel which could be borne by one man, unless it was their purpose to make a display of might, against which the complainant's lone opposition, whether right or wrong, could scarcely be expected to prevail. That these men abused their authority after gaining entrance to the premises is too plain for discussion. Once it was made clear to them, as indeed it was, that they would not be suffered to remove the television set without resistance, they grossly exceeded and abused their rights when they persisted in carrying out their project of abducting the television receiver, using force for the purpose if necessary. They thus became trespassers even if their original entry was lawful, a point which, on the evidence, is itself not free from doubt.

The learned Deputy Attorney-General contends that by force of the provisions of s. 38(2) of the Cr. Code alone, quite apart from the actual physical force applied by the respondents to the person of the complainant, they must be held to have committed an assault without justification or provocation. Section 38(2) reads:

(2) Where a person who is in peaceable possession of movable property lays hands upon it, a trespasser who persists in attempting to keep it or take it from him or from any one lawfully assisting him shall be deemed to commit an assault without justification or provocation.

Also by s. 38(1) the person in peaceable possession of such property is justified in preventing a trespasser from taking it if he does not strike him or cause him bodily harm.

In my view of the facts, the conduct of the respondents towards the complainant Chappell while exercising their purported right to repossess the television set in question by force is in itself sufficient to support a charge of common assault against them. I agree, however, that if it were necessary for the Crown to rely upon the provisions of s. 38(2) of the Cr. Code, those provisions might successfully be invoked against the respondents.

Appeal allowed.

NOTES AND QUESTIONS

1) The issue before the court in *Doucette* was the criminal liability of the secured creditor's agents. Does a decision that the conduct of the accused was criminal also mean that the seizure was a violation of the debtor's property rights or that the secured creditor could be held liable in conversion or trespass? What criminal or civil liability would a secured creditor incur if, without the knowledge of the debtor, but after being told by the debtor to stay off his property, the secured creditor took possession of collateral in the form of an automobile that was parked in the debtor's driveway at the time of repossession? (Assume that the security agreement expressly gave the secured party a right to effect seizure in this way.)

2) What alternative measures are available to a secured creditor in cases where self-help repossession is likely to result in a breach of the peace? See *Courts of Justice Act*, SO 1990, c. C.43, s. 104 and rule 44 of the *Rules of Civil Procedure*. See also OPPSA s. 67(1). However, in *Bank of Nova Scotia v. Siver* (2002), 2 PPSAC (3d) 278 (Ont. SC), the court refused an order directing the police to assist a secured party. Wright J concluded at 282:

> I have grave doubts whether s. 67 of the *Personal Property Security Act* clothes the court with jurisdiction to order the police to act in this manner. ... Police officers are not normally charged with the enforcement of civil remedies. Under the circumstances, in order to avoid any misapprehension of the respective rights of the parties, the bailiff should be left to attempt seizure on his own. In the event that resistance is met his duty is to retreat and have the issue placed before the courts.

If this occurs and the "issue is placed before the court," what can the court do?

3) Where the collateral is an intangible, chattel paper, or an instrument, enforcement of the security interest is quite easy. See OPPSA s. 61. However, s. 244 of the *Bankruptcy and Insolvency Act* may apply.

4) OPPSA s. 17 addresses the custodial obligations of the secured party while in possession of the collateral (whether after seizure or when the security interest has been perfected by the secured party being in possession of the collateral).

5) Section 17.1 provides that, unless otherwise agreed and despite s. 17, a secured party having control of investment property as collateral: (a) may hold as additional security any proceeds received from the collateral, (b) must either apply funds received from the collateral to reduce the secured obligation or remit the funds to the debtor, and (c) may create a security interest in the collateral; in addition, the secured party may deal with the collateral as provided in the security agreement.

6) The repossessory rights of a secured party on the debtor's bankruptcy are governed by conflicting provisions in the BIA, which have engendered strong differences of opinion among courts. See BIA ss. 69.4 and 81, and *R v. Ford Motor Credit of Canada* (1990), 78 CBR (NS) 266 (Ont. SC). An automatic stay on repossessory rights also applies under BIA ss. 69 and 69.1, where a debtor gives notice of intention to file a proposal under s. 50.4 or files such a proposal under s. 62(1). These stays are essential to allow an insolvent debtor an opportunity to develop a plan for the reorganization of its business.

7) Under s. 11 of the *Companies' Creditors Arrangement Act*, a court has wide-ranging power to order a stay of proceedings, and such orders are made readily (and usually *ex parte*) on the debtor's application. These provisions give a distressed debtor some leverage in renegotiating the terms of security agreements with its creditors.

IV. VOLUNTARY FORECLOSURE

Angelkovski v. Trans-Canada Foods Ltd.
[1986] 3 WWR 723 (Man. QB)

WRIGHT J: The primary issue in this case is whether the defendant, by taking possession of chattels given as security under a chattel mortgage, after default by the plaintiff, and utilizing the chattels in a certain way, thereby terminated any rights the defendant may have had to any other claim for the moneys secured.

The principal of the defendant is one Patrick Cory. The defendant at one time owned and operated the Red Barn Restaurant, 882-884 Main Street, Winnipeg. In 1978 the restaurant was sold to the male plaintiff (Angelkovski) and a partner. The balance of the purchase price was secured by a chattel mortgage of all the chattels in the restaurant, in the amount of $155,230, repayable $2,500 per month with interest at 12 per cent per annum.

Collateral security in the form of a promissory note for the same amount and on the same terms was also provided by the purchasers. As additional security Angelkovski and his co-plaintiff, his wife, gave the vendor a real property mortgage on their home for $55,000, also repayable at $2,500 a month and on the same interest terms as the other security.

After making the payments required through September 1978 to December 1981 the plaintiff and his partner defaulted, and on or about 20th January 1982 the defendant had a bailiff seize the chattels under the chattel mortgage. The seizure was effected by padlocking the premises, which were leased, per authority provided in the chattel mortgage.

Subsequently in March a sale of some sort was organized through the bailiff but proved abortive. Very little evidence was presented as to this sale. It was not suggested that any other effort was made to sell the chattels until the following July.

Following the abortive bailiff's sale the defendant took control of the premises and the chattels. Cory decided to reopen the restaurant, and in the name of the defendant applied for and by June obtained a new liquor licence and opened for business.

Cory had to make some repairs to certain of the chattels and to clean up and partially redecorate the premises. In a letter dated 26th August 1982, to the plaintiff's solicitor, his lawyers said the cost of the work was about $3,150.

Cory continued to operate the restaurant until 4th January 1983, when a fire occurred in the restaurant and the chattels were destroyed.

In the meantime the plaintiffs had issued a statement of claim dated 17th August 1982, but not served until 1st September 1982. As indicated at the outset of these reasons, the main allegation in the claim was that the defendant by its action elected to receive the chattels in full satisfaction of the debt owed, and therefore the plaintiffs had (and have) no further obligation to the defendant.

The exact amount outstanding on the chattel mortgage as of the date of seizure was not precisely established at trial, but as of 29th February 1982 it was no more than $112,179.71 and perhaps it was less.

If it were not for the provisions of the Personal Property Security Act (Manitoba) (which I will come to shortly), the law in Manitoba in respect of this issue would be, in my opinion, the same as the general law applicable to chattel mortgage seizures in Ontario. Subject always to any special provisions in a particular chattel mortgage (which does not apply in the instant case) in Ontario the courts have held that if it can be demonstrated a chattel mortgagee has appropriated the pledges to his own use, following default by the mortgagor and a proper seizure, he must then be found to have taken them for the debt: *McDonald v. Grundy* (1904), 8 OLR 113; *Gladman v. Hothersall*, [1936] OWN 358 (HC); *Miller v. Budreau*, [1954] OWN 274 (HC); and *Greenberg v. Rapoport*, [1970] 2 OR 349, 10 DLR (3d) 737 (HC).

...

To the extent any of the cases that I have cited above in support suggest a chattel mortgagee cannot sell the pledged goods without losing his right to claim for any deficiency I am not in agreement. Most chattel mortgages provide for a right of sale, either public or private, and protect the mortgagee's right to sue for any deficiency. There is provision to that effect in the present chattel mortgage. There is also a clause confirming the defendant's right to utilize the chattels for his own use if desired, which serves to protect the defendant (the mortgagee) from any further claim by the mortgagor relative to the chattels in the event that the defendant (mortgagee) decides to take the chattels in satisfaction of the debt. Whether the defendant here had done this or not is a question of fact to be determined at least in part by identifying his intention and purpose after seizure.

If the facts show the defendant intended to reopen the restaurant to sell the chattels as part of an ongoing business in order to improve their sale value, with the primary purpose of recovering the balance of the debt owing, then I do not think an appropriation of the chattels can be found. On the other hand if it can be concluded the defendant reopened the restaurant with the essential purpose of operating it himself, or of reselling it, so as to make more money than the amount owing on the debt, with no intention of accounting to the plaintiff and his partner for any surplus, then the court could reasonably conclude the chattels were appropriated in full satisfaction of the debt.

From the facts, I have decided in favour of the second alternative.

...

If it were not for the provisions of the Personal Property Security Act (the PPSA), the plaintiffs would be entitled to a declaration that they have no further obligation to the defendant in connection with the original debt. However, the PPSA, which applies to chattel mortgages, provides as follows:

> 61(1) At any time before the secured party has disposed of the collateral by sale or exchange or contracted for the disposition under section 58 or before the secured party shall be deemed to have irrevocably elected to retain the collateral in satisfaction of the obligation under subsection (2) of section 60, the debtor, or any person other than the debtor who is the owner of the collateral, or any secured party in possession, may, unless he has otherwise agreed in writing after default
>> (a) redeem the collateral by tendering fulfillment of all obligations secured by the collateral; or
>> (b) reinstate the security agreement by paying the sums actually in arrear, exclusive of the operation of any acceleration clause, or by curing any other default by reason whereof the secured party intends to dispose of the collateral;
> together with a sum equal to the reasonable expenses of retaking, holding, repairing, processing, preparing the collateral for disposition and in arranging for its disposition, and, to the extent provided for in the security agreement, the reasonable solicitor's costs and legal expenses.

This subsection brings into play s. 60(2) which in turn relates to s. 60(3). These two subsections provide that a secured party in possession of the collateral may, after default, propose to retain the collateral in satisfaction of the obligation secured, upon giving notification to that effect to the debtor. If the debtor objects within 15 days, the secured party must proceed in such a manner as to protect any realized surplus for the debtor, on the disposition of the collateral. If there is no objection within the 15 days, the collateral is no longer subject to any claim of the debtor.

In this context I interpret s. 61(1) to mean that until there has been compliance with the provisions of s. 60(2) and (3) the debtor retains the right to redeem. In other words, the statute makes it *impossible* for the secured party to appropriate the collateral for his own use free and clear of any claim of the debtor unless s. 60(2) and (3) has been followed. The effect of these statutory provisions then is to preclude any actual or deemed appropriation of the collateral according to the general law principles I earlier identified. The intention and objective of the secured party is no longer of importance. That does not mean to say a secured party does not have to account for the chattels and may be subject to a claim by the debtor for damages in that regard (*cf.* s. 62(2)), but—be that as it may—unless there has been compliance with the procedure under s. 60(2) and (3), the secured party is free to pursue any perceived deficiency.

Counsel for the plaintiffs submitted that it can be inferred from the evidence in the present case the defendant gave the notification required under s. 60(2) to the debtor. Counsel pointed out that the definition of notification in the PPSA simply means "coming to the attention of the debtor" [s. 1r], and argued Angelkovski had that kind of notification. However, I disagree. It may be possible to infer Angelkovski knew the defendant was retaining the collateral but I do not believe the evidence is at all clear he knew the purpose was to retain it *in satisfaction of the obligation secured*. I think in view of the wording in s. 60(2) and (3) the notification should be in clear and precise terms. In any event, I am unable to conclude on the preponderance of evidence that the debtor had the required notification.

The plaintiffs are not entitled therefore to a general declaration that they have no further obligation to the defendant.

...

NOTES AND QUESTIONS

1) Rather than selling seized collateral, a secured party may "propose to retain the collateral in satisfaction of the obligation secured." See OPPSA s. 65(2). The secured creditor's right to keep the collateral in return for cancellation of the debt arises by default if the persons who are entitled to object (see OPPSA s. 65(2)) fail to do so within the prescribed time and in the prescribed manner. See OPPSA s. 65(6).

2) Under the OPPSA (but not under the Acts based on the CCPPSL model), where the collateral is consumer goods and the debtor has paid at least 60 percent of the "indebtedness secured," the secured party is not entitled to retain the collateral if the debtor "has not signed, after default, a statement renouncing or modifying his rights under the Part." See OPPSA s. 65(1). The section appears to require a general renunciation of "rights under this Part." Would a specific surrender of rights under s. 65(1) not be sufficient? Consider the cumulative effect of OPPSA s. 65(1) and s. 25 of the Ontario *Consumer Protection Act*, above in the Notes to *Waldron*.

3) Someone other than the debtor may have an interest in seeing that the collateral is sold and not retained by the secured party. A subordinate security interest is extinguished along with that of the debtor when the debtor's rights in the collateral are surrendered. See OPPSA s. 65(6). However, under ss. 65(2) and 65(3) a person with a security interest in the collateral can force a sale of it only if the collateral is other than consumer goods or, if consumer goods, only when more than 40 percent of the secured indebtedness remains owing. What justification is there for this distinction?

4) What is the result under OPPSA s. 65(7) if a person buys the collateral in good faith for value before the expiry of the period mentioned in s. 65(6)?

5) The court in *Angelkovski* found that there had been an appropriation of the collateral by the secured creditor to its own use, yet also found the debtor still liable for a deficiency (reduced by any amount of damages the debtor could establish he had suffered as a result of the defendant's illegal conduct). The court made no mention of the Manitoba equivalent of OPPSA s. 17(5). Should it have?

6) Do you agree that the legislative purpose of OPPSA s. 65 is to prevent a debtor from relying on the common law rule that a secured creditor that appropriates collateral to its

own purposes is treated, at the debtor's election, to have taken the collateral in full satisfaction? Is there any way that OPPSA s. 65 can be read so as to preserve this aspect of the common law?

7) How does OPPSA s. 65 operate in the context of a situation in which the secured party
wishes to retain *some* of the collateral in return for cancellation of *part* of the obligation
secured?

V. DISPOSAL OF THE COLLATERAL

Copp v. Medi-Dent Services Ltd.
(1991), 2 PPSAC (2d) 114 (Ont. Gen. Div.)

HOILETTE J: The relevant facts, which are distilled from the material filed, are hereafter
briefly summarized.

Starting in early 1984 Doctors Copp and Piccininni established a dental practice in
premises located at College Park here in Toronto.

At the commencement of their practices Doctors Copp and Piccininni formed a management company, Dentistry and Anaesthesia Management Limited, which company
has, at all material times held the lease to the premises occupied by the two dental practices as well as the leases to virtually all the equipment used by the dentists in their respective practices. So far as the equipment is concerned there are five leases, numbered
376770, 378711, 381615, 381616 and 391287.

Acrimony, it is not an exaggeration to say, has been the dominant characteristic of the
relationship between the two dentists since about early 1987.

The acrimony between the two dentists reached one of its peaks when in the summer
of 1989 Dr. Piccininni stopped making his share of the payments due under the leases to
Medi-Dent. Dr. Copp for some time contributed more than his agreed upon share in order to maintain the leases in good standing but when the impasse between him and Dr.
Piccininni remained unresolved he too held back on his payments. The result was that
the leases fell into default. In consequence of the default, Medi-Dent served notice of intent to sell, pursuant to s. 63(4) and (5) of the *Personal Property Security Act*, SO 1989,
c. 16 (PPSA). The notice of intent to sell, dated April 18, 1990, reports arrears in the
amount of $31,151.97 on the leases, and concludes, among other things, that,

> Unless the Collateral is first redeemed, the Collateral will be disposed of by private disposi-
> tion or public sale after May 14, 1990.

It is common ground that the above notice of intent to sell was served upon Dentistry
and Anaesthesia Management Limited, Dr. Copp and Dr. Piccininni, on or about the
date it bears, April 18, 1990. Dr. Piccininni responded to the notice of intent to sell by in-
structing his solicitors on or about April 20, 1990 to redeem the security. The result was
an agreement of purchase and sale, dated May 15, 1990, entered into between Dr. Piccininni and Medi-Dent for the purchase of the leased property for a purchase price of
$31,151.97; the amount of the arrears outstanding on the leases. The agreement provided

for, among other things, a closing date of May 15, 1990 (clause 3); and, in clause 6(a) that:

> (a) The Purchaser acknowledges that this Agreement is subject to the expiry of the redemption period provided to the Debtor under the Leases and the *Personal Property Security Act.*

A companion bill of sale to the agreement of purchase and sale forms Exhibit "C" to the affidavit sworn by Dr. Piccininni, and a release, executed on behalf of Medi-Dent Services, forms Exhibit "D" to Dr. Piccininni's affidavit.

Dr. Copp, seemingly because of the long-standing dysfunctional relationship between him and Dr. Piccininni, suffered a form of decision-making paralysis and it was not until May 14, 1990 that his solicitors, acting on his instructions, contacted Medi-Dent with a view to pursuing the redemption. It is not explicit from the material filed if May 14, 1990 was the date of Dr. Copp's instructions to his solicitor; what is clear, however, is that it was at the eleventh hour, having regard to the May 14, 1990, redemption deadline. Suffice it to say that the last minute attempts by Dr. Copp's solicitor, Mr. David Wingfield, to make meaningful contact with Medi-Dent or their solicitors, proved abortive. The letter, Exhibit "A" to Mr. Wingfield's affidavit, sworn May 29, 1990, among other things, speaks of his abortive attempt at communicating with Medi-Dent and confirms their telephone conversation of May 17, 1990, in which he was informed of the sale of the security that had been consummated on May 15, 1990.

The following other points are worth mentioning: The sale to Dr. Piccininni was without notice to Dr. Copp, there was no appraisal, independent or otherwise, of the items sold, and there was no advertisement of the securities sold in any relevant publications. Finally, the only independent opinion of value is that reported by one Roy Brown, who in his affidavit describes himself as a "professional business valuator specializing in valuing medical and dental practices. I have been so engaged for over 17 years." Mr. Brown's affidavit, sworn September 13, 1990, forms Tab 1 to the "supplementary application record" and the report itself, dated June 25, 1990, though not formally made an exhibit in these proceedings, was filed without objection. The report places a value of $79,030.00 on the dental equipment that is in issue.

···

Fundamental to a resolution of the issues raised, in my view, is a determination as to whether or not the sale consummated between Dr. Piccininni and Medi-Dent was a "commercially reasonable transaction."

Steele J in his oral reasons for judgment in the unreported decision in *National Bank of Canada v. Marguis Furs Ltd.*, December 3, 1987, Doc. No. 780/86, Ont. HC, summarized the applicable test at page 5 of his reasons:

> Generally there are two tests that may be applied to the conduct of a sale as referred to by the Court of Appeal in *Wood v. Bank of Nova Scotia et al.*, 14 RPR 1. One is the less stringent test which is that the creditor who sells must act in good faith. The plaintiff has clearly complied with that test. The other test is the more stringent one, that the creditor must take reasonable care that the proper value is obtained. While it is not a trustee for the debtor it cannot act negligently in the sale. I adopt the principle as stated in *Debor Contracting Ltd. v.*

Core Rentals Ltd. and Parks, 44 CBR 9 (a *Mechanics' Lien action*) that the creditor must "act a role somewhat akin to that of an agent or fiduciary for the purpose of a sale." This is a higher standard than that referred to in *Kimco Steel Sales Ltd. v. Latina Ornamental Iron Works Ltd.*, 1984 3 PPSAC 237, at page 241 where the test was that the sale be in good faith and not be in a recklessly improvident manner calculated to result in a sacrifice of the equipment.

In my opinion, the proper test under the PPSA is the more stringent one that I have enunciated.

Whether a sale is commercially reasonable is a *question of fact in every case.* ...

In the particular case Steele J found that the test had been met, but the point should be made that on the facts before him, without canvassing the details, there had been advertisements in several locations and in relevant publications aimed at the relevant market.

In the instant application I have no difficulty in concluding that not even the most generous test of reasonableness could be met. There was no attempt at advertisement or publicity. What we had was a private sale to a party clearly adverse in interest to the joint debtor. Those circumstances are aggravated by the fact that there was no attempt at obtaining any opinion of value of the security, let alone an independent appraisal. The only measure of the sale price was the amount of the debt outstanding to the lessor and when one considers that the only independent evaluation places a value on the security more than twice the amount of the sale price, the conclusion is inescapable, in all the circumstances, that the impugned transaction was not a "commercially reasonable" one.

The foregoing reasons are sufficient to dispose of this application favourably to the applicant. There are, however, other equitable considerations which fortify me in that conclusion. They are:

1. Neither of the parties has come to this Court with perfectly clean hands.

2. Regardless of the true nature of the relationship between Doctors Copp and Piccininni, which it is not here necessary to decide, it was such, in my view, as to carry with it certain moral, if not legal, obligations such as not to allow one to score what, in my view, was clearly an unfair victory over the other. Equitable considerations dictate that Dr. Piccininni should not be allowed to profit from what was essentially a private, if not secret, deal between him and Medi-Dent.

⋯

There is an obvious need for an accounting between the two dentists, in respect of which, if they cannot arrive at an agreement, I am prepared, upon further representation, to order a reference.

The moving party should be indemnified by the respondents in respect to any loss consequential upon what was not a proper "disposition" under the provisions of the PPSA.

[The court granted an order containing, *inter alia*, a declaration that the transfer of the collateral to Dr. Piccininni is not a disposition under the PPSA and that Dr. Piccininni "continues to have duties to the secured party to the collateral."]

Application granted.

NOTES AND QUESTIONS

1) A secured creditor who has seized collateral may elect, or may be required, to sell the collateral. Under OPPSA s. 63(3), the secured creditor may delay disposition for such period of time as is commercially reasonable. Failure of the secured party to proceed expeditiously or properly is remediable by court order. See OPPSA s. 67.

2) OPPSA s. 63(7)(c) excuses the notice, where, *inter alia*, "the collateral is of a type customarily sold on a recognized market." The provision does not provide guidance as to what constitutes a "recognized market." Experience in the United States with a very similar provision has generated considerable litigation and differences in judicial opinion as to the meaning of this term. The prevailing view is that a "recognized market" is one in which neutral market forces, as opposed to competitive bidding, determine the price, and where the prices paid in actual sales of comparable property are currently available by quotation. See, for example, *Cottan v. Heppner*, 9 UCC Rep. Serv. 805 (Utah SC 1989). Accordingly, bonds and commodities traded on public exchanges would be types of collateral sold on "recognized markets." Where the collateral is fungible property sold on national or international exchanges, its market value can be determined immediately by reference to quoted prices for property of the same kind without the need to offer the particular items of collateral for sale at the highest price.

While the test is easy to state, it is more difficult to apply in peripheral situations. For example, it is possible to determine on the basis of published information the "value" of an automobile of specified make, model, age, and condition. However, the prevailing US view is that automobiles do not fall within the exception. See, for example, *Community Management Association v. Tousley*, 505 P2d 1314 (Colo. Ct. App. 1973). In each case the outcome will depend upon whether or not at the date of seizure it is possible to get a reliable indication of the market value of the collateral at the place of its location without offering it for sale. If there are factors in the local market that affect the price, there is no "recognized market" for the collateral in the sense in which the term is used in the Act. The Acts based on the CCPPSL model provide that a notice is unnecessary where "the collateral is a security or instrument that is to be disposed of by sale on an organized market that handles large volumes of transactions between many different sellers and many different buyers." See, for example, SPPSA s. 59(16)(e). Does this provision remove the uncertainty associated with the Ontario formulation?

3) The disposition "may be by public sale, private sale, lease or otherwise" (OPPSA s. 63(2)). Under OPPSA ss. 63(9) and 63(10) it appears that the position of a *bona fide* purchaser of the collateral varies depending upon whether the sale has or has not been conducted in accordance with the section, and, in the latter case, whether the sale is a public sale or is otherwise than a public sale. But are the standards of ss. 63(10)(a) and 63(10)(b) different? If so, which is the more demanding?

4) Under OPPSA s. 63(2), "every aspect of the disposition" of the collateral by the secured party must be "commercially reasonable." How is this standard to be applied in the following situations?

a) The evidence establishes that if the collateral had been held for two months longer, a higher sale price would have been obtained because of predictable increased demand for the type of goods involved. The secured party did not hold the collateral because it had a cash flow problem and was in need of cash at the date of the sale.

b) The evidence establishes that if the secured party had incurred the not unreasonable expense of transporting the collateral to a place some distance from the place of seizure and had offered it for sale there, a higher sale price for the collateral would have been obtained.

c) The evidence establishes that if the secured party had spent small amounts of money to make the collateral more presentable for sale, a higher sale price would have been obtained. See OPPSA s. 63(1) and *Donnelly v. International Harvester Credit Corp. Ltd.* (1982-83), 2 PPSAC 290, at 298 (Ont. Co. Ct.).

5) In *Copp*, the court accepted the proposition, as an aspect of a commercially reasonable sale, that the collateral's "proper value is obtained." There is generally a difference between the wholesale price and the retail price of goods. Assume a bank seizes a car and sells it to a used car dealer at "wholesale price." Has the standard been violated if it is established that, had the bank advertised the car for sale and sold it privately, a higher price would have been obtained?

6) The right to recover damages for non-compliance with Part V is set out in OPPSA s. 67(2). How does one characterize the "illegal" conduct of a secured party who does not comply with Part V? Does the party's non-compliant seizure and/or sale of the collateral amount to conversion or trespass? If so, is the measure of damage recoverable different from that suggested by s. 67(2)? Could the court award punitive damages?

7) OPPSA s. 67(1)(f) has no counterpart in the Acts based on the CCPPSL model. Note that it empowers the court to require "a secured party to make good any default in connection with the secured party's custody, management or disposition of the collateral of the debtor." What does this add? Does it provide the debtor with an additional remedy and a different measure of recovery than under s. 67(2)? Note also that the section gives power to the court to "relieve the secured party from any default on such terms as the court considers just, and to confirm any act of the secured party." Does this mean that a court can deny a debtor the recovery in an action brought under s. 67(2)?

VI. DEFICIENCY CLAIMS AND GUARANTORS' LIABILITY

NOTES

1) The PPSAs provide a statutory right to a "deficiency" (that is, the difference between the debt owing, including disposition costs, and the net amount recovered on sale of the collateral). See, for example, OPPSA s. 64(3). The right to a deficiency has become an issue in the context of cases where there has been non-compliance with Part V. The question that has been debated in the Ontario cases is whether or not (and, if so, to what extent) failure to comply with a requirement of Part V results in a loss or diminution in the amount payable by the debtor as a deficiency. The legal position with respect to the right to recover a deficiency was clarified by the Court of Appeal in *Bank of Montreal v. Featherstone* (1989), 9 PPSAC 139. In a *per curiam* judgment, the court stated at 142-43:

> In our opinion, the failure of the respondent to give the s. 59(5) notice to the appellants does not result in its being deprived of the right to claim the deficiency owing. Each side before us has relied on the judgment of this Court in *Royal Bank v. J. Segreto Construction Ltd.* (1988), 63

OR (2d) 502, 8 PPSAC 43, 38 BLR 134, 67 CBR (NS) 168, 47 DLR (4th) 761, 25 OAC 297 in support of its position on this issue. In our view the reasoning in this decision supports the respondent. In holding that the bank in that case had no right to claim the deficiency owing because of failure to comply with s. 59(5), the Court indicated that this conclusion would have been otherwise if the bank had "shown [a] contractual right to sue for the deficiency" (at p. 509). The Court contrasted the case where the creditor is obliged to rely upon the statute as the basis of its right to recover the deficiency. In the present case the respondent relies upon its contractual right to sue for the deficiency. In the light of this conclusion it is not necessary to pursue the issue further as to whether the right to claim the deficiency in the present case could be based on common law principles. In this respect it may be noted that at common law it was only in the case of a conditional sale contract that the creditor, in the absence of an agreement to the contrary, was not entitled to recover the deficiency upon the repossession and resale of the property sold. See *Delta Acceptance Corp. v. Redman* (1966), 2 OR 37 at 46-7, 55 DLR (2d) 481 (CA).

Accordingly, it is our opinion that failure to give notice does not of itself afford a defence to the claim for a deficiency. In some circumstances it may give rise to an award of damages under s. 63(2) of the Personal Property Security Act. No claim for such an award is made in this case. This is understandable in light of the trial Judge's findings, which are not challenged by the appellants, that the appellants suffered no damages as a result of the failure to give notice and that the respondent acted reasonably in selling the assets.

(Note that *Featherstone* was decided under the old Ontario Act.)

2) Is the distinction between the right to a deficiency given by statute and one given by contract a justifiable distinction? Should a secured party that ignores the debtor's rights under Part V be in a better position because the secured party happens to have included a "boilerplate" deficiency clause in its security agreement?

3) Note that in *Featherstone*, the Court of Appeal concluded that, in some circumstances, the failure to give a notice to the debtor may result in a successful claim for damages. See also OPPSA s. 67(2). What are these circumstances likely to be? Must the debtor show that, if he or she had received the notice, steps would have been taken that would have avoided the loss to the debtor? In Ontario, which gives only a very limited right of reinstatement, the only meaningful steps would likely be to redeem the collateral by paying the total amount owing under the security agreement. How often would the debtor be able to establish that he or she had sufficient resources to redeem the collateral? If a debtor simply loses the use of the collateral (but does not go to the expense of replacing it), what damages has the debtor suffered? If the collateral was sold for its fair market value, would the debtor suffer anything other than nominal damages? Note that the value of the collateral would have been applied by the secured party to the debt with the result that the net position of the debtor would not have changed. See the final sentence of the comment in *Featherstone*, above in Note 1. Does it follow from the aforesaid that in many cases a secured party can ignore a debtor's rights under Part V with impunity? For further discussion of these and related issues, see Ziegel, Comment (1988-89), 3 *BFLR* 196.

Where the collateral is consumer goods, the debtor need not prove actual damages to recover $500. See OPPSA s. 67(2). Can a court "relieve a secured party" under s. 67(1)(f) so as to deny the debtor his or her right of recovery of $500 under s. 67(2)?

4) For the US position with respect to deficiency claims, see Ziegel, "Standard of Care in Realization: Obtaining the Best Possible Price" (2007), 13 *BFLR* 165, at 179-80:

> American courts have long approached deficiency claims from a different perspective. Their concern has been not about the presence or absence of a deficiency clause in the security agreement but the inadequacy of remitting consumers to a claim for damages where the secured party failed to comply with the disposition and notice provisions in Part 5 of old Article 9. Consequently, one group of cases held that a creditor that had violated its obligations under Part 5 should be barred from a deficiency claim as a matter of law. According to another group of cases, there was a rebuttable presumption that the value of the collateral was equal to the debtor's liability unless the secured party proved otherwise. A third group of cases made no presumptions at all but remitted the debtor to having to prove her damages. New Article 9 has changed the old position in two important ways [UCC 9-626(a)(2), (3)]. First, it adopts a rebuttable presumption rule for *business transactions* about the debtor's damages. Second, it adopts no position with respect to the consequences of the secured party's breach in *consumer* cases but leaves it to the court to continue to fashion an appropriate remedy.

5) The Acts based on the CCPPSL model have not completely severed the link between compliance with Part V and the recovery of a deficiency. In addition to providing for "deemed damages" in an amount prescribed by regulations as a penalty for non-compliance with specified provisions of the Act (a remedy also given in OPPSA s. 67(2) where the collateral is consumer goods), ss. 67(3) and 67(4) of the APPSA provide:

> (3) In an action for a deficiency, the defendant may raise as a defence the failure on the part of the secured party to comply with the obligations of section 17, 18, 60 or 61, but non-compliance shall limit the right to a deficiency only to the extent that it has affected the right of the defendant to protect the defendant's interest in the collateral or has made accurate determination of the deficiency impracticable.
>
> (4) Where a secured party fails to comply with obligations in section 17, 18, 60 or 61, the onus is on the secured party to show that the failure,
>
> > (a) where the collateral is consumer goods, did not affect the debtor's ability to protect his interest in the collateral by redemption or reinstatement of the security agreement, or otherwise, or
> >
> > (b) did not make the accurate determination of the deficiency impracticable.

Does this provision place an impossible burden of proof on the secured party? If you were advising a secured party, what measures would you suggest be taken to enable your client to meet the burden of s. 67(4)(a) if the need to do so arises?

6) Whether the right to claim a deficiency, even on compliance with the "commercially reasonable" requirement, should exist at all, was once a hotly debated issue in Canada and the United States: see, for example, British Columbia Law Reform Commission, *Working Paper No. 4, Deficiency Claims and Repossession* (May 1971); and P. Shuchman, "Profit or Default: An Archival Study of Automobile Repossession and Resale" (1969-70), 22 *Stan. L Rev.* 20. Arguments against the right to deficiency point to the potential for abuse, the unfortunate position of a debtor who is forced to pay for goods he or she no longer enjoys, and the business community's ability to internalize losses as well as screen debtors before extending credit to them. The anti-deficiency lobby has won many adherents. Statutory provi-

sions extinguishing deficiency claims have been enacted in several provinces. Most of these require secured sellers to elect between seizing the collateral and pursuing judgment for the amount owing by defaulting buyers. See, for example, Alberta's *Law of Property Act*, RSA 2000, c. L-7, ss. 51-54. In British Columbia, the "seize or sue" principle also applies to both PMSI and non-PMSI secured lenders as well as to PMSI sellers. See BCPPSA s. 67. In Saskatchewan, subject to a few enumerated exceptions, a secured seller is only allowed to repossess the goods (that is, he or she cannot elect to sue): see the *Limitation of Civil Rights Act*, RSS 1978, c. L-16, s. 18. The seize or sue principle has also been adopted in Manitoba, Quebec, and Newfoundland and Labrador.

7) When the amount of a deficiency is calculated, must the secured creditor account for any unearned interest charges resulting from acceleration of payments under an installment credit contract? See *Consumer Protection Act*, RSO 1990, c. C.31, s. 28. What is the position apart from such a statutory provision? Can the creditor's claim to unearned interest be treated as an unenforceable penalty or does it depend on whether or not the interest is precomputed and becomes part of the principal debt? See *The Protector Endowment Loan and Annuity Co. v. Grace* (1880), 5 QBD 592.

Bank of Montreal v. Charest
(2001), 52 OR (3d) 497 (SCJ)

CULLITY J: The plaintiff has sued to enforce a personal guarantee given by Steven Charest, and an agreement to provide a guarantee by his spouse, Barbara Charest. The guarantee and the agreement relate to indebtedness of a corporation, Dynamic Steel Sales and Distributors Inc. (the "Corporation"), of which Steven Charest was, at all material times, an officer, director and shareholder. The defendants moved before me for summary judgment dismissing the action.

Between 1992 and 1997 the plaintiff provided credit facilities to the Corporation. Security was provided over the Corporation's present and future, tangible and intangible, assets—including equipment, inventory and accounts receivable—pursuant to two general security agreements dated June 25, 1992 and June 25, 1996, and chattel mortgages relating to specific properties.

On August 18, 1995, Steven Charest signed a personal guarantee of "all present and future debts and liabilities direct or indirect or otherwise, now or at any time and from time to time hereafter due or owing to the Bank from or by the [Corporation] ... ." Liability under the guarantee was limited to $250,000. By a "Letter of Acknowledgement" dated June 25, 1996, the Corporation gave certain covenants to the plaintiff in consideration of further financing. The concluding paragraph of the letter reads:

> If the above covenants are not within compliance as at August 31, 1996, Barbara Charest is to sign a guarantee jointly and serverally [sic] with Steve Charest in the amount of $250,000.

The letter was signed on behalf of the Corporation by Steven Charest and also signed and acknowledged by him and Barbara Charest personally.

By letter dated June 2, 1997, the plaintiff demanded payment of principal amounts of $372,300.18 (Can.) and $1,059,000 (US), plus accrued interest, that are alleged to be owing by the Corporation. The letter enclosed a notice of the plaintiff's intention to enforce security which was stated to be served on the Corporation pursuant to the *Bankruptcy and Insolvency Act*, RSC 1985, c. B-3. The letter was addressed to Steven Charest in his capacity as president of the Corporation.

In August, 1997 the Corporation filed an assignment in bankruptcy. Later in the same month, the plaintiff issued a notice pursuant to s. 63(4) of the *Personal Property Security Act*, RSO 1990, c. P.10 ("PPSA") notifying the persons designated in a schedule that the Bank intended to dispose of the undertaking, property and assets of the Corporation unless such security was redeemed. The schedule indicates that the notice was to be sent to the Corporation marked to the attention of Steven Charest. While in his affidavit sworn for the purpose of this motion, Mr. Charest states that the Corporation was not served with the notice, the evidence provided by the plaintiff is to the contrary. Whether service on the Corporation was effected is not in issue on this motion as counsel for the defendants submitted that his clients are entitled to judgment in any event. In consequence, I will deal with the motion on the basis that the requirements with respect to notice to the Corporation were satisfied and, if the defendants are unsuccessful, this is an issue that may be raised at the trial.

It is not disputed that the PPSA notice was not served on either of the defendants in their capacities as obligors if this is required by s. 63(4)(b) of the Act. No attempt has been made to prove that the notice allegedly served on the Corporation came to the attention of Steven Charest "under circumstances in which a reasonable person would take cognizance of it" so that, by virtue of s. 69(a), he would be considered to have received notice. It is also not disputed that the plaintiff has subsequently disposed of all or part of the security. No details with respect to this are included in the motion record.

In support of the defendants' motion for summary judgment, Mr. Basman advanced two arguments—one on behalf of each of the defendants and the other for Barbara Charest alone. The first argument was based on the plaintiff's failure to give notice to the defendants of its intention to dispose of the security; the second relied on the effect of the *Statute of Frauds*, RSO 1990, c. S.19 on the plaintiff's ability to enforce the concluding paragraph of the Letter of Acknowledgment against Mrs. Charest.

Notice

In Mr. Basman's submission, the failure to give notice to the defendants of the plaintiff's intention to dispose of the security is fatal to its claims against them. My first impression was that the correctness of this submission depended entirely on the resolution of two issues relating to the interpretation of the PPSA: namely, (a) whether the plaintiff was required to give notice to the guarantors pursuant to s. 63(4)(b); and (b), if so, what consequences are attached by the statute to its failure to do so. Although the answer to neither of these questions is provided expressly in the statute, my tentative conclusion with respect to the first was that the words of s. 63(4)(b), read literally, support an affirmative answer. If notice is required, I would have thought that the answer to the second question is provided in s. 67(2), which confers a right to compensation for any reasonably foresee-able loss or damage caused by a breach of the obligations imposed by Part V. I have found nothing in the legislation that would suggest that it was intended that a failure to give notice will, *ipso facto*, discharge a guarantor from liability. The question is discussed in J.S. Ziegel and D.L. Denomme, *The Ontario Personal Property Security Act*, 2d ed. (Markham, Ont.: Butterworths, 2000), at pp. 528-29. Counsel have persuaded me that, in view of previous decisions of this court, the Divisional Court and the Court of Appeal, this relatively straightforward approach is not open to me, although the end result would be the same as in two decisions of the Court of Appeal in which there was a failure to give notice to a guarantor.

Mr. Basman submitted that a guarantor is an "obligor who may owe payment or per-formance of the obligation secured" within the meaning of para. 63(4)(b) of the PPSA and, in consequence, is a person to whom a creditor must give notice of an intention to enforce a security with respect to the guaranteed obligation. The statutory language is, *prima facie*, broad enough to apply to a guarantor and the words I have quoted may have been added in response to the suggestion of the CBAO that the paragraph should be ex-tended to include guarantors: see Ziegel and Denomme, above, at p. 519, footnote 22. Counsel's submission is, moreover, in accordance with the decision of Spiegel J in *Bank of Nova Scotia v. Antoine* (1998), 13 PPSAC (2d) 231, 159 DLR (4th) 365 (Ont. Gen. Div.). The decision of the learned judge was affirmed by the Divisional Court on appeal and his reasons were expressly approved: [1999] OJ No. 2931 (Quicklaw). I must, there-fore, accept this interpretation. I did not understand Mr. Schwartz to take issue with the conclusion, although one to the contrary would avoid some of the problems with respect to the relationship between the provisions of the PPSA and the common law and the ex-tent to which the former can be overridden, or the rights they confer can be waived or ignored because of the terms of the contract between the parties. In *Bank of Montreal v. Korico Enterprises Ltd.* (2000), 50 OR (3d) 520 at p. 525, 190 DLR (4th) 706 the Court of Appeal found it unnecessary to decide "whether the provisions of Part V of the PPSA also apply to guarantors."

Mr. Basman then submitted that, having failed to give notice as required by the PPSA, the plaintiff is disentitled to enforce the guarantee as the guarantor had lost the opportu-nity to exercise its right to receive a transfer of the collateral pursuant to s. 2(1) of the *Mercantile Law Amendment Act*, RSO 1990, c. M.10. This, he submitted, was an impair-ment of the security sufficient to discharge the guarantor. I note, also, that if guarantors are entitled to be given notice under s. 63(4)(b), a statutory right to redeem the collateral is conferred on them by s. 66(1). In view of (a) the disparity between the amounts alleged-ly owing and the limitation on the amounts guaranteed; and (b) the fact that it would be a prerequisite to a guarantor's right to enforce a transfer under either provision that all obligations of the debtor had been paid, the right may well be illusory on the facts of this case.

I believe some support for Mr. Basman's argument can be found in the reasoning of the Court of Appeal in *Royal Bank of Canada v. J. Segreto Construction Ltd.* (1988), 63 OR (2d) 502, 67 CBR (NS) 168.

There it was held that a creditor who had not given notice could not claim against the principal debtor for a deficiency that existed after realization of security. The provisions of the security agreement in that case were not before the court and the creditor's claim was treated as one that depended on the existence of an implied right conferred by the PPSA to sue for a deficiency. The court held [at pp. 508-09 OR] that any such statutory right could be enforced only by a creditor who had complied with the provisions of the Act dealing with realization of a security after a default by the debtor.

> It may well be that it is inherent in the nature of some security agreements covered by the PPSA that the principal debt survives any seizure of assets. But if the security holder is rely-ing on the PPSA and nothing else, surely he must comply generally with its provisions deal-ing with default and sale, and in particular with [para. 63(5)(f)] which deals with deficiencies. ...
>
> In my opinion the appellant cannot succeed. It has shown no contractual right to sue for the deficiency and it is apparent that no such right exists at common law. It cannot rely on the PPSA as evidencing an implied right to recover the deficiency because it is not in com-pliance with the notice provisions of that statute. In short, it is reduced to complaining that the respondents are receiving a windfall while neglecting the corollary, that they were also deprived of an opportunity to redeem their own property.

Segreto was decided prior to the enactment of s. 64(3) of the PPSA, which was in force at the relevant times in respect of the transactions I am concerned with and which pro-vides that where a creditor has disposed of security,

> [u]nless otherwise agreed in the security agreement, or unless otherwise provided under this or any other Act, the debtor is liable for any deficiency.

If I am correct in understanding the Court of Appeal to have held that rights against a debtor impliedly conferred by the Act on a creditor who has disposed of security are, in effect, contingent on the latter's compliance with the statutory conditions relating to notice, the decision on the facts of the case would presumably have been the same if s. 64(3) had been in force at the relevant times: *Antoine*, above, at p. 241.

On the analogy of *Segreto*, it would seem that any attempt by the plaintiff to enforce the guarantee on the basis of its statutory right to sue the principal debtor for the defi-ciency—a right whose existence I must assume for the purpose of this motion—might be met with the response that, having failed to perform its statutory duty to give notice to the guarantor, it is not entitled to rely upon the statutory right.

However, in Mr. Schwartz' submission, neither the decision in *Segreto* nor the PPSA has any relevance to the facts of this case where the plaintiff relies on contractual rights that are said to exist independently of the statute. It is implicit in his submission that such rights are not restricted by the provisions of the PPSA. For this purpose, he relies not only on the provisions of the security agreements and the implication in the reasons of the Court of Appeal that the decision was affected by the absence of any evidence of a contractual right to sue for the deficiency, but also on the subsequent decisions of the same court in *Bank of Montreal v. Featherstone* (1989), 68 OR (2d) 541, 58 DLR (4th) 567 (CA) and *Canadian Imperial Bank of Commerce v. Moshi* (1992), 3 PPSAC (2d) 86, 55 OAC 230 (CA), in which failure to give notice to guarantors of an intended realization of security was held not to prevent an action against them for a deficiency. In the first of these cases, it was held that the creditor had contracted for a right to sue the principal debtor for any deficiency and that the terms of the guarantee covered whatever debts and liabilities were still owing by the latter to the former when it claimed against the guarantor. The court was prepared to assume, for the purpose of the appeal, that the predecessor to s. 63(4) required notice to be given to a guarantor. Its conclusion was as follows [at p. 544 OR]:

> In our opinion, the failure of the respondent to give the [s. 63(4)] notice to the appellants does not result in its being deprived of the right to claim the deficiency owing. Each side before us has relied on the judgment of this court in *Royal Bank of Canada v. J. Segreto Construction Ltd.* ... in support of its position on this issue. In our view, the reasoning in this decision supports the respondent. In holding that the bank in that case had no right to claim the deficiency owing because of failure to comply with [subsection 63(4)], the court indicated that this conclusion would have been otherwise if the bank had "shown [a] contractual right to sue for the deficiency." ... The court contrasted the case where the creditor is obliged to rely upon the statute as the basis of its right to recover the deficiency. In the present case the respondent relies upon its contractual right to sue for the deficiency.

Essentially the same analysis was applied, and the same conclusion reached, in *Moshi*, where it was held that the trial had proceeded on the basis that the debtor was liable to the creditor for the deficiency and that the appeal should be dealt with on the same basis. Like *Featherstone*, *Moshi* was decided on the basis of the provisions of the PPSA that have been replaced by those of the legislation now in force and, as in the earlier decision, it was assumed—although I think it was not decided—that the creditors had a statutory obligation to give notice to the guarantor.

While, in neither case, was there any dissent from the finding in *Segreto* that a failure to give notice to the debtor will prevent a creditor from enforcing rights conferred on it by the PPSA—a conclusion also reached by the Court of Appeal in *Canadian Imperial Bank of Commerce v. Cassidy* (1992), 55 OAC 357, 3 PPSAC (2d) 90 (CA)—the decisions appear to permit a creditor to ignore the statutory requirements by relying on rights that exist contractually independently of the statute. In view of s. 59(5) that provides that the rights of a debtor and the duties of a secured creditor under ss. 63-66 shall not be waived or varied, this is, perhaps, a surprising result—at least where, as in *Segreto* and *Cassidy*, the correlative rights and duties of the debtor and creditor are in question. I note that, although decided under the previous legislation, the decisions were considered to be of continuing application in *Antoine*—which, as I have mentioned, was affirmed by the Divisional Court—notwithstanding the indication in s. 72 that the law of contract is intended merely to supplement the provisions of the PPSA and will be overridden to the extent of any inconsistency. I will return to this point at the conclusion of this part of my reasons.

I believe it is implicit in *Featherstone* and *Moshi* that failure by a creditor to give the statutory notice of an intended realization of a security will not prevent the creditor from enforcing the guarantee if: (a) the creditor has a contractual right to sue the principal debtor for the deficiency; (b) the terms of the guarantee purport to make the guarantor liable for the balance of any liabilities owed by the debtor to the creditor at the time the creditor seeks to enforce the guarantee; and (c) the relevant documentation between the parties does not give the guarantor a contractual right to receive notice. It appears also to be implicit in the decisions that s. 59(5) of the PPSA, which precludes a waiver of the statutory duties of a secured creditor, but which does not refer to the rights of guarantors or obligors other than debtors, does not apply to duties owed by the creditor to a guarantor at least where the former is not seeking to rely on rights conferred by the PPSA.

The first of the three requirements I have mentioned gives rise to the most difficulty on the facts of this case. In the two chattel mortgages, the right to sue for any deficiency after the security has been realized is explicit. Each contains a provision in the following terms:

> After payment out of the net proceeds of such sale of all amounts due to the Bank hereunder the Bank shall pay over to the Mortgagor or such other person who may be entitled thereto any surplus but if such proceeds are not sufficient to pay all amounts due to the Bank hereunder the Mortgagor will pay the deficiency to the Bank.

However, there is no similar express provision in either of the general security agreements. The question is, therefore, one of implication and there is a threshold question whether the implication must be found in the intentions of the parties revealed by the terms of the agreements without reference to any presumption of common law or equity. This question appears to have been left open by the Court of Appeal in *Featherstone* where, immediately after the passage I have quoted above, the court states [at p. 544 OR]:

> In the light of this conclusion is not necessary to pursue the issue further as to whether the right to claim the deficiency in the present case could be based on common law principles. In this respect it may be noted that at common law it was only in the case of a conditional sale contract that the creditor, in the absence of an agreement to the contrary, was not entitled to recover the deficiency upon the repossession and resale of the property sold: see *Delta Acceptance Corp. v. Redman*, [1966] 2 OR 37, at pp. 46-7. ...

As the last sentence indicates, in loan transactions with collateral security, a creditor has, *prima facie*, a right to sue the debtor for a deficiency. The contrast with conditional sales contracts was noted in *Delta Acceptance Corp. v. Redman*, [1966] 2 OR 37, 55 DLR (2d) 481 (CA) where Laskin JA regretted that the prevailing authorities in this country had refused to apply the same analysis to them and had preferred a construction that treated realization as a termination of the contract of sale [at p. 46 OR]:

> Unless the seller protected himself by contract, repossession alone, not to speak of both repossession and resale, could be construed at common law as an election to terminate the contract: ...
>
> Thus, at strict common law, unless there was contractual respite, the seller who repossessed or who repossessed and sold could not sue for the price or for any deficiency, nor could the buyer claim a right to redeem. ... These harsh results were a consequence of a reluctance to treat the conditional sale as what it in essence was, that is, a security transaction on the analogy of an absolute sale and a mortgage back.

Clear statements of the right of a mortgagee to sue for a deficiency after realization of a security can be found in *Halsbury's Laws of England*, 4th ed., Volume 32, para. 815 and in W.B. Rayner and R.H. McLaren, *Falconbridge on Mortgages*, 4th ed. (Toronto: Canada Law Book, 1977), at pp. 443-44. The same principles are applicable to mortgages and charges of personal property: see, for example, *American Express International Banking Corp. v. Hurley*, [1985] 3 All ER 564 at pp. 568-69, [1986] BCLC 52 (QBD) per Mann J.

The basis of the principle that, *prima facie*, a secured creditor can sue for a deficiency—and, surely, the reason why no reference to such a right is found in the otherwise comprehensive security agreements provided by the plaintiff and by the large financial institutions involved in some of the other cases—is set out very clearly by Professor Jacob S. Ziegel in a case comment on *Segreto* in (1989), 3 BFLR 196, at p. 199:

> ... debentures and other secured loan agreements often do not contain a deficiency clause, and for good reason. It is fundamental to the concept of a secured loan that the security is only collateral to the debt and that the primary obligation remains intact until the debt has been fully discharged.

No question relating to conditional sales contracts arises here. I am dealing with secured loans, and if, as the latest decisions of the Court of Appeal indicate, the relevant provisions of the PPSA are not to be construed as derogating from the contractual rights of the parties, I do not see how rights that principles of common law or equity would treat as necessary incidents of the contract should be excluded unless spelt out expressly. Such rights must, I believe, be regarded as implied contractual terms in a sufficient sense.

I am necessarily troubled by passages in the judgment of the Court of Appeal in *Segreto* that seem to contemplate that, *prima facie*, a secured creditor has no right to sue for a deficiency at common law. These passages were referred to with apparent approval in *Cassidy* and they were followed in *Antoine*. In the former, however, the creditor had not sought to rely upon the existence of any continuing liability at common law and, in *Antoine*—as in *Segreto*—the court had not been provided with the provisions of the security agreement. The continued existence of the otherwise well-established distinction between conditional sales contracts and loans with collateral security was confirmed in *Featherstone* and, as it was decided after *Segreto* and is the only subsequent case in which the point has been considered, I believe I should adhere to the traditional analysis.

I have found nothing in the general security agreements in this case that is inconsistent with the plaintiff's right to sue the Corporation for any deficiency remaining after the security has been realized. Although, as I have indicated, there are no express words that stipulate, or refer to, the existence of such a right, there is general language that is broad enough to encompass such a right. Paragraph 10 of each agreement provides that upon "any default under the security agreement, the bank may declare any or all of the obligations to be immediately due and payable and may proceed to realise the security hereby constituted and to enforce its rights by entry" or by a variety of other methods including the appointment of a receiver or by leasing or selling the secured assets. The paragraph concludes with a stipulation that no remedy for the realization of the security "or *for the enforcement of the rights of the Bank* shall be exclusive of or dependent on any other such remedy, but any one or more of such remedies may from time to time be exercised independently or in combination" (italics added). Para. 11 of each agreement reads as follows:

> Any and all payments made in respect of the Obligations from time to time and moneys realised from any securities held therefore (including moneys realised on any enforcement of this Security Agreement) may be applied to such part or part of the Obligations as a [sic] the bank may see fit, and the Bank shall at all times and from time to time have a right to change any appropriation as the Bank may see fit.

It is, I believe, probably implicit in these provisions that realization of the security and the appropriation of the proceeds to certain of the liabilities of the debtor does not discharge its liability with respect to any obligations remaining after all of the proceeds have been appropriated in this manner. Whether or not that conclusion is correct, the right to sue for the deficiency is, in my opinion, *prima facie* implied in the security agreements and, as I have indicated, there is nothing in their provisions to displace this *prima facie* presumption. It follows that the first of the three requirements mentioned above has been satisfied. I note, again, that, for the purpose of this motion, the question whether the Corporation received notice of the intention to realize the security is not in issue.

As far as the second requirement is concerned, the words of the guarantee given by Steven Charest do not appear to be materially different from those that were held by the Court of Appeal in *Featherstone* and *Moshi* to make the guarantor liable for the balance of any remaining liability of the debtor after security had been realized. It is provided that the agreement is to provide a continuing guarantee and is to cover and secure "any ultimate balance owing to the bank." It is also provided that the plaintiff was entitled to proceed against the guarantor without seeking recourse against the Corporation or any security it might hold.

As I have found nothing in the provisions of the guarantee to suggest that the plaintiff agreed not to realize on the security without giving prior notice to the guarantor, I am in agreement with Mr. Schwartz' submission that the case is not distinguishable in principle from the decisions of the Court of Appeal in *Featherstone* and *Moshi*. While, without the guidance they provide, I might well have failed to draw the necessary sharp distinction between rights arising under the PPSA and those arising by way of contract and common law—and while I believe there would otherwise be considerable force in the view that the issue in this case should be considered to depend essentially on the interpretation of the PPSA—I am bound by the decisions of the Court of Appeal and I am satisfied that this is sufficient to dispose of the first ground on which summary judgment was sought.

· · ·

Order accordingly.

VII. ENFORCEMENT OF SECURITY INTERESTS BY RECEIVERS AND RECEIVER-MANAGERS

Generically, receivership involves the appointment of a person with authority to take possession or control of the property of another for the benefit of a third person. Receiverships are used in many situations, the most significant of which are:

- As a method to enforce a judgment by appointing a receiver to take control and liquidate specified property of the judgment debtor. In this context, the receiver is appointed by and acts on the instructions of the court.
- As a method of taking control of property for the purposes of protecting it from destruction or dissipation pending the completion of proceedings. A specific example of this is found in s. 46 of the *Bankruptcy and Insolvency Act*, RSC 1985, c. B-3, as am. 1992, c. 27. However, the use of this type of receivership is not confined to bankruptcy. For example, a receiver can be appointed to preserve property of an estate pending probate or administration or to protect the interest of disabled persons. Here again, receivers in this category are appointed by the court.
- As a mechanism for enforcement of security interests in real and personal property. It is this use of the receivership that is the focus of the following materials.

The appointment of receivers originated in the latter part of the 16th century as a remedy of the Courts of Chancery. The remedy was designed to provide a means whereby property could be preserved pending judicial determination of conflicting claims. Occasionally, it was used to supplement common law and statutory judgment enforcement remedies. The use of receivers to enforce mortgages was developed by Chancery as a special feature of equitable mortgages that compensated for the absence of a right in the mortgage (a right enjoyed by legal mortgagees) to take possession of the mortgaged property. After the merger of the equity and common law courts in 1873 under the *Supreme Court of Judicature Act*, the power to appoint a receiver was no longer confined to Chancery proceedings. See now *Courts of Justice Act*, RSO 1990, c. C.43, s. 101(1).

Originally, court-appointed receivers only had authority to receive or take possession of property and to dispose of it in accordance with the powers vested in them. However, by the beginning of the 20th century, the judicial practice of appointing a receiver and manager (now frequently referred to as a receiver-manager) had developed so as to permit receivers to take over and manage the business of a debtor pending disposition of the assets of the business. This became particularly useful and common where the entire undertaking (all of the property) of a business corporation was taken as security under an equitable floating charge and a fixed mortgage.

The practice of making provision in security agreements for the extra-judicial appointment of a receiver also developed during the 19th century and was later expanded to include receiver-managers.

Until the advent of modern legislation (*circa* 1965) dealing with receivers and receiver-managers, a clear distinction existed between court-appointed receivers and receiver-managers and privately-appointed receivers and receiver-managers. While some aspects of this distinction remain, it is no longer as significant as it once was.

Standard Trust Co. v. Turner Crossing Inc.
(1993), 4 PPSAC (2d) 238 (Sask. QB)

MATHESON J: The defendant, Turner Crossing Inc. ("Turner"), has applied for an order setting aside the appointment by the plaintiff of a receiver and manager of the business of Turner.

Turner acquired property in the City of Regina in February 1989, for the purpose of constructing a shopping mall complex. The project was to be financed by Standard Trust Company. Agreements were executed as security for the funds to be advanced, consisting of a first real property mortgage in the amount of $5,646,000; a second participation mortgage; a purchase money security agreement; and an assignment of leases and rental.

Phase I of the shopping mall complex was completed by March 1991. However, problems developed with respect to Phase II. Turner has alleged Standard Trust Company refused to provide additional funding. In any event, on May 2, 1991, Standard Trust Company was ordered by the Ontario Court of Justice to be wound up, and Ernst & Young Inc. was appointed permanent liquidator.

In November 1991, the liquidator informed Turner that it was in default under the mortgage. The alleged default was apparently not remedied, and on December 23, 1991, the liquidator appointed a "Receiver and Manager of the business of Turner Crossing Inc." The plaintiff then applied for, and was granted, leave to commence this action, wherein the principal claims are for judgment against the defendants and foreclosure of the mortgaged premises.

The defendants filed a statement of defence, and Turner filed a counterclaim against the plaintiff. The defendants did not really deny that they were in default under the mortgage, but one of the assertions in the counterclaim is that the appointment of the receiver and manager was unlawful.

···

The plaintiff purported to appoint the receiver and manager pursuant to the purchase-money security agreement and assignment of leases and rental. However, in the event that the appointment was not authorized by those documents, the plaintiff has argued that it had a statutory right to appoint a receiver and manager.

There is no disagreement between the parties with respect to the basic facts. Turner has acknowledged that it executed the security agreements and that it defaulted in making the payments required of it pursuant to the first real property mortgage. If, in those circumstances, the plaintiff was entitled by statute to appoint a receiver and manager, the resolution of that question entails only the interpretation of the appropriate statute, or statutes, which is solely a matter of law. But the form of appointment states that it was made pursuant to a purchase-money security agreement and assignment of leases and rental. It must first be determined from the provisions of those documents whether the appointment was authorized. The documents speak for themselves.

···

Division VIII of the Business Corporations Act, RSS 1978, c. B-10 (also CCSS, c. B-10), encompassing ss. 89 to 96, is entitled "Receivers and Receiver-Managers." There is no provision in any of those sections empowering a creditor to appoint a receiver or receiver-manager. It is quite clear from the initial words of s. 91—"if a receiver-manager is appointed by a court or under an instrument"—that the functions and duties of receivers and receiver-managers, set out in the Act, related to court appointments or those made pursuant to agreements between the debtor and creditor.

The plaintiff has suggested that s. 56 of the Personal Property Security Act, SS 1979-80, c. P-6.1 (also CCSS, c. P-6.1) ("PPSA") empowered it to appoint the receiver and manager. However, subs. (1) of s. 56 states that "A security agreement may provide for the appointment of a receiver or a receiver-manager and, except as provided in this Act, prescribe his rights and duties." Subsection (2)(a) of s. 56 states that a court may appoint a receiver or a receiver-manager. No right is given to a creditor, by that statute, to appoint a receiver or receiver-manager.

The appointment of the receiver and manager was in the following terms:

STANDARD TRUST COMPANY, by its liquidator, ERNST & YOUNG INC., being the registered holder of a security interest under a Purchase Money Security Agreement and an Assignment of Lease(s) and Rental with Turner Crossing Inc. both dated February 24, 1989, in favour of STANDARD TRUST COMPANY (the "Security Agreements") and which said security interests were registered under the provisions of The Personal Property Security Act of Saskatchewan on the 29th day of May, 1989 as Instrument Number 03258370, hereby appoints McClocklin Real Estate Corp. with an office in the City of Saskatoon, in the Province of Saskatchewan, pursuant to the powers conferred upon STANDARD TRUST COMPANY, *to be the Receiver and Manager of the business of Turner Crossing Inc.* with full power and secured by the Security Agreements upon the terms and with and subject to the powers, provisions and conditions in the Security Agreements.

(Emphasis added.)

A notice of appointment of receiver and manager was filed with the Director of Business Corporations on February 3, 1992, as required by s. 96(a) of the Business Corporations Act. That requirement is not without significance, because s. 91 of the Business Corporations Act states:

91. If a receiver-manager is appointed by a court or under an instrument, the powers of the directors of the corporation that the receiver-manager is authorized to exercise may not be exercised by the directors until the receiver-manager is discharged.

The purchase-money security agreement does not contain any provision whereby Turner agreed, upon default, that the plaintiff would be entitled to appoint a receiver, or a receiver and manager, of any assets of Turner. Counsel for the plaintiff so acknowledged, but stated that the authority for the appointment of the receiver and manager was derived from the assignment of leases and rentals ("the assignment").

The assignment contains the following clause:

3. THAT at any and all times when there shall be default under any of the provisions contained in the mortgage, *the Assignee shall be entitled to* enter into possession of the mortgaged premises and collect the rents and revenues thereof and distrain in the name of the Assignor for the same, and *appoint its agents to manage the mortgaged premises* and pay such agents reasonable charges for their services and charge the same to the account of the

Assignor; and that any agents so appointed by the Assignee shall be and are hereby authorized and empowered;

(a) To make any lease or leases of the mortgaged premises or any part thereof, for not more than three years, at such rental or rentals and in all other respects on such terms as the Assignee in its discretion may direct or agree to;

(b) *To manage generally the mortgaged premises* to the same extent as the Assignor could do;

(c) Without derogating from the generality of the foregoing:

(i) To collect the rents and revenues and give good and sufficient receipts and discharges therefor, and in their discretion distrain in the name of the Assignor for such rents;

(ii) To pay all insurance premiums, taxes, necessary repairs, renovations and upkeep, carrying charges, rental commissions, salary of janitor or caretaker, cost of heating, and any and all payments due on the mortgage to the Assignee;

(iii) To accumulate the rentals in such agents' hands in a reasonable amount to make provision for maturing payments of interest and principal on the mortgage, and for the payment of taxes, insurance, heating, repairs, renovations and upkeep and other expenses or carrying charges connected with the mortgaged premises.

(Emphasis added.)

The foregoing is the clause pursuant to which the receiver and manager was appointed. The plaintiff has submitted that the authorization granted to it to appoint agents "to manage the mortgaged premises" is synonymous with an authorization to appoint a receiver or a receiver and manager.

The distinction in law between a receiver and manager was set out by Jessel MR in *Re Manchester & Milford Railway Co.; Ex parte Cambrian Railway Co.* (1880), 14 Ch. D 645, 49 LJ Ch. 365, 42 LT 714 (CA) when he was considering the meaning of an agreement to "the appointment of a receiver and, if necessary, of a manager." At p. 653 Ch. D he pointed out that a "receiver" is a term which was well known in the Court of Chancery, as meaning a person who receives rents or other income. But a receiver did not have the power to manage the business of the debtor. He stated that if it was desired to continue the trade of the debtor, it was necessary to appoint a manager, or a receiver and manager.

In Frank Bennett, *Receiverships* (1985), it is stated, at p. 109:

The appointment of a receiver will usually coincide with the appointment of a manager. In this dual role, the receiver and manager may operate the debtor's business pursuant to the terms of his appointment. Initially, such terms may authorize the receiver and manager to preserve the debtor's business. Subsequently, the receiver and manager may be authorized to liquidate or sell the business as a going concern.

If the security instrument does not charge the debtor's goodwill, only a receiver can be appointed. However, *if the security instrument covers all the debtor's property and effects whatsoever*, the court will infer that the goodwill was included in order to permit the appointment of a receiver and manager.

(Emphasis added.)

The terms "receiver" and "receiver and manager," and the differences between the two terms, obviously have a distinct meaning in law. Both the Business Corporations Act and the PPSA distinguish between the two terms. But the assignment contains no reference whatever to an entitlement granted to the plaintiff, upon Turner's default, to the appointment of either a "receiver" or a "receiver and manager." The authority was confined to the plaintiff collecting rents and revenues from "the mortgaged premises" and to the appointment of agents to manage the "mortgaged premises." Instead of exercising the powers granted to it in the terms of the assignment, the plaintiff purported to appoint a "Receiver and Manager of the business of Turner Crossing Inc." Nowhere in either the appointment, or notice of appointment which became a matter of public record, is it stated that the authority of the appointee is confined to the "mortgaged premises."

The material on file does not reveal the extent of the business of Turner. Nevertheless, one can imagine the furore which would be created if an international developer defaulted in payment of but one mortgage, but then was faced with the appointment of a receiver and manager of its "business," notwithstanding that the mortgagee's rights were confined to the mortgaged premises.

The notice of appointment of receiver and manager, filed with the Director of Business Corporations, is even more misleading than the notice of appointment itself:

> NOTICE IS HEREBY GIVEN pursuant to Section 96 of The Business Corporations Act that on the 23rd day of December, 1991, STANDARD TRUST COMPANY, by its liquidator, ERNST & YOUNG INC., appointed McCLOCKLIN REAL ESTATE CORP. *as Receiver and Manager of the business of TURNER CROSSING INC. with full power and authority over all of the premises, chattels and undertakings of TURNER CROSSING INC.*, pursuant to the terms of a Purchase Money Security Agreement and Assignment of Lease(s) and Rental (the "Security Agreements") given by TURNER CROSSING INC., in favour of STANDARD TRUST COMPANY both dated February 24, 1989, and which security interests were registered under the provisions of The Personal Property Security Act of Saskatchewan on the 29th day of May, 1989, as Instrument Number 03258370.

(Emphasis added.)

On the basis of the wording contained in clause 3 of the assignment, it seems quite incredible that anyone could have, other than deliberately, drafted the appointment of receiver and manager, and notice of appointment, in the terms which they contain. However, that is a question which will no doubt be pursued at trial if Turner proceeds with its counterclaim. In the meantime, Turner is effectively prevented from carrying on business by virtue of the clearly unlawful appointment of a receiver and manager of its "business." To allow that situation to continue until trial, when there was no legal justification whatever for the appointment of the receiver and manager, would be patently unjust.

There will therefore be an order setting aside the appointment of the receiver and manager and vacating the notice of appointment of receiver and manager filed with the Director of Business Corporations.

Application granted.

NOTES AND QUESTIONS

See OPPSA s. 60 and the definition of "secured party" in s. 1(1). Note that s. 60 refers to both privately-appointed receivers (and receiver-managers) and court-appointed receivers (and receiver-managers) but the definition of "secured party" refers only to "receivers and receivers and managers." Must a court-appointed receiver (hereafter read "receiver" as including a receiver-manager unless otherwise indicated) comply with the requirements of Part V applicable to secured parties unless the court-appointed receiver obtains an order under s. 67(1)(b) or (d)? Is there any reason why a court-appointed receiver should be exempt from these requirements? For further discussion of this issue in the context of the Acts based on the CCPPSL model, see the Notes and Questions following the next case.

Ostrander v. Niagara Helicopters Ltd.
(1974), 40 DLR (3d) 161 (Ont. HC)

[Ostrander was the founder and principal shareholder of the defendant corporation. The defendant borrowed money from Roynat Limited and gave as security a debenture under a trust deed arrangement encumbering its assets. Upon default, Roynat appointed Bawden as receiver-manager of the defendant. Roynat sold most of the assets of the defendant after receiving two tenders.

Ostrander brought an action to regain possession of the defendant and to set aside the sale of its assets. He alleged improper conduct on the part of Bawden. As part of his case, Ostrander argued that Bawden was acting in a fiduciary capacity with respect to the defendant and that his conduct amounted to a breach of trust. In dealing with this aspect of the case, STARK J observed:]

My decision might well be otherwise if I had come to the conclusion that Bawden as receiver-manager was acting in a fiduciary capacity. I am satisfied that he was not. His role was that of agent for a mortgagee in possession. The purpose of his employment was to protect the security of the bondholder. Subsequently his duty was to sell the assets and realize the proceeds for the benefit of the mortgagee. Of course he owed a duty to account in due course to the mortgagor for any surplus; and in order to be sure there would be a surplus he was duty bound to comply with the full terms of the conditions of sale set out in the debenture, to advertise the property and to take reasonable steps to obtain the best offer possible. Certainly he owed a duty to everybody to act in good faith and without fraud. But this is not to say that his relations to Ostrander or to Niagara or to both were fiduciary in nature. A very clear distinction must be drawn between the duties and obligations of a receiver-manager, such as Bawden, appointed by virtue of the contractual clauses of a mortgage deed and the duties and obligations of a receiver-manager who is appointed by the Court and whose sole authority is derived from that Court appointment and from the directions given him by the Court. In the latter case he is an officer of the Court; is very definitely in a fiduciary capacity to all parties involved in the contest. The borrower, in consideration of the receipt by him of the proceeds of the loan agrees in advance to the terms of the trust deed and to the provisions by which the security may be enforced. In this document he accepts in advance the conditions upon which a sale is to be made, the nature of the advertising that is to be done, the fixing of the amount of the reserve bid and all the other provisions contained therein relating to the conduct of the sale. In carrying on the business of the company pending the sale, he acts as agent for the lender and he makes the decisions formerly made by the proprietors of the company. Indeed, in the case at hand, Mr. Bawden found it necessary to require that Ostrander absent himself completely from the operations of the business and this Ostrander consented to do. As long as the receiver-manager acts reasonably in the conduct of the business and of course without any ulterior interest, and as long as he ensures that a fair sale is conducted and that he ultimately makes a proper accounting to the mortgagor, he has fulfilled his role which is chiefly of course to protect the security for the benefit of the bondholder. I can see no evidence of any fiduciary relationship existing between Ostrander and Bawden. Mr. Papazian in his able argument put it very forcibly to the Court that the duties and obligations of a receiver-manager appointed by the Court and a receiver-manager appointed under the terms of a bond mortgage without a Court order, were in precisely the same position, each being under fiduciary obligations to the mortgagor. I do not accept that view and I am satisfied that the cases clearly distinguish between them. A good example of the obligation placed upon the Court-appointed receiver-manager is provided by *Re Newdigate Colliery, Ltd.*, [1912] 1 Ch. 468. That case was authority for the proposition that it is the duty of the receiver and manager of the property and undertaking of a company to preserve the goodwill as well as the assets of the business, and it would be inconsistent with that duty for him to disregard contracts entered into by the company before his appointment. At 477 Buckley LJ described the duties of the Court-appointed receiver and manager in this way:

> The receiver and manager is a person who under an order of the Court has been put in a position of duty and responsibility as regards the management and carrying on of this business, and has standing behind him—I do not know what word to use that will not create a misapprehension, but I will call them "constituents"—the persons to whom he is responsible in the matter, namely, the mortgagees and the mortgagor, being the persons entitled respectively to the mortgage and the equity of redemption. If we were to accede to the application which is made to us, and to allow the receiver and manager to sell the coal at an enhanced price, the result would be that the enhanced price would fall within the security of the mortgagees and they would have the benefit of it; but, on the other hand, there would be created in favour of the persons who had originally contracted to purchase the coal a right to damages against the mortgagor, the company, with the result that there would be large sums of damages owing.

Lord Justice Buckley then continued with language which further accentuates the difference between the two classes of receiver-managers [at 447-48]:

> It has been truly said that in the case of a legal mortgage the legal mortgagee can take possession if he choose[s] of the mortgaged property, and being in possession can say "I have nothing to do with the mortgagor's contracts. I shall deal with this property as seems to me most to my advantage." No doubt that would be so, but he would be a legal mortgagee in possession, with both the advantages and the disadvantages of that position. This appellant

is not in that position. He is an equitable mortgagee who has obtained an order of the Court under which its officer takes possession of assets in which the mortgagee and mortgagor are both interested, with the duty and responsibility of dealing with them fairly in the interest of both parties.

It appears to me unfortunate that the same terms "receiver-manager" are customarily applied to both types of offices, when in fact they are quite different. The difference is well pointed out in the case of *Re B. Johnson & Co. (Builders) Ltd.*, [1955] 1 Ch. 634, where it was held that a receiver and manager of a company's property appointed by a debenture holder was not an officer of the company within the meaning of the *Companies Act*. The language of Evershed MR, at 644, is in point:

The situation of someone appointed by a mortgagee or a debenture holder to be a receiver and manager—as it is said, "out of court"—is familiar. It has long been recognized and established that receivers and managers so appointed are, by the effect of the statute law, or of the terms of the debenture, or both, treated, while in possession of the company's assets and exercising the various powers conferred upon them, as agents of the company, in order that they may be able to deal effectively with third parties. But, in such a case as the present at any rate, it is quite plain that a person appointed as receiver and manager is concerned, not for the benefit of the company but for the benefit of the mortgagee bank, to realize the security; that is the whole purpose of his appointment. ...

Again, at 662, Lord Justice Jenkins stated:

The company is entitled to any surplus of assets remaining after the debenture debt has been discharged, and is entitled to proper accounts. But the whole purpose of the receiver and manager's appointment would obviously be stultified if the company could claim that a receiver and manager owes it any duty comparable to the duty owed to a company by its own directors or managers. ...

The duties of a receiver and manager for debenture holders are widely different from those of a manager of the company. He is under no obligation to carry on the company's business at the expense of the debenture holders. Therefore he commits no breach of duty to the company by refusing to do so, even though his discontinuance of the business may be detrimental from the company's point of view. Again, his power of sale is, in effect, that of a mortgagee, and he therefore commits no breach of duty to the company by a bona fide sale, even though he might have obtained a higher price and even though, from the point of view of the company, as distinct from the debenture holders, the terms might be regarded as disadvantageous.

In a word, in the absence of fraud or mala fides (of which there is not the faintest suggestion here), the company cannot complain of any act or omission of the receiver and manager, provided that he does nothing that he is not empowered to do, and omits nothing that he is enjoined to do by the terms of this appointment. If the company conceives that it has any claim against the receiver and manager for breach of some duty owed by him to the company, the issue is not whether the receiver and manager has done or omitted to do anything which it would be wrongful in a manager of a company to do or omit, but whether he has exceeded or abused or wrongfully omitted to use the special powers and discretions vested in him pursuant to the contract of loan constituted by the debenture for the special purpose of enabling the assets comprised in the debenture holders' security to be preserved and realized.

Similar principles are to be found in the case of *Deyes v. Wood et al.*, [1911] 1 KB 806.

Action dismissed.

NOTES AND QUESTIONS

1) The traditional approach to the role of a court-appointed receiver is that, as an officer of the court, the receiver takes possession and control not only for the benefit of the secured party, but for the benefit of other creditors with a claim to the property as well. *Royal Bank v. Vista Homes* (1984), 57 CBR (NS) 124 (BCSC). The receiver's authority derives from the order appointing the receiver. A privately-appointed receiver is essentially an agent of the secured party appointing the receiver. The receiver draws authority to act from the security agreement.

2) Each type of receivership has advantages and disadvantages. The advantages of a privately-appointed receiver include speed, efficiency, and the control that the secured party can exercise through the receiver. Since no court order is required, a receiver can be appointed immediately upon the debtor's default under the security agreement. However, this does not mean that the collateral can be seized immediately. See *Bankruptcy and Insolvency Act*, ss. 243(2) and 244 and *Waldron v. Royal Bank*, above in Part II. The judicial appointment of a receiver under Ontario law requires an interlocutory application to a court as part of an action brought against the debtor. This may involve delay and expense. Under the Acts based on the CCPPSL model, a receiver may be appointed by a court on application without the need to commence an original action against the debtor. See, for example, BCPPSA s. 66(1). An important advantage of a court appointment is that, because the receiver is acting under the instructions and authority of the court, the receiver and the secured party are shielded (although not completely immune) from liability and attack by those who disapprove of the conduct of the receiver. But see OPPSA s. 67(2).

3) It is possible for a receiver, initially appointed under a security agreement, to be appointed by a court. However, when this occurs, the receiver's authority derives solely from the court and he or she cannot revert to acting under the terms of the security agreement. *Price Waterhouse Ltd. v. Creighton Holdings Ltd.* (1984), 54 CBR (NS) 116 (Sask. QB).

4) The traditional distinction between court-appointed and privately appointed receiverships may be breaking down. This is particularly so in the provinces whose PPSAs are based on the CCPPSL model (see below). However, the erosion may also be happening in Ontario. This is because OPPSA s. 60(2) applies "with respect to a receiver or receiver and manager, however appointed." Are the powers given to the court by OPPSA s. 60(2)—especially ss. 60(2)(b) and (d)—consistent with the traditional view of the position of a privately-appointed receiver as agent of the secured party? If a court-appointed receiver is subject to the same standard of conduct when dealing with the collateral (for example, s. 60(2)) as is a privately-appointed receiver, does the reasoning used in *Ostrander* have any relevance in the context of a receivership to which the OPPSA applies?

5) The homogenization of rules applicable to court-appointed and privately-appointed receivers has gone much further in provinces whose PPSAs are based on the CCPPSL model. Most of these Acts contain extensive regulatory provisions applicable to receivers. See, for example, BCPPSA ss. 64 to 66. This legislation sets out the minimum qualifications for receivers, basic bookkeeping and extensive disclosure requirements, and gives to the court wide supervisory jurisdiction over receivers. The PPSA regulatory scheme applies to receivers of both personal and real property. (See *Law and Equity Act 1996*, RSBC 1996, c. 253, s. 64.) All receivers are subject to the overriding obligation to exercise and discharge their duties and obligations under the security agreement and under the Act or any other applicable law "in good faith and in a commercially reasonable manner." See BCPPSA s. 68(1). Does this mean that the standard of conduct of a receiver in these provinces is the same whether the receiver is court appointed or privately appointed? The same approach appears to be incorporated in the BIA, RSC 1985, c. B-3, ss. 245-252, esp. s. 247.

6) In a security agreement providing for the appointment of a receiver, it is standard practice to insert a clause similar to the following:

> Any receiver or receiver-manager appointed hereunder shall be deemed to be the borrower's agent and the borrower shall be solely responsible for his act, defaults and remuneration.

In *Peat Marwick Ltd. v. Consumers' Gas Co.* (1978), 83 DLR (3d) 450 (Ont. HC), a receiver-manager sought an injunction against the defendant utility company requiring it to supply gas to the business under the receiver-manager's control. The company in receivership was indebted to the defendant, which was the reason the defendant refused to supply additional gas to it. Under s. 59 of the *Public Utilities Act*, RSO 1970, c. 390, the defendant was entitled to cut off supply to any person who neglected to pay the amount owing for the supply of gas. It was argued by the receiver-manager that he was representing the charge holder who had appointed him and not the defendant company and, therefore, s. 59 provided no basis for the defendant's refusal to supply gas to the company under his control. In rejecting the receiver-manager's argument, Osler J observed:

> In practice, however, the debenture in such cases, as here, provides expressly that the receiver shall be deemed to be the agent of the company. Obviously, this is done for the purpose of making it apparent to third parties that the receiver has authority to deal with and manage the affairs of the company. That being so, it is not surprising that the defendant in the present case should look to the receiver for payment of its account and refuse to enter upon a new contract unless it is paid. This was the result in two English cases dealing with similar situations under very similar legislation, namely: *Re Smith*, [1893] 1 QB 323; and *Paterson v. Gas Light & Coke Co.*, [1896] 2 Ch. 476.

See also *Sperry Inc. v. Canadian Imperial Bank of Commerce* (1985), 50 OR 267 (CA). In this case, the court concluded that when a receiver took possession, this could not amount to perfection by possession under former OPPSA s. 24 because, by the terms of the security agreement, the receiver-manager was the agent of the debtor: see Chapter 5, Part II.

7) An additional reason for including agency clauses in security agreements providing for the appointment of receivers is to protect the secured party that appoints the receiver from liability for misconduct or negligence of the receiver. To the extent that the agency clause is recognized as protecting the secured creditor in this way, the secured creditor has

the best of all worlds: the receiver or receiver-manager must act in its interests, but it is insulated from liability for the misconduct of the receiver. The Acts based on the CCPPSL model, in effect, have addressed this practice. For example, SPPSA s. 64(8)(e) provides that, upon application of an interested person, a court may

> (e) notwithstanding anything contained in a security agreement or other document providing for the appointment of a receiver, make an order requiring a receiver, or a person by or on behalf of whom the receiver is appointed, to make good a default in connection with the receiver's [or receiver-manager's] custody, management or disposition of the collateral of the debtor or to relieve the person from any default or failure to comply with this Part.

The implication of the provision is that, ordinarily, a secured party is not liable for the misconduct of a receiver appointed by it (to the extent that the misconduct relates to custody, management, and disposition of the collateral), but that, in appropriate circumstances, a court may hold the secured party responsible.

VIII. DEEMED SECURITY INTERESTS

A. Introduction

OPPSA s. 57.1 provides that, except as otherwise provided in Part V, Part V applies to a security interest only if it secures payment or performance of an obligation. In other words, Part V does not apply to a non-security assignment of accounts or chattel paper or a true lease, even though these transactions are subject to the other parts of the statute by virtue of s. 2: see Chapter 2, Part V.B. The reason is that the remedies in Part V presuppose an actual security agreement. For example, s. 63 provides that upon default under a security agreement, the secured party may dispose of the collateral and use the proceeds to pay down the secured obligation. Likewise, s. 66 allows the debtor to redeem repossessed collateral by paying out the obligations secured by the security interest. These provisions make no sense unless there is an actual secured obligation.

B. True Leases and Security Leases Distinguished

As noted in Chapter 2, following amendments made in 2006, the OPPSA now applies to a lease of goods for a term of more than one year, whether or not it secures payment or performance of an obligation and this reform brings the OPPSA into line with the other provinces. The purpose is to avoid litigation on whether a lease is a true lease or a security lease. OPPSA s. 57.1 resurrects the issue, but only in the context of Part V, and so, while there is still scope for litigation, the number of cases should be substantially reduced.

Nevertheless, the net result of these developments is that the lease classification issue retains its full vitality to determine the parties' rights and obligations where the debtor has defaulted on his lease obligations and the lessor seeks to enforce its contractual rights. If (a) the court determines the lease is in substance a security agreement, the parties' rights and obligations will be determined under Part V of the PPSA and by related legislation, such as the "seize or sue" provisions obtaining in the Western provinces (with the exception of Saskatchewan) and in Newfoundland and Labrador; but (b), if the court concludes the lease agreement is a true lease, the parties' rights and obligations will be determined by common law principles and not Part V. This is because none of the common law provinces have so far adopted a comprehensive law governing personalty leases comparable to Article 2A of the Uniform Commercial Code. The following judgments and discussions are designed to illustrate the practical importance of this bifurcation in current Canadian law.

In *DaimlerChrysler Services Canada Inc. v. Cameron* (2007), 279 DLR (4th) 629, the British Columbia Court of Appeal was called upon to consider whether the trial judge, V. Gray J, had been correct in characterizing as a security lease a lease agreement concerning a pickup truck, which contained the following provisions as summarized in Kirkpatrick JA's judgment at paras. 10-18:

[10] In the instant case, the lease was on a printed form. The term of the lease was 48 months, ending 5 October 2006. Pursuant to the lease, Mr. Cameron was obliged to pay $1,092.30 monthly. He was also required to pay $0.12 per kilometre if the truck was driven over 2,000 kilometres monthly.

[11] Mr. Cameron was required to maintain the truck in good condition and operating order, and to make all requisite repairs. Further, the lease imposed restrictions on Mr. Cameron's use of the vehicle: he was obliged both not to use the truck unlawfully or inappropriately and to keep the truck free of others' claims.

[12] The lease did not include a down-payment or trade-in allowance.

[13] Mr. Cameron had an option to purchase the truck at the expiration of the lease term for $29,851.20. The option purchase price (to which the parties refer as the truck's "Residual Value") was 54 percent of the manufacturer's suggested retail price of $55,280 before the dealer installed accessories. The figure of 54 percent was derived from a table prepared by Daimler to forecast various vehicles' values at the end of their respective lease terms.

[14] Mr. Cameron had the right to terminate the lease anytime before the end of the lease term. However, if he invoked this right, he was required to either exercise the option to purchase or pay an early termination liability and return the vehicle to Daimler.

[15] If Mr. Cameron exercised the option to purchase prior to the expiration of the lease, he had to pay the Residual Value plus the unpaid monthly payments for the balance of the lease term, plus any other charges payable under the lease, less unearned lease charges on an actuarial calculation method.

[16] If Mr. Cameron terminated the lease without exercising the option to purchase, he had to pay the early termination liability, which the lease defined as all past due monthly amounts, plus all monthly payments not yet due, plus any amounts due under the lease, plus the Residual Value, minus the net amount that Daimler received in a reasonable sale, minus any insurance monies received by Daimler, minus any unearned lease charges.

[17] Mr. Cameron was also required to pay the early termination liability if Daimler terminated the lease. Regardless of who terminated the lease, Mr. Cameron's ensuing payment obligation would ensure that Daimler obtained at least the Residual Value.

[18] Upon default, Daimler could take immediate possession of the truck, obtain the early termination liability and sue for damages to be calculated in accordance with the terms of the lease described above.

The trial judge held, (2006), 32 CBR (5th) 188, that while some of the terms of the lease indicated a true lease and other terms were equivocal, the default terms indicated a security lease. Part V of the BCPPSA therefore applied to the lease.* In reaching this conclusion with respect to the characterization of the lease, V. Gray J relied particularly on the Master's judgment in *Re Bronson* (1995), 34 CBR (3d) 255, aff'd. [1996] BCJ No. 1597, esp. at para. 47:

> It strikes me that it is clear from the default clause that this agreement secures the payment of the lease payments and the option price. If default occurs, the full amount of the lease payments become due, the option price becomes due and the lessee will be given credit for the net sale price, but if that is insufficient to cover the amount due, it will still be liable for a portion of the residual price. The lessee will be given credit for the residual value if the net sale proceeds are less than the residual value. In that case the lessee would only be liable for the lease payments, not the residual value portion and the lessor would have sustained the loss.

In *DaimlerChrysler*, writing for a unanimous court, Kirkpatrick JA dismissed this reasoning on the following grounds (paras. 39-41):

> [39] It appears to me unhelpful to focus on default provisions and render them determinative of whether a lease is a security lease. The fundamental question is whether a lease secures payment or performance of an obligation.
>
> [40] The decision in *Child & Gower Piano Co. v. Gambrel*, [1933] 2 WWR 273 (Sask. CA) articulates this point at 281-82:
>
> > In *Stroud's Judicial Dictionary*, vol. 3, p. 1815, it is stated that a security is "anything that makes the money more assured in its payment or more readily recoverable." Security for a debt, in the ordinary meaning of the term, carries with it the idea of something or somebody to which, or to whom, the creditor can resort in order to aid him in realizing or recovering the debt, in case the debtor fails to pay; the word implies something in addition to the mere obligation of the debtor. When a person buys goods from a merchant, his promise to pay, whether express or implied, is not security, nor does the promise to pay become security merely because it is reduced to writing.
>
> [41] In my view, it cannot be said that the default provisions in the lease in question create any separate security. They simply represent the calculation of the amounts owing by the lessee upon a breach of the agreement.

The *DaimlerChrysler* decision has been followed in subsequent BC cases and is also the subject of a favourable comment by Peter Lee in (2007), 24 *Nat. Insolvency Rev.* 23-24. Nevertheless, Professor Ziegel has expressed the view that the BC Court of Appeal's decision was mistaken because Kirkpatrick JA misunderstood the essential feature of a security interest, as defined in all the PPS legislation, and its relationship to a financial lease. If the terms of the lease ensure that, come what may, the lessor will be entitled, or be able, to recover the full price plus the implicit finance charge, it becomes indistinguishable from a purchase-money security interest and the lease should be treated as a security lease. (Kirkpatrick JA's

---

* V. Gray J's judgment does not indicate what difference the applicability of Part V made to the plaintiff's claim. Section 67 in Part V of the BCPPSA contains a seize or sue clause in respect of consumer goods. In *Daimler-Chrysler*, however, the vehicle was a pickup truck, so presumably it did not satisfy the test of consumer goods.

judgment does not refer to the BCPPSA definition of PMSI.) See J. Ziegel, "Security Interests and Continuing Challenges in Characterization of Equipment Leases" (2009), 47 *CBLJ* 283.

Those commentators who support the decision in *DaimlerChrysler* do so on the ground that there is a basic distinction between an "open-end" and a "close-end" lease. The distinction is said to be that, in a close-end lease, the lessee is only obliged to make the required payments during the basic leasing period. He is not responsible for any deficiency the lessor may suffer if the residual value of the vehicle is less than the balance that would have been owing if the lease had been structured as an installment (conditional) sale.

The opposing view is that the risk to the lessor of suffering this loss may be minimal (particularly since the lessor is in the best position to determine the risk when drafting the leasing terms) and that the dominant features of the lease in *DaimlerChrysler* were the heavy liabilities imposed on the lessee if the lease was terminated by the lessor before the basic leasing period had expired.

Ziegel also notes (op. cit., at 293-94) that the history of the "seize or sue" provisions in the BC legislation shows that the provisions were intended to apply to leases with an option to purchase as well as to conditional sale agreements. In his view, there were no reasons to believe that the BC legislature intended to change this feature of BC law when incorporating the seize or sue provisions in Part V of the BCPPSA, and he believes that the BC Court of Appeal should have been willing to give the provisions the broader reach they enjoyed under the earlier BC *Sale of Goods on Condition* legislation.

C. The Measure of Damages for Breach of a True Lease

Keneric Tractor Sales Ltd. v. Langille
(1988), 79 NR 241 (SCC)

WILSON J: The issue in this appeal is how damages are to be calculated for breach of a lease of chattels. Central to this issue is whether the reasoning of this Court in *Highway Properties Ltd. v. Kelly, Douglas and Co.*, [1971] SCR 562; 17 DLR (3d) 710, a case dealing with the method of calculation of damages for breach of a lease of land, should be extended to cover leases of chattels.

1. The Facts

The appellants, Eric and Paul Langille are farmers. During the summers of 1981 and 1982 the respondent Keneric Tractor Sales Limited ("Keneric") leased ten pieces of farm equipment to the Langilles. The 1982 leases called for ten semi-annual payments over a five-year period. The sum of these semi-annual payments was equal to 120% of the original purchase price. A separate agreement gave the Langilles an option to purchase the equipment for 25% of the original purchase price. The option was exercisable at the end of the five year period. If the option was not exercised the equipment would revert back to Keneric. The 1982 leases were structured the same way but the semi-annual payments were higher and the option to purchase was set at 30% of the original purchase price.

Keneric has bought the farm equipment in question from Allis-Chalmers Canada Inc., the manufacturer. In order to finance the purchases the leases taken from the Langilles were assigned to Allis-Chalmers Credit Corporation of Canada, Ltd. Keneric guaranteed the Langilles' performance under the leasing agreements and agreed to act as agent for the recovery of amounts due to Allis-Chalmers Credit Corporation.

In March 1983 the Langilles advised Keneric that they would have trouble making the lease payments. Negotiations failed to resolve the problem. The Langilles defaulted under the leases and Keneric seized the equipment. After due notice Keneric sold the seized equipment. Keneric then commenced the present action claiming damages resulting from breach of the leases.

...

3. The Issue

Counsel for the appellants submit that the Nova Scotia Court of Appeal erred as to the proper method of assessing damages for default under the equipment rental agreements. Two sub-issues must be examined in order to determine the principal issue. These are (a) what are the general rules governing damages for breach of a lease of chattels? and (b) did the resale by Keneric satisfy its duty to mitigate its damages?

(a) The General Rules

The most recent discussion of the relevant law is found in the Manitoba Court of Appeal's decision in *Canadian Acceptance Corp. Ltd. v. Regent Park Butcher Shop*, [(1969), 3 DLR (3d) 304 (Man. CA)]. That case involved the lease of a cash register. After the lessee failed to make several payments the lessor repossessed and sold the cash register. A clause in the leasing contract stipulated a particular level of damage payable upon breach. The Court of Appeal held that the sum stipulated in the clause was not a genuine pre-estimate of liquidated damages and therefore the clause was a penalty and unenforceable. The court then examined the case law dealing with the damages recoverable for breach of a chattel lease.

Dickson J (as he then was), speaking for the Court examined the Canadian case law on the subject and concluded at p. 314:

> There being no uniform pattern emerging from the Canadian decisions we feel free to approach the matter afresh according to our best judgment. It is our considered opinion that the rationale of the series of cases beginning with *Bridge v. Campbell Discount Co. Ltd.*, [1962] 1 All ER 385, provides the proper approach and we propose to apply it. In one of the cases of that series, *Financings Ltd. v. Baldock*, [1963] 1 All ER 443, Lord Denning MR said at p. 445:
>
>> It seems to me that, when an agreement of hiring is terminated by virtue of a power contained in it and the owner retakes the vehicle, he can recover damages for any breach up to the date of termination, but not for any breach thereafter, for the simple reason that there are no breaches thereafter. I see no difference in this respect between the letting of a vehicle on hire and the letting of land on a lease. If a lessor, under a proviso for re-entry, re-enters on the ground of nonpayment of rent or of disrepair, he gets the arrears

of rent up to date of re-entry and damages for want of repair at that date, but he does not get damages for loss of rent thereafter or for breaches of repair thereafter.

And at p. 446:

In applying this principle, I asked counsel for the plaintiffs: What were the breaches by the hirer up to the termination of the hiring? He could only point to the simple failure to pay the two instalments of rent. In these circumstances, the only moneys which the plaintiffs can recover are those two instalments which are in arrear and unpaid with the interest thereon. If the plaintiff could prove damages for breach of contract to repair, they could recover them, but no more ...

If, however, there is no repudiation, but simply, as here, a failure to pay one or two instalments (the failure not going to the root of the contract and only giving a right to terminate by virtue of an express stipulation in the contract), the owners can recover only the instalments in arrear, with interest, and nothing else; for there was no other breach in existence at the termination of the hiring.

Thus, a lessor who terminates a chattel lease by virtue of a provision in the lease allowing him to do so is limited in his remedies to the rent due at the time of the termination plus any proceeds from resale.

Both *Regent Park* and *Baldock* on which Dickson J relied proceed by analogy to the common law of damages for breach of a lease of land. As Dickson J pointed out at p. 315 of his reasons:

If a landlord re-enters land for nonpayment of rent he may bring an action for arrears of rent on the express or implied covenant to pay rent but he cannot recover rent falling due after the date of re-entry. No authority has been given us to show why the position of a lessor of a chattel should be stronger than that of a lessor of land.

Indeed, if the law in this area is to be coherent and principled it would make good sense to abolish artificial legal distinctions between leases of land and leases of chattels. However, the pursuit of consistency today mandates a different result in this case because the decision of this Court in *Highway Properties* has intervened and shifted the jurisprudential foundation upon which the *Regent Park* decision was based.

In *Highway Properties* the Court addressed the issue of the landlord's right to damages flowing from the repudiation of a lease of shopping centre space by a tenant. The landlord claimed both for the loss suffered to the date of repudiation and for the prospective loss resulting from the tenant's failure to carry on business in the shopping centre for the full term of the lease. An application of the traditional approach reflected in *Regent Park* would have defeated the second half of the landlord's claim. Laskin J, speaking for the whole Court, noted at p. 570 that up until that point:

The developed case law has recognized three mutually exclusive courses that a landlord may take where a tenant is in fundamental breach of the lease or has repudiated it entirely, as was the case here. He may do nothing to alter the relationship of landlord and tenant, but simply insist on performance of the terms and sue for rent or damages on the footing that the lease remains in force. Second, he may elect to terminate the lease, retaining of course the right to sue for rent accrued due, or for damages to the date of termination for previous breaches of covenant. Third, he may advise the tenant that he proposes to re-let the property on the tenant's account and enter into possession on that basis.

What was not possible at common law before *Highway Properties* was for the landlord to terminate the lease, relet the property, and make a claim for damages that included a claim for unpaid future rent less the actual rental value of the unexpired period.

Highway Properties changed this. Laskin J examined the applicable English, Australian and American authorities. He paid particular attention to the decision in *Buchanan v. Byrnes* (1906), 3 CLR 704 (H. Ct. Aust.). In that case the tenant, in breach of covenant, abandoned hotel property which he had leased. The landlord succeeded in a claim for damages over the unexpired term of the lease despite the surrender. The approach to the damages issue taken by the High Court is summarized in two passages from the judgment (the first from the reasons of Griffith CJ at p. 715 and the second from the reasons of Barton J at p. 719):

> Then the question arises—to what damages is he entitled? There is a covenant the performance of which will extend over a term of 15 years, and it is unequivocally broken. The natural damage is the loss likely to be sustained by the plaintiff during the period for which the covenant ought to be kept; just as in the case of a contract to engage a servant for a term of years, paying him monthly wages. If the contract is unequivocally broken by the employer, the servant can bring an action at once. He cannot, of course, recover anything in the form of wages; he recovers damages, which are assessed usually upon the basis of the wages that he would have received; but he must on the other hand give credit, and the jury must give the employer credit, for whatever the servant might reasonably be expected to have earned during the period for which the contract would have been in existence. Prima facie, the damages, therefore, would be the value of the term to the lessor, that is, the difference between the benefit which he would have derived from the premises being kept as a going hotel for 15 years at the agreed rent, being kept in repair, and so on, and the value of the premises as they were thrown on his hands.
>
> But it is said that the conduct of the plaintiff in resuming possession under the circumstances estops him from suing upon the covenants. It must not be taken to hold that it has that effect as to the covenant to pay rent. But, however that may be, can it estop him as to the other covenants which relate to the keeping the premises as an inn throughout the term, and the doing of the other things necessary for that purpose? Conduct, to constitute an estoppel, must have caused another to believe in the existence of a certain state of things, and have induced him to act on that belief so as to alter his own position. How can that be said to be the effect of the plaintiff's conduct, when the act of the defendant, so far from having been induced by it, has preceded it? In my judgment the doctrine of estoppel cannot be applied against the plaintiff ...

Laskin J noted that *Buchanan v. Byrnes* was applied by the Supreme Court of Australia in *Hughes v. N.L.S. Pty., Ltd.*, [1966] WAR 100. He concluded at pp. 575-576:

> The approach of the High Court of Australia commends itself to me, cutting through, as it does, artificial barriers to relief that have resulted from overextension of the doctrine of surrender in its relation to rent. Although it is correct to say that repudiation by the tenant gives the landlord at that time a choice between holding the tenant to the lease or terminating it,

yet at the same time a right of action for damages then arises; and the election to insist on the lease or to refuse further performance (and thus bring it to an end) goes simply to the measure and range of damages. I see no logic in a conclusion that, by electing to terminate, the landlord has limited the damages that he may then claim to the same scale that would result if he had elected to keep the lease alive.

Laskin J then expressly adopted the Australian approach.

The Court in *Highway Properties* justified its decision by an appeal to both principle and practicality. In principle it made no sense to regard a commercial lease of land as "simply a conveyance and not a contract." This historical anomaly could only be corrected by assessing damages in breach of land lease cases on general contract principles. Practicality supported the change as well since the new approach avoided the potential for multiplicity of actions inherent in the old approach. Both these factors suggest that the same change should be made in the law applicable to breaches of chattel leases.

In addition to these two considerations the need for consistency within the law militates in favour of a change in the rules relating to breach of chattel leases. As was noted in both *Baldock* and *Regent Park* there is no essential difference between a lease of land and a lease of chattels that is material to the ascertainment of damages on breach. They are both contracts. Thus the spirit of *Regent Park*—the harmonizing of the law relating to the leasing of chattels with the law relating to the leasing of land—is best given effect today by a different result in a chattel lease case. The damages flowing from the breach of a chattel lease, like the damages flowing from the breach of a land lease, should be calculated in accordance with general contract principles. To the extent that *Regent Park* reflects a different approach it should not be followed.

Counsel for the appellants, however, point out that *Highway Properties* was a case of express repudiation by the lessee. The present case, they argue, is distinguishable in that there was no express repudiation. Assuming that the appellants could establish the factual basis for this distinction, is there any reason why the rule laid down in *Highway Properties* should not logically extend to all cases involving a lawful termination by the lessor?

In order to answer this question we must go back to first principles in the law of contract. If a party to a contract breaches a term of sufficient importance the other party has the right to treat the contract as terminated and consider himself discharged from any future obligations under it: *Pigott Construction Co. v. W.J. Crowe Ltd.* (1961), 27 DLR (2d) 258 (Ont. CA), at pp. 269-272; *Alkok v. Grymek*, [1968] SCR 452, at p. 456; *Hongkong Fir Shipping Co. v. Kawasaki Kisen Kaisha Ltd.*, [1962] 2 QB 26 (CA), *per* Diplock LJ at pp. 65-66, 71; *Cehave NV v. Bremer Handelsgesellschaft n.b.H. The "Hansa Nord,"* [1976] QB 44 (CA). An identical right arises where one party to a contract by words or conduct indicates to the other party that he does not intend to perform his contractual obligations. In the latter instance the first party is said to have repudiated the contract: see Sir W.R. Anson, *Law of Contract* (26th ed. by A.G. Guest), pp. 470-484; G.C. Cheshire, C.H.S. Fifoot and M.P. Furmston, *Law of Contract* (11th ed. 1986), pp. 521-533. The question at hand is whether the assessment of damages in a case of termination based on breach of a term of the contract should be any different from the assessment of damages in a case of termination based on repudiation.

Laskin J in *Highway Properties* seemed to assume that the answer to this question was no. His analysis in that case focussed on the "courses that a landlord may take where a tenant is in fundamental breach of the lease or has repudiated it entirely." I would respectfully agree with Laskin J that damages should be assessed in the same way in both cases. Repudiation may be triggered by either the inability or the unwillingness of a party to perform his contractual obligation. The same is true of a breach of contract that gives rise to a right to terminate; it may be the result of inability or unwillingness to perform. The breach and the repudiation are merely subdivisions within a general category of conduct, i.e., conduct which gives the innocent party the right to treat the contract as terminated. Thus, there is no conceptual difference between a breach of contract that gives the innocent party the right to terminate and the repudiation of a contract so as to justify a different assessment of damages when termination flows from the former rather than the latter. General contract principles should be applied in both instances.

The trial judge in this case correctly found that the Langilles' default constituted a breach of lease that gave Keneric the right to terminate. Keneric accepted the breach and terminated the leases. It is not necessary to determine whether the Langilles also repudiated the leases. For the reasons given above such a finding would make no difference to the assessment of damages.

...

Appeal dismissed.

NOTE

Justice Wilson's assertion that there is no conceptual distinction between the innocent party's right to terminate the agreement and claim damages because of repudiatory conduct by the guilty party and a right to claim damages because of a termination clause in the agreement is controversial and is not consistent with the English Court of Appeal's reasoning in *Financings Ltd. v. Baldock*, [1963] 1 All ER 443. Nevertheless, Justice Wilson's position has been justified on the ground that the British approach in the hire-purchase cases was artificial and provided no meaningful protection to consumers. Her approach to the measurement of damages is also unusual since it relies on the first rather than the second rule for the measurement of damages in *Hadley v. Baxendale* (1854), 9 Exch. 341. See Ziegel, "Measurement of Damages for Breach of a Chattel Lease: The Supreme Court of Canada Liberalizes the Rules," [1988] *Lloyd's Maritime Comm'l Law Quar.* 276. Part 5 of Article 2A of the Uniform Commercial Code contains a more sophisticated and refined series of rules for measuring the lessor's damages where the equipment has been repossessed by the lessor. Note, too, that while in the Canadian PPSAs, Part V contains detailed enforcement rules, largely for the benefit of debtors, there is no comparable regime in Canada for the protection of lessees in true leasing agreements. Is the distinction justifiable?

CHAPTER FOURTEEN

Conflict of Laws

I. INTRODUCTION

The conflict of laws (also often referred to as private international law) is the branch of civil law that determines which law applies where a transaction has multiple-state contacts. A security agreement may have connections to more than one province. For example:

- The secured party is located in Ontario and the debtor is located in British Columbia.
- The secured party and the debtor are located in Ontario, but the collateral is located in British Columbia.
- The secured party and the debtor are located in British Columbia and so is the collateral. The debtor moves to Ontario and brings the collateral with him.

In cases like these, which PPSA applies: Ontario or British Columbia? More particularly:

1. Whose law governs the validity of the security agreement? Jurisdictions often have different validity rules, particularly so far as consumer transactions are concerned. Many civil law jurisdictions also impose restrictions on the availability of non-possessory security interests as collateral in commercial transactions. (For example, Quebec law does not generally permit the creation of non-purchase-money, non-possessory security interests in consumer goods.)

2. Whose law determines whether and when a security interest has attached to collateral and the requirements for perfection of the security interest?

3. Whose law determines priority among competing security interests and the effect of an unperfected security interest?

4. What is the effect of tangible collateral—for example, goods—being moved, after the security agreement is made, to another jurisdiction with or without the secured party's knowledge or consent? What is the effect of the debtor changing its location to another jurisdiction after the signing of the original security agreement?

5. If the debtor defaults, whose law governs the secured party's enforcement rights?

Some of these problems were already familiar under the pre-PPSA conditional sales law, particularly where a vehicle subject to a conditional sale agreement concluded in province A was taken by the debtor to province B without the seller's knowledge, and there resold or

527

traded in by the debtor to an unsuspecting third party. In response to the problem, many of the provincial conditional sales acts required the seller to reperfect the conditional sale agreement in the second province as a condition of the conditional sale agreement being recognized there. See further J.S. Ziegel, "Conditional Sales and the Conflict of Laws" (1967), 45 *Can. Bar Rev.* 284.

The original OPPSA addressed some of the issues described above much more systematic-ally than was true of the conditional sales legislation. Further changes and refinements were incorporated in ss. 5 to 8 of the 1989 revised Act. The Ontario provisions are similar, but not identical to, the provisions in the other PPSAs. Revised Article 9 has introduced important conflict of laws changes to the 1972 Article 9 rules, some of which are currently being con-sidered for adoption in Canada. The principal features of the current Ontario rules are as follows:

1. Section 5(1) prescribes which law governs the validity, perfection, and effect of per-fection of a security interest in goods and a possessory security interest in other types of collateral, and continues the long-established *lex situs* rule.

2. Section 5(2) determines the status in Ontario of goods brought into the province while subject to a security interest created under the first *lex situs*. Section 5(5) is particular to Ontario and continues a provision in the old Ontario *Conditional Sales Act* involving goods sold by a Quebec seller and subject to an unpaid seller's right of revendication under the Quebec *Civil Code*. See Falconbridge, *Conflict of Laws*, 2d ed. (1984), c. 19.

3. Section 6 incorporates an important exception to the *lex situs* rule where the parties to a security agreement understand at the time the security interest attaches that the goods will be kept in another jurisdiction and the goods are removed to that other jurisdiction within 30 days after the security interest attaches.

4. Section 7 deals with the choice of law rule governing the creation and perfection of a security interest in collateral other than goods, and of a possessory security inter-est in documentary intangibles. (Note that s. 7(1)(a)(ii) also applies to non-consumer mobile goods—that is, goods that are normally kept in more than one jurisdiction.) These types of collateral are governed by the law of the debtor's loca-tion at the time the security interest attaches. Section 7(4) indicates how that loca-tion is to be determined. If the debtor changes its location, then the security interest must be reperfected: s. 7(2). Section 7.1 deals with the choice of law rules relating to the validity, perfection, effect of perfection, and priority of a security interest in in-vestment property.

5. Finally, s. 8 determines the law governing the enforcement of a security interest and distinguishes between the procedural and substantive aspects of the secured party's enforcement rights. The cases and commentary that follow partially illustrate some of the policy and constructional issues raised by these provisions.

II. SECURITY INTERESTS IN GOODS: INITIAL VALIDITY AND PERFECTION

OPPSA s. 5(1) provides:

> 5(1) Except as otherwise provided in this Act, the validity, perfection and effect of perfection or non-perfection of,
> (a) a security interest in goods; and
> (b) a possessory security interest in an instrument, a negotiable document of title, money and chattel paper,
> shall be governed by the law of the jurisdiction where the collateral is situated at the time the security interest attaches.

Consider the following example:

D is a retailer. Its head office is in Toronto. D has four other stores in Ontario and one in New Brunswick. SP and D enter into a security agreement. The collateral includes the inventory in D's New Brunswick store. SP perfects its security interest by registering a financing statement in Ontario. D becomes bankrupt. D's trustee in bankruptcy disputes SP's claim to the New Brunswick store inventory.

Assuming the disputed New Brunswick store inventory was located in New Brunswick at the time SP's security interest attached, New Brunswick law applies. The governing provision is the New Brunswick equivalent of OPPSA s. 20(1)(b): an unperfected security interest is ineffective against D's trustee in bankruptcy. SP's security interest is unperfected in New Brunswick because, although SP registered a financing statement in Ontario, it failed to do so in New Brunswick. To perfect in New Brunswick, SP must register a financing statement there.

As this example demonstrates, if D carries on business in more than one province or territory, SP may need to register a financing statement in each province. Likewise, a prospective secured party or the like may need to conduct separate searches in each province or territory. Multi-provincial registrations and searches would not be necessary if there was a national PPS register, but at present this seems to be a remote prospect. Part of the problem is that there are differences between the provinces relating to the form and content of financing statements, the relative merits of exact match and close similar match search facilities and other matters (see Chapter 6), and these would have to be resolved before the provinces could contemplate moving to a unified register.

A national register would remove the need for multiple registrations and searches, but it would not avoid all potential conflict of laws problems at the interprovincial level. To achieve this outcome, the provinces would also have to make their PPSAs uniform. While most of the provincial and territorial PPSAs are substantially uniform, Ontario and Quebec remain outside the common scheme and there is no immediate prospect of their joining the fold. The most the provinces have been able to agree on is uniform conflict of laws rules. Uniformity at this level is important because it avoids the risk of different laws applying depending on the jurisdiction in which the dispute happens to be litigated. For example, assume that in the above hypothetical case the action between SP and D's trustee is brought in Ontario. To determine the choice of law issue, an Ontario court would be obliged to apply the Ontario choice of law rule, namely OPPSA s. 5(1). Correspondingly, if the action is brought in New Brunswick, the New Brunswick court would be obliged to apply the New Brunswick choice of law rule. If this happened to be different from the Ontario rule, the court might arrive at a different conclusion from the one an Ontario court would reach if it was the decision-maker. Fortunately, though, the New Brunswick and Ontario choice of laws rules are the same and so the problem is avoided.

III. RELOCATION OF GOODS

Consider the following case:

> D runs a small manufacturing business in Alberta. SP has a security interest in D's factory equipment that is perfected by registration in Alberta at all relevant times. D relocates the business to Ontario and on January 1 the factory equipment is moved there along with everything else. On February 1, D sells an item of equipment to T without SP's consent. SP learns about D's move on February 15 and immediately registers a financing statement in Ontario. SP later finds out about the unauthorized sale and claims the equipment from T.

OPPSA s. 5(1) provides that perfection issues are governed by the law of the jurisdiction where the goods are situated when SP's security interest attached. If this provision applied, then Alberta law would govern and, under Alberta law, SP's claim would succeed: SP has a security interest perfected in Alberta and a perfected security interest is effective against a transferee for value unless the secured party authorized the sale or unless the sale was in the ordinary course of D's business: see Chapter 11. However, s. 5(2) displaces s. 5(1). It provides as follows:

> 5(2) A security interest in goods perfected under the law of the jurisdiction in which the goods are situated at the time the security interest attaches but before the goods are brought into Ontario continues perfected in Ontario if a financing statement is registered in Ontario before the goods are brought in or if it is perfected in Ontario,
>
> > (a) within sixty days after the goods are brought in;
> >
> > (b) within fifteen days after the day the secured party receives notice that the goods have been brought in; or
> >
> > (c) before the date that perfection ceases under the law of the jurisdiction in which the goods were situated at the time the security interest attached,
>
> whichever is earliest, but the security interest is subordinate to the interest of a buyer or lessee of those goods who acquires the goods from the debtor as consumer goods in good faith and without knowledge of the security interest and before the security interest is perfected in Ontario.

Section 5(2) implies that Ontario law governs the dispute between SP and T in our example and, on this basis, it provides for the perfection of SP's security interest in Ontario. In summary, SP must register a financing statement in Ontario, subject to a grace period. During the grace period, SP is deemed to have a continuously perfected security interest in Ontario. The grace period is the shortest of the three periods listed in s. 5(2), paras. (a), (b), and (c).

The closing words of s. 5(2) make an exception for consumer transactions. Consider the following example:

D lives in Alberta. SP has a purchase-money security interest in D's home entertainment system. SP's security interest is perfected by registration in Alberta. D moves to Ontario on March 1, bringing the system with her. On March 15, D sells the system to T for T's personal use. On March 30, SP learns about D's move and immediately registers a financing statement in Ontario. On May 1, SP learns about the sale and claims the system from T. The closing words of s. 5(2) apply and so, provided that T acquired the system in good faith and without knowledge of SP's security interest, she gets clear title even though SP's security interest is deemed to have been perfected in Ontario at the time of the purchase.

The rule in the main part of s. 5(2) is not the only possible response to the relocation problem. For example, the statute might have provided instead that even if the debtor moves the goods to Ontario, the other province's law still applies. If that was the rule, the risk of the relocation would fall entirely on searchers. The only sure way of avoiding the risk would be for the searcher to search in every province. Again, instead of s. 5(2), the statute might have provided that if the debtor moves the goods to Ontario, Ontario law applies immediately. If that was the rule, the risk of the relocation would fall entirely on the secured party. The only sure way of avoiding the risk would be for the secured party to register in every province. Section 5(2) steers a middle course between these two extremes. It distributes the risk of relocation between the secured party and the searcher. The secured party is at risk if it registers outside the grace period and so it has to decide upfront whether the risk justifies registering in all provinces or not. The searcher is at risk if the secured party registers inside the grace period (unless the consumer goods exception applies) and so the searcher has to decide whether the risk justifies searching in all provinces or not. The exception for consumer goods is because consumers presumably are less able to quantify the risk. More specifically, the exception reflects the view that it is unrealistic to expect a consumer to make inquiries about the origins of second-hand goods and to search the PPSA register in the province of origin. The OPPSA is more limited than the other PPSAs in this regard: in the other provinces, the exception applies to any buyer or lessee, not just consumers.

The following cases, both decided under the former OPPSA, deal with aspects of s. 5(2) (old s. 7(2)).

Re Adair; Re General Motors Acceptance Corporation
(1985), 4 PPSAC 262 (Ont. CA)

GOODMAN JA: ... This is an appeal by Ward Mallette Inc., trustee in bankruptcy (the trustee) from an order [reported at 48 CBR (NS) 214] pronounced on October 11, 1983 by the presiding Judge in bankruptcy on an application by General Motors Acceptance Corporation (GMAC) for an order declaring that GMAC has a security interest in a 1982 Chevrolet van in accordance with a security agreement made between the bankrupt and GMAC in priority to the trustee in bankruptcy of Alice Marie Adair (Adair).

The undisputed facts which gave rise to these proceedings are as follows. Adair purchased the Chevrolet van and financed its purchase under a conditional sales agreement which was executed in Florida on September 8, 1982. This agreement was assigned to GMAC which duly perfected its security interest in the van in accordance with the law of the State of Florida at a time prior to the date upon which the van was brought into Ontario by Adair, *viz.* April 21, 1983.

The van remained in Ontario on and after that date.

On May 26, 1983, Adair made a voluntary assignment in bankruptcy and the trustee herein was appointed as the trustee in bankruptcy of her estate. At that time at least two creditors of her estate had no knowledge of any security interest of GMAC in the van.

On May 31, 1983, notices in the prescribed form were mailed by the trustee to all known creditors of the estate of Adair including GMAC in Jacksonville, Florida. The parties agree that pursuant to the Rules of Practice and the Bankruptcy Rules, GMAC is deemed to have received the notice on the fourth day following that on which it was mailed, *viz.* June 4, 1983.

On June 15, 1983, GMAC filed a proof of claim with the trustee claiming the van pursuant to the terms of its conditional sales agreement. On June 17, 1983, the trustee mailed to GMAC a notice of disallowance of claim as a secured creditor on the basis of "No evidence of registration under the Personal Property Security Act," and accepted the claim as that of an unsecured creditor for the amount claimed.

On June 28, 1983, GMAC filed a financing statement with respect to the van pursuant to the provisions of the Personal Property Security Act, RSO 1980, c. 375 (PPSA).

The parties have agreed that the van had a value of $8,000 net of costs of disposition. On consent the van, at some time after October 15, 1983, has been exported by GMAC and the sum of $8,000 has been deposited in the name of the solicitors for GMAC in an interest bearing account with Guaranty Trust of Canada pending disposition of this appeal and the determination of entitlement.

On these facts the learned Judge in bankruptcy made an order with short reasons as follows [at 214]:

> Order to go declaring that General Motors Acceptance Corporation has priority to the trustee with respect to the van in question. This order is based upon a consideration of *Re Johnson* (1979), 30 CBR (NS) 210 (Ont. SC), and a consideration of *Trans-Can. Credit Corp. v. Bachand* (1980), 1 PPSAC 185 (Ont. CA). This latter decision did not involve bankruptcy. I am also relying on the provisions of s. 7(1) of the Personal Property Security Act, RSO 1980, c. 375, together with ss. 22(1)(a)(iii) and 22(2) of that Act. The applicant and trustee are entitled to their costs forthwith after taxation thereof.

The parties are in agreement that for the purpose of the determination of the issue in this appeal, regard must be had in particular to the provisions of s. 7 and s. 22 of the PPSA [*cf.* ss. 5 and 20 of the current OPPSA]. The relevant portions of those sections are as follows:

> 7(1) Subject to section 5, a security interest in collateral already perfected under the law of the jurisdiction in which the collateral was when the security interest attached and before

being brought into Ontario continues perfected in Ontario for sixty days and also thereafter if within the sixty-day period it is perfected in Ontario.

(2) Notwithstanding subsection (1), where the secured party receives notice within the sixty-day period mentioned therein that the collateral has been brought into Ontario, his security interest in the collateral ceases to be perfected in Ontario unless he registers a financing statement in the prescribed form within fifteen days from the date that he receives such notice or upon the expiration of the sixty-day period, whichever is earlier.

(3) A security interest that has ceased to be perfected in Ontario due to the expiration of the sixty-day period may thereafter be perfected in Ontario, but such perfection takes effect from the time of its perfection in Ontario. ...

22(1) Except as provided in subsection (3), an unperfected security interest is subordinate to,

> (a) the interest of a person,
>> (i) who is entitled to a priority under this or any other Act, or
>> (ii) who, without knowledge of the security interest and before it is perfected, assumes control of the collateral through legal process, or
>> (iii) who represents the creditors of the debtor as assignee for the benefit of creditors, trustee in bankruptcy or receiver; and ...

(2) The rights of a person under subclause (1)(a)(iii) in respect of the collateral are referable to the date from which his status has effect and arise without regard to the personal knowledge of the representative if any represented creditor was, on the relevant date, without knowledge of the unperfected security interest.

There is no doubt that if GMAC had perfected its security interest in Ontario within the 60-day period mentioned in s. 7(1) or within the 15-day period mentioned in s. 7(2), whichever expired the earlier, it would have had a security interest in the van in priority to the interest of the trustee. The parties are agreed that the 60-day period referred to in s. 7(1) expired on June 21, 1983 and the 15-day period referred to in s. 7(2) expired on June 19, 1983. It is common ground that GMAC did not register a financing statement in prescribed form within 15 days from the date it received notice that its collateral had been brought into Ontario nor did it perfect its security interest in the collateral (the van) within the 60-day period after it was brought into Ontario.

It was the submission of GMAC that the failure to perfect its security interest within the appropriate time period specified in s. 7 did not affect the priority of its security interest over the claim of the trustee. GMAC claimed that its security interest continued perfected in Ontario for the 60-day period, if s. 7(1) were applicable or for the 15-day period following notice, if s. 7(2) were applicable. It then submitted that under s. 22(1)(a)(iii) and s. 22(2) the rights of the trustee were fixed as of the date of its appointment, *viz.*, May 16, 1983, and that on that date, GMAC's security interest having continued to be perfected in Ontario, it was entitled to priority over the interest acquired by the trustee.

It appears that the learned Judge in bankruptcy accepted this reasoning. There is some support for this viewpoint from the academic realm and in the United States courts. Professor Jacob S. Ziegel in an article published in 4 *CBLJ* 54 (1979-80), commenting on the trial decision of His Honour Judge Staniszewski in *Bachand v. Trans-Can. Credit Corp.* May 2, 1979 [now reported 1 PPSAC 41, at 83 (Ont. Co. Ct.)] said:

> The question the court should have asked itself in the present case was whether the lapse of the 60-day period without reperfecting by Trans Canada *retroactively* invalidated Trans Canada's security interest and cured plaintiff's defective title.
>
> A literal reading of PPSA, s. 7(1) leads to the conclusion that the secured party has an unqualified perfected security interest during the 60-day period. American case law decided under the pre-1972 version of UCC [Uniform Commercial Code] 9-103(3) supports this reading as does an important line of cases decided under the analogous (but not identical) provisions of the prior provincial Conditional Sales and Chattel Mortgages Acts. The Article 9 Review Committee criticized the American jurisprudence for failing to consider the effect of the subsequent lapse of the security interest. In any event, UCC 9-103 was amended in 1972 to make it clear that if the foreign security interest is not reperfected in the jurisdiction to which the collateral was removed before the expiration of the period of perfection in the foreign jurisdiction or within four months [60 days under PPSA s. 7(1)] after the collateral is brought into the forum, whichever occurs first, it is thereafter deemed to have been unperfected "as against a person who became a purchaser after removal." Such an amendment should also be considered in Ontario to prevent the anomalies that may otherwise arise.

The facts in the *Bachand* case, *supra*, are very similar to the facts in the present case except that the contest in *Bachand* was between an assignee of a conditional sales agreement and a subsequent purchaser, whereas the contest in the present case is between an assignee of a conditional sales agreement and a trustee in bankruptcy.

The facts in *Bachand* were that on February 26, 1976, L. Company in New Brunswick sold a motor vehicle on conditional sales terms to one M. The agreement was assigned to T.C.C. Corp. and registered in New Brunswick. On May 20, 1976, T.C.C. Corp. learned that the vehicle was located in Alberta and registered the agreement in that province. On August 13, 1976, the vehicle was registered by M. in Ontario. The registration permit for the vehicle was then transferred to the H. & J. Auto Centre who resold the vehicle to the plaintiff on September 3, 1976. T.C.C. Corp. registered a financing statement in Ontario on October 27, 1976 (more than 60 days after the vehicle was brought into Ontario). On December 13, 1976, bailiffs acting on T.C.C. Corp.'s instructions, seized the vehicle while it was in the plaintiff's possession. The issue before the Court was whether the plaintiff had obtained a good title when he purchased the vehicle. Judge Staniszewski upheld the plaintiff's claim and found that the 60-day registration on October 27 was "inoperative and null and void."

Professor Ziegel in his article said at 82-83 in commenting on this conclusion:

> The soundness of the decision is open to serious question. In the first place, the learned Judge was mistaken in holding that Trans Canada's registration was a nullity. PPSA s. 7(3) provides that a security interest that has ceased to be perfected in Ontario because of the expiration of the 60-day period may thereafter be perfected in Ontario but that such perfection only operates from the time of perfection in Ontario. This provision is quite inconsistent with the notion that a foreign security interest becomes "null and void" if it is not reperfected within 60 days. In fact, the Act throughout consciously eschews use of the

terminology of nullity because of its misleading character; "unperfected" is the Act's characterization of a security interest that has not been perfected and the effect of an unperfected security interest is to "subordinate" the security interest to the interest described in PPSA s. 22.

In the second place, the learned trial judge overlooked the effect of s. 7(2) conferring a perfected status on the New Brunswick security interest for a 60-day period. That period had not expired on September 3rd when the plaintiff purchased the vehicle from H. & J. Auto Centre. Prima facie, therefore, it was the plaintiff who had committed the act of conversion.

Professor Ziegel then posed the question which I have quoted above. Professor Ziegel's article was written prior to the time this Court heard an appeal by the defendant from the decision of Judge Staniszewski.

The judgment in that appeal is reported as *Trans Can. Credit Corp. v. Bachand* (1980), 30 OR (2d) 405, 1 PPSAC 185, 12 BLR 247, 117 DLR (3d) 653 (Ont. CA). On that appeal the appellant took the position that the perfection mentioned in s. 7(1) was absolute and although the holder of the security interest did nothing thereafter, if an innocent purchaser buys the goods during that 60-day period, the transaction is liable to be vitiated at any time thereafter; if he still has possession of the goods innocently purchased they can be seized, or, in any event he will be liable for their money value if he has disposed of them. The appellant relied on a decision of the New Jersey Supreme Court in *First Nat. Bank of Bay Shore v. Stamper*, 3 UCC Reporting Service 949, 225 A2d 162 (Sup. Ct. NJ 1966), which followed a decision of the New York Supreme Court, Appellate Division in *Churchill Motors Inc. v. A.C. Lohman Inc.*, 16 AD 2d 560, 229 NY 2d 570 (App. Div. 1962). In the latter case it was held that the four-month period provided in the Uniform Commercial Code for recording a conditional sales contract in a state to which property has been removed is not a grace period for filing, but is an absolute period of protection of vendor's security interest designed to give him time to locate the property. At 577 Justice Halpern said:

> Under the provisions of the Uniform Commercial Code, the conditional vendor's interest continued to be perfected interest for four months. At the end of the period, it ceased to be a perfected interest and became an unperfected one but there is no provision which forfeits the four month period of protection because of failure to file prior to its expiration.

The provisions of the UCC at the time of these decisions was similar in nature to those contained in s. 7(1) of the PPSA except that the period of protection was four months instead of 60 days. In *Trans Can. v. Bachand* this Court refused to follow the American line of cases. MacKinnon ACJO said at 408 [30 OR (2d)]:

> I can only say that I am not persuaded by the reasoning in that case and note that it is subject to some editorial criticism in the report.
>
> The appellant was given 60 days within which to locate the property covered by its security interest and perfect that interest in Ontario. If he perfects it within the 60-day period it continues to be perfected after the expiration of that period. But, if he fails to perfect it within the 60-day period but perfects it thereafter then under s. 7(3) "such perfection takes effect from the time of its perfection within Ontario." It clearly does not relate back to the

day when the collateral is brought into Ontario. To hold that the 60-day perfection is absolute without need for any subsequent action by the security holder could lead to obvious injustice to innocent parties. They would never be secure.

The appeal was accordingly dismissed. As previously mentioned the facts in *Trans Can. v. Bachand* are similar to those in the present case except that the grace period involved in the present case is the 15-day period allowed under s. 7(2) rather than the 60-day period allowed under s. 7(1) which does not affect the principle enunciated and except for the further fact that the present case involves a trustee in bankruptcy rather than a subsequent purchaser.

The appellant trustee in the present case relies on the decision of this Court in *Trans Can. v. Bachand*. GMAC, on the other hand, submits that the rationale in *Trans Can. v. Bachand* was that bona fide purchasers within the 60-day period should be protected from being dispossessed by a previously unknown secured party after the 60-day period has expired and that that is not a consideration in a bankruptcy case. In my view the submission of GMAC cannot prevail. In *Trans Can. v. Bachand* and in the present case financing statements were filed in Ontario after the expiration of the appropriate period of grace. The effect of the decision in *Trans Can. v. Bachand* was to treat a conditional sales agreement, properly perfected as a security interest in a foreign jurisdiction but not perfected in Ontario during the 60-day period after the collateral was brought into Ontario, as an unperfected security interest until the date of filing of the financing statement and accordingly the holder of the agreement had an unperfected security interest which was subordinated to the interest of a subsequent purchaser pursuant to the provisions of s. 22(1)(a)(i). Such subsequent purchaser acquired such priority as of the date of his purchase of the collateral.

In my view the principle enunciated in the *Trans Can.* case is that a security interest in collateral perfected under the law of jurisdiction in which the collateral was when the security interest attached and before being brought into Ontario becomes an unperfected security interest as of the date upon which the collateral is brought into Ontario if the person who owns such security interest fails to perfect it in Ontario within the times limited by s. 7(1) and (2), whichever is applicable, and it remains an unperfected security interest unless and until it is perfected as provided by s. 7(3). In my view this principle applies regardless of the manner in which the claimant, who claims an interest in priority to that of the unperfected security interest, has obtained his interest. The only question that remains to be decided in such a case is whether the claimant has obtained priority over the other contending party's security interest under the provisions of the PPSA.

It is of some interest to note that Minister of Consumer and Commercial Relations Advisory Committee on the Personal Property Security Act, presented to the Minister in April, 1984, a draft Personal Property Security Act. It is provided in s. 5(2) of that draft Act, which pertains to goods which have been brought into Ontario from another jurisdiction, as follows:

> 5(2) A security interest in goods perfected under the law of the jurisdiction in which the goods are situated at the time the security interest attaches but before the goods are brought into Ontario continues perfected in Ontario if it is perfected in Ontario,
>
> (a) within sixty days after the goods are brought into Ontario;

(b) within fifteen days after the day the secured party receives notice that the goods are brought into Ontario; or

(c) … whichever is the earliest.

This proposed sub-section is a revised version of s. 7(1) and (2) of the present Act and is in accord with the decision of the Court in *Trans Can. v. Bachand*.

In the present case, following this Court's decision in *Trans Can. v. Bachand*, the security interest of GMAC must be deemed to have been unperfected until June 28, 1983. The interest of the trustee was acquired therein on May 26, 1983 as provided by s. 22(2) of the PPSA. Accordingly, by virtue of the provisions of s. 22(1)(a)(iii), the unperfected security interest of GMAC in the van is subordinate to the interest of the trustee therein.

The appeal is therefore allowed, the order of the learned Judge in bankruptcy is set aside, and an order will go declaring that the security interest of GMAC in the 1982 Chevrolet van evidenced by a conditional sales contract dated September 8, 1982 is subordinate to the interest of the trustee therein. The trustee shall have its costs of this appeal and of the application in Bankruptcy Court.

Appeal allowed.

QUESTION

Re Adair was decided under the old OPPSA. Would it have been decided differently under s. 5(2) of the current Ontario Act?

Re Claude A. Bedard
(1983), 46 CBR (NS) 172 (Ont. SC)

SMITH J: This application is by the trustee for an order that the security interest claimed by the Banque Nationale du Canada in a 1982 Buick Serial No. 1G4AW69YOCH436461 is subordinate to the interest of the trustee.

The parties are completely *ad idem* on the facts. The assignment in bankruptcy was made on 10th September 1982. The bank filed a secured claim based upon a conditional sales contract acquired by the bank when it supplied the purchase moneys for the purchase by the bankrupt of the said automobile on 16th May 1982.

The security attached in the province of Quebec on the date of purchase. The parties agree however that there is no statutory framework for an act of registration or perfection in Quebec as there is under the Personal Property Security Act, RSO 1980, c. 375, in Ontario. The partial statement of facts, to which the parties agreed in writing and filed with the court, also states that the conditional sales contract between the two parties is binding against third parties in Quebec.

On the basis of the foregoing, the bank invites the court to conclude that the security interest was perfected in Quebec so as to enable it to take advantage of the conflict of laws provisions embodied in s. 7 of the Personal Property Security Act [cf. s. 5 of the current OPPSA]. They read as follows:

7(1) Subject to section 5, a security interest in collateral already perfected under the law of the jurisdiction in which the collateral was when the security interest attached and before being brought into Ontario continues perfected in Ontario for sixty days and also thereafter if within the sixty-day period it is perfected in Ontario. ...

(3) A security interest that has ceased to be perfected in Ontario due to the expiration of the sixty-day period may thereafter be perfected in Ontario, but such perfection takes effect from the time of its perfection in Ontario.

The collateral was brought into Ontario on 17th May 1982. The financing statement was registered by the bank on 20th July 1982, namely, 65 days after the security interest attached and 64 days after the vehicle was brought to Ontario.

Subject to the provisions of s. 7(2), to which I will turn in a moment, and leaving aside any question that may arise under s. 6, the bank is seeking a pronouncement by this court on the question of whether perfection of the security interest in the province of Quebec had occurred in the circumstances recited above on the theory that the bank in Quebec had acquired the greatest bundle of rights possible. I am prepared to accept that the principle of comity suggests, and the Act implies, that a functional equivalence will suffice. I need not pass upon the question however, nor would I be inclined to do so in the appropriate case, in the absence of additional expert evidence as to the state of the law of Quebec regarding protection of third parties.

The point is academic, for I am of the view that s. 7(2) disposes of the issue in this case. It reads:

(2) Notwithstanding subsection (1), where the secured party receives notice within the sixty-day period mentioned therein that the collateral has been brought into Ontario, his security interest in the collateral ceases to be perfected in Ontario unless he registers a financing statement in the prescribed form within fifteen days from the date that he receives such notice or upon the expiration of the sixty-day period, whichever is earlier.

The secured party knew that the car was for personal use and that the residence of the debtor was Ontario. It thereby *received notice* in the sense which must be ascribed to those words of *acquiring* notice. The interest accordingly ceased to be perfected after the expiration of 15 days and by virtue of s. 22 of the said Act it became subordinated to the interest of the trustee.

Application granted.

NOTES

1) As will be noted, Smith J did not find it necessary to decide whether a conditional sale concluded in Quebec is deemed to be a perfected security interest in Ontario. The Ontario Advisory Committee thought the position should be clarified. Section 8(2) of the current OPPSA provides:

8(2) For the purposes of this Part, a security interest shall be deemed to be perfected under the law of a jurisdiction if the secured party has complied with the law of the jurisdiction with respect to the creation and continuance of a security interest that is enforceable against the debtor and third parties.

Is the result too favourable to foreign secured parties? Should the extraprovincial security interest be treated as unperfected in Ontario unless the jurisdiction from which the goods are brought has a public register that a third party can consult to determine the existence of security interests, or would this result in Ontario imposing its chattel security law concepts on other jurisdictions?

2) The new Quebec *Civil Code*, which came into force in 1994, while adopting important elements of an Article 9 system, does not treat title retention agreements—that is, conditional sales—as creating a security interest in movables, that is, as a *hypothec*. Nevertheless, the Code requires conditional sale agreements to be perfected by registration. Presumably this avoids the hiatus between perfection requirements for conditional sale agreements in Ontario and Quebec that previously existed as illustrated by *Bedard*, above.

However, the same problem may arise between Ontario and other PPSA jurisdictions in Canada or between those jurisdictions and one of the American states with respect to non-security leases. Assume that a three-year lease for a trailer is concluded in North Dakota (an Article 9 state) between a lessor and lessee. The lease is treated as a non-security lease under North Dakota law. The lessee brings the trailer into Manitoba where it is seized by a creditor of the lessee. Because the lease is for more than a year, it will be deemed a security lease under the Manitoba PPSA and will be subject to reperfection requirements under the Act even though the lease is not a security lease under North Dakota law.

In addition, the lease may not be treated as a perfected security interest in Manitoba for the first 60 days or any other period after the trailer is brought into Manitoba because of the requirement in s. 7(4) of the Manitoba Act that the foreign security interest will be subordinated to an interest in the "goods" acquired in Manitoba if the extraprovincial jurisdiction does not provide for public registration or recording of the security interest or the filing of a notice relating to it. (Section 7(4) may be satisfied in this hypothetical situation if North Dakota has a certificate of title law applicable to trailers.) Cf. *Juckes (Trustee of) v. Holiday Chevrolet Oldsmobile (1983) Ltd.* (1990), 60 DLR (4th) 142 (Sask.) and J.S. Ziegel, Comment (1991), 17 *CBLJ* 303.

3) The obverse of the scenario discussed in Note 2, above, arose in *Re TCT Logistics Inc.* (2004), 70 OR (3d) 321 (CA). SP and D entered into a non-security lease of truck trailers for a term of more than one year. At the time, the OPPSA only applied to security leases. D's principal place of business was in Alberta. SP registered a financing statement there, but it got the debtor's name wrong. SP never registered a financing statement in Ontario because it assumed, correctly, that the Act did not apply. D went into bankruptcy and SP and the trustee both claimed the trailers. The case was litigated in Ontario.

The trustee argued that the mobile goods rule in OPPSA s. 7(1) applied (see Part IV, below) and so the governing law was the law of D's location; that is, Alberta. SP's Alberta registration was ineffective and so it was unperfected in Alberta. SP argued that OPPSA s. 7(1) did not apply because there was no "security interest" as defined in the Act. In the absence of a statutory choice of law rule, the common law applied and, at common law, Ontario law would have governed.

The court rejected SP's argument, holding that the references to "security interest" in the PPSA conflicts provisions are not limited to a security interest as defined in the Act. The rationale was that otherwise there might be different results, depending on where the case was litigated. For example, if the case was litigated in Ontario, then the outcome might be the one SP was arguing for. But if the case was litigated in Alberta, the Alberta court would have to apply the Alberta conflicts rules. The Alberta equivalent of s. 7(1) *would* apply because a non-security lease for a term of more than one year does create a security interest within the meaning of the Alberta PPSA. For a critical comment on the case, see Jacob S. Ziegel, "Ontario PPSA Choice of Law Rules and Ambulatory Definition of Security Interest: *GMAC Commercial Credit Corp. v. TCT Logistics Inc.* (2004), 40 *CBLJ* 412. What is the significance of *TCT Logistics* now that the Ontario PPSA applies to any lease for a term of more than one year?

IV. THE DESTINATION OF GOODS RULE AND THE MOBILE GOODS RULE

Consider the following case:

> D owns a newspaper business in Ontario. On March 1, D buys a printing press from Seller in Saskatchewan. D borrows money from SP1 to pay for the press. SP1 takes a security interest in the press and registers a financing statement in Saskatchewan. On March 15, Seller delivers the press to D's plant in Ontario. On April 1, D gives SP2 a general security interest and SP2 registers a financing statement in Ontario. On April 15, SP1 registers a financing statement in Ontario. D defaults against both SP1 and SP2 and they both claim the press.

OPPSA s. 6(1) may apply. It provides as follows:

> 6(1) Subject to section 7, if the parties to a security agreement creating a security interest in goods in one jurisdiction understand at the time the security interest attaches that the goods will be kept in another jurisdiction, and the goods are removed to that other jurisdiction, for purposes other than transportation through the other jurisdiction, within thirty days after the security interest attached, the validity, perfection and effect of perfection or non-perfection of the security interest shall be governed by the law of the other jurisdiction.

OPPSA s. 6(1) is an exception to the rule in s. 5(1). Where s. 5(1) applies, the law of the other jurisdiction governs until the goods are brought into Ontario. For s. 6(1) to apply, there has to be an understanding between SP and D that the goods will be kept in the other jurisdiction. Is this requirement satisfied in our example? Assuming that it is, what will be the outcome of the dispute?

The so-called "mobile goods rule" is in OPPSA s. 7(1), which provides in relevant part as follows:

> 7(1) The validity, the perfection, the effect of perfection or non-perfection and the priority,
>> (a) of a security interest in, ...
>>> (ii) goods that are of a type that are normally used in more than one jurisdiction, if the goods are equipment or inventory leased or held for lease by a debtor to others ...
> shall be governed by the law of the jurisdiction where the debtor is located at the time the security interest attaches.

OPPSA s. 7(4) provides that the debtor is deemed to be located at its place of business, if there is one, at the debtor's chief executive office if there is more than one place of business, and otherwise at the debtor's principal place of residence. The 2006 amendments have made some changes to the conflict of laws provisions, including a new test for the debtor's location. The new test provides that if the debtor is an individual, she is located at her principal place of residence, regardless of where she carries on business, and if the debtor is a corporation incorporated under provincial law, it is located in its province of incorporation. The new provision goes on to specify rules for the case where the debtor is a corporation incorporated under federal law, where the debtor is a US corporation, and where the debtor is a partnership or trust. The main aim of the new provisions is to bring the PPSA conflicts rules more closely into line with the Article 9 conflicts rules. The advantage of the place of incorporation test is that it is more certain than the place of business and location of executive office tests. The new conflicts provisions have not yet been proclaimed because Ontario is waiting for the other provinces to enact corresponding provisions.

Gimli Auto Ltd. v. BDO Dunwoody Ltd.
(1998), 160 DLR (4th) 373 (Alta. CA)

CÔTÉ JA:

A. Issues

[1] This is a priority dispute over motor vehicles, between two lessors and the lessee's trustee in bankruptcy. The issues argued were where to register, and the constitutionality of letting a trustee in bankruptcy prevail. (Since then, the second issue has become obvious.)

B. Facts

[2] The bankrupt was in the business of renting out trucks with campers on them to tourists for short periods. It did not own three pickup trucks. It in turn leased them for three years from their owner, the appellant Gimli. Gimli carries on business in Manitoba, and the lease was apparently entered into there. At that time Manitoba statutes did not require registration of pure leases (though that law is now being changed). The leases of the three trucks were not registered anywhere. The bankrupt company brought the three trucks to Alberta, where its head office and chief place of business was. It apparently used them in Alberta as part of its tourist rental business.

[3] The bankrupt had a branch of its business in Surrey, British Columbia. There it made a long-term lease of a passenger vehicle owned by the appellant Eagle Ridge. The bankrupt lessee kept the auto in British Columbia, and apparently its staff used it; it was not rented out farther. That car lease was registered in British Columbia, but not elsewhere.

[4] Since bankruptcy occurred before any registration in Alberta, the trustee in bankruptcy has rejected the claims of these two lessors. (Claims respecting other vehicles have since been compromised.)

C. Priorities Legislation

[5]   Alberta's *Personal Property Security Act* (PPSA) in effect provides that the interest of a lessor for over a year is "not effective" against a trustee in bankruptcy if that interest is not perfected before bankruptcy: see RSA c. P-4.05 55. 1(qq)(ii)(C) and 20(1)(b)(i). If that legislation is constitutional, and if Alberta law applies, it is common ground that therefore the trustee will prevail and the lessors will lose the vehicles. That is plainly correct.

[6]   That is because if Alberta law applies, it requires registration in Alberta, and there was none. On the other hand, if British Columbia law applies to the automobile, the lessor Eagle Ridge will prevail because that lease was registered in British Columbia. And if Manitoba law applies to the three trucks, then the lessor Gimli will prevail because Manitoba's PPSA did not require registration, as it did not apply to pure leases. The Supreme Court of Canada now discusses that at length in *Re Giffen* ... . [See Chapter 5.] It holds that the PPSA replaces common-law rules such as *nemo dat*, and title versus possession, with new statutory priority rules.

D. Conflict of Laws

[7]   Therefore, the first issue is conflict of laws. One does not even reach the issue of whether part of Alberta's PPSA is constitutional, unless Alberta law applies to at least some of the vehicles in issue.

[8]   One need not consider common-law choice-of-law rules, because Alberta's PPSA replaces them with new statutory choice-of-law rules. (So do all the other PPSAs, and they are very similar, though that probably does not matter much here.)

[9]   Nor need one consider a choice-of-law clause in a lease, for the statute sets which law applies. Nor is this a suit between two parties to a contract. The whole point of the PPSA is to overrule certain contractual or property rights: *Re Giffen*, supra. The lessor and lessee could not, by contracting that the lease would be valid even if not registered, bind others. This is legislation on priorities: ibid.

[10]   The appellant's argument relied on s. 8 of Alberta's PPSA. But I am satisfied that that section only governs rights of enforcement as between the original parties to the lease (or their assigns), such as seizure and sale. It has nothing to do with priorities contests. The textbooks agree. See, for example, Cuming and Wood, *Alberta Personal Property Security Act Handbook* 108 (3d ed. 1996).

[11]   Sections 5 through 7 do deal with which law governs perfection or priorities. Section 5(1) begins "Subject to this Act ... ," so if it conflicts or overlaps with s. 6 or s. 7, the latter must govern. Section 6 is not on point, for it refers to goods to be removed from the jurisdiction. That plainly does not apply to the automobile. Whether it could apply to the three trucks is unclear, but s. 6 is expressly subject to s. 7. Therefore, if s. 7 applies, it prevails.

E. The Three Gimli Trucks

[12]   Section 7(2)(a)(ii) of Alberta's PPSA [Ont. s. 7(i)(a)(ii)] applies to "goods that are of a kind that are normally used in more than 1 jurisdiction, if the goods are equipment or are inventory leased or held for lease by the debtor to others. ..." The three

IV. The Destination of Goods Rule and the Mobile Goods Rule 543

trucks were plainly such inventory, leased out to tourists. So whether they were also "equipment," I need not decide.

[13] Most trucks are equipment of a type that is used in more than one jurisdiction. They are easily capable of crossing a provincial or national border. Indeed, trucks often do so as part of the business of carrying goods. One case holds that they fit within s. 7 (or its equivalent): *Ens Toyota v. Megill Stephenson Co.* (1989) 81 Sask. R 22, 9 PPSAC 169. (I do not suggest that it is enough that trucks are capable of crossing borders and being driven on both sides.)

[14] The issue is not how these three particular trucks were actually used, or even the intention of this lessee (though rental to tourists would seem to qualify). Rather the issue is how trucks in general (or pickup trucks in general) "are normally used."

[15] Lest the paucity of authority in Canada, or its reasoning, cause unease, one may look at the United States' Uniform Commercial Code. Its s. 9-103(3)(a) expressly says that "motor vehicles" are an example of equipment of a type normally used in more than one jurisdiction. (There is an exception for vehicles whose very title is registered under a sort of Torrens system, as many American vehicles are, but that does not apply here.)

[16] That American Code is very relevant, for two reasons. In the first place, the Canadian PPSAs were closely modelled on the American legislation, and specifically on the UCC s. 9: Cuming and Wood, *Alberta Personal Property Security Handbook* 1-5 (3d ed. 1996). So copying the precise words "of a type normally used in more than one jurisdiction" implies that the American meaning would guide us. (Changing the word "type" to "kind" seems immaterial.) And in the second place, one of the major reasons to enact PPSAs was to make the law uniform, and so facilitate doing business in more than one jurisdiction: Henson, *Handbook on Secured Transactions* 4 (2d ed. 1979); McLaren, *Secured Transactions in Personal Property in Canada* 1.01 (pp. 1-3 to 1-6) (1989). It is therefore undesirable to interpret part of Alberta's PPSA in a way different from the established American meaning of the same or similar words. That is doubly true of conflict of laws sections. Such inconsistent interpretations would defeat one of the major purposes of these statutes. And it might defeat settled expectations and transactions based on them.

[17] Therefore, section 7 applies to the three pickup trucks, and Alberta law governs. That is because the debtor (lessee) had its chief executive office in Alberta, and so s. 7 deemed the debtor (lessee) to be in Alberta. There was no registration at all, so the lessor's interest was not perfected. So the trustee in bankruptcy of the lessee prevails under s. 20 (if it is constitutional).

F. *The Eagle Ridge Automobile*

[18] Priority over the automobile is not so straightforward.

[19] There is no Canadian authority directly on the subject of passenger automobiles, so far as I know. But for reasons given above, I conclude that all motor vehicles are goods of a type used in more than one jurisdiction. I adopt the American view.

[20] Motor vehicles cross every border thousands of times a day. As many sedans cross borders as do trucks. Almost every sedan crosses provincial, state or national borders in its operational life. Even a private passenger vehicle kept in Calgary or Edmonton probably does so every one or two years.

[21] Furthermore, only Alberta and Newfoundland have large cities hundreds of miles from any border. None of the other provinces or states do. Most centres of population in Canada (and the USA) are very close to provincial, state or national boundaries. There a sedan which rarely or never crosses a border must be very unusual.

[22] Therefore, I conclude that all passenger motor vehicles are "of a kind that are normally used in more than one jurisdiction."

[23] But that does not complete the test in s. 7(2)(a)(ii). It also speaks of equipment or inventory leased or held for lease by the debtor to others. I take that to refer to a further (sub) lease, not to the very lease which is the security interest. So this automobile was not leased or held for lease to others.

[24] However, the two branches of s. 7(2)(a)(ii) are alternative: the references to equipment and to leased inventory are separated by the word "or." Furthermore, they are also separated by the word "are," so it is plain that "equipment" need not be held for re-lease.

[25] Section 1(o) defines "equipment" as any goods held by the debtor which are neither inventory nor consumer goods. This company car plainly does not fit within the definition of "inventory" in s. 1(w). And "consumer goods" are defined in s. 1(h) as "goods used or acquired for use primarily for personal, family or household purposes." Plainly the car is not a consumer good, and so it is "equipment." Therefore, it satisfies the first branch of s. 7(2)(a)(ii).

[26] Therefore, s. 7(2) says that the governing law is the law of the jurisdiction where the debtor was located. Section 7(2) says that law includes conflict rules. The reference to conflicts rules could in theory create a renvoi (reference back), but as the British Columbia and Alberta statutes appear to contain the same rules, that becomes academic. It was argued that the chambers judge appealed from created a renvoi respecting the automobile. Since the two laws are the same, that ceases to be a concern.

[27] Where the debtor is located is defined by s. 7(1) to be his place of business. If he has more than one place of business, as this lessee did, then it is "his chief executive office." The evidence here clearly indicates that that was in Alberta, and the chambers judge so found. Aside from a suggestion of misrepresentation, that fact finding was not challenged on appeal. So Alberta law would apply if there was no misrepresentation. As there was no registration in Alberta, the lessor's interest was not perfected before bankruptcy, and by s. 20 the trustee would prevail.

G. Misrepresentation

[28] The lessor has another argument against that result. It contends that the bankrupt misrepresented its chief executive office as being in British Columbia, because the place in the printed lease form for chief executive office was not filled in, but left blank. The clause began by saying that the lessee declared its chief executive office was located at the address filled in in the heading, or at the place in the blank. The address filled in in the heading was the address of the local Surrey BC branch office of the lessee. The lessor appellant contends that that is a misrepresentation, and that the trustee in bankruptcy cannot take clear of the bankrupt's misrepresentation. (I doubt the last *nemo dat* proposition, given *Re Giffen*, supra.)

[29] Even if that proposition is correct, a chambers application is a poor place to try questions of misrepresentation. Who filled in the address blank on the lease? Who was supposed to fill in the chief executive office blank? Did the lessor know that that information was incorrect? Did the lessor rely upon that information? Did it suffer any detriment? Is that blank in the lease why it registered in British Columbia and not in Alberta? Any evidence on that subject before the chambers judge was third-hand hearsay, and he properly refused to admit it.

[30] Yet misrepresentation would ordinarily require a representation of fact by the lessee or its authorized agent. It would not have legal effect unless it was made either carelessly or with a certain state of mind. And there would be no effect without detrimental reliance by the lessor. I have no way of telling whether those conditions are met here. I repeat my rhetorical questions above.

[31] I would send the misrepresentation issue alone back to the same judge to hear oral evidence and try that one issue. (If he is unable or unwilling to act, then any Queen's Bench judge can try the issue.) Title to the car awaits the result of that. The trustee in bankruptcy will prevail unless operative misrepresentation is found. But this issue has no effect on title to the three Gimli trucks.

H. Constitutional Question

[32] The other objection by the lessor was the constitutionality of s. 20 of the PPSA. The Supreme Court of Canada in *Re Giffen*, supra, has now reversed the British Columbia Court of Appeal, and held that the equivalent section in British Columbia's PPSA is constitutional. Indeed, the provincial PPSA does not even conflict with the federal *Bankruptcy and Insolvency Act*, says the Supreme Court of Canada. The former is valid priorities legislation, and it defines the property rights which the trustee has.

...

Judgment for the trustee with respect to the three trucks.

NOTE

The mobile goods rule avoids the need for SP to register in every province if the collateral is mobile. Where the rule applies, SP only has to register in D's home province. Likewise, the rule avoids the need for a searcher to search in every province.

Given these benefits, is there a case for making the debtor's location the general choice of law rule? As it happens, this is more or less what the Americans have done in Revised Article 9. The reason the United States moved to a universal debtor location rule was to save on registration and search costs. There are 50 American states and so, under a location of the goods test (*lex situs*), a secured party or searcher wanting to guard against the risk of relocated goods would have to file and search up to 50 times. It is true that under a location of the debtor rule, there is a risk that the debtor might relocate. However, debtors relocate less often than goods do and so the risk is smaller. The issue is a less pressing one in Canada, given the smaller number of provinces.

V. SECURITY INTERESTS IN INTANGIBLES, ETC.

Section 7(1) provides in part:

> 7(1) The validity, the perfection, the effect of perfection or non-perfection and the priority,
>
>> (a) of a security interest in,
>>
>>> (i) an intangible, or
>>>
>>> (ii) ... and
>>
>> (b) of a non-possessory security interest in an instrument, a negotiable document of title, money and chattel paper,
>
> shall be governed by the law of the jurisdiction where the debtor is located at the time the security interest attaches.

For goods and other tangibles, the general rule is s. 5; in other words, the test is the location of the collateral when the security interest attaches. For obvious reasons, a location of the collateral test will not work if the collateral is intangible and so the statute substitutes the debtor location test.

The debtor location test applies to non-possessory security interests in instruments, documents of title, money, and chattel paper because these types of collateral are all highly mobile, and so the rationale is the same as for the mobile goods rule.

VI. SECURITY INTERESTS IN INVESTMENT PROPERTY

John Cameron, "Secured Transactions Under Ontario's Security Transfer Act, 2006"
(2007), 22 *BFLR* 309, at 349-51 (footnotes omitted)

The new conflict of laws rules in section 7.1 deal with the validity of a security interest in investment property separate from the perfection and priority of a security interest in investment property.

(a) Validity

The validity of a security interest in investment property is addressed by section 7.1(1), the material portion of which provides that:

> (1) The validity of a security interest in investment property shall be governed by the law, at the time the security interest attaches,
>
>> (a) of the jurisdiction where the certificate is located if the collateral is a certificated security;
>>
>> (b) of the issuer's jurisdiction if the collateral is an uncertificated security;
>>
>> (c) of the securities intermediary's jurisdiction if the collateral is a security entitlement or a securities account; ...

Clause 7.1(1)(a) and 7.1(1)(b) deal with the direct holding system, and clause 7.1(1)(c) deals with the indirect holding system. The issuer's jurisdiction is determined under section 44 of the STA, and the securities intermediary's jurisdiction is determined by section 45 of the STA, each of which is discussed below.

(b) Perfection and Priority

Simplifying the rules slightly:

- *Registration*—The perfection by registration of a security interest in investment property is governed by the location of the debtor. The location of a debtor is defined in section 7(3) by reference to the traditional PPSA test which looks to the debtor's chief executive office in the case of a debtor with more than one place of business.
- *Certificated security*—Apart from perfection by registration, the perfection and priority of a security interest in a certificated security is governed by the location of the certificate.
- *Uncertificated security*—Apart from perfection by registration, the perfection and priority of a security interest in an uncertificated security is governed by the issuer's jurisdiction, discussed below.
- *Security entitlement*—Apart from registration, the perfection and priority of a security interest in a security entitlement is governed by the securities intermediary's jurisdiction, discussed below.
- *Issuer's jurisdiction*—Apart from Crown issuers (whose securities would not be uncertificated unless held in a clearing system such as CDS, in which case the jurisdiction of the securities intermediary is the only relevant jurisdiction in day-to-day practice), section 44(5) of the STA defines an "issuer's jurisdiction" to be the jurisdiction in which a Canadian federally incorporated issuer has its registered or head office (or if permitted by federal law, another jurisdiction specified by the issuer), and otherwise is the jurisdiction in which an issuer is incorporated or organized (or if permitted by the law of that jurisdiction, another jurisdiction specified by the issuer).
- *Securities intermediary's jurisdiction*—Section 45(2) defines the securities intermediary's jurisdiction according to a series of rules which apply in sequence until a particular rule addresses the facts. In essence, these rules allow the agreement between the securities intermediary and entitlement holder to specify the jurisdiction which is to be the securities intermediary's jurisdiction. Failing that choice, then the law governing the securities account agreement is the securities intermediary's jurisdiction. The vast majority of situations will fall into one of these first two rules; so the other rules are not likely to be relevant and are not summarized here.

Sections 7.1(6) and 7.1(7) of the PPSA contain rules to address a change of debtor location, and a change of the issuer's jurisdiction or securities intermediary's jurisdiction, each of which require that steps be taken to perfect in the new jurisdiction within specific periods of time.

VII. ENFORCEMENT

Cardel Leasing Ltd. v. Maxmenko
(1991), 2 PPSAC (2d) 302 (Ont. Gen. Div.)

ADAMS J: The issue in this matter centres on whether a vehicle leasing company with its head office in Ontario can enforce in Ontario an agreement with a resident of British Columbia and essentially performed in that province where British Columbia law would preclude such enforcement but where the parties to the agreement have chosen Ontario's law and courts.

The parties have agreed to the following Statement of Facts:

1. The Defendant entered into an agreement (the "Agreement") dated June 30, 1987 with the Plaintiff for the lease of a 1986 Volvo automobile (the "Automobile").

2. The Agreement was signed by the Defendant in British Columbia and at the time that it was signed the Defendant was a resident of British Columbia.

3. According to the Agreement, the monthly payments were $645.00 plus sales tax of $38.70.

4. There was a deposit held by the Plaintiff equal to one month's payment (including taxes) of $683.70.

5. The Agreement also contained a buy out provision in the amount of $8,000.00 plus provincial sales tax.

6. The Plaintiff was at the material times a company with its head office in Ontario and pursuant to paragraph 25 of the Agreement, the Agreement became effective at the time of its acceptance by an officer of the Plaintiff at Toronto.

7. In or about February of 1988, the Plaintiff considered that the Defendant's lease payments to the Plaintiff had fallen into arrears.

8. On or about April 12, 1988, the Automobile was repossessed by the Plaintiff's agents in British Columbia and sold there. At the time, the Defendant was a resident of British Columbia.

9. It is alleged by the Plaintiff that the Automobile was sold by the Plaintiff to a car dealership for $20,300.00.

10. The Agreement contained, inter alia, the following provision:

CHOICE OF LAW (25) This Agreement shall not be effective unless and until accepted by an officer of the Lessor at Toronto, Ontario. This Agreement shall be governed by and construed in accordance with the laws of the Province of Ontario. If, however, any provision herein in any way contravenes the laws of any Province or jurisdiction where this Agreement is to be performed so as to be invalid or unenforceable, such provision shall be deemed not to be part of this Agreement, but such an event shall not void or affect any remaining provisions of this Agreement; and no action shall be brought to construe or enforce this Agreement or otherwise with respect to it except in the Courts of the Province of Ontario, to whose jurisdiction the Customer hereby attorns.

11. Clause 16 of the Agreement provides, inter alia, that the Plaintiff is entitled to repossess the Automobile.

12. That aspect of performance of the Agreement in repossessing the Automobile took place in British Columbia.

13. Clause 18 of the Agreement provides that the Plaintiff is entitled to damages as follows:

> Damages (18) The Lessor may, without notice, but shall not be obliged to, sell such vehicles, or any of them at public or private sale or sales, upon such terms as it may deem advisable, and in the event of such sale or sales the Lessor shall in addition to all other rights or remedies hereunder, be entitled to retain as liquidated damages and not as penalty all proceeds of any and all such sales, and to recover from the Customer, all additional rents in respect of the vehicles sold, determined in respect of each vehicle as provided in Article (11). The Lessor may bid for or purchase any or all of said vehicles at any such sale. Upon default of the Customer, the Lessor may retain all rents, payments, deposits, downpayments and resale proceeds theretofore received, including refunds and other sums, if any, otherwise payable to the Customer hereunder, and the Lessor shall be entitled to recover from the Customer, as liquidated damages and not as penalty:
>
> (a) the proceeds of any and all sales of the vehicles in accordance with the preceding paragraph; and in addition thereto;
>
> (b) any and all losses incurred by the Lessor on the resale of the vehicles; and
>
> (c) a cancellation fee equivalent to three months' rental at the rate provided in Schedule "A"; and
>
> (d) any and all unpaid monthly rents for the balance of the rental terms of the vehicles, and all additional sums, if any, due and unpaid; together with costs and expenses, including legal fees and expenses, incurred by the Lessor in the enforcement of its rights and remedies under this or any other provision of this agreement, it being expressly understood and agreed that these remedies are cumulative, and that the Lessor shall not be obliged to elect any one remedy, but is entitled to recover damages under all of the heads of damage aforesaid.

14. The provisions of the Agreement described in paragraphs 11 and 13 above which permit the Plaintiff to repossess the Automobile and at the same time pursue other remedies to collect damages are contrary to the laws of British Columbia as follows.

15. Subsections 19(1) and 19(2) and section 22 of the Sale of Goods on Condition Act. RSBC 28, Eliz. 2, 1979, c. 373 provided at the material time the following:

> 19(1) Subject to subsection (4) and section 23, a seller may enforce his right to recover money due and owing under a conditional sale either
>
> (a) by taking possession of the goods, on a surrender or pursuant to the contract; or
>
> (b) by suing the buyer for the money due and owing,
>
> but not both.

19(2) Where the seller takes possession of the goods, the buyer's obligations and the obligations of the guarantor or indemnitor under the contract and in any instrument granting collateral security are extinguished.

22 A waiver or release of any benefit given by sections 19 to 24, except if given by a corporation, is void.

16. These provisions referred to in paragraph 15 were in effect at all the material times during the currency of the Agreement.

17. There is no similar provision in an Ontario statute.

Mr. Summers, on behalf of the plaintiff, agreed that suing and seizing is not permitted under British Columbia law but asserted that clause 25 of the agreement provides that Ontario law is to govern and that Ontario does not require an election between these two remedies. While the last sentence of clause 25 contemplates the possibility that a provision of the agreement may contravene the laws of another province so as to be invalid and unenforceable, counsel submitted that this action is in an Ontario court; is subject to Ontario law; and that nothing has happened to render any clause in the agreement invalid or unenforceable. Mr. Summer's second submission was that the second sentence of clause 25 is quite specific in limiting its effect to the contravention of a law "where this agreement is to be performed." He submitted that the aspect of performance now complained of by the defendant is this action for damages which is being "performed" in Ontario and where there is no law precluding the bringing of such a law suit. It was further argued that this agreement does not in any way offend British Columbia law because the agreement does not require Cardel to seize and sue but rather permits it to do so. Finally, it was submitted that, while the plaintiff could not sue in the courts of British Columbia because of the "procedural effect" of section 19(1) of the Sale of Goods on Condition Act, this "procedural" provision can have no effect before an Ontario court as in *243930 Alberta Ltd. v. Wickham* (1967), 61 OR (2d) 731, a decision of Mr. Justice McKeown.

On behalf of the defendant, it was submitted that this court should not permit an action which would give effect to a contractual provision where its performance is illegal in the place of performance. Mr. Rosenhek argued that clause 18 of the agreement is illegal or unenforceable by the laws of British Columbia which foreclose the option of suing upon electing repossession of the vehicle. He further submitted that section 19(2) of the Sale of Goods on Condition Act is clearly substantive in that it explicitly extinguishes the buyers obligations under the agreement following repossession. It was pointed out that the plaintiff, in drafting the agreement, contemplated that laws of another province could have application and specifically provided for this event. Alternatively, counsel contended that because the contract was drafted by the plaintiff it was subject to the doctrine of contra proferentum whereby any ambiguity in clause 25 must be construed against the interests of the plaintiff.

Mr. Summers, in reply, emphasized that the defendant had agreed to the application of Ontario law and that this choice of law governs in accordance with *Vita Food Products Inc. v. Unus Shipping Co. Ltd.*, [1939] AC 277.

I have decided the action is to be dismissed.

Where the parties to a contract expressly stipulate that an agreement shall be governed by a particular law, that law will generally be the proper law of the contract. See *Vita Food Products Inc. v. Unus Shipping Co. Ltd.*, supra, at p. 290. This freedom of choice, however, is subject to certain limitations. As Lord Wright in the *Vita Food Products* case observed, the selection must be bona fide and legal and there must be no reason for avoiding the choice on the ground of public policy. As an example, Professor Castel points out in his treatise that where a law is expressly chosen to evade the provisions of the system of law with which the transaction, objectively, is most closely connected, that choice will be disregarded. See J.-G. Castel, *Canadian Conflict of Laws*, 2nd ed. (1986), at p. 531. The learned author also notes at page 554 that there is substantial weight of authority in support of the proposition that a contract illegal by the law of the country where it is to be performed will not be enforced notwithstanding the explicit choice of law of the contracting parties. Examples of this exception are: *Ralli Bros. v. Compania Naviera Sota y Aznar*, [1920] 2 KB 287 (CA); *Kleinwort Sons and Co. v. Ungarische Baumwolle Industrie AG*, [1939] 2 KB 678 at 697; *Regazzoni v. K.C. Sethia (1944) Ltd.*, [1958] AC 301 at 319.

The second sentence in clause 25 of the agreement explicitly anticipates application of something akin to these principles by providing:

> If, however, any provision herein in any way contravenes the laws of any Province or jurisdiction where this Agreement is to be performed so as to be invalid or unenforceable, such provisions shall be deemed not to be part of this Agreement. ...

It is the defendant's position that clause 18 contravenes subsections 19(1) and 19(2) and section 22 of the Sale of Goods on Condition Act in British Columbia and that the performance of the agreement was in that province. The plaintiff submits that it is the performance of the provision being challenged that must be within British Columbia and that clause 18, in light of clause 25, contemplates performance in Ontario (i.e. the recovery of any and all unpaid monthly rents for the balance of the rental term of the vehicle). I find the defendant's position more closely accords to the meaning of the contract and the policy of conflict of laws analysis in cases of this kind.

The contract is styled "Vehicle Lease Agreement." The defendant leased the vehicle from the plaintiff in British Columbia and enjoyed the use of the car there. The defendant was resident throughout the term of the agreement in British Columbia. He did not purchase it in Ontario and then move to the west. The car was seized and sold in British Columbia when the defendant failed to honour the payments in that province. Presumably a demand for the balance of the payments was made upon him in British Columbia pursuant to clause 18. In the light of these facts, I find that British Columbia was the place of performance of the contract and that the contract has its most substantial connection with that province notwithstanding the technical effect of the first sentence of clause 25.

This being the case, subsections 19(1), 19(2) and section 22 of the British Columbia Sale of Goods on Condition Act rendered unenforceable and, indeed, extinguished the plaintiff's entitlement to recover the unpaid monthly rents upon it taking possession of the vehicle which it has admitted it did. Section 22 of the Act specifically precludes contracting out of the benefits accorded to an individual by sections 19 to 24. Unlike the situation in *243930 Alberta Ltd., v. Wickham*, supra, where this court found an Alberta law limiting the right of a mortgagee to sue on a covenant to be procedural and thus not applicable in Ontario, subsection 19(2) actually extinguishes the buyer's obligations under the contract when a seller takes possession. For this reason, the combined effect of subsections 19(1), 19(2) and section 22 is not simply "a procedural limitation." Rather, section 19(2) amounts to a "substantive" elimination of a debt and together all of these provisions render clause 18 of the agreement invalid or unenforceable within the meaning of clause 25 insofar as the former clause contemplates the plaintiff having the right to seize the vehicle as well as the right to demand the payment or recovery of outstanding rental payments. See *Alberta Treasury Branches v. Granoff* (1984), 15 DLR (4th) 295 and the cases cited therein. Further, as a matter of comity between provincial systems of laws, this decision is fuelled by a reluctance to ignore the consumer oriented policy expressed by section 22 of statute in question when the performance of the contract is so substantially connected with British Columbia save for clause 25.

Finally, while the plaintiff's proposed interpretation of clause 25 is a possible one, the broader meaning of "performance" proposed by the defendant is, at least, equally tenable. Applying the contra proferentem rule of construction, the defendant's interpretation is to be preferred. ...

Action dismissed.

NOTE

The immediate ground of the decision in *Cardel* was the third sentence of the choice of law provision in clause 25 of the agreement. However, the judgment implies that, even in the absence of this sentence, the court would have found in the defendant's favour: "I find the defendant's position more closely accords to the meaning of the contract *and the policy of conflict of laws analysis in cases of this kind*" (emphasis added). The judgment seems to suggest that the courts should not give effect to a choice of law clause in a consumer contract if the consequence is to displace the law of the place where the agreement is to be performed. Is there any basis in OPPSA s. 8(1)(b) for such an approach? How would Adams J have approached the case if it was *Ontario*, not British Columbia, that had the seize or sue provision?

CHAPTER FIFTEEN

Federal Security Interests

I. INTRODUCTION

Personal property security interests for the most part are governed by provincial laws. The PPSAs establish comprehensive regimes for the creation, registration, priority, and enforcement of personal property security interests. However, federal laws also play an important role. For example, *Bank Act*, SC 1991, c. 46, s. 427 establishes a special regime for security interests in inventory and other goods given to banks by retailers, traders, and manufacturers and also in farming, fishing, mining, and forestry concerns. The antecedents of *Bank Act* s. 427 go back to the early days of Confederation at a time when provincial chattel security law was very cumbersome and not lender friendly. The interaction between *Bank Act* s. 427 and the provincial PPSAs raises complex and difficult questions.

Patent Act, RSC 1985, c. P-4, s. 51 establishes a registration system for patent assignments. Insofar as the provision covers security assignments, there is a potential for overlap with the provincial PPSAs and the relationship between the two regimes has yet to be determined. *Copyright Act*, RSC 1985, c. C-42, s. 57(3) provides for the registration of copyright assignments. This provision raises similar issues to *Patent Act* s. 51 in terms of its relationship with the provincial PPSAs. See also *Plant Breeders' Rights Act*, SC 1990, c. 20, s. 31(3); *Industrial Design Act*, RSC 1985, c. I-9, s. 19; *Trade-marks Act*, RSC 1985, c. T-13, s. 48(3); and *Integrated Circuit Topography Act*, SC 1990, c. 37, s. 21—all of which raise more or less similar issues.

Other examples of federal involvement in personal property security law include the *Canada Shipping Act, 2001*, SC 2001, c. 26, which establishes a regime for the registration and enforcement of ship mortgages, and the *Canada Transportation Act*, SC 1996, c. 10, which deals with security interests in rolling stock and other railway company assets.

Part II of this chapter deals with *Bank Act* s. 427, Part III deals with the federal intellectual property statutes and their interaction with the PPSAs, Part IV gives a short account of the interaction problems that arise in relation to ship mortgages, and Part V addresses international developments.

II. THE BANK ACT SECURITY INTEREST

Roderick J. Wood, "The Nature and Definition of Federal Security Interests"
(2000), 34 *CBLJ* 65, at 71-75 (footnotes omitted)

The Bank Act security system is the most complete of the federal statutes governing security interests in personal property. Unlike the other federal provisions dealing with security interests in personal property, the Bank Act security provisions are not premised on the terminology and concepts of Victorian era, Anglo-Canadian chattel security law. In many respects, the Bank Act security device was far ahead of its time in introducing innovative features into the law of secured financing. Because of this, there is a greater degree of conceptual affinity between the approach to secured financing adopted in the Bank Act and the approach of the *PPSA*. These features, which are familiar to those who are acquainted with the *PPSA*, are summarized below.

(a) *Notice Filing System:* The early provincial chattel registries were document registration systems in which the actual security documents were filed at the registry. The Bank Act security system in 1923 became the first personal property registry system in Canada to adopt a notice filing system. Instead of registering the security document, a bank registers a document called a notice of intention in the Bank of Canada registry.

(b) *Centralized Registry System:* The Bank Act registry system was more highly centralized than its provincial counterparts. At a time when local filings in the county or district were the norm, the Bank Act provided a single registry within the province. In addition, multiple registrations or searches of the different Bank of Canada registries will not generally be required because the notice of intention is only required to be registered at the Bank of Canada registry in the province in which the principal place of business of the debtor is located.

(c) *Fixed Security in After-Acquired Property:* The Bank Act permits the granting of a fixed security interest in the collateral. The security attaches automatically to the debtor's after-acquired property, but does not carry the inferior priority status of an equitable interest or the subtle complexities of a floating charge.

(d) *Future Advances:* The Bank Act permits the lender to tack further advances. It thereby abandoned the rule in *Hopkinson v. Rolt* in favour of a rule that promotes inventory financing by recognizing the efficacy of a security interest in circulating assets to secure a revolving credit facility.

(e) *Fixture Provisions:* The Bank Act contains fixture financing provisions that permit the bank to remove a fixture from real property to which it has become affixed. However, in order to have priority over subsequent real property interest holders, the bank is required to register a notice of it in the provincial land registry system.

(f) *Commingled Property Rule:* The Bank Act provides that if the collateral is used to manufacture or produce goods, the security continues in those goods. It does not, however, attempt to work out a system of priorities governing competing security in the product or mass.

(g) *Wage-Earner and Agricultural Product Priority:* There has been an ongoing and long-standing debate in Canada concerning the inferior priority status of wage-earners and agricultural producers who sell their livestock or crops to the debtor. The Bank Act introduced creative approaches to these problems by providing for wage-earner and agricultural product priority. Canadian bankruptcy law is still attempting to find an acceptable approach to the resolution of these issues.

Although the Bank Act possesses many of the features of secured financing law found in the *PPSA*, there are some elements that are noticeably absent and areas where the legislation is incomplete. As well, the legislation has a number of highly idiosyncratic features. The following summarizes the areas where there is a marked divergence from the approach of the *PPSA*:

(a) *Limited Scope:* Bank Act security is limited in that it can only be given to banks and it can only be given by certain classes of debtors on the security of certain types of collateral. The list of eligible loans and eligible forms of collateral reflects a now outdated view of areas considered to be of particular importance to the Canadian economy in which secured lending by banks is viewed as legitimate and is sought to be encouraged.

(b) *Antediluvian Anti-Fraud Provisions:* The Bank Act security interest evolved at a time when there was still a widespread suspicion of the chattel mortgage as a species of fraudulent conveyance. The Bank Act was purposely drafted in a manner designed to differentiate it from the less reputable chattel mortgage. One measure used to reinforce this distinction was a provision that prevented Bank Act security from being used to secure past unsecured advances. Although the general suspicion against security interests that secure past advances has since dissipated, this feature of the Bank Act lives on.

(c) *Obscure Language:* The Bank Act contains a number of provisions that use outdated or obscure language. For example, there is an express priority rule that provides that the bank has priority over an unpaid vendor unless the vendor had a lien on the property and the bank acquired the property without knowledge of it. This has led to considerable debate on whether the provision covers conditional sales agreements or if it merely covers an unpaid seller's lien provided under sales law. In some cases, the Bank Act gives the bank a "first and preferential lien and claim," while in other cases this right is not given. The effect of this lien and the reason why it is given in some cases but not others is unclear.

(d) *The Document of Title Fiction:* The rights obtained by a bank that holds a Bank Act security interest are deemed to be the same as if it had acquired a bill of lading or warehouse receipt covering the property. This feature has spawned a line of cases that espouse the proposition that the bank thereby becomes the owner of the goods and that the debtor has a mere right to possession of the goods. Although this notion is increasingly out of step with current jurisprudence, it is still being used to argue that the security should not be treated the same as other forms of security interests.

(e) *Lack of a Complete Priority System:* The Bank Act does not directly link priorities to the state of the registry, nor does it adopt a first-to-register rule of priority. Lack of registration has a negative effect in that it deprives the secured party of the priority it would otherwise enjoy. The Bank Act contains a number of priority rules, but these are incomplete. In addition, the Act is silent on the question of proceeds. This incomplete framework makes it necessary to speculate upon the nature of the law that will be used to fill in the gaps in the legislation.

(f) *Lack of a Comprehensive Enforcement System:* The Bank Act does not contain a comprehensive system of rules and principles that govern the enforcement of the security. This incompletely specified enforcement regime has created a number of problems concerning the applicability of provincial law.

Royal Bank of Canada v. Sparrow Electric Corp.
[1997] 1 SCR 411

GONTHIER J: ... [58] The earliest authority to comment upon the nature of BAS [Bank Act Security] is the decision of this Court in *Royal Bank of Canada v. Workmen's Compensation Board of Nova Scotia*, [1936] SCR 560. That case involved a priority competition between security under s. 88 of the Bank Act, RSC 1927, c. 12, the predecessor of s. 427, and a lien created by s. 79(2) of The Workmen's Compensation Act, RSNS 1923, c. 129. In his concurring judgment, Davis J observed the effect of s. 88 security as follows, at p. 567:

> ... the security [does] not operate to transfer absolutely the ownership in the goods but ... the transaction [is] essentially a mortgage transaction and subject to the general law of mortgages except where the statute has otherwise expressly provided. ... Section 88 set up by the Bank Act enables manufacturers, who desire to obtain large loans from their bankers in order to carry on their industrial activities, to give to the bank a special and convenient form of security for the bank's protection in the large banking transactions necessary in the carrying on of industry throughout the country. Until the moneys are repaid, the bank is the legal owner of the goods but sale before default is prohibited and provision is made for the manufacturer regaining title upon repayment. To say that Parliament did not use language to expressly provide that the bank shall have a first lien on the goods is beside the mark. The bank acquires ownership in the goods by the statute.

[59] More recently, this Court had occasion to consider the attributes of Bank Act security in [*Bank of Montreal v.*] *Hall*, [1990 CanLII 157 (SCC), [1990] 1 SCR 121]. In that case, La Forest J underlined this Court's previous ruling in *Workmen's Compensation Board of Nova Scotia, supra*, that BAS gives to the lender legal title in the collateral. At pp. 133-34, La Forest J stated:

> By section 178(2) [now s. 427(2)], a bank may take security in property owned by the borrower at the time of the loan transaction, and any property acquired during the pendency of the security agreement. The rights and powers of the bank with respect to the secured property are set out in s. 178(2)(c). By the terms of s. 178(2)(c), these rights and powers are stated to be "the same rights and powers as if the bank had acquired a warehouse receipt or bill of lading in which such property was described." These powers are defined, in turn, in s. 186 [now s. 435] of the Act where it is specified that any warehouse receipt or bill acquired by a bank as security for the payment of a debt, vests in the bank all the right and title to goods, wares and merchandise covered by the holder or owner thereof.
>
> The nature of the rights and powers vested in the bank by the delivery of the document giving the security interest has been the object of some debate. Argument has centred on

whether the security interest should be likened to a pledge or bailment, or whether it is more in the nature of a chattel mortgage. I find the most precise description of this interest to be that given by Professor Moull in his article "Security Under Sections 177 and 178 of the Bank Act" (1986), 65 *Can. Bar Rev.* 242, at p. 251. Professor Moull, correctly in my view, stresses that the effect of the interest is to vest title to the property in question in the bank when the security interest is taken out. He states, at p. 251:

> The result, then, is that a bank taking security under section 178 effectively acquires legal title to the borrower's interest in the present and after-acquired property assigned to it by the borrower. The bank's interest attaches to the assigned property when the security is given or the property is acquired by the borrower and remains attached until released by the bank, despite changes in the attributes or composition of the assigned property. The borrower retains an equitable right of redemption, of course, but the bank effectively acquires legal title to whatever rights the borrower holds in the assigned property from time to time.

[60] It follows from the comments of this Court regarding the ownership rights in inventory conferred by the Bank Act that security taken under that Act must be considered to be in the nature of a fixed and specific charge. As stated above, the concept of the fixed charge is correlative to the notion of a creditor's having legal proprietary rights in the collateral. I add that this view has been adopted by academic literature in this area: R.J. Wood, "Revenue Canada's Deemed Trust Extends Its Tentacles: Royal Bank of Canada v. Sparrow Electric Corp.," [(1995), 10 *BFLR* 429], at p. 433; and William D. Moull, "Security Under Sections 177 and 178 of the Bank Act" (1986), 65 *Can. Bar Rev.* 242. I find this following passage, at p. 251, from the article written by Professor Moull which was cited with approval by this Court in *Hall, supra,* particularly persuasive:

> Because of its scope and flexibility, some commentators have suggested that section 178 [now s. 427] security is in the nature of a floating charge. This can be misleading, however. Because the bank effectively acquires legal title, section 178 security is really in the nature of a fixed charge on the present and after-acquired property of the borrower assigned to the bank. One attribute that section 178 security may be said to share with a floating charge is its application to all property of a specified class held by the borrower from time to time. But while a floating charge may apply to all property of a specified kind held by the borrower from time to time, it does not affix itself specifically upon any particular item of property until it crystallizes upon default by the borrower. Conversely, a section 178 security is a fixed charge on each item of assigned property held from time to time whether or not the loan is in default. This gives a bank significantly greater rights than it would hold under a floating charge debenture on inventory.

[61] For these reasons, I consider the security interest of the bank in the form of BAS to be in the nature of a fixed and specific charge with a licence to sell the inventory.

Innovation Credit Union v. Bank of Montreal
2009 SKCA 35

JACKSON JA:

I. *Introduction*

[1] This appeal concerns a priority dispute between a prior unregistered security interest taken under *The Personal Property Security Act, 1993* (the "*PPSA*") in agricultural equipment and a subsequent security interest taken and registered under the *Bank Act* in the same collateral. Both security agreements are valid and the debtor had proprietary rights in the collateral when the *Bank Act* security came into effect. The central issue is which security interest takes priority in these circumstances.

[2] Sections 427(2) and 435(2) of the *Bank Act* apply to resolve this dispute. On a proper interpretation of these sections, they provide that the prior *PPSA* interest defeats the *Bank Act* security on the basis that the Bank acquired its interest subject to the prior interest regardless of the fact it was unperfected. Applying this priority rule to the facts of this appeal necessarily results in the appeal being allowed, and the proceeds of the sale of the collateral being granted to the Credit Union.

II. *The Facts*

[3] The facts in this case are succinctly stated in the judgment of the learned Chambers judge. It must be noted, however, that this appeal does not concern collateral claimed as after-acquired property. Unlike the companion appeal involving Radius Credit Union [2009 SKCA 36; extracted below], the debtor had proprietary rights in the collateral in question before the *Bank Act* security came into existence.

[4] A Saskatchewan farmer, James Buist, granted a security interest in all of his present and after-acquired personal property (mostly farm equipment) to the Innovation Credit Union, pursuant to a General Security Agreement dated October 7, 1991. The Credit Union did not register its security interest in Mr. Buist's property in the Personal Property Registry until June 28, 2004.

[5] Meanwhile, beginning in 1998 and continuing until January of 2004, the Bank of Montreal loaned Mr. Buist money secured on the same collateral that had been used to secure the Credit Union's loans. Mr. Buist did not disclose to the Bank that he had already granted a General Security Agreement to the Credit Union. It is common ground that the Bank took the necessary steps to register the requisite notices under s. 427 of the *Bank Act*, and followed its usual practice of searching the Personal Property Registry prior to doing so.

[6] In 2004, Mr. Buist defaulted on repaying his loans to the Credit Union and to the Bank, and the latter seized and sold collateral comprised entirely of agricultural equipment and some hay. It is the proceeds from the sale of that collateral, less costs of sale, which are the subject of the priority dispute in this case. The amount that is in dispute is $32,891.31.

[7] Mr. Buist owed $58,856.36 to the Credit Union, as of December 15, 2004, which is a date close in time to the date of the Bank's seizure of the collateral. At the time of enforcement of its interest, Mr. Buist was indebted to the Bank for an operating loan that had a balance of $72,609.97. The Bank also held equipment loans, but those are not the subject of this appeal.

III. Decision of the Chambers Judge

[8] The learned Chambers judge recognized the legal dilemma before him: the allocation of priority between two security interests, in the same collateral, each taken pursuant to a fundamentally different secured transactions regime. He resolved this dilemma by constructing a bridge between the two systems, so as to permit the Bank to rely on the other secured creditor's failure to perfect its security interest. ... The issue, of course, is whether statute law or common law permits a bank, as the holder of *Bank Act* security, to rely on a *PPSA* secured creditor's failure to perfect its security interest.

IV. Questions to Be Answered

[9] The central issue in this case gives rise to these subsidiary questions:

1. What is the proper framework of analysis to resolve the priority dispute in this case?
2. Does the priority rule created by s. 428(1) of the *Bank Act* apply?
3. If not, do ss. 427(2) and 435(2) of the *Bank Act* apply to resolve this priority dispute?
4. If so, what right or title did the debtor retain after the Credit Union acquired its security interest in the collateral?

V. What Is the Appropriate Framework of Analysis?

[10] Before turning to an examination of the legislation and the jurisprudence, I must acknowledge the difficult exercise faced by counsel and the Chambers judge in this case, and by courts in general, when faced with a conflict between *PPSA* and *Bank Act* security. As Professor Ziegel writes: "when a court is required to determine priorities between a s. 178 [now s. 427] security interest and a security interest governed by PPS legislation it may be engaging in the logically impossible task of comparing apples and oranges or trying to square the proverbial circle." The courts are, however, assisted in this task by a large body of academic literature, reference to which will be made both in this case and in the companion decision involving Radius Credit Union.

[11] The Chambers judge's intentions are clearly laudable. In the best traditions of the common law, he sought a solution to a continuing problem. In my respectful opinion, however, his chosen solution will create other problems, including further litigation, and is contrary to existing jurisprudence and to the existing legislative base, such as it is.

[12] It is common ground that the *PPSA* cannot derogate from the rights accorded to the Bank under the *Bank Act*. Relying on *Bank of Montreal v. Hall* [[1990] 1 SCR 121], the trial judge correctly stated that "[t]o the extent that a conflict exists between the

Bank's rights to enforce *Bank Act* security and provincial statutes restricting enforcement rights, the federal statute prevails." The Bank, however, did not pursue any argument based on federal paramountcy. Indeed, there is no "actual conflict in operation" between the two systems of law, nor does "compliance with the federal statute necessarily entail defiance of its provincial counterpart." In *Hall*, it was found that the bank was restricted by provincial legislation with respect to the enforcement of rights that had been conferred upon it by the *Bank Act*.

[13]   Resolution of the dispute in the instant case, however, does not require compliance by the Bank with provincial law. Enforceability of the Bank's interest is not restricted. Furthermore, as will be seen later in these reasons, the *Bank Act* itself looks to the general law of the province to determine what "right or title" of the debtor is acquired by a bank when it takes security pursuant to that *Act*.

...

[20]   The overall significance of the majority's decision in [*Rogerson Lumber Co. v. Four Seasons Chalet Ltd.* (1980), 113 DLR (3d) 671 (Ont. CA)], for the purposes of the appeal before this Court, cannot be overstated. The equivalent of s. 428(1) of the *Bank Act* did not apply, notwithstanding the fact that the interest of the seller was subsequent to that of the bank. The *PPSA* did not apply so as to grant priority to the bank, notwithstanding the fact that the *PPSA* interest was unperfected. The unregistered *PPSA* interest was not subordinated to the *Bank Act* interest, as the bank security was not one of the types of interests falling within the protection of the provincial legislation. Priority was accorded to the subsequent unregistered interest based on an application of the principles of property law, the vendor having, in effect, retained full title, and in a jurisdiction that in 1980 had adopted a modern personal property registration system.

[21]   Some seven years later, this Court in [*Bank of Montreal v. Pulsar Ventures Inc.* (1987), 58 Sask. R 224] considered a priority competition between a *Bank Act* security and a subsequently taken and perfected *PPSA* security interest in the same collateral. The principal issue was whether the assignment of a security interest in present and after-acquired property, granted pursuant to s. 178 [now s. 427] of the *Bank Act*, takes priority over a perfected security interest in the same after-acquired property granted subsequently under the *PPSA*. To resolve this question, the Court, like the Court in *Rogerson*, had to address the question of the appropriate analytical framework, but this time to resolve a priority dispute between federally and provincially created security interests, in after-acquired property. The issue was complicated by the fact that the bank had also registered its interest under the *PPSA*.

[22]   ... [T]he court in *Pulsar* set aside the priority rules of the *PPSA*, and looked to the *Bank Act* to resolve the dispute. Since both interests attached simultaneously, s. 179(1) [now s. 428(1)], which refers to "subsequently" acquired interests, however, could not apply. The Court concluded that "[w]hat is of significance in determining priority here is the time at which the respective security interests were entered into."

[23]   The next decision, in this line of jurisprudence, is [*Bank of Nova Scotia v. International Harvester Credit Corp.* (1990), 73 DLR (4th) 385)], where the Ontario Court of Appeal considered a priority competition between an imperfectly registered conditional sales contract and a subsequent *Bank Act* security. When the debtor defaulted, the bank applied for a declaration that its interest had priority over the prior unperfected security

interest. As in *Pulsar*, the case was complicated by the fact that the bank had registered its claim under the *PPSA*, as well as under the *Bank Act*. In consequence, all three judges wrote, with differing approaches and emphasis. Nonetheless, the result is clear: judgment was granted in favour of the prior unperfected provincially created security interest.

· · ·

[25] The significance of *International Harvester* for the instant appeal is that the Court accorded priority to a "prior unregistered provincially created interest." The bank attempted to rely on the provincial registration of its federally created interest as a means of defeating that interest. Like the case before this Court, if the bank had taken and perfected a provincially created interest, that interest would have prevailed. The Ontario Court of Appeal, however, had no difficulty in rejecting the bank's approach to resolving the dispute.

[26] *International Harvester* is not squarely on all fours with the instant appeal, however, because the prior unperfected interest in that case was in the form of a traditional title retention security agreement, i.e., a conditional sales contract, whereas in the present case, the prior unperfected interest takes the form of a general security agreement. Nonetheless, the decision is significant because the Court held, as it did in *Rogerson*, that the bank could not acquire, by registration under the *PPSA*, anything more than its security documentation, and the *Bank Act*, had already given it. The Court found that the *Bank Act* gave to the bank only that which remained after the prior unperfected security interest had been given, or in other words, *nemo dat quod non habet*.

[27] Building on the analysis of these decisions, we reach another decision from this Court: *Agricultural Credit* [*Corporation of Saskatchewan v. Royal Bank of Canada* (1994), 120 Sask. R 205]. This decision concerned a registered and, therefore, perfected *PPSA* security agreement, and a subsequent *Bank Act* security registered under the *Bank Act*, both claiming an interest in the same collateral. To resolve this dispute, Bayda CJ summarized what he found to be the state of the law regarding the appropriate approach to resolving a priority dispute between provincially and federally created interests. He wrote, for the Court:

> In a priority dispute between a s. 178 *Bank Act* security and a security interest that is perfected or is perfectible under the PPSA, there are, generally speaking, three basic rules to follow for determining the priority: (1) set aside the PPSA from the analysis and determine the priority as if the PPSA did not exist; (2) determine the priority pursuant to ss. 178, 179 and 180 of the *Bank Act* (and such other provisions as may be applicable to the circumstances) to the extent it is possible to do so; (3) where appropriate, apply the first-in-time priority rule. ...

Bayda CJ noted that the foregoing conclusion was "in complete consonance with this court's decision in *Pulsar*" where "the first-in-time priority rule applied and the bank succeeded." He noted, however, that in the case before him the same rule resulted in a different outcome, because "all of the advances by the bank to the debtor and the governing assignments creating the securities in respect of those advances were made *after* the security interest created by the security agreement entered into by the opposing claimant (ACS)." ... The Court concluded that the *PPSA* security, taken and registered prior in time, had priority over the subsequently taken and registered *Bank Act* interest.

[28] Finally, in [*Royal Bank of Canada v. Moosomin Credit Union*, [2004] 5 WWR 494], Lane JA summarized this Court's approach to the resolution of disputes between provincially and federally created security interests:

> [38] This Court, in *Royal Bank v. Agricultural Credit Corp. of Saskatchewan* puts it clearly that the common law must be resorted to in order to resolve the priority in such disputes [between *Bank Act* and *PPSA* security].

In the same decision, Sherstobitoff JA, concurring with Lane JA on this point, held that when a prior executed *Bank Act* security interest has attached pursuant to an after-acquired property clause and the *PPSA* interest has later attached, both the common law principle of *nemo dat quod non habet* and the principle of "first-in-time" provide priority to the first taken security interest.

...

[30] It is within this jurisprudential framework that the instant appeal must be decided. The issue is whether the result changes by virtue of the fact that the Credit Union's prior interest was unperfected at the time the Bank took delivery of its security documentation.

VI. Does the Priority Rule Created by s. 428(1) of the Bank Act Apply?

[31] The Chambers judge interpreted s. 428(1) as creating a priority rule in favour of prior rights, and then decided that those prior rights had to be registered in order to defeat a subsequent *Bank Act* interest. In addition to implying a priority rule into the section, this interpretation rests on an understanding that the purpose of registration is one of "notice to all." Registration, in the context of the *PPSA*, does not serve this purpose. While its incidental purpose is to permit prospective creditors to search debtor names, and certain types of personal property by virtue of serial numbers, the fundamental effect of registration is to establish priorities by virtue of the time of registration, and for the purposes of the *PPSA* only. Registration no longer constitutes actual or constructive notice in the context of the *PPSA*. Section 47 of the *PPSA* abolishes that concept.

...

[38] With much respect, the Chambers judge has interpreted s. 428(1) so as to grant priority to *Bank Act* security over a prior, unperfected *PPSA* security interest and thereby created a new priority rule. This is a reading of s. 428(1) that cannot be given to it and is contrary to all past authority. Further, such a priority rule would permit the Bank to rely on the Credit Union's failure to register, which is contrary to the intent of s. 4(k) of the *PPSA*. As will be seen, s. 428(1) may be used to support an interpretation that the *Bank Act* relies on provincial law to determine what a bank acquires when it takes s. 427 security, but it does no more than that *vis à vis* a security interest taken prior to the *Bank Act* interest. In summary, s. 428(1) of the *Bank Act* does not apply to resolve the instant dispute.

VII. Do ss. 427(2) and 435(2) of the Bank Act
Apply to Resolve This Priority Dispute?

[39] The issue at this point is whether some other rule in the *Bank Act* applies, or whether we have reached the point in the analysis, referred to in *Agricultural Credit*, where the first-in-time or other common law or equitable priority rule is applied.

[40] The section of the *Bank Act* to be considered first is s. 427(2). ... This section makes two important statements relevant to the within appeal.

[41] First, it states that the bank receives a "first and preferential lien and claim thereon for the sum secured and interest thereon." Second, it states that the bank acquires "the same rights and powers in respect of the property as if the bank had acquired a warehouse receipt or bill of lading in which the property was described."

[42] The reference to the creation of a "first and preferential lien" does not increase the priority position of a bank *vis à vis* another secured creditor of personal property for this reason: it is contrary to the other, explicit priority rules contained in the *Bank Act*. Thus, this aspect of s. 427(2) has been interpreted, not as a priority rule *per se*, but as a statement of the nature of the interest acquired, and for the purposes of addressing conflicts between a bank and the holder of an underlying interest in real property upon which agricultural equipment or crops are affixed, for example. ...

[43] The second aspect of s. 427(2) states that the bank acquires "the same rights and powers in respect of the property *as if* the bank had acquired a warehouse receipt or bill of lading in which the property was described." This has been labeled the "document of title fiction."

[44] The document of title fiction arises in this manner. The *Bank Act* describes what a bank acquires when taking a warehouse receipt or bill of lading. ... It then must be determined what interest a bank acquires in personal property secured by a s. 427 interest, by reference to what a bank acquires by taking a warehouse receipt or bill of lading, both of which are themselves documents of title.

[45] With few exceptions, judicial authority and the commentators are agreed that s. 435(2) is to be given its plain meaning: a bank acquires only the "right and title" of the person from whom the interest is taken, and leaves to the law of the province to determine what that means.

• • •

[52] At bottom, this is an exercise in statutory interpretation, which requires recourse to the general principles of statutory interpretation, including the need to read the words to be interpreted in their entire context. It is clear that the *Bank Act* provides no express priority rule *vis à vis* prior security interests. To read a priority rule into the *Bank Act* in favour of prior interests, and thereby defeat *Bank Act* security in all cases would have far-reaching ramifications. It would raise, for example, the question as to what types of prior interests would have such effect, which was the conundrum faced by the Chambers judge in the approach that he took.

[53] A conclusion that the *Bank Act* relies on provincial law to determine the consequences of holding a warehouse receipt or bill of lading avoids this problem. Such a conclusion is in keeping with the history of the *Bank Act*, and the wording of the sections under consideration. It enhances credit, but not at the expense of prior interests duly

taken and valid under the provincial system of secured transactions. It is consistent with s. 428(1), which accords priority to *Bank Act* security over "rights subsequently acquired," but to make this statement does not import into the section a priority rule in favour of prior rights. If Parliament did not intend to defer to provincial property law principles, there would be no mechanism to resolve this dispute in the *Bank Act*, and in consequence, the courts would be thrust back upon a consideration of the principles of the general law of the province including the common law and equity in any event.

[54] In summary, a bank, by virtue of the document of title fiction, acquires whatever interest the debtor has in the property at the time the bank acquired its interest. This, of course, brings us to the question of what the debtor owned in this case when the Bank acquired its interest under the *Bank Act*, and this, in turn, necessarily takes us to provincial law governing proprietary interests.

VIII. What Right or Title Did the Debtor Retain After the Credit Union Acquired Its Security Interest in the Collateral?

[55] The corollary of the question, what did the Bank acquire by virtue of the document of title fiction, depends on an analysis of what interest the Credit Union had already acquired in the debtor's property before the delivery of the security documentation to the Bank.

[56] The General Security Agreement between the Credit Union and Mr. Buist states that he "GRANTS, CHARGES AND RESERVES to the [Credit Union] A SECURITY INTEREST ... IN ALL OF THE DEBTOR'S PRESENT AND AFTER-ACQUIRED PROPERTY, including but not limited to: Goods, Inventory, Equipment (all kinds and types), Accounts, Money, Chattel Paper, Intangibles, Documents of Title, Instruments, Securities, Fixtures, and the property described on the Schedules(s) hereto (all of which property, together with the proceeds as hereinafter described, is herein referred to as the "Collateral")." The Agreement goes on to provide that "[t]he Security Interest granted by the Debtor to the Credit Union secures the performance or payment and satisfaction of any and all obligations, indebtedness and liability of the Debtor to the Credit Union ... ."

[57] According to the *PPSA*, an agreement in these terms creates a security interest in the property with respect to which it is granted. Clause 2(1)(qq)(i) of the *PPSA* defines a security interest as "an interest in personal property that secures payment or performance of an obligation." There can be no doubt, based on the terms of the General Security Agreement mentioned above, that Mr. Buist granted to the Credit Union *a security interest* in all his personal property.

[58] The *PPSA* refers to both "attachment" and "perfection." Since the security interest, in this case, was not registered and therefore not perfected, that leaves for consideration whether it was attached. ... Section 10, which is referred to in s. 12, provides that a security interest becomes enforceable when the debtor has signed a security agreement that contains a description of the collateral, including a claim to all present and after-acquired property. In this case, it is common ground that the Credit Union gave value, Mr. Buist had rights in the collateral before the *Bank Act* interest arose, and the requirements of s. 10 were met. Thus, the Credit Union held an attached security interest in the collateral.

[59] The *PPSA* gives full effect to the concept of attachment and to an attached security interest. Contrary to prior law, a failure to register does not affect the validity, or the enforceability, of the interest. For example, priority among competing unperfected security interests is determined by the order of attachment (see s. 35(1)(c)).

...

[61] Applying s. 427(2), read in conjunction with s. 435(2), means that the Bank acquired its interest in the collateral subject to the proprietary rights of the Credit Union. By the time the Bank acquired its interest in the property, the Credit Union already had real rights in the collateral through the attachment of its security interest. Thus, on an application of the *Agricultural Credit* framework, priority must be accorded to the Credit Union.

...

[67] In short, in the within appeal, the Bank cannot insist on registration under a system of which it is not a part and that it has not adopted. The Credit Union is entitled to priority over the Bank of Montreal by virtue of the Credit Union's prior security interest. The priority rule, resting as it does on ss. 427(2) and 435 of the *Bank Act* and provincial law, does not depend on whether the prior security interest is perfected.

Sherstobitoff and Smith JJA concurred.

Appeal allowed.

Radius Credit Union Limited v. Royal Bank of Canada
2009 SKCA 36

JACKSON JA:

I. Introduction

[1] This is a companion appeal to *Innovation Credit Union v. Bank of Montreal* [2009 SKCA 35; extracted above]. The priority dispute in this appeal, however, is with respect to collateral that is after-acquired property for the Radius Credit Union under its security agreement taken pursuant to *The Personal Property Security Act, 1993* (the "PPSA"), and for the Royal Bank under its valid security taken and registered under the *Bank Act*. The Credit Union's security interest was unperfected when the Bank's interest came into existence under the *Bank Act*, but the Credit Union's security agreement was executed before that time.

[2] Since the *Bank Act* does not provide a rule to address this priority dispute, it is necessary to resort to the ordinary law of the province. As a matter of law, both security interests are legal interests and both attached simultaneously to the collateral when the debtor acquired his interest in it. Notwithstanding that the competing interests are legal interests and the Credit Union's interest was unperfected at the time of the acquisition of the *Bank Act* interest, the priority rule to apply is *qui prior est tempore potior est jure* (whomever is first in time is first in right), and this rule should apply according to the date of execution of the respective security agreements. In the result, the Credit Union's prior unperfected security interest takes priority over the interest of the Bank.

II. Facts

[3] In this appeal, a Saskatchewan farmer, Mr. Wayne Hingtgen, executed a General Security Agreement with the Credit Union on January 24, 1992 and granted a security interest on all present and after-acquired property. On January 22, 1996, the Bank first registered its Notice of Intention to take security and began loaning money to Mr. Hingtgen in 1997. The Credit Union registered a financing statement in the Personal Property Registry on September 24, 1998. It also registered a second financing statement on June 14, 1999.

[4] When the Credit Union registered its security interest in 1998, it claimed a security interest in a 1991 GMC ½ ton truck, a 1991 Bergen stock trailer, as well as a general property interest in "ALL PRESENT AND AFTER ACQUIRED PROPERTY. ALL PROCEEDS." The financing statement was amended on January 16, 2003, September 3, 2003, and February 5, 2004, in each case to extend the expiry date of the registration. It was amended on March 3, 2005 to add a specific item of serial numbered property: a 2001 New Holland TM 125 Tractor. The following was also added, by way of amendment at the same time, under the heading "General Property" and follows the claim to all present and after-acquired property:

> 2003 JIFFY BALE PRO 920 SHREDDER SER #JSB20010424 2001 NEW HOLLAND 688 BALER SER #12945 2003 NEW HOLLAND 1475 MOWER CON. HAYBIND SER #1140526 2003 NEW HOLLAND 2316 HEADER SER #1110728 PURCHASE MONEY SECURITY INTEREST. ALL PROCEEDS, ALL GOODS, CHATTEL PAPER, DOCUMENTS OF TITLE, INSTRUMENTS, MONEY, SECURITIES AND INTANGIBLES. ALL PRESENT AND AFTER ACQUIRED CATTLE AND LIVESTOCK OF EVERY NATURE AND DESCRIPTION. ALL PROCEEDS.

(While this financing statement indicates a claim for a purchase-money interest, the evidence does not support such a claim, and such a claim was not pursued in the Queen's Bench or in this Court.)

[5] The second registration filed by the Credit Union on June 14, 1999 claimed an interest in "ALL PRESENT AND AFTER ACQUIRED CATTLE AND LIVESTOCK OF EVERY NATURE AND KIND AND DESCRIPTION. ALL PROCEEDS PURCHASE MONEY SECURITY INTEREST. ALL PROCEEDS: ALL GOODS, CHATTEL PAPER, DOCUMENTS OF TITLE, INSTRUMENTS, MONEY, SECURITIES & INTANGIBLES." This interest was amended twice, on April 6, 2000 and on January 16, 2003, for the purpose of extending the registration's expiry date.

[6] The security interest granted to the Bank was in "all crops growing or produced upon the farm, all products of agriculture, all livestock, and all implements" pursuant to a s. 427 assignment dated June 10, 1997, a subsequent "application for credit and promise to give security" and "agreement as to loans and advances" dated June 10, 1997, an assignment taken pursuant to s. 427 dated December 21, 1999, an agreement as to loans and advances dated December 21, 1999, an assignment under s. 427 dated December 18, 2001, and an agreement as to loans and advances dated December 18, 2001. The Bank registered Notices of Intention on January 22, 1996, February 10, 1999 and March 27, 2002. No questions were raised with respect to any aspect of the Bank's claim.

[7] The Credit Union is owed approximately $550,000 secured on both real and personal property. The Bank is owed approximately $100,000 in advances.

[8] The Bank seized and sold the collateral that is the subject of this appeal. The most valuable collateral is the 2001 New Holland TM 125 Tractor S/N 164831B, a 2001 New Holland 688 Baler S/N 12945, a 2003 Jiffy Bale Pro920 Shredder S/N JSB20010424, and a 2003 New Holland 1475 Mower Con. Haybine S/N #1140526. Importantly, all of this equipment is after-acquired property for the purposes of both the Credit Union and the Bank interests. The total value of the collateral seized and sold is $65,125.

III. Framework of Analysis

...

[10] The proper framework of analysis is, however, that set out in *Royal Bank of Canada v. Agricultural Credit Corp. of Saskatchewan* [(1994), 120 Sask. R 205], which concerned a registered *PPSA* security agreement and a subsequent *Bank Act* security registered under the *Bank Act*. ...

[11] While this framework applies, the analysis in the within appeal must proceed along different lines than that pursued in *Innovation Credit Union*. Mr. Hingtgen's property became subject to the *Bank Act* and *PPSA* security interests by virtue of an after-acquired property claim asserted by both creditors. This fact dictates that the analysis must take a somewhat different form.

...

IV. When Did the Security Interests Taken Under the PPSA and Bank Act, Respectively, Attach?

[16] The answer is straightforward in relation to the interest created by the *PPSA*. ... It is common ground that the Credit Union gave value at the time the security agreement was entered into, and it is obvious that Mr. Hingtgen did not acquire rights in the collateral until each of the items of personal property were purchased by him. Thus, the Credit Union's interest attached to the collateral when Mr. Hingtgen purchased it.

[17] With respect to the *Bank Act* security, the matter is more complicated. ...

...

[20] In order to determine when *Bank Act* security attaches, it is necessary to construe s. 427(2) of the *Bank Act*. ... Specifically, the issue is whether these words address the issue of attachment and, if so, whether "vesting" of after-acquired property is backdated to the time of first delivery of the document giving security.

[21] The [provision], like much of what must be considered in this area, [is] not as specific as one might like. In construing any legislation, however, a court must be guided by the Supreme Court of Canada's direction to read "the words of an Act ... in their entire context and in their grammatical and ordinary sense harmoniously with the scheme of the Act, the object of the Act, and the intention of Parliament." Parliament has not been explicit in stating when a security interest in after-acquired property attaches, notwithstanding an expansion both of the banks' lending rights with respect to such property, and with respect to the types of property against which security may be taken. Viewed against the backdrop of provincial personal property security regimes designed

to create similar rights, it is reasonable to assume that the banks' interests would emulate such interests. Provincial law, as I have already indicated, is clear: a security interest does not attach until the debtor acquires rights in the collateral.

···

[23] The resolution of this appeal that fits best with the ordinary law of this Province is that an after-acquired property clause, taken under the *Bank Act*, attaches when the debtor acquires rights in the collateral. Any other result would be anomalous. If the *Bank Act* interest in after-acquired property attaches as of the date of the creation of the interest, it would defeat intervening purchase money security interests, whether perfected or not, which would be in direct conflict with this Court's reasoning in *Pulsar* [*Bank of Montreal v. Pulsar Ventures Inc.* (1987), 58 Sask. R 224] and the Ontario Court of Appeal's decision in *Rogerson* [*Lumber Co. v. Four Seasons Chalet Ltd.* (1980), 113 DLR (3d) 671].

···

[25] Thus, I conclude that the *Bank Act* security attaches to after-acquired property when the debtor acquires an interest in the property, which in this case is when Mr. Hingtgen purchased it. Since the Credit Union's interest also arose upon the debtor's acquisition of his interest in the property, i.e., at the time of purchase, it necessarily follows that the interests of the Credit Union and the Bank arose simultaneously.

[26] That brings us to the next issue, which is the application of the principle of *qui prior est tempore potior est jure*.

V. Should the Principle of Qui Prior Est Tempore Potior Est Jure Be Applied in the Context Presented by This Appeal, and If So, How?

[27] Since the *Bank Act* does not contain a priority rule with respect to competing interests arising in after-acquired property, this is not an exercise in interpreting that *Act*. ... [I]t is necessary to determine the source of the applicable law to fill the gap and resolve the dispute at hand. ...

[28] As this Court held in *Innovation Credit Union*, the priority rules contained in the *PPSA* do not apply to resolve a dispute between *PPSA* and *Bank Act* interests. In this case, unlike in *Innovation Credit Union*, the *Bank Act* is silent as to the appropriate means to resolve the dispute. Given this, the Court must look to the ordinary law of the jurisdiction, which encompasses the common law and the rules of equity, as well as applicable statute law.

···

[30] These maxims require a consideration of the nature of the interest held by each of the secured creditors in this case. In [*Royal Bank of Canada v. Sparrow Electric Corp.*, [1997] 1 SCR 411], Gonthier J quotes approvingly from Professor Moull to the effect that a bank taking security under s. 427 of the *Bank Act* "effectively acquires legal title to the borrower's interest in the present and after-acquired property assigned to it by the borrower."

[31] A security interest taken under the *PPSA* is also a legal interest in that it is created pursuant to statute law and is accorded a status according to that law. ...

[32] In this case, the *PPSA* interest was not perfected when the debtor executed the *Bank Act* security. The lack of perfection, however, is irrelevant to the determination of whether an interest is a legal interest or an equitable one. The time of perfection, or the lack of perfection, under the *PPSA*, determines which of two or more competing security interests takes priority. It does not determine the status of the interest as legal or equitable. Legal status is determined by the statute creating the interest. ...

[33] The *PPSA* gives full effect to the concept of attachment and to an attached security interest. Contrary to prior law, a failure to register does not affect the validity, or the enforceability, of the interest. For example, priority among competing unperfected security interests is determined by the order of attachment (see s. 35(1)(c)). Thus, I conclude that the failure to perfect a security interest does not affect its status as a legal interest.

[34] The question then becomes whether the principle of first-in-time can be used to determine priority among legal, as opposed to equitable, interests.

...

[37] Counsel for the Bank argued that the principle of first-in-time should not be applied to resolve the priority conflict in this case, or if it is applied, it should relate to who registered, or perfected, first, so as not to "reward" the Credit Union for having failed to register. As Professor Berger and *Snell's Equity* [31st ed. (Toronto: Thomson Carswell, 2005)] have indicated, there would be nothing inherent in the first-in-time principle that requires it to be applied to grant priority to the first party to execute a security agreement, and, as has been noted, this principle was developed to resolve a priority dispute between two "equitable" interests. It would be equally consistent with the first-in-time principle to develop a rule that would grant priority to the first creditor to have registered under the governing registry system. The Court is being asked to establish a priority rule where neither the statute law nor binding precedent has established one.

[38] The argument for a rule based on the date of registration would be that it provides greater certainty for banks loaning money in individual cases. The arguments against such a rule, however, are three-fold.

[39] First, a rule insisting on compliance with the registration requirements of the *PPSA*, in order to be able to assert priority over a *Bank Act* security interest, appears contrary to the legislature's intention in enacting s. 4(k) of the *PPSA*. Section 4(k) declares that the *PPSA* does not apply to "a security agreement governed by an Act of the Parliament of Canada that deals with the rights of parties to the agreement or the rights of third parties affected by a security interest created by the agreement, including an agreement governed by sections 425 to 436 of the *Bank Act*." As a consequence, a bank holding *Bank Act* security cannot participate in the priority structure created by s. 35 of the *PPSA*, which grants priority to perfected security interests over unperfected interests. To apply the first-in-time principle to the date of registration would, in effect, establish a priority rule that the legislature has stated should not be applied to resolve this dispute. It would also allow the Bank to benefit from the *PPSA* without being bound by it.

[40] Second, and in any event, to introduce such a refinement would add yet another level of complexity to an already overly complex system. As this Court stated in *Innovation Credit Union*, and as counsel for the Credit Union has correctly pointed out, if the

system were such that the banks were entitled to insist on the perfection of the *PPSA* interest, the following non-exhaustive additional list of priority issues will arise:

1. If the provincial security interest is perfected at the same time the bank reserves its s. 427 security interest, must the provincial interest continue to be perfected thereafter?
2. If the bank searches a debtor's name and receives actual notice of a security interest registered by a provincial lender, but the registration is deficient in a manner prescribed by the regulations to the *PPSA*, can the bank still rely on the "objective test" of a "seriously misleading error" provided by the *PPSA* to challenge the registration, even when the bank was not misled?
3. If, in the case at hand, the credit union had registered a security interest in "all farm machinery" but had failed to describe the serial number of a tractor (as required by the regulations to the *PPSA*) would the bank have enjoyed priority to the tractor, but not the remaining machinery?
4. Are all rules of perfection applicable including perfection by possession?
5. Do the *PPSA*'s rules of temporary perfection apply when, for example, goods are moved from one jurisdiction to another?

Given the result in *Innovation Credit Union*, where it has been decided that an unperfected security interest in collateral, in which the debtor already has proprietary rights, defeats a subsequent *Bank Act* interest, one would be hard-pressed, in the interests of simplicity and certainty, to recognize a different result in this case.

[41] Third, there will be cases where what appears to be an unjust result will arise no matter which rule is chosen. In this case, for example, one could argue that the "equities" favour the Credit Union. The Credit Union has been the debtor's principal lender throughout, and it registered its financing statement before the Bank incurred any significant liability. The Bank did not loan the bulk of the money presently owed to it until after the Credit Union had registered its interest in 1998. It also must be remembered that we are dealing here with after-acquired property, such that the expanded asset base may, in certain cases, have little to do with the prior security that has been granted. Both a "first to register" and a first-in-time rule can lead to a windfall for the "first" creditor. All of this is, in my view, irrelevant to the proper resolution of this appeal, and is mentioned only to demonstrate how balancing equities is a difficult task even if the rule were based on the first to register. Given this, and in the absence of a more fundamental, legislated solution to the problem, it appears preferable to opt for the certainty of a first-in-time rule that is consistent across all types of security interests, both perfected and unperfected, granting priority to the first security agreement to be executed.

[42] Clearly, this is what this Court had in mind in *Pulsar*. While decrying the absence of an effective registration system that would integrate all types of security, the Court was, nonetheless, motivated to provide a simple, and certain, priority rule.

···

[44] In summary, where valid *Bank Act* and *PPSA* security interests are asserted in after-acquired property, priority is to be determined as of the date of execution of the respective security agreements. This rule applies even if the *PPSA* interest is unperfected.

Sherstobitoff and Smith JJA concurred.

Bank of Nova Scotia v. International Harvester Credit Corp.
(1990), 73 DLR (4th) 385 (Ont. CA)

McKINLAY JA: The appellant, International Harvester Credit Corporation of Canada Limited ("IHCC"), now known as Navistar Financial Corporation of Canada Inc., is assignee of the rights of a vendor of farm equipment under two conditional sales contracts. It appeals the judgment of the learned trial judge, reported in 36 DLR (4th) 278, 58 OR (2d) 493, 7 PPSAC 1, which declared its interest in the equipment to be subsequent in priority to the interest of the respondent bank under its security taken pursuant to s. 178 (now s. 427) of the *Bank Act*, SC 1980-81-82-83, c. 40 (Part I, s. 2).

In 1981 financing statements were registered by IHCC pursuant to the provisions of the *Personal Property Security Act*, RSO 1980, c. 375 ("PPSA"), for the purpose of perfecting its security interest in the equipment. The financing statements named the debtor as "Richard Howe."

Subsequent to these registrations, the Bank of Nova Scotia registered with the Bank of Canada a notice of intention from Mr. Howe to give the bank security pursuant to s. 178 of the *Bank Act*. Some two years later he did in fact give security over all farm equipment of which "the undersigned [Howe] is now or may hereafter become the owner." The bank also registered a financing statement pursuant to the provisions of the PPSA, describing the collateral as "all farm machinery and the proceeds thereof," and naming the debtor as "Richard Howe."

The full name of the debtor is Richard Glen Howe. It is conceded by both parties that pursuant to the provisions of the PPSA and the regulations thereunder at the time of these registrations and at the time of trial, as interpreted by this court in *Re Gibbons* (1984), 8 DLR (4th) 316, 45 OR (2d) 664, 51 CBR (NS) 235 (CA), a security interest remained unperfected where the middle initial of the debtor (if he had one) was not included in the debtor's name on the financing statement.

On June 8, 1984, approximately one year after filing its original financing statement, the bank registered a financing change statement naming the debtor as "Richard G. Howe." The decision of the learned trial judge that this registration did not result in the perfection of the bank's security appropriately is not appealed.

On June 15, 1984, solicitors for the bank obtained an order ex parte, under s. 64 of the PPSA extending the time for registration of a financing statement and pursuant thereto, registered a financing statement on June 21, 1984, naming the debtor as "Richard G. Howe."

Following default by Mr. Howe, the bank obtained a default judgment against him on October 16, 1984, in the amount of $163,335.38.

On November 20, 1984, IHCC repossessed the machinery pursuant to the provisions of the conditional sales contracts between it and Mr. Howe. It then notified the bank of its intention to sell the machinery if Mr. Howe's indebtedness to it was not satisfied by December 7, 1984. Although the bank notified IHCC of its claim to priority, IHCC sold the equipment and applied the proceeds against Mr. Howe's indebtedness to it.

Many issues apparently argued before the trial judge were not addressed before us.

...

The numerous problems resulting from inconsistencies between the provisions of the PPSA and the *Bank Act* have been the subject of a number of learned treatises, but the subject of very little in the way of judicial interpretation. Of the cases which have addressed the problems, most were decided prior to the enactment of modern personal property security legislation, and dealt primarily with questions of title to the property involved, and the possible invalidity of conditional sales contracts and chattel mortgages resulting from non-registration pursuant to the relevant provincial statutes. Title to collateral is, for most purposes, irrelevant under the PPSA, and priority, rather than possible invalidity, is now the major issue: see s. 2(a).

The conflict between these two Acts should be looked at in the light of the history of bank lending against personalty. Prior to 1967, the *Bank Act* prohibited the lending against personalty. Prior to 1967, the *Bank Act* prohibited the lending of money on the security of "goods, wares and merchandise" except by way of security pursuant to ss. 87 and 88—the predecessors of ss. 177 and 178 of the present Act—(see SC 1953-54, c. 48, s. 75(2)(d), and see SC 1966-67, c. 87, ss. 75(1)(c) and (3)). One of the results of this broadening of the bank's security taking powers has been the practice of many banks of taking security pursuant to the provisions of s. 178 of the *Bank Act*, and, in addition, taking security in the form of a general security agreement covering all of the assets of the same debtor and registering a financing statement under PPSA with respect thereto. That was not done in this case, but rather, the bank purported to treat the s. 178 security itself as a "security interest" within the terms of the PPSA.

The procedure followed by the bank in this case raises the following series of questions:

(i) Does the s. 178 security of a chartered bank fall within the definition of "security interest" in s. 1(y) of the PPSA, and, if so, is the giving of s. 178 security a transaction to which the PPSA applies?

(ii) What interest does the bank take from its debtor under the provisions of the *Bank Act* and of the s. 178 security document?

(iii) If the PPSA applies to s. 178 security, can the bank attain, as a result of prior registration of a financing statement under the PPSA, an interest in the collateral which neither the *Bank Act* nor the security document may have given it?

There can be no doubt that by virtue of taking s. 178 security a bank obtains "an interest in goods ... that secures payment or performance of an obligation"—a "security interest" within the meaning of s. 1(y). Whether or not the transaction is one to which the PPSA applies is governed by s. 2(a), which reads:

2. Subject to subsection 3(1), this Act applies,
(a) to every transaction without regard to its form and without regard to the person who has title to the collateral that in substance creates a security interest ...

The relevant portion of s. 3(1) reads:

3(1) This Act does not apply,
(a) to a lien given by statute or rule of law ...

Section 178(2)(d) of the *Bank Act* (which is quoted under question (ii) below) vests in the bank "a first and preferential lien and claim" upon the property which is the subject of the s. 178 security. That lien being "given by statute" to the bank falls within the exception in s. 3(1) of the PPSA, and consequently that Act does not apply to it. However, s. 178 in addition thereto vests in the bank "the same rights and powers in respect of the property as if the bank had acquired a warehouse receipt or bill of lading in which the property was described." Thus, the PPSA applies to rights vested in the bank pursuant to that provision.

(ii) What interest does the bank take from its debtor under the provisions of the *Bank Act* and of the s. 178 security document?

In an attempt to answer this question, it is necessary to consider the following provisions of the *Bank Act*:

[Sections 178(1)(c); 178(2)(a), (b), (d); 179(1), (2), (7), (9)]

The security in this case was given in a form "to ... like effect" to that set out in Sch. VI of the Act (see s. 178(1)). The relevant portions of the security document read:

> ... the undersigned hereby assigns to the Bank as security for the payment of the said loan or advance or renewals thereof or substitutions therefor and interest on such loan or advance and on any such renewals and substitutions, the property hereinafter described of which the undersigned is now or may hereafter become the owner, to wit—all farm machinery that is now or may hereafter be in the place or places hereinafter designated, to wit—Lots 3 and 4 Concession 1 and Lot 2 Concession 2, Harris Township, District of Temiskaming ...
> *This security is given under section 178 of the Bank Act.*

(Emphasis added.)

It should be noted that, pursuant to the security document and pursuant to s. 178(2)(a) and (b), the debtor must, when the security is given or before it is released, be the "owner" of the property described therein before any of the statutorily given rights vest in the bank. Nowhere in the Act is the word "owner" defined, but for the purposes of this case it is sufficient to say that a conditional purchaser is an "owner" within the meaning of s. 178(2)(a) and (b): *Royal Bank v. Hodges*, [1930] 1 DLR 397, [1929] 3 WWR 605, 42 BCR 44 (CA); *Mutchenbacker v. Dominion Bank* (1911), 21 Man. R 320, 18 WLR 19 (CA); *Grouse Mountain Resorts Ltd. v. Bank of Montreal* (1960), 25 DLR (2d) 371 (BCSC).

...

Section 178(2)(d) vests in the bank "a first and preferential lien" for the debt secured plus interest, and also "the same rights and powers ... as if the bank had acquired a warehouse receipt or bill of lading in which the property was described." The provisions of s. 179(1) and (2) expand and elaborate upon the priority rights of a bank holding s. 178 security. Section 179(1) gives the bank priority over all subsequently acquired rights in the property. That portion of s. 179(1) is inapplicable to the facts of this case, since the rights of IHCC pre-dated the taking of the bank's security. However, that section also gives the bank priority over "the claim of any unpaid vendor." In the *Rogerson* case, Arnup JA made no reference to s. 179(1) (then s. 89(1)). Houlden JA simply stated at p. 682: "In my opinion, the word 'vendor' should not be interpreted to include a person who sells goods to a purchaser pursuant to a conditional sales contract."

···

The holder of s. 178 security, by virtue of that provision, gets only the right and title to the equipment that the owner of the equipment had. Therefore, the conditional purchaser being an owner, the bank gets priority under s. 179(1) over the claim of a conditional vendor only to the extent of the right and title of its customers—the conditional purchaser—which in the *Rogerson* case could have been no more than a right of possession until payment of the purchase price, none of which had been paid.

According to the majority's reasoning in that case, it appears that if a conditional purchaser had paid some of the purchase price, the bank's priority over the vendor's rights would be limited to the rights provided the conditional purchaser by the conditional sales contract.

(iii) If the PPSA applies to s. 178 security, can the bank attain, as a result of prior registration of a financing statement under the Act, an interest in the collateral which neither the *Bank Act* nor the security document may have given it?

One of the frequently stated objectives of the PPSA was to do away with the concept of title which permeated the numerous and confusing statutory and common law interests which vendors and other financers of personal property could obtain. As stated above, s. 2 of the Act provides that the Act applies to "every transaction without regard to its form and without regard to the person who has title to the collateral that in substance creates a security interest ... ."

I have no doubt that the PPSA can apply to security taken pursuant to s. 178 of the *Bank Act* where the bank elects to utilize the provisions of the Act. In so stating, I wish to lodge the caveat that no consideration has been given in these reasons of the complications that would arise should there be a competition between a s. 178 security which has not been registered under the PPSA and other security interests in the same collateral which are so registered.

The learned trial judge appears to have assumed that once it was established that s. 178 security constituted a security interest under the PPSA and was registered under that Act, it was entitled to the collateral in priority to the holder of an unperfected security interest in the same collateral. That conclusion arises as a result of the application of the general priority rule set out in s. 35(1)(a) of the Act. Section 35(1)(a) states:

> 35(1) If no other provision of this Act is applicable, priority between security interests in the same collateral shall be determined,
>
> (a) by the order of registration ...

Section 9 of the Act reads:

> 9. Except as otherwise provided by this or any other Act, a security agreement is effective according to its terms between the parties to it and against third parties.

The provisions of s. 35 in no way give to a secured party anything that has not been given to that party by the security document itself. Consequently, the provisions of s. 9 apply and the security agreement remains effective according to its terms between the parties and against third parties. In this case, neither the provisions of the *Bank Act* which provide for the security nor the provisions of the security document itself give to the bank anything other than the interest which Howe had in the equipment. Of course, most documents which would come within the definition of "security agreement" under the PPSA would not be so limited in their terms.

Consequently, I am of the view that the bank's prior registration under the PPSA does not, on the facts of this case, give it any right in the equipment, or in the proceeds from its sale, other than the rights that its customer might have had.

HOULDEN JA: While I agree with McKinlay JA's proposed disposition of the appeal, I would like to set out briefly my own reasons for arriving at that conclusion.

I agree with McKinlay JA that s. 64 of the Personal Property Security Act, RSO 1980, c. 375 ("PPSA"), is of no assistance to IHCC. The "rights" protected by s. 64 are rights which have been acquired under the PPSA prior to the order permitting late registration. The only right which IHCC had prior to the perfection of the respondent's security interest was that of the holder of an unperfected security interest. Any prejudice suffered by IHCC was caused, not by the late registration, but by IHCC's failure to perfect its security interest.

Counsel for IHCC conceded that the agreement creating the s. 178 security was a "security agreement" and gave rise to a "security interest" as those terms are defined in the PPSA. However, he submitted that the provisions of the *Bank Act*, SC 1980-81-82-83, c. 40 (Part I, s. 2), for registration and validation of a s. 178 security interest were incompatible with the provisions of the PPSA and, hence, "security interest" under the PPSA would be nugatory, and IHCC, on the basis of this court's decision in *Rogerson Lumber Co. Ltd. v. Four Seasons Chalet Ltd.* (1980), 113 DLR (3d) 671, 29 OR (2d) 193, 12 BLR 93 (CA), would have priority over the bank.

In support of his submission that the provisions of the *Bank Act* were incompatible with the provisions of the PPSA, counsel for IHCC relied on the following differences in the two statutes:

(a) To have a valid security under s. 178 as against other creditors, a bank must comply with the registration requirements of the *Bank Act*. To have a valid security interest under the PPSA as against other creditors, a creditor must perfect its security interest in accordance with the PPSA; this can be accomplished by registration of a financing statement or by taking possession of the collateral.

If the definition of "security interest" under the PPSA is interpreted so as to include a security interest under s. 178 of the *Bank Act*, then it would include a s. 178 security interest which was not registered in accordance with the *Bank Act*. Such a security interest would be unenforceable under the *Bank Act* but could be perfected under the PPSA by taking possession of the collateral. Counsel for IHCC contended that it was not the intention of the legislature in enacting the PPSA to create a process whereby an otherwise unenforceable security interest created by federal statute would become enforceable by operation of provincial law.

With respect, I do not agree. Under the PPSA, a security interest in certain defined collateral may be perfected by possession. If the bank's s. 178 security interest creates a security interest in collateral coming within those defined categories, I see no reason why the bank should not be able to perfect its security interest by taking possession of the collateral, even though the bank has failed to comply with the registration provisions of the *Bank Act*. The security interest of the bank would be invalid under the *Bank Act*, so that the bank would be unable to claim the benefit of the priority provisions of that statute; but it would be perfected under the PPSA, and the bank, like any other holder of a security interest, could claim the benefit of the priority provision of that statute.

(b) The priority rules under the two statutes are different. If a bank is permitted to take advantage of both statutes, it can claim, counsel for IHCC submitted, the benefit of the priority rules under the *Bank Act* as well as the benefit of the priority rules under the PPSA. While this is undoubtedly true, I do not believe that this is a valid reason for holding that "security interest" under the PPSA is not intended to include a security interest created by s. 178 of the *Bank Act*. If a bank has validly perfected its security interest under both statutes, the bank should be able, in my opinion, to claim the benefit of the priority rules of both statutes.

(c) The enforcement procedures under the two Acts are different. If a bank is permitted to register under both Acts, it could, counsel for IHCC contended, rely on the perfection of its interest under the PPSA to achieve priority, but utilize the enforcement procedure of the *Bank Act* in realizing its security. This is not the problem that arises in this case, and I, therefore, prefer to express no opinion on it. Suffice it to say, that the existence of this difficulty—if there is a difficulty—is no reason, in my opinion, to interpret "security interest" in the PPSA as not including a security interest created by s. 178 of the *Bank Act*.

There may be, as Cuming and Wood point out in their article "Compatibility of Federal and Provincial Personal Property Security Law" (1986), 65 *Can. Bar Rev.* 267 at p. 284-6, difficulties in permitting a s. 178 security interest to be registered under the PPSA. If there are such difficulties, then the solution is legislative action, not judicial stretching of the plain words of the PPSA.

•••

Watt J, like McKinlay JA, held that the respondent's security interest under s. 178 of the *Bank Act* could be registered under the PPSA [36 DLR (4th) 278, 58 OR (2d) 493, 35 BLR 299]. Having done so, he turned his attention to the question of priorities, and after reviewing the matter, he found that the bank's perfected security interest had priority over the unperfected security interest of IHCC. I agree with McKinlay JA that he erred in so finding. If the security agreement which gives rise to the bank's security interest were not given pursuant to s. 178 of the *Bank Act*, Watt J would be clearly right. If, for example, instead of s. 178 security, the bank had taken a general security agreement covering all the farm machinery of Howe and had properly perfected its security interest under the PPSA, the bank would have had priority over the unperfected security interest of IHCC. But the bank's security agreement was given pursuant to s. 178 of the *Bank Act*, and it is essential, therefore, to turn to that statute to see what rights are given to the bank by its security agreement[.]

•••

GRANGE JA: I have no doubt that the bank intended and tried to get priority over the IHCC collateral but to succeed in that endeavour it would have had to use a document which purports to give it security on the whole and not just one which on its face and under the *Bank Act*, SC 1980-81-82-83, c. 49 (Part I, s. 2), gave it security only on the borrower's interest in the whole.

...

Appeal allowed.

Jacob S. Ziegel and David L. Denomme, *The Ontario Personal Property Security Act: Commentary and Analysis*, 2d ed.
(Markham, ON: Butterworths, 2000), 52-55 (footnotes omitted)

Does the Ontario Act apply to s. 427 *Bank Act* security interests? In attempting to answer this question it is important to distinguish between two quite separate scenarios. The first involves a situation in which only one agreement is concluded between the parties—the customer's agreement to give the bank a s. 427 security interest—but the bank files a financing statement under the provincial Act as well as complying with the s. 427 registration requirements. The second situation involves the bank taking a security assignment and also concluding a *separate* security agreement with the customer covering part or all of the same collateral as under the s. 427 assignment. It is further supposed that the s. 427 assignment and the general security agreement are respectively perfected under the *Bank Act* and the Ontario Act.

Situation 1. In principle, where the debtor has signed only an agreement to give a s. 427 security interest, the bank should not be free to invoke the provincial Act to take advantage of its more favourable provisions. Yet the contrary was held by the Ontario Court of Appeal in its controversial decision in *Bank of Nova Scotia v. International Harvester Credit Corporation*. The Saskatchewan Court of Appeal appears to have reached the same conclusion in two earlier judgments, neither of which was referred to in *International Harvester*. In *International Harvester*, McKinlay JA and Houlden JA relied on the fact that the definition of "security interest" in the Ontario Act is wide enough to include a s. 427 interest and that the Ontario Act did not expressly exclude a security interest created under federal law. Houlden JA admitted that applying the two regimes in tandem might create difficulties in some cases, but he was satisfied there was no such conflict on the facts before the court. Even if he was correct on this point (which is debatable), both his and McKinlay JA's reasoning is open to the following objections:

(a) It overlooks Arnup JA's holding in *Rogerson Lumber Co. v. Four Seasons Chalet Ltd.* that the reference in s. 22(1)(a)(i) of the old Ontario Act to "any other Act" is only a reference to other Ontario legislation. By a parity of reasoning, the definition of security interest in s. 1 of the Ontario Act as an interest in personal property must mean interests which fall within provincial jurisdiction. This conclusion is supported by s. 73 of the current Act (formerly s. 69), which provides that where there is a conflict between the OPPSA and any other Act, the OPPSA is to prevail. The Ontario legislature would not presume to override a constitutionally competent federal Act, but this intention must be imputed to it if "security interest" includes a security interest created under federal law;

(b) The rationales and history of the old and new Acts offer no support to an intention by the Ontario legislature to exercise concurrent jurisdiction with the federal Bank Act over the same collateral, particularly given the almost complete incompatibility between the two statutory regimes;

(c) If the Ontario Act applies, it must apply throughout, yet McKinlay and Houlden JJA (like the Saskatchewan courts before them) appear to have assumed that a bank with a s. 427 interest is free to elect whether (and presumably to what extent) it wishes to adopt the provincial rules.

Situation 2. It has long been customary for banks to take a provincial security interest as well as a s. 427 assignment in all or substantially all of the same collateral so as to overcome the narrow reading of the s. 427 priority rules given in *Rogerson Lumber*. Given that Situation 2 assumes a separate agreement covering the provincial security interest, the difficulties that confronted the court in *International Harvester* do not arise, but the problems of reconciling two overlapping security interests governed by incompatible statutory regimes still persist. Assuming the parties are rational actors, how would they have wished to avoid the conflict? Cuming and Wood have recommended the adoption of a "quantum" theory, *i.e.*, the proposition that where two security agreements cover the same collateral the debtor intends to create two *consecutive* interests, of which the s. 427 interest will ordinarily be the earlier and senior of the two. This is an ingenious attempt to reconcile the two agreements, but we believe it is too artificial and that it cannot fairly be supposed to reflect the debtor's intention in the usual boiler plate type of agreement.

In our view, a better approach is to read down the provincial agreement so that collateral already subject to a s. 427 interest is excluded entirely. If this approach is adopted, the result in most cases will be substantially the same as under the Cuming-Wood construct but it would be less metaphysical. Another solution, given the incompatibility between the s. 427 and the provincial security interests, would be to put the bank to its election. That election should ordinarily be deemed to be made when the first security interest is taken by the bank unless there is persuasive evidence that the parties intended a different result. Whichever of these approaches is preferred, it should be clear that none of them permits the bank to opt in and out of the provincial legislation as its interests may dictate.

With a view to overcoming the foregoing difficulties, the Alberta, British Columbia and Saskatchewan PPSAs contain a provision excluding from the scope of the Act any security agreement governed by federal legislation and, in particular, any security agreement governed by Division B of Part V of the *Banks and Banking Law Revision Act 1980*. This takes care of the *International Harvester* type problem, but it does not address the situation where the debtor has given two security interests covering the same collateral. So far, the Ontario government has shown little interest in adopting a similar provision.

For many years the federal government has been urged to revise s. 427 to make it more compatible with the provincial Personal Property Security Acts, to improve and clarify its drafting and to remove its many anomalies. It seems unlikely that the federal government will meet these concerns in the near future. The federal government did, however, commission a study by Mr. Derrick Tay and several of his then colleagues at

Osler, Hoskin & Harcourt, and this was given a limited circulation in 1991. The study recommended repealing s. 427 and its companion sections and replacing them with a federal Personal Property Security Act. The Act would govern all security interests taken by banks, and, it would appear, banks would no longer be free to make use of provincial security interests. These recommendations have encountered considerable criticisms. In any event, they do not represent federal government policy.

In 1997 the Commercial Law Section of the Canadian Bar Association made a submission to the federal Minister of Finance arguing that since all the common law provinces had adopted, or were about to adopt, a PPSA and that since Quebec had also modernized its chattel security law there was no longer any need for a federal s. 427 law, and that those provisions of the *Bank Act* should be suspended so long as the provincial legislation was not changed to discriminate against the banks. Regrettably, the Minister of Finance's reply was unhelpful and it does not look as if the *Bank Act* will be changed in the foreseeable future to resolve the conflict between s. 427 and the provincial PPSAs.

Law Commission of Canada, *Modernizing Canada's Secured Transactions Law: The Bank Act Security Provisions*
(Ottawa: Government of Canada, 2004), at 26-30 (footnotes omitted)

The third option would eliminate the federal security system by repealing sections 427 to 429 of the *Bank Act*. Banks that wished to take security interests in the personal property of their debtors would do so by taking provincial or territorial security interests.

A major advantage of this option is that it results in a more efficient and less complex legal environment. All of the legal uncertainty problems associated with the co-existence of both provincial/territorial and federal personal property security systems would be eliminated. This option would also have the important effect of reducing the transaction costs of secured financing by reducing search and registration costs. A third party wishing to acquire an interest in the personal property of another would no longer need to undertake dual searches of both the provincial/territorial and the federal registries to determine if property is encumbered. A buyer or lender would only need to conduct a search of a provincial or territorial registry system.

Another major advantage is that it creates a fairer system. One criticism of the *Bank Act* system is that it creates an uneven playing field that favours banks and disadvantages non-bank credit granting institutions. Banks are able to take both *Bank Act* security and provincial or territorial security interests to secure their loans, while credit unions, small loan companies and other non-bank lenders are able to take only provincial or territorial security interests. This may allow banks to obtain an enhanced priority position over competing non-bank financial institutions.

Repealing the *Bank Act* security provisions would, therefore, produce significant benefits that the other reform options do not achieve. It would

- eliminate legal uncertainty,
- reduce transaction costs, and
- establish equal treatment of institutional lenders.

Are there any disadvantages that would militate against implementing this option? We conclude that although the *Bank Act* security played an important role in the Canadian economy at one time, it no longer serves this purpose. When we examine other justifications for retaining it, we conclude that they are weak and do not justify the continued existence of the *Bank Act* security device.

The original justification for the *Bank Act* security was that it would promote certain identified sectors of the Canadian economy. At one time, banks were not permitted to take provincial or territorial security interests to secure their loans. This restriction was later removed, but at that time provincial and territorial secured transactions law was in a disordered state and did not provide a fully effective secured transactions regime. This impediment has now been eliminated. In every province and in every territory, a modern secured financing regime has been put into place. Therefore, the original justification for the *Bank Act* security is no longer valid.

It might be argued that repealing the *Bank Act* provisions would result in a loss of a long-standing secured financing regime and that eliminating it would make banks change their lending practices. A review of registration statistics provides convincing evidence that this would not be the case. The number of *Bank Act* registrations effected in Canada is relatively small in comparison with the number of provincial or territorial registrations. Banks are well acquainted with the operation of the provincial/territorial secured transactions regimes and regard the provincial or territorial security agreement as their dominant security device. The *Bank Act* security is viewed merely as a secondary or back-up security device that will be used only if a problem is encountered with the provincial or territorial security interest. It is, therefore, highly unlikely that eliminating the *Bank Act* security provisions would result in any significant change in bank lending practices.

The final argument that might be made for maintaining a separate federal secured transactions regime is that it permits banks to make secured loans in jurisdictions that have restricted the enforcement remedies of secured parties. In particular, it might be argued that eliminating the *Bank Act* security regime would cause banks to reduce the availability of credit to the agricultural sector. To secure their loans, banks would rely on provincial or territorial security interests and would be subject to farm protection legislation that restricts the enforcement remedies of secured parties. The flaw with this argument is that the federal government is constitutionally limited in its ability to formulate a legislative policy that can effectively regulate the credit marketplace. Parliament only has the ability to legislate banks. Pre-empting provincial or territorial legislation will only be effective in relation to banks and not in relation to any non-bank lenders such as caisses populaires or credit unions. This will simply result in a distortion in the market by conferring a benefit on only one class of lenders. To be effective, the regulation must apply to all financial institutions. Only the provinces and territories have the legislative competence to deal with all market participants engaged in secured lending.

Legal experts who have studied the matter have similarly concluded that repealing the *Bank Act* security provisions is the best option. Surveys of commercial lawyers indicate that this is their preferred option. On April 7, 1997, the Personal Property Security Law Sub-Committee of the Canadian Bar Association—Ontario made a submission proposing the suspension or repeal of the *Bank Act* security regime. In August 2003, the Secured Transactions Working Group of the Uniform Law Conference of Canada recommended the abolition of the *Bank Act* security provisions, and at the Annual Meeting of the Conference it was resolved that the President of the Uniform Conference of Canada should write the federal ministers of Justice, Finance and Industry recommending repeal of these provisions. In June 2003, a study paper was prepared for the Department of Justice which also proposed repealing the *Bank Act* security provisions as the preferred option.

The Commission believes that this option best meets the criteria of the three guiding principles. We believe that repealing the *Bank Act* security provisions is most likely to create greater certainty in legal outcomes and a more efficient and effective secured transactions regime. This option is best able to take account of the bijural nature of Canadian commercial law. It is also the option that does not frustrate legitimate legislative measures of general application within the provinces and territories.

Recommendation 1

The Law Commission of Canada recommends that Parliament eliminate the *Bank Act* security regime by repealing sections 427 to 429 of the *Bank Act*.

NOTE

This recommendation has not been acted on and the federal government remains resistant to overtures from the proponents of reform. Apart from the Law Commission's Report, the Business Law Section of the Canadian Bar Association also adopted a resolution, concurred in by the Canadian Conference on Personal Property Security Law, urging the federal government to repeal or suspend the operation of s. 427 of the *Bank Act* in favour of the provincial PPS legislation. The federal ministers of finance responded twice to these submissions. The first response came from Finance Minister Paul Martin on April 7, 1998. The second response was from Finance Minister James M. Flaherty on March 12, 2007. Both responses, although they contain some qualifications, were essentially negative. Mr. Flaherty's letter said in part:

> The government decided that, given the benefit of a national security regime and the uncertainty with respect to potential market outcomes resulting from its removal, the *Bank Act* special security regime would not be substantially altered at this time.

See Jacob Ziegel, "Ottawa Rejects Reform of Section 427 of the Bank Act" (2007), 45 *CBLJ* 123, at 126. Are you persuaded by Mr. Flaherty's reasons? If the s. 427 security interests are so valuable, why are the banks also regularly resorting to security interests under the provincial PPSAs?

III. INTELLECTUAL PROPERTY SECURITY INTERESTS

Roderick J. Wood, "The Nature and Definition of Federal Security Interests"
(2000), 34 *CBLJ* 65, at 100-6 (footnotes omitted)

Patents, copyrights, trade marks, industrial designs, plant breeder's rights and integrated circuit topographies are forms of personal property whose creation is governed by federal statute. In this sense, they can be regarded as examples of federal property interests, *i.e.*, property interests whose attributes are given definition by statutes of the Parliament of Canada. However, it is neither correct nor meaningful to claim that a security interest in such property is a federal security interest.

For the most part, the federal statutes do not concern themselves with the regulation of security interests in intellectual property. Although the Bank Act security provisions and the Canada Shipping Act mortgage are not complete statutory codes, they do provide a legal framework for the regulation of these federal security interests. The intellectual property statutes are different in their structure. Their presence, where there is a presence at all, is limited to a provision which permits assignments to be registered, and another which provides a single priority rule for competitions between competing assignees.

Section 57(3) of the Copyright Act provides:

> Any assignment of copyright, or any licence granting an interest in a copyright, shall be adjudged void against any subsequent assignee or licensee for valuable consideration without actual notice, unless the prior assignment or licence is registered in the manner prescribed by this Act before the registering of the instrument under which the subsequent assignee or licensee claims.

Section 50 of the Patent Act provides that a patent is assignable and sets out the formalities that are required before the assignment can be registered. Section 51 goes on to provide:

> 51. Every assignment affecting a patent for invention, whether it is one referred to in section 49 or 50, is void against any subsequent assignee, unless the assignment is registered as prescribed by those sections, before registration of the instrument under which the subsequent assignee claims.

Section 31(3) of the Plant Breeders' Rights Act similarly provides that an assignment of a plant breeder's right is void against a subsequent assignee for value and without notice. As with the other provisions, the subsequent assignee must be the first to register the assignment in order to obtain this priority. The Industrial Design Act, the Trade-marks Act and the Integrated Circuit Topography Act permit the registration of transfers, but do not provide a priority rule for competitions between assignees.

There are four distinct questions that concern the interaction between provincial and federal law in this context:

(1) Do the federal provisions have any application at all to security assignments (*i.e.*, assignments that are not absolute, but are only intended by way of security)?

(2) If yes, does the form of the transaction have an effect on the applicability of the federal provisions? In other words, will the provisions apply to all secured transactions that create a security interest in the intellectual property right? Or will it apply only where the secured transaction is in the form of an assignment?

(3) Is there anything in the *PPSA* which limits its scope such that it does not apply to security assignments of intellectual property?

(4) If both the federal registration provisions and the *PPSA* apply to a security interest in intellectual property, to what extent, if any, does the federal provision pre-empt the application of the *PPSA*?

The starting point is to determine if the federal provisions apply to assignments that are not absolute, but are by way of security. There is very little authority on this point. A decision of the Alberta Court of Appeal in *Colpitts v. Sherwood* dealt with a competition between two assignments, both of which were of a patent given as security for a debt owed to a creditor. The Court read into s. 51 of the Patent Act the requirement that the subsequent registered assignee must take the interest without knowledge of the prior registered assignment in order to take the advantage of the statutory priority. The case lends support for the view that security assignments are governed by the federal provision. However, this question was not directly addressed in the decision. Other textual arguments provide some additional support for the view that security assignments are covered. Many, though not all, commentators believe that security assignments are covered. In any event, given the fact that there is uncertainty on this issue, prudent lawyers will typically operate on the assumption that security assignments of intellectual property are caught by the section.

The second question looks to the form of the secured transaction. Under pre-*PPSA* law, the form of the transaction was of fundamental importance. The characterization of a security interest as a mortgage, charge, conditional sale, floating charge or assignment determined which body of rules were to be applied to the transaction. Under the *PPSA*, these categories are no longer significant. The Act looks to the substance of the transaction. The Act will apply to any transaction that in substance creates a security interest without regard to its form and without regard to the person who has title to the collateral. The *PPSA* therefore does not distinguish between a mortgage, charge or assignment.

The federal statutory provisions were drafted in a different era, and have not been amended to reflect the changes in secured transaction law. They adopt the older language and categories of Anglo-Canadian chattel security law. This may not pose a problem if the security agreement deploys the traditional property conveying terminology in the security agreement. However, a controversy will arise if one or both of the competing interests are drawn up in a form that does not involve a conveyance of title to the intellectual property right. Does this bring the transaction outside of the operation of the federal provision? A security agreement that does not convey title to the secured party is typically characterized as a charge under traditional common law property principles. If the *PPSA* security agreement is characterized in this manner, it would fall outside the definition of an assignment.

The significance of this point can be illustrated in the following example:

A debtor (D) gives SP1 a security interest in a patent. The security agreement merely grants the secured party a security interest in the collateral and does not purport to assign or convey title to it. The security interest is registered under the *PPSA*. D later gives SP2 a security interest in the same patent. The security agreement provides for an assignment of the collateral. SP2 registers the assignment in the Patent Office, and also registers under the *PPSA*.

Section 51 of the Patent Act creates a first-to-register rule of priority. But if that section does not apply because SP1's security agreement was not in the form of an assignment, priorities will presumably fall to be determined by the *PPSA*. SP1 will therefore obtain priority because SP1 was the first to register under the *PPSA*. This result would seriously undermine the utility of federal registration of assignments. Nevertheless, this conclusion may be difficult to escape given the clearly understood definition of an assignment, and the distinction that has always been drawn between an assignment and a charge under traditional property law concepts.

The third question asks if there is anything in the *PPSA* itself which might limit its application where a security interest is taken in intellectual property. The scope provisions of the *PPSA* are clearly broad enough to cover such a security interest. The Act covers any transaction that creates a security interest in personal property. An intellectual property right falls within the definition of an "intangible," which is one of the seven categories of personal property defined by the Act. The issue arises because many of the statutes provide a limitation on the application of the Act where federal security interests are involved. The *PPSA* does not apply to a security agreement governed by an Act of Parliament if that statute "deals with rights of parties to the agreement or the rights of third parties affected by a security interest created by the agreement."

The section was designed to ensure that the *PPSA* would not apply to Bank Act security and Canada Shipping Act mortgages. However, it might be interpreted to extend as well to the federal statutes that provide a priority rule to resolve priorities between competing assignees. This interpretation would produce peculiar results. Some of the federal statutes permit the registration of transfers or assignments, but do not provide a priority rule to resolve competitions between assignees. Here, the *PPSA* would govern a security interest taken in these kinds of assets. Federal statutes that contain a priority rule for such competitions would be excluded from the Act, and issues dealing with validity, priorities and enforcement of the security interest would be determined by traditional common law chattel security principles. A more reasonable approach is to hold that the federal statute must be one that purports to create a statutory regime governing the enforcement or priorities of security interests. The fact that the federal provision governing competing assignments may also cover a security assignment as well should not result in the complete non-application of the *PPSA*.

Assuming that federal registration provisions and the *PPSA* apply to a security interest in intellectual property, it becomes necessary to determine the extent to which the *PPSA* is pre-empted or otherwise affected by the federal provision. It is interesting to note that a very similar controversy arose in the United States in *Peregrine Entertainment Ltd. (Re)*. The United States Copyright Act provided for the recordation of a transfer or mortgage of a copyright. The court decided that the Copyright Act pre-empts any state recordation system pertaining to copyrights. Registration of a security assignment in the United States Copyright Office was held to be the exclusive means by which a security interest in a copyright could be perfected. The failure to register the security interest pursuant to Article 9 therefore did not result in the invalidation of the security interest as against the trustee in bankruptcy. This did not result in the complete pre-emption of state law. Article 9 continued to govern the secured transactions on matters that did not involve the registration system.

In reaching its decision, the court expressed concern over the problems of duplication and overlap of state and federal registration systems:

> A recording system works by virtue of the fact that the interested parties have a specific place to look in order to discover with certainty whether a particular interest has been transferred or encumbered. To the extent there are competing recordation schemes, this lessens the utility of each; when records are scattered in several filing units, potential creditors must conduct several searches before they can be sure that the property is not encumbered.

The fundamental problem with this approach is that it becomes necessary to register the security interest against each separate copyright. The secured financing of businesses that owned a large inventory of copyrights has become cumbersome and more expensive since a single filing covering all the inventory could no longer be used to perfect the security interest.

It is doubtful that the *Peregrine* approach would be followed in Canada. The practical problems that came to light in the aftermath of the decision undermine its policy justification. More significantly, the approach to federal pre-emption differs. In the United States, state law will be pre-empted if the federal enactment is so pervasive so as to indicate that "Congress left no room for supplementary state regulation" or that "the federal interest is so dominant that the federal system will be assumed to preclude enforcement of state laws on the same subject." In Canada, the concept of federal paramountcy utilizes a test of operational conflict rather than negative implication. Mere duplication or overlap does not constitute a conflict.

Further support for the concurrent operation of federal and provincial law is found in *Poolman v. Eiffel Productions S.A.* The dispute was between a prior assignment and a subsequent unregistered assignment which was entered into before the prior assignment was registered. Section 57(3) of the Copyright Act invalidates a prior unregistered assignment against a subsequent registered assignment. It covers only this scenario and does not create a general first-to-register rule of priority. Pinard J held that the federal provision does not immunize the transaction from the general laws applicable to property and civil rights in the province. It therefore appears to support the position that provincial law will govern all matters that do not strictly fall within the priority rule of the federal statute.

It seems likely, therefore, that in Canada the federal statutes governing intellectual property and the provincial *PPSAs* operate concurrently. Registration of a financing statement in the *PPSA* registry is required to protect the security interest against a trustee in bankruptcy. With a single registration, a secured party will also be able to perfect its security interest in a large inventory of intellectual property rights, including after-acquired rights. Registration under the *PPSA* alone will carry a somewhat greater level of risk. The security interest will be defeated by a competing transferee or secured party who registers in the federal registry. To be able to take advantage of this federal priority rule, the competing party must be without notice. However, registration under the *PPSA* does not constitute constructive notice. Therefore, registration in both the federal and provincial registries will be necessary if a secured party wants to obtain the maximum level of protection.

NOTE

The relevant part of the judgment in *Poolman v. Eiffel Productions S.A.* (1991), 35 CPR (3d) 384 (FC) reads as follows (at 392 per Pinard J):

> At the hearing, counsel for the plaintiff argued that subsection 57(3) "is a complete rebuttal of the argument based on article 1488 of the Civil Code." I disagree. This provision of the Copyright Act states only that a prior assignment of an interest in a copyright must be adjudged void against any subsequent assignee unless such prior assignment is duly registered before the registering of the instrument under which the subsequent assignee claims. This does not mean that the interest of such first assignee in a copyright, even though registered before the registering of the instrument under which the subsequent assignee claims, is immune from legal challenge under the general laws applicable to property and civil rights in the provinces of Canada. In principle, the registering of the instrument under which an interest in a copyright is granted is not compulsory and, except as expressly provided for the benefit of a subsequent assignee in subsection 57(3) above, creates nothing more than a presumption of ownership of such interest, which is rebuttable.

Law Commission of Canada, *Leveraging Knowledge Assets: Reducing*
Uncertainty for Security Interests in Intellectual Property
(Ottawa: Government of Canada, 2004), at vii-xvi and 94-96

Executive Summary

Part 1: Introduction

Secured credit is an efficient form of lending that, when implemented in a proper legal and institutional framework, can reduce transaction costs associated with borrowing and thus stimulate economic activity. Historically, the reform of laws and institutions associated with specific types of property has tended to mirror changes in their economic importance. Land was one of the first types of property used as collateral, but as the economy shifted from farming to manufacturing, movable assets such as equipment and inventory became increasingly important forms of security, as did intangible assets such as accounts receivable. Today, with the growing importance of intellectual property, it is not surprising that there is mounting pressure to improve the framework for securing loans with intellectual property rights (IPRs). Enterprises in the technology sector would not be the only ones to benefit from this reform. Any modern enterprise, from manufacturing to the service sector, holds significant intellectual property assets, ranging from business software to licence rights. This report examines the legal and institutional reforms needed to facilitate IPR-secured lending.

The report draws a distinction between IPRs that fall within federal legislative jurisdiction and those that fall within provincial authority. It focuses on the most important federally regulated IPRs, namely patents, copyrights and registered trade-marks. The need for reform is most urgent for these IPRs since the existence of federal title registries for patents, copyrights and trade-marks is a significant obstacle to IPR secured financing. Provincial IPRs, on the other hand, can be accommodated within the existing provincial secured lending systems with relatively minor reforms. The measures recommended in this report anticipate the ongoing creation of new forms of federal IPR. The ability to leverage them for credit will render these rights all the more valuable to their owners.

The main challenges to secured lending based on IPRs are valuation difficulties and deficiencies in the legal and institutional framework for secured lending.

Part 2: Inherent Valuation Challenges

Many IPRs are potentially valuable as collateral, either individually or when pledged *en masse*, but they pose unique valuation risks for secured creditors compared with other types of movable and immovable property. First, most IPRs have a statutorily limited lifespan. Next, and even more important, the economic value of an IPR is susceptible to erosion by the next generation of innovation. Moreover, because the value of an IPR is often linked to a specific application in a specific company, its liquidation value may be significantly lower than its use value. IPRs are also subject to legal challenge, which introduces a discount as well as uncertainty into the valuation process.

In general, this valuation risk cannot be reduced by changing the legal incidents and attributes of IPRs without unacceptably compromising fundamental policies of intellectual property law. The greatest potential for reducing the valuation risk associated with IPRs lies in improving valuation techniques. Those techniques will become more reliable as assessors gain practical experience in evaluating IPRs. Thus, eliminating other barriers to the use of IPRs as collateral will also indirectly reduce valuation risks.

Part 3: Uncertainties in the Current Federal Registration and Priority Framework

The law relating to security interests in IPRs is uncertain. Before considering security interests themselves, any secured creditor, or more broadly, any potential assignee, must ascertain the debtor's title to the asset being offered as collateral. Although title registries exist at the federal level for all federal IPRs, these are not reliable for purposes of title investigation. Under three of the federal intellectual property acts—the *Trade-marks Act*, the *Industrial Design Act* and the *Integrated Circuit Topography Act*—registration of an assignment in the federal title is merely permissive; examination of the title register does not provide authoritative information regarding title. Under the remaining three acts— the *Patent Act*, the *Copyright Act* and the *Plant Breeders' Rights Act*—an unregistered assignment is void against a subsequent assignee without notice [of] who registers first. Even so, details of existing law mean that the registry is not entirely authoritative. In particular, the first-registered assignee must take the property without actual knowledge of the prior unregistered assignment. This qualification creates residual uncertainty and has been eliminated in modern registry design in other contexts. Moreover, the courts have held that priority established by mere registration is subject to the exceptions to first-in-time priority embodied in certain principles of provincial property law, thus further undermining the value of the registry as a source of title information.

When security interests are added into the mix, the uncertainty increases dramatically. Virtually all aspects of priority contain uncertainty. First, it is not clear which secured transactions fall within the scope of the federal registration provisions. Are all secured transactions federally registrable, or only those that are formally cast as assignments? It may be that none are registrable. Even if registration of a security interest does not establish priority of its own effect, annotation of such a registration may serve as notice or constructive notice and so establish priority indirectly.

In addition to this legal uncertainty, current registry practices are not sensitive to the information needs of either prospective secured creditors or prospective assignees of federal IPRs. The patent, copyright and trade-marks databases are currently accessible online, but these online resources were designed for other purposes, such as searching prior patents. They are not adequate for financing- or purchasing-related due diligence searches since they may be incomplete or out of date.

This uncertainty increases direct costs because lenders are routinely advised to register under both federal intellectual property law and provincial secured transactions law and to observe the formal requirements of both systems. Yet even this practice does not eliminate priority uncertainty of federal registration. And the interaction and potential conflict between federal statutes and provincial secured transactions laws undermine the confidence of secured creditors in the quality of IPR collateral relative to other movable assets. This increases both the initial risk and the ongoing monitoring burden for secured creditors, inconveniences for which debtors ultimately pay in the form of less accessible and costlier secured credit.

For many years, lawyers with expertise in intellectual property law have recognized that there is uncertainty in secured transactions involving intellectual property. In 1998, after the matter was studied by the National Intellectual Property Section, the Canadian Bar Association urged the Government of Canada to enact a national scheme for the registration of security interests in personal property.

Although the benefits of a reformed legal framework for IPR-based secured financing are difficult to quantify, the current uncertainties are so well documented and so pervasive that the cost savings are bound to justify the investment. The case for reform is especially pressing in view of the expected increase in demand for IPR-based secured financing that will accompany improved access and reduced costs.

Part 4: Reform of the Ownership Disclosure Function of the Federal Intellectual Property Registries

Reform of the title aspects of federal intellectual property registries is an essential prerequisite to any approach to reform of security interests in IPRs. Title-level reform will facilitate the efficiency of all types of commercial transactions in federal IPRs, including secured transactions, by providing commercial parties with a cheap, efficient and reliable source of information about the current ownership of IPRs. However, the statutes as currently drafted not only fail to achieve this potential, they actually create confusion.

To resolve this deficiency in the title aspects of the federal intellectual property registries, we recommend that the assignment and registration provisions of all six federal intellectual property statutes be strengthened to provide for the registrability of all transfers of ownership in federal IPRs. The amendments should also give conclusive legal effect to registered transfers as against unregistered transfers. In particular, we recommend that successive assignments or transfers of the same IPR by the same assignor be ranked on a strict first-to-register basis, subject to an exception where fraudulent conduct is involved. We further recommend that the scope of registrable transfers include assignments and licences. Structural and operational reform of the registries themselves to allow reliable online title searching is needed to support these substantive reforms.

Part 5: Choice of Law Approach

The reforms recommended in Part 4 would improve the ability of prospective secured creditors to investigate a prospective debtor's legal title to the collateral, thus reducing one important source of the legal uncertainty identified in Part 3. But further reforms are needed to address the uncertainties in the priority of claims to the same federal IPR, both as between competing secured creditors and between a secured creditor and a federally registered assignee. Part 5 outlines a "choice of law" approach to this second problem, while Parts 6 and 7 discuss a "federal" approach.

Under the choice of law approach, the federal government would recognize the law of the debtor's location as the legal regime applicable to the registration, the effects of registration or non-registration, and the priority of security granted in any federal IPR. For Quebec debtors the relevant provisions of the *Civil Code of Québec* would apply; for debtors located in the other provinces and territories, reference would be made to the relevant personal property security act. For non-Canadian debtors, foreign secured transactions law would govern; for example, French law would govern French debtors.

If this approach is adopted, we recommend that it be implemented by a federal choice of law rule explicitly designating the law of the debtor's location as the applicable law. The alternative would be to have the law remain silent on this point and allow the choice of law rules of the litigation forum to determine the applicable law. For cases litigated in Canada the applicable law would therefore be the law of the debtor's location, but there is sufficient variation among provincial statutes that this approach would still result in uncertainty and potential conflict over the applicable law. For similar reasons, we recommend that a federal statutory provision be created that ranks assignees and secured creditors according to the order in which they registered their interests in the relevant federal intellectual property registry and the secured transactions registry of the province or territory where the debtor is located.

One of the features of the choice of law approach is that it invokes more than one legal system: the law of the debtor's location applies to the registration and priority status of security rights, while determinations relating to ownership and assignment of the IPRs are subject to federal law. This has two main disadvantages, the first of which is the chain-of-title problem. To ascertain priority, a prospective secured creditor must search the chain of title to the IPR federally and then search all the various registries corresponding to the location of the prior owners disclosed by that title search to determine whether those prior owners had granted prior security interests. Thus the existence of the federal title register makes it more complicated for a prospective creditor to ascertain priority of security interest in a federal IPR than in a more traditional form of personal property. Moreover, the lack of uniformity in debtor/owner name rules between provincial and federal registries means that valid security interests granted by prior owners may remain invisible, even after a full search. The only way to eliminate this source of uncertainty would be to implement uniformity in provincial debtor name rules. This in itself would be a major law reform undertaking. "Gateway" searching (a process whereby a single online portal automatically queries multiple registries) could relieve some of the technical burden of searching multiple jurisdictions, but it would not eliminate the need for multiple searches, nor could it eliminate the problems arising from lack of uniform debtor names.

The second main disadvantage of the choice of law approach is the foreign debtor problem. Under the choice of law approach, security interests in Canadian IPRs granted by foreign owners would be valid encumbrances if adequately publicized according to the law of the debtor's location. This means that verifying encumbrances affecting an IPR could necessitate searching a foreign registry (and gateway searching would obviously not be possible). Worse still, many countries outside North America do not operate general encumbrance registries of the kind established by the provincial and territorial secured transactions regimes in Canada and by Article 9 of the *Uniform Commercial Code* in the United States. Thus, valid prior security interests might be entirely undiscoverable.

Part 6: Federal Substantive Approach

The alternative to the choice of law approach is a federal approach under which the federal intellectual property statutes would be amended to explicitly provide for the federal registration of security rights in federal IPRs. Priorities between a secured creditor and an assignee, or between competing secured creditors, would then be governed by the order of federal registration. That is, security interests as well as outright assignments would be registrable federally, and once so registered would have priority over any competing assignment or security that was not so registered.

While we refer to this as a federal approach, the reach of federal law would be limited. First, it would apply only to federal IPRs. Provincial IPRs would be treated as general intangibles under existing provincial secured transactions law. Further, only security interests in federal IPRs themselves would be subject to the federal regime; security interests in IPR-related rights, particularly security interests in rights to royalty payments, would be excluded. And even with respect to security interests in federal IPRs themselves, the registration and priority rules of the secured transactions law in effect in the debtor's home province or country would be pre-empted only for the purposes of resolving a contest involving at least one federally registered claimant. Furthermore, although a provincially registered security interest in a federal IPR would be subordinated to any federally registered interest in that IPR, the provincially registered interest would, nevertheless, take precedence over any interest that was not registered federally, and over the debtor's insolvency administrator.

Part 7: *Structural and Operational Reforms of the Federal Intellectual Property Registries to Accommodate the Federal Approach*

Some legal and structural reforms to the federal registry system are necessary or potentially desirable to accommodate the federal registration of security interests. As discussed in Part 4, the title aspects of federal intellectual property registries could be modernized through various design and legal reforms. Part 7 looks at how federal registries might be modified to implement the federal approach to security interests in IPRs. It recommends the enactment of a statutory provision enabling the federal registration of security interests. This reform should be very minor if carried out with the title-side reforms discussed in Part 4.

A registration could be implemented in one of two ways—through document-filing or notice-registration. In a document-filing system, the actual security documentation would be filed, whereas in a notice-registration system only a notice need be registered, setting out the barest factual particulars needed to alert third parties to the potential existence of a security interest. Experience at the provincial registry level has proven that the notice-registration system is far superior to the document-filing system, and we strongly recommend that it be adopted for federal registration of security interests. It would also be easier to implement than document-filing.

It is sometimes suggested that, because the federal registries are indexed and searched according to each specific item of IPR, adoption of a federal priority regime would impede creditors who hold security in the whole of a debtor's present and after-acquired movable assets from effectively perfecting their security in the debtor's after-acquired federal IPRs so as to ensure priority over competing claimants. We believe this concern is ill founded. In fact, it is easier to deal with after-acquired property under the federal approach than under the choice of law approach. The most basic solution would be to create a separate federal name-indexed registry for security interests and similar encumbrances. A searcher would first search the federal ownership registry to determine the chain of title to the relevant IPR and then search the federal encumbrance registries for encumbrances granted or registered against all owners in the chain. This would be simpler than under the choice of law approach because it would be necessary to search only two registries, and the problem of nonuniform names would be avoided.

Part 8: *Implementation Strategy*

Secured lending based on IPRs faces challenges both because of valuation difficulties and because of the inadequate legal regime governing security interests in IPRs. Governments can reduce the valuation risk by encouraging the development of expertise in the valuation of IPRs and the development of best practices in this domain. By sponsoring research and disseminating knowledge, governments can foster a climate that is more receptive to the use of IPRs as collateral.

Meanwhile, the legal expertise to support such reforms is dispersed among two types of specialists. Intellectual property lawyers are knowledgeable about IPRs, while commercial lawyers are knowledgeable about the creation of security interests. Unfortunately, there are very few lawyers well versed in both. As lenders increase their reliance on IPR-based collateral, lawyers will need to become conversant with *both* intellectual property law and commercial law. The Canadian Bar Association, the Intellectual Property Institute of Canada and the provincial law societies can help their members make this transition by creating the necessary education programs and materials.

Part 9: Conclusion

The federal government should modernize the legal regime governing security interests in IPRs. The current framework is fraught with uncertainty. Modernizing and rationalizing the rules governing security in IPRs will improve access to secured credit based on IPRs and lower its cost. Such reforms will also indirectly improve valuation techniques, as growing demand for IPR-based security increases lender familiarity with IPR collateral. Formal government action to strengthen the ability of financiers to evaluate intellectual property collateral is not required. Valuation expertise will be developed by the private sector as the importance of intellectual property assets increases.

Of the two basic approaches to law reform discussed in this report, we recommend the federal approach. The choice of law approach faces an unresolvable problem in the form of invisible foreign debtors in the chain of title. And their numbers are likely to grow in an increasingly global economy. Under the federal approach, only two registries need be searched—the federal title registry and the federal security interest registry. Debtor name variation and the accompanying uncertainty would be eliminated. The foreign debtor problem would also disappear since foreign creditors, like any other creditor, would be required to register federally in order to establish their priority.

· · ·

List of Recommendations

Recommendation 1

Parliament should improve the legal framework governing federal intellectual property rights to reduce the legal uncertainty associated with taking such rights as collateral.

Recommendation 2

All of the federal intellectual property statutes should create true title registries so that registration of a transfer of a registered federal intellectual property right will be conclusive evidence of legal title against any unregistered transfer.

Recommendation 3

The federal intellectual property registries should be governed by a strict first-to-register rule of priority in which knowledge of a prior unregistered interest is irrelevant, except in the case of fraud or bad faith.

Recommendation 4

The federal intellectual property registration regimes should permit the registration of all transfers, grants of interests or interests in applications for grants in federal intellectual property, irrespective of whether those grants of interests are by assignment or licence.

Recommendation 5

The federal intellectual property registration systems should be overhauled to ensure that they support reliable, current, online searching of the full chain of title of all federal intellectual property rights.

Recommendation 6

To resolve the priority claims of secured creditors to federal intellectual property rights, Parliament could enact a federal choice of law rule that designates the law of the debtor's location as the law applicable to registration and priority. Because this approach makes it more difficult to search a chain of title and creates problems where foreign debtors are involved, it should be regarded as a second-best solution and should be adopted only if Parliament thinks that it is unable to implement a federal substantive approach to the problem.

Recommendation 7

Parliament should amend the intellectual property statutes to provide for the federal registration of security interests in the intellectual property registries.

Recommendation 8

The federal registry system for security interests in intellectual property should apply only to federal intellectual property rights. Security interests in royalty payments should be excluded from the scope of the federal system.

Recommendation 9

To have priority over other interests subsequently registered in a federal intellectual property registry, a security interest would have to be registered in the federal intellectual property registry system. However, registering a security interest in a federal intellectual property right in the provincial registry system would be effective to establish priority over any interest that was not registered federally, including the debtor's insolvency administrator.

Recommendation 10

The federal registry system for security interests in intellectual property should adopt a notice-registration system.

Recommendation 11

The federal registry system for security interests in intellectual property should provide a separate federal name-indexed registry for security interests and should permit a secured creditor to register an interest in after-acquired intellectual property rights.

Recommendation 12

Governments should encourage the development of expertise in the valuation of intellectual property rights and facilitate the development of best practices in this domain.

Recommendation 13

The Canadian Bar Association, the Intellectual Property Institute of Canada, law schools, business schools and law societies should support the development of educational materials and courses dealing with security interests in intellectual property and promote expertise in commercial and intellectual property law.

IV. SHIP MORTGAGES

Roderick J. Wood, "The Nature and Definition of Federal Security Interests"
(2000), 34 *CBLJ* 65, at 86-89 and 94-95 (footnotes omitted)

The Canada Shipping Act (hereafter "*CSA*") ship mortgage provisions were drawn largely from the British Shipping Act, 1894. The recent amendments to this statute modernize the language of the ship mortgage provisions and provide for the centralization of the ship registry, but for the most part the amendments were not intended to introduce any major substantive changes to the law governing statutory ship mortgages.

The *CSA* provides a system for the registration of the ownership of ships or of shares in a ship. Transfers of ownership are recorded in this registry, as are mortgages of the ship or a share of it. The registry also permits the recording of mortgages against ships that are under construction. These mortgages will be referred to as statutory ship mortgages in order to distinguish them from other types of security interest that can be granted in a ship. A statutory ship mortgage can only be granted if the ship is registered under the *CSA*. The *CSA* does not require that all ships be registered. Smaller vessels are not required to be registered, but registration is permitted if the owner wishes to effect it. There are approximately 47,000 ship registrations under the *CSA* and 22,000 registered mortgages. In many cases, a ship is subject to more than one registered mortgage.

The *CSA* adopts a form of document registration system in relation to ship mortgages. The mortgage must be prepared in the proper prescribed statutory form. This single page document contains only the barest of details concerning the contractual terms of the mortgage. It sets out the following:

(a)   the official number and name of the ship, time and date of registration, its place of registration and a few details concerning its dimensions and tonnage;

(b) the name and address of the debtor;

(c) the name and address of the secured party;

(d) the amount secured by the mortgage; and

(e) the signature or other form of execution of the debtor.

The details concerning the terms of the mortgage (the representations, warranties, covenants, events of default, acceleration clauses and remedy provisions standard in personal property security agreements) are typically included in a collateral loan agreement which is not registered. It is the usual practice for the statutory mortgage to make reference to the collateral loan agreement, but likely a failure to do so is not of any legal significance.

Until recently, the executed statutory mortgage was filed with the registrar of the ship's port of registry. The *CSA* now provides a single, centralized registry system. This eliminates the risk that a searching party may inadvertently conduct a search at the wrong registry. The unique name and number of registered ships eliminates the similar name problem that arises under other *PPSA* registration systems. The registrar records the mortgages in the order in which they are produced and assigns a number, time and date to the registration. The *CSA* provides that priority between registered statutory mortgages is to be determined on the basis of the order of registration "notwithstanding any express, implied or constructive notice." Although the section only purports to deal with priority competitions between registered statutory mortgages, it seems to be accepted that the registered statutory mortgage will also have priority over a prior or subsequent unregistered security interest in the ship. The amendments to the *CSA* permit an alteration to the priority ranking if all mortgagees file their written consent.

The *CSA* contains further provisions for a discharge of a mortgage and a transfer of a mortgage. The mortgagee is not considered to be the owner by virtue of the mortgage except to the extent necessary to make the ship or share available as security under the mortgage.

Registration of a security agreement not in the form of a statutory mortgage is not permitted. The one exception to this rule is created by s. 428(5) of the Bank Act which provides for the registration of a s. 427 Bank Act security covering a fishing vessel in the *CSA* ship registry.

The *CSA* ship mortgage provisions have very little to say about the enforcement of the statutory ship mortgage. The *CSA* gives the holder of a registered ship mortgage a statutory power of sale, and provides that the power of sale cannot be exercised if there are prior registered mortgagees unless their consent to the sale is obtained. Other than this, it is silent on the question of enforcement remedies.

...

The *CSA* provides only a skeletal framework for the regulation of statutory ship mortgages. On many issues, it will be necessary to fill in the gaps in the federal statute. Here we discover that a fundamentally different approach will be taken. In other areas, the presumption is that provincial law will govern. This does not hold true in the case of statutory ship mortgages. There is a body of non-statutory federal law that will provide the suppletive law. It is called Canadian maritime law.

...

If a secured party takes security in the form of a statutory ship mortgage, the *PPSA* will not apply to the transaction. Most of the provinces include in the *PPSA* an express exclusion of statutory ship mortgages. Even in the absence of such a provision, the *PPSA* cannot apply to statutory ship mortgages on constitutional grounds. The *CSA* looks to Canadian maritime law and not to provincial law to fill gaps in the statute. The issue that arises is whether a *CSA* statutory ship mortgage and a Bank Act security in a fishing boat are the only means by which it is possible to create a security interest in a ship. Is it possible to create a *PPSA* security interest in a ship that is registered under the *CSA*?

There is nothing in the *CSA* to invalidate a ship mortgage that does not take the form of a statutory ship mortgage. Nor is there anything in the *PPSA* that would prevent it from applying to a security interest in a ship that is not in the form of a statutory ship mortgage. Indeed, the *PPSA* registration systems in most provinces expressly provide for the registration of security interests in ships that are registered under the *CSA*. Therefore, if it is not possible to create a *PPSA* security interest in a registered ship, it can only be on constitutional grounds. Although there is at least one case that has applied the *PPSA* to security interests in registered ships that were not in the form of a statutory ship mortgage, the constitutionality of the provincial legislation was not in issue.

[Professor Wood goes on to argue the case for the PPSAs to apply in the case of a security interest in a registered ship that is not in the form of a statutory ship mortgage.]

V. INTERNATIONAL DEVELOPMENTS

This chapter is mainly about the interaction between Canadian provincial and federal laws governing personal property security interests and proposals for the harmonization of laws at the two levels. There are also significant moves afoot for the harmonization of personal property security laws at the international level. These moves are a response in part to the globalization of trade and finance and in part to the need in developing countries for a modern and workable set of commercial laws to encourage and facilitate business transactions within their borders. The following extract from a recent report by the Department of Justice Canada to the Uniform Law Conference of Canada on the Department's activities on the private international law front provides an overview of recent international initiatives in which Canada has been involved. The Goode extract, which comes next, provides a more detailed account of the Convention on International Interests in Mobile Equipment, while the Note following the Goode extract provides a little more information about the Convention on the Assignment of Receivables in International Trade.

Department of Justice Canada, *Activities and Priorities of the Department of Justice in International Private Law—Report of the Department of Justice Canada*
Uniform Law Conference of Canada, Civil Section
(Quebec City, Quebec, August 2008), at 8-14*

Project on Harmonised Substantive Rules Regarding Indirectly Held Securities (Unidroit)

At Unidroit, intersessional work continued on the first element of its project on transactions on transnational and connected capital markets; that is, the creation of clear and consistent rules for the taking of securities, especially securities held indirectly through intermediaries in multi-tiered holding patterns and evidenced by book entries in the investor's account, as collateral. This Unidroit project is complementary to the *Convention on the Law Applicable to Certain Rights in Respect of Securities Held with an Intermediary*, adopted under the auspices of the Hague Conference on Private International Law in December 2002.

Four meetings of governmental experts have been held on this project: May 2005, March 2006, November 2006 and March 2007. The text is now well-developed and will take the form of a convention. A diplomatic conference to finalize the instrument will be hosted by Switzerland in Geneva from September 1-13, 2008.

Given the relatively recent enactments in several Canadian jurisdictions of legislation based on the Uniform Securities Transfer Act [USTA], it will continue to constitute the main point of reference for Canada's position on the substance. Consultations will be held to develop Canada's position for the diplomatic conference and will include provincial and territorial authorities, the Uniform Law Conference of Canada (ULCC) Working Group on the Uniform Securities Transfer Act, federal departments and agencies, the private bar, academics and non-governmental organizations.

•••

Convention on International Interests in Mobile Equipment and Aircraft Protocol (Unidroit/ICAO)

The Convention provides a framework for the creation of international interests in mobile equipment and an international registry in which these interests can be registered. Each type of mobile equipment is the subject of a specific protocol under the Convention. There are no limitations on the categories of mobile equipment for which a protocol could be adopted. In addition to aircraft equipment, the Convention could apply to registered ships, oil rigs, containers, railway rolling stock, agricultural equipment, mining equipment, space property, and other objects that could be identified in the future.

The Convention entered into force internationally on April 1, 2004, after its third ratification. It only enters into force as regards a specific category of objects to which a Protocol applies as of the date of the entry into force of that Protocol. The Aircraft Protocol entered into force at the international level on March 1, 2006 after the eighth instrument

---

* The full text of the report is available at www.ulcc.ca under Proceedings of Annual Meetings, Civil Section Documents.

of ratification or accession required for its entry into force was deposited. Canada signed the Convention and Aircraft Protocol in March 2004.

The ULCC adopted a uniform implementing act in 2002. Canadian jurisdictions have been asked to consider adopting legislation to implement the Convention and Aircraft Protocol. Legislation implementing the Convention and Aircraft Protocol has been adopted at the federal level as well as in Ontario, Saskatchewan, Nova Scotia, Alberta, Newfoundland and Labrador, and Quebec.

The federal government is in a position to consider ratifying the Convention and Aircraft Protocol given the support for ratification that has been expressed by the adoption of implementing legislation in the provinces and territories. The Department has worked with provinces and territories to develop a proposed list of uniform declarations. Although it is up to each province and territory to determine the nature of the declarations it wishes to have made on its behalf, there seems to be consensus on almost all of the proposed declarations at this time. The Department will continue to work with the Department of Transport Canada towards ratification in the near future. The federal government will continue to encourage provinces and territories to consider adopting legislation to implement the instruments.

...

Convention on the Law Applicable to Securities Held by Intermediaries (Hague)—ULCC Uniform Act

Canada actively participated in the negotiations of the *Convention on the Law Applicable to Certain Rights in Respect of Securities Held with an Intermediary.* The Convention was finalized and adopted during the Diplomatic Session held from December 2 to 12, 2002 in the Hague.

This Convention is a first attempt worldwide to draft cross-border rules on the law applicable to securities held with an intermediary. The objective is to enable financial market participants in the global market to ascertain readily and unequivocally which law will govern the proprietary aspects of transfers and pledges of interests in respect of securities held through indirect holding systems. This Convention is intended to provide certainty and predictability on a limited but crucial aspect of such transactions.

...

In 2004, the ULCC agreed that the Canadian Securities Administrators (CSA) authorize the Task Force to prepare a uniform implementing statute for the Convention once the Explanatory Report for the Hague Convention was finalized, which occurred in late 2004. Securities Administrators approved the CSA Task Force pursuing Convention implementation work in April 2005.

Since then, Canadian experts have continued to focus on USTA implementation as a priority with the result that no progress has been made on a uniform act to implement the Convention apart from informal discussion suggesting that implementation might be accomplished via a small addition to USTA legislation. We hope to see a convention implementation Working Group making progress on uniform implementing legislation over this coming year. Note that the United States and Switzerland signed the Convention on July 5, 2006 and Mauritius on April 28, 2008.

...

Convention on the Assignment of Receivables in International Trade (UNCITRAL)

In July 2001, UNCITRAL adopted the *Convention on the Assignment of Receivables in International Trade* after six years of development. The Convention was opened for signature in December 2001. The rules are intended to facilitate financing by removing uncertainty encountered in various legal systems as to recognition and effects of assignments in which the assignor, the assignee and the debtor are not in the same country. Canada was an active participant in the development of this Convention.

...

The ULCC Working Group on Assignments of Receivables prepared a draft uniform implementation act and a final report, presented at the annual meeting of the ULCC in 2006. This work was part of a joint project with the then US National Conference of Commissioners on Uniform State Laws (NCCUSL) and the Mexican Uniform Law Centre. At the 2006 annual meeting, the adoption of the draft uniform act was postponed to allow the joint project to proceed. The Uniform Act was adopted by the Conference in 2007.

Internationally, the Convention's importance continues to be recognized. The United States has indicated that it anticipates taking the steps necessary for ratification. The European Commission, by letter of June 22, 2006 to UNCITRAL, stated its intention to ensure coherence between the Convention and the Rome I Regulation and to facilitate the ratification of the Convention by EU Member States.

Roy Goode, *The Cape Town Convention on International Interests in Mobile Equipment and Its Protocols*
(paper presented at the 14th Biennial Meeting of the International
Academy of Commercial and Consumer Law, Bamberg, Germany,
July 31-August 3, 2008), Parts I-X (footnotes omitted)

I Introduction

It is rare for an international convention in the field of transactional commercial law to attract the degree of enthusiasm and support accorded to the Convention on International Interests in Mobile Equipment (the Cape Town Convention) which, with its Protocol on Matters Specific to Aircraft Equipment (the Aircraft Protocol), was concluded at Cape Town on 16 November 2001. Even one of the most successful international instruments, the 1980 UN Convention on Contracts for the International Sale of Goods, attracted a mere five signatures at the time of its making and took nearly eight years to come into force. By contrast the Cape Town Convention and Aircraft Protocol were both signed on the final day of the Cape Town Diplomatic Conference by no fewer than 20 States, and in the ensuing 6½ years 25 States have ratified the Convention and 23 the Protocol. This is all the more striking in that the ratifying States have not so far included any Member State of the European Union except Ireland, and this because of a diplomatic problem between two Member States which held up progress towards adoption by the European Community for several years but has now been resolved, so that we can expect the number of ratifications to increase significantly in the not too distant future. A second Protocol (the Luxembourg Protocol), relating to railway rolling stock, was concluded in Luxembourg on 23 February 2007, and a third, covering space assets, is in course of preparation and if all goes well will be adopted at a Diplomatic Conference in 2010.

These are not minor instruments. The Convention runs to 62 Articles, the Aircraft Protocol 37 Articles and the Luxembourg Protocol 34 Articles. It is not possible in a paper of this kind to do more than give an outline of the objectives and main provisions. ...

II The Background

The project began with a proposal from the Canadian government to the International Institute for the Unification of Private Law (UNIDROIT) in June 1988 to build on the UNIDROIT Convention on International Financial Leasing, concluded a month previously, by providing an international regime for the protection of security interests in mobile equipment generally. The object of the proposed convention would be to deal with the types of problem encountered when the rights of secured parties in mobile equipment arising under security agreements created under the laws of one State come into conflict with rights created under the laws of another State. Professor Ronald Cuming of the University of Saskatchewan prepared a major comparative law study of security interests, which drew on responses by commercial law experts from different countries to a set of questions on the adequacy of national laws. The study showed widespread agreement that rules of private international law were inadequate to deal with problems arising from the movement of equipment of high value from one jurisdiction to another. The selection of the *lex situs* (*lex rei sitae*) as the governing law worked well enough for equipment that remained in one jurisdiction but was profoundly unsatisfactory for equipment regularly moving across national borders and therefore having no fixed situs. Moreover, even if a suitable conflicts rule could be devised, the lack of uniformity in substantive law would still leave creditors exposed to the risk of a hostile legal environment at the enforcement stage.

The study proposed a convention covering security and title retention interests in equipment of a kind normally moved from one State to another and consisting partly of conflict of laws rules—in particular, recognition of a security interest constituted under the law of the State of the debtor's principal place of business—and substantive rules governing default remedies and priority. But priority would depend on compliance with the public notice requirements (if any) of the law of the above State.

A questionnaire prepared by Professor Cuming and attracting about 100 responses showed agreement on the need for a convention of this kind. The restricted exploratory working group agreed that the project was not only feasible but useful. However, as the work progressed, three crucial deviations from the original scheme were agreed. First, it became clear that a functional approach to the concept of security based on Article 9 of the American Uniform Commercial Code, which treats conditional sales and certain types of leasing agreement as security agreements, would not be acceptable in Europe, so that security, title reservation and leasing agreements should be treated as distinct categories. Secondly, it was decided to focus on three categories of high unit value equipment capable of unique identification: aircraft objects, railway rolling stock and space assets. Thirdly, rather than providing for recognition of a national interest, the Convention should create an entirely new international interest possessing the characteristics given by the Convention itself and protected by registration in an international registry, registration being against a uniquely identified asset rather than against the debtor. These bold ideas for a wholly new international interest and an international asset-based registration system, endorsed by the Governing Council of UNIDROIT when authorising the project to proceed, were to become central to the Convention and Protocol.

III Key Features of the Convention

The lack of an international legal regime governing security interests in high-value mobile equipment has resulted in the instability of creditors' rights. In the first place, some legal systems are hostile to non-possessory security interests in tangible movables, so that a creditor taking security under the law of one jurisdiction cannot be sure that its rights will be recognised in others. Secondly, the exercise of default remedies, which are liberally treated in most common law jurisdictions, may be significantly restricted in others. Thirdly, there has hitherto been no mechanism for securing international priority for a security interest created under national law. The Convention, with its associated Protocols, is designed to address all these problems in the following ways:

- By providing for the constitution of an international interest under a security agreement, a title reservation agreement or a leasing agreement, its perfection by registration in an International Registry and its priority over subsequently registered interests and unregistered interests.
- By conferring on the creditor a set of basic default remedies, including speedy relief pending final determination of the claim.
- By ensuring the effectiveness in the debtor's insolvency of an interest registered before the commencement of the insolvency proceedings.
- By providing for the assignment of associated rights to payment or other performance under the agreement, registration of the assignment and priority.

Reflecting its complexity, the Convention contains an unusually large number of definitions—40 in all—to which the Aircraft Protocol adds 16 definitions and the Luxembourg Protocol five definitions. So in relation to aircraft objects the texts have to be read in the light of no fewer than 56 definitions, and in relation to railway rolling stock, 45 definitions.

IV The Two-Instrument Structure

At a fairly early stage in the drafting certain things became clear. First, there were significant definitional problems which could not be resolved by a Drafting Committee. How, for example, was an aircraft to be defined? What qualifying features should be introduced to exclude light aircraft? Answers to these questions would require intensive examination by experts in the aviation industry. Secondly, was there a method by which we could avoid cluttering up the text of the Convention with technical data arising from the definitions? Thirdly, what was the best way of resolving problems arising from the fact that on some aspects the three sectors involved—aviation, rail and space—had different needs?

There were three possible approaches to the resolution of these problems. One was to have a single Convention containing all the provisions required for all three categories, one part containing equipment-neutral provisions while each of the others would be devoted to the particular category concerned. But such an instrument would have been lengthy and complex. Moreover, adoption of this approach would mean that if different sectors proceeded at different speeds, conclusion of the Convention would be delayed until the work on the slowest had been completed. A second approach was to have a separate Convention for each of the three categories of object. This certainly would have the advantage of enabling work in relation to different categories to proceed at different speeds. But there were also serious disadvantages. In the first place, most of the provisions of the Convention were likely to be equipment-neutral, so that there would be not merely duplication but triplication of effort. Moreover, the drafting of different Conventions by different hands at different times was likely to result in divergences in the text even as regards equipment-neutral provisions which would undermine the unity of the project and inhibit a uniform interpretation of such provisions. Finally, a single Convention would inhibit the ability of a Contracting State to select only the particular category of object for which it needed the Convention.

The Aviation Working Group (AWG), set up to co-ordinate responses of the aviation industry and co-chaired by Boeing and Airbus, had become increasingly frustrated by the slow progress resulting from the attempt to cover all three industries in parallel, and on behalf of the AWG, Boeing invited the International Air Transport Association (IATA) to propose a means by which the project could be moved forward in relation to aircraft objects without being held up by the fact that work on railway rolling stock and space assets was proceeding at a much slower pace. Lorne Clark, then General Counsel of IATA, came up with the imaginative idea of a two-instrument approach: a Convention consisting entirely of equipment-neutral provisions and then separate Protocols for each of the three categories of object, the Protocols being able to modify the Convention to meet the particular needs of the industry sector involved. This novel use of a Protocol not merely to supplement but to control a Convention was seen to possess several advantages. The Convention itself would be shorter and free from technical data. Its equipment-neutral provisions would apply across the board, so that interpretation of a provision affecting one category of object would be equally applicable to the others. And the different sectors could proceed at different speeds. This proposal, submitted to UNIDROIT by IATA and the AWG, was adopted by UNIDROIT, at whose invitation an Aircraft Protocol Group (APG) was established to prepare a protocol for aircraft objects, IATA and the AWG being joined by the International Civil Aviation Organization (ICAO), which was to co-sponsor the Diplomatic Conference with UNIDROIT.

Even so, the two-instrument approach was not without its opponents. While a strong majority of delegations at the 31st Session of the Legal Committee of ICAO in Montreal in August and September 2000 favoured such an approach, there were those who advocated an aircraft-only Convention. Only on the first day of the Diplomatic Conference in

Cape Town in November 2001 did it become clear that there was overwhelming support for the Convention-Protocol approach, which was then adopted. That settled the issue not only for aircraft objects but for rail and space. It was, however, agreed that for the convenience of the aviation industry the Secretariats of UNIDROIT and ICAO should produce a Consolidated Text combining the provisions of the Convention and Aircraft Protocol. The resulting text is widely used but has no legal status.

The Convention and Aircraft Protocol were concluded and signed at the same time on 16 November 2001; more than five years were to elapse before conclusion of the Luxembourg Protocol relating to railway rolling stock—a striking vindication of the two-instrument approach. Most of the provisions of the Convention and Aircraft Protocol entered into force on 1 March 2006; those provisions of the Convention unrelated to objects—including the final clauses, covering such matters as signature, ratification, declarations, etc.—entered into force on the conclusion of the Convention on 16 November 2001.

V Sphere of Application

In order for the Convention to apply, the following conditions must be satisfied:

(1) Equipment

The equipment must belong to one of the following categories of object:

- (a) aircraft objects, that is, airframes, aircraft engines and helicopters, as defined by the Aircraft Protocol;
- (b) railway rolling stock as defined by the Luxembourg Protocol;
- (c) space assets, prospectively defined by the draft Space Protocol.

Because it is not uncommon to finance aircraft engines separately from airframes, the Convention treats them as separate categories. It is therefore not possible to take an international interest in an aircraft as a whole. By contrast, an engine installed on a helicopter is part of the helicopter and cannot be the subject of an international interest, though it is possible to take a prospective international interest in a helicopter engine which will become an international interest the moment the engine leaves the helicopter.

(2) Designation in a Protocol

The object must not only fall within one of the above three categories but the category must be one which is designated in the relevant Protocol. The Convention cannot come into force as regards an object until the Protocol relevant to that object has itself come into force. The Protocol is thus crucial to the operation of the Convention.

(3) Unique identification

The Convention applies only to uniquely identifiable objects. This is because the registration system is asset-based, so that it must be possible to identify the asset from the registered particulars. This precludes an international interest in after-acquired property and also in general proceeds, though an international interest in an object will extend automatically to its insurance proceeds or the proceeds of confiscation, condemnation or requisition. The identification criteria must be prescribed by the Protocol and/or by regulations made pursuant to the Protocol.

As regards aircraft objects, the requirement of identifiability applies not only to the registration of the interest but also to its constitution. However, at the Diplomatic Conference leading to the Luxembourg Protocol a member of the Canadian delegation asked why it was necessary to be so strict as regards the creation of an international interest. Why should a fresh security agreement have to be taken every time a new item of rolling stock was given in security? Curiously enough, it had never occurred to anyone to ask this question before! So Article V of the Luxembourg Protocol allows an international interest to be taken not only over an individually identified object but over categories of object or over all objects or all objects other than excluded categories. The draft Space Protocol currently under consideration follows this approach.

(4) Nature of interest

The interest must be one which is granted by the chargor under a security agreement or is vested in a person who is the conditional seller under a title reservation agreement or the lessor under a leasing agreement. The interest of a buyer under an outright sale is not an international interest and is not registrable under the Convention, though in the case of an aircraft object the Aircraft Protocol extends the Convention's registration and priority provisions to outright sales.

"Security agreement," "title reservation agreement" and "leasing agreement" are all defined terms. So for the Convention to apply at all, the agreement must fall within one of the three definitions. Assuming it does it is then for the applicable law to determine into which category the agreement falls. This may lead to recharacterisation. For example, under Article 9 of the American Uniform Commercial Code a title reservation (or conditional sale) agreement constitutes a security agreement. So if proceedings are brought in New York in respect of a title reservation agreement, a New York court will apply the default provisions of the Convention governing default by a chargor under a security agreement, whereas a Paris court would apply the different provisions governing default by a conditional buyer or lessee. Of course, even under New York law the agreement, though characterised as a security agreement, is still a title reservation agreement. So to avoid duplication of categories the Convention provides that an interest arising under a security agreement does not also fall to be treated as arising under a title reservation or leasing agreement.

(5) Connecting factor

The final condition is that the debtor is situated in a Contracting State at the time of conclusion of the agreement creating or providing for the international interest. To give maximum scope for the application of this connecting factor, Article 4 provides a number of different ways in which the situation test can be satisfied. As regards a helicopter, or an airframe pertaining to an aircraft, the Aircraft Protocol provides as an alternative connecting factor the registration of the aircraft in the aircraft register of a Contracting

State which is the State of registry as defined by the Protocol. The situation of the creditor is irrelevant.

VI The International Interest and National Law

Nature of the international interest

The international interest is a construct of the Convention. Once the conditions for the constitution of the international interest have been satisfied, it takes effect by force of the Convention in any Contracting State, whether or not it is of a kind recognised by the law of that State. This does not mean that the interest is wholly independent of national law, for this continues to govern the question whether certain constitutive elements of the international interest, such as the existence of the agreement as a contract, are present. But the international interest is an autonomous interest and, once registered, usually trumps any interest created by national law. In many cases, fulfilment of the conditions for the creation of an international interest will also be sufficient to create a national law interest, so that the two will co-exist.

A new international interest may arise from an amendment of the agreement for the existing international interest. This will occur, for example, in the case of an amendment which substitutes a new item of equipment, extends the period of a lease, brings in a new or additional party as grantor or grantee of a security interest, changes the category of agreement (as by adding an option to purchase to a lease so as to lead to recharacterisation of the agreement as a security agreement under the applicable law) or extends a security interest to cover an obligation previously unsecured. In all these cases a new international interest arises which needs to be registered, though this does not affect the validity of the existing registration.

The Convention and national law

There is a fear in some quarters that the Convention may undercut regulatory law and even facilitate money laundering and the like. This is a misconception. The Convention operates in the field of private transactional law. It has no impact on criminal or regulatory law. But within its sphere of application, the Convention, though providing for an autonomous international interest, does not operate in a legal vacuum. It specifically refers a number of issues to national law, including (re-) characterisation, additional remedies, legal and contractual subrogation and the treatment of items installed on or removed from an object.

VII Constitution of the International Interest

The formal requirements for the constitution of an international interest are relatively simple. The agreement creating or providing for the international interest must be in writing, must relate to an object of which the chargor, conditional seller or lessor has power to dispose, must enable the object to be identified in conformity with the Protocol and, in the case of a security agreement, must enable the secured obligations to be determined, but without the need to state a sum or maximum sum secured. "Power to dispose" is broader than "right to dispose," covering any situation in which, under the applicable law or the Convention itself, the disposing party has the ability to make a disposition which is binding on the owner of the object, as where an agent sells an asset of its principal without actual authority to do so but in the course of its apparent authority. While the power to dispose usually arises under the applicable law it may also arise under the Convention itself. For example, it is implicit in the rules governing the registration and priority of the interest held by a lessor that a lessee has a power to dispose for the purposes of the Convention, for if that were not the case there would be no point in making the lessor's interest registrable.

VIII Default Remedies

The Convention provides a set of basic default remedies which, subject to certain mandatory rules, can be expanded or modified by agreement. These include, in the case of security agreements, taking possession or control of the object, selling or granting a lease of it, collecting or receiving any income or profits arising from its management or use, and taking the object in or towards satisfaction of the debt, and, in the case of title reservation and leasing agreements, termination of the agreement and the assumption of possession or control of the object. Also important is the right conferred on the creditor, on adducing evidence of default, to speedy relief pending final determination of its claim on the merits. The forms of relief to which the creditor is entitled are preservation of the object and its value, possession, control or custody of the object, immobilisation of the object or lease or management of the object or the income therefrom. Sale is not one of the forms of relief available, though it is a remedy provided by the Aircraft Protocol if at any time the debtor and the creditor specifically so agree. Because the breadth of these remedies and the fact that there is no judicial discretion to refuse them may run counter to the policy of some States, it is open to a Contracting State not to apply Article 13, wholly or in part. The Protocols add other remedies.

IX The International Registry

The International Registry system

Central to the Convention is the International Registry. By registration the holder of an international interest or any other registrable interest can give notice of that interest to third parties and secure priority over competing interests. There will be a separate International Registry for each category of object. The International Registry for aircraft objects has been operational since the Convention and Aircraft Protocol entered into force on 1 March 2006. The International Registry for railway rolling stock is in the course of being established in Luxembourg under the aegis of the Preparatory Commission set up pursuant to a Resolution of the Luxembourg Diplomatic Conference, so the following remarks are confined to the aircraft Registry. This is based in Dublin and is run by the Registrar, Aviareto (a joint venture company of SITA SC and the Irish Government), with a small staff and technological support from SITA.

The International Registry is wholly electronic. Applications for registration are made and consents to registration transmitted on-line by computer and are processed by computer at the International Registry without human intervention. Similarly, searches are made and search certificates issued electronically. The risk of error in the description of the aircraft object is greatly reduced by the fact that free-texting is not normally allowed. The manufacturers of aircraft objects supply details of all their airframes, aircraft engines and helicopters to the International Registry, and registrants are required to select the relevant data from drop-down menus. There is, of course, the possibility of error in the registration of such data as the names of the parties, but since the registration system is asset-based, not debtor-based, any such error is unlikely to have significant consequences.

It is important to note that the International Registry is not a title registry; its function as regards international interests is simply to record the apparent existence of a security interest or a right held by a conditional seller or lessor without regard to the quantum of that right or, indeed, the question whether it exists at all. Even in relation to outright sales of aircraft objects the International Registry merely records the sale, without regard to the title of the seller or that acquired by the buyer. Registration is therefore no guarantee of the validity or existence of the interest to which it relates.

Registration cannot usually be effected without the consent in writing of the party affected. Regulations made pursuant to Article 18(1) provide for the prior electronic transmission of a consent.

Fees are required to be set by the Supervisory Authority on a cost-recovery basis, not with a view to providing a profit either to the Supervisory Authority or to the International Registry. Currently the fee for a registration is US$100 and for a priority search US$35. There are also user and controlled entity set-up fees.

The registration system is not confined to international interests. Also registrable are: a prospective international interest, a registrable non-consensual right or interest, an assignment or prospective assignment of an international interest, the acquisition of an international interest by legal or contractual subrogation under the applicable law, a notice of a national interest and a subordination of an interest. The registration system also accommodates amendments, extensions and discharges of a registration. The ability to register a prospective international interest in a uniquely identified object is particularly useful. Among other things, it enables a prospective creditor with whom the debtor is negotiating for an advance on the security of the object to protect its priority by registering a prospective international interest so that, when this takes effect as an international interest, it will have priority as from the time of registration of the prospective international interest. The need for a fresh registration when the international interest comes into existence is avoided by a provision that a search certificate shall state merely that the creditor named in the registration information has acquired or intends to acquire an international interest in the object without indicating whether what is registered is an international interest or a prospective international interest, even if this is ascertainable from the relevant registration information.

Registrable transactions

Another case in which the registrability of a prospective international interest is of importance concerns helicopter engines. While an international interest can be acquired in an engine before its installation on or after its removal from a helicopter, it is not possible to acquire an international interest in an engine while it is installed on a helicopter. This is because an installed engine is part of the helicopter, not an independent object under the Convention. This could have caused difficulties for financiers of installed engines. However, by registering a prospective international interest the financier can ensure that as soon as the engine leaves the helicopter an international interest arises and has priority as from the time of registration of the prospective international interest.

Liability of the Supervisory Authority and the Registrar

The Supervisory Authority is given international legal personality where not already possessing it and enjoys such immunity from legal or administrative process as is specified in the Protocol. The Aircraft Protocol gives ICAO such immunity as is provided under the rules applicable to it. As a specialised agency of the United Nations ICAO possesses an international legal personality and enjoys immunity. By contrast the Registrar is strictly liable not only for its errors and omissions but also for system malfunction except where this is "caused by an event of an inevitable and irresistible nature which could not be prevent[ed] by using the best practices in current use in the field of electronic design registry and operation, including those related to back-up and systems security and networking." It is only in exceptional cases that this exemption from liability is likely to apply. There is no limit of liability.

X Priorities

National legal systems usually have quite complex rules governing the priority of competing security interest. But those involved with the preparation of the Cape Town Convention took the decision to strip the priority rules down to their essentials. Simplicity rather than refinement was seen as essential to an international priority system. Apart from some rather complex rules governing the priority of assignments of associated rights, all the priority rules are gathered together in a single Article and are clear and uncomplicated.

The basic rule is that a registered interest has priority over any other interest subsequently registered and over an unregistered interest. In the interests of simplicity Article 29(2) goes on to provide that the above priority applies even if the holder of the first registered interest had actual knowledge of the other interest and even as regards value given by the holder of the first registered interest with such knowledge. The idea, which is also found in national registration systems, is to avoid factual disputes as to whether a party did or did not have knowledge of an interest. Moreover, the priority given over unregistered interests applies even if they are not interests registrable under the Convention at all. So an interest given by national law but not of a kind to which the Convention applies or registrable under it will be displaced by a registered international interest.

To this basic rule there are five principal exceptions.

(1) An outright buyer acquiring the object before registration of the international interest takes free from it. Since outright purchase is so common and the buyer's interest is not registrable it was felt necessary to carve out this exception to the general rule. However, it does not apply in relation to aircraft objects, sales of which are registrable by virtue of the Aircraft Protocol.

(2) A conditional buyer or lessee acquires its interest free from an interest registered after the registration of the interest held by its conditional seller or lessor. So if a conditional buyer registers its title reservation agreement and then charges the object to a third party to secure a loan, the charge being registered, the conditional buyer or lessee is not affected by the charge. The rationale for this exception is that by searching the International Registry, an intending chargee can ascertain the existence of the title reservation or leasing agreement.

(3) The priority of competing interests can be varied by agreement between the holders of those interests, though any subordination agreement has to be registered if it is to bind an assignee of the subordinated interest.

(4) A non-consensual right or interest covered by an effective declaration under Article 39 has priority even over a registered international interest.

(5) As stated above, where a prospective international interest is registered, then upon the international interest coming into existence it is to be treated as registered from the time of registration of the prospective international interest.

Any priority in an object extends to proceeds, but as indicated earlier these are narrowly defined and do not cover general proceeds.

[Professor Goode goes on to discuss the provisions relating to security interests in insolvency, assignments of associated rights, non-consensual rights and interests, jurisdiction, and the Protocols.]

NOTE

The following is an overview and assessment of the UNCITRAL Convention on the Assignment of Receivables in International Trade. It is extracted from a report by the Committee on Foreign and Comparative Law of the Association of the Bar of the City of New York, dated December 21, 2001, which is available at http://www.abcny.org/pdf/report/IntroV7 .pdf:

In order to address, as far as possible, the needs and desires of the participating States and retain compatibility with various legal systems, it was necessary for the Convention to focus on areas where broad agreement was possible. Among the more important concepts adopted by the Working Group are:

Rules Relating to Receivables Transactions. The Convention provides specific rules that set forth when the debtor may be notified of an assignment and who the debtor must pay, following assignment, in order to obtain a discharge of the receivable. The debtor's setoff and recoupment rights are generally preserved. Furthermore, agreements of a debtor not to assert claims and defenses against an assignee are generally validated.

Bulk, Future and Partial Receivables. The Convention recognizes the validity of assignments of receivables in bulk, present assignments of future receivables, and assignments of partial or undivided interests in receivables. The Convention does not require each receivable to be described in the contract of assignment and does not require a new contract of assignment when a future receivable, which is already subject to an existing assignment, is created.

Anti-Assignment Clauses. The Convention generally overrides contractual clauses that restrict assignments of receivables arising from the sale or lease of goods, credit card receivables or receivables arising out of the licensing of intellectual property.

Choice of Law for Priority. The Convention provides that the perfection and priority of an assignee's interest in a receivable is determined by the law of the State in which the assignor is located. That law also determines whether the assignment is a "true" sale or, rather, a secured transaction. If an insolvency proceeding is commenced by or against the assignor in a State other than the State in which the assignor is located, the insolvency tribunal may not refuse to apply the priority rules of the State of the assignor's location unless those rules are "manifestly contrary to the public policy of the forum State." The insolvency court may, however, charge the receivables with preferential claims if otherwise required under the forum State's insolvency laws.

Proceeds. The Convention gives the assignee a substantive interest in the proceeds of an assigned receivable that are paid to the assignee directly or that are held by the assignor on instructions by and for the benefit of the assignee in a segregated lock box or in any other manner in which the proceeds are segregated from the assets of the assignor.

Optional Provisions. The Convention sets forth optional choice of law rules to be applied in cross-border assignments of receivables even if the Convention would not otherwise apply. The Convention also sets forth in its Annex three alternative substantive priority rules that a State may choose to apply, including a priority rule based upon a notice filing system. In addition, the Annex contains general rules for the operation of such a notice filing system.

Notwithstanding these accomplishments, the Convention could have done more. The most serious deficiency in the Convention is that it lacks a single substantive rule for determining the priority of competing claims to the same receivable. Although the alternative adopted in the Convention, a choice of law rule, is by no means a negligible accomplishment, it is something of a disappointment for those legal practitioners and businesspeople who operate in States which have filing systems and who were hoping to see such a system established worldwide. One of the purposes of the Annex is to provide a framework for future development of such a worldwide system. Perhaps if a few States create an international filing system, others will be able to observe its merits in action.

Considering the diversity of the world's economic and legal systems, however, the Convention remains a remarkable achievement. Time after time, the Working Group was divided, not between the haves and the have-nots but between civil law and common law countries. Even a requirement which seems as basic (to a common law practitioner) as requiring an assignment to be in writing was stricken from the Convention because some European countries have no such rule. As negotiated and drafted, the Convention is substantially compatible with the existing laws of Working Group countries, including Revised Article 9 of the Uniform Commercial Code.

Added to these issues of divergent economic and legal systems was the worldwide tendency of lawyers to favor precedent over novelty. The legal profession is properly resistant to change. For any legal system to function properly, the people who are subject to its strictures must be able to order their lives according to predictable rules and any major alteration of those rules disrupts thousands of transactions within that legal system. That the Working Group was willing to entertain the revolutionary concepts embodied in the Convention is a tribute to both the achievement of the Convention's proponents and the importance of the issue for the global economy.

Different philosophies also affected the outcome. The concept of receivables financing is alien to many legal systems and a threat to some. The perceived threat to countries with relatively fixed social classes cannot be discounted: allowing unknown upstarts to use their customers' credit rating in order to help grow into viable competitors to established entities is nothing short of revolutionary. It is only a slight exaggeration to say that a sort of Catch-22 exists in some countries: you can't borrow money from a bank unless you have a long relationship with the bank, but you can't establish such a relationship without borrowing money. The dynamism of the lava lamp society creates as many losers as it does winners and forces all players to maximize their efficiency and productivity.

The issues on which the Working Group agreed far outweigh the issues on which no consensus was reached and set the stage for the resolution of those unresolved issues in the future. The list of achievements is long, among them: recognition of bulk and future receivables and partial assignments, a set of rules outlining the relationship between debtor, assignor and assignee, the override of anti-assignment clauses and the recognition of an assignee's right to proceeds. Nearly all of these achievements represent a long and hard effort to achieve consensus within the Working Group. That it was in some ways an educational process was very clear to those who followed the Working Group, and it was encouraging to see delegates from legal systems in which receivables financing is unknown develop a sophisticated and enthusiastic knowledge of the concept over the course of the sessions.

There are other, more abstract, contributions that the Convention brings. The concept of receivables financing will become more visible to many countries for whom it would have otherwise remained a vague concept. In particular, countries which adopt the Convention will gain a familiarity with its format and may soon find it to be a useful tool for domestic purposes as well.

For a fuller account of the Convention, with comparisons to the Canadian PPSAs and discussion of the modifications that would be required to Canadian laws for Canada to implement the Convention, see J. Michel Deschamps and Catherine Walsh, *United Nations Convention on the Assignment of Receivables in International Trade: Pre-Implementation Report* (Uniform Law Conference of Canada Annual Meeting, St. John's, Newfoundland, August 2005), available at www.ulcc.ca.

Forms of Agreement in Secured Transactions*

1. Canadian Imperial Bank of Commerce, *Conditional Sale Agreement.*
2. Canadian Imperial Bank of Commerce, *Chattel Mortgage Agreement.*
3. Canadian Imperial Bank of Commerce, *General Assignment of Accounts.*
4. Canadian Imperial Bank of Commerce, *Demand Debenture.*
5. Canadian Imperial Bank of Commerce, *Pledge Agreement.*

---

* Several of the forms have had to be reduced in size to accommodate them to the size of the casebook pages.

Form 1

CONDITIONAL SALE AGREEMENT

CANADIAN IMPERIAL BANK OF COMMERCE

ORIGINAL

ORIGINAL SIGNATURE REQUIRED ON FIRST FOUR COPIES

DATE _____ 19 ___

	DATE OF BIRTH			SEX
	DAY	MONTH	YEAR	M/F

Insert full name of Buyer(s); if not an individual, full business or corporate name

FULL NAME OF BUYER

ADDRESS: Street number and name, apt. no. if any, OR lot, concession and township | City, Town or Village (and rural route if any) | Prov./Terr.

	DATE OF BIRTH			SEX
	DAY	MONTH	YEAR	M/F

FULL NAME OF CO-BUYER(S)

ADDRESS: Street number and name, apt. no. if any, OR lot, concession and township | City, Town or Village (and rural route if any) | Prov./Terr.

FULL NAME OF SELLER

ADDRESS: Street number and name, apt. no. if any, OR lot, concession and township | City, Town or Village (and rural route if any) | Prov./Terr.

NAME OF BUYER (IF MORE THAN ONE) DESIGNATED FOR INSURANCE UNDER PARAGRAPH NINE (9) OF THE TERMS AND CONDITIONS HEREOF

Buyer hereby purchases from Seller, on the terms and conditions herein set forth, the property described below complete with all attachments and accessories (herein called the "property"), delivery and acceptance of which in good condition and as ordered is hereby acknowledged by Buyer.

MANUFACTURER AND DESCRIPTION OF PROPERTY (INCLUDING MAKE & BODY STYLE)	NEW OR USED AND YEAR	MODEL NO.	SERIAL NO.	NO. CYL	MOTOR NO. (IF MOTOR VEHICLE)	LICENCE NO. (IF MOTOR VEHICLE)	PRICE

CHECK ACCESSORIES AND INSERT COST	RADIO	AUTO-TRANS	POWER STEERING	POWER BRAKES	POWER SEATS	POWER WINDOWS	AIR CONDIT.	OTHER (ITEMIZE)	
$	$	$	$	$	$	$	$		$ $ $

Itemize all services for which separate charge is made, e.g. delivery, installation and inspection

1.	BASIC CASH PRICE	(a) PROPERTY		$	
		(b) SERVICES		$	
				$	
			TOTAL	$	$
2.	PLUS PROVINCIAL SALES TAX				$
3.	RETAIL CASH PRICE (1 + 2)				$
4.	OFFICIAL FILING OR REGISTRATION FEES PAYABLE BY SELLER AT BUYER'S REQUEST				$
5.	INSURANCE PREMIUM PAYABLE BY SELLER AT BUYER'S REQUEST INSURING FOR ACCIDENTAL PHYSICAL DAMAGE TO THE PROPERTY. (CHECK INSURANCE COVERAGE INCLUDED) COVERAGE APPLICABLE TO PROPERTY				$

Term _____ months. Effective date _____ 19 ___

$ _____ □ Comprehensive | Deductible Collision □ Fire and Theft | NO BODILY INJURY OR PROPERTY DAMAGE LIABILITY INSURANCE INCLUDED

Insert particulars of obligation paid.

6.	TOTAL CASH PRICE (3 + 4 + 5)		$
7.	A. GROSS TRADE-IN ALLOWANCE	$	
	B. AMOUNT PAYABLE TO _____ BY SELLER AT BUYER'S REQUEST FOR _____	$	
	C. NET CREDIT FOR TRADE-IN (A-B)	$	
	D. CASH DOWN PAYMENT	$	
	E. TOTAL DOWN PAYMENT (C + D)	$	$
8.	BALANCE OF TOTAL CASH PRICE (6-7E)		$
9.	COST OF BORROWING-ANNUAL PERCENTAGE RATE OF _____ % OF BALANCE OF TOTAL CASH PRICE		$
10.	TOTAL AMOUNT PAYABLE (HEREIN CALLED THE "UNPAID BALANCE") (8 + 9)		$

	COMPLETE IN P.E.I. & N.S. ONLY	11.	OFFICIAL FEES PLUS INSURANCE PREMIUMS (4 + 5)	$
	COMPLETE IN ALTA, NB, NFLD, P.E.I. & N.S. ONLY	12.	RETAIL CASH PRICE LESS TOTAL DOWN PAYMENT (3-7E)	$
	COMPLETE IN MAN. ONLY	13.	COST OF BORROWING PLUS TOTAL CASH PRICE (9 + 6)	$

The Unpaid Balance shall be paid by Buyer to Canadian Imperial Bank of Commerce, *
as follows: $ _____ on the _____ day of _____ , 19 ___ and _____ equal consecutive payments of
$ _____ each on the _____ day of each month commencing on the _____ day of _____ , 19 ___ ,
and ending on the _____ day of _____ , 19 ___ , totalling $ _____ ; with interest after maturity
on each instalment at the rate of _____ % per annum and upon default in any such payment, all remaining instalments shall forthwith become due and payable without notice.

PAYMENT OF THE UNPAID BALANCE MAY ALSO BE ACCELERATED UNDER THE TERMS AND CONDITIONS ON THE REVERSE HEREOF WHICH CONSTITUTE PART OF THIS AGREEMENT.

BUYER ACKNOWLEDGES RECEIPT OF A COMPLETE EXECUTED COPY OF THIS AGREEMENT.

DATED this _____ day of _____ , 19 ___

WITNESS: _____

SIGNATURE OF BUYER _____

SIGNATURE OF CO-BUYER (IF ANY) _____

Seller hereby agrees to the foregoing and assigns the within contract to Canadian Imperial Bank of Commerce upon the terms and conditions of the Assignment and Transfer set forth on the reverse hereof and Buyer acknowledges and accepts such Assignment and Transfer and undertakes to make payment to the Bank at

DATED the _____ day of _____ , 19 ___

VOID

Signature of Buyer _____

VOID

Signature of Co-Buyer (if any) _____

VOID

Signature of Seller _____

VOID

By _____

* FILL IN COMPLETE ADDRESS

Form 1—*Continued*

<u>TERMS AND CONDITIONS</u>

The following terms and conditions form part of the Agreement set forth on the face hereof:

1. The title to and ownership of the property shall not pass to Buyer on delivery thereof bu. shall remain in Seller at Buyer's risk until the Unpaid Balance together with interest and all other amounts payable by Buyer hereunder is paid in full.

2. Destruction of or damage to the property shall not release Buyer from liability hereunder and Buyer will keep the property insured in favour of Seller against such risks as Seller may require for an amount sufficient to secure the interest of Seller therein. If Buyer fails to keep the property insured, Seller may so insure (but shall be under no obligation to do so) and charge the amount of the premium to Buyer who shall pay the same forthwith.

3. Buyer shall keep the property free of all liens, charges and encumbrances and if any such lien, charge or encumbrance is created, Seller may pay off the same and any amount so paid with all costs and expenses shall be paid forthwith by Buyer.

4. No notice, demand or mise-en-demure shall be required to put Buyer in default under this agreement and if Seller shall grant or tolerate any extension or delay for the payment or performance of any obligations of Buyer, no such extension, delay or tolerance shall be deemed an acquiescence by Seller in such default, or a waiver of any of Seller's rights or recourse under this agreement.

5. Buyer shall keep the property in good repair.

6. If Buyer makes default in payment or fails to perform any obligation hereunder or if Seller deems itself insecure (of which Seller shall be sole judge) or if Seller has reasonable cause to believe that its security is in jeopardy or if any proceeding in bankruptcy, receivership or winding up be taken by or against Buyer or if Buyer fails to insure the property and Seller does not place such insurance forthwith or if the Buyer parts with possession of the property or removes the same for more than 20 days from the county or district within which Buyer resides at the time the property is delivered to Buyer hereunder or uses the property for hire without the written consent of Seller, the amount of the Unpaid Balance and all other amounts then outstanding hereunder shall immediately become due and payable and Seller may enter upon any premises where the property may be and repossess and remove the same without legal process; provided that if the rights of the parties hereunder with respect to the property are subject to the laws of the Province of Manitoba, Buyer may so remove the property within the Province of Manitoba or may charge his interest in the property if Buyer shall have given to Seller by delivery or registered mail at the address specified on the reverse hereof at least ten (10) days' prior written notice of his intention to do so, specifying the place within Manitoba to which the property is to be removed or the person in whose favour any such charge is to be created.

7. In the event that the property is repossessed under paragraph 6 hereof and is not thereafter redeemed in the manner and within the period prescribed by law, or within 30 days, whichever is greater, all or part of the property may from time to time be sold at public or private sale at the option of Seller, and after deducting the costs and expenses of sale, of taking and keeping possession and of repair and legal fees, the net proceeds of sale shall be applied on the amount then owing by Buyer and any surplus shall be paid to Buyer and any deficiency shall be forthwith paid by Buyer.

8. This agreement and all rights of Seller including the right to repossess the property may be assigned and transferred to Canadian

Imperial Bank of Commerce (herein call the "Bank") and such assignment (and any further assignments) shall not be subject to any equities as between Buyer and Seller unless otherwise required by law.

9. Buyer consents to life insurance being arranged under a Group Life Insurance Policy with The Canada Life Assurance Company, such insurance to be owned and paid for by and payable to the Bank, be effective as of the date of assignment of this contract to the Bank, and be subject to such terms and conditions as may be agreed upon between the Bank and said insurer, but the amount of insurance shall not exceed the amount of the Unpaid Balance. The name of Buyer (if more than one) whose life is to be insured is specifically designated on the face hereof. Such insurance shall terminate upon such terms and conditions as may be agreed upon between the Bank and said insurer. If the insurance becomes payable prior to such termination, the Unpaid Balance and all other amounts then outstanding hereunder shall be repaid to the extent possible from the insurance proceeds. Failure of the Bank to obtain or keep in force any or sufficient insurance for any reason shall not limit or lessen the liability of Buyer hereunder.

10. If the rights of the parties hereunder with respect to the property are subject to the laws of the Province of Saskatchewan, Buyer (if a body corporate) agrees that The Limitation of Civil Rights Act of Saskatchewan shall not apply to this contract or to any security for the payment of money made or created by or pursuant thereto or any agreement or instrument renewing or extending or collateral to this contract and any of the benefits of the said Act are hereby specifically waived.

11. Buyer expressly waives the benefit of every statute or law which prevents or restricts Seller from recovering a deficiency from Buyer after resale by Seller following repossession of the property, and without limiting the generality of the foregoing, if the rights of the parties hereunder with respect to the property are subject to the laws of the Province of Alberta, Buyer expressly waives the benefit of Section 19 of The Conditional Sales Act of Alberta.

12. Any term or condition or part thereof of this agreement which is prohibited or unenforceable by the law of any province shall, as to that province, be ineffective to the extent of such prohibition or unenforceable without invalidating the remaining terms and conditions of this agreement.

13. There are no representations, conditions, warranties, guarantees or collateral agreements, express or implied, statutory or otherwise, in respect of the property or this agreement, other than as set out herein, and without limiting the generality of the foregoing, if the rights of the parties hereunder with respect to the property are subject to the laws of the Province of Ontario, the implied conditions, warranties and guarantees contained in Section 13, 14, 15 and 16 of The Sale of Goods Act of Ontario are expressly excluded from this agreement.

14. This agreement shall ensure to the benefit of and shall bind the respective heirs, executors, administrators, successors and assigns of Buyer and Seller.

15. In the event that this agreement is signed by more than one buyer then "Buyer" wherever it appears in this agreement shall be read and construed as "Buyers" with all grammatical changes thereby rendered necessary, and the liability of such persons under this agreement shall be joint and several.

<u>ASSIGNMENT AND TRANSFER</u>

FOR VALUE RECEIVED Seller hereby assigns and transfers to Canadian Imperial Bank of Commerce,
                                                    *

(herein called the "Bank") the within contract, all rights, claims and moneys payable thereunder, all right, title and interest in and to the property therein described and the benefits of insurance upon the same and warrants that the contract is genuine and is not subject to rescission and that the property has been delivered to and accepted by Buyer, in default of which the agreement set out below in the paragraph entitled With Recourse shall apply.

Seller's liability hereunder shall not be affected by any extension, indulgence, compromise, security, variation of the contract or release of Buyer or other interested person whether by operation of law or otherwise. This assignment is supplemented by the agreement set out below in the paragraph initialled by Seller and these provisions shall apply to and bind the heirs, executors, administrators, successors and assigns of Seller and shall enure to the benefit of and be enforceable by the Bank, its successors and assigns.

Initial applicable paragraph:

☐ WITHOUT RECOURSE: Save as to the warranties set forth above, this assignment is without recourse to the Seller.

☐ WITH RECOURSE: Seller unconditionally agrees to repurchase the within contract forthwith upon demand, for the Unpaid Balance and all other amounts outstanding under the contract at the date of demand whether or not the contract shall then be in default.

☐ REPURCHASE: If within 90 days after any default which is not cured the property described in the within contract is repossessed by the Bank and delivered to Seller, Seller shall forthwith pay to the Bank the Unpaid Balance and all other amounts then outstanding under the contract regardless of the condition of the property, and Seller also agrees to repurchase the property for such amount after expiration of the said 90 day period provided the Bank institutes legal action to repossess the property within such period and the property is delivered to Seller within 30 days after the Bank has obtained legally indisputable possession thereof.

☐ LIMITED REPURCHASE: The above paragraph entitled Repurchase shall apply provided that the obligation of Seller thereunder shall terminate upon payment by Buyer to the Bank of the first   monthly instalments within 15 days of their respective due dates.

☐ OPTIONAL PURCHASE: If the Bank repossesses the property described in the within contract Seller shall have the option after demand by the Bank either to pay the Bank $ or to buy the property in its then condition and location from the Bank for the Unpaid Balance and all other amounts then outstanding under the contract.

* fill in complete address

Form 2

DL 30-83
For use in Ontario,
Manitoba, Saskatchewan
FIXED RATE OR FLOATING RATE

CANADIAN IMPERIAL BANK OF COMMERCE - SECURITY AGREEMENT (Chattel Mortgage)

BRANCH DOMICILE	DATE

BORROWER(S)

FIRST GIVEN NAME	INITIAL OF SECOND GIVEN NAME	LAST NAME	FIRST GIVEN NAME	INITIAL OF SECOND GIVEN NAME	LAST NAME

DATE OF BIRTH	DAY	MO	YR	SEX ☐ M ☐ F	DATE OF BIRTH	DAY	MO	YR	SEX ☐ M ☐ F
FULL ADDRESS					FULL ADDRESS				

(In this Agreement, the words "I", "me" and "my" mean each borrower who signs it and the word "Bank" means Canadian Imperial Bank of Commerce.)

Complete appropriate box.

NEW LOAN (Insert principal amount)
The Bank has made me a new loan of $ _____ (Note(s) dated _____ 19 _____). As a condition of my loan I agreed to sign this Security Agreement.

EXISTING LOAN (Insert original principal amount)
I have an existing loan from the Bank (Note(s) dated _____ 19 _____ for a total original principal amount of $ _____). The balance of my loan is now due. In return for the Bank not requiring me to repay my loan immediately, I am giving the Bank this Security Agreement.

SUBSTITUTION OF SECURITY FOR EXISTING LOAN (Insert original principal amount)
I borrowed $ _____ from the Bank and gave it my Note(s) dated _____ 19 _____ and a security agreement (chattel mortgage) on the following property:

In return for the Bank agreeing to release its interest in that property, I am giving it this Security Agreement.

SECURITY INTEREST
I now give the Bank a security interest in the following Property and all proceeds of it (and transfer my title in the Property and proceeds to the Bank) as security for the payment of my loan, interest on it, my Note(s), any replacement notes and all other amounts payable under this Agreement:

MANUFACTURER AND DESCRIPTION (INCLUDE BODY STYLE)	MODEL YEAR	SERIAL NO.	MOTOR NO. (IF MOTOR VEHICLE)	LICENSE NO (IF MOTOR VEHICLE)

Use headings or fully describe the Property

I agree with the Bank as follows:

PAYMENTS
1. Payments required by my Note(s) and each replacement note, as amended from time to time, will be made by me when due.

OWNERSHIP AND POSSESSION
2. I own the Property and I will not sell, lease or give up possession of it without the Bank's consent.

OTHER CLAIMS
3. The Property will be kept clear of all mortgages, liens and other claims except any I have already reported to the Bank in writing. If it is not, the Bank may (but does not have to) pay all or part of them.

INSURANCE
4. The Property will be kept insured by me for the amount and against the risks the Bank reasonably requests. If it is not, the Bank may (but does not have to) insure it and pay the premiums. As additional security, I transfer to the Bank my right to receive the insurance proceeds and it may apply them to the amount I owe (whether or not that amount is then due).

REPAIR AND INSPECTION
5. The Property will be kept in good repair by me. The Bank may inspect it at any reasonable time and may (but does not have to) make and pay for any reasonable repairs.

CHANGE OF RESIDENCE
6. I will tell the Bank before I move from any Province or Territory where I now or may later live so that it can register this Agreement where necessary.

BANK'S RIGHTS ON DEFAULT
7. The balance of my loan and accrued interest will become payable immediately if I breach any of my obligations under this Agreement, or if, without the Bank's consent, the Property is about to be sold or removed from Canada, or if proceedings are started by or against me under any insolvency or bankruptcy law, or if anything else happens which the Bank believes endangers the Property or affects my ability to pay the amounts that may become payable under my loan. In any such case the Bank may from time to time, in any order and in any lawful way, and after giving any notice required by law, do any one or more of the following:

(a) take possession of all or part of the Property, wherever it is;

(b) store, sell or lease all or part of the Property;

(c) sue me for any amount I owe; and

(d) exercise any other rights the Bank may have.

Sale or lease proceeds may be applied to the amount I owe, including the expenses mentioned in paragraph 8, and I will pay any amount still owing.

EXPENSES AND INTEREST
8. I will immediately repay all amounts the Bank is permitted to pay under this Agreement and all expenses, including legal fees, paid by it in exercising its rights. I will pay interest, at the rate shown in my Note(s), on such amounts and expenses from the date they are paid by the Bank until they are repaid by me.

GENERAL
9. This Agreement does not replace any other security held by the Bank or my Note(s). If more than one borrower signs this Agreement, each is separately liable and all are jointly liable under it.

COPY OF AGREEMENT
10. I have received a signed copy of this Agreement.

VOID

_____   _____
WITNESS   BORROWER

void

_____   _____
WITNESS   BORROWER

Form 3

73-83

GENERAL ASSIGNMENT OF ACCOUNTS, ETC.

....
(Branch Designation)

FOR VALUABLE CONSIDERATION the undersigned [1]

(1) Insert
full name
of assignor.

....
(Name)

of ....

(Street number and name, apt. no. OR lot, concession and Township)   (City, Town or Village and rural route)   (Prov./Territory)

hereby assign(s) and transfer(s) all debts, accounts, claims, moneys and choses in action which now are or which may at any time hereafter be due or owing to or owned by the undersigned, and also all securities, bills, notes and other documents now held or owned or which may be hereafter taken, held or owned by the undersigned or anyone on behalf of the undersigned in respect of the said debts, accounts, claims, moneys and choses in action or any part thereof, and also all books and papers recording, evidencing or relating to said debts, accounts, claims, moneys and choses in action or any part thereof (all of the foregoing being herein called the "assigned premises") to CANADIAN IMPERIAL BANK OF COMMERCE (herein called the "Bank") as a general and continuing collateral security for payment of all existing and future indebtedness and liability of the undersigned to the Bank wheresoever and howsoever incurred and any ultimate unpaid balance thereof, and as a first and prior claim upon the assigned premises.

2. The Bank may collect, realize, sell or otherwise deal with the assigned premises or any part thereof in such manner, upon such terms and conditions and at such time or times as may seem to it advisable and without notice to the undersigned (except as otherwise required by any applicable law), and may charge on its own behalf and pay to others reasonable sums for expenses incurred and for services rendered (expressly including legal advices and services) in or in connection with collecting, realizing, selling or obtaining payment of the assigned premises and may add the amount of such sums to the indebtedness of the undersigned.

3. The Bank shall not be liable or accountable for any failure to collect, realize, sell or obtain payment of the assigned premises or any part thereof and shall not be bound to institute proceedings for the purpose of collecting, realizing or obtaining payment of the same or for the purpose of preserving any rights of the Bank, the undersigned or any other person, firm or corporation in respect of the same.

4. The Bank may grant extensions of time and other indulgences, take and give up securities, accept compositions, grant releases and discharges and otherwise deal with the undersigned, debtors of the undersigned, sureties and others and with the assigned premises and other securities as the Bank may see fit without prejudice to the liability of the undersigned or the Bank's right to hold and realize this security.

5. All moneys collected or received by the undersigned in respect of the assigned premises shall be received as trustee for the Bank and shall be forthwith paid over to the Bank.

6. All moneys collected or received by the Bank in respect of the assigned premises (whether by virtue of paragraph 5 hereof or otherwise howsoever) may be applied on account of such parts of the indebtedness and liability of the undersigned as to the Bank seems best or in the discretion of the Bank may be released to the undersigned, all without prejudice to the Bank's claims upon the undersigned.

7. The undersigned shall from time to time forthwith on request furnish to the Bank in writing all information requested relating to the assigned premises and the Bank shall be entitled from time to time to inspect the aforesaid securities, bills, notes, books, papers and other documents or take temporary custody thereof and for such purposes the Bank shall have access to all premises occupied by the undersigned.

8. The undersigned shall from time to time forthwith on the Bank's request do, make and execute all such financing statements, further assignments, documents, acts, matters and things as may be required by the Bank of or with respect to the assigned premises or any part thereof or as may be required to give effect to these presents, and the undersigned hereby constitutes and appoints the Manager or acting Manager for the time being of the above mentioned branch of the Bank, or any other branch at which this security is held, the true and lawful attorney of the undersigned irrevocable with full power of substitution to do, make and execute all such statements, assignments, documents, acts, matters or things with the right to use the name of the undersigned whenever and wherever it may be deemed necessary or expedient.

9. The provisions hereof shall enure to the benefit of the successors and assigns of the Bank and shall be binding upon the respective heirs, executors, administrators, successors and assigns of the undersigned.

WITNESS the hand and seal of the undersigned this........ day of .... 19.......

Witness:

SEAL

SIGNATURE

RECEIPT OF A COPY OF THE WITHIN SECURITY AGREEMENT IS HEREBY ACKNOWLEDGED.

DATE

(To be completed for registration in Manitoba, Ontario and Saskatchewan)

If an individual(s), first given name, initial of second given name, if any, then surname. Record full address including postal code.	FULL NAME AND ADDRESS OF ASSIGNOR(S)	If given by individual(s) record				For Manitoba only Driver's License No. (If Available)
		Initials of ASSIGNOR(S)	Date of Birth For Ontario Day / Month / Year		Sex M/F	
			For Manitoba Year / Month / Day			

Form 4

DEMAND DEBENTURE

Form 1073-79

PRINCIPAL SUM   Dollars
($)   Date

(Delete inapplicable clause)

INTEREST (a) nominal annual rate of _____ %
RATE (b) _____ % per annum, being a nominal annual rate _____ percentage points above the Minimum Lending Rate (the "MLR") of Canadian Imperial Bank of Commerce (the "Bank") in effect on the date hereof; provided that if and whenever the MLR is varied by the Bank the interest rate hereunder shall also be varied, effective on the day such variation in the MLR comes into effect, so that at all times the interest rate hereunder shall be the said number of percentage points above the MLR then in effect. The certificate of a Vice-President or Assistant General Manager of the Bank as to the MLR in effect at any time shall be accepted as conclusive evidence thereof for all purposes hereof.

BANK BRANCH AND ADDRESS

1.1 ....
incorporated under the laws of _____ (the "Company") for value received hereby acknowledges itself indebted and promises to pay on demand to or to the order of CANADIAN IMPERIAL BANK OF COMMERCE (the "Bank") the above mentioned principal sum in lawful money of Canada on presentation and surrender of this debenture at the Bank's branch mentioned above, or at such other place as the Bank may designate by notice in writing to the Company, and in the meantime to pay interest thereon from the date hereof at the above mentioned rate in like money at the same place monthly on the last day of each month; and, should the Company at any time make default in the payment of any principal or interest, to pay interest on the amount in default both before and after judgment at the same rate in like money at the same place on the same dates.

SECURITY

(Delete inapplicable provisions)

2.1 As security for the due payment of all moneys payable hereunder, the Company as beneficial owner hereby:

(a) grants, assigns, conveys, mortgages and charges as and by way of a first fixed and specific mortgage and charge to and in favour of the Bank, its successors and assigns:

(i) all lands and premises now owned by the Company and described or referred to in Schedule A hereto, including all appurtenances, buildings and fixtures now or hereafter situate thereon, and all other lands and premises, including buildings and fixtures, hereafter acquired by the Company; and

(ii) all machinery, equipment, plant, vehicles, goods and chattels now owned by the Company and described or referred to in Schedule B hereto and all other machinery, equipment, plant, vehicles, goods and chattels, hereafter acquired by the Company; and

(b) charges as and by way of a first floating charge to and in favour of the Bank, its successors and assigns, all its undertaking, property and assets, both present and future, of every nature and kind and wherever situate (other than such as are at all times validly subjected to the first fixed and specific mortgage and charge hereby created) including, without limitation, its franchises and uncalled capital.

In this debenture, the mortgages and charges hereby consituted are called the "Security" and the subject matter of the Security is called the "Charged Premises".

2.2 Until the Security becomes enforceable, the Company may dispose of or deal with the subject matter of the floating charge in the ordinary course of its business and for the purpose of carrying on the same provided that the Company will not, without the prior written consent of the Bank, create, assume or have outstanding, except to the Bank, any mortgage, charge or other encumbrance on any part of the Charged Premises ranking or purporting to rank or capable of being enforced in priority to or pari passu with the Security, other than any mortgage, lien or other encumbrance upon property, created or assumed to secure all or any part of the funds required for the purchase of such property or any extension or renewal or replacement thereof upon the same property if the principal amount of the indebtedness secured thereby is not increased, or any inchoate liens for taxes or assessments by public authorities.

2.3 The Security shall not extend or apply to the last day of the term of any lease or agreement therefor but upon the enforcement of the Security the Company shall stand possessed of such last day in trust to assign the same to any person acquiring such term.

2.4 The Bank is the person entitled to receive the money payable hereunder and to give a discharge hereof.

ENFORCEMENT

3.1 In the event that the Company makes default in the payment of principal or interest hereunder the Security shall become enforceable.

3.2 Whenever the Security has become enforceable, the Bank may realize upon the Security and enforce its rights by the following remedies:

(a) entry into possession;

(b) proceedings in any court of competent jurisdiction for the appointment of a receiver (which term as used in this debenture includes a receiver and manager) of all or any part of the Charged Premises;

(c) proceedings in any court of competent jurisdiction for sale or foreclosure of all or any part of the Charged Premises;

(d) filing of proofs of claim and other documents to establish its claims in any proceeding relative to the Company;

Form 4—*Continued*

    (e)   appointment by instrument in writing of a receiver of all or any part of the Charged Premises and removal or replacement from time to time of any such receiver; and

    (f)   any other remedy or proceeding authorized or permitted hereby or by law or equity.

Such remedies may be exercised from time to time separately or in combination and are in addition to and not in substitution for any other rights of the Bank however created.

3.3 Any receiver appointed by instrument in writing shall have power to:

    (a)   take possession of, collect and get in all or any part of the Charged Premises and, for that purpose, to take proceedings in the name of the Company or otherwise and to make any arrangement or compromise;

    (b)   carry on or concur in carrying on all or any part of the business of the Company;

    (c)   borrow or to raise money on all or any part of the Charged Premises in priority to this debenture or otherwise for such purposes as may be approved by the Bank; and

    (d)   sell or concur in selling all or any part of the Charged Premises without notice and in such manner as may seem advisable to the receiver, and to effect such sale by conveying in the name and on behalf of the Company or otherwise.

The receiver shall be vested with such other discretions and powers as are granted in the instrument of appointment and any supplement thereto. The receiver shall for all purposes be deemed to be the agent of the Company and not of the Bank, and the Company shall be solely responsible for his acts or defaults and for his remuneration. All moneys from time to time received by the receiver may be applied as follows: first, in discharge of all operating expenses and other outgoings affecting the Charged Premises; second, in keeping in good standing all charges and liens on the Charged Premises having priority over the Security; third, in payment of the remuneration and disbursements of the receiver; fourth, in payment to the Bank of the moneys payable hereunder; and the balance, if any, shall be paid to the Company.

EXPENSES

4.1 The Company agrees to pay to the Bank forthwith on demand all costs, charges and expenses, including all legal fees, (on a solicitor and his own client basis), incurred by the Bank in connection with the recovery or enforcement of payment of any moneys owing hereunder whether by realization or otherwise. All such sums shall be secured hereby and shall be added to the principal hereof and bear interest at the rate in effect hereunder at the date hereof.

PLEDGE OF DEBENTURE

5.1 This debenture may be deposited or pledged by the Company as collateral security for its indebtedness and liabilities and, when redelivered to the Company or its nominees, shall be forthwith cancelled; but this debenture shall not be deemed to have been redeemed by reason of the account of the Company having ceased to be in debit while this debenture was so deposited or pledged and no payment shall reduce the amount owing under this debenture unless specifically appropriated to and noted on this debenture at the time of payment.

NEGOTIABILITY

6.1 This debenture is a negotiable instrument and all rights created hereunder are exercisable by any holder hereof.

WAIVER

7.1 No consent or waiver by the Bank shall be effective unless made in writing and signed by an authorized officer of the Bank.

NOTICE

8.1 Any notice to the Company may be given by prepaid registered mail to the Company at its head office and any notice so given shall be deemed to have been duly given on the day on which the envelope containing the notice was deposited prepaid and registered in a post office.

IN WITNESS WHEREOF the Company has duly executed this debenture.

                                         (Company name)

By: _____ **VOID**

                                   (Signature and Title)

                                   VOID   c/s

                                   (Signature and Title)

Form 5

Form 1076-79

PLEDGE AGREEMENT

Description of Debenture

Principal Amount: _____

Date: _____

^(delete inapplicable clause) Interest Rate:
(a) Nominal annual rate of _____%
(b) A variable nominal annual rate _____ percentage points above the Minimum Lending Rate of Canadian Imperial Bank of Commerce from time to time.

The undersigned hereby assigns, deposits with and pledges to CANADIAN IMPERIAL BANK OF COMMERCE (the "Bank") the debenture created by the undersigned and described above (the "Debenture") to be held by the Bank as a general and continuing collateral security for the payment of all present and future indebtedness and liability of the undersigned to the Bank however incurred and any ultimate unpaid balance thereof (the "Indebtedness").

In the event of any default in payment of any part of the Indebtedness or in the performance of any other obligation of the undersigned to the Bank, the Bank may at any time during the continuance of any such default realize upon the Debenture by sale, transfer or delivery, or exercise and enforce all rights and remedies of a holder of the Debenture as if the Bank were absolute owner thereof, without notice to or control by the undersigned, and any such remedy may be exercised separately or in combination and shall be in addition to and not in substitution for any other rights of the Bank however created; provided that the Bank shall not be bound to exercise any such right or remedy.

The proceeds of the Debenture may be applied by the Bank on account of such part of the Indebtedness as it chooses without prejudice to the Bank's claim upon the undersigned for any deficiency.

The Bank may grant extensions of time or other indulgences, take and give up securities, accept compositions, grant releases and discharges and otherwise deal with the undersigned and with other parties, sureties or securities as the Bank may see fit without prejudice to the liability of the undersigned or the Bank's rights in respect of the Debenture.

Payment to the Bank of interest for any period in respect of the Indebtedness shall be deemed payment in satisfaction of the interest payment for the same period under the Debenture.

The Debenture shall not operate by way of merger of any of the Indebtedness and no judgment recovered by the Bank shall operate by way of merger of or in any way affect the security of the Debenture which is in addition to and not in substitution for any other security now or hereafter held by the Bank.

The provisions hereof shall be binding upon and shall enure to the benefit of the undersigned and the Bank and their respective successors and assigns.

In witness whereof the undersigned has duly executed this instrument the day of   , 19   .

_____
(Company name)

_____ *V oiD*
(Signature and title)

V oiD   c/s
(Signature and title)